The Archaeology of Western Iran

SMITHSONIAN SERIES IN ARCHAEOLOGICAL INQUIRY

ROBERT McC. ADAMS AND BRUCE D. SMITH, SERIES EDITORS

The Smithsonian Series in Archaeological Inquiry presents original case studies that address important general research problems and demonstrate the values of particular theoretical and/or methodological approaches. Titles include well-focused, edited collections as well as works by individual authors. The series is open to all subject areas, geographical regions, and theoretical modes.

ADVISORY BOARD

THE ARCHAEOLOGY OF WESTERN IRAN

SETTLEMENT AND SOCIETY FROM PREHISTORY TO THE ISLAMIC CONQUEST

Edited by Frank Hole

SMITHSONIAN SERIES IN ARCHAEOLOGICAL INQUIRY

Smithsonian Institution Press   Washington, D.C.   London

© 1987 BY SMITHSONIAN INSTITUTION
ALL RIGHTS RESERVED
PRINTED IN THE UNITED STATES OF AMERICA

LIBRARY OF CONGRESS CATALOGING-IN-PUBLICATION DATA
THE ARCHAEOLOGY OF WESTERN IRAN.

  (SMITHSONIAN SERIES IN ARCHAEOLOGICAL INQUIRY)
  BIBLIOGRAPHY: P.
  INCLUDES INDEX.
  1. IRAN—ANTIQUITIES. 2. EXCAVATIONS (ARCHAEOLOGY)—
IRAN. I. HOLE, FRANK. II. SERIES
DS261.A73 1987   935   86-42576
ISBN 0-87474-526-8

THE PAPER USED IN THIS PUBLICATION MEETS THE MINIMUM
REQUIREMENTS OF THE AMERICAN NATIONAL STANDARD FOR
PERMANENCE OF PAPER FOR PRINTED LIBRARY MATERIALS
Z39.48–1984.

Contents

List of Figures

List of Figures

List of Tables

Preface

The gestation of this book began in the spring of 1977 when a number of archaeologists met at the School of American Research to hold the Advanced Seminar, Patterns of Settlement and Cultural Development in Western Iran. We recognized that it was time to take stock after nearly twenty years of active archaeological effort by scholars representing many countries, institutions, and special interests. But we did not know then that most of us would not immediately have the opportunity to resume research to test the many ideas generated during the seminar. Our era of archaeological research ended, at least temporarily, with the fall of the Pahlavi Dynasty in January of 1979. This volume has taken a long time to produce, yet the delay resulted in part from our deliberate attempt to start afresh after the seminar to write chapters that we had not previously planned. Some of us were unable to follow through with this task immediately; others found that words which had come so spontaneously in the vigorous discussions of the seminar were much harder to put into print. Nonetheless, the present volume does not suffer from the delay; indeed, it may have profited from the longer gestation. The papers in this book provide a baseline against which future work can be measured and from which future research can be planned.

There have been several great regional historical traditions in the Near East that have maintained a geographic and cultural coherence over millennia. Among these we can cite both southern and northern Mesopotamia, Egypt, Palestine, and western Iran. The shaded area in figure 1 illustrates roughly the region of western Iran dealt with in this volume and its geographical relation to other regions in the Near East.

Table 1 outlines the archaeological chronologies for these different regions. In spite of ease of travel between these regions and demonstrated exchange of goods through trade and other means, in many ways each has always remained distinct in its cultures and cultural manifestations. Thus, to understand the Near East one must grasp the differences between regions and seek the factors that have tended to keep them apart. No differences in the Near East are more sharply expressed in ancient historic writing than those between southern Mesopotamia and western Iran, home of a number of separate, often hostile political entities. But from the viewpoint of southern Mesopotamia, the cultures of western Iran were collectively regarded as hostile and difficult, if not impossible, to subdue. Potts (1982:35) refers to the "deep-seated, mutual hatred and endemic warfare between the populations of Elam [Susiana in lowland western Iran] and the Zagros, and the cities of Mesopotamia." Such hatred is expressed well during the third millennium B.C., but Potts (1982) makes a case that a barrier has stood between the two regions since the time of the first sedentary villages in the eighth millennium. This barrier is expressed in prehistoric times in the distributions of different types of artifacts on either side of a line roughly following the present border between Iran and Iraq (figure 1). During historic times, much the same situation prevails but the border between the lowlands and uplands shifts in response to current conditions. Despite the differences displayed by western Iran with respect to southern Mesopotamia, a great deal of internal regionalization took place within western Iran, a point that is made in much detail in the following chapters.

Western Iran occupies a crucial place in the development of trade between the resource-poor peoples of southern Mesopotamia and the resource-rich mountain and plateau region of Iran and beyond to the east. Because of this, peoples of the Zagros Mountains could abet or frustrate ambitions of lowland peoples, even those who were able to mount major military expeditions. It is this ability to maintain independence from—and often to exert influence on—neighboring peoples that makes western Iran an archaeological laboratory for studying the processes of culture and history in the Near East. Yet heretofore there has not been a comprehensive and systematic attempt to present the archaeological picture in more than a cursory fashion. We examine some 8,000 years of archaeological history (table 1), and we are able to do this in the compass of a single book only by narrowing our view to matters concerning settlement patterns and the inferences one can derive from them about cultural-historical questions. The authors here did not directly address the question of the differences between Iran and Mesopotamia, a problem that requires a fundamentally different theoretical perspective and a global regional approach. As we look to the future, a consideration of regional differentiation and tradition might well serve as the basis for another similar work.

This volume is as up-to-date as we can make it. Since there has been little archaeology done in Iran since the seminar, apart from that conducted by some of the authors themselves, the articles represent the latest findings. But one should not assume from this book that all of the significant research on Iranian archaeology has been done by the authors—quite the contrary. However, it is the case that the authors have worked in all of the relevant periods and most have participated in a series of colloquia and exchange visits sponsored by the Centre National de la Recherche Scientifique (CNRS) and the National Science Foundation (NSF) which have enabled us to exchange information and ideas freely with our French colleagues. The first of these colloquia was held at Susa in 1977, the results of which were published in *Paléorient* 4:133–244. Subsequently, with aid of a joint CNRS-NSF grant, many members of the French and American teams visited collections and colleagues in France, the United States, and Canada. Finally, in the summer of 1985, another jointly sponsored seminar, The Development of Complex Societies of Southwest Iran, was held in Bellevaux, France. As a result of this latest seminar, which included the full range of time covered in this volume, many of the conclusions reached in these pages were discussed and debated in the light of different theories and sources of data emanating from recent analyses. Thus, as nearly as it is possible, the material presented here is current, even if there remains a lack of consensus on many matters of interpretation.

We have not attempted a comprehensive review of all information; rather, we have concentrated on regional settlement patterns for the insight they give us into traditional archaeological problems. Collectively we have engaged in surveys and excavations the length and breadth of western Iran, so that a regional geographic focus is natural. It is an approach that has been developed successfully in the work of Robert McC. Adams for neighboring Mesopotamia so there is a ready source of comparative material. However, we do not dwell on cross-regional comparisons because our attention is focused on the ties that interrelate regions within western Iran. This geographic approach, with an emphasis on settlement patterns, illustrates the diversity of some periods and the unity of others. Sometimes the explanations for these differences are apparent; in other cases they are speculative and provide a series of hypotheses that the next generation of archaeologists may test.

Iran's rich historical traditions have encouraged archaeological investigations for well over one hundred years, but the importance of the country to archaeologists must be seen in part as a result of modern political circumstances. For most of this century, archaeology in Iran was carried out annually only by the French archaeological mission, while some occasional work was sponsored by American museums. During and after the 1950s, archaeologists from a number of countries including Great Britain, Japan, Denmark, West Germany, Belgium, Canada, and the United States converged on Iran. Their interest in the virtually untapped potential of Iran was abetted by the receptive attitude of the Iranian government toward archaeological work. Throughout the 1960s and 1970s, Iran was among the most favorable countries in Southwest Asia in which to carry out significant, problem-oriented archaeology where travel to gain broad geographic overviews and the use of specialists in ancillary fields are required. The Iranian government was unusually responsive to requests to carry out these nontraditional kinds of research, with the result that archaeological progress in the last generation was more accelerated in Iran than in neighboring countries. All of us who have worked in Iran are especially grateful for the research conditions, and with this general volume as well as the numerous specialist reports that we have published, we hope to repay in some small measure the great debt we owe to Iran.

Within Iran we focus on the western region because historically it has been the cultural center of the country and most of the archaeological research has been here. Further, in ways that will become apparent, western Iran has a historical coherence that makes it a suitable frame of reference for an overview. It was also in western Iran, namely in the lowland province of Khuzistan and in the intermontane valleys near Kermanshah that Robert McC. Adams and Robert Braidwood carried out the systematic surveys in 1959 and 1960 which stimulated much of the work that we describe.

When the seminar was organized we hoped to generate discussion on many topics. Rather than soliciting formal papers for discussion during the five days that we met, I decided to request a broad range of background material from each participant with the idea that out of this we could achieve results of cultural-historical, methodological, and theoretical importance.

Although our interests were diverse, each of us had experience in regional surveys and we had distributional maps of sites, analyzed by period of occupation. These basic data became the point of departure for our discussions, enabling us to quantify our impressions and to discuss changes in number and sizes of sites, patterns of occurrence, and differences in types of settlements period by period, region by region. This approach to archaeological investigation was first successfully realized in the work of Gordon Willey in the Viru Valley of Peru in 1953. Since then it has been a standard procedure of American archaeologists, at least in broad principle. In Iran, although many surveys had been run at various levels of intensity, many of the results had not yet been published so that a wealth of important data remained to be incorporated into our body of general knowledge. This fact led me to propose a seminar that would focus on the geographic aspects of culture history in Iran.

In my initial letter to participants, I wrote:

As I now conceive it, the Seminar will emphasize 1) the specific overviews of human history which are provided by survey, 2) means of conducting surveys, and 3) of using survey data more effectively. Thus the Seminar will consider practical problems, theoretical implications, and substantive results which can be viewed in both their historical and comparative aspects.

In a subsequent letter prior to the seminar I emphasized that we should deal with the

overall culture history and of the processes that underlie it. To pursue these objectives effectively at the Seminar, we need to deal with substantive matters of survey, geographic coverage, techniques of analysis, and other somewhat mundane topics and to present an outline of our principal findings period by period. Out of this we should be able to reach some consensus on comparable periods and to begin comparing the sequences in the various regions through time.

It seemed to me then that we could give coherence to our seminar most effectively by dealing with regional perspectives as these are gained through survey, and by addressing the issue of changes with comparisons of each region with others through time. This perspective ultimately became the topic of this volume.

At the seminar our first task was to create a common language of discourse. This language took the form of a rough chart of chronological equivalences and stages of development which later formed the basis for the organization of this book. When we considered the entire range of time encompassed by our individual research (from the terminal Paleolithic to the seventh century A.D.), we recognized fundamental changes in the direction and composition of cultures, as well as in the archaeological approaches to them. The agricultural revolution changed hunters and gatherers into food producers; the agriculturalists in turn diversified their subsistence and economy and set in motion circumstances that resulted in social stratification; early forms of states quickly arose and with them the requirements for and stimulus to effective literacy.

At the threshold of history, archaeologists customarily forgo the tedium of artifactual analysis and concentrate on single major sites, historical reconstructions, the recovery of monumental architecture and art objects, and the translation of texts. Preoccupation with mundane villages and common artifacts, patterns of settlement, and mode of subsistence are often eschewed by archaeologists who work with the advantage of history. Although such disjunction in academic orientation may occur when history begins, we found that because we had gathered our historical, survey, and other data in the typical manner of prehistorians, we could deal with historic periods in much the same terms that we use for the prehistoric.

Continuing the historical progression, the advent of empires was another important change. And while the Achaemenians deserved their chapter, we recognized that even in the time of empires, cultures are seldom uniform and that interplay between cultures on the frontiers is important in shaping the development of empires. Thus the review of the first millennium B.C. deals extensively with northwestern Iran.

Finally, we review the Iranian peoples who came under the influence of the Greek and Roman worlds of classical antiquity. Although the Persian Empire fell to the advancing Greeks, a resurgence of Persian culture took place subsequently under the Sasanian kings. Indeed, much of Iran prospered as never before, and we can still see vestiges of the vast irrigation works, cities, and thousands of sites built in this era.

To state our outline in this manner suggests that the task of compiling a book was easy, and so it would have been had we dealt, each in his own way, with his data alone. We decided on the more difficult course. Each participant accepted an assignment that required him to assess the relevant data that every other person had provided from his own region of investigation. We attempted to deal with these data in common terms: number of sites; their pattern on the landscape; hierarchies among settlements; evidence of stratification, trade, and commerce; relations between areas; major changes in economic or political affairs; and so on. In short, each of us attempted to provide a narrative that placed a period of cultural development into its proper historical and geographical context. We hoped in this way to produce a book that would read as a series of interconnected essays about cultural development in western Iran as it is revealed through archaeological remains and, to the extent that they are available, historical texts.

We did not entirely dismiss technical and theoretical matters. Concepts concerning settlements and their spatial relations, and their implications for estimating size of population and integration of the settlement system are also explained. A number of authors also deal with problems of doing survey and of using data derived from surface collections from sites. These provide us with the common frames of reference needed to ensure continuity of expression and purpose in the chapters. Each chapter is also illustrated with a series of maps that graphically express the information under discussion. Our original conception was to publish a complete set of maps showing the locations of all sites discussed in the text. However, because the sites are so widely spread and infrequent in much of western Iran, to publish complete maps would require an excessive amount of space without contributing much to our understanding of settlement. We recognize the necessity of publishing maps so that archaeologists may use them for various purposes, but this is best accomplished in original site reports rather than in syntheses such as these. Accordingly, we publish in this volume only maps of regions where the density and distribution of sites is sufficient to provide a useful visual impression. Readers who wish detailed documentation on the locations of sites should consult the relevant site reports and survey reports cited in the text.

The seminar met in Santa Fe from March 14–18, 1977, with the following participants: Henry Wright, Robert Wenke, William Sumner, Elizabeth Carter, Robert Schacht, James Neely, Louis Levine, Gregory Johnson, Frank Hole, and Kent Flannery. Several members of the seminar did not write papers following our meeting. Although we regret the lack of these direct contributions, the indirect effect of all the participants is very much felt in the contents of the chapters of this book, and in all cases data were shared among authors and participants so that the story is as complete as we could reasonably make it. To help bridge gaps in coverage during the second and third millennia, John Alden, who was not a member of the seminar, has contributed a short chapter on the Susiana Plain, and Robert Henrickson has provided previously unpublished data from the central Zagros.

It would be ungracious to fail to recognize the contributions to this book of persons whose names would not otherwise appear. First, the helpful criticism of anonymous reviewers encouraged us to strive to place western Iran into a broader historical perspective, and they recognized numerous instances where a few words of clarification would add immeasurably to general understanding. There were many times during the past several years when it seemed unlikely that we would actually produce a final set of papers and a coherent volume. Much of the credit for keeping us on course must go to Gregory Johnson, whose periodic telephone calls and exhortations eventually helped us cross the final hurdles. The production of the final manuscripts required enormous effort, as any editor can attest, but mine was considerably alleviated by the excellent help of Laura Trawick and Bonnie Hole, who compiled and typed the master bibliography. The mechanical aspects of the final revision, which included the redrafting of most of the illustrations, were coordinated by Bonnie Hole. Most of the maps were redrafted by Heidy Fogel. The result of all of these unheralded efforts is that the book has become more than a collection of papers and has achieved a measure of consistency and overall coherence. As named editor, my debt to all these persons is profound, and I am certain that the authors will appreciate more readily than the readers, who see only the final product, how much the book has been improved because of their efforts.

Finally, we are grateful to Douglas Schwartz for extending the invitation to attend an advanced seminar and to the School of American Research and its members and benefactors who created the intellectual and institutional setting in which the seminar could take place. It is probably true that one must experience a seminar to truly appreciate it. Those of us who have can attest to the unique synergism that arises from prolonged and intense interaction.

Frank Hole

Publisher's Note: Figures and tables are found at the end of relevant chapters. For multiply referenced figures, consult the List of Figures.

Table 1. An Outline of Archaeological Chronologies for Selected Regions of the Near East

Date AD/BC	Western Iran	Southern Mesopotamia	Northern Mesopotamia Assyria	Palestine	Egypt
600	Islamic	Islamic	Islamic	Islamic	Islamic
0	Sasanian	Sasanian	Sasanian/Byzantine	Byzantine	Byzantine
	Parthian	Seleucid-Parthian	Seleucid	Seleucid-Ptolemaic	Ptolemaic
500	Achaemenian Median	Achaemenian	Persian Sargon II	Persian	Persian
	Neo-Elamite	Neo-Babylonian	Neo-Assyrian		Late Period
1000	Middle Elamite	Mid-Babylonian	Mid-Assyrian	Hebrew Conquest Iron Age	Amarna Period New Kingdom
1500		Cassite		Late Bronze	
	Old Elamite III (Sukkalmah Dynasty)	Old Babylonian	Old Assyrian		
2000					Middle Kingdom
	Old Elamite II (Shimashki Dynasty)	Ur III-Larsa	Ur III Dynasty	Middle Bronze	
		Akkadian	Akkadian		1st Intermediate
2500					
	Old Elamite I (Awan Dynasty)	Early Dynasty I–III	Early Dynasty I–III		Old Kingdom
	Proto-Elamite				
3000	Late Uruk	Jemdet Nasr Late Uruk	Late Gawra	Early Bronze	Early Dynastic
3500	Early Uruk	Early Uruk	Early Gawra / Late Ubaid	Ghassoulian	
4000	Late Village	Late Ubaid			
4500	Middle Village		Early Ubaid	Pottery Neolithic B	Pre-Dynastic
5000		Ubaid / Eridu	Halaf/Samarra	Pottery Neolithic A	
6000	Early Village		Hassuna	Pre-pottery Neolithic B	
7000			Jarmo		
8000	Initial Village		Zawi Chemi	Pre-pottery Neolithic A	

Note: Column 1 is not uniformly leaded to represent time intervals.

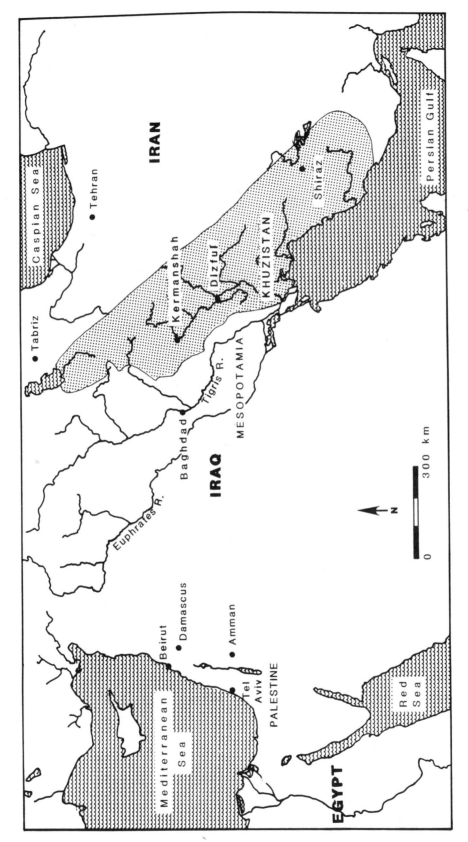

Figure 1. The Near East. The shaded region is roughly the area of western Iran discussed in this volume. The western edge of the shaded area is the modern political border between western Iran and eastern Iraq.

Chapter 1

Themes and Problems in Iranian Archaeology

FRANK HOLE

Introduction

Archaeologists investigate the ruins of ancient cultures attempting to understand their changes and variations. Often—perhaps usually—they must work with incomplete sequences, discontinuous geographic coverage, and uneven data when they approach these fundamental concerns of change and variability. It is regrettably true that much archaeology has been carried out piecemeal, sometimes with little forethought, and only rarely by grand design. Exceptions to this generalization are few, the most notable in the Near East being the work of Robert McC. Adams in southern Mesopotamia where he has carried out reconnaissance of vast regions and temporal span, from the inception of settled life to modern times. The coherence and direction of his projects was ensured by his single-handed and single-minded pursuit of certain limited objectives. However, as he is the first to admit, his coverage of most regions was not intensive and lacks the firm control of chronology that only stratigraphic excavations can yield.

Our situation in Iran is different. In western Iran, a multitude of individual projects have been carried out over a number of years with various methods and purposes, combining survey and excavation. In this book we attempt to unify the results of these disparate projects by focusing on a common denominator, the geographic distributions of sites. Beyond simple observations of this kind, we use whatever data—archaeological or historical—are available to attempt to characterize some of the central features of ancient life. And, when appropriate, authors employ concepts and methods derived from fields such as geography to help interpret the settlement and other data.

This book cannot present all the data available from the many excavations and surveys of western Iran. For the most part, these data are published, but some are presented or systematically compiled here for the first time.

An archaeological framework within which to pursue studies of change and variability over a span of some eight thousand years is rare; a framework that begins with the earliest sedentary agricultural societies is unique. The chronological sequence in Iran is longer than that present in some other key agricultural regions: in southern Mesopotamia, we have about seven thousand years; in Mesoamerica and the central Andes, about four thousand years; in the American Southwest, about two thousand years. Most other parts of the world are known in much less detail. In western Iran, we can provide a reasonably consistent outline of settlement and society from the earliest villages around 8000 b.c. to the time of the Islamic conquest in the seventh century A.D. Our papers outline this framework, forthrightly stating the nature and limits of the evidence and making a variety of interpretations.

No other large region of the Near East has been examined systematically over the great sweep of time that is encompassed in either western Iran or southern Mesopotamia. These two sets of studies provide an unusual opportunity to examine the factors that affect change and variability, as well as to characterize these differences in social and historical terms. There is much in these pages that will stimulate additional studies. Ultimately, many dissertations should emerge from the background and suggestions set forth here, for with the data organized systematically, one can see that problems worthy of investigation abound. With the benefit of hindsight, the haphazard development of archaeology in Iran has become clear. If this book becomes a point of departure for more coordinated efforts to develop coherent pictures of ancient Iran or elsewhere, it will have served a lasting purpose.

The treatment of the various periods in each of the chapters varies widely despite the common goal of presenting a geographic framework for the archaeology. These differences reflect the state of archaeological knowledge, the regions incorporated within certain social and political entities, and the personal predilections of each author. In the first two chapters, Hole reviews most of western Iran because the data are more complete and there are several distinct, important enclaves of settlement and development. Other authors do not reach so widely geographically except for the historic periods when the polities were larger than the modern state of Iran. Thus, both Levine and Wenke, drawing heavily on historic material, place the Iranian sites into a broader geographic and political perspective.

Some authors restrict their coverage to one geographic region. Johnson focuses exclusively on the Susiana Plain in his discussion of fourth millennium Uruk because only this region has been well investigated. Alden, who has recently published elsewhere (1982) a detailed paper outlining early third millennium developments, also restricts his coverage to this plain. Wright centers his discussion on Susiana but ranges more widely in search of evidence for pastoralism. Schacht discusses developments during the third and second millennia, focusing on the three major geopolitical regions of Iran and relating history to archaeology. His chapter is supplemented by Henrickson's discussion of the chronology of the central Zagros as revealed at Godin Tepe, and the historical implications of settlement distributions in the many small valleys.

It should be evident that in dealing with a long sweep of human history, where the quantity and quality of data from different periods vary widely, there may be no possibility of developing unifying themes beyond such mundane points of departure as settlement patterns. In fact, one can recognize themes that run through all the contributions here, but the authors have treated problems that are currently relevant to their periods, rather than a common set of issues. This enables each author to capitalize on the strengths of his data, but it points up problems of research interest for future investigators. For the most part, such research will require additional fieldwork, but much can still be done by reworking basic survey and excavation data from new points of view.

Reading the chapters in this volume, one is struck by the common themes, some of them traditional archaeological problems, that must be addressed anew for each period in each region: environment, chronology, distribution and nature of settlement, differences and similarities between regions, and appropriate models and methods of interpretation. For the most part the analyses and interpretations have grown out of concerns with geography, environment, ecology, and systems and information theory—concerns that require quantified data. This volume makes a first step toward providing some of that quantification, but it is apparent that much more remains to be done.

It is convenient here to review the problems and themes that underlie this volume so that readers can better appreciate the differences between the chapters both in coverage and interpretation. The problems fall into three general categories: the quality of the data; geographic, geomorphic, and climatic factors; and major cultural-historical issues.

Quality of Data

Archaeological data have both perceived and intrinsic qualities. Intrinsically, a site that once existed is either present or absent and we may actually know which situation obtains. But more often, we have no way of knowing the presence or location of former sites unless they stand obviously at the surface and have been surveyed by an archaeologist. Knowing the pattern of location of some sites often enables us to predict where others might be, so that we can base our survey strategies on this perception. However, the sites that have been found may not be a good guide to those that remain undiscovered if the obvious sites are atypical. Thus, numerically numerous small campsites or villages of very short duration may be missed altogether in most surveys. The former because they are located away from roads or villages and consequently may not be in the path of routine archaeological surveys; the latter because they are not visible at a distance or perhaps not visible at all owing to burial or erosion (Kirkby and Kirkby 1976). In areas of heavy erosion, sites that remain are atypical if most of the others have disappeared—as would happen if they lay in the center of an eroding valley, whereas the sites we find are on its edges (Brookes, Levine, and Dennell 1982). As a general rule, large sites in easily accessible areas are more likely to be reported. When this happens it confirms our a priori expectation that people used to live in places that are today most suitable for settlement. But for the most part this conclusion is unverified. The issue is critical many times in this volume when changes in density of sites are reported, sometimes with the comment that nomadic people may have occupied certain stretches that appear to be vacant, or when an apparent population flux raises the possibility that there was a shift between settled and mobile life (Wright, chapter 5, this volume).

It has been demonstrated many times that the first surveys of an area tend to record only the most obvious sites. With each subsequent survey the detail grows, both in number of sites and in the precision of dating the sites or in estimating areas of occupation. Nevertheless, the older a site is, the less likely it is to be found through surface survey. Indeed, Kirkby and Kirkby (1976) estimate that without reoccupation or subsequent disturbance, a site will become invisible to surface survey after about a thousand years, as a result of the gradual flattening of the mound through erosion and the dispersal of the artifacts. Also, after a thousand years, a site that has been reoccupied to a depth of five or more meters, will fail to show evidence of the occupations in its lowest levels. Fortunately, there are enough disturbances that we are often able to find sites that fit both of these conditions. The issue of erosion is particularly apt, however, in a case such as Ali Kosh where we recovered only a handful of eroded sherds of the Chogha Mami Transitional phase on the surface and none whatsoever beneath the surface. Here the site had been abandoned for some seven thousand years and it is not unlikely that evidence of other phases subsequent to the Mohammad Jaffar (which we were able to excavate in part) had also disappeared. Clearly pottery fired to high temperature has a greater chance of surviving prolonged exposure than ceramics which are less well fired.

Kirkby and Kirkby emphasize that finds such as those at Ali Kosh are fortuitous to a much greater extent than archaeologists have been willing to assume. They show that population trends derived from numbers of sites per period, may partly, if not wholly, reflect age (Kirkby and Kirkby 1976:249). That is, fewer older sites will be discovered, even though they may have been as numerous as more recent sites. The authors of this volume have not dealt in detail with the implications of the geomorphic processes that act on site visibility, as these have been outlined by Kirkby and Kirkby, but it is safe to say that future work will have to take them into account. We do know, however, that there is considerable variability in the rates and specific processes in the various regions that we discuss here so that no single model of attrition will suffice to characterize our data collectively.

Although the problems of site visibility are difficult, when a site has been found, we have yet to devise a means (short of excavation) for establishing ages independent of recognizing changes in the artifacts found on the surface. And even with excavation, unless artifacts that are likely to be found on the surface change relatively quickly, we will still not gain appreciable accuracy. The dating problem is most acute when we wish to estimate sizes of populations or assess rates of change. Paradoxically, we are often on much more secure ground in dating the earlier prehistoric periods

with their elaborately decorated pottery than we are in dating the historic periods when the bulk of the ceramics are unpainted and manufactured with monotonous repetition. It is important to emphasize that, in fundamental respects, even during "historic" periods, problems of chronology remain. This is the central issue dealt with by Henrickson and in another sense by Schacht who outlines (appendix, chapter 7) the historical and stratigraphic data that are utilized by scholars concerned with the early historic periods.

Another aspect of quality of data concerns the degree to which excavations and surveys have been published. For example, we have a series of site reports that describe excavations at a number of prehistoric villages, but there are no comparable publications as yet for key sites of some other periods. On the other hand, despite a prevailing lack of detailed site reports on a period such as Uruk, a series of detailed analyses of such data as exist for this period have been published. Thus, Johnson (chapter 4) is able to provide an essentially interpretive chapter rather than one that presents basic data.

Approaches to the prehistoric and historic eras differ in essential ways, reflecting the differences between historical and archaeological data. In an important summary volume, Carter and Stolper (1984) have addressed the historical and archaeological evidence for the Elamite Period separately, drawing on the very different sorts of information available. Both authors carefully evaluate the quality of their data and then outline the period in terms appropriate to history and archaeology, respectively. No attempt at complete reconciliation of these two approaches is offered because the evidence is not strictly compatible. However, when historic sources are available, there is a tendency to try to relate them to sites and places. For instance, a lively debate continues concerning the places named in Elamite texts. Vallat (n.d.) has recently attempted to locate the regions known as Shimashki, Marhasi, Su, Awan, and Elam, in central western and southern Iran, but although this general region is accepted, other scholars find the details of his arguments unconvincing (Stolper 1984:4, 20; Carter 1984:140). The problems are similar to locating the cities and places named in the Old Testament, a task that has occupied generations of biblical scholars and whose success will depend on excavation at likely places and probably on chance finds.

Clearly, as Wenke (chapter 10) discusses, there is no need to infer from distributions of sites or types of artifacts that the Sasanians had a highly centralized government that expended unprecedented amounts of capital in agricultural development. But it is precisely the nature of governance in Uruk and, to a lesser but significant extent, in the early historic periods such as Elamite, that is at issue. Thus, archaeological data from different periods may be used for quite different purposes, depending on ancillary information. For the Sasanian Period, archaeology supplements the historical information, enriches it with examples, and contributes much information on regions that are poorly recorded historically. But inferences from the nonverbal data must take the place of history for the earlier periods. It is understandable, therefore, that typically a shift occurs in archaeological method and interest when one crosses the threshold of history.

But history does not answer all questions. There are several problems. First, the older the writing, the less straightforward is its translation into modern terms. Historically useful texts begin only about 2500 B.C., although Proto-Elamite writing goes back to 3200 B.C. Second, writing in all periods tends to reflect concerns of elite groups and rulers whose biases and veracity cannot be accurately assessed. And many texts are merely lists of goods and economic transactions which have little historical value in the normative sense. Finally, much of the "history" of Iran derives from Mesopotamian rather than from indigenous sources (Stolper 1984:5). Thus, although history adds an enormous dimension to our potential for understanding, written sources as we know them today are not in any sense full pictures of the world we wish to describe.

Traditionally, archaeologists have eschewed meticulous observations of pottery and concern with diet when they have works of art, clay tablets, and fine tombs to occupy their attention. What we have done in this volume, as Robert McC. Adams has done previously, is call attention to the relevance of settlement data even in historic contexts. We find then that there are common frames of reference across all the millennia which help us understand the nature of shifts in human orientation, albeit in numerical and spatial terms that abstract the essence of density and pattern.

To some extent, as each chapter illustrates, the quality of the data determines the methods of analysis and interpretation. Each author provides fundamental, comparable data on the location, number, and sizes or other characteristics of settlements. Beyond that, the authors adopt a framework for interpretation that suits their own particular interests and the availability of models that can be invoked to elucidate the data. The models archaeologists use depend on how they perceive life in the past: what were the major human or social problems that required solutions? Most authors favor models that emphasize economic behavior, and consequently they find models derived from geography and economics most satisfying. There is a notable disregard in most of the chapters of the role of religion or even of individuals, although these are usually treated in detail in the historic periods. This neglect reflects the materialist view of human behavior favored by most of the authors, a view that currently is strong in American archaeology and, to a lesser extent, in anthropology generally. The important point for a reader to remember, however, is that this volume displays basic data as well as their interpretation so that others can apply their own models or interpretive philosophy.

Geographic, Geomorphic, and Climatic Factors

Geography defines the physical setting in which the sites of western Iran occur. We have each made use of geographic factors to define a region or regions of interest. In doing so, we have implicitly treated geography as both an active and a passive factor. That is, we often take an area such as the Susiana Plain to be a self-evident, geographically circumscribed area that is a natural unit of analysis. At other times we look at the archaeological data and conclude, on the basis of similarities in artifacts, that sites in a certain area go together. Thus we draw a boundary around a region on the basis of the distribution of pottery, so that in this instance, geography is the passive factor. The question of the proper unit of analysis has not yet been solved, for even those who focus narrowly on the Susiana Plain recognize that it receives much sustenance in goods and materials from other areas. The practical problems are (a) to define the reasons for outlining an area, and (b) to establish accurate evidence of the limits of interaction as they relate to a specific problem.

We all recognize that any particular landscape has its unique qualities that cannot fail to exert an active influence on the distribution of sites: extent of arable land, amount of rainfall, availability of fuel. Techniques such as site catchment analysis have been devised to help inventory the local resources. The further step of definitively relating these resources to particular cultural developments or events has not been taken, perhaps because most archaeologists doubt that geography is the active agent it was once considered to be. According to this view, human enterprise and ingenuity can, and usually do, overcome geographic limitations.

Despite such a viewpoint, most would agree that mountains are barriers which affect both travel and climate, that accessible water is essential, that broad flat areas are generally more desirable for agriculture than steep rocky ones, that certain ecotones afford unusual opportunities, and so on. These are truisms that govern carrying capacity, the intrinsic ability of the land to support people or other forms of life. However, archaeologists in Southwest Asia have been slow to construct models of cultural development that take regional resource variability or environmental potential into account. How, for example, does the geography of the Mahidasht Plain in the mountains affect people differently from that of the Susiana Plain in the lowlands? Why has the latter seen the highest development? Stated differently, are there geographic reasons why cultures of the highland valleys developed more slowly and to a lesser degree than their counterparts in the lowlands?

Geography also involves climate, a topic that is not frequently addressed in this volume although it hovers as a kind of latent specter in our consciences. Most would agree that climate as such may have been an active factor only during the prehistoric era and that, since then, it has been essentially stable. From roughly ten thousand to five thousand years ago, there may have been substantially increased precipitation in parts, if not all of Southwest Asia (Flohn 1981; Kutzbach 1981:59; Street and Grove 1979; Van Zeist and Bottema 1982). Butzer (1975:393) infers that "the southern sectors of Iran were apparently wetter and certainly cooler" than today. If this were indeed the case, it could help explain the rapid development of cultures in the wetter southern areas as compared with the north of Iran. Although this fact was noted by Hole (chapter 2), it does not explain why *both* the southern and northern mountain regions lag appreciably behind the central Zagros and the lowland plains. A significant shift in rainfall and temperature could also help account for the change in regime of the rivers in the lowlands that was noted by Kirkby (1977:286) as occurring between the end of the Pleistocene and about 3,000 years ago. As he saw it in the lowlands, the shift was from alluviation to downcutting, effects that had their earlier counterparts in the upper reaches of the rivers. The causes of these changes are difficult to determine but they may have involved both natural and cultural events (Kirkby 1977:283). For our purposes, the fact that severe environmental changes have occurred is at least a warning that there may have been some cultural responses which could be manifest in such events as shifts in settlement, changes in agricultural technology, and changes in the mix of farming and herding.

Erosion and deposition are geomorphic processes that affect the preservation of sites as well as the lives of the people who lived in them; hence, quality of data is affected. When 4 meters of alluvium have been deposited on a plain since people first lived there in villages, we can guess that some small, short-term sites may have been buried. Equally, the plains and slopes from which that 4 meters of alluvium were derived may have been stripped of sites (Brookes, Levine, and Dennell 1982). The other principal geomorphic processes affecting western Iran are tectonics and landslides. Earthquakes occur at frequent intervals and claim a heavy toll of mud houses, but

what compensatory human reactions were taken remain to be determined. Landslides are relatively rare on a large scale although the Saimarreh landslip, reportedly the largest in the world, dammed the Saimarreh River and stopped about half the flow into the Karkheh, one of the principal rivers of the Susiana Plain (Oberlander 1965). Although the date of this catastrophe is uncertain, it surely had a profound effect locally on human settlement. But perhaps equally serious was the breaching of the dam and the gradual erosion of the trapped sediments, a process that has taken its toll of archaeological sites (Hole, chapter 2).

Tectonics are also known to have affected ground water supplies. Travelers to western Iran are familiar with springs that have dried up following tremors and some believe that levels of rivers have been profoundly affected as well (Stein 1940:215). Again, such effects may have had chiefly local consequences, but they may be seen in the kinds of data we present in this book. The problem is that we are unable to assess with any accuracy when tectonic events took place. Suffice it to say that our appreciation of cultural factors could not help but be enhanced by more accurate data on geographic and geomorphic factors in our areas of concern.

Major Cultural-Historical Issues

A problem addressed in each of the chapters is that of the proper geographic units of analysis. We speak of regions, districts, areas, and zones, all without precise definition or with consistency from one author to another. The inconsistency stems from divergent conceptions of our frame of reference. On the one hand we treat a region as a geographic entity; on the other as a social, administrative, or economic unit. Inconsistency also derives from history, in that the regions with historical or archaeological coherence change from period to period. Because the meanings shift depending on our perspective, there may be some slight advantage for the present in using ambiguous terms. For the moment, it would be best to treat terms derived from geography as well as those that describe presumed characteristics of spatial entities such as "interstitial," "core area," or "central place," in their colloquial senses, unless specific definitions are given.

Beyond the matter of terminology are the questions of how an entity can be defined archaeologically and what such an entity implies in terms of human organization. Standard practice is to compare artifacts between sites with the implicit understanding that the more similar they are, the greater the intensity of interaction. Stated in this form, the proposition is unassailable on a common-sense level, but what we often do not make clear are our standards for pronouncing that sites are similar or different. Here, quality of data and quality of interpretation are both involved in our ability to spell out just what is similar or different. In practice, we find that familiarity with data breeds discrimination: at first everything looks the same; eventually we distinguish differences and, with diligence, we may even come to understand the nature of the differences.

There are a number of ways to assess relations among areas, apart from examining artifacts. For example, geographic factors may imply interaction for products that are not available locally. In such cases one may find sites near sources of raw material and along routes of travel. Another kind of interaction occurs when pastoral people move seasonally with the growth of fresh pasturage and equable weather. The presence of these mobile people also raises the possibility of interactions with settled farmers for agricultural products in exchange for animal products, and it raises the specter of conflict in which the mobile herders raid the farmers. There is, thus, a strong concern over the nature of lowland-highland interaction in many of the papers. Unfortunately, in spite of the fact that most highland regions were probably occupied by transhumant people, there is little to say about interaction except to mention the possibility, for there are few sites or data to shed light on any presumed relations (Wright, chapter 5, this volume). Another aspect of this interaction is glossed "rural-urban," statuses that enter our picture only with the growth of cities or "centers."

The nature of relations within any one defined area is also a matter for interpretation. Johnson (chapter 4) goes to considerable lengths to illustrate how physical spacing of sites, coupled with minimal information on other attributes, can be used to infer the nature of relations among them or, as he puts it, "systems integration."

Schacht addresses broad historical questions of the interaction among political entities during the mid-third to mid-second millennia by combining distributional data, techniques for evaluating the intensity of interactions among sites called gravity and rank-size analysis, and historic sources. He is thus able to use independent means to assess historical inferences and to test gravity analysis, in particular, against instances where the historical data are secure. Henrickson deals with a narrower aspect of these data, following a more traditional archaeological approach in which he constructs a detailed chronology for a region based on the excavation of Godin Tepe. He can then utilize this framework to look at site distributions throughout what Schacht calls the central Zagros region in his less detailed review. While

Schacht presents the more general historical problems, their solution will ultimately depend on studies such as that by Henrickson. Thus we can view these two chapters as complementary approaches to the same body of data and set of historical problems.

Wenke also experiments with techniques for assessing interrelations among sites. His approach is to use multidimensional scaling (MDS) which is based upon a matrix of similarities in artifacts between sites to help interpret the patterns of settlement. By different means, this approach accomplishes the same ends as gravity analysis in that it measures differences between sites which may relate to geographic distances.

Johnson, Schacht, and Wenke have all made ingenious use of relatively sparse data to provide convincing assessments of the hierarchical and social organization of the Susiana Plain. Nevertheless, we have, as yet, few independent historical means of verifying these interpretations.

As a whole, the authors of this volume are concerned with change: change in size, spacing, density, mode of adaptation, and so on. We begin at the time of the first significant change, when agriculture replaced hunting and gathering. Hole (chapters 2 and 3) carries the story to the threshold of the state, but it is Johnson (chapter 4) who develops the arguments for state formation in Uruk. Wright (chapter 5) addresses the problems of determining patterns of pastoralism in the early periods. The expanding polities of the early historic period are discussed by Alden, Schacht, Henrickson, and Levine (chapters 6 through 9), while the next higher level of integration, that of empire, is treated by Wenke (chapter 10). Along with discussions of changes in the state of organization, the authors review changes in interrelations among areas. One particularly interesting case is that of the highlands of the central and southern Zagros and their relations with the lowlands. Inevitably, the larger social context that includes Mesopotamia must often be brought into discussion as the peoples of Iran were affected by that area in different ways throughout history (e.g., Carter 1984:117).

The bare data of settlement suggest changes in population and shifts of people from one area to another. Periodically, based on our distributional data, we find that the apparent size of overall population changes markedly in a very short time. For instance, at the end of the fifth millennium, the number of sites declines dramatically; then, following a buildup of population again, a rapid and then a long period of decline occurs from the late fourth to late first millennia. The rise began in Uruk and the fall, starting in Middle Elamite, continued through Achaemenid and Seleucid times. In the centuries surrounding the birth of Christ, populations grew to unprecedented numbers, as we see in the remarkable Parthian and Sasanian constructions. This development collapsed, in part abetted by the Islamic conquest, and since that time population has gradually rebounded.

Although it is conventional to infer gross changes in the sizes of populations from changes in the numbers of sites, it is not at all clear how such changes might have come about or whether there were repeated shifts from settled to nomadic life and back again in response to environmental or economic conditions of which we are now ignorant.

The difficulty we have explaining the changes only points up that we have been preoccupied with the "rises" of civilization rather than with "falls," although this is an issue Wenke addresses. Clearly we have some sort of an oscillation in population throughout history, but we are unable to assess it in the absence of fine chronology and more accurate estimates of the sizes of populations. Nor will we be able to do so with any confidence until we are able to estimate the sizes of mobile populations. Neither possibility will be easy to achieve, especially without further work in the field. Wright focuses on this problem explicitly, but he is able to make only relatively weak inferences based on negative information and on the geographic location of a few sites.

One traditionally assesses the number of sites in a period by counting all those that share the same chronologically diagnostic pottery. Thus, we see a rather sharp decline in number of sites during the late Susiana period that carries over into Early Uruk before a significant rise is seen again. In some regions, such as Mahidasht and the Hamrin region of Iraq (Oates 1983), we know that people using different pottery lived essentially side by side so that the question of whether there may be coexisting cultures (in a ceramic sense) must be addressed. In the case of Susiana, we would have to consider whether Late Susiana and Early Uruk were contemporary, were sequential, or whether a shift to new and subsequently short-lived settlements left most of these sites buried and out of view. Leaving the geomorphic problem aside, Johnson would argue strongly against contemporaneity of sites with different ceramics, but the issue can be solved definitively only when stratigraphic excavations show them to be successive. Unfortunately, relatively few sites appear to contain both terminal Susiana and Early Uruk in contexts where postdepositional mixing can be ruled out.

If the problem of contemporaneity and succession is difficult on the Susiana Plain, it is even harder when we try to compare one region with another. There is good reason to believe that there was a substantial lag in the diffusion of certain ceramic styles, particularly in the highlands of Iran where, for example, painted

buff-ware pottery appears later and continues in use longer than in the lowlands. As yet we are unable to specify what, if any, implications this has for aspects of life other than material culture.

For the Future

Despite the wealth of data and attempts at systematic coverage displayed in this volume, quality of the basic data remains our most serious problem, because our attempts to reconstruct the culture history of western Iran inevitably depend on these basic data, whatever theoretical models we may wish to employ.

The empirical studies of the Mahidasht by Brookes, Levine, and Dennell (1982) and of Deh Luran and the Susiana Plain by Kirkby (1977) show the severity of the problems of alluviation and deposition, but the case of Hulailan and perhaps the Harsin area show quite different circumstances (Mortensen 1975; Smith and Mortensen 1980). A matter of high priority must be a careful assessment of the processes that have affected each of the settled areas. In areas where deposition has been excessive, we must make use of some form of subsurface sampling to test for sites. One such method may be to use ground penetrating radar (Morey 1974), an instrument that has been used to good effect at both prehistoric and historic sites in the United States (Vickers and Dolphin 1975; Bevan and Kenyon 1975). As these systems are potentially capable of rendering profiles of the upper 20 meters of soil, they would be extremely useful in identifying buried mounds as well as traces of former streams and canals. Once having identified the presence of a site, one could either dig or use a coring device to obtain samples for age assessment. Although these methods are, needless to say, costly and perhaps inapplicable to local circumstances, the technology to achieve higher quality survey data is not the limiting factor.

Remote sensing is more often thought of in relation to aerial surveys, either from aircraft or satellites. Wenke (1975–76) has shown the efficacy of this method when sites are visible at the surface, but one might do still better by selecting different spectra that emphasize ground anomalies. Again, although the technology for this exists, it is not necessarily available in the resolution required for archaeological purposes. Low-level aerials in the traditional black-and-white form still have much potential, especially for mapping traces of ancient sites, terraces and irrigation systems, and remains of roads and bridges. Just as this has proved to be of great value in Iraq (Adams 1965, 1981; Adams and Nissen 1972), it could pay high dividends in Iran.

Remote sensing may yield impressive results, but intensive surface survey is proven and would unquestionably repay the effort, as many have shown in limited areas. Coupled with careful examination of all disturbed areas such as wells, canals, road cuts, and erosion gullies, it might help to resolve the questions about site burial, particularly where alluviation is suspected. The major drawback to such examination is finding an adequate spacing of cuts. Intensive surface survey combined with careful geomorphological study should be carried out at an early stage in future archaeology in some selected areas where previous work has shown high potential. Such an area would certainly be in the margins of the Mahidasht Plain system in the central Zagros, such as Harsin; the study might equally examine a lowland plain like Deh Luran or the older, more stable slopes at the verge of the Zagros Mountains and the alluvial plain below.

Environmental change is implied in the geomorphic processes outlined by the Kirkbys, but the specific causes of changes in these processes derive from anthropogenic and climatic factors. Therefore we need much more detailed climatic information on the Holocene than is presently available from the single core from Lake Zeribar, near Marivan, about 60 kilometers northwest of Kermanshah (Van Zeist 1967). To do this it may be necessary to sample sediments that are less than optimum, and it is not precluded to take samples directly from archaeological sites or their immediate environs (Woosley and Hole 1978). It may also be possible to make climatic inferences from stable isotopes in wood or bone from sites but this is a project that will require considerable fundamental research (Epstein and Yapp 1976; Yapp and Epstein 1977). In the short range, it will be best to concentrate on assessing the differential changes in geomorphic processes in each of the various regions under study. Such changes will be apparent in the landforms and sediments, and it may be possible to relate them to changes in temperature and rainfall, as well as to activities associated with the human use of the land.

We have made considerable strides in charting dietary changes, particularly through the use of flotation and palynology, but neither of these two methods has been universally applicable. Here we may be aided by methods of analysis involving trace elements and stable isotopes of carbon and nitrogen, although, as yet, these have been applied only infrequently to human bone material (Brown 1981; Chisolm et al., 1982). Such analyses may also shed some light on the keeping of livestock (De Niro and Epstein 1978, 1981).

Excavation will naturally remain central to our understanding of the archaeological past of Iran, and here too, there are some projects that must have high priority. One of these is to reexamine key sites—insofar as they remain suitable for examination—such as Giyan, Sialk, or Musiyan. Each site has provided primary archaeological data for its area, yet each was dug by methods that are far too coarse for modern purposes. As these were in their time among the largest sites in Iran, they indubitably have features that are not duplicated at hamlets and villages. The reexamination should take at least the form of the type of careful stratigraphic cuts that have been carried out by the French with such notable success at the Susiana sites Jowi, Bendebal, Jaffarabad, and Susa acropole (Le Brun 1971; Dollfus 1978, 1983). Nevertheless, the hamlets and villages are the most accessible to archaeological excavation because of their smaller size so that extensive excavations here are warranted. In particular, we need a number of relatively large exposures (such as the one at Tepe Zagheh by Malek Shahmirzadeh 1977) to help us assess the nature of the settlements themselves, both as spatial entities and as loci for activities. Only in this way will we gain control over the factors by which we must estimate sizes of populations. Such excavations will also enable us to assess definitively the degree of social differentiation manifest, let us say, in an Uruk community with wall cones as opposed to one that has none. Again, the differences in community integration before and after the rise of the state would be illuminating.

Ideally, we would have cemeteries from each of the periods and regions so that we could assess the multiplicity of things that may be revealed by burials; status and sex differences, diet and nutrition, pathology, and perhaps climate. To find cemeteries it will obviously be important to look off the sites, perhaps around their perimeters or in a nearby abandoned site (Dollfus 1983b:289). Looking off the mounded sites will also enable us to examine agricultural practices, perhaps to see canals and even plow marks. Chemical and geomorphological studies of the soils may provide useful information on the spatial distribution of activities.

Chemical and physical studies should also be applied systematically to the identification of sources of raw materials so that we can use these data to trace out the subsequent distribution of artifacts through trade or other mechanisms. Again, the technology to accomplish these ends is available: what is lacking are the source surveys and the subsequent analyses.

Ethnographic studies of the kind carried out by Hole (1978a, 1979), Kramer (1979b, 1983), and Watson (1979) help greatly by showing how people today in the same environments, using similar techniques, carry out subsistence food production. Other similar studies, particularly those that quantify their data, will help us assess land use and its relation to settlement, to social hierarchy, and to cultural divisions between regions. A combination of aerial photography and ethnographic reconnaissance could accomplish much along these lines. From the archaeological point of view it is unfortunate that even the most remote of the tribal people have long been dependent on some contact with markets, but in spite of this, it is evident that in certain cases such things as migration patterns, form of dwelling, and many subsistence practices, have changed scarcely at all in many millennia. There is, therefore, still room for penetrating ethnographic studies that can interrelate archaeological concerns with ethnographic observations.

To summarize, in future archaeological research in Iran (as elsewhere in the Near East), we must strive to obtain the fullest contextual information for each site during each period. In particular we need to pay much more attention to the circumstances of the finds: where they are located in sites; their relationships to one another; the nature of the deposits; how the material came to be deposited where it was found; the processes that may have degraded the archaeological picture, etc. The efficacy of this approach has been brilliantly illuminated by Alain LeBrun (n.d.) in his reconstruction of successive occupations of a single house unit over a period of several generations at the site of Susa. Here we can glimpse the actual uses to which rooms were put and see how these uses changed through time. This small window into the activities of one household reveals much about relationships between the accounting devices—carved seals and impressed sealings, bullae and inscribed tablets—and domestic activities. Such reconstruction requires painstaking excavation and analysis but results in entirely new interpretive possibilities about matters that previously had been subjects only of speculation based upon essentially contextless objects quarried out of sites. This sort of attention to context is essential for all periods, whether prehistoric or historic, and it is particularly important in helping to understand the implications of such things as botanical and faunal remains (Miller and Smart 1984). When this kind of recovery is practiced on large-scale excavations, we will begin to bring into focus a markedly sharper picture of life in ancient times.

Through the years a great deal of archaeological material has been removed from Iranian soil, much of it studied in only very preliminary fashion, and all of it candidate for more intensive examination. Restudy of this material, as in the case of the Susiana burial ceramics (Hole 1982, 1983, 1984) or Le Brun's (n.d.) contextual analysis at Susa may be more productive than conducting further excavations, particularly when these data are of unusual importance and cannot be duplicated.

Finally, each of the authors has speculated about some aspect of the archaeology of his period. In effect, these speculations are hypotheses that can and should be tested by carefully designed programs of survey, excavation, and analysis.

As we look back on two decades of research in Iran, we find it hard to recall how little we knew at the beginning and, consequently, how much has been learned. It is our nature, though, to emphasize the tasks that remain undone and restlessly to seek after answers to a multitude of cultural-historical and scientific problems. When political and economic circumstances change, there is little doubt that the present authors and many others will once again turn toward Iran for answers to some of the basic questions concerning human development in the Near East.

Chapter 2

Archaeology of the Village Period

FRANK HOLE

Introduction

The long span of time, from roughly 8000 to 4000 b.c., saw the establishment of the first sedentary villages, the development of effective agriculture and animal husbandry, and the emergence of social complexity in western Iran and in Southwest Asia. Although the inception and pace of development varied from region to region, the agricultural areas of greater Mesopotamia moved through successive stages of development in remarkably similar fashion. Generally, a number of widely scattered villages represent initial sedentism, exhibiting evidence for the use of both wild foods and domesticates. Later, these villages multiply, spreading rapidly and steadily throughout areas of rain-fed agriculture. Subsequently, irrigation is introduced along with the opening of the vast, fertile tracts of the Mesopotamian lowlands. Finally, large settlements with religious architecture emerge in several favored areas. By this time, social hierarchies and specialist roles in society are evident. This is the threshold of the political state with its literacy, widespread economic relationships, military competition, and urban clusters. Western Iran fits neatly into this order as a contributing and constituent element, even as its varied and remote locales display unique characteristics.

This sequence of development most closely describes Mesopotamia and its fringing mountain regions in Iraq, central and eastern Anatolia, and Iran. The Levant and western Anatolia differ more and will not be considered here (A. Moore 1985). The coherence of the greater Mesopotamian cultures derives largely from geographic propinquity, ecological similarities, and perhaps from the necessity of inter-regional transfer of products. Nevertheless, one should bear in mind the prevailing isolation of the separate areas, which prohibited constant contact and allowed individuality to develop as reflected in the material remains described in the following discussion.

This chapter is organized geographically around "core areas," which are agricultural plains of sufficient size and quality to sustain substantial numbers of villages and to participate in some significant aspects of social change. There are four such areas: (1) the lowland steppe, (2) the Azerbaijan region, (3) the valleys of the central Zagros, and (4) the mountain plains of the southern Zagros in Fars (figure 2). To the east of Mesopotamia, the lowland steppe at the base of the Zagros Mountains includes the Susiana and Deh Luran plains (figure 6). To the north, the Azerbaijan region is the area around Lake Urmia, including the Solduz Valley (figure 11). The central Zagros area includes the area along the Khorasan Road, or Great High Road, which is the natural route from Baghdad to Hamadan (figure 12). It contains many small mountain valleys at elevations which decline as one travels through the Zagros Mountains down to the Mesopotamian Plain. In the province of Fars, the southern Zagros area includes the broad Marv Dasht Plain, northeast of Shiraz (figures 2,3).

In addition to these main areas, there are smaller areas which have been investigated. These include valleys that fringe the Susiana Plain. Among these are the Izeh, Dasht-e Gol, and Iveh plains. Several small valleys, including the Khana Mirza and Shahr-e Kord, lie along routes between the lowlands of steppe and Behbehan and the Isfahan region higher up on the Iranian plateau. By far the greater proportion of land is left to the category of "marginal" or "interstitial," chiefly mountainous terrain or plains of low agricultural potential. Among these, the mountains of Kurdistan and Luristan are discussed below.

The limits of the available data force us to focus on sedentary life, although we have reason to believe that substantial pastoral populations coexisted with the villages, occupying much of the marginal terrain. Little can be said about these people whose specter haunts our estimates of population and our interpretations of changes in settlement and population.

For each area I will review the history of archaeological investigations, outline the excavations, and provide maps for cases where sufficient sites are known from survey to show changes. In chapter 3, I will examine the broader implications of the data.

Because each region of Iran manifests distinct archaeological sequences and has been investigated independently, it is difficult to delineate precise correspondences among them. Indeed, it is often impossible to obtain consistent counts within regions of the numbers of sites of any given period for several reasons. First, different archaeologists hold different opinions regarding the status of individual sites. Second, archaeologists continually revise their assessments of chronology and their interpretations of the appropriate boundaries for given regions. Third, new evidence, in the form of surveys and excavations as well as reanalyses, changes these assessments, adding or deleting occupations attributed to specific periods. Thus the data base is not a static body of site names and known periods of occupation, but a changing one that reflects the state of combined knowledge at a specific moment in time.

Most authors use the terms "Neolithic" and "Chalcolithic" to refer to the earlier and later aspects of the early villages, but to use these terms conflates chronology and cultural development. Others prefer to use the names of local periods or phases, but these become quite confusing to the nonspecialist. I have adopted another course, dividing the long span into four parts where the evidence permits this kind of subdivision: the Initial, Early, Middle, and Late Village periods. These terms clearly imply relative chronological position. They are devoid of cultural implications, so that the local terminology can be readily incorporated into the system. This system allows us to look at four slices of time for purposes of cross-regional comparisons, while retaining the ability to examine development and change within each region.

For reference to the periods and their local manifestations, see table 2. For a complete list of radiocarbon dates for the Village periods, with corrections where applicable, see table 3.

The Initial Village Period

The earliest villages of Iran are characterized by houses made of mud with rectangular rooms. In their architectural form, community patterning, and spacing on the landscape, villages of the type described here have characterized the settlement of western Iran since the seventh millennium B.C. Once established, this fundamental village plan proved remarkably resistant to change, and even today it continues to satisfy the requirements of a mixed farming and herding way of life.

Within Southwest Asia as a whole, initial villages range in size from small rural communities to large settlements with public, ceremonial, and even defensive architecture. The range is illustrated by Abu Hureyra (Moore 1975), Jericho (Kenyon 1960), Mureybat (Cauvin 1972), Catal Huyuk (Mellaart 1967), Umm Dabaghiyah (Kirkbride 1974), and Yarim Tepe (Merpert and Munchaev 1976), as shown in figure 4. None of these represents the "typical" early farming village that was postulated by Childe (1952) or Braidwood (1952, 1958, 1973); rather this ensemble of villages displays the "idiosyncratic progress of technology" (Oates and Oates 1976a:80) and regional styles, for no two early villages are identical. To be sure, many sites approximate the model of relatively isolated and self-sufficient communities, but others—by virtue of evidence of craft specialization, the presence of exotic goods, and geographic location—probably played key roles in both intraregional and interregional activities.

Despite their differences in technological and social complexity, the early villages of Iran display certain similarities. For the most part, they are recognized on survey by the presence of "soft-ware" ceramics (chaff-tempered) and sometimes by chipped stone tools. When not covered by later occupations, the sizes of these sites can be measured. Few are larger than a hectare or two.

Most writers who deal with the Initial Village Period focus on agriculture, for the question of its origins has stimulated much writing (e.g., Childe 1952; Braidwood and Braidwood 1953; Braidwood 1958; Reed 1977b; Moore 1982; and Flannery 1973 for reviews of previous work). As archaeological knowledge from the many distinct regions of Southwest Asia has grown in recent years, there have appeared a number of good reviews of the Neolithic. For example, for Southwest Asia as a whole, see Mellaart (1975), Oates and Oates (1976a), Burney (1977), and Moore (1985); for Mesopotamia, Smith (1972c) and Oates (1972b, 1973); for Iran, Hole and Flannery (1968), Smith and Young (1972), and Pullar (1975, 1977).

Our knowledge of the Initial Village Period in Iran comes from excavations at some ten widely scattered sites and from surveys that have discovered more than two hundred other sites of similar age (roughly 8000 to 5000 b.c.). Closely related information comes from another half-dozen excavations and some surveys in eastern Iraq. Considering that the period under review encompasses as much as three thousand years and covers a belt of land about 1,000 kilometers long and 150 kilometers wide from Azerbaijan to Fars, the paucity of evidence is striking. To put the matter at its worst, we know of about one initial village for every 1,000 square kilometers. Of course the situation is not quite so bad as it might appear, for most of the land in question is mountainous and much was forested so that it held few villages of any age; moreover, most of this terrain has never been systematically surveyed for sites.

Nevertheless, we know vastly more about many details of the Initial Village Period than any other period, chiefly because most of the excavations have been carried out in recent years with refined techniques of recovery. Our evidence of subsistence in Iran is matched at only a few other places in Southwest Asia. We have a great deal of information on all categories of small objects that can be recovered only through the use of the slower, more tedious methods of excavation. We also have extensive evidence of settlement distributions, but in comparison with some later periods, we may have substantially poorer information because of the effects of erosion, alluviation, and burial by later occupations. On balance, there is enough information to make some general remarks but not enough to validate them.

The Later Village Periods: The Early Village Period, the Middle Village Period, the Late Village Period

The fundamental patterns of agriculture and animal husbandry that characterized Iran into the twentieth century were established during the Early to Late Village periods. Looking at it another way, if the political and economic superstructure of later eras were stripped from rural Iranian settlements of subsequent eras, what would remain would be essentially like the Late Village Period. In this sense, the period provides the foundation on which all later Iranian civilizations were built.

The later village periods are frequently called the "Chalcolithic," which is usually heralded by the appearance of well-made, usually buff-colored painted ceramics, such as Halaf and Ubaid wares, that were fired in kilns to relatively high temperatures. Although pottery is a convenient archaeological marker of change, it is only symptomatic of other changes that are harder to detect archaeologically, especially through survey. And, despite changes in ceramics, in most areas there is little evidence for cultural discontinuities from the initial villages. At its earliest, this buff ceramic emerges around the beginning of the sixth millennium, but it starts as late as the fifth millennium in some areas (see table 2 for the local chronologies). The end of the period is more readily defined but perhaps less well understood: it is distinguished by the appearance of unpainted, mass-produced ceramics, such as Uruk wares, that quickly, if not immediately, replace the distinctive earlier wares. Stratigraphically, the change in ceramics is found between levels 22 and 23 of the Acropole sounding at Susa, to which we can assign a date early in the fourth millennium. The later village periods thus last for about two thousand years.

Culturally, the later village periods are compared most commonly with the Ubaid, named after a site in southern Mesopotamia, but the term refers more generally to ceramics that feature designs painted in black on a buff fabric. Variants on this ceramic ware are found in sites from Syria to Iran, roughly following the arc of lowland Mesopotamia and penetrating some distance into the mountain valleys, especially along the Iranian side. Wherever there have been careful surveys, it is evident that the number of sites gradually increases through the Early and Middle Village periods and then, in some key areas, it declines. During the latter part of the later village periods, there is clear evidence of the emergence of exceptionally large sites among the small villages. In southern Iraq, these develop into temple centers such as Eridu and Ur, where the pattern of raising large platforms as foundations for temples began with the Early Village Period. Because of the paucity of excavations into the deep levels of these large sites, we can say relatively little about the organization of Ubaid society in any particular region. But we infer that the foundations of urban civilization lay in this period. The transformations leading to the first political states are poorly understood and can be perceived only faintly in dramatic changes in the pattern of settlement and in shifts in ceramic technology, the use of writing, and the symbols on seals that were pressed into clay.

From an Iranian perspective, we can say a great deal in some areas about demographic changes and variability. Excavations in a few of the smaller sites allow insight into some of the organizational underpinnings of local society. We have a few rare glimpses of social dynamics among people who had begun to display the kind of differences in artifacts and spatial distribution that we associate today with local groups. We are thus able to make some judicious use of ethnographic analogy in helping to understand this evidence.

Whatever we can say with certainty pales before that about which we have no knowledge. A chief purpose of reviewing the disparate evidence is to establish precisely a foundation upon which we can build by asking questions and designing projects that will move us toward understanding. The status of Iranian archaeology is better than in many other areas and not distinctly worse than for any other region of Southwest Asia. Our pictures are composed from evidence that was gathered without overall central purpose, so that regional gaps and chronological omissions are to be expected. One should bear in mind too that the archaeology of this region is relatively new with most projects in their initial stages of discovery when fieldwork ceased, and we still lack publications describing many of the key sites. Rather than belabor the shortcomings of our data, which are painfully obvious to those of us who work with them, the goal of this review is to elucidate overall patterns of change and development, and to convey a sense of emerging distinct social groups, the developing centralization and hierarchization of society in some areas, and the salient problems that might be targeted for future research.

Western Iran is largely mountainous with relatively small, discontinuous agricultural plains nestled in the midst of mountain ridges (figures 12,13). Only the lowland Susiana steppe (Khuzistan), the eastern edge of the Mesopotamian plain, contains a really broad, arable, and irrigable expanse that is comparable to southern Mesopotamia, and it was here that the first complex society of Iran arose (figure 6).

The review that follows deals with each of the major plains for which a reasonable amount of evidence for the period exists. We begin with the Deh Luran Plain on the lowland steppe where we have detailed information about the earliest villages, and turn next to the Susiana Plain where there is the best information on the emergence of complex society, comparable with that of southern Mesopotamia. Next we move into the mountains where there is evidence of nomadic pastoralism. Our review then considers Azerbaijan where we encounter the Dalma ceramics and then follow these wares into the Karkheh drainage with its large mountain plains. Here we find a co-mingling of a local Ubaid, the Dalma, and a ceramic derived from Halaf, a pre-Ubaid ware, best known from northern Mesopotamia. Finally we review Fars, in the southern Zagros. This geographic spread enables us to look at specific changes in each region and to compare regions at the same time. This approach indicates clearly which areas were central to development, and it raises questions about the delays that other areas experienced. Finally, we see in this some semblance of the local groupings mentioned earlier.

Background to Settled Life

Before we review the evidence for villages it is useful to discuss briefly what we know of antecedent cultures.

Mortensen (1975) was the first to verify the presence of a Lower Paleolithic in the Zagros, since Braidwood's (1960a,b) survey team discovered a single hand axe near Kermanshah; however the nature of this early presence is difficult to assess in the absence of any excavation. The major lesson to be learned from the Paleolithic at this time is that it has been more severely affected by geomorphic processes than later periods so that there are no safe grounds for generalizing about any aspect of life during the Pleistocene, including the matter of population sizes (Hole 1971).

In 1967, Hole and Flannery published a review of the Paleolithic of western Iran, based to a large extent on surveys and excavations in the central Zagros. Using evidence on density and ages of surveyed sites, artifact inventories, and ethnographic analogy, the authors concluded that there were essentially three types of sites: base camps, transitory camps, and special purpose sites such as butchering stations and quarries. Since then, there has been relatively little work on the Paleolithic to change that picture. Gotch (1968), Zagarell (1975a, 1978), and Wright (1979, n.d.; Wright et al. 1976) have worked in the southern parts of the Zagros and extended information on the geographic range of Epipaleolithic industries. Solecki (1969) surveyed the northwest region of Iran with largely negative results. The most important Paleolithic recoveries have come from the Hulailan region where Mortenson (1974a, b), employing very intensive methods, located a number of sites that are essentially surface concentrations, in contrast to the layered deposits in caves or shelters. When excavated, such sites should provide supplementary information to enhance our understanding of the activities of the hunters and gatherers who roamed the Zagros during the Pleistocene.

It appears that the hunters and gatherers of the Pleistocene and early Holocene lived in relatively low density, moving the locations of their camps regularly (Hole and Flannery 1968).

The only such camp that has been excavated is Asiab near the city of Kermanshah on the broad Mahidasht Plain at an elevation of about 1,500 meters (figure 5). Only through fortuitous circumstances was this site discovered, for no mound rose above the floor of the plain here; only flint tools scattered over a plowed terrace of the Qara Su River indicated the presence of the site. The excavation revealed a deposit some 2 meters in depth, at the base of which was a semi-subterranean structure about 10 meters in diameter. Two skeletons stained with red ochre were buried beneath the structure. The artifacts consisted largely of flint tools, with some "beads, pendants, and bracelet fragments of marble, and numerous small clay objects, including a few enigmatic figurines" (Braidwood et al. 1961:2008). On comparison with Zawi Chemi Shanidar, a site in eastern Iraq where round structures were also found, a date between 11,000 and 9,000 years ago was assigned Asiab (Braidwood et al. 1961:2008), a date later verified by radiocarbon (Protsch and Berger 1973:236). Since the site has considerable depth of deposit, and it has not been published, we cannot be certain whether the artifacts mentioned extend throughout the site, or are particular to some strata. The bones, likewise undifferentiated by strata, have been studied by Bökönyi (1977) who reports an early occurrence of domestic goat (cf. B. Hesse 1978:64), but much more impressive evidence for the hunting of wild goats, sheep, red deer, and pigs. For the most part, the specimens are of very large, fully adult animals. Bökönyi (1977:11,13,36–37) infers that the inhabitants ranged widely to obtain game from various environments during their winter stays. Seasonality was determined from bones of the corn crake (*Crex crex*) which winters in Iran, but could have been obtained late in the fall or spring. Thus occupance during mid-winter need not be presumed. Unfortunately, we know no other sites from Iran of the same age so we are uncertain whether it establishes the pattern of life of the times or is merely a special, atypical site. The earliest subsequent sites are as much as 2,000 years later and have mud architecture and evidence of domestication.

In view of the burials in the depression and the domestic debris, the structure must have been some sort of shelter, perhaps with boughs for a roof to shield the occupants from the sun. The round house form corresponds with early architecture in Southwest Asia and elsewhere, according to Flannery (1972a) who sees the eventual shift to rectangular houses as corresponding to shifts in economy and social organization when agriculture replaced the more mobile hunting and gathering way of life and the sizes of communities grew.

We cannot yet determine what became of the Pleistocene hunters. All we can say is that the Zarzian, the terminal Epipaleolithic industry of the Zagros, ceases sometime at or after the end of the Pleistocene, but it is likely that hunters maintained their ways of life alongside the early villagers for considerable time in some areas. If this was the case, there must have been mutual influences, some cooperative, some antagonistic. Among the former, hunters may have played an important role in trade and exchange. Of the latter, hunters poaching herds or stealing stored crops may have stimulated nucleation of settlement and eventually the construction of defensive structures. At present, the early Iranian villages give us no information on either of these matters.

One would like to know what role, if any, the hunters played in the acts of domestication themselves, but again the record is silent (Hole 1985). No unequivocal transition from the Zarzian camps to the early villages has been demonstrated, despite certain superficial similarities, such as those seen in the chipped stone tools and the use by early villagers of caves for penning animals. Nor is there a ready transition in settlement, for we have no actual huts or houses of hunters to compare with the round structures of the earliest villagers (whom some think do effect a transition). Moreover, the camps of the hunters for the most part are in places frequented by animals such as hilly, craggy country which may or may not have fertile soil nearby, whereas villages are located on or adjacent to arable land. We cannot assess the significance of this apparent difference in most regions because excessive deposition of alluvium may have buried short-term camps on arable land.

Deh Luran

The lowland steppe lies at the base of the Zagros Mountains and includes such regions as the Deh Luran Plain, the Susiana Plain, and the Ram Hormuz Plain (figure 6). This is a land of climatic extremes. Summers in this region are extremely hot and dry, with temperatures reaching 130°F (50°C). Winter lows seldom drop to freezing, but cold north winds and overcast skies maximize the chilling effect during the brief winter season. Rain, which falls only during the winter months, is highly variable from year to year. In general, rainfall increases with elevation and proximity to the mountains. The upper part of this lowland steppe receives an average of 300 millimeters of rain annually, peaking during December and March. This amount is sufficient for dry farming in an average year, but insufficient if the timing of the rains does not accord with the agricultural cycle. Kirkby (1977:269) estimates that crops will succeed about 50 percent of the time if rainfall is not supplemented with irrigation.

The parts of the steppe that concern us here are the Deh Luran and Susiana plains. The Susiana Plain was named after Susa, its most prominent archaeological site. Some 60 kilometers to the west of Susa at a slightly higher average elevation is the Deh Luran Plain (Hole, Flannery, and Neely 1969:19–22; Kirkby 1977) whose geographic characteristics are similar to those of Susiana. To the southeast of Susiana, the lowland steppe extends down to Ram Hormuz which figures primarily in the Late Village Period. Wherever sweet water flows in any abundance across these flat lands, there are agricultural settlements. Such fertile locales are intermittent and relatively smaller than Susiana itself, but they provide a view of variability in lowland cultures and, at certain times, a direct link with sites in eastern Iraq.

The Deh Luran Plain (figures 6–8) lies essentially between the Mehmeh and Daiwairij rivers (with a few sites outside), and between the base of the Zagros Mountains and the Jebel Hamrin, a low anticlinal ridge at approximately the border with Iraq. Although today the major rivers are both incised deeply into their beds, at the time of concern here, they flowed at the surface. Since human occupation began, some 4 meters of alluvium have accumulated on the plain, changing appreciably its physical characteristics (Kirkby 1977).

This plain has achieved archaeological prominence owing to the small excavations into five sites: Ali Kosh, Chagha Sefid, Tepe Sabz, Farukhabad, and Musiyan. Deh Luran was first visited by archaeologists in 1903 when the French team of Gautier and Lampre (1905) put soundings into Musiyan, Khazineh, and Tepe Mohammad Jaffar (later called Ali Kosh). Hole and Flannery visited the plain nearly sixty years later, carrying out limited survey and testing Ali Kosh (Hole 1962; Hole and Flannery 1962). They returned in 1963, along with James Neely, to dig further at Ali Kosh, to put another pit into Musiyan, and to make a stratigraphic cut into Tepe Sabz (Hole, Flannery, and Neely 1969). In 1968–69, Hole returned to excavate at Chagha Sefid and Neely conducted an intensive survey of the plain (Hole 1969a; Neely 1969, 1970). At this time, Michael Kirkby investigated the geomorphology (Kirkby and Kirkby 1969; Kirkby 1977). In 1968, Henry Wright excavated at Tepe Farukhabad and did additional survey. Finally, in 1973 Hole searched for nomad camps on the north part of the plain. The various surveys have covered most of the plain intensively but only parts of it with systematic traverses (Neely 1970). On this plain our information on sites which are visible on the surface is as complete and accurate as on any other plain in Iran.

Although Deh Luran is a distinctly separate agricultural plain, ceramics found there resemble closely those found in Susiana, thus allowing us to divide time in similar ways. The excavations in Deh Luran have all been published, using phase terms that are particular to the region.

The Initial Village Period: Bus Mordeh, Ali Kosh, Mohammad Jaffar, Sefid, and Surkh Phases

The local sequence has been revealed at two sites, Ali Kosh and Chagha Sefid, each of which was founded before the use of pottery. Since the information on the phases in Deh Luran is easily available (Hole and Flannery 1968; Hole, Flannery, and Neely 1969; Hole 1977a), it suffices here to give only the briefest outline of their characteristics and contents (table 4).

Five phases, distinguished stratigraphically and on the basis of changes in artifacts and architecture, are relevant to the Initial Village Period. From earliest to latest, they are Bus Mordeh and Ali Kosh (both preceramic), Mohammad Jaffar, Sefid, and Surkh. The latter three phases exhibit varieties of soft, chaff-tempered pottery. The Bus Mordeh settlers subsisted largely on wild plants and animals, although they carried out some farming and animal husbandry. By the Mohammad Jaffar Phase, both the animal and plant domesticates were well developed morphologically. At Chagha Sefid, a greater emphasis was placed on domesticated herds and correspondingly less on hunted animals. This difference is not readily understood in view of the propinquity of the two sites and their contemporaneity during the Ali Kosh and Mohammad Jaffar phases.

Architectural forms change through the sequence, but the small size of the trenches does not allow us to elaborate on this topic. Stone-founded structures replaced those made solely of mud by the late Sefid Phase. At that time, the first of two substantial, but enigmatic, mud brick platforms appears. Both platforms were 7 to 10 meters on a side and stood over 1 meter in height. The limited extent of the excavation and the fact that both platforms were just below the surface of the site, prevented us from ascertaining how they related to other structures or whether they had served as the bases for buildings.

The phases of the Initial Village Period display gradual change and continuity within a distinctly local tradition, but the presence of an alabaster "bell" and phallic representation (Hole, Flannery, and Neely 1969:203, 233) and some "Samarran" sherds (Hole 1977a:138; Oates 1983:261) indicate contact with eastern (Iraqi) Mesopotamia.

On the Deh Luran Plain, only two sites, Ali Kosh and Chagha Sefid, are known which have the characteristic early soft-ware sherds. One other mound has flints that may be from a preceramic component, and there are three surface scatters of early flints in the vicinity of the tar seep at the north central edge of the plain. That these may be nomad camps is suggested by their location on gravelly slopes, the lack of mounded deposits, and the absence of artifacts other than flint.

Considering the 300 square kilometers of the Deh Luran Plain, we can conclude that settlement was sparse in the Initial Village Period. But we should bear in mind that, since villages were first founded there, some 3–4 four meters of alluvium have built up over the surface of the plain. Therefore, some—perhaps many—early villages may have been buried. Frankly, little can be said about settlement except that both excavated village sites were situated close to water sources: Ali Kosh lay alongside a marsh and Chagha Sefid may have been along a seasonal stream. In contrast, the other sites occur on land best suited today to grazing.

The dynamics of interregional interaction during the Initial Village Period are suggested by the changing patterns of obsidian supply in Deh Luran. To follow Renfrew's terms, most of the obsidian came from source *4c,* located near Lake Van in eastern Anatolia. Another source, also in the vicinity of Nemrut Dag, called *1g,* supplied a lesser quantity. Renfrew has suggested that the earliest phases were characterized by down-the-line exchange in which obsidian was passed in successively smaller amounts from one village to another. According to this scheme, the farther a village is located from the source, the less obsidian it will obtain. Ali Kosh fits this model well (Renfrew 1977; Renfrew and Dixon 1976). Interestingly the picture changes during the Sefid Phase when group *1g* obsidian increases markedly at the same time as the supply of obsidian reaches its peak. The following Surkh Phase sees a steady and rapid decline in the amount of obsidian reaching Deh Luran. Renfrew proposes that, by this time, obsidian was being redistributed through central places which were in competition with one another. From this time onward, obsidian occurs only in low frequency in Deh Luran which, in Renfrew's view, is not one of the central places. Considering that contemporary developments in Iraq (the Hassuna-Samarra sequence) seem advanced over Deh Luran, Renfrew's scenario has some merit. One might add to this, however, that the supply may have failed to keep pace with the growing populations of northeastern Iraq where a great many sites and some very large communities such as Tell es-Sawwan are known to be contemporary with the Sefid and Surkh phases.

The Initial Village Period is represented as far south in eastern Iraq as the Mandali Plain (Oates 1972b). Other sites are probably to be found farther south still, wherever there are arable land and suitable sources of water for both agriculture and domestic uses. The former limits sites to approximately the 250 millimeter rainfall isohyet, and the latter requires perennial streams. Owing to modern political boundaries which have made reconnaissance difficult, disproportionately more is known about the Iranian than about the Iraqi side, but we should not construe from this that the distribution of prehistoric sites also coincides with the border.

The Early Village Period: Chogha Mami Transitional, Sabz, and Khazineh Phases

The Chogha Mami Transitional (CMT), named after the coeval period at Chogha Mami in the Mandali Plain of eastern Iraq (Oates 1968, 1969), marks the end of the Initial Village Period. On the Deh Luran Plain, the CMT has been exposed so far at only Chagha Sefid although the pottery is found at five sites on the plain, including Ali Kosh, where a few sherds on the surface hint that a small settlement there may have eroded away entirely (Hole 1977a:12–13)—(figure 7).

The CMT signals both a change in economy and an increase in the number of known sites. The traditional local economy changes with the introduction of six-row hulled barley, free-threshing hexaploid wheat, large-seeded lentil and flax, and domestic cattle and dogs. The new crops are thought to be associated with irrigation agriculture and probably with changes in social organization. The CMT also introduces a disconformity in the ceramics, which implies a change in manufacturing techniques and, possibly, the movement of new people to the plain. As I have reconstructed the events, people exploiting irrigation moved into regions that were suitable for this intensive agriculture, displacing the traditional local economies (Hole 1977a:35–36). At the moment, continuities in other artifacts throughout the sequence suggest that the dramatic economic shift took place without completely disrupting local traditions. Dollfus (n.d.) reports a similar situation in Susiana. However, more extensive exposure of the CMT at the point of contact with the previous Surkh Phase would help clarify this issue.

Subsequently there is essential continuity in the ceramic—and by implication, cultural—development through the remainder of the Village Period. Thus, although we can distinguish phases based on changes in ceramics, we must remember that one phase grades into the next.

The Sabz Phase occurs in Chagha Sefid where it was exposed in only limited fashion. It also appears at the base of Tepe Sabz where, in 1963, Neely excavated a 3-meter-wide step-trench into the steeply eroded south face of the site (Hole, Flannery, and Neely 1969:50–64). The trench provided the first stratified sequence of Village Period material from the area. Although it was not clear at the time, the four phases delineated at Tepe Sabz were equivalent only to the Early and Middle Village periods. Later, Wright's work at Farukhabad clarified the Early Late Village Period, but the final phases, coeval with Susa A and Terminal Susa A (locally called the Sargarab Phase), have not yet been excavated on the plain.

Materials dating to the Sabz Phase occurred at the base of Tepe Sabz. The site is important for its evidence (fortuitously preserved by fossilization) of irrigation, as inferred from the large flax seeds, seeds of six-row hulled barley, hexaploid wheat, lentils, and domesticated dogs, domestic cattle, and Susiana buffware pottery (Hole, Flannery, and Neely 1969:55–57; Helbaek 1969:408). In the narrow trench, the 1.5 meters of Sabz Phase deposit consisted exclusively of midden without traces of architecture. Among changes in artifacts was the replacement of the previously fine technique of chipping chert with a relatively crude method based on different source material, and the concomitant reduction in amount of chipped stone. Little obsidian is found in these deposits, suggesting a cessation of whatever trade or exchange networks had served the area for the previous two millennia (Renfrew 1977:307). Eight sites, five of them on the western side of the plain, are attributed to the Sabz Phase.

The Khazineh Phase is revealed in 3 meters of deposit, about half of which is midden. The remainder exhibit traces of stone-founded architecture, but no coherent plans of rooms. For the most part, there is continuity in the ceramics and here we find the first local evidence of coiled basketry, a technique found much earlier in northern Mesopotamia.

The Middle Village Period: Mehmeh, Bayat, and Farukh Phases

Each of the phases contributes information of interest even though the excavated areas are all small. Mehmeh deposits, which have been dug at both Tepe Sabz and in a small sounding at Musiyan, illustrate well the uniformity of the ceramic changes on either side of the plain. The agricultural components of the two sites, including irrigation, were essentially identical: linseed, lentil, and hexaploid wheat (Helbaek 1969:411). Unlike the situation in the Initial Village Period, different sites did not follow substantially different mixes of subsistence activities (Hole, Flannery, and Neely 1969:361–63).

A Mehmeh Phase house was also found on the surface of a site near Tepe Sabz where that phase was exposed by erosion of the surface of the site. The stone-founded building was easily mapped and proved to have the same kind of construction and layout, insofar as that could be determined at Tepe Sabz, as the short segments of walls found in the excavation. In general plan the layout resembles that of a tent rather than a mud-walled house (Hole 1974), although clearly mud walling accounts for a substantial component of the height of Tepe Sabz. This raises again the question of transhumant pastoralists on the plain and perhaps their seasonal residence at settled villages, a practice found in the area today. Without more exposure of these deposits, we have no secure grounds for further inferences. Certainly a fully effective and quite modern-looking agriculture and stock-herding was practiced. By this time the crudely chipped stone hoes of the Mohammad Jaffar and Sabz phases are being replaced with finely chipped and polished implements, presumably now to break clods and perhaps to dig small canals.

The Bayat Phase is most notable for documenting the final occupation of Tepe Sabz, an event that is made more meaningful through the botanical remains. According to Helbaek (Hole, Flannery, and Neely 1969:364; Woosley and Hole 1978), environmental deterioration in the vicinity of the site may have contributed to its abandonment, a situation similar to that he found at Ali Kosh. The inference is that two thousand years of continued use of the site and the surrounding premises led to a buildup of salts, for the plants most in evidence at the end are those that are most resistant to saline conditions. Although Kirkby (1977:255) maintains that the plain is not usually subjected to salinization, Helbaek (1969:406) points out that the irrigation water for Tepe Sabz came from the spring above Deh Luran, a source which may be considerably more saline than water derived from the large rivers or more ephemeral surface run-off.

In the excavation at Farukhabad, carried out in 1968 under the supervision of Henry Wright, deposits of the Farukh Phase were exposed in two trenches, separated by 45 meters (Wright 1981b:figure B). The trenches, whose widths were 5 meters each, were cut into the steep, eroded face of the site overlooking the Mehmeh River. Trench A, which penetrated into late Bayat levels (33–37), included a long series of Farukh Phase (levels 23–31). Trench B contained only Farukh Phase in its lowest levels (37–47). Earlier deposits on the site were not excavated.

Although little architecture is exposed, in the Farukh levels of Trench A, there is a thick-walled building on a brick platform in levels 32–29, which Wright (1981b:19) regards as a "public" building. At least one other structure in Trench A (layers 23–22) was also founded on a brick platform, apparently in contrast to the thinner-walled buildings of Trench B. Thus there is a suggestion, further supported by the finding of conical cups in a hallway of the large building, of elite activities in Trench A. These unbroken cups were found in a building that had been well cleaned in antiquity (Wright 1981b:19). Another line of evidence pointing to elite activities in the Farukh Phase is the fact that gazelle bones were unusually abundant in Trench A, whereas equid bones were found chiefly in Trench B (Redding 1981:259). Wright thinks the building with thick walls found in Zone A3 at Tepe Sabz (Hole, Flannery, and Neely 1969:figure 18, 61–64) is an earlier manifestation of an elite residence or public building.

The Late Village Period: Susa A and Terminal Susa A/Sargarab

The major deficiency in our knowledge of Deh Luran now is the lack of any excavation of a Susa A site. From Susiana, we know what to expect in the ceramics, but it would be helpful to excavate one or more of the local sites. Musiyan would be particularly interesting, because it was a large site and perhaps a temple center. Information from Musiyan might contribute to an understanding of the hierarchical social relations of the time and of the circumstances that led to the drastic reduction of local population at the end of the period. Some sherds from this site are identical to the early burial wares from Susa, but it is not clear whether the final Susa A is represented.

Chronologically the next archaeological remains are found at two small sites in the upper piedmont steppe zone of the plain. Neither has been excavated. One of the sites, Sargarab, exposed at the surface, was a small community (Wright et al. 1975: figure 3) that had made extensive efforts to control water and erosion with terraces and check dams. The ceramics here have highland affinities and Wright et al. (1975) have suggested that highland people actually intruded, perhaps forcibly, into Deh Luran at the end of the Susa A Phase. Whatever the case, these Sargarab sites have nothing evident to do with the previous local traditions and they seem to mark the transition into the Early Uruk. Wright et al. (1975:111–12) regard the Sargarab sites as Terminal Ubaid or, in Susiana terms, Terminal Susa A because of the continuation of certain vessel forms. However, the dominant aspect is one of difference from Susa A, particularly in the lack of painted decoration and in the presence of finger-impressed wares.

Settlement History

Figures 7, 8, and table 5 illustrate the changes and continuity in settlement during the Village Period. We have briefly mentioned the gradual increase in numbers of sites that began with the CMT, but it is worth looking more closely at the changes, especially those occurring in the Middle and Late Village periods. The CMT is found at five sites, of which four are on the eastern side of the plain; Chagha Sefid is the lone exception. During the subsequent Sabz Phase, the western side of the plain is also occupied; and by the Khazineh Phase, the twenty villages are scattered across the entire plain. Most of these are small and only one is a terminal occupation at its location. The same situation occurs during the Mehmeh Phase, but during the Bayat the pattern changes: for the first time, two of the sites are larger than 3 hectares in extent. Another large site is on the Chikad River some 25 kilometers to the east. (This site is outside the area shown in figures 7, 8.) On the plain itself, Tepe Sabz and Musiyan are the centers of population. During the succeeding Farukh Phase, for which we have thirteen sites, there are large centers at Farukhabad and Musiyan and again at the site on the Chikad River. At a small site near Farukhabad, Wright found a stamp seal which suggests the possibility that the site had been the location of an elite residence. As Wright (1981b:67) reconstructs it, Farukh Phase society has "settlements varying from a few very small ones without ranking figures [people of high social rank] through a greater number of larger settlements which often have ranking figures to a few even larger centers which always have ranking figures."

During the Susa A Phase there are only five sites. Musiyan and a small site a short distance to the north probably contained the bulk of the population. Across the Daiwairij River from Musiyan are two adjacent small sites of Susa A age. The remaining site is in the Shakkar Ab Plain just west of the Mehmeh River. Settlement thus appears to be concentrated in the east, but the most impressive shift has been in the reduction of the number of sites. The location of the few sites suggests that they may have been drawing water off the rivers for irrigation. The site along the Chikad River was no longer occupied.

Table 5 shows a steady decline in the number of sites from a peak in the Khazineh Phase. In part this loss may be offset by an increase in the sizes of a few sites, so that the total population may have remained nearly constant until Susa A. At that time, unless a massive Susa A settlement underlies Musiyan—an unlikely possibility in view of intensive surface survey (Wright 1981b:70)—we must accept that there was a decline in sedentary population. Interestingly, all five Susa A sites had been occupied during the preceding Farukh Phase, so that Susa A is the only phase in which new sites were not founded. A parallel reduction in numbers of sites occurred in Susiana and appears to be part of a widespread phenomenon that we do not yet understand.

Finally, in the Sargarab Phase there are only two sites, both in the upper central steppe near the town of Deh Luran where there had previously been little settlement. Wright et al. (1975:111) suggest highland affinities for these sites which may have intruded upon a nearly empty plain or, alternatively, may represent a separate, contemporary component that coexisted with Susa A.

The changes in settlement during the Village Period may have come about for environmental, social, or technological reasons. Whatever specific factors may have led to the dramatic decline in numbers of sites at the end of the period, this effect was only symptomatic of an underlying instability of settlement in which more than 20 percent of the sites in each period changed status (table 5). The sites averaged 2.5 periods of occupation each, and only a few sites were occupied through as many as five phases (table 6).

We know little about environmental change, except as it pertains to the immediate vicinity of a few sites. Kirkby (1977:253) maintains that the plain can sustain irrigation agriculture without becoming excessively saline, but the botanical remains of the Bayat Phase indicated to both Helbaek (1969:422) and Woosley (Woosley and Hole 1978:66) that degradation of the immediate environment occurred. In spite of this, there should have been ample room on the plain for continued successful agriculture if people had simply moved their sites periodically. Shifting settlement within rather strict environmental boundaries was the norm, a practice that is consistent with the hypothesis that the people practiced irrigation agriculture.

The need for irrigation required the placement of villages near potential sources of water from canals. The first sources in the CMT and Sabz phases were apparently the natural channels carrying rain water from the piedmont. As early as the Khazineh Phase and continuing through the Farukh, we see probable use of canals carrying water from the Mehmeh and perhaps Daiwairij rivers, as well as continued use of the natural runoff channels elsewhere on the plain. By Susa A, the latter may no longer have been sufficient. The Sargarab pattern is a radical change and must represent an entirely different kind of agricultural economy. At this time the flat, fine-grained alluvial soils were eschewed for relatively rocky, granular locations on the upper plain, much less favorable for agriculture than any of the previous by occupied sites.

To suggest a natural—as opposed to man-induced—environmental change is appropriate even though the means to test the idea are presently beyond us. Deh Luran is marginal agricultural land today because of the lack of rainfall; more particularly, because of variability in the quantity and annual onset and distribution of rainfall. Slight changes from year to year can have dire consequences for people who depend on rainfall agriculture, and these changes can be equally serious for irrigators whose canals depend on runoff channels. During years of low rainfall, the Mehmeh and Daiwairij rivers are extremely saline even during the growing season (Hole, Flannery, and Neely 1969:20).

A shift toward somewhat drier conditions, as some have posited, could have rendered much of the Deh Luran Plain unsuitable for settled agriculture and accelerated any potential development of the herding sector. Until environmental changes have been ruled out, they would seem the most likely causes of the decline in number of sites and (apparently) in overall population during the fifth millennium and continuing into the first half of the fourth.

Whatever natural environmental changes may have occurred, one cannot ignore social factors as evidenced in the emergence of large sites (centers). This happened first in the Bayat Phase, when we also have our first evidence of emerging status differences in the form of thick-walled buildings and seals and their impressions. There appears to be a center with satellite villages on each side of the plain. The growth of a similar site on the Chikad River, not to mention the

centers in Susiana itself, signals a new demographic and social situation. In Bayat times, the massive constructions at Chogha Mish on the Susiana Plain and the later ones at Susa demonstrate that the days of the undifferentiated, self-sufficient villages on Khuzistan had passed.

The Susa A phase on the Deh Luran Plain is the last expression of this social system whose roots were in the Initial Village Period. The remaining population clustered around Musiyan, a thriving Susa A settlement, replete with monumental architecture and some of the Susa burial pottery. The remainder of the plain may well have been taken over by pastoralists so that settlement may have been as it was in the mid-twentieth century: a townlike center, a few villages, and the sites of numerous seasonal pastoral camps. In the long run, for environmental reasons, this is an enduring system.

In chapter 4, Johnson discusses changes in Uruk Period settlement in Susiana which are superficially similar to those of earlier Deh Luran. There, competing centers emerged as Susa became the preeminent site. In Deh Luran there may have been competition between sites in the two halves of the plain, but it is not at all clear that those on the west side "lost" to the rising fortunes of Musiyan. Rather it seems as if half of the system simply disappeared. The villagers could not have emigrated to Susiana because that plain also suffered a decline in population despite the brilliance of Susa itself.

The Susiana Plain

The oil-rich province of Khuzistan is also the most productive agricultural plain of Iran. This plain, a smaller Mesopotamia, lies between the Karkheh and the Karun rivers at an elevation of between 40 and 170 meters above sea level (figures 6, 9, 10). For the periods of concern here, its upper boundary merges with the first major range of the Zagros Mountains, while the lower edge is defined by the Haft Tepe ridge. In all, this area encompasses some 1,500 square kilometers.

This major agricultural plain has seen archaeological investigations for more than one hundred years. Rawlinson (1839) and Loftus (1857) preceded the French who took up residence at Susa in 1897, and carried out a survey of the western part of the plain and adjoining areas such as Deh Luran (Morgan 1900). Following the initial surveys, which were usually augmented with soundings, the French devoted most of their efforts to historic periods at Susa and Chogha Zanbil, leaving further work at the prehistoric villages to a few seasons of investigations at Jaffarabad, Jowi, Bendebal, and Bouhallan (Mecquenem 1928; LeBreton 1947, 1957). Recently the first three of these sites have been reexcavated to clarify their stratification and architecture (Dollfus 1978, 1983).

Robert McC. Adams (1962) initiated the modern era of investigations with his extensive survey of the entire plain. Hole followed up on Adams's work (1969b) explicitly to try to find early prehistoric sites. Since then, other major surveys have been conducted by Wenke (1975–76), Wright (unpublished), Carter (1970, 1971), Schacht (1976), and Johnson (1973), each focusing on different periods. In addition to these investigations, an American team under the direction of the late Pierre Delougaz and Helene Kantor has dug extensively at Chogha Mish and made smaller soundings at two nearby sites, Boneh Fazili and Chogha Bonut. As yet, little has been published of this work. Hole (1974, 1975b) briefly tested a pastoral tent site called Tula'i, and Harvey Weiss (1972) excavated at a village site in the northeast quadrant of the plain.

Despite the wealth of sites (some 150 pertinent to the Village periods, many of them of impressive size), and despite the long history of investigations, relatively little of substance has yet been published of most excavations. Nevertheless, the excavations provide invaluable information on chronology that enables us to make use of the survey data to reconstruct a picture of changes in settlement and society over some 2,500 years (table 7).

For purposes of illustration here, I have divided the Susiana sequence into four parts, corresponding to accepted periodization of the plain and to the broad periods that I use to describe changes in each of the surveyed regions. We should regard this chronological picture for Susiana as only a rough indication, for a considerably refined periodization is currently under development by Hole and Dollfus. The general picture will remain the same, but we will be able to see the onset of changes more clearly in the projected version.

The four parts of the sequence encompass the first sedentary villages, the growth of population, the spectacular temple center at Susa, and the subsequent abrupt demise of the society that built it. The Initial Village Period, known locally as the Archaic, was defined by Kantor (1974) to accommodate deposits that contained a soft-ware pottery. She recognized three distinct ceramic phases and one preceramic within this period. Next comes the Jaffarabad (our Early Village Period), during which the buff wares that came to characterize the Susiana Plain were first produced. From this time onward, we find a marked increase in the numbers of villages. The Jaffarabad Phase is followed by the Chogha Mish Phase (our Middle Village Period), a transition distinguished by changes in ceramics. During this span, the number of sites reaches its maximum and a central place, Chogha Mish,

emerges. The Late Village Period, the Susa Phase, is also defined on the basis of ceramic changes, and it sees a decline in the number of sites and the shift of the center from Chogha Mish to Susa. By 4000 B.C., this period was entering its terminal phase. The last expression of the well-known Black-on-Buff ceramics is found in a handful of sites that we call Terminal Susa A. After this, a complete change of ceramics, of settlement pattern, and of site hierarchies replaces the previous patterns. This episode, known as the Uruk Period, is discussed in chapter 4.

Although there are some striking changes in material remains over this span of 2,500–3,000 years, one is impressed most by the evident continuity of culture as it is expressed in the ceramics and settlement patterns. Indigenous development rather than abrupt changes are characteristic despite some suggestions at one time or another of exogenous influences, particularly in the form of traded goods.

The Initial Village Period

At present, four early sites have been excavated: Chogha Mish, Boneh Fazili, Chogha Bonut, and Tula'i. Chiefly through the work of Delougaz and Kantor (Kantor 1974), we are able to discern two ceramic phases within the early sites, and at least one preceramic phase. Because little of the material from these sites has yet been published, we can refer to them only as ceramic styles.

Tula'i (Hole 1974, 1975b), which was only briefly tested, is a herders' camp. Whether it represents full-scale nomadic life completely separated from villages is problematic, but at the least, it is a seasonal camp. Pires-Ferreira (1975–1977) suggests that it was a "village based fallow herd" camp where a group of livestock were kept separated from the "subsistence herd" at a village. Her interpretation was based upon the survivorship curves of animals at Chagha Sefid and Tula'i, in particular the low infant mortality at Tula'i. The small number of bones in her analysis from Tula'i are, unfortunately, lumped from several loci, and Pires-Ferreira is evidently not aware that livestock in Iran can have two distinct breeding seasons. The implication that Tula'i represents a nomad fallow herd camp is, therefore, suspect.

In all, there are twenty-five sites on the Susiana Plain that have ceramics of one or another of the periods; three more sites are suggested only by flints (figure 9). These early sites are more widely dispersed than are sites of the later Susiana phases, but we can make little of this distribution because there is high probability that we have overlooked many sites, for the same reasons as in Deh Luran. Although the time encompassed by these early villages with ceramics may be 1,500 years or more, the paucity of diagnostic sherds makes it difficult to tell from surface indications alone when, during this period, the sites were occupied.

In view of the potential of the Susiana Plain for early agricultural settlement, it is disappointing that the excavations have not provided more definitive information. A faunal report was written for Tula'i and a brief botanical one for the two sites near Susa, but none of these reports is definitive (Miller 1983, Pires-Ferreira 1975–77) because of problems with sample sizes and contexts. Chogha Mish has a large settlement, as do the nearby sites of Chogha Bonut and Boneh Fazili. Nowhere else in western Iran have we found three thriving sites of the Initial Village Period in such close proximity, although this may be simply an accident of discovery.

The Early Village Period: Jaffarabad Phase

The Jaffarabad Phase, first revealed in Levels 6–4 at the eponymous site, has also been uncovered at Jowi (Dollfus 1977, 1983a), and Chogha Mish and Boneh Fazili (Delougaz and Kantor 1971, 1972, 1974, 1975). The only coherent plans published so far come from Jaffarabad (Dollfus 1975, 1983b), where the early settlement covered about 2,000 square meters. This settlement saw three major rebuildings; the latest of which, level 4, was considerably reduced in size. At about the time Jaffarabad was abandoned, Jowi was founded some 3 kilometers to the north, perhaps by people from Jaffarabad. At present count, sixteen sites on the plain have pottery like that at Jaffarabad.

The architecture of this phase is defined by large dwelling rooms or halls associated with smaller storage facilities in a highly nucleated settlement (Dollfus 1975: figures 6–8;1983), leaving very little open space in the site. Some of the building complexes had buttressed walls, features also seen in the contemporary Late Samarran of eastern Iraq and CMT of Deh Luran; but the buildings and artifacts are those associated with ordinary domestic activities. A kiln for making pottery and a possible figurine workshop are the only evidence of craft activities. Simple potter's marks appear on the bottoms of some vessels, but these are more common later at Jowi (Dollfus and Encreve 1982). While silos or storage bins imply well-developed agriculture, the report on the botanical remains does not inform on the question of irrigation.

There are burials of two infants and one child, possibly placed in the corners of abandoned structures at Jaffarabad. The bodies were extended and oriented north-south. One of the infants had large sherds of common pottery under its head and the other was covered with red ochre. The lack of interments in the villages during this phase implies burial practices that are presently beyond our ability to perceive.

The settlement at Jowi covered approximately 1 to 1.5 hectares and consisted of buildings similar to those at Jaffarabad and Chogha Mish. At Chogha Mish, the largest site on the plain at 3.5–4.5 hectares (Kantor, personal communication), in the midst of large multi-room houses, Delougaz and Kantor (1975:95) found a brick platform of uncertain use, 8 by 6 meters in extent. Despite the lack of complete plans of the villages other than Jaffarabad, an underlying similarity is evident in construction techniques and agglomeration of rooms in the architectural units with contemporary dwellings at Sawwan and Chogha Mami. Dollfus (1983b) infers that extended families lived in these multi room houses.

The Middle Village Period: Chogha Mish Phase

During the Chogha Mish Phase, the number of sites on the Susiana Plain reached a maximum. At this time solid evidence exists of nondomestic architectural units and of functional differentiation among sites. Jaffarabad, Chogha Mish, and Bendebal provide the information; here we will consider that Qabr Sheykheyn is transitional to the Susa Phase.

During the Chogha Mish Phase at Jaffarabad, the site may have been used solely for manufacture of pottery, for it contains only pottery kilns and some fragmentary traces of architecture (Dollfus 1975). According to Kantor (personal communication), the pottery that was fired at Jaffarabad is identical to that recovered from an adult's grave at Chogha Mish (cf. Delougaz and Kantor 1975:94).

At Chogha Mish, buildings of the phase covered the entire site making it, at 11 hectares, the largest site of its time in Susiana. In several trenches these deposits have revealed mostly domestic architecture with associated pottery kilns (Delougaz and Kantor 1972:89–91, 1975:95). However, in Trench IX, there is a monumental building and perhaps much more extensive architectural remains that were destroyed by an intense fire. The area has been only briefly tested and is not yet well described except for the plan of the large building (Kantor 1976:27–28, figure 11). This building, whose exterior walls are 1–2 meters thick, may have been buttressed and may have had a second story. Along one side, solid brickwork extending some 15 meters may have been a platform or terrace adjacent to the building. The building is at least 10 by 15 meters with many small rooms inside. One of these rooms was filled with stacked ovoid storage jars and "eighteen complete unpainted bowls were clustered at the base of the structure's western wall, on the exterior side" (Kantor 1976:27–28). A large quantity of flint nodules and some blades suggest the use of one room for working flint.

Although they are sparse, the published findings imply that Chogha Mish was a center of regional importance. It remains to be determined how large and

Frank Hole

extensive the elaborate architectural precinct is and precisely what activities occurred there. Uses as an administrative and temple center have been suggested (Kantor 1976:28), but neither can be demonstrated on the basis of presently available evidence. The conflagration, which preserved walls up to near ceiling height, occurred at the end of the Chogha Mish Phase. Subsequent occupation of the site was confined to the high northern eminence.

The recent work at Bendebal has also revealed deposits of Chogha Mish Phase, chiefly of domestic structures, some with kilns (Dollfus 1983b:figure 8). Among these layers are seven tombs, all of infants or children, probably interred in abandoned rooms or open spaces, but further information on these is not yet available. Beneath the levels that have been sounded by Dollfus, a cleaning of Mecquenem's trench shows a massive brick construction of earlier Chogha Mish age. It is impossible at present to say whether this structure corresponds with the burned complex at Chogha Mish, but the slight evidence suggests that Bendebal is somewhat earlier.

There are a number of burials in sites of the Chogha Mish Phase, all of them apparently late in the phase. At Jaffarabad an adult, accompanied by a goblet and small jar, was interred in a brick tomb. Similar burials occur in Bendebal and Jowi, evidently with the same kinds of grave goods (Dollfus 1975:48, footnote 34; 1977:171; 1983a:141–43, figure 53). Another grave of the same age, at Chogha Mish, has an adult in an extended position accompanied by an unpainted beaker and a small jar (Delougaz and Kantor 1975:94, figures 3, 4). At Qabr Sheykeyn—also Late Chogha Mish/Early Susa Phase—Weiss (1972) reports finding an adult, extended on its back with a buff cup and a red pot; two infants also occurred in the deposits.

The pottery accompanying all of these burials is late Chogha Mish Phase, an important fact in consideration of the later Susa Phase burials: for the only adults so far reported from the Susa Phase are in the cemetery at Susa, but the style of burial is the same as for children. The late Chogha Mish Phase interments seem to mark the beginning of a consistent style of burials for certain adults and children which is manifest best at Susa—a tomb of sun-dried bricks, and a body extended on its back accompanied by pottery.

The Late Village Period:
Susa A and Terminal Susa A

Qabr Sheykheyn bridges the transition between the Chogha Mish and Susa phases. Harvey Weiss (1972) excavated this site in 1971 to test the hypothesis that certain sites consisted of a single architectural unit on an eminence. I suggested that these might be analogous to "Khan's houses" (Hole 1969a). A report on

the excavations has not been published, but Weiss's preliminary report indicates that a single large domestic structure occupied the site. Dollfus (1983b:297), however, questions whether other buildings may have eroded away. Thus, the actual nature of this house remains to be determined.

The Susa Phase is best known architecturally from Jaffarabad where there was a small domestic settlement of twenty-five to thirty persons contemporary and similar to a village at nearby Bendebal. For this period, Dollfus (1983b:299) infers nuclear family residences. The architecture at Jaffarabad consists of a series of rooms with fireplaces and kitchen debris surrounding a central court. Two children were buried in bricked tombs. One of the tombs contained three ceramic vessels and a seal; the other, a single vessel. Mecquenem (1935:102) reported finding pottery in tombs of children, as well as a copper disk, but copper has not yet been found in any of the recent excavations.

Although the architecture at Jaffarabad appears to be mundane and domestic, the site contains fine painted ceramics (but not in the tombs), seals, figurines, pointed ceramic rings, and "clous," perforated ceramic cones. These items are found also at Bendebal and Susa in contemporary layers and may relate to special elite or cultic activities. In view of the large buildings of the Chogha Mish Phase, to say nothing about the imposing edifice at Susa in the Susa Phase (see below), one can hardly deny elite activity in Khuzistan; but demonstrating the association of any particular set of objects with it is not easy. The modest domestic context at Jaffarabad, if anything, argues against the association with rank distinctions, but not necessarily against ceremonial or cultic activities.

At Susa itself, the high platform stands alone among the ancient monuments of its time. This platform, which was partially destroyed in the earlier work of Morgan, is some 10 to 11 meters high and roughly 70 meters on a side. As the interior has not been penetrated, it is not clear whether the platform is the result of one or of many periods of construction. This platform was built upon thin debris of the first settlement of Susa. Adjacent to it was a cemetery that contained an estimated one thousand or more burials (Morgan 1912:7), most of which contained pottery. The platform itself was faced with brick into which were set four rows of ceramic cylinders with flared, pierced heads ("clous"). At some time during its use, the platform was destroyed by fire, its facade crumbling and covering over the cemetery area. During the Susa Phase, there was apparently a domestic settlement at the site and some structures atop the platform itself (Stève and Gasche 1971); but neither of these has yet been excavated over a large enough area to enable a reconstruction of the settlement or the uses of the buildings, and the structures atop the platform were largely destroyed by later occupants.

The cemetery at the base of the platform is near its southwest corner, but as only one face of the platform has been exposed at all, it is possible that more burials can be found. At any rate, the ceramics from the burials date to the earlier part of the Susa Phase (Hole 1983). For the moment, this is the only cemetery as such from a settlement of this period in Iran, although the two cemeteries of Hakalan and Parchineh (probably those of transhumant pastoralists) are of similar age, and there are cemeteries at other major sites such as Eridu in Mesopotamia (Lloyd and Safar 1947, 1948; Safar et al. 1981). Whatever the status of this cemetery at Susa in relation to the isolated burials in the villages, it clearly contained bodies representing a wide social spectrum, from those who had ordinary, coarse cooking pots, to those with extraordinary pieces of ceramic art and hordes of copper. A full publication of the material from this cemetery is in progress (Hole).

The only other excavated site of importance for this phase is Chogha Mish. The occupation here is said to have been confined to the highest part of the site (and this was much reduced from its previous size), but little has yet been published of this (Delougaz and Kantor 1971:39).

A "Terminal Susa A" has been advanced by Johnson (1973:68) and Wright and Johnson (1975) on the basis of excavations in the Acropole at Susa and at Tall-i Ghazir, near Ram Hormuz. At both sites there are levels in which the fine painted wares are found in association with coarse wares that anticipate the forms of Early Uruk. Johnson (1973:82) lists eighteen sites with this ceramic complex.

The Late Village Period Settlement

Until the results of the careful stratigraphic work at Jaffarabad, Jowi, and Bendebal have been incorporated into the analysis of sherds from survey (a project now in progress by Hole and Dollfus), it is premature to attempt a detailed discussion of changing settlement for the entire Village Period. However, we can examine the Late Village Period relatively closely. During the transitional period between the Chogha Mish and Susa phases (conventionally known as Susiana d), 86 sites dotted the plain (figure 9). During the earlier and later parts of the Susa Phase, there were 58 and 31 sites, respectively; and in Terminal Susa A, only 18 sites (Hole 1977b; Johnson 1973:68)—(figure 8). In other words, beginning with the end of the Chogha Mish Phase, the number of sites declined markedly and steadily until, during Terminal Susa A, it had dropped to its lowest point since the Early Village Period. Since all of the sites except Susa were very small, it is clear that the sedentary population was markedly reduced. This naturally raises the question of a transhumant population but, as Wright discusses (chapter 5), there is little direct evidence one way or the other.

My analysis of the changes in settlement during the Susa Phase reveals some informative aspects. First, sites were often occupied for only short periods, then abandoned for a time and reoccupied. About half the sites changed status from occupied to unoccupied or vice versa in each of my distinguishable subperiods, implying that settlements were unstable and that land was not particularly scarce and therefore not valuable (table 8). Second, with the exception of Susa and Chogha Mish, the sites were uniformly small, well under two hectares, although there is a slight tendency for sites that were occupied longer to be larger (table 9). Finally, at many sites the distinctive fancy ceramics of the types found in the burials appear to be missing. Assuming that these ceramics imply an elite status, these statuses were not present at each site. The fact that these ceramics occur at even the smallest sites indicates, however, that size of site does not automatically inform on the nature of the social distinctions within.

Despite the impressive changes in numbers of sites during the Village Period, there are no appreciable differences in distribution of sites, but there are some trends in terms of location on the Susiana Plain (table 10). We can illustrate this by dividing the plain into three roughly equal parts, bounded on the west by the Karkheh, on the east by the Karun, on the north by the rocky upper plain (roughly the present Dizful-Shushtar highway), and on the south by the Haft Tepe ridge. The central part is bounded by the Diz and Shur rivers (figure 9). Beyond this central area, there are also sites on the northern and southern peripheries, and west of the Karkheh.

In order to illustrate the trends in settlement, I have tabulated the occurrence of sites in each region from the Early Village through Uruk periods. The major trend is the increase in proportion of sites in the western zone and the compensatory decline in sites in the central and eastern regions. The peripheral areas were never important. If we look more closely at the subperiod breakdown, the move toward the western zone occurs principally in the Susa Period, whereas earlier there had been a much more uniform distribution across all three zones of the plain. This change, which continues to be expressed throughout the Uruk, may relate to a changing emphasis on irrigation agriculture and pastoralism, for the eastern zone is the least suited to irrigation because of a rolling topography, but it is well suited to herding and dry farming on a limited scale. Thus, an intensification of irrigation would have favored increased settlements in the central and western zones, whereas herding would have been expanded most readily in the east where it did not compete with irrigation agriculture.

Admitting the uncertainties about estimating site sizes from surface occurrences, with a few possible exceptions, I estimate that all of the sites were well under 2 hectares and often less than a hectare. The major exceptions are Chogha Mish and Susa in their successive phases. These sites were in the range of 15 hectares and qualify both as centers and as primate sites (see chapters 4 and 6 for further discussion of these terms). Sometime after Chogha Mish burned, the site was essentially abandoned and Susa was founded. Its temple also burned but was rebuilt and eventually went out of use. As a center, Susa is odd for it is located on the edge of the plain rather than, as Chogha Mish, near its geographical center (albeit on the northern end). This raises the possibility that both sites served interests that are not represented solely in the villages of the plain, such as a pastoral population along the banks of the Karkheh and along the northern steppe fringing the mountains.

On the basis of survey data alone, it is difficult to interpret the nature of a relatively dispersed settlement system. It is clear that there was a temple center at Susa but it is quite unclear what its effect was on any individual settlement. With a "span of control" (see Johnson, chapter 4) of fifty to seventy sites (the number of sites under its "authority") and considering the distances to remote sites, its leaders could have effected only the most minimal control on the region generally, although as a shrine it may have commanded devout allegiance. Local leadership must have been, as it is in many societies today, vested in the heads of households. At this time, as I remarked in regard to instability of settlement, land was not scarce and could not have been held for economic and political advantage (C. Smith 1976). Therefore, leaders would probably have been elders with large families. Such persons might reside in a large and prominent dwelling of the type called today "Khan's house." The earlier burnt house at Chogha Mish and the large house at Qabr Sheykeyn conform with this idea, but it remains to be seen whether buildings of this sort occur in isolation on the tops of certain sites as I proposed (Hole 1969b).

To continue with the settlement system, we have a center at Susa and elite residences at scattered sites. Other sites, for the most part, are therefore residential and nonelite. I propose that there are also "manufactories," sites at which certain crafts such as pot making or basket making, flint knapping, cheese making, and so forth were practiced (Hole 1983). A site of this type would be Jaffarabad during the Chogha Mish Phase when it consisted solely of ceramic kilns. Depending on the distribution of raw products and the development of market proclivities, there might have been a large number of such specialist sites which could, of course, have occurred at residential villages and herding camps as well. Finally, we must consider the pastoral component. Although we lack any direct evidence of it during this period on the Susiana Plain, a well-developed pastoral economy in western Iran is implied by the tombs in the mountains of Pushti-Kuh.

We are thus able to enumerate a series of plausible components in a settlement system without yet being able to delineate the ties between them as seen in archaeological evidence. Nor, despite the evident eminence of a Susa or Chogha Mish, are we able to infer accurately whether there existed any sort of formally recognized governing body over the Susiana Plain. Although the evidence is fundamentally deficient, it would seem to me that it is most economical to argue for a loosely organized social system in which there were significant differences of status among individuals, but in which villages were largely autonomous (Hole 1983, and chapter 3, this volume). The Uruk system as outlined by Johnson in chapter 4 is a drastic reformulation of late Susiana organization.

The Mountains of Kurdistan and Luristan

Falling roughly between the Lake Urmia basin and the broad plains of Mahidasht, these mountains have been traditional grazing lands for Kurdi tribes that have few permanent settlements (figures 2, 3).[1] This region has been surveyed only lightly. The few sherds recovered from the Initial and Early Village periods pertain to cultures that are well known from Azerbaijan (Dyson 1961, personal communication; Young, personal communication). Intensive survey might be rewarding, but the region has been largely inaccessible because of the lack of roads and generally unstable political situation.

The Middle to Late Village Period

South and west of the Kurdi area is the Pushti-Kuh region of Luristan and southern Kurdistan (figures 5,6), which falls between the lowland plain of Deh Luran and the western sector of highland plains such as Hulailan and Saimarreh (figures 12, 13). No archaeological settlements have been reported from this mountainous terrain, but Louis Vanden Berghe directed a series of annual campaigns from 1965 until the Iranian revolution, searching for Bronze Age tombs that had escaped looters. In the course of this work he discovered two cemeteries of the Middle to Late Village Period, Hakalan and Parchineh. The latter is quite outside the zone of settlement today, whereas the former is located near the small modern agricultural village of Sarab Maimeh. This rugged region is unsuited to large-scale agriculture and permanent settlement, although small fields can be planted in many places nearby and throughout the Zagros. At neither cemetery is there a prehistoric village so that the bodies interred were almost certainly those of transhumant herders.

Another site, Qaleh Nissar, in what today is Kurdish-speaking territory, contained a Bronze Age cemetery, but the excavators also exposed the stone foundations of a structure that resembles a modern nomad tent site in mode of construction and layout. One room, paved entirely with rough stones, may have been used as a pen for lambs and kids. Vanden Berghe's brief reports on this site attribute the buffware pottery to the late Chalcolithic, roughly equivalent with the Late Village Period (Vanden Berghe 1970a, 1971, 1973b).

These two cemeteries and house constitute our only evidence from this area for the Middle to Late Village herding peoples, but they suggest that it may still be possible to recover a great deal more information. Although the people of Hakalan and Parchineh practiced burial customs similar to those of Susa, their ceramics were stylistically unlike those found at any known village. This implies that they were locally made and that the system in which these people lived was effectively self-sustaining, certainly not requiring trade or exchange of ceramics. If the population was relatively low, cereal needs could have been provided by harvesting wild stands or planting small fields in advantageous spots.

Parchineh, where 156 tombs were opened, is a large burial area whose extent has not yet been determined, but Vanden Berghe (personal communication) estimates that as many as one thousand graves remain to be opened. The tombs consist of stone lined and covered cists large enough to contain an adult lying extended. The cemetery was used for a considerable time, as evidenced by changes in the ceramics and by somewhat different orientations and spacing in different parts of the cemetery; however, the entire occupation was in the range of the Middle to Late Village periods.

Nearly half the tombs lacked any grave goods; the remainder had generally one or more pots and rarely other artifacts such as seals, mace heads, axes, rubbing stones, flints, or beads. There are differences between the two excavated parts of Parchineh, but relatively few tombs stand out for having an unusual quantity of material. A few of the skulls had been trephined: holes 1.5–2.0 centimeters in diameter, were found in five skulls but no other evidence of surgery or pathology was reported.

It is apparent that a few tombs signify high status. For example, B72 contains two alabaster jars, a large pedestaled ceramic bowl, a plain ceramic bowl, and two small stone celts. Both the quantity of goods and the fact that some vessels were of stone make this tomb stand apart from the others. But the implications of this relative richness are by no means clear, for this tomb, like many others, may have been used for more than one burial. When multiple interments occurred, the skeletons of the earlier burials were not always preserved so that accurate body counts cannot be made. Indeed, in most tombs no bones were preserved at all.

At Hakalan, where thirty-six cist tombs in two areas were excavated, considerably higher proportions of these tombs contained artifacts, mostly painted ceramics. In general, the same range of material exists at Hakalan as at Parchineh and some vessels at the two sites are nearly identical. It appears as if Parchineh begins somewhat earlier than does Hakalan but that they overlap for a time, after which Parchineh continues alone. Inasmuch as neither cemetery was entirely dug, this difference in age may be only an artifact of sampling.

There are reasons to believe that the two cemeteries were in the territory of one group. Apart from the obvious similarities in ceramics, the fact that Hakalan is at 1,200 meters and Parchineh 900 meters above sea level suggests that they are close to either end of an annual migration. This does not imply that pastoralists remained in the vicinity of either cemetery for half a year at a time, only that the cemeteries were close enough to summer and winter camping areas, respectively, to render them accessible during those seasons.

Together these sites may imply that some mountainous areas were occupied by herding people who had no permanent villages and came into direct contact with settled farmers only infrequently. The mace heads and small axe-like celts could imply hostile proclivities, but it is equally probable that the maces were most often used against nonhuman predators and the celts to work wood. There is no evidence from this era for the use of pack or riding animals.

Azerbaijan

Surrounding salty Lake Urmia are the mountains and plains which empty their waters into this internal drainage or into the Caspian Sea (figures 2, 11). At an elevation of 1,300 meters, the lake is situated in relatively flat, sometimes marshy, low-lying land which extends back as much as 30 kilometers from its shores.

The Initial Village Period: Hajji Firuz Period

The major excavated site of this period is Hajji Firuz, first visited by Stein (1940:382–404) and later by Burney, Young, and Voigt (all reported in Voigt 1983). Five other excavated sites have Hajji Firuz material at their bases, but little of these has been reported. These sites include Dalma Tepe (Young 1962:707), Hasanlu (Dyson 1967:39), Yanik Tepe

(Burney 1964), and Tepe Seavan (R. S. Solecki 1969). Three of these sites lie on the Solduz Plain, south of the lake. Tepe Seavan lies on the west side, and Yanik Tepe is on the east side of Lake Urmia. Counting sites found on surveys, there are only about a dozen villages of the Hajji Firuz Period, seven of which are in the Solduz-Ushnu Valley. We cannot yet assess how closely the material from either Tepe Seavan or Yanik Tepe compares with Hajji Firuz or, for that matter, what the ages of these sites are. Kearton (1969:189) reports that soft-ware ceramics of the same genre as those at Hajji Firuz "but with significant local variation of surface treatment and design are found throughout western Azerbaijan."

Voigt (1976:279–81) has discussed problems of finding these early sites in Solduz. Burney (1964:55) reports that 4 meters of alluvium have covered the plain surrounding Yanik Tepe since that village was founded. In view of consistent evidence for alluviation around Lake Urmia, it is likely that many sites are buried. Some early sites may be under mounds such as Hasanlu, where Hajji Firuz sherds turned up only in a deep sounding.

Like some other settlements in the Solduz Valley, Hajji Firuz may have been situated on elevated strips of land on an otherwise poorly drained plain (Voigt 1983:281). The village consisted of small, rectangular, separated, single-family dwellings of farmers and herders (for full details see Voigt 1977; 1983:chapter 5). The dead were buried inside the houses, usually after flesh had decomposed. Few goods were associated with the bodies, and there is little sign of wealth or status differences. Only villages, of an estimated one hectare size, are known from this period; no camps or special activity sites have been found.

The economy was mixed farming and herding, including the keeping of pigs, and grain was stored in large pithoi sunk into the floors of houses. Agricultural fields were probably the muddy shores of seasonally filled fresh water basins surrounding the site. Today, irrigation is not essential for farming on the hillside slopes, although grain is usually irrigated on the plain. Young (personal communication) says that local people today prefer the taste of dry-farmed bread wheat but that yields are much lower than for irrigated wheat.

Voigt (1983:324) regards the Hajji Firuz occupations as closely related to the Hassuna of Iraq, but as differing in being more transhumant and generally more conservative. In fact, she argues that there is substantial culture lag in the Solduz region in spite of the demonstrable intercourse (as seen in sherds) between Hassuna sites and Hajji Firuz (Voigt 1983:324). The evidence suggests that there are close resemblances between Hassuna sites and Hajji Firuz in ceramics and houses, although in the high proportion of pigs and in burial practices there appear to be major differences with the Hassuna sites which themselves are not yet published in detail.

On the basis of excavations at Hajji Firuz and Yanik Tepe, the Hajji Firuz Period is dated to about 5200–5500 b.c. A single date obtained by Hole and Flannery from an exposed face of a site near Hajji Firuz (NQ-6) is 6084 ± 216 b.c., clearly out of the range of the other Hajji Firuz and Hassuna dates. The late sixth millennium dates mean that Hajji Firuz is exactly contemporary with Hassuna, as expected from the artifacts.

The low plains around Lake Urmia are generally excellent qishlaq (winter pasture) because snow rarely accumulates in significant depth and the plains are wet enough to support lush vegetation, especially for cattle. Consequently, it is somewhat surprising to find a high proportion of sheep, goats, and pigs but no domestic cattle at Hajji Firuz (Meadow 1983:401). However, this finding is not inconsistent with the idea that Hassuna people who had permanent villages in the lowlands of Iraq moved seasonally into the mountains to graze their sheep and goats. If this practice was followed, some of the people might have settled down eventually, making Solduz their permanent home.

The focal point of Hajji Firuz settlement, as presently known, is the Solduz-Ushnu Valley which is a natural locale for transhumant people because of its routes to the lowlands (Voigt 1983:269–70). In view of this it would be desirable to conduct intensive surveys in border valleys such as Qaleh Paswah. Young (personal communication) reports finding some early sites along the border but that some of the pottery is stylistically different from that known in Solduz.

The Middle Village Period: Dalma Period

Curiously, there appear to be no sites to fill the apparent temporal gap between Hajji Firuz and Dalma, a gap estimated to be on the order of one thousand years. In a report on soundings in Dalma Tepe, Hamlin (1975:120) assigned a date between 5000 and 4000 B.C. to the period, thus taking care of a "gap," but this does not accord with the radiocarbon dates which clearly put Hajji Firuz in the sixth millennium B.C. and Dalma in the fifth. Although the excavations were too small to reveal much about the settlements themselves, they documented a change from predominantly painted ceramics in the lower levels to increasing proportions of wares with impressed, incised, punched, or appliquéd surfaces. A radiocarbon date places the Dalma Period in the late fifth millennium (4036 ± 87 b.c.).

Although the various soundings in Solduz are fairly small, they provide some information on the subsequent development of societies and offer tantalizing hints at future possibilities for investigation. The architecture at Dalma consists of freestanding common domestic structures, within which Young found fourteen burials. "These primary burials consisted of tightly contracted single infants placed in ceramic vessels . . . remains of adult occupants of the Dalma settlement were never found" (Hamlin 1975:115). This suggests the beginning of a pattern of interring adults outside settlements which we see elsewhere (e.g., Yanik Tepe, Burney 1964:56) at the same time.

The Dalma Period is important in western Iran because of the anomalously wider geographic spread of its ceramics in comparison to other ceramic styles. It is confined to the northern and central Zagros Mountains, but it occurs alone in such widely separated mountain plains as the Urmia basin and the Mahidasht and the Kangavar regions. It also occurs in combination with typical Ubaid and Halaf pottery in the Hamrin region of eastern Iraq (Oates 1983:261), and Hamlin (1975:120) points to other wider, but more tenuous ties. Solecki and Solecki (1973) suggest that it was spread by transhumant pastoralists, but this is a hypothesis that must be tested.

The Late Village Period: Pisdeli Period

Following the Dalma sequentially, but not at Dalma itself, is the Pisdeli Period, named after another small mound in the Solduz Valley that was sounded in 1957 and 1958 (Dyson and Young 1960). The Pisdeli ware is a chaff-tempered buff ceramic with designs and shapes in the general style of (Mesopotamian) Ubaid from which it is usually considered to be derived. A somewhat later phase of the tradition occurs at Geoy Tepe where another small sounding penetrated Pisdeli levels at the base of the large mound (Burton-Brown 1951:264). The range of corrected radiocarbon dates for the Pisdeli Period is 4500–3900 B.C. (table 3). Overlying the Pisdeli painted wares, a series of gray wares denote the end of the Village Period and the beginning of traditions which, by virtue of their close relationships with Anatolia and Transcaucasia, will not be discussed in this volume.

Burton-Brown (1950:66) described a find at Geoy Tepe that hints of major differences among coeval sites and of changes in social organization:

> The Ubaid level contained large houses with long storerooms, in one of which was found a row of six buff-ware pithoi whose collars were decorated with a row of dark triangles. Many saucers and several small jars of buff or red ware, the latter sometimes painted with black, were found. Two interesting features were the existence of very large baked bricks and two seal impressions, one of a stamp depicting a deer and its young.

It is well to note that the Ubaid levels are some 17 meters below the summit of the site whose base was never reached. Geoy Tepe clearly was a major site in several periods, a precedent that apparently began as early as the late Pisdeli Period.

These scraps of information indicate that the Urmia basin participated in the same general trends of change and development that characterized the central and southern Zagros, and indeed, Mesopotamia, at the same time.

The Mahidasht Region of the Central Zagros

This region consists of a series of valleys along the western half of the Khorasan Road, or Great High Road, which is the natural route from Baghdad to Hamadan: Shahabad, Zibiri, Mahidasht, and Kermanshah (figures 12, 13). To these we should add the Hulailan and Shian valleys, just to the south of Mahidasht and Shahabad, respectively. This area includes southern Kurdistan and the buffer between it and Luristan, inhabited today in part by people who speak Laki. The valleys of the Mahidasht region range in elevation from 1,300 meters (Kermanshah) to 900 meters (Hulailan).

This region has been visited intermittently by archaeologists since Stein's week-long survey of the Kermanshah Plain in 1936 (Stein 1940:412–21). In the same year, Schmidt (1940:46–7, 80–91) landed on the Mahidasht Plain during his aerial reconnaissance of Iran. The first systematic surveys were carried out under the direction of Braidwood during the 1959–60 season. His survey teams collected only Village Period sites and worked quickly through the Karind, Shahabad, Shian, Zibiri, Mahidasht, and Kermanshah plains (Braidwood 1960a, 1960b, 1961; Braidwood, Howe, and Negahban 1960; Braidwood, Howe, and Reed 1961). The most recent work has focused on the Mahidasht (Levine and McDonald 1977) where the Royal Ontario Museum has carried out surveys, small excavations, and geomorphological studies (Brookes, Levine, and Dennell 1982).

The Initial Village Period: Neolithic

Initial Period settlements have been found in only the following valleys: Kermanshah, Mahidasht, Shahabad, Shian, and Hulailan. In these, only three sites, Sarab, Guran, and Siahbid, have been excavated, and only Guran has been published in detail. Stein (1940:413) dug into what he called a preceramic site near Kaisarwand to the northeast of Kermanshah, but no further information has been published, nor has the site been visited since. Asiab, a preceramic site near Kermanshah was discussed earlier.

Sarab has been an enigma for many years. Rather than mud-walled architecture, its deposit consisted of broad layers of ash derived from the burning of quantities of reeds and other vegetal material (Braidwood

Frank Hole

1960a, 1960b, 1961; Braidwood, Howe, and Reed 1961). This picture changed somewhat in the summer of 1978, when members of Louis Levine's team extended Braidwood's excavation of Sarab and found an earlier and a later Neolithic deposit. Appearing on the eastern part of the site, the late Neolithic displayed some fragmentary evidence of mud architecture. This same late Neolithic pottery with architecture was also found at Siahbid, a site some 4 kilometers to the northeast, which was first tested by Frederick Matson as part of Braidwood's project in 1960 (Braidwood et al. 1960).

The most reasonable interpretation is that the early levels at Sarab (6200–5800 b.c.) represent the remains of seasonal campsites by transhumant herders whose houses were constructed of reeds. A close analogy to this can be seen today among people who move from their lowland pastures to camp near Kermanshah in the summer. In the summer camp they construct huts of reeds, which they burn when they leave in the fall. The result is a camp area covered annually with ash.

The later deposits at Sarab are more problematic inasmuch as some traces of thin mud walling have been found (McDonald 1979:312). If the settlement followed the pattern observed at Guran in the Hulailan valley, it is possible that the people became more sedentary. From his analysis of the age distribution of mammals and the presence of migratory fowl, Bökönyi (1977:36–37) has stated that the site was occupied the year round (see Hesse 1978 for a different interpretation). However, McDonald (1979:254) has suggested that Bökönyi may have derived this evidence from the late part of the site. Unfortunately his analysis does not distinguish bones from the separate parts of the site. Stratification aside, the severity of winters on the Kermanshah Plain (we recorded below 0°F, or −20°C) renders implausible the notion that people lived there all year in flimsy shelters.

Tepe Guran, a small contemporary site on the Hulailan Plain, provides much more information than Sarab (Mortensen 1964). Guran, like Jarmo (Braidwood et al. 1960:40), has a preceramic component (levels T-V). On this basis both sites appear to begin earlier than Sarab. This suggestion is corroborated by a radiocarbon date (6700 b.c. for level U at Guran). Mortensen (1972:294–96) thinks that the first settlers at Guran were herders who lived in wooden huts during the winter and that the village became permanent around 6400 b.c., about the time mud houses first came into use there (Mortensen and Flannery 1966). The idea that the site was used in the winter season is supported by the finding of bones of migratory fowl and by the fact that, at 900 meters above sea level, Hulailan is good winter pasture.

Through the combined efforts of the survey groups

of Levine and Braidwood, some thirteen sites with Sarab-like pottery have been found in the Mahidasht Plain (Levine and McDonald 1977:43). Two sites were found in Shahabad, one in Shian, an extension of the latter valley, and one in Zibiri. Mortensen has conducted intensive surveys of the Hulailan Plain and its surrounding flanks, finding three additional initial villages, one open site (a fishing station), and three caves, all with early ceramics (Mortensen 1974a, 1975). These results strongly imply that a careful search of all land surfaces might yield a number of early sites whose remains are not evident at a distance. The geomorphic situation in Hulailan seems to be different from that in Mahidasht, where many sites have been buried by alluvium (Levine 1974:488; Levine and McDonald 1977:46; Brookes, Levine, and Dennell 1982). By contrast, there is little alluvium in Hulailan so that Mortensen's results may be hard to duplicate elsewhere. It should be emphasized that the initial villages span considerable time, for Levine has distinguished four types of early ceramics that are found stratified at Sarab, Guran, or Siahbid, but whose absolute dates have yet to be determined. Generalized similarities for the Middle Neolithic at Sarab are found in Hassuna in Iraq and Hajji Firuz in Azerbaijan; and sherds of Late Neolithic with white paint (and black or red) are in secondary context at Seh Gabi Mound C near Kangavar (Levine and Hamlin 1974:211–13) and at Chagha Sefid (Hole 1977a: figure 54). The latter, in the Surkh Phase, are probably roughly contemporary with the sherds in Mahidasht. The chief importance of this is to show that there are stylistic similarities between distinct areas by the time of the late Neolithic, but we are unable as yet to ascribe any particular mechanism, such as transhumance or trade, to account for them.

The Early Village Period

Siahbid, east of Kermanshah, and Chogha Maran, on the northwest edge of the Mahidasht, have both been sounded and reveal deposits of the Village Period. Siahbid was first tested by Matson, but little was published (Braidwood, Howe, and Reed 1961; Braidwood 1961; see Bökönyi 1977 for an analysis of the fauna). It was retested later by members of Levine's team (E. Henrickson 1983; Levine and McDonald 1977). For both sites our best information concerns the succession of ceramics, an invaluable aid in understanding the survey data.

In the Mahidasht, the Initial Village Period ends with the appearance of "J-ware," a ceramic that is in the Eastern Halafian Tradition (Levine and McDonald 1977:42). The J-ware is found stratigraphically immediately above the Late Neolithic at Siahbid and Chogha Maran (E. Henrickson 1983). Levine and McDonald (1977: figure 3) list sixty-one J-ware sites in Mahidasht; Braidwood noted three sites in Shahabad and one in Shian, a geographic distribution similar to that of the Sarab-related wares. Figure 14 illustrates the general distribution of J-ware sites in the Qara Su River basin. One sherd turned up in Hulailan, but Young (personal communication) says that no Halaf is present in the Kangavar region. On the other hand, Halaf is found at sites in the Hamrin and Mandali regions of eastern Iraq which is part of the lowland steppe. The chief distribution of Halafian pottery is in northern Mesopotamia where the sites have internally consistent, exclusively Halafian pottery. Thus the presence of Halaf mixed with Ubaid and Dalma suggests a movement of peoples and perhaps an ethnic intermixing rather than trade (cf. Copeland 1979:269–70; Oates 1983).

The distribution of these wares also implies a movement up the Khorasan Road into Mahidasht, but this raises questions about the political or economic basis of the movement and the fate of the earlier villagers. It is perhaps relevant that the version of Halaf represented by J-ware lacks the most elaborate painted styles and vessel shapes of the lowland Halaf, thus suggesting that it had pushed well beyond its primary sustaining area. To excavate some of these sites would be particularly rewarding, for at least one of them in Mahidasht is greater than 5 hectares in size, providing us the first indication of a settlement hierarchy in the mountains.

The Middle and Late Village Periods: Dalma and Ubaid "Periods"

The next phase in the local sequence features a combination of different wares, predominantly in the Black-on-Buff style commonly referred to as Ubaid (figure 14). This ceramic is found at both Siahbid and Chogha Maran, stratigraphically above the J-ware, and at Maran below later wares. Occurring with this Black-on-Buff ware at Maran was Dalma "Ubaid" Painted ware. A small amount of Dalma Incised Impressed ware was recovered from both excavations along with the Black-on-Buff ware. Thus, in these two sites, there are three distinct but contemporary wares: a preponderance of Black-on-Buff and small amounts of Dalma "Ubaid" Painted and Dalma Impressed. No Dalma Painted, a ware found with the Dalma Impressed in Azerbaijan, was found in the Karkheh drainage.

Although the excavation at Siahbid has not been well reported, the ceramics from Matson's excavation were studied by Robert Santley (1974:figure 13b) who illustrates a vessel in a style identical to that of the Susa cemetery (Hole 1984). The possibility of direct contact between Susa and Siahbid is thus raised. Levine and McDonald (1977: figure 3) report 117 Ubaid sites in the Mahidasht, but we have no current

information on the numbers of these sites in other valleys, except Hulailan: here Mortensen (1975:5) has found twenty-three villages with painted buff pottery in what he calls the Susiana style (i.e., Ubaid). Only two of these sites are as large as 2 to 3 hectares, and the average distance between them is about 2.5 kilometers. No longer, as in the earlier period, are these sites situated on springs or rivers; rather they are scattered evenly across the plain, suggesting the possibility of irrigation. Although Mortensen has not yet published a breakdown of sites by subperiod, he has indicated that settlement drops abruptly toward the end of the "Susiana" sequence; by the start of the succeeding period, only four sites can be counted. Two mounds, Kazabad A and B, seem to have the entire sequence under consideration and would probably repay excavation (Mortensen 1974b:33–45).

The chronology of the Middle and Late Village periods cannot be resolved easily (Oates 1983:261–62). The fact that the Dalma Impressed and "Ubaid" Painted wares occur on fewer than a dozen sites in Mahidasht, in comparison with the 117 sites of Black-on-Buff, implies either that the latter ware lasted for a much longer time or that the two Dalma wares were traded infrequently into the area. In view of the narrow distribution of Dalma wares from Azerbaijan to the Kangavar region, passing by way of Chogha Maran, their rare occurrence in Mahidasht and absence in other valleys of the Kermanshah region is probably an indication that Dalma settlements as such were not present there. In other words, there was some trading involving the movement of pottery from Dalma regions into Mahidasht, but for the most part the two traditions remained spatially separate. There are no dates from Mahidasht itself to elucidate the duration of any of these wares. For this information we must turn to the Kangavar region.

The Kangavar Region of the Central Zagros

This sector of the mountains, known as Pish-i Kuh, consists of a series of valleys at high elevations to the northeast of the Kuh-i Sefid, a wall-like mountain range extending nearly 160 kilometers. The most prominent of the valleys are the Kangavar-Asadabad-Sahneh cluster, Nehavand-Khawa, Harsin, Borujerd, and Alishtar (figures 12, 13). Intensive survey has been carried out in the Kangavar group, but the remaining valleys have seen only cursory reconnaissance.

The Kangavar group has been surveyed in conjunction with the Godin Project (Young 1966, 1975a,b); Young and Smith (1966) worked just to the south in the Gamas-ab basin; Goff (1968, 1971) ranged widely through Pish-i Kuh; Stein (1940:277–86) visited Alishtar; Young (1966) visited Borujerd; and Godard

(1931) and Smith and Mortensen (1980) surveyed near Harsin in 1977. Although more than three hundred sites of various ages are now known from this region, only the immediate Kangavar enclave is relatively well surveyed.

Excavations have also been widely scattered, beginning chronologically with Giyan near Nehavand (Contenau and Ghirshman 1935), which does not appear to contain the earliest village material. Godin likewise lacks truly early deposits as does the nearby site of Seh Gabi Mound C, where the Shahnabad phase (approximately 5000 B.C.) is the earliest known occupation (Hamlin 1973, 1974b), although some late Neolithic sherds were found there in secondary context. Ganj Dareh in the Gamas-ab basin is a village with very early pottery (P. Smith 1976b). Some 75 kilometers east-southeast of Ganj Dareh, Abdul Hosein appears to be largely aceramic (Pullar 1975; McDonald 1979:510–12), following excavation in 1978. Apart from these sites, the earliest known material is found on surveyed sites.

The Initial Village Period: Neolithic

The most important site of the period is Ganj Dareh, a small mound some 40 kilometers east of Kermanshah at an elevation of about 1,400 meters. But in a careful survey of a region surrounding this site, Smith and Mortensen (1980) discovered three other preceramic sites. One of these, Tepe Kasemi, was much larger than Ganj Dareh, but the other two are so badly disturbed by agriculture and the building of a fortress, respectively, that their original condition cannot be determined. Tepe Kasemi proved in soundings to have more than 1 meter of deposit which yielded two burials. Another site, Tepe Geneel, contains pottery in the Sarab Linear style (Middle Neolithic) at the top and preceramic settlements below. These three sites are within a two-to-three hour walk of Ganj Dareh, and they are considered to be roughly contemporary.

The oldest settlement at Ganj Dareh is without parallel. The first traces are of "fire pits," but the lack of architecture suggests that the site was a campground. According to Hesse (1978; 1982:412–13), the bones imply that the site was used for specialized hunting. At this time agricultural tools are lacking although one crude sherd and cultivated barley were recovered from this context. The date of this settlement (level E) is probably in the middle of the eighth millennium, making it the oldest site in Iran with pottery and about the same age as Mureybet in Syria, where early pottery and similar fire pits were found (Cauvin 1972). Warm season occupation only is implied by the rodent remains (Hesse 1979). Within level D, there is solid mud-walled architecture and abundant evidence of ceramics. A number of large storage vessels, formed in place inside the small rooms, were inadvertently fired when the houses burned. Additionally many small, portable, unpainted vessels of clay are represented in numerous sherds in this and succeeding levels. In level D, appears the first evidence of tools associated with agriculture: sickles and grinding stones. Some of the houses were of two stories with small bin-like cubicles on the lower floor. In one room of level D were two pairs of wild sheep skulls and horns set into a plastered niche, a practice reminiscent of the "shrines" at Çatal Hüyük in Anatolia.

At 1,400 meters elevation, Ganj Dareh is among the highest of the early villages, and it may lie above the zone of distribution of the wild cereals. One suspects, therefore, that from the beginning agriculture was practiced, perhaps in small plots, by people who herded goats in the area seasonally. It is abundantly clear that from level D onward, the animals were domestic (Hesse 1982:413). Thus there is a suggestion that Ganj Dareh holds evidence of the shift from hunting and gathering to an economy based on domesticates.

Tepe Abdul Hosein on the Khawa Plain was first visited by Goff and Pullar (1970) and later excavated by Pullar in 1978. About 75 kilometers east-southeast of Ganj Dareh, this site is at about 1,600 meters elevation. According to McDonald (1979:511–12), there are two architectural levels in the aceramic: a lower with curvilinear walls and a later one with well-built rectilinear walls. The site contained artifacts suggesting agriculture, including mortars set in mud stands. Emmer wheat seeds were recovered. McDonald suggests that the site may be contemporary with Sarab rather than with Ganj Dareh, despite its lack of pottery.

In the Malayer Valley to the east, R. Howell reports finding four sites with Late Neolithic pottery, similar to that from Seh Gabi C, and McDonald (1979:561) suggests that the sites may have been those of transhumant people.

The Early Village Period: Shahnabad and Dalma Phases

The primary archaeological sequence for the Village Period comes from the Kangavar Valley in which the earliest deposits yet uncovered are from the base of Seh Gabi C, in the Shahnabad levels which date to around 4200 B.C. (McDonald 1979:348). A few sherds of Late Neolithic hint at a still earlier occupation which was not uncovered (McDonald 1979:413). The site was excavated by Levine in 1971 and 1973, as part of the Godin Tepe Project (Young and Levine 1974). The most complete description of its contents during the Shahnabad Phase is given in McDonald (1979). She concludes that the people were settled cultivators who kept pigs as well as sheep and goats and enjoyed a few exotic materials such as copper.

The durability of the architecture and its prolonged use give further suggestion of year-round sedentism. Although Young (1975a,b:192) reported two other sites in Kangavar with the Shahnabad ware, McDonald (1979:533) casts doubt on the identification. At the very least, sites of this age are rare and settlement was sparse.

The Middle Village Period: Seh Gabi and Taherabad Phases

The recently completed excavations at Godin Tepe and Seh Gabi provide us with the best information from the entire central Zagros for the Early to Late Period villages. Although all of the details have not yet been worked out, we can present a reasonably complete sequence based on stratified material from the several mounds at Seh Gabi and Godin itself. In terms of the Godin system of numbering periods, the Shahnabad Period precedes anything on Godin and hence is earlier than Godin XI. Godin XI, the Kucheh Period, is known only from some sherds and it may be similar to, or a stage of, the Shahnabad. Dalma occurs in Mound B at Seh Gabi and also Godin X. This is followed by the Seh Gabi Period, Godin IX, a local version of the Ubaid. The terminal Ubaid is called Godin VIII, the Taherabad Period, which ends around 3600 B.C. (Levine and McDonald 1977:46). For purposes of this chapter, Godin VII, a local post-Ubaid set of ceramics, called the Hoseinabad Period, is the end of our concern. But we should note that there appears to be essential continuity from Godin VII into Godin VI, at which point Uruk types of pottery appear in the local collection. This implies that there was some lag in ceramic changes in Kangavar as compared with Susiana. The actual interplay between peoples during the developed village period is impossible to discern, although larger excavations at Seh Gabi might go a long way toward answering the questions in this locale.

The work at Seh Gabi was confined to two seasons of soundings at the various mounds, of which Mound B (the largest) and Mounds A and E have provided the most information. Mound B has an excellent sequence of Dalma at the bottom and Seh Gabi in the upper levels. Continuity between these two is suggested but not conclusively demonstrated (Young and Levine 1974:11). No coherent architecture was found in the 4-by-4-meter exposure of Dalma levels but several rebuildings of houses in the Seh Gabi strata were revealed. The houses themselves are probably typical domestic structures.

In the Seh Gabi Period, probably placed under house floors, were eight burials, all of which "were very young infants or perhaps even fotuses. In the well-preserved examples, the body was always in a tightly contracted position, and in a bowl. No adult burials were found that can be connected with the Seh Gabi period, or for that matter, with any period represented at Seh Gabi" (Young and Levine 1974:10). This find is especially interesting in view of the near identity of the Dalma ceramics at Seh Gabi and Dalma, sites which are 400 kilometers apart. In view of this it may not be entirely coincidental that all of the burials at Dalma in Azerbaijan were infants buried in pots. This raises the possibility that the Dalma levels at Seh Gabi may also yield burials, and that there is continuity of the practice into the Seh Gabi Period.

The Late Village Period: Hoseinabad Phase

Mounds A and E both have deposits of Godin VIII. In Mound A, the architecture is remarkably well preserved, consisting of a large building with at least eight rooms, some of which contain cruciform hearths with central holes. These structures were multistoried; one is said to have had three stories. Evidence for the upper rooms is found in the supporting posts that were embedded in the lower walls. Clearly there is great promise at the site for further excavation inasmuch as doorways and windows are preserved intact (Hamlin 1974b:275).

Mound E, which is apparently contemporary, has very different preservation and architecture. The exposure shows three unconnected rooms around a courtyard. Each room has a cruciform hearth and the same floor features as in the large building of Mound A. Again, further excavation seems warranted for the possible information on differences within settlements.

Some hints of elite activities at Seh Gabi are found in the stamp seals in Mounds A and B and the copper in Mound A. Seals and sealings of Dalma age in Mound B and of Godin VII–VI in Mound E imply storage and perhaps administrative dealings. The copper, which occurs in a Godin VII context, includes fragments of crucibles and pieces of molds. In addition, the presence of kiln wasters indicates that pottery was fired there. There is, therefore, the possibility of a small workshop site with an elite residence at Seh Gabi.

Following the excavations in 1974, members of the Godin team carried out survey of the Kangavar Valley. After the poorly represented Shahnabad Period, the team found twenty Dalma Period sites. The total area occupied was about 13 hectares, and none of the sites was larger than a single hectare. The succeeding Seh Gabi Period saw seventeen sites occupying about 10 hectares; again, none was greater than 1 hectare in area. The Taherabad Period, Godin VIII, was absent from surface collections, thus raising the possibility that it is a spurious period, having been defined at Godin on the basis of too small a sample. The Hoseinabad Period, Godin VII, is recorded at twenty-three sites which have a total surface exposure of 16 hectares. Of these, ten are between 1 and 2 hectares.

The other plains in the Kangavar region have been surveyed only cursorily by Young (1966) and must be resurveyed to provide comparable data. By way of comparison, Young's initial survey of Kangavar produced only four occupations of the developed Village Period whereas the recent survey found thirty-nine. Similar changes would be expected in the other valleys.

The first major excavation in Luristan was made at Tepe Giyan near Nehavand by Contenau and Ghirshman (1935) in 1931 and 1932, who found that the site had already been badly damaged by farmers digging for fertile soil to put on their fields. Unhappily this practice has continued to the present day so that virtually nothing is left of this site which once was among the largest in all of Luristan. By means of "trenches" of somewhat irregular shape, the excavators sounded the stratification of the mound. The work was coarse by modern standards, but it provided the basis for all comparative work until Young's team excavated Godin and Seh Gabi. Apparently the entire later Village Period was represented at Giyan.

It is important to note that although no architectural information was recorded, the excavators found objects of copper, including an axe like those found in the cemetery at Susa, and some seals, one of which is engraved with goats (Contenau and Ghirshman 1935:66, plate 38:21). Amiet (1980:plate 4) also illustrates some seals from level V. These objects tell us only that Giyan was probably an exceptional site during the Late Village Period and would deserve modern excavation if a satisfactory block of undisturbed deposits remains.

The Khorramabad Region of the Central Zagros

Nestled between a series of folded mountain ranges within the drainage area of the Saimarreh and Kashgan rivers, lie narrow, fertile valleys ranging in elevation from 700 to 1,500 meters (figures 12,13). These valleys are bounded on the southwest by the Kabir Kuh and on the northeast by the Kuh-i Sefid. To the southeast of the Kashgan River segments of similar valleys extend within a territory which is a tangle of mountains known as the Bala Gariveh. Traditionally this territory is used by transhumant Luri peoples rather than farmers. Included in the southern sector are Saimarreh, Tarhan, Rumishgan, Kuh-i Dasht, and Khorramabad, situated at the end of Kuh-i Sefid.

This area has seen extensive rather than intensive surveys. Stein (1940:190–265) visited the prominent valleys and other less well-known areas; Schmidt (1940) made both aerial reconnaissance and some ex-

cavations; Morgan (1895a:3–6) visited Saimarreh and Rumishgan; Hole and Flannery traversed rapidly most of the valleys (Hole 1962); Goff (1971) covered much of the territory; and Young (1966) visited the Khorramabad region.

The Early Village Period

The earliest ceramics in this region are from Bog-i No, near Khorramabad. Hole and Flannery took a radiocarbon sample and a large collection of the pottery from a section through the site that had been cut by workers who were mining brick soil. The ash contained wheat, other cereal grains, melon, lentils, pistachios, and zizyphus fruit pits (Helbaek 1969:399) and small fish bones, turtle carapace, sheep/goat bones, and cattle. According to Helbaek, the grains are naked barley and hexaploid wheat.

Flannery and Hole found this ceramic on at least six more sites in the Khorramabad Plain. A few sherds are in Kunji Cave along with other early sherds (Hole and Flannery 1968). Young (1966) reports three other sites, one just east of Khorramabad and the other two at opposite ends of the Borujerd Valley. Goff (1971:figure 2) found other sites in the Kuh-i Dasht Valley to the west of Khorramabad. Other wares (coarse, plain, straw-tempered) that might be included in the Early Village Period, but for which there is neither accurate dating nor accurate definition of the types, have been reported by Young (1966:230–31). The distribution of these wares overlaps that of the Bog-i No painted. It seems probable that the straw-tempered wares change to grit or grit- and straw-tempered wares which continue to be painted in a style derived from Bog-i No, yet without excavations it is difficult to be more precise.

In all, therefore, the earliest settlements are found in the Khorramabad–Kuh-i Dasht plains around the south end of the Kuh-i Sefid at elevations of about 1,200 meters and in the higher valley of Borujerd at about 1,500 meters. It is surprising that such sites have not yet been reported from Alishtar, because the distribution of sites implies a distinct enclave of people who may have been involved in transhumance as some people in the region are today. We have already seen that sites in Malayer at 1,800 meters have pottery related to Shahnabad, and again the implication is of seasonal transhumance to these higher valleys.

The Later Village Period

Owing to the lack of excavations and the inconclusive nature of most surveys, following Bog-i No, we can point only in the most general terms to ceramic parallels between valleys in this sector and elsewhere. Part of the reason for this is that many of the valleys are deficient in surface water (Stein 1940:220; Hole 1962), making them unsuitable for permanent settlement until after wells were put into use. Also there is reason to believe that natural changes in the ground water table have altered the character of some of the valleys. For instance, in Saimarreh I found that erosion had removed much of the land surface during or subsequent to the time under consideration here, for Ubaid-style sherds occurred in eroded gravels several meters below the present surface. Major sites such as Kozagaran are now atop erosional remnants, their surrounding landscape having largely disappeared. Our major hope for understanding this region comes from careful surveys of areas where old land surfaces are still intact, and excavations of some of the key sites that remain.

Goff (1971:137–39) reviewed the evidence for settlement in this region and provided a rough idea of the relative chronology. Between her review and my surveys, we can account for twenty-four sites of all periods. We recall that Khorramabad had nine sites with Bog-i No pottery, but there are only seven sites with the later buff wares. Remarkably the number of sites actually decreases during a period when it generally increases elsewhere. This is particularly noteworthy inasmuch as the Bog-i No period is probably of much shorter duration. Two of the later sites are between 1 and 2 hectares, and the remainder are all well under 1 hectare in extent. The Kuh-i Dasht Plain has five sites with painted buff pottery, all of them well under 1 hectare in size.

The two remaining valleys are Tarhan and Rumishgan. Tarhan lacks prehistoric sites, but Rumishgan has three that have been tested. Erich Schmidt excavated at Chigha Sabz and Kamtarlan, and Stein (1940:218–20) dug at Chagha Bal where he found painted pottery at the base. None of these has been published sufficiently to give more than the most general impression of age.

Of all the valleys in the Khorramabad region, Saimarreh has been the most important historically, a judgment reinforced by the presence of sites ranging from early to late in our present sequence. Stein (1940:196–215) made observations of the geology; trenched the two sites of most interest, Taikhan and Kozagaran; and visited three other sites where he found painted sherds. My survey found another site or two which date somewhere within the "Ubaid" range.

Kozagaran is interesting on two counts: it consists of a small settlement with numerous burials, and it sits atop an erosional remnant. The erosion has left very little of this site which is on "a completely isolated narrow ridge of clay rising to about 100 feet above the patches of flat ground below" (Stein 1940:198). No more than 2 meters of deposit, often less, was encountered on this ridge and it appears that much of the site may have disappeared down the slope. Several vessels contained evidence of burials and even cremation: "A large vessel containing fragmentary human remains, including pieces of adult skull, ribs, legs and arms, partly perished, was found under a row of rough stone blocks." In another section Stein found two burial pots

> close together within a rough enclosure formed by stones. . . . Both were found with their mouths turned to the ground. Small bone fragments mixed with ashes filled portions of the inverted pots. . . . Two more burial pots came to light in close vicinity to those mentioned above. . . . In both were found plenty of small pieces of human bones, including skull fragments, and also ashes (Stein 1940:202–3).

The illustrations of sherds from this site show that it encompassed a later "Ubaid" span, but the most striking thing is sherds that are stylistically identical to those from the Susa cemetery (Hole 1984). This, with Siahbid and Musiyan, is one of only three certain cases where Susa pottery has been discovered outside Susiana itself. It suggests an introduction into a local context, perhaps funerary in nature. Stamp seals round out the similarities with Susa.

As there is abundant evidence of massive erosion in Saimarreh and the strong possibility of similar erosion elsewhere, coupled with changes in the water table in this sector, it is clear that there is more to the regional prehistory than can ever meet the eye. Consequently, it seems necessary to delay inferences about such matters as settlement until after thorough studies of the geomorphology have been made.

The Mountain Plains of the Southern Zagros-Fars

Because this province of southern Iran (figures 2, 15, 16) has been surveyed recently and relatively intensively, at least some outlines of settlement history have emerged. But unfortunately, despite excavations at early sites, there is still no solid evidence for chronology even in the central Marv Dasht, some 60 kilometers northeast of Shiraz. Fars is too large to be examined at a single glance. At a minimum we must distinguish the Marv Dasht-Sadatabad Plain, the Shiraz-Sarvestan area, Fasa and Darab in eastern Fars (150 and 250 kilometers southeast of Shiraz, respectively), and Kazerun to the west. In addition, small mountain valleys between the major agricultural plains contain sites.

The principal focus of prehistoric settlement in Fars is northeast of the present city of Shiraz on the broad plain known as the Marv Dasht. The Marv Dasht is circumscribed by northwest-southeast trending anticlinal ridges which enclose a relatively flat alluvial basin at an elevation of about 1,600 meters above sea level (Sumner 1972:7–15). Although precipitation here averages about 340 millimeters annually, the plain is watered by many springs and the Sivand and Kur rivers. In fact, part of the plain is subject to seasonal inundation as marshy areas become lakes. The temperatures here reach freezing during the winter and are hot and dry in the summer, following the same pattern as western Iran generally.

Sir Aurel Stein visited the principal valleys in 1934 (1936). Henry Field examined some caves (1939), and the Marv Dasht was explored through survey and sondage over a number of years by Vanden Berghe (1954, 1959). The modern era of survey was initiated by Gotch (1968, 1969), followed by Sumner (1972) and Miroschedji (1973). Some work in eastern Fars on the Paleolithic was carried out by Krinsley (1970:224) and Piperno (1972, 1974).

The Initial Village Period

Throughout this region we find a soft ware, or wares, apparently followed by the buff wares characteristic of the later village periods. Unfortunately, the radiocarbon dates from Tepe Mushki span some five thousand years and are clearly unreliable. Thus one can say only that the Early Village Period predates the fifth millennium, based on dates from the Shamsabad Phase at Bakun. Sumner (1972:52; 1977:299) and the excavators (Fukai, Horiuchi, and Matsutani 1973) believe that the Mushki wares precede those of Jari A III and B, a conclusion that runs counter to Vanden Berghe (1954:400) and to Miroschedji (1973:5). The unfortunate truth is that one cannot be sure which is correct in spite of excavations at the three key sites, Mushki (Fukai, Horiuchi, and Matsutani 1973) and Jari A and B (Egami 1967).

Sumner recognizes five varieties of soft ware and suggests that some of the differences may relate to geographic rather than to chronological factors. The Mushki wares are found in the Kur River basin at six sites (figure 16a) and at two sites in Shiraz and Sarvestan. They occur as well at two sites in mountain valleys to the west of Kazerun. Jari wares, which I take to be the later, occurs at forty-nine sites in the Kur basin (figure 16b) and at five in the Shiraz-Sarvestan plains. Shamsabad wares, which seem to be a later version of Jari, occur at 102 sites in the Kur basin (figures 16c).

In Fasa and Darab, the problems of relative chronology are even worse. Jalyan wares, which occur in Fasa (fifteen sites) and at Darab (five sites), resemble more closely the early painting styles such as Mohammad Jaffar, Guran, and Sarab, rather than Mushki, with which it has been compared (Miroschedji 1973:5). The Bizdan wares occur only in Darab (five sites), and they have tenuous stylistic relations to Jari. Thus they might be later than Jalyan, although Miroschedji (1973:5) suggests the reverse. Once again, the answer depends on which is earlier, Mushki or Jari.

Another early ware, Kutahi, is mentioned by Sumner (1977:295), but its description is not published. Found near Shiraz, Sarvestan, and Kazerun, this ware vaguely resembles Jari and thus may fill the gap there following the local Mushki wares. Clearly, little satisfactory information can be gained from surface survey at such widely scattered locales. We can now state only that occupation probably began in the late seventh millennium and people continued making varieties of soft wares until the first half of the fifth millennium when Bakun B1 wares spread and the early period comes to an end (Langsdorff and McCown 1942).

According to Sumner (n.d.:8), "Mushki sites are almost invariably located near large springs and a similar association has been reported for Bizdan and Jalyan wares" (Miroschedji 1973:1). Although Jari sites occur in a number of places that could not be watered by springs, Sumner (1981) infers that the villagers practiced dry farming. He believes that the expansion into irrigable areas in the Shamsabad Phase is the first good evidence of irrigation.

From the final report on Mushki (Fukai, Horiuchi, and Matsutani 1973), we gain some additional information about the Initial Village Period. The report on Jari B is too brief to be of much value (Egami 1967).

Mushki today has a depth of only 1.7 meters, in which five levels have been distinguished. The lowest of these, which was exposed over about 50 square meters, contained remains of a rectangular building. In the top of Level 1, traces of buildings with curvilinear walls were exposed. Although the architecture in the upper level is by no means clear, it does seem as if changes in architecture occurred throughout the occupation of the site. Change is also reflected in the buff wares, which increase in frequency from early to later deposits. In other respects, the material is thought by the excavators to be essentially homogenous.

For our purposes, some of the rarer artifacts are interesting. Particularly striking are the 391 earspools, most of which were made of clay: nearly all came from the upper two levels. Their abundance raises questions. Are they actually earspools? If so, were they worn by occupants of the site, or were they being manufactured for export? This abundance is unprecedented and the possibility of craft specialization should be investigated when Mushki or another site of its age is excavated.

Twenty-six pieces of obsidian, of uncertain source, occur in Levels 2–5; none was found in Level 1. The obsidian from Mushki has not been analyzed for source, but obsidian from Bakun is reported to be of Group 3, from the vicinity of Lake Urmia (Renfrew 1977:291). In view of the implications for trade, it is essential to obtain analyses of this material. Trade with regions to the south and west is indicated in the presence of seashells of types found in the Red Sea or Persian Gulf (dentalium and cowrie). Some turquoise beads and a number of copper objects were recovered, both of which suggest contact and exchange with the plateau to the north and east.

Subsistence is poorly documented because of the absence of any plant remains and the lack of a report on the fauna. When I visited the site during excavation, I noted quantities of sheep/goat bone and those of a large ungulate, probably *Bos*. Interestingly, few grinding stones were recovered, suggesting that processing of cereal grains was not a major occupation. Less than one percent of the chert blades were sickles (as distinguished by the presence of sheen).

Although the data are inconclusive, the following facts suggest that Mushki may have been an impermanent campsite: (1) the thin mud walls may have served only as the bases of thatched houses or tents; (2) the range of artifacts more closely approximates those of transhumant than of permanently settled people; and (3) Marv Dasht is above the zone of natural habitat for cereals, but it is a fine grazing land; agriculture there today is practiced chiefly with the aid of irrigation.

The Middle to Late Village Period

The best-known site is Tall-i Bakun, excavated by Herzfeld (1929) and reported in detail by Langsdorff and McCown (1942). This site is composed of two mounds, A and B. At site A, nearly one thousand square meters were exposed, providing substantial evidence of a village. Level III, which includes four architectural levels, contains a number of multiroom storage and dwelling complexes. Some of the rooms contained domestic remains, others storage vessels, intimating thereby the uses of the structures. All of the levels contain generally the same kind of pottery, although Dyson (1965a:242–44) thinks they can be subdivided stylistically into chronological subphases, and Langsdorff and McCown (1942:59) implicitly recognize this.

Ceramic kilns stood outside the domestic buildings, perhaps for communal use. By contrast, each house had its own storage rooms and exclusive domestic space. One room in level IV is identified as a workshop for chipped stone (Langsdorff and McCown 1942:20). The small finds are similar to objects in other contemporary sites: knives, sickles, figurines, and an especially nice series of engraved seals, sealings, and tags. Chests and jars of ash found in some rooms raise the possibility of cremation, although no bones were reported from the ash (Langsdorff and McCown 1942:12–13). In fact, no burials of any type were found. A number of the storage vessels contained remains of food, including fish and animal bones (Langsdorff and McCown 1942:15,16). It is apparent that careful analysis of the finds in the various rooms would be of value, as would further excavation by modern techniques of other parts of this 2-hectare site.

Apart from the excavations at Bakun, there have been a number of other small soundings into various sites. Many of these are by Vanden Berghe (1952, 1954). Both Tall-i Jari and Tall-i Gap have been excavated by the Japanese Archaeological Mission. At the site of Jari A, the uppermost level contained pottery painted in the general Bakun style (Egami 1967; Egami et al. 1977). At Tall-i Gap, two mounds, A and B, had painted pottery, again resembling that from Bakun itself. The excavators have designated the levels with this pottery as Gap II (Egami and Sono 1962; Sono 1967). Finally, near Pasargadae, Clare Goff excavated at Tall-i Nokhodi, where levels III–IV contained painted ceramics in the Bakun style (Goff 1963, 1964). None of these excavations has been reported in great detail.

Sumner (1981) provides a summary of the settlement in both of the periods of concern here, Bakun and Lapui, based on his own survey (1972) and those of Stein (1936, 1937, 1940), Gotch (1969), Miroschedji (1973), and information provided by Donald Whitcomb and David Freidel.

A total of about 250 sites are known to have Bakun painted wares. (Figure 16 indicates the distribution of sites located in the Kur River basin.) These will probably be divided eventually among several subphases; there is no implication that all sites were occupied simultaneously. We have little information on many of these sites but we can make use of Sumner's report (1981) on the Kur River basin. He reports some 146 sites with Bakun pottery and 103 with Lapui wares. In all cases he found a multiplicity of small villages; those of Bakun Period had a mean size of 1.2 hectares, whereas those of Lapui were about 1.0 hectare. Most impressive is the fact that three of the Bakun Period sites exceed 5 hectares. Their unusual size (no other site is larger than 3.5 hectares) implies that they played a special role in society of the time. Unfortunately, none of these sites has been excavated, so that this suggestion is untested.

The Lapui Phase brings a disruption in the local sequence. The number of sites shrinks, and settlements are often found adjacent to natural pasturage, suggesting herding rather than agriculture. No site larger than 5 hectares has been identified (Sumner 1981).

Not surprisingly, Fasa and Darab exhibit a sequence similar to that in Marv Dasht, but none of the sites has been excavated. Miroschedji (1973) reports finding 67 sites of the Bakun Period, 42 in Fasa, and 25 in Darab. One of the sites in the latter valley is about 7 hectares in area. In each valley, sites close to rivers or to springs are larger than sites farther away from those sources of water. Contemporary with the Lapui Period, Miroschedji has 18 sites: 12 in Fasa and 6 in Darab which have red wares that he names Vakilabad. One variety of this ware is painted, unlike

Frank Hole

Lapui; but the overall similarities between the two areas are notable, at least in sharing the absence of the Bakun buff wares. Miroschedji feels that Vakilabad pottery may be partly contemporary with Banesh in Marv Dasht, an uncertainty about chronological relationships that is shared in the latter region by Sumner (Miroschedji 1973:7).

A vast tract of rugged mountain land separates Khuzistan from the southern plateau of Fars province. With numerous trails, but few good routes and little arable land, this tract has traditionally belonged to the Bakhtiari tribespeople. Understandably, there have been few archaeological surveys of this potentially interesting region, and none provides more than an outline of the archaeological history. The single excavation reveals only local details of the chronology, with little information on the matter of sedentism versus pastoralism. Yet despite the nature of the evidence, our knowledge has been gained more systematically by survey here than in the mountains of Kurdistan, and it provides some interesting comparisons with what was happening on the Susiana Plain and in Fars. We shall now consider surveys in the following four areas: Izeh-Malamir, Dasht-e Gol, and the Khana Mirza and Shahr-e Kord plains.

Izeh

Situated along the edge of the Zagros overlooking the central Susiana Plain southeast of Shushtar, is the important plain of Izeh (figures 3,6). The first systematic survey was undertaken in 1976, when the Iranian Centre for Archaeological Research conducted a training program here under the direction of Henry Wright. During a two and one-half month survey, they recorded 168 sites of periods ranging from Upper Paleolithic to recent (Wright 1979).

The plain itself stands some 750 meters above sea level, an elevation which provides sufficient rain for dry farming. Because of the internal drainage of the basin, some 20 kilometers are occupied by seasonal lakes and salt flats, leaving about 75 square kilometers of good agricultural land. Springs issue from only the southwest side of the plain, thus limiting irrigation and the number of people who can be supported year round. Summer irrigation of large tracts is impossible with only the natural sources. Although snow rarely falls on the plain, vegetation dies during the winter and optimum grass is available chiefly during the spring and early winter. The plain has traditionally been a center of Bakhtiari pastoralists, although some forty-five modern settlements, three-quarters of which are seasonal, were recorded. During the spring, many of these people travel into the mountains by means of well-established trails toward Shahr-e Kord, which is just to the northwest of the Khana Mirza Plain.

Since the Izeh-Malamir Plain is close to Khuzistan where some of the nomads spend the winter, it is one of the crucial areas for investigation of relations between agriculturalists and nomads. Events in Khuzistan may be mirrored in Izeh; or, conversely, under certain conditions such as political instability, the people of Izeh might become politically disruptive, if not dominant, in Khuzistan (see chapter 5).

The Initial Village Period

There is one possible preceramic site. Ten other sites have pottery in the Archaic styles of Chogha Mish or related wares (Shahideh 1979:42). These sites average 1.4 hectares in extent with a range of 0.5 to 3.0 hectares; thus they are larger than the average mounded site in Susiana. Because of lack of water during this period, Wright infers that most sites were temporary encampments of transhumant people with a few permanent settlements.

The Early to Late Village Periods

A single site represents the introduction of the buffware ceramics and is equivalent in age to basal Jaffarabad. The next ceramic style, "Susiana b," is found at six villages, one of which is about 5 hectares in extent and another which is nearly 4 hectares.

The Middle Village Period is represented by six villages, none of which exceeds 2.1 hectares. From this point the population declines, following the pattern in Susiana. The Susiana d time is represented by only three sites, the largest of which is 3.1 hectares. The Late Village Period is seen at three Susa A sites, the largest of which is 1.9 hectares, and Terminal Susa A is thought to be at two sites of 1.5 and 3.1 hectares, respectively (Shahideh 1979:54). Except for the large size of the villages, the general pattern of a rise and then a fall in the number of sites parallels Susiana, to which Izeh is closely related insofar as ceramics are concerned.

Dasht-e Gol and Iveh

Surveys of two small valleys along the middle Karun river drainage were carried out in 1975 by Henry Wright and Yahya Kossary; and in 1976 by Wright, Kossary, Ismail Yaghma'i, and Mansur Sadjadi. Each survey lasted four days. Dasht-e Gol and Iveh both have small plains at elevations between 400 and 500 meters above sea level. The valleys are occupied by Bakhtiari pastoralists who make use of trails leading from the lowlands of Khuzistan to the plateau (Wright et al. 1976:430–31; Wright and Kossary 1979; Wright and Yaghma'i 1979).

During the Initial Village Period "there are at least three large open air campsites, two small camps marked by surface scatters of tools and a possible occupation in a rockshelter" (Wright et al. 1976:431). Soft-ware sherds were found at only two of these sites which are said to be "either the seasonal camps of lowland villagers or the camps of herding groups closely related to these villagers" (Wright et al. 1976:434). At one of these are stone footings for some sort of buildings; at the other, some accumulation that may have resulted from mud construction. Unfortunately, these sites are now covered with the waters impounded behind the Dez River Dam. No sites pertaining to the Early to Late Village Period were found in either valley.

Khana Mirza and Shahr-e Kord

Scarcely more than dots on a map of western Iran (figure 3), several small valleys were explored from 1974 to 1978 by Allen Zagarell (1982a:11–17). In 1975, Nissen and Zagarell (1976) tested several of the sites to help establish a chronological sequence. The importance of these small plains is that they lie astride migration routes between the lowlands of Khuzistan and Behbehan and the Isfahan region on the Iranian plateau. This extremely rugged terrain is today the homeland of transhumant Bakhtiari pastoralists.

Zagarell has identified interesting projects for future excavation, but he has only scratched the surface of research in this vast region; thus although any attempts at a detailed reconstruction of settlement history would be premature, some tentative conclusions may be drawn. The two major plains are Khana Mirza, 80 kilometers south-southwest of Isfahan at an elevation of 1,800 meters, and Shahr-e Kord at about 2,100 meters. Both plains are well suited for grazing but are less desirable for agriculture because of elevation, lack of surface water, and poor soils.

Of the Initial Village Period, the Shahr-e Kord plain contains six small sites, whereas Khana Mirza has only one certain site. This site, Qaleh Rostam, was sounded by Nissen and Zagarell (1976) and proved to have an aceramic component at the base. The upper part of the site, Phase I, contained boulder-built houses and sickles, grinding stones, and whorls for spinning, thus suggesting a sedentary agricultural village (Zagarell 1982a:57). However, such a village may have been occupied for only part of the year, presumably during the summer. The same six sites were occupied during Phase II in Shahr-e Kord, the time of maximum population.

The Early to Late Village Period is represented by the Early and Middle Chalcolithic. There is an apparent decline in the number of sites from the first settlement through Phase I, as defined at Qaleh Rostam. This decline is continued into the Early Chalcolithic where two very small sites are positively identified in Khana Mirza and only one in Shahr-e Kord (Zagarell 1982b:58–59).

The Late Village Period is represented by nineteen sites in Khana Mirza, with an average size of only 0.5 hectares; but some appear to be large enough to suggest a hierarchy of sites. The picture in Shahr-e Kord is similar in that, of four sites, two are distinctly larger (Zagarell 1982a:60).

The value of these data lies not in their completeness, but in the proof they provide of extant sites containing useful information about patterns of pastoralism going back as far as the preceramic. To some degree the data suggest parallels in settlement with the fertile lowland plains, but in other respects the people of the mountains forged their own style of life and settlement that will be difficult to interpret without excavation.

Notes

1. Well after this chapter had been completed, "An Updated Chronology of the Early and Middle Chalcolithic of the Central Zagros Highlands, Western Iran" was published by E. Henrickson (1985). This article reviews in detail the ceramic and other evidence for a chronological ordering of sites in the central Zagros and adjacent areas. In large part this article is based on her dissertation (1983) which was consulted during the preparation of this chapter.

Table 2. Relative Chronology of Regions during the Village Period

Period	Deh Luran	Susiana	Azerbaijan	Kangavar	Karkheh Drainage	Fars	Southern Mesopotamia	Northern Mesopotamia
Post Village Period	Early Uruk	Early Uruk 3750–3500		Godin V 3300–2800	Late Chalcolithic	Banesh 3400–2600	Early Uruk	Gawran/Uruk
Late Village Period	Sargarab Susa A	Terminal Susa A Susa A 4200–4000		Godin VII (Hosseinabad) 3600–3200	Middle Chalcolithic	Lapui 3900–3400	Terminal Ubaid Ubaid 4 (Late Ubaid)	Ubaid
Middle Village Period	Farukh 4400–4200 Bayat 4600–4400 Mehmeh 4800–4600	Susiana d (Chogha Mish Phase) Susiana c	Pisdeli 4700–3900	Godin VIII (Taherabad) Godin IX (Seh Gabi) 4400–3800		Bakun 4800–3900	Ubaid 3 (Early Ubaid)	Ubaid Late Halaf
Early Village Period	Khazineh 5000–4800 Sabz 5200–5000 CMT 5400–5200	Susiana b (Jaffarabad Phase) Susiana a Archaic III	Dalma 5200–4700	Godin X 4500 Godin XI Shahnabad 5200–5000	Early Ubaid Early Chalcolithic J-Ware	Shamsabad 5500–4800	Ubaid 2 (Hajji Mohammad) Ubaid 1 (Eridu) Samarran/CMT	Early Halaf 5500–5200
Initial Village Period	Surkh 5700–5400 Sefid 6000–5700 Mohammad Jaffar 6300–6000	Archaic II Archaic I	Hajji Firuz 6100–5400		Late Neolithic 5500 (Bog-i-No, Siahbid) Early Neolithic 6000 (Sarab)	Jari 6000–5500 Mushki 6000		Hassuna Jarmo
Pre-Ceramic	Ali Kosh 6700–6300 Bus Mordeh 7500–6700	Preceramic			Ganj Dareh 7500–7000 Asiab 8000			Early Jarmo Karim Shahir Zawi Chemi 8000

Note: All dates are approximate according to the best calibration. No entry is made when Carbon 14 dates are not available.

Table 3. Radiocarbon Dates Pertinent to the Village Period

The Lowland Steppe		Laboratory	B.P. 5568 hl	B.C.: 95% Confidence	b.c.: B.P. × 1.03−1950±1000
Susa	Acropole A1	Brussels	5093±105	4120−3660	
	Acropole A2	GrN 6054	5280±80	4400−3860	
	Acropole A2	GrN 6052	5370±40	4410 −3900	
	Acropole II	TUNC 58	5665±121	4725−4385	
	Apadana 6 (=A2)	P-912	5581±72	4550−4155	
Jaffarabad	1 (2m)	TUNC 3	5062±68	4085−3665	
	2 (3.2m)	TUNC 4	5166±72	4135−3785	
	2 (4.1m)	TUNC 5	5246±71	4340−3865	
	2 (4.5m)	TUNC 6	5238±72	4335−3860	
	3	TUNC 43	4966±84	3925−3550	
	3	TUNC 44	5096±121	4120−3660	
	3	TUNC 46	5141±122	4140−3675	
	3	TUNC 48	5133±94	4135−3670	
Tall-i-Ghazir	5, 6 (=d/A)	P−930	7762 ± 98		6045±1000
Farukhabad	B 45	M−2153	5760±200	5175−4160	
Tepe Sabz	A1	I−1499	6050±140	5285−4570	
	A1	SI−203	6170±200	5455−4585	
	A2	SI−204	6060±200	5330−4555	
	A2	I−1503	5860±230	5220−4410	
	A2	SI−205	5700±250	5040−4120	
	A3	SI−156	5770±120	4945−4425	
	A3	I−1502	6060±140	5290−4575	
	A3	UCLA−750A	6070±100	5300−4575	
	B1	I−1500	5410±160	4540−3885	
	B3	I−1493	6470±160	5710−5090	
	C1	I−1501	7460±160		5734±1000
	C3	UCLA−750B	6925±200	6285−5360	
	C3	SI−206	7200±1000		5466±1000
	D	I−1497	6740±190	6060−5265	
	D	UCLA−750C	9050±160		7372±1000
Ali Kosh (MJ Phase)	A2	I−1495	7220±160		
	A2	SI−160	8920±100		9188±1000
	A2	I−1494	7820±190		8055±1000
(AK Phase)	B1	SI−207	7740±600		7972±1000
	B1	I−1491	8100±170		8343±1000
	B1	I−1490	9950±190		10249±1000
	B2	0−1845	8250±175		8498±1000

Table 3. (Continued)

The Lowland Steppe		Laboratory	B.P. 5568 hl	B.C.: 95% Confidence	b.c.: B.P. × 1.03−1950±1000
	B2	0−1848	7770±330		
	B2	0−1833	8425±180		
	B2	0−1816	8425±180	same sample	8678±1000
	B2	Shell 1246	8410±200		
	B2	Shell 1174	8850±210		9115±1000
	C1	I−1496	7380±180		7601±1000
(BM Phase)	C2	I−1489	7670±170		7900±1000
	C2	UCLA−750D	9900±200		10197±1000
Chogha Mami		BM−483	6846±182	6200−5325	
The Karkheh Drainage					
Seh Gabi (Mound C)	(Shanabad Period)	SI−2668	6220±280	5380−4935	
	(Shanabad Period)	SI−2669	6195±105	5350−4920	
	(Shanabad Period)	SI−2670	6055±80	5260−4730	
Seh Gabi (Mound B)	(Godin IX)	SI−4909	5495±60	4520−3980	
	(Godin IX)	SI−4910	5020±70	4115−3685	
	(Godin IX)	SI −4911	5240±55	4335−3860	
	(Godin IX)	SI−4912	5175±50	4135−3785	
	(Godin IX)	SI−4913	5430±50	4425−3940	
	(Godin IX−X)	SI−4914	5155±85	4305−3675	
	(Godin X)	SI−4915	5625280	4705−4150	
Seh Gabi (Mound A)	(Godin VII)	SI−4917	4690±50	3755−3195	
	(Godin VII)	SI−4918	4470±60	3470−2945	
Godin Tepe	(Godin VII)	GaK−1074	4729±120	3780−3185	
	(Godin VII)	GaK−1073	5699±99	4885−4405	
Sarab	SI−4	P−465	7605±96		5883±1000
	SI−5	P−466	7956±98		6245±1000
	SI−1	P−467	7644±89		5923±1000
Guran	Level U	K−1006	8410±200		6712±1000
	Level H	K−879	7760±150		6043±1000
Ganj Dareh	Level B (2.1−2.4m)	P−1486	8888±98		6679±1000
	Level C (4.5m)	P−1485	9239±196		7566±1000
	Level D (6.2m)	P−1484	8968±100		7287±1000
	Level E (6.7−6.8m)	SI−922	8570±310		6877±1000
	Level E (7.5−7.6m)	SI−923	8625±195		6934±1000
	Level E (7.6−7.8m)	SI−924	8640±90		6949±1000
	Level E (7.6m)	SI−925	8385±75		6686±1000

Table 3. (Continued)

The Lowland Steppe		Laboratory	B.P. 5568 hl	B.C.: 95% Confidence	b.c.: B.P. × 1.03−1950±1000
	Base of mound	GaK−807	10400±150		8762±1000
	1m above GaK−807	GaK−994	8910±170		7227±1000
Asiab	120−140 cm	1714C	8700±100		7011±1000
	140 cm	1714B	8900±100		7217±1000
	below 140 cm	1714F	9050±300		7371±1000
	1.65 −1.70 m	BrN6413	9755±85		8098±1000
Siabid		P−442	5815±83	5020−4435	
		QU−1035	5870±120	5080−4545	
Bog-i No		I−1492	6200±140	5420−4895	
Southern Zagros-Fars Bakun	B1 (Shamsabad Period)	P−438	5990±81	5230−4575	
	B1 (Shamsabad Period)	P−931	6264±70	5395−4990	
Mushki		Tk 35b	6800±600	6005−5370 (bone)	
		Tk 35a	3610±110	2305−1720 (bone)	
		Tk 34	8640±120	(charcoal)	
Nokhodi	(Late Chalco.)	BMI-171	5050±150	4130−3570	
Tall-i Gap	2	Gak−198	5440±120	4525−3915	
	1	Gak−197	5870±160	5195−4435	
Azerbaijan Yanik Tepe	(Pisdeli period?)	P−1245	5090±56	4100−3675	
	(Pisdeli period?)	P−1246	5267±73	4355−3870	
Pisdeli	I (Pisdeli period)	P−157	5460±160	4555−3900	
	II,5 (Pisdelli period)	P−504	5518±81	4550−3970	
	II,10 (Pisdelli period)	P−505	5638±85	4715−4365	
Rezaiyeh Road Tepe	(Pisdeli period)	P−866	5445±72	4430−3945	
RY-2	(Pisdeli period)	Shell Dev	5730±190	5065−4135	
Hajji Firuz	H12 (6) (H.F. Period)	P−1843	6870±100	6120−5385	
	V:4 (H.F. Period)	P−502	6895±83	6160−5400	
	D15 (H.F. Period)	P−455	7269±86	5538±1000	
	68-S-70 (Pisdeli Period)	P−1841	5450±80	4535−3930	
	68-S-73 (Pisdeli Period)	P−1842	5370±80	4425−3890	
Yanik	P7 (Late Neolithic)	P−1244	7035±69	6295−5470	
	P5 (Late Neolithic)	P−1243	6926±80	6195−5410	
Sayid Hammadani	(H.F. Period)	Shell Dev	7800±210	6084±1000	
Dalma IV	(Dalma Period)	P−503	5986 + 87	5230−4575	

Note: 95% confidence intervals based on Klein et al. (1982) calibration tables. For publication of dates, see *Radiocarbon*, vols. 1, 5, 8, 9, 10, 11, 12, 14, 15, 16; Oates 1972; Hole, Flannery, and Neely 1969; Hole 1977; for Seh Gabi A,B, Henrickson 1983; for Fars, Sumner, pers. comm.; for Asiab, Howe 1983:116.

Table 4. Excavated Strata and Total Number of Sites in Each Deh Luran Phase

Text Period	Phase	Ali Kosh	Chagha Sefid	Tepe Sabz	Musiyan	Farukhabad	Total Sites	"Centers"
Late Village Period	Sargarab						2	none
	Susa A						5	Musiyan
Middle Village Period	Farukh					X	13	Farukhabad
	Bayat			X		X	16	Sabz,
								Musiyan
	Mehmeh			X	X		18	
Early Village Period	Khazineh			X			20	
	Sabz		X	X			8	
	Chogha Mami Transitional		X				5	
Initial Village Period	Surkh		X				1	
	Sefid		X				1	
	Mohammad Jaffar	X	X				3	
	Ali Kosh	X	X				2	
	Bus Mordeh	X					1	

Table 5. Changes in Status of Sites during the Later Village Periods in Deh Luran

	Early Village Period			Middle Village Period			Late Village Period	
	Chogha Mami Trans.	Sabz	Khazineh	Mehmeh	Bayat	Farukh	Susa A	Sargarab
Number of Occupied Sites	5	8	20	18	16	14	5	2
From Occupied to Occupied		3	7	14	12	7	5	0
From Occupied to Not		2	1	4	6	9	9	5
From Not to Occupied		5	13	4	4	7	0	2
Number That Change Status		7	14	8	10	16	9	7
Percent Occupied	14	23	57	51	46	40	14	6
Percent That Change		20	40	23	29	46	26	20

Table 6. Occupational History of Sites on the Deh Luran Plain

Number of Periods Occupied	Number of Sites	Total Periods Occupied	
1	10	10	
2	11	22	
3	5	15	
4	4	16	
5	5	25	
	35	88	Average 2.5 periods/site

Table 7. Chronology of Strata in Excavated Sites on the Susiana Plain

Text Period	Phase	Susa	Jaffar-abad	Chogha Mish	Qabr Shekheyn	Bende-bal	Jowi	Chogha Bonut	Boneh Fazili	Tula'i
Late Village Period	Terminal Susa A	X								
	Susa	X	X	X	X	X				
Middle Village Period	Chogha Mish		X	X	X	X	X	X	X	
Early Village Period	Jaffarabad		X	X			X		X	
Initial Village Period	Archaic III			X					X	
	Archaic II			X					X	
	Archaic I			X				X	X	X
	Pre-Ceramic							X		

Table 8. Changes in Status of Sites during the Susa Period in Susiana

	Middle Village Period	Late Village Period	
	Susiana d	Early Susa A	Late Susa A
Number of Occupied Sites	87	82	53
From Occupied to Occupied		60	40
From Occupied to Not		27	42
Number that Change Status		49	55
Percent Occupied	76	71	46
Percent That Change		43	48

Table 9. Mean Sizes in Hectares of Measurable Late Village Period Sites in Susiana during One or More Subperiods

Phases Occupied	All Periods	Late Susa A	Early Susa A	Susiana d	"Centers"
All Periods	2.0				
Late Susa A		.7	1.7	1.8	Susa 15 ha.
Early Susa A			1.0	1.4	Susa 15 ha.
Susiana d				1.2	Chogha Miṣh 15 ha.
Number of Sites Measured	30	4	14	47	3

Note: 98 of 115 sites were measurable.

Table 10. Proportion of Sites in Each Region of the Susiana Plain during the Village and Uruk Periods

Text Periods	Phases and Alternate Names	West of Karkheh	Karkheh to Diz	Diz to Shur	East of Shur	North of Road	South of Haft Tepe Ridge	N
Uruk	Late Uruk	0	50	36	0	7	7	14
	Middle Uruk	1	44	33	10	10	2	52
	Early Uruk	2	47	33	6	10	2	49
	Total	2	47	32	8	9	2	133
Late Village Period	Terminal Susa A	0	55	28	11	6	0	18
	Late Susa A (=Susa)	4	36	26	38	2	4	53
	Early Susa A	3	25	31	31	9	0	77
Middle Village Period	Susiana d (=Chogha Mish)	2	28	30	31	2	6	86
	Susiana b-c			data not available				
Early Village Period	Susiana a (=Jaffarabad)	6	38	44	12	0	0	16
	Total	3	31	31	28	4	3	250
Initial Village Period	Archaic	4	29	46	13	0 ·	8	25
	All Periods	3	35	32	21	6	3	389

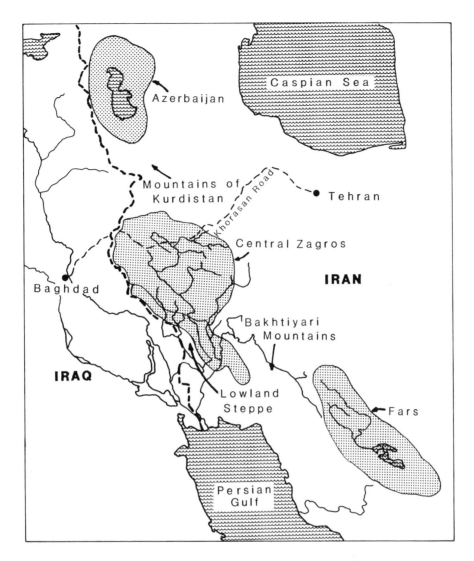

Figure 2. Locations of four principal regions of western Iran: the lowland steppe, Azerbaijan, the central Zagros, the mountain plains of Fars.

Figure 3. Cities in western Iran. Many of the regions mentioned in the text, such as valleys and agricultural plains, are called by their associated cities.

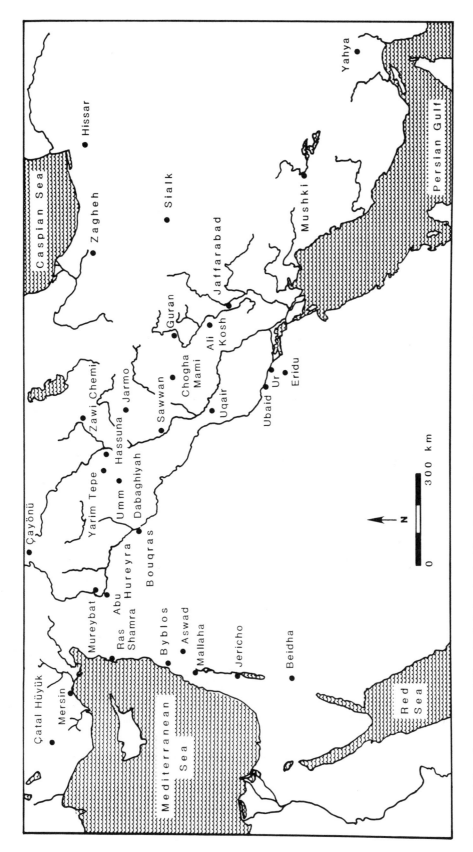

Figure 4. Selected prominent Village Period sites in the Near East, with emphasis on those located outside Iran.

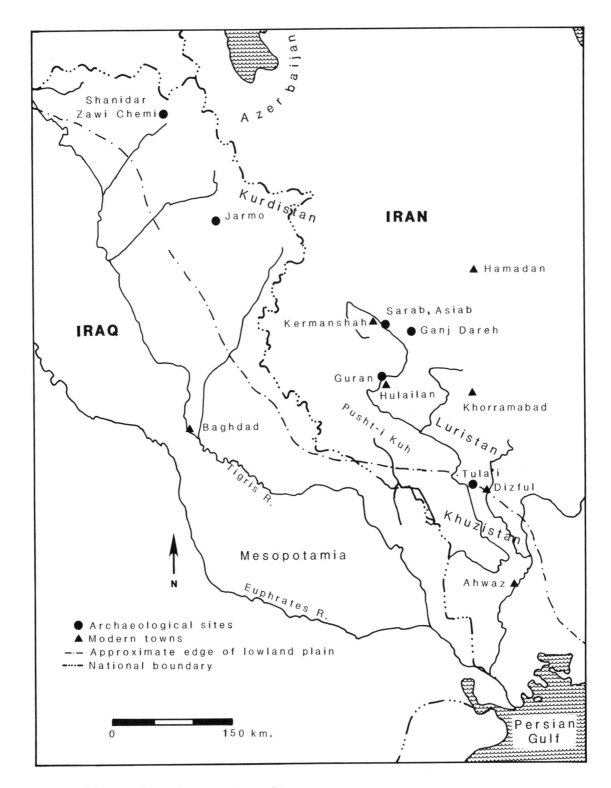

Figure 5. Selected early sites in western Iran and Iraq.

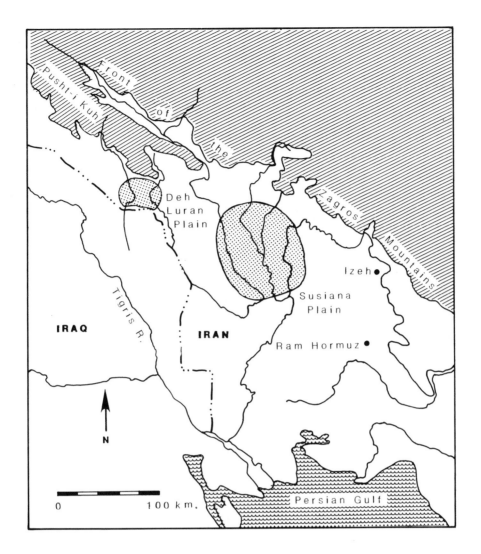

Figure 6. The lowland steppe of western Iran, including the Deh Luran, Susiana, Ram Hormuz, and Izeh plains.

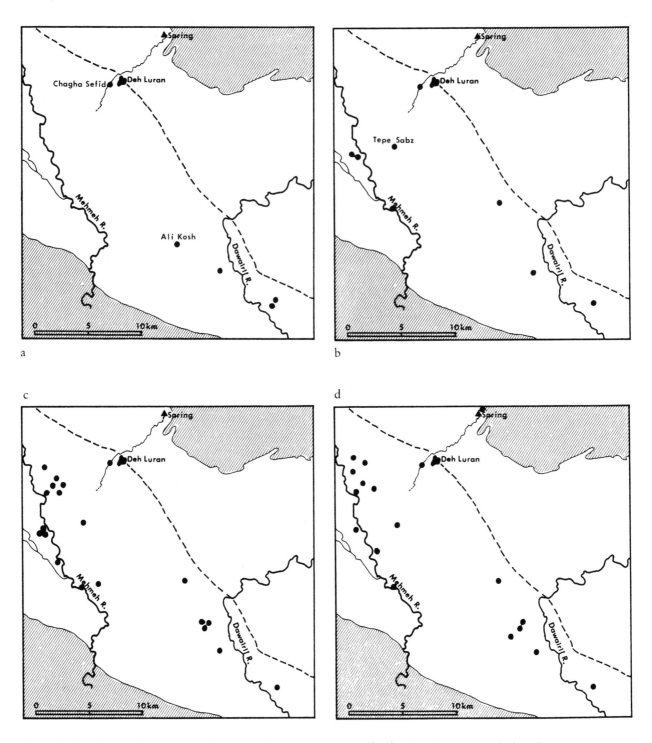

Figure 7. Distribution of sites on the Deh Luran Plain, by phase: (a) Chogha Mami Transitional, (b) Sabz,
(c) Khazineh, (d) Mehmeh.

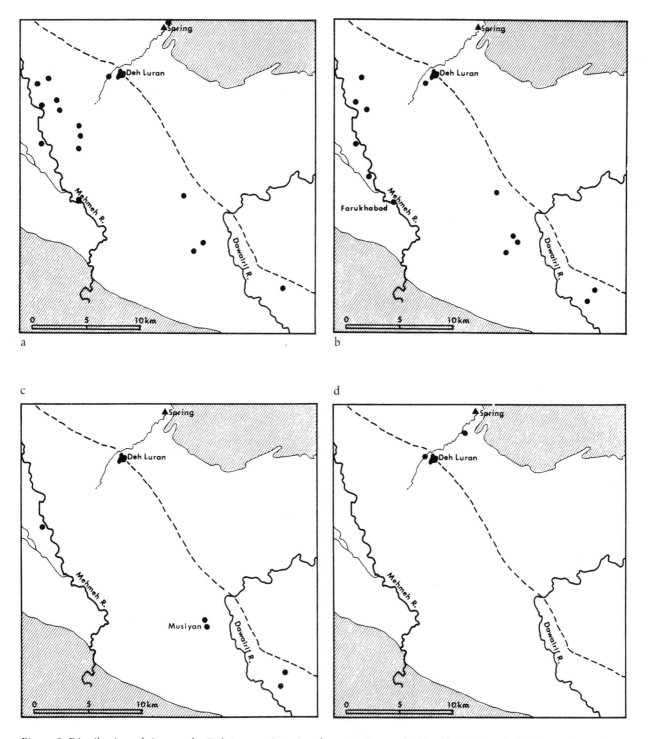

Figure 8. Distribution of sites on the Deh Luran Plain, by phase: (a) Bayat, (b) Farukh, (c) Susa A, (d) Sargarab.

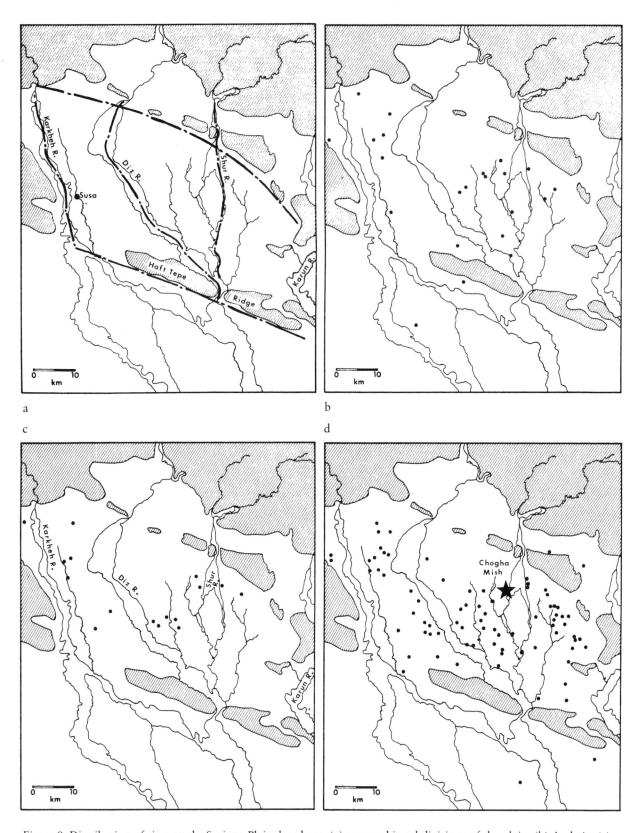

Figure 9. Distribution of sites on the Susiana Plain, by phase: (a) geographic subdivisions of the plain, (b) Archaic, (c) Jaffarabad, (d) Susiana d. The sites indicated on the map are those located within the map area, for which data were available. Thus all of the known sites attributed to each phase may not be depicted on the map.

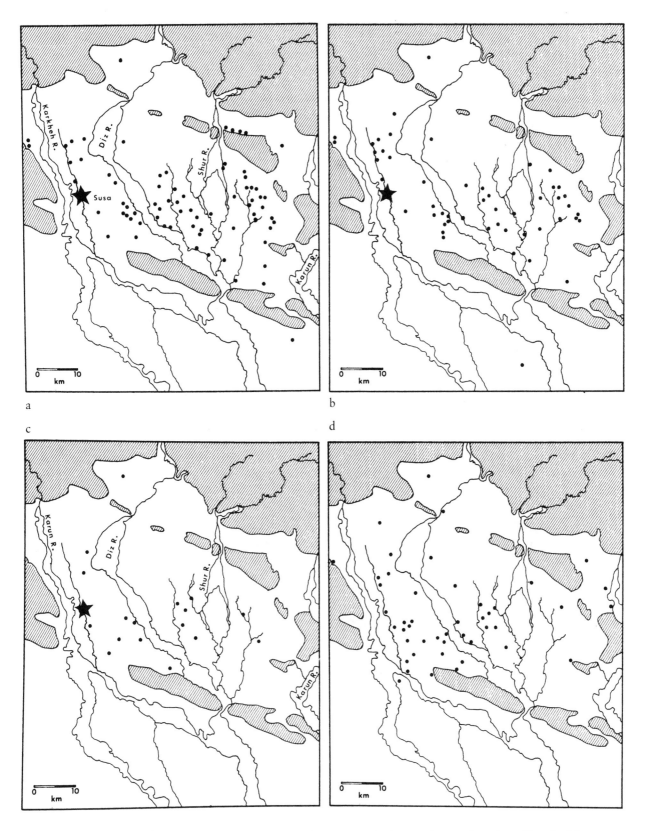

Figure 10. Distribution of sites on the Susiana Plain, by phase: (a) Early Susa A, (b) Late Susa A, (c) Terminal Susa A, (d) Early Uruk. The sites indicated on the map are those located within the map area, for which data were available. Thus all of the known sites attributed to each phase may not be depicted on the map.

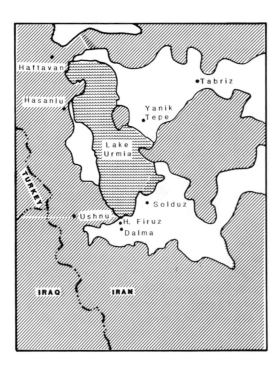

Figure 11. Map of the Azerbaijan region surrounding
Lake Urmia.

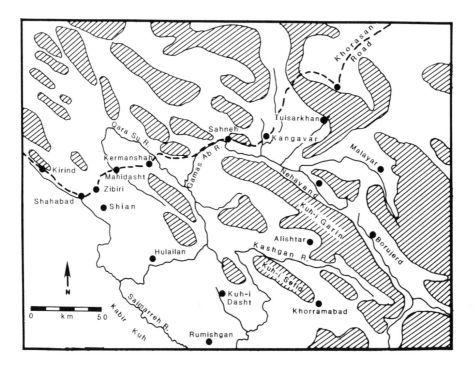

Figure 12. Map of the central Zagros area, indicating modern towns after which
surrounding valleys are named. The dashed line is the Khorasan Road, or Great
High Road, leading from Hamadan on the Iranian plateau down to Bagdad on the
plains below.

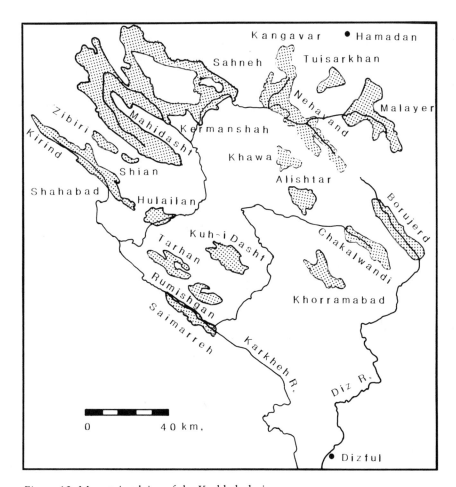

Figure 13. Mountain plains of the Karkheh drainage.

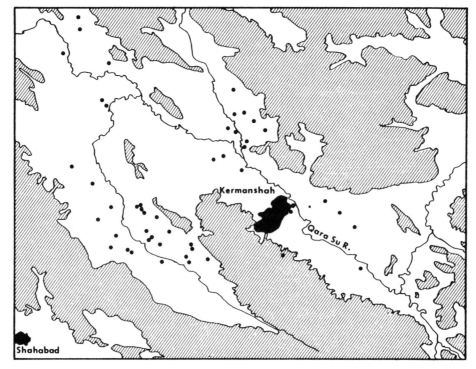

a

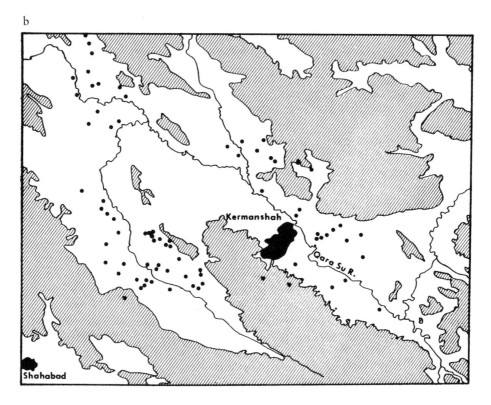

b

Figure 14. Distribution of sites in the Mahidasht, by period; (a) J-ware and Dalma, (b) Ubaid. The sites indicated on the map are those located within the map area, for which data were available. Thus all of the known sites attributed to each phase may not be depicted on the map.

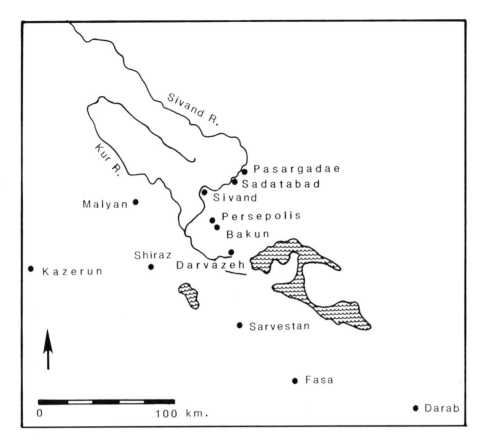

Figure 15. The Marv Dasht region in the southern Zagros region of Fars.

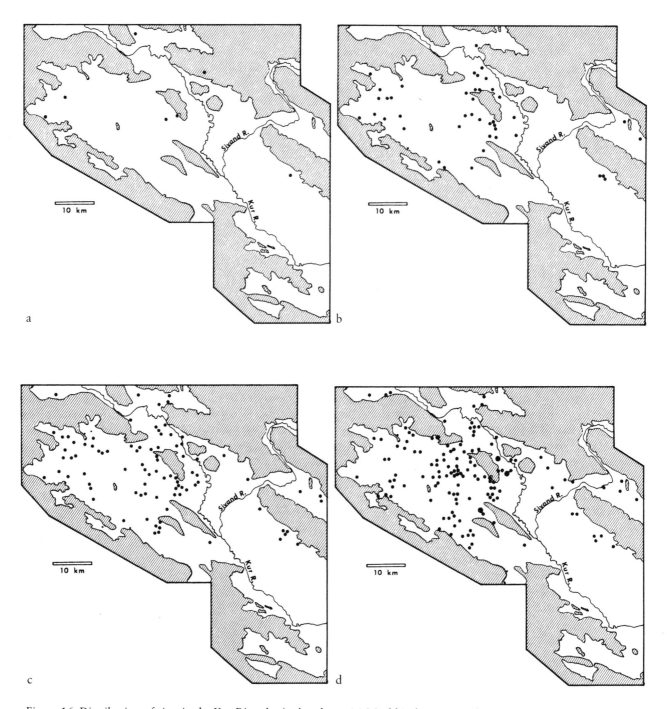

Figure 16. Distribution of sites in the Kur River basin, by phase: (a) Mushki, (b) Jari, (c) Shamsabad, (d) Bakun. The sites indicated on the map are those located within the map area, for which data were available. Thus all of the known sites attributed to each phase may not be depicted on each map.

Chapter 3

Settlement and Society in the Village Period

FRANK HOLE

Introduction

The data presented in the previous chapter provide a chronological outline of the sedentary occupations in the major regions of western Iran, and a sense of changes in the distribution and number of settlements up to the beginning of the fourth millennium B.C. In some areas, the outline is reasonably detailed. Nevertheless, survey coverage has been uneven and there are few published excavations that provide information beyond chronology. The data base, therefore, consists largely of settlement data, supplemented by information gained through excavation. All in all, even by archaeological standards, it is a meager base from which to derive inferences about the culture history of the region, but it is no poorer than the data for most other regions of the Near East. It does provide us with the opportunity to examine some questions of general interest in a comparative way and to reconstruct some elements of the histories of particular regions.

It has become customary in archaeology to make a distinction between questions of process and those of culture history. By means of the former, one attempts to discover the reasons underlying the facts of regional differences and similarities, and changes within and between regions. By means of the latter, one attempts a kind of paleo-ethnography in which elements of the way of life of the time are reconstructed. Culture history is less an explanatory exercise than a chronicling of events. Of course, the two approaches may be merged and this is what we attempt to do here.

A host of possible "causes" for historical events has been proposed under the general rubric of "prime movers." Some of these are socially regulated, such as warfare, trade, ideology, and technological innovation; others are independent or exogenous factors, such as population pressure, diffusion, and the potential of the natural environment for expansion in space or in intensity of exploitation. A number of essays criticizing these unicausal factors have been written. Two recent examples are Blanton et al. (1981:14–16) and Price (1982), who argue, as do many archaeologists today, for a systemic or multicausal approach in which the single prime movers are merely elements acting in concert with others. There is consensus among the systemicists that the most important (or core) factors have to do ultimately with food—or energy, to use a more general form of expression. Price (1982:709) puts it this way: "Those behaviors which harness, or encapsulate, relatively more energy will be relatively more important systemically." Blanton et al. (1981:16) focus on "the way people or whole systems survive (or not)," emphasizing such fundamental matters as energy balances and survival. They believe that questions of "why" can be resolved ultimately by referring to these core factors.

A goal of archaeological investigation is to "understand similarities, differences, and changes in human societies" (Price 1982:9). Price approaches this through a rigorous cultural materialism; Blanton et al. use an approach they call evolutionism, that is, the changes in cultural systems: "Cultural evolution, like biological evolution, probably moves opportunistically, solving only today's problems, proceeding rather blindly, without a predetermined course, into the future" (Blanton et al. 1981:13).

Blanton et al. provide some operational means by

which one can investigate cultural evolution through the use of archaeological data. They propose to study scale, integration, and complexity. In essence, scale refers to the size of the unit of study; integration refers to the relative independence of units; and complexity to the diversity of functions found in either vertical or horizontal integration. This is a systemic approach. Price adds a useful concept to the discussion: adaptation, in which the fittest survive the rigors of natural selection. This concept then enables us to make direct use of settlement pattern data:

> Settlement pattern (is) a virtual isomorph of infrastructure and political economy, which records and preserves the most significant features of energy production and flow. Since Darwinian adaptation is by definition operationalized on grounds of population numbers and distributions, the paradigmatic mandate is direct and overwhelming. Despite the customary strictures concerning the use of negative evidence, one can say that what is not observable or reliably recoverable from this class of data was probably of negligible systemic importance (Price 1982:728).

One need not agree wholly with Price's optimistic assessment to see the advantages conferred by survey data, and we shall have occasion to refer again to her arguments.

Underlying both approaches outlined above is the belief that, although there are a multiplicity (essentially infinite) of special circumstances that may converge in any particular region, there are only a limited number of structural responses—greater or lesser scale, integration and complexity, whose success (adaptation) is measured by survival and growth. If one tracks the organizational bases of ancient societies, one necessarily charts changes in these variables. The first part of this chapter, therefore, deals with matters of systemic change in settlement, within and between regions.

To discuss only factors that can be demonstrated through a limited range of empirical data, however, omits much of interest. We shall therefore address some of the traditional problems of culture history, and, finally, provide some more speculative reconstructions of life during the Village Period. The problems of culture history have to do with subsistence (agricultural sedentism and pastoral transhumance), questions of interaction and isolation, the relative rates of change in different areas, the organization of Susiana society, and the emergence of social complexity.

Our reconstructions confront certain human problems that require social solution. We can enumerate these as follows: (1) shortage of food resulting from such factors as drought, flood, crop or livestock diseases, fire, insects, warfare, and raiding; (2) the variable quality of land and resources; (3) environmental degradation; (4) mediation of interpersonal strife; (5) mediation with the supernatural world; (6) human mortality and morbidity; and (7) interethnic strife. Rather than take up this list serially, I incorporate comments on the various factors into the sections that follow.

Subsumed in this list is the problem of communication or, as some have put it, "information processing," whether this be communication with the physical, biological, social, or supernatural worlds. According to one approach, evidence of the integration of society—another way of saying "effectiveness of communication"—is in the scale and organization of its constituent units. This approach has been outlined by Johnson (1982b, n.d.; chapter 4, this volume), with the interesting conclusion that organizations that are nonhierarchical must be relatively small. After compiling a variety of empirical data on performance, he finds that six equivalent decision-making units is about the size that a small egalitarian group can sustain effectively. When the number of these units grows larger, the system will incur "scalar stress" and either split or become hierarchical. We shall see later how we can use these ideas to help interpret the nature of Susiana society from settlement data.

Variation and Change in Settlement

An outline of settlement region by region is given in chapter 1. Here I attempt to assess the variability from one valley or region to another, and changes from period to period. Each region is put into sharper perspective by this comparative approach because we look at the similarities and differences. However, before we deal with the settlements themselves, it is useful to review the nature of the data.

An intrinsic limitation of settlement data is the effect of differential preservation and exploration. Not all sites in any single region have been found; indeed, we have only initial surveys in some regions with the consequent high probability that the number of known sites would be increased twofold or more by subsequent work. In such cases it is usually the smaller sites that are overlooked, but early sites buried by later occupations may also not be noticed during rapid reconnaissance. Within our principal regions, Hulailan (figures 12, 13) in the central Zagros has seen the most intensive work, but only for a portion of that small valley. The Deh Luran and Susiana plains on the lowland steppe (figures 7–10) have both been surveyed with the use of aerial photos and closely spaced transects, so that most of the visible sites must have been discovered. Much of the Kur River basin in Fars

Frank Hole

(figures 15, 16) has also seen this level of investigation, which ranks as among the most complete in the Near East.

The situation is worse in the Mahidasht in the central Zagros (figures 12, 13), where only parts of the valley system were reexamined by the Royal Ontario Museum team, and Shahabad and Shian were not reexamined. The Kangavar Valley has been carefully searched, but this represents only a small part of the larger Kangavar region. The other valleys within the Karkheh drainage have seen only superficial survey in which the more obvious sites have been recorded. Only the Solduz-Ushnu valleys within Azerbaijan (figures 2, 11) have been carefully and systematically examined, leaving the greater part of this region with only superficial reconnaissance. The mountainous regions of Kurdistan, Luristan, and Bakhtiari country (figure 2) are essentially unexplored in spite of some attention to locations along trails or roads.

An additional complicating variable is the state of preservation of sites. We know in Deh Luran and Susiana that as much as 4 meters of alluvium has covered the plains since the first settlements; thus there is high probability that many, if not most, early sites are buried and invisible at the surface. In this region, settlement at some sites continued over thousands of years so that early small components are often hidden beneath massive later constructions. At the moment we can do nothing about these problems except to recognize that our distributional data for the earlier periods have little meaning in terms of a settlement system. The situation may be similar in parts of the Mahidasht, but not everywhere. The central part of that valley alongside the major rivers has been affected the most, but relatively little alluviation occurred in Kangavar or in Hulailan, and we do not know the situation in the remainder of the valleys of the Karkheh drainage. The Saimarreh Valley, potentially a choice location, has been heavily eroded, leaving a few sites on remnant land surfaces. Alluviation has little affected sites in Fars so that data there should be relatively good for the early as well as later periods.

A problem identified by Kirkby and Kirkby (1976) and later discussed by Brookes, Levine, and Dennell (1982), that of deflation, has been inadequately assessed for the variety of conditions in western Iran. In essence, deflation refers to the fact that sites, like hills, erode and consequently become shorter and broader with time. It is implied that the older a site is, the less likely it will still retain a mounded appearance.

Finally, as nearly all surveys have focused on agricultural plains, we are able to say next to nothing about settlement in the intervening regions, or even on the lower slopes of the plains. These crucial areas constitute the primary grazing lands and the places where camps of herders would be found. In the absence of solid information on mobile people, we cannot hope to construct more than a rudimentary picture of what a settlement system during any period might constitute.

Having enumerated a number of discouraging things about our data base, I shall now list some factors that may be at the root of actual differences and changes in such settlement as has been discovered. First, settlement must relate to the local resources. Without invoking the nebulous concept of carrying capacity, it is both intuitively obvious and empirically demonstrated that settlements are denser in "richer" areas. The quality of the area depends on certain intrinsic properties such as rainfall, soils, climate, and on the ability of people to make use of them. Thus, technology, in the broad sense of types of domesticates, herding and farming techniques, and dependable distribution of scattered resources by social means, all come into play. Second, settlement is related to changes in the environment induced by natural and anthropogenic factors. Changing climate following the Pleistocene may well account for the sequence of initial settlement and some of its changes later throughout western Iran, but once people were in an area, their damage to the landscape through alteration of the natural vegetation because of farming and grazing and cutting trees for fuel, and salination as a result of irrigation, had effects on the location and duration of settlements. Finally history itself was a powerful force in determining the location of settlements. After the Initial Period, there were no empty plains to colonize, so that new sites were placed in relation to those that already existed and to the camps of herders or hunters who may have interacted with the sedentary farmers.

Some idea of the way prehistoric settlements compare with modern villages can be gained from examination of tables 11 and 12 (also see Dollfus 1983b). Although modern villages reflect both ecological and political factors that may be different from those affecting the prehistoric villagers, the figures give a sense of relative densities that seem to accurately reflect the relative agricultural potentials of the valleys.

We must imagine Iran not as a small-scale two-dimensional map, but as it is—an extensive, rugged, topographic region, cut by rivers and gorges, interrupted by mountain ridges, covered with forests, and composed of gypseous, boulder-strewn slopes. Rarely does one settle in this tangled landscape on a flat, well-watered plain, and these little oases are often widely separated. The prevailing scarcity of good agricultural land is one of the facts of western Iran, despite the potential, in places, to support large populations. The major part of western Iran is not suited to permanent settlement in agricultural villages, even though it is suitable for grazing and for supporting the wild cereals. Much of the land is or was forested, providing opportunities for harvesting food, but serving as a barrier to both agriculture and herding. This is a landscape in which the typical enclave of settlement was isolated (more than a day's walk) and out of direct contact with any other. Under the circumstances, these enclaves must have been largely self-sustaining and, therefore, separate and independent settlement systems.

The nomadic people must be the links between the various systems. The distances and barriers described above are of little moment to herders who, in the course of a year, may circulate very widely, impinging on several settled enclaves. Geography figures importantly in their movements only insofar as it creates barriers that are impassable and creates seasonal pasturage. In these instances, mountain passes assume overriding importance and may determine the direction of movement and interaction. Unfortunately, we know little about former migration patterns, particularly about the distance any group might travel. That distance must have depended on density of settled and nomad populations, accessibility of suitable pasturage, distribution of forests or other barriers, and portability of the ménage. After studying modern transhumant people I concluded that the early pastoralists probably moved only short distances (Hole 1978a). If that were the case, it would have been rare for any nomadic group to have reached more than one settled enclave and many may have been out of routine touch of any at all (e.g., Hakalan and Parchineh). Under such circumstances, one might find greatly divergent rates of development and change in the various enclaves.

The Initial Village Period

The shift to sedentism in relatively permanent villages is not explicitly recorded in Iran, although there are suggestions of the process, especially in basal Ganj Dareh and Guran (figure 5) where the initial settlements consisted of temporary camps that were utilized seasonally. These deposits lack the mud-walled architecture and conform most closely to the style of hunters' huts made of perishable materials. Following closely on these in both instances are rectangular mud-walled houses, perhaps occupied permanently. The shift in degree of sedentism and in architecture follows the pattern discussed by Flannery (1972a) in his comparative study of the Near East and Mesoamerica, where he attributed the change in architecture to a change in the organization of society. Johnson's recent research sheds some light on the factors that may have underlain the change in social organization. According to Johnson (chapter 4), when an egalitarian group reaches a size of six or more equivalent units (e.g., families), scalar stress sets in (disputes, etc.) which

encourages fissioning. A way to overcome this tendency and still enjoy the company of more people is to enlarge the basal organizational units from nuclear to extended families. By such a process, village size might increase fourfold without incurring scalar stress or the need to organize hierarchically. In effect, the shift from round to rectangular houses signals a corresponding shift from the nuclear family to the potential for housing an extended family in rectangular houses whose modular nature permits easy modification of the space. If Johnson is correct, when we find houses large enough to hold extended families (see Dollfus 1983b), the society must already have passed through an episode of scalar stress. This reconstruction says nothing about why the societies grew; for this we must turn to other fundamental matters such as ability to capture energy.

We are not safe in regarding our data on site numbers as other than an indication of where the first settlements occurred. The Hulailan Valley may hold the best indication yet found of the nature of early sedentism in that it indicates that Epipaleolithic and Neolithic sites are in the same locations. The Neolithic villages were sited along the river, but within easy access to the caves that the people continued to use. This distribution implies an emphasis on herding (or hunting and collecting) and accords well with our finding of early sherds in caves of Khorramabad (but so far no villages to go with them) and with the implications of transhumance in Deh Luran and Mahidasht as indicated at Ali Kosh and Chagha Sefid, and Sarab. In the initial stages of sedentism in the Zagros, agriculture may have been of less importance than herding (Hole 1985). The situation of Asiab in this picture remains ambiguous, but Ganj Dareh seems to fit the pattern. One thus sees the heartland of early sedentism as being in the mountains and perhaps in the adjacent lowland winter pastures. Why one finds no similarly early sites in Azerbaijan or Fars, or, for that matter, in most of the valleys of the Karkheh drainage, is difficult on present evidence to determine. The various surveys in the Bakhtiari Mountains hold promise also of establishing a link with the Epipaleolithic and the first sedentary villages, again implying the primacy here of herding rather than of agriculture.

There is a thin scatter of sites with soft-ware pottery, corresponding to what McDonald (1979) calls the Middle Neolithic. Like Mortensen (1964), she sees the ceramics of the Karkheh drainage as being part of a Zagros group, including the site of Jarmo and others known from survey in Iraqi Kurdistan (Braidwood et al., eds. 1983). Many of these sites are at lower elevations than those in Iran and they are also larger, perhaps reflecting the richer environment (McDonald 1979:551).

The Late Neolithic is represented by more sites, and a seeming expansion into new and higher areas. McDonald (1979:552) points to the evident clustering of these sites in the Mahidasht in groups of three to four. From excavation data from Sarab, Guran, and Seh Gabi C, she infers that there was greater sedentism than in the Middle Neolithic (McDonald 1979:556–57). Despite the apparent greater density and the colonization of new lands, the early villages are scattered and widely separated from one another, leaving plenty of space around each village to accommodate gathering of wild foods, grazing for the village flocks, and agriculture. One would suspect that living space was freely available. However, caution is in order because it is likely that we have failed to find evidence of the actual density: we are glimpsing only the tip of a settlement iceberg which has either eroded away or lies under seas of alluvium. Moreover, a substantial element of the population during the period may have lived in tent sites such as Tula'i whose traces are difficult to recognize and have seldom been found.

Although it may not be useful to speculate on the nature of an Initial Period settlement system, a suggestion by Mortensen (personal communication) clearly has merit. In his view, the early villages occur in groups, each group widely separated from the next. We have already seen how this is true in Mahidasht, and Mortensen cites the following additional examples: the group in Susiana, Chogha Bonut, Boneh Fazili, and Chogha Mish; the western Hulailan group of Guran, Tepe Faisala, Asiabian, and others; and Ganj Dareh and other nearby sites. Let us assume that these early settlements did tend to cluster and that the sites mentioned exemplify this tendency. Why should this be so? There is at least one very practical social reason: the viability of the local groups. That is, it would have been difficult for the inhabitants of a village of one hundred or so persons to supply marriageable pairs continually; thus marriage partners must have been supplied from outside. Among people today who live at low density, the figure of five hundred comes up as the minimum size necessary to maintain a viable social system (Birdsell 1973:337–38; Wobst 1974). Assuming a system of some five hundred persons in the Initial Village Period, it must have been the case that any particular village was closely allied through marriage and other social ties to at least three or four others: hence, a "cluster." In areas such as the Deh Luran Plain, where surveys indicate a "shortage" of people, we may need to look beyond the geographic boundaries of survey (into Iraq) or look to herding peoples to supplement the group.

One would expect ceramics to be nearly identical within a closely related group, and this is what the clusters show. This notion of the relation between site clusters and social systems also provides an explanation of the differences between regions in that direct exchange of people (potters) would have been much reduced as compared with ingroup movement through marriage and for other reasons.

The Early Village Period

This period is well expressed in all regions and is marked by a substantial increase in the number of sites so that we may, for the first time, be able to infer something of a system; certainly we are on more secure ground in recognizing differences and similarities. The lack of precision in radiocarbon and stratigraphic dating in all regions makes it impossible to compare the trajectories of change in much detail, but there are some striking differences. In table 12, we see that the increase in number of sites over the Initial Period is rather low and probably gradual in the major lowland plains to the south and Azerbaijan to the north (which got a late start). Continuity of settlement and "budding off" of surplus population is thus indicated. By contrast, Mahidasht in the central Zagros sees a sudden intrusion of a foreign ceramic representing an apparently rapid filling of the plain. A similar situation is seen in Kangavar where Dalma sites appear in large numbers, making this plain the "other" center of that ware. It is evident that both J-ware and Dalma originated outside the Mahidasht and Kangavar, presumably in northern Mesopotamia and Azerbaijan, so that actual movement of exogenous peoples bearing these wares is indicated.

The situation in Fars in the southern Zagros (figures 2, 15, 16) is somewhat different in that, although Jari pottery suddenly appears on a large number of sites, it is compatible with the previous Mushki tradition and is probably of local origin. With better control over chronology, a situation more like that of the lowland plains would probably become apparent here. Occupation of the remaining plains of Fasa and Darab, southeast of the Kur River basin, begins effectively at the Jari time and probably represents a diffusion of population into these more remote valleys, but the surveys have been too cursory to go beyond this initial assessment.

We see essentially two patterns: indigenous development and continuity of settlement (without discounting the effects of some immigration such as the Chogha Mami Transitional [CMT] into Deh Luran); and the initial settlement of regions by people whose origins were elsewhere. The former shows as gradual increases in the number of sites; the latter as discontinuities in the population curves.

During the Early Village Period, there is some suggestion of a hierarchy of sites in Mahidasht, but not elsewhere. At the least, one is on safe ground to postulate differentiation between sites that are situated to take advantage of irrigation waters, and those that depend on rainfall (see below); still others may turn out, upon excavation, to have been more dependent on herding than on agriculture. McDonald (1979:-556–71) sees a tendency toward more sedentism in the Karkheh region from the Late Neolithic onward, as this is expressed in tool kits from the excavated sites and in the lack of sites (e.g., in Hulailan) that are situated for grazing. She also observes that good sources of flint are lacking in some valleys, such as Nehavand (figures 12, 13), so that settlement there in the sixth millennium may have been prevented by that fact. In the fifth millennium, a lessened dependence on flint and more efficient distribution of blades may have alleviated this problem. Nevertheless, in this period specialist sites have yet to be identified. At the moment, we can describe the settlement pattern as dispersed. According to rough calculations (subject to the caveats about discovery and preservation mentioned earlier), 15 to 96 square kilometers are available, on average, for each village to exploit. The greatest density of sites is in Deh Luran during the Khazineh Phase where only 15 kilometers are available; the least appears to be in Darab with one village for every 96 square kilometers. By any stretch of the imagination, such densities are well below the level that any of these plains will support even by crude agriculture. When we add that it is unlikely that all villages were occupied simultaneously during any identified phase (e.g., Dalma which lasted from 5200–4500 b.c.), we see that the density decreases further still. This exercise in estimating density is useful primarily for the patterns that develop in the following periods.

The Middle Village Period

In the lowland regions there is demonstrable continuity in settlement with the previous period, as seen both in the distributions of sites and in the ceramics. It is also the period during which the maximum number of sites occurs in Susiana, thereafter to decline. In Deh Luran, the peak had already been reached at the end of the Initial Period, and the Middle Period sees a progressive decline. Part of the explanation for the decline must be that larger sites develop so that the actual population may have remained substantially the same, but at present we cannot be definite about this. In Deh Luran the sites of Tepe Sabz, Musiyan, and Farukhabad all seem larger than normal, but the differences are not great: they are perhaps twice as large. In Susiana, on the other hand, Chogha Mish grew to 11 hectares, about eleven times the size of typical villages surrounding it. To complicate the issue of counting residential sites, we know that some sites, such as Jaffarabad, were locations of ceramic workshops rather than villages.

The other regions are not yet effectively subdivided so that for a long period we can present only totals. It is not surprising, therefore, that the largest number of sites occur at this time, but it is important to note that the locations of these sites are sometimes different from those of the earlier period.

In the central Zagros in Mahidasht, Levine and McDonald (1977:49–50) report that the Early Period J-ware sites are on wadis or small streams, whereas Ubaid sites display no such dependence on ground water and irrigation. Some 35 percent of the J-ware sites are on poorly drained soil and, since "virtually every 'J' ware site is located on a wadi or small stream bed . . . we can assume that a reasonable and consistent water supply was of some importance in site location." This contrasts with the Ubaid in which 34 percent of the sites are now on uplands, well removed from the possibility of irrigation. Levine and McDonald attribute this shift to a change in climate. According to their interpretation, as conditions grew wetter during the fifth millennium, it became more feasible to grow crops by rainfall and allowed the Ubaid people to spread out of optimum areas for irrigation.

A growing dependence on irrigation is also implied by the data from Fars where Sumner (1981) has outlined the regions of settlement by phase (figure 16). One of these, known as the Soon irrigation area, saw particularly dense settlement during the Village Period. Sumner traces the use of the Soon region from Jari times when eighteen of the forty-six sites are here and the remainder are where spring-fed streams could have been used. Actual canalization in the Soon area began, according to Sumner, in Shamsabad times when 31 percent of the sites are in the Soon region, occurring at twice the density of sites in other parts of the Kur River basin. Many of these are far enough from any source of surface water to suggest "that the Soon system was first constructed in Shamsabad times" (Sumner 1981:11).

During Bakun times, the number of sites in the Soon region nearly doubled and the areas of these sites approached 45 percent of the total for the period, giving a density four times as great as for any other region. In addition, the three unusually large sites are found clustered in the Soon region. Unfortunately, one can say nothing about their role and, as Sumner says, they may be simply large villages.

Although irrigation is implied beginning in the Early Village Period in some regions and possibly only in the Middle Village Period, if at all in others, it is obvious that not all sites are located with primary concern for surface water. Moreover, it is impossible, on present evidence, to distinguish between a site alongside a stream that practices dry farming from one that uses irrigation. Only when sites cannot be reached by canals can we be certain that irrigation was not used. On the other hand, with modern climate, most of the mountain region can be farmed by rainfall alone and

Frank Hole

the upper parts of the lowland steppe can also be cultivated without irrigation.

Densities of sites during the Middle Village Period are hard to interpret when we lack precise chronological data. However, it is striking to see (table 12) similar density figures from widely separated valleys. On plains that have been carefully surveyed, densities are about one site per 13 to 20 square kilometers when we calculate on the basis of the entire plains and not just separate regions as Sumner did for the Kur River basin. Presumably any valley has its specially dense areas, and these are submerged in the overall statistics.

The Late Village Period

Now we see a dramatic shift. The number of sites drops quickly in the lowlands, first being apparent in Deh Luran and at a slower rate, but no less drastically, ultimately in Susiana. For practical purposes these regions both appear to have been essentially emptied of people by the end of this period. By now, the modern climatic regime was established, giving, if anything, enhanced opportunity for the spread of villages into newly favorable areas. But what we see is not expansion, but a general contraction as it is expressed in the numbers of sites.

To facilitate comparisons, chapter 2, table 10 provides data on the locations of sites on the Susiana Plain by geographic subdivision and by phase. It is immediately apparent that there is a great deal of consistency in the location of sites from phase to phase in that the central part of the plain is always most important and the marginal regions are relatively insignificant. There is a perceptible shift of sites from the Diz River-to-Shur River region to the Karkheh River-to-Diz River region at the time of Susa A, corresponding to the rise of Susa as a temple center. Prior to that, there were relatively more sites in the vicinity of Chogha Mish, the Middle Period center in the Diz-to-Shur region.

In Susiana, settlement distribution appears to be more affected by sheer numbers of sites than by geographic region. In any case, there is no evident shift away from good irrigation areas toward the end of the Village Period. The general shift toward the western side of the plain continues into the Uruk Period, a distribution that may have more to do with purely social factors (nomadic people may be implicated) than with climatic or environmental change.

The decline on the Deh Luran Plain sees a shift in settlement towards the east, and then the abandonment of the plain by the Susa A people whose territory was marginally "invaded" by the Sargarab sites. Effectively, the plain was abandoned for agriculture at the end of the Village Period. The hypothesis that societal conflict caused the sudden drop in population in Deh Luran has been advanced by Wright (1981b:7) who once saw the Sargarab intrusion into Deh Luran

as evidence that highland peoples had forced the Deh Luranis out of their homeland (Wright et al. 1975). Wright now doubts that highland peoples, without substantial help from a nomadic component, could have effected such a demographic shift, but he raises the possibility that conflict between populations in Mesopotamia and Susiana could have made "life on the intermediate Deh Luran plain precarious" (Wright 1981b:70). However, he admits that there is no evidence of conflict in either area in this era. At this time, I judge the conflict hypothesis to be very weak indeed.

The population decline in Iran occurs at about the same time as the great increase in Mesopotamia, manifest in Early to Late Uruk, which Adams (Adams and Nissen 1972:11) believes may have required an influx of people from outside the immediate area. The issues hinge in part on the dates of Early Uruk in Mesopotamia versus Late Susiana, which may overlap if the Uruk began earlier in Mesopotamia than in Iran. If Iranian villagers migrated to the Mesopotamian alluvium toward the end of our Late Village Period, it would account for the decline in sites, but not explain the movement itself.

The single exception to a reduction in number of sites in the Late Period is Kangavar where sites reach their maximum number at the end of the Late Village Period. This anomaly is as difficult to explain as is the decline in sites elsewhere. Henrickson (1983) interprets the expanding Kangavar settlement on the basis of changing climate. During the Early and Middle Village periods it was drier than today, thus accounting for the location of most sites on the valley bottom where water could be obtained for irrigation. In the Late Village Period, settlement expanded toward the drier piedmont areas where dry farming could be practiced under wetter climatic conditions. Nevertheless, during the entire Village Period, sites in Kangavar remained small, "typically well under a hectare in size." She concludes that it had poorer agricultural potential than Mahidasht.

If we grant the accuracy of these inferences about the reasons behind the expansion of sites in the Late Village Period, we must question why other areas, intrinsically more favorable, did not witness the same growth. However convenient it may seem in the Kangavar instance, climatic change cannot explain a simultaneous decline in sites in all the other parts of western Iran.

In the Kur River basin in Fars, Sumner sees a dramatic change with the Lapui Phase.

Every major trend observed in the sequence was radically reversed in the Lapui Period. It is apparent that the requirement for irrigation water was no longer a major factor in the location of settlements. The greater dispersion of sites, and the tendency for new settlements to be founded in regions adjacent to natural pasturage, suggest an increased reliance on herded animals (Sumner 1981).

Sumner suggests, as reasons for this shift, a gradual deterioration in soils due to salinization, a slight climatic change toward more favorable conditions for dry farming, and political instability. That the latter reason may be of some consequence is suggested by the fact that the settlement system changes again in the Banesh Phase toward clustering of sites and nucleation of population in one urban center, Malyan. That herding may have played a role in the Lapui settlement pattern is also suggested by the Banesh picture where significant numbers of sites are found adjacent to good pasturage in areas that today are used as campgrounds by transhumant pastoralists.

The data from other regions are so sparse as to discourage any attempts at interpretation. Information about the increasing role of pastoralists, suggested by settlement data in some valleys, is augmented by the cemeteries in northeastern Luristan which were used for a considerable time and indicate in their ceramics and other artifacts that these people were relatively isolated from the sedentary villagers. It would seem unlikely that the decline in villages is to be accounted for by an increase in herders, but the option of shifting between these two modes is well attested in early historic Mesopotamia (Adams 1978).

In a general sense, Iran was thinly settled throughout the Village Period, with concentrations of sites in the richer agricultural valleys, and the whole perhaps somewhat interconnected by transhumant pastoralists. Within this overall region we can conceive in only the most general terms of specific elements in a settlement system, using purely the distributional data. But we can augment our understanding considerably by examining in more detail information from excavations that bears on specialist activities and hierarchical relations among sites and individuals.

Specialization, Status, and Hierarchy

From a settlement perspective, we are interested in identifying sites that stand apart from the others by displaying evidence of specialized activities, high status of their residents, or a special position within the hierarchy of sites, such as might be revealed by size or another characteristic. Understandably, since few excavations augment the survey data, most of what can be said is inferential. Nevertheless, we can, at the least, target sites of potential interest for possible future excavation.

Specialization

Evidence of craft specialization during the Initial Village Period has been found at sites in the Near East generally, but little in Iran itself. Outside the immediate area of concern are the artisans' workrooms at Beidha (Kirkbride 1966); the copper working at Çayönü (Çambel and Braidwood 1970; Braidwood et al. 1971); the copper and lead smeltin at Çatal Hüyük (Mellaart 1967) and Yarim Tepe (Merpert and Munchaev 1976:64); and the large pottery kilns at the latter site (figure 4). None of this proves "commerce," nor does it even prove that objects from these sites were intended for use elsewhere. But the fact that similar remains have not been found in the Iranian early villages implies a difference.

Direct evidence of craft activities is sometimes found in the presence of ceramic kilns or of kiln wasters. These criteria allow us to identify sites at which production took place. But negative evidence is not so convincing because of the many problems involved in discovery and preservation. The only excavated site that is apparently nothing more than a ceramic workshop is Jaffarabad during the Middle Village Period. At least some of the production at Jaffarabad was for vessels of types that occur in burials. But kilns or kiln wasters have been found at so many other sites on the Susiana Plain as to suggest that local production was the norm. However, one surmises that the fine Susa A ceramics were made at Susa itself, although the excavation reports contain no direct evidence for this: once mentioned, the kilns at Susa were not further reported.

Sumner (1981) notes three ceramic workshops in the Soon irrigation region of the Kur basin, but these are known only from survey. Bakun, the site for which the ware is named, had kilns in the residential area. In the area excavated, about 8 percent of the total site, it appears as if only one kiln was in use at any time (Langsdorff and McCown 1942:figures 2,4).

Beyond ceramics, there are only hints of other craft production. Although we have found flint workshops as early as the Bus Mordeh Phase in Ali Kosh, we cannot tell whether these served more than the immediate needs of the village (Hole, Flannery, and Neely 1969:36). The quality of the chipping in the Initial Village Period is quite remarkable, indicating a high level of proficiency and suggesting the possibility that some individuals specialized in this kind of work. Sollberger and Patterson (1983) argue that a simple machine may have been used to effect the extremely delicate work that is displayed in the microliths. Certainly by the Middle Village Period, there is evidence of the importation of flint blades to Deh Luran (Hole, Flannery, and Neely 1969:87). A site known to have been a flint chipping station is the Middle Period village of Murian in the Mahidasht located near an outcrop of fine quality gray flint (Braidwood 1960a:696). In view of the quality of this raw material, it is likely that it was exported to regions such as Deh Luran, where the local chert was relatively poor (Wright 1981b:69).

Most of the small items we find in sites were probably manufactured locally, but the unusual concentration (391 examples) of earspools at Mushki raises the possibility that they were being made for export. They were undoubtedly manufactured at the site, as broken examples were found in various stages of finishing (Fukai, Horiuchi, and Matsutani 1973:58). Interestingly, most of the examples are of clay, only fifty-two being of stone.

Copper must have been acquired near its sources on the Iranian plateau, and sites such as Sialk are likely to have held specialist producers. However, the quantity of copper found in sites is very low, suggesting that there may not have been any sites within our area of concern that handled the material in other than finished form. On the other hand, at Mushki the excavators found a small sheet of copper that may have been the remnant stock from which beads and pins were made (Fukai, Horiuchi, and Matsutani 1973:67–68). The copper axes found in the Late Village Period at Susa and Giyan were probably imported as finished goods. They were cold-hammered out of nearly pure native copper from the Iranian plateau and were apparently destined to be used in ceremonial contexts.

Wright (1981b:270) speaks of the export of bitumen from Farukhabad in the Late Uruk Period. We suspect that this product was also widely disseminated throughout our time of concern because it was used to bind flint tools to their hafts and to waterproof baskets. Sites on the Deh Luran Plain may have been involved in the extraction, boiling, and distribution of this material, but we have certain knowledge only of its local use and not of its export (Wright 1981b:70).

The suggestion that goods were moving from one site to another is strengthened by the finding of seals, in the form of incised stamps or beads, and sealings. The former were used to impress a pattern into the soft clay of jar stoppers, or into the sealings over knots on bundles or sacks of goods. The seals appear first during the Middle Village Period, and they are widely distributed throughout western Iran during the Late Village Period. The two seals and four stoppers from the Bayat Phase at Tepe Sabz (Hole, Flannery, and Neely 1969:247) imply that goods were opened at the site, but we do not know where they were sealed. Amiet (1972, 1980) has published comprehensive reviews of the seals and sealings from Iran and Mesopotamia from a stylistic point of view, but most of the examples are without provenience.

The sum of our information on specialist production during the entire Village Period is relatively sparse. The quality of the workmanship in flint chipping, ceramics, and polished stone suggests a high level of skill which may not have been universally shared. But specialist production requires a means of disseminating the goods. On this topic we are in the

dark despite evidence for the movement of many products throughout western Iran and the implications of seals and stoppers (Amiet n.d.).

Trade—a generic term for social interaction that results in the movement of goods from one party to another—is manifest from the Initial Villages onward in obsidian, copper, seashells, and some other decorative objects. During the Initial Period in Deh Luran, we also have evidence of exotic sherds whose origin is northeastern Mesopotamia (Samarra). The Early Village Period sees the intrusion of whole ceramic complexes: Chogha Mami Transitional (and sherds derived from Tepe Sialk) in Deh Luran, J-ware and Dalma in Mahidasht, and Dalma in Kangavar. These major complexes might best be considered evidence of movements of people bearing new traditions rather than trade or sporadic contact.

In the Middle and Late Village periods, a number of examples of exotic ceramics occur in local assemblages. In Deh Luran, several distinct, nonlocal wares made their appearance during the Bayat Phase (Hole, Flannery, and Neely 1969:167–69). A black-on-red ware, whose origin is usually thought to be in the mountains, is found in low frequencies in Susiana and throughout the Karkheh drainage during the Late Village Period, implying intermittent contact of low intensity. Pots made in the style of the Susa cemetery are found at Musiyan in Deh Luran, at Siahbid in Mahidasht, at Kozagaran in Saimarreh, and possibly at Kazabad in Hulailan. Whereas the distribution of the black-on-red ware suggests movement of pastoral peoples and perhaps of goods moving in these pots, the Susa cemetery vessels may have been exchanged among members of an elite group, or simply be souvenirs brought home by people who visited the temple (C. Kramer, ed. 1982:261).

The best documented example of a commodity from known sources is obsidian. Pieces from the same source (4c) in eastern Anatolia have been found as far apart as Tell Ramad in Syria and Ali Kosh! Whether or not the underlying nature of the exchange has yet been interpreted correctly, one cannot fail to be impressed by the transmission of this material over such distances during the Early Village Period. It matters little whether other artifacts made such journeys: the potential for the transmission of knowledge remains, and that may have been the most significant effect (Renfrew 1977:310; Kohl and Wright 1977:275).

In addition to obsidian, other exchanged commodities found in Early Villages include cowrie and dentalium shells from the Mediterranean or Red Sea. Copper has been found in a number of villages, and it is probably present in most. There are at least two major sources of native copper; one in central Iran near Anarak, the other in central Anatolia. Although trace element analysis can reveal sources, such metals are usually corroded beyond identification and, in any case, they are presently too rare to provide much of a pattern of distribution. The same could be said for turquoise, carnelian, and various kinds of stone, semi-precious or otherwise.

This assembled evidence points not to a complex, well-regulated interchange of goods among regions of western Iran, but rather to a low level of infrequent interaction that may have involved many different processes. On the other hand, our tangible evidence is surely just symptomatic of a much greater volume and intensity of interaction that left few, if any, traces. On present evidence, trade is unlikely to have been a major factor in the social development of the region, but the evidence is largely negative, and it is apparent that all regions were open to at least sporadic interregional contact.

Status

Status is manifest principally in objects that signal the importance of an individual or of his role in the community. One may infer such roles and their attendant status from architecture, personal objects, the quality of goods, and burial treatment. Again, although evidence would be much fuller from excavation than survey data, we have some hints pertaining to these matters.

It seems clear from all the excavations of Initial Villages that the groups were effectively egalitarian. The objects found in the burials are personal ornaments of little distinction (table 13). Beneath the floors of houses or in houses, the burials themselves imply continuity of residence and lineage. In comparison with later periods, these burials stand out because they contain bodies of all ages and both sexes. In short, it appears as if all members of the community were interred beneath the floors of their houses.

Some major changes in burial practices become evident with the Early Village Period, after which adults are rarely found buried in habitation sites. The sample for the Early Period is small but consistent with later periods, and it shows some continuity with previous practices in the use of ochre and some personal ornaments.

The Middle and Late periods can be considered together. Now with a larger sample, the lack of adults and of personal ornamentation are much more striking. Nearly all the burials from these two periods are of infants or fetuses, increasingly, as time passes, found with one or more pots. Second, nearly all the burials are in tombs of either mud brick or of stone. The exceptions to this occur in the eastern valleys of the Karkheh drainage where Giyan, Seh Gabi B, and Kozagaran infants were placed in pots, and at Dalma Tepe where the eight fetuses or infants were tightly flexed and placed in bowls under floors. The possibility that this practice was carried to Kangavar with the spread of Dalma pottery and then continued in use into the Middle and Late periods is thus raised. Most of the burials of these periods seem to have been put into abandoned rooms or in vacant parts of sites rather than being systematically interred in dwellings as had been the earlier practice.

We know primarily from the two cemeteries in Luristan—Hakalan and Parchineh—that formal, systematic disposition of the dead in traditional burial grounds had become customary during the Middle Village Period. To judge from the sizes of the tombs, nearly all held adults rather than infants. These cemeteries are striking for the relative poverty of most of the burials and by the rather ordinary appearance of the richest. At most one can distinguish age and sex differences (and not too well at that), so that the cemeteries seem to reflect a relatively egalitarian population. Whether this situation would hold in the rich agricultural regions remains to be seen when some cemeteries there have been discovered and excavated.

In the Late Village Period the cemetery at Susa is the most interesting; however, in the absence of inventories of grave lots one cannot make claims other than that some individuals had extraordinarily fine pottery, perhaps in association with copper disks and axes. I have argued elsewhere (Hole 1983) that although priestly roles are represented, the society was not highly stratified.

It is relevant here to consider also the contemporary cemetery at Eridu, a temple center in southern Mesopotamia where the burials took the same form as at Susa (mud-brick tombs with two to three ceramic vessels). Here where inventories of the tombs are recorded, there is little to distinguish one from another (Safar and Lloyd 1981). Thus, at a parallel site whose function as a temple center is more clearly delineated than is Susa's, there is little, if any evidence in the burials of significant status differences.

The settlement data from Susiana give other clues to status. During my survey of the plain (Hole 1969b), I recognized that certain sites had unusual buildings on their north ends and I suggested that they might be "Khan's houses," using an analogy with modern times where local leaders sometimes set their houses apart from the village either spatially or vertically. Qabr Sheykeyn may have such a house, but since sites of this kind could be identified only when they had no later overburden, the sample I noted must be an underestimate. While there is some possibility that Chogha Mish was this sort of site in the Late Period, the relevant part of the site has not been excavated. The difficulty in identifying sites of this type precludes any attempt to study their spatial distribution in relation to districts within the plain.

Assuming that my interpretation is correct, certain sites were home to persons of higher than average status. However, because such sites may be no larger than others and display no universally identifiable characteristics, we can probably not identify them from surface indications alone. Henry Wright (1981b:67) suggested that a site near Farukhabad on the Deh Luran Plain, where he found a seal on the surface, might be such a site. The problem with seals is that they are difficult to find on the surface and, to judge from the Susa cemetery, they were not usually placed with the burials, although one or two turned up in the Luristan cemeteries and one occurred with a child's burial in Jaffarabad.

Wright also points to the relatively heavy construction of buildings at Tepe Sabz and Farukhabad as evidence of elite structures. If so, they are analogous to the house at Qabr Sheykheyn and suggest that such buildings and elite statuses may not be infrequent. However, much more salient to the discussion and sobering to consider is that the houses at Jaffarabad, the site closest to Susa, do not display any unusual architecture, although fine ceramics, seals, copper, and other artifacts imply status.

Hierarchy

The traditional way of establishing the importance of sites is to measure their sizes to see what sort of distribution (tiers or levels in a settlement hierarchy) they exhibit (see chapter 4). Although the difficulties of establishing sizes of sites are considerable, the exercise of examining the distribution of sizes is not altogether fruitless because it gives us an opportunity to consider what the causes of any size differences might be.

The distribution in Susiana differs from all others during the Middle and Late periods in that there are two "primate" sites, settlements much larger than all others; there is no curve, only small sites and a large site. By the usual interpretations these are centers, and we have already identified Susa as such for religious purposes at least. It is not clear what purposes the constructions at Chogha Mish during the Middle Period served. Although the burned house is probably secular, it is likely that a religious precinct was also at this site. A hierarchy is clearly implied in Susiana, yet it remains a mystery what direct effect these sites had on the lives of the populace that must have sustained them. In view of the low density of settlement on the Susiana Plain, it is not unreasonable to assume that those resident at these two centers produced their own food, but one expects that at least the religious functionaries drew on the collective population of Susiana to support religious activities.

Although quite a number of sites in western Iran stand out as unusually large, there are no other sites on the same scale as Susa (table 14). On the Deh Luran Plain, the sites of Tepe Sabz, Musiyan, and Farukhabad may have been no more than a few hectares each,

suggesting that they were large villages rather than centers. Presently, we do not know whether they were organized differently from the smaller villages. In the Late Village Period, this picture may change at Musiyan but the full extent of its settlement has not been determined; if there is a "center" in terms of sheer size, this site would be the only possibility. Deh Luran, having only one-fifth as much land as Susiana, might have featured correspondingly smaller centers—2 to 3 hectares as compared with 11 seems about the right proportion.

The Saimarreh Valley may have contained a substantial population and some large sites; only Kozagaran stands out today, in part because it is one of the few sites outside Susiana at which Susa ceramics have been found. This site is some 110 kilometers from Susa (this and other distances are straight-line measures). Tepe Giyan, 175 kilometers from Susa, is another large site (maximum 3 hectares) in the Nehavand Valley. A copper axe identical to those found at the Susa cemetery was recovered there, but none of the ceramics match those of Susa. If Giyan was a center, it may well have controlled trade along the copper route from the plateau to the lowland plain and its constituency probably included a large number of nomadic people.

About 200 kilometers from Susa, the Mahidasht features three sites of at least 5 hectares in the J-ware and Ubaid phases. The Kur River basin, 400 kilometers from Susa, has three large sites (3 to 7 hectares) in the Soon irrigation region. Darab has a site of 7 hectares. Tepe Kazabad in Hulailan appears to be a site of some 5 hectares. Sherds of Susa type also appeared at this site which has been badly disturbed by looters of Bronze Age graves.

These "centers" are widely spaced, although large sites (villages?) may be clustered as they are in the Mahidasht and the Kur River basin. Looking beyond Iran toward the west we see the burgeoning temple centers of southern Mesopotamia—Ur, Eridu, and Warka—all more than 200 kilometers from Susa. One can conclude from this distribution that the really large sites must have an adequate sustaining population, which is satisfied in Iran only by having large amounts of territory.

However, it is worth comparing this situation with southern Mesopotamia where we find a number of large sites but relatively small numbers of smaller ones. There are problems with preservation and discovery in this region that are difficult to assess, but as the principal surveys were carried out by Adams who initiated the work in Susiana, the results are to some degree comparable. We must take his assertion (Adams 1981:60), that settlement during the Ubaid Period is denser in Susiana than in Mesopotamia, as an indication of real differences. To quantify this impression, I have calculated the densities of Late Ubaid in the Warka region and in the Ur-Eridu region (cf. table 12). In an area of 1,415 square kilometers, there are eighteen sites in the Warka region, 475 square kilometers and eight sites in the Kish-Uqair enclave; and in an area of about 1,100 square kilometers in the Ur-Eridu region, there are seven to eleven sites. The latter region has three large sites, whereas the former has only one. The largest site, Eridu, is estimated to be about 12 hectares (Wright 1981a:338), whereas the largest site in the Uruk region is about 10 hectares and the remaining sites are under 1 hectare (Adams and Nissen 1972:9). The densities in these two regions are as great as one site per 157 square kilometers in the Ur-Eridu region, one site per 79 square kilometers in the Warka region, and one site per 59 square kilometers in the Kish-Uqair enclave. Surprisingly, because these centers later developed into the cities of Sumeria, the apparent densities in the Late Ubaid of Mesopotamia are more comparable with the Early than with the Late Period in Iran. In Mesopotamia, sheer size of local sedentary population cannot in itself be invoked as a factor underlying the growth of these large sites. As a matter of fact, distinctly large sites begin in Mesopotamia during the Early Period when densities are even lower than in the Late Ubaid.

The large sites in Mesopotamia were undoubtably temple centers (Adams 1981:66), some with cemeteries, implying a structural relationship with Susa. The other large sites in Iran may also have supported some religious activities, but their political and social roles during the Village Period are presently unclear. Certainly we have seen how small, unobtrusive sites have refined ceramics, seals and sealings, and substantial architecture, which we argue imply status. The implication that these small sites housed people of importance makes one careful in jumping to conclusions about the levels of hierarchy displayed only by size distributions of sites. According to conventional analysis, the Village Period has a two-level site hierarchy by the Middle Period, a status reached somewhat earlier in Mesopotamia. Nevertheless, unless we can determine how these sites actually functioned in a system, one should not treat the notion of hierarchy too seriously.

While the factors that result in sites of greatly different sizes are quite uncertain at this time, several lines of investigation might be pursued. In all cases, the research will require acquisition of new data.

First, one would expect that sizes of villages relate to beneficence of resources, but the upper limit on size may equally relate to social factors, such as the avoidance of conflict. Johnson (1982b), who has dealt with this topic in detail, sees limits on the ability of people to process information, rather than environmental constraints, as determining the sizes of the basal residential units. Measuring these social factors is beyond our current ability.

Second, if the environment is stable, there is more likelihood that villages will grow to greater size or appear to do so because of debris from continuous occupation. We have seen how settlement was relatively unstable in Susiana, and this situation may have been common throughout western Iran. What we cannot assert is that environmental instability forced abandonment of villages, although this seems likely, either because of periods of unfavorable climate or because of progressive degradation of the environs resulting from continued occupation. In no instance is the density of sites so great that local production of food by the residents of the largest sites would not have been feasible; we are not yet talking about urban concentrations during the Village Period either in Iran or in Mesopotamia.

Finally, the relation between size and function needs closer investigation. It is likely that the small sites, however homogeneous they may appear in their unexcavated form, actually harbor a great deal of diversity, perhaps more than the large sites, at least those that focus on religious activities. If the large sites began as specialist locations (shrines), gradually growing through repeated buildings, and adding functions of residence and craft manufacture, they may actually be more similar to one another than their size differences would imply.

In the attempt to generalize, I have no doubt ignored much interesting diversity, but essential differences among sites will be revealed ultimately only through well-considered excavations that seek information on the nature of the regional systems by testing and excavating several key sites. To suggest how this might be pursued in one area, I consider the Susiana case in some detail.

Organization of Susiana during the Late Period

Only from the Susiana Plain do we have enough survey information, supported by excavations, to allow us to attempt a reconstruction of a settlement and social system. Here I shall focus on the period during which the step platform at Susa was constructed, but first it will be useful to review the geography of the plain and its potential for agriculture.

Upper Susiana includes some 1,500 square kilometers of relatively flat, undifferentiated land (figures 9,10). The present physiography poorly reflects the probable appearance of the land during the Susiana Period when it was a rich, grassy, steppe parkland which supported herds of wild ungulates and a natural biotic assemblage including many plants useful to humans. For the prehistoric periods, the limits of Susiana are defined by the Karkheh and Karun rivers which bound the western and eastern edges of the plain. Although today these rivers provide important sources for irrigation water, the chief artery for irrigation traditionally has been the Diz River which, like the others, flows out of the Zagros Mountains that define the upper edge of the plain. The arable plain begins some distance out from the mountains and, so far as primitive farming is concerned, it terminates at about the Haft Tepe ridge (figure 9), a low anticline crossing the plain transverse to the rivers. Within this irregular space delimited by rivers and mountains, the land is fairly flat, but it is cut by numerous broad, gravelly watercourses that drain waters from flash floods. In wet years, grain can be grown without irrigation on nearly every part of the plain, but with even simple irrigation, agricultural success is greatly enhanced. Nevertheless, agriculture is risky because of periodic flooding, prolonged droughts, severe winter cold, unseasonable early searing summer winds, insects, and fire. In principle, Khuzistan possesses great agricultural potential: in practice, it disappoints as often as it rewards.

As a complement to agriculture, animal husbandry is practiced, chiefly by transhumant herders who winter in Khuzistan and take their flocks to higher pastures during the hot summer. Archaeological evidence from as far back as the late seventh millennium indicates that both herding and farming were practiced in the area (Hole 1974). Little evidence exists concerning the details of what was almost certainly a complex mosaic of differing subsistence strategies. We know at least that the essentials of a modern agricultural regime based on irrigated (?) hybrid wheats and barleys and domesticated animals had been established early in the sixth millennium. In addition, there may have been gardens of vegetables, perhaps some fruits, and the keeping of bees. Despite this potential diversity, subsistence agriculture supplemented with hunting and gathering was probably the norm. We do not yet know whether production much beyond basic need occurred. I argue that excess production to support an elite group is unlikely during the Susiana Period, in spite of evidence of social ranking.

Settlement and Interaction

Although it is easier to locate sites on the plain than to define the intangible relations among them, we can hope to reconstruct the latter if we recognize some diversity among the sites themselves. Unfortunately, we lack sufficient informative excavation to assess the specific kinds of activities that occurred at any particular site, even though we may identify a series of types of sites whose functions in a settlement system may have differed.

Let us begin with the ceramic evidence. Remarkably, within the 1,500 square kilometers of Khuzistan

that were settled during the fifth millennium, the ceramics are essentially identical stylistically and readily distinguishable from those of surrounding regions: no local variants in ceramic styles, no isolated enclaves exhibiting idiosyncracies, have been recognized. This pervasive homogeneity suggests that ceramics were made in few places and then widely distributed. However this inference may be wrong, for Dollfus (n.d.) finds many sites with kiln wasters (twisted, overfired sherds), implying that production of even single types of ceramics was widespread, but not necessarily at every site.

In view of trade demonstrated elsewhere in both Halafian and Ubaid wares (Davidson and McKerrell 1976, 1980; Oates et al. 1977) and the extensive trade in obsidian that had been carried out over great distances for more than 2,000 years up to the time of Susiana (Renfrew and Dixon 1976), trade in ceramics should not be surprising. But if trade in ceramics was widespread and voluminous in Khuzistan, how was it organized, and what commodities were exchanged in return? Most researchers assume that exchange in the fifth millennium was not a market activity, and they search for other redistributive mechanisms serving in its stead. Theoretically, one might postulate a range of economic transactions from balanced reciprocity among kinsmen to intervillage trading partners, to centralized redistribution through a chief, to formal markets. Clearly, additional information is necessary to enable effective evaluation of these alternatives because they depend on our assessment of the level of political integration as well as regional diversity. However, we can consider several concrete pieces of evidence: the size of population, the diversity of the plain, and the sites themselves.

By various estimates, the size of the settled population in the Late Village Period is between 8,500 and 25,000. (The figure of 200 persons per hectare of settlement is often used in these calculations [Dollfus 1983].) Considering this size and the number of villages, it appears unlikely that marriage and interfamilial exchange of purely local domestic production could account for so thorough a diffusion of the complex and highly specific compositions of designs on these vessels. Therefore we should look to other mechanisms for the pervasive exchange.

The subsistence economy is one place to look. Susiana society consisted of settled agriculturalists and mobile pastoralists on a plain containing diverse and scattered resources, a situation in which there was potential for fruitful exchange in products grown or manufactured entirely locally. It is not necessary to consider interregional exchange, for the necessities of life were available on the plain or at its margins. Only luxury or exotic goods, such as copper, need have come from afar. Ceramic evidence as well as common experience suggests that local centers of production, or manufactories, existed and at least some goods—such as pottery, matting, wool, milk products, bitumen, flint tools, and so on—were distributed from these points. Elements of a model of the settlement system should therefore include manufactories and possibly trading posts.

Let us now turn to the settlements themselves. One is struck by the overwhelming size of Susa and the uniformity of the remaining small villages. In geographers' terms, this is a primate distribution with one site much larger than all the rest. Such a large site is usually considered to be a "center," a reasonable attribution in view of the large temple-platform and surrounding settlement at Susa. However, Susa is not "central" in the more ordinary sense of the word, for it is situated at the extreme western edge of the Khuzistan Plain (figure 10). Clearly the location of Susa does not conform to any notion of a central place in a network of surrounding satellite villages unless most of the Khuzistan Plain is excluded from the sphere of influence of the site, or if its interaction is with other centers outside Susiana.

Among the remaining sites, the small villages, at least four variants are recognizable. At Jaffarabad, not far from Susa, a ceramic workshop was operated during a hiatus in the domestic occupation of the site (Dollfus 1975). In my terms, this is a manufactory. Another type of site is the "Khan's house," a term I coined to describe certain sites that appeared to contain a single building on the highest part of the mound. Excavation of such a house by Harvey Weiss (1972) confirmed its large size and solitary location. I suggest that these sites were residences of local headmen whose constituents may have included pastoralists and farmers. A third type of village, thus far not attested through excavation, is the trading post, a site that might have been useful in my postulated economic system, but not necessarily essential, in mediating transactions between herders and farmers or between artisans and customers. I suspect that any such sites might have been situated near sources of raw material where bulky craft activities such as ceramic production, basketry, or mat making were carried on. The fourth type of village is the agricultural settlement. The spacing and size of these sites are consistent with the idea that they represent economically self-sufficient entities with adequate arable and fallow land surrounding them to meet their needs for subsistence. Additionally, we must presume the presence of herding camps, either established as entities separate from the agricultural villages or as units detached seasonally. In view of evidence that nomad camps date back to 6000 B.C., I favor the notion that substantial populations of tent-dwelling herders lived seasonally on the plain during the late Susiana Period, but so far we have no direct proof of this.

In reconstructing the settlement system, one further matter, permanence of settlement, requires discussion. When we study the settlement system with reasonably accurate control over chronology, it is apparent that settlements shift. A tree diagram of the settlement histories of the late Susiana sites reveals that each has about a fifty-fifty chance of lasting from one phase to the next (figure 17). Translating this into years, one finds that the average life expectancy of most villages was somewhere around one hundred years; thus, although a site might be occupied intermittently over a span of several thousand years, any single village on it might endure for only a few generations before the site was abandoned for several more generations, a process called "cyclical reoccupation" (Adams and Nissen 1972:30).

The shifting nature of settlement in the Susiana Period is important for two reasons. First, it implies that estimates of population based on total numbers of sites on the plain are inherently suspect and probably too high, because sites are founded and abandoned through time and not all sites of a phase are occupied simultaneously. Second, it implies that land was not particularly scarce and therefore that specific territory was not highly valued, at least not in the sense of property or inheritance. This suggestion is corroborated by the relatively low density of population. Even at peak density during the Susiana Period, there were probably fewer than ten inhabitants per square kilometer, an area that might support several times that many by agriculture (Adams and Nissen 1972:29).

My reconstruction of the Susiana settlement system thus consists of three "levels" without any suggestion that a controlling political or economic hierarchy is operative. Susa figuratively, and perhaps literally, heads the settlement system. The next level consists of agricultural villages and herding camps, which are full-range domestic and economic units. The third tier holds the specialist communities: the Khan's houses, craft manufactories, and possibly trading posts. Most of this diversity is evidenced in excavations or inferred from survey, but to define types does not enable us to specify how many of each type may be present or to exclude the possibility that a single site may have served several functions.

An important aspect of this reconstruction is the degree of specialization and extent of exchange that is implied. If this reconstruction is accurate, by analogy with modern economic models, one would suppose that market centers would arise to mediate this business. One could view Susa, or its immediate predecessor, Chogha Mish, as a possible market center, although no indications of market facilities have been found at either site. One problem with ascribing the status of a market center to either of these major sites is that neither is well situated for receiving or distributing goods in any bulk, even though both sites are within walking distance of a determined villager. Sited at the edge of the plain, Susa was some 50 kilometers from the farthest village and Chogha Mish about half that distance. At a relatively primitive level of transportation, it is more probable that consumers took themselves to many manufacturing or distribution sites where wool, reeds, milk products, grain, vegetables, honey, oils, ceramics, and other materials could be obtained. These sites might be termed manufactories or "demand markets," operating not continuously but only when required or when demand was anticipated according to a seasonal cycle. Such a system accords well with both the simple level of technology and with the essentially subsistence economy implied in the multiplicity of small villages. If longer distances were involved, one might postulate either a peddler system or itinerant craftsmen, but neither appears necessary in the Susiana case.

Notwithstanding decentralization of economic functions, the potential complexity of the system of Khuzistan is impressive. If there were producers of fine ceramics, there may well have been specialists in many of the other crafts. Sumerian vocabularies list dozens of occupations, a later hyperdevelopment of practices that may have been emerging in Khuzistan and southern Mesopotamia during the later Village periods.

As I see it, an organic interdependence, a "pluralistic collectivism" to use Geertz's phrase (1964:30), based on periodic exchange may have knitted the many small villages of Khuzistan together without either overriding political or economic motivators or controllers. Indeed, in view of the low density of population and shifting settlement, it is improbable that such control could have been effectively implemented during the Susiana Period. On the other hand, geographic propinquity and common ideological bonds, in the absence of divisive threats, may have sufficed to sustain a largely unmanaged but not unstructured system.

So far, this reconstruction has omitted consideration of the site of Susa itself, the focal point of settlement in Khuzistan. Let us now address that issue.

The Nature of Centrality

During the Late Village Period, a great step-platform was built at Susa. Constructed of unbaked mud bricks, it measured some 70 meters along each side of its base and stood 15 meters above the plain. Although no structures associated with the platform have been recovered, there is little reason to doubt that the platform was the base of a temple (Hole 1983). Many writers would regard the temple itself as evidence of political centralization and, following evolutionary typology (Service 1962; Fried 1967; Renfrew 1973) of evidence that Susa was the seat of a chiefdom. As the use of the term has itself undergone an evolution, its connotations differ widely among authors. I use it here for purposes of discussion in the sense employed by Renfrew (1978:100) who said that the most distinctive feature of chiefdoms

> in the archaeological record is the presence of central places. The central person, who is the permanent chief, is generally situated at the central place, even if this be a periodic one. . . . The central place was usually dignified by special buildings pertaining to the chief and sometimes by monumental ones relating to ceremonies of life or death.

The chief, then, coordinated "economic, social, and religious activities" (Renfrew 1974:73). In the theorizing of evolutionists about chiefdoms, a central concept is that of emerging control, the seizing of power by an elite group which can then use this power to obtain perquisites such as elite residences and luxury goods. In this regard, the Late Village Period is critical, for the Uruk Period, only a few hundred years later, sees the emergence of a functional state. (See Johnson, chapter 4, for a discussion of the Uruk Period.) According to some views, this state was the natural outgrowth of a ranked society during the Late Village Period (Johnson 1973; Wright and Johnson 1975).

In pursuing these ideas, we need not become fixated by Renfrew's definition of "chiefdom," for there is ample evidence that human societies display, and have undergone variability that cannot be accommodated easily by a simple typology. Nevertheless, all would agree that "chieftancy," if it is more than a figurehead position, requires control of critical resources, whether these be food, labor, commodities, access to water, or to the supernatural. Depending on the degree of control over these resources, a chief may retain for himself a greater or lesser proportion of the good they can confer, "spending" the rest directly on his constituents in the form of feasts and gifts, or indirectly in the form of public works. These are forms of redistribution. According to George Dalton (1969:73)

> Redistribution entails obligatory payments of material items, money objects, or labour services to some socially recognized centre, usually king, chief, or priest, who reallocates portions of what he receives to provide community services (such as defense or feasts) and to reward specific persons.

Sahlins (1972:190) carried the argument further, saying that, in a logical sense, redistribution

> sustains the community. . . . At the same time, or alternatively, it has an instrumental function: as a ritual of communion and of subordination to central authority, redistribution sustains the corporate structure itself. . . . Chiefly pooling generates the spirit of unity and centricity, codifies the structure,

stipulates the centralized organization of social order and social action.

As chieftancy depends in a sense on redistribution, a center should display evidence of its nature. If commodities were redistributed, a center should possess facilities to handle the pooling of goods and their subsequent dispersal. Thus storage facilities would be one sign of redistribution. However, any substantial contribution of material to a redistribution agent implies either acceptance of the system on the part of the donors or the exercise of authority on the part of the agent. In the case of Susiana, Susa could not have exercised very tight control over the multitude of villagers and pastoralists for the simple reason that it, the sole center, was far removed from the face-to-face interaction with the bulk of the populace. In Johnson's terms (chapter 4) there was a wide "span of administrative control." Since Susa stood alone, perforce it must have possessed sole responsibility for all of Susiana, a region in which 10,000 or more people may have resided in a multitude of separate communities.

The concept of span of control forces us to consider just how broad a territory a chief could effectively administer. According to Johnson, six units (separate villages) might approach the limits that could be closely controlled, although more could be overseen in a looser sense. However, the effectiveness of Susa in administering the countryside could have been greatly enhanced if it dealt directly only with "khans," each of whom spoke on behalf of a half dozen or so villages. This would be an example of what Johnson (1982b) calls a "sequential hierarchy" in which decisions are made by spokesmen for increasingly larger units: head of family for family, head of village for village, khan for group of villages. The organization may be non-hierarchical, but it accomplishes the same end, namely reducing the number of individuals that must be dealt with by any other individual.

It is difficult to think of prehistoric Susiana as a ranked society with a chief who participated in other than limited ceremonial activities, even should it be demonstrated that khans were employed as intermediaries. A strong reason for this is that ethnographic literature contains only examples of multiple chiefs and subchiefs, never isolated holders of title. Evidently, chiefdoms thrive where competition between chiefs inspires emulation and creative use of persuasion over constituencies. Had a political chief emerged at Susa or elsewhere, I suspect that many more would have sprung up, quickly carving up the plain among themselves and displaying their ascendancy by emulative behavior.

Undoubtedly, one function of large sites may be to house the multifarious activities required to administer a complex state or a chiefdom. However, large sites need not necessarily be internally diversified or to have served more than one function. Nor must a large site be associated in some way with administration in either an economic or political sense. The important issue is whether chieftancy as a distinct organizational paradigm had been invented and recognized yet during the Village Period. I would maintain that it had not and that although chieftancy is an idea which once grasped is powerful, before the fact it has no meaning. In other words, chieftancy is not an inevitable consequence of circumstances, but an idea that formed the basis of a new social paradigm which subsequently underwent its own core development and rationalization, an idea suggested by Wallace (1972) in a different context.

I have already mentioned reasons why Susiana society is unlikely to have been administered in any profound sense. I proposed that Khuzistan was knitted together by essentially ad hoc exchange and a tendency toward craft specialization and demand manufacturing. Importantly, there is no comparable region close by which might easily have competed for the same resources of land and raw materials. Here the isolation of Khuzistan from other potential and competitive centers must be emphasized. Khuzistan is 200 kilometers from Ur and Eridu, 75 from Musiyan, and 175 from Giyan where a copper axe like those from Susa was found. The distances are well beyond the average ranges of 30 to 70 kilometers reported separating centers of chiefdoms and early states by Renfrew (1975:14; 1978:103), not to mention the centers in southern Mesopotamia that were within sight of one another. Thus the role of threat from abroad or "competition" between chiefs in unifying Khuzistan appears unlikely, as does threat by pastoral groups which also occupied the plain. This reconstruction is admittedly speculative and the force of the argument must depend in part on the role played by Susa in such a system. Can we determine what this role was?

In addition to the monumental platform at Susa, excavators have uncovered a cemetery at its base and traces of residential structures which have not yet been excavated in an informative manner. Thus Susa appears to be a temple center with residential housing, similar to contemporaneous sites in southern Mesopotamia such as Eridu and Ur. Artifacts reported from domestic areas at these sites are identical to those found in small villages of the period. But the cemetery contains unique information and perhaps the most important clues to the nature of Susiana society. Let us first deal with the temple platform.

If a chief resided at Susa, the temple was probably a vehicle for symbolizing chiefly sanctity, perhaps through ancestor worship (Service 1975:78). But if, as I argue, chieftainship is not necessarily operative at

Susa, what purpose did the temple serve? It seems clear that it must have served as the locus of rites concerning fertility, perhaps under the aegis of a tutelary deity. All early historic evidence points to this conclusion (Adams 1966:123; Jacobsen 1976), as does the environmental situation (Adams and Nissen 1972:85–87; Adams 1974:4–7; Oates and Oates 1976b) in which uncertainty was the norm. In fact, my postulated hyperdiversification of specializations within a subsistence economy may have been one way of contending with the unpredictability of fertility and regeneration. By this means, populations might have been able to buffer stresses through an economic interdependence that necessitated exchange of even petty articles, a situation found today in some subsistence communities.

The notion that specialization could arise out of an essentially noncentralized, subsistence economy may seem strange to those who regard specialization as a kind of spin-off from economic centralization, a way for the elite to dispose of their raw commodities through patronizing the workshops. There are those who would question whether the fine workmanship implied by the painted pottery of Late Susiana Period did not require patronized craftsmen, artisans who owed their support to consumers of their products. Gordon Childe addressed this question many years ago in reference to other fine wares.

> Indeed, such is the technical and artistic perfection of Halafian pottery that some think it must have been produced by professional craftmen. Perhaps these authorities underestimate the general high level attained in domestic arts and crafts, like embroidery, among peasant societies today and would have to conclude that 'Persian rugs' were manufactured by full-time specialists who bought their goods in shops (Childe 1952:111).

Economic surpluses may be invested in support of craft industries, but the opposite may hold, as I believe it did in the Late Period. In many societies today, people use marriage alliances to accomplish economic interdigitation, but there is no inherent reason why a more open system, in which interaction takes place according to diversified need and production, might not have worked equally well. Such a system provides ultimate flexibility and requires only consensus about its operation to succeed. We have something like this today with our money economy.

Although an economic argument can be made for the desirability of developing specialization to enhance both the quantity and quality of production in either a centralized or noncentralized society, specialization may also enable people to derive social benefits such as leisure and the social intercourse that attends it. An example of such a situation occurs among the Greek villagers of Vasilika described by Ernestine Friedl:

> Vasilika's farmers and shepherds consider themselves specialists; they view themselves with pride as experts in farming and sheepherding, and assign the same dignity to the expertness of others. . . . They do not expect a man to know how to do anyone else's work. One speciality is considered enough" (Friedl 1962:35).

As a result, when their jobs are finished, the men of Vasilika congregate socially instead of spending additional time puttering around with repairs and other tasks. I might add that this degree of specialization is not uncommon in the world today.

If a primary motivation for specialized diversification in Khuzistan was to ameliorate the effects of variable resources and agricultural unpredictability, another rational and obvious solution to the same problem was to enhance the ability of mortals to plead their cases before the whimsical forces of nature which capriciously meted out their agricultural blessings. This would explain the emergence of specialized shamans or priests to conduct the services, and the establishment of a stable, monumental edifice in which to perform these rites. I see the platform at Susa as having been constructed specifically for such rites. The center thus formed was a single-purpose, specialized site, not in its original conception a village and certainly not a political center.

The essentially sacred nature of the site is corroborated by several factors. First, it was founded on the western edge of the plain where no site had previously stood. In fact, no site had ever been located very close for Susa was founded in an empty quarter of the plain. Second, Susa alone of the excavated sites contains a cemetery. The association of a large site with a sacred cemetery is similar to that at Ur, Eridu, and probably other temple sites. Finally, rare ceramic vessels from the cemetery, and impressions of seals from Susa contain images of persons dressed in sacerdotal garb performing rites (Hole 1983). In these seals, religious functionaries of some sort are clearly implied. However, as yet, there is no suggestion of secular leaders in these depictions. Therefore, I conclude that Susa served as a temple center which was also the residence of priests. The community may well have included elements of a standard village which seems to have grown unusually large.

The construction of the platform provides evidence of massive cooperative labor, but in itself this does not imply any particular level of organization. The burials which contain fine pottery, large copper axes, and copper disks are certainly evidence of differential statuses, but I argue that these are graves of priests rather than of secular leaders. However, except for the copper symbols of their sacred roles, the graves of priests differ only in slight degree from those of the laity among whom they were buried in undifferentiated tombs. Clearly we have here a society with some elaboration of roles and statuses, but there is no compelling reason to think that political or economic control was attached to any of these statuses. If that is a correct assessment, the best analogy to Susa is that of a modern religious shrine which is supported by the local populace out of piety, but which exercises no direct control over the people except as they subscribe to its admonitions for monetary or other support. A monumental shrine on an otherwise flat landscape would have stood as an awesome reminder of man's inherent dependence on the gods. If such sensibilities could have been mobilized by administratively creative priests to further their own ends, true political advantage could have emerged in the clergy. But there is no evidence that this happened. Nor is there evidence that clerical sanctions were employed to further the aims of secular leaders. In short, I see a system that had achieved a certain level of sophistication through specialized diversification, but one in which social relations were regulated largely on a familial level and the roles such as priesthood were a normal reward of elderly status. At death the priests took the copper symbols of their roles with them.

The closest analogy among social organizations known ethnographically occurs among the acephalous, noncentralized societies of Africa such as the Ibo and Tiv (Middleton and Tait 1958). Residential units in these societies may be based on kinship or territory or both, but segments are equivalent in status. These acephalous systems are particularly prevalent where settlements shift so that social alignments are fluid. Locally autonomous villages are united through territorial propinquity and networks of relationships that derive from kinship, differential access to resources, and so on. Even populations numbering in the tens of thousands may regard themselves as a single people under this loose kind of affiliation.

In conclusion, I envision Susiana in the Late Village Period as composed of a series of independent, shifting communities occupying a large territory in common, with little or no hostile competition. Interaction among these communities was regulated by need, and opportunity enhanced by relatively well-developed specialization that took advantage of variability in local resources and modest entrepreneurial activity. In this system, consumers sought out sources of supply which were then made available by local artisans or producers. The result was a high level of craftsmanship, secured by increasing economic interdependence among the producers and consumers.

Diversification through local specialization may have been largely inadvert, but its effect was to buffer unpredictabilities of natural origin, such as unseasonable weather, and its consequence was further elaboration of the system. There was a primary concern with fertility and regeneration of crops, a problem met through diversified specialization and through the development of rituals carried out by mortal intermediaries at sites specially designed for the purpose. Thus Susa served as the ritual center, deriving its support from the constituent population of Khuzistan whose labor was used to build the platform and whose gifts of products may have been used in religious rites. The association between people and priests was voluntary, in support of firmly held beliefs that proper maintenance of ritual was essential to continued prosperity.

Powerful ideas lay fallow in this relationship, ideas that could later be mobilized by priest administrators to further their own goals as well as the goals of society. These later developments most likely took place in the context of competitive emulation as separate, territorially based societies came to impinge on one another, probably first in southern Mesopotamia. From there the new social paradigm became a tool in a struggle for competitive advantage. During the Uruk Period, this paradigm culminated in the theocratically rationalized city states whose concerns remained with fertility, but which now conceived of man as servant of the gods and put the individual cottage craftsman into collective workshops or factories whose production served societal as well as individual needs.

By this time, the paradigm on which the old Susiana system had been based no longer sufficed to satisfy the needs of a burgeoning populace. By taking the step of statehood, human society crossed a threshold, leaving behind an archaic form which is no longer represented among modern societies and whose record can be traced only archaeologically.

Systemic Implications

After having reviewed various aspects of our data, we can now return to the theoretical positions with which we began. We have not reached our goal of explaining the variability and change in the archaeological histories of regions except in terms of culture history in certain instances. We have left unexplained, or at least unverified because the means of testing are not at hand, the causes underlying these episodes. Frankly, at this point there is no consensus about where one should seek explanations, although those who favor a scientific approach based on empirical data turn to some form of materialist explanations. What is the evidence favoring a cultural materialist interpretation? First, if as Price (1982:728) maintains, settlement pattern is "a virtual isomorph of infrastructure and political economy, which records and preserves the most significant features of energy production and flow," then for most of the time under observation here, there was little, if any, asymmetrical energy flow between the prevailingly and uniformly small, dispersed sites. Susa and the Mesopotamian centers display prodigious use of energy in the construction of temples, but beyond these examples, there is little to point out that is indicative of unusual expenditure of energy. Even the "Khan's houses" could well have been built by an individual although it is unduly cautious to hold to such a strict position. By the Late Period, cooperative effort (Khan's houses) on the local level and temples on the regional level are strongly suggested. However, the potential and apparent self-sufficiency of each village is striking. Insofar as materials are concerned, unusually fine ceramics are a hallmark of the Susa A Period, but they are not to be found elsewhere in western Iran or, for that matter, in Mesopotamia. These may well have been more "costly" in a real sense and were certainly not universally available. Some of these functioned in ceremonial contexts, both religious and secular, as well as in burial ceremonies. When these vessels or copper axes and disks were placed in graves, they were removed from the living system, creating a need for more goods with their attendant costs, so that some conspicuous consumption of sumptuary goods was a part of life. These facts suggest some production of surpluses to use in the acquisition of these goods but do not inform on the identity of the producers or the relations between them and the consumers.

The vicissitudes of adaptation in the Susiana region are well chronicled in succeeding chapters of this book. According to Price, the adaptive value of the behavior we detect archaeologically can be measured by its survival and by the sizes of the systems employing it. In terms of adaptation, most of the specific customs of the Village Period have disappeared, although the pattern of a relatively dispersed population in small villages remains to the present day. However, in particular regions, the systems were not successful, as we have discussed in regard to the decline in population in the Late Period. It is hard to see the failure of these systems in terms of maladaptation to energetic needs, although there may have been some environmental explanations of particular instances. Rather, it seems more likely that the declining populations reflect different opportunities, perhaps in Mesopotamia, or in the expansion of herding, or in newly competitive social situations. I have argued that the Chogha Mami Transitional intrusion into Deh Luran was a case where larger groups, using irrigation, forced their way into new territories that were especially favorable for irrigation. A similar explanation has been advanced for the J-ware entry into Mahidasht. An Uruk "intrusion" (whether by people or

new techniques and ideas) at the end of our period is probably different, empowered this time not by better technology but by a more complex social organization that was able to mobilize the populace more effectively to implement collective goals.

The temple at Susa, like those in Mesopotamia, focused on fertility and regeneration, the two most pressing problems for people practicing subsistence agriculture before the inception of the social institutions of mass storage and redistribution. As the largest, most costly, and most impressive structures of their times, the temples clearly reflect the idea that "those behaviors which harness, or encapsulate, relatively more energy will be relatively more important systemically" (Price 1982:709). One need not accept all the tenets of cultural materialism to see the relationship here.

Throughout this chapter I have reviewed the aspects of scale, integration, and complexity that Blanton and Johnson have advanced. It has been useful to consider these parameters because they give us a ready means to compare regions and then to seek causes of variability. Unfortunately, our data are too limited to enable us to track these variables very accurately, but our attempt has pointed up places where future research should be applied. During the Village Period, we have little in the way of systemic change, and this is expressed only in the largest of the regional systems. By the Middle Village Period, a two-level size hierarchy of sites, and the possibility that temples and other public or private elite structures may have been present, are our chief evidence of growth in system complexity. Were we to continue with Blanton's approach throughout this volume, we should see marked changes. As it is, in the Village Period we catch only a glimpse of cultural evolution, perhaps, moving "opportunistically, solving only today's problems, proceeding rather blindly, without a predetermined course, into the future" (Blanton et al. 1981:13). Until we have, in fact, tracked these courses, it will be difficult to assess whether they follow an opportunistic, a predetermined, or some other course. And it will be necessary to consider, more seriously than we have, what geographic range our observations should encompass.

It may be that an evolutionary paradigm is not particularly appropriate or necessary even though in some gross sense we can measure systemic growth. Perhaps a more neutral attempt to explain change and variability in their own terms, as was recently attempted for European prehistory (Renfrew and Shennan 1982), is a preferable approach. Renfrew (1982:4) expresses the view of many of the authors in this volume in that "most of the fruitful approaches . . . can be reduced, in effect, to the study of the effect of two processes upon social structure and upon each other, and of the influence of social structure upon both. The processes in question are the intensification of production, and the interaction between polities." The immediate problem for us with this approach is the lack of data, but one sees how current archaeological—and quite diverse—thought centers on the development and exploitation of food and other energy sources that can be manipulated through social means. With our focus so clearly on these factors, the direction of future research is equally clearly indicated.

Frank Hole

Table 11. Area (in Square Kilometers) per Village in Selected Valleys of Iran and Iraq

Region and Valley	Area (sq. km.)	Number of Villages	Sq. km. per Village	Sources of Data
Lowland Steppe				
Deh Luran	298	3	99.3	1/4″ Series
Susiana (pilot project area)	223	55	4.1	[Gremliza 1962: 38, Table 5]
Azerbaijan				
Solduz	203	26	7.8	1/4″ Series
Ushnu	149	7	21.3	1/4″ Series
Karkheh Drainage of the Central Zagros				
Mahidasht			5	[McDonald 1979: 116, 1]
Kangavar			5	[McDonald 1979: 116, 1]
Nehavand			5	[McDonald 1979: 116, 1]
Shahabad			8	[McDonald 1979: 116, 1]
Huilailan	91	7	13	1/4″ Series
Rumishgan	129	2	65	1/4″ Series
Kuh-i Dasht	234	14	16.7	1/4″ Series
Khorramabad	104	13	8	1/4″ Series
Saimarreh	128	10	12.8	1/4″ Series
Kangavar-Asadabad	1040	96	10.8	[Kramer 1982: 157]
South Zagros-Fars				
Kur River Basin	2502	108	23.2	[Sumner 1972: 174–5]
Fasa	133	17	7.8	1/4″ Series
Northeast Iraq				
Chemchemal	934	64	14.6	[Kramer 1982: 186–7]

Notes:
Sources of information on Kangavar and area examined by McDonald and Kramer differed.
The Susiana Pilot Area stretches south from Dizful, encompassing the best irrigation land between the Diz and the Shur Rivers.
The 1/4″ Series maps are British Army, 1/4″ to the mile, dated 1942. Areas of valleys calculated by planimeter from the 1/4″ Series enclose the Village Period sites and modern villages. This area may differ significantly from areal figures given by other authors.
McDonald does not give the number of villages or the area of the valley.

Table 12. Summary of Numbers and Densities of Village Period Sites

	Deh Luran			Susiana			Mahi Dasht			Kangavar		
	Phase	#	Density	Phase	#	Density	Phase	#	Density	Phase	#	Density
Uruk	Late Uruk	2	149.00	Late Uruk	14	104.07	no data		[decline in #, increase in size]	Godin V		no data
	Mid Uruk	8	37.25	Mid Uruk	52	28.02						
	Early Uruk	6	49.67	Early Uruk	49	29.73						
Late Village Period	Sargarab	2	149.00	TSA	18	80.94				Godin VI	39	26.67
					53	27.49				Hosseinabad		
	Susa A	5	59.60	Susa A	77	18.92				Godin VII	23	45.22
Middle Village Period	Farukh	12	24.83	Susiana d	86	16.94				Taherabad		
	Bayat	14	21.29				Ubaid	134	13.76	Godin IX		
	Mehmeh	18	16.56	Susiana c		no data				Seh Gabi	17	61.18
Early Village Period	Khazineh	20	14.90	Susiana b			(Dalma)	16	115.25	Godin X		
	Sabz	8	37.25	Susiana a	16	91.06				Dalma	20	52.00
	OMT	5	59.60	Archaic III			J-ware	70	26.34	Shanabad	1	1040.00
Initial Village Period	Surkh	1	298.00	Archaic II								
	Sefid	1	298.00									
	Mohammad J	2	149.00	Archaic I	25	58.28	Neolithic	10	184.40			
	Ali Kosh	2	149.00	Preceramic								
	Bus Mordeh	1	298.00									

Note: Areas in square kilometers—Deh Luran 298; Susiana 1457; Mahi Dasht 1844; Kangavar 1040; Kur River 2502; Fasa 525; Darab 480; Solduz-Ushnu 352.

Kur River			Fasa			Darab			Solduz-Ushnu		
Phase	#	Density	Phase	#	Density	Phase	#	Density	Phase	#	Density
Banesh	41	61.02	Kheyrabad & Zohak	8	65.63	Juzjan & D.29	5	96.00		no data	
Lapui	103	24.29	IV–III mill Vakilabad	12	43.75	IV–III mill Vakilabad	6	80.00	Pisdeli		
Bakun	146	17.14	IVth Bakun	42	12.50	IVth Bakun	25	19.20	Pisdeli	20	17.60
Shamsabad	95	26.34									
Jari	46	54.39	Vth Jalyan & Bizdan	15	35.00	Vth Jalyan & Bizdan	5	96.00	Dalma [Gap?]	15	23.47
Mushki	6	417.00									
									Hajji Firuz	7	50.29

Table 13. Summary of Burials during the Village Period

Period	Site	Age	Disposition	Container	Grave goods	Number
Late Village Period	Susa	?	secondary	brick tombs	pottery, copper axes and disks	1000+
	Jaffarabad	infant	extended	mud box lined with mat	3 pots, seal	1
						1
	Jaffarabad	infant	extended	mud box lined with mat	bowl and jar	3
						2
	Giyan	infants	flexed	in jars	2 in painted, 1 in plain jar	
	Seh Gabi B	children	tightly flexed	extramural in large pots	none; textiles?	
Middle Village Period	Qabr Sheykheyn	infant	?	?	bracelet of paste beads	1
	Qabr Sheykheyn	infant	?	?	none	1
	Qabr Sheykheyn	adult	extended		plain red and plain buff pots, sling missile	1
	Jaffarabad	foetus	?	in trash	none	1
	Jaffarabad	infant	extended	brick tomb	goblet and small jar	1
	Bendebal	infant	?	brick tomb	painted jar	1
	Bendebal	infant	?	brick tomb		6
	Bendebal	infant	?	mud box		1
	Chogha Mish	adult	?	brick tomb	plain cup and jar	1
	Jowi	infants	?	brick tombs	conical goblets	2
	Dalma	infants or foetuses	?	under floors in bowls	?	?
	Hakalan	?	extended	stone tombs	pottery; a few with other objects	36
	Parchineh	?	extended	stone tombs	pottery; a few with other objects	162
	Kozagaran	infant		in a jar	plain jar with lid	1
	Seh Gabi	infants/ foetuses	tightly contracted	under floors?	each in a redware bowl	8
	Jari	adults	flexed	?	bowl	2
Early Village Period	Seh Gabi	infants	?	not in pots	some beads	several
	Jaffarabad	child	extended	under floor	ochre, micro-adze	1
		foetuses	?	?	sherds	2
	Chogha Mish	?	?	?	none; one stone pendant	5

Table 13. (Continued)

Period	Site	Age	Disposition	Container	Grave goods	Number
Initial Village Period	Ali Kosh (Ali Kosh Phase)	adult	tightly flexed	subfloor in matting	necklace with one bead	6
		child		subfloor in matting		1
		foetus		subfloor in matting		1
		adult	extended	subfloor in matting		2
		child	extended	subfloor in matting		1
		infant	extended	subfloor in matting		1
	Ali Kosh (Mohamad Jaffar Phase)	adult	semiflexed	?	labrets, bracelets, pendants	5
	Chagha Sefid (Sefid Phase)	adult	extended	disturbed;	none; ochre	3
		child		matting disturbed		
	Chagha Sefid (Surkh Phase)	child		disturbed	ochre	1
	Hajji Firuz (Phases F-A)	adults and children	secondary and primary	ossuaries in bins and platforms; some subfloor pits and jars	pottery, spindle whorls, ochre	>50
	Hajji Firuz (Phases J,H)	children, adult	tightly flexed	subfloor pits	none	3

Sources:
Ali Kosh—Hole, Flannery, and Neely 1969: 248–255
Bendebal—Dollfus: personal communication; 1977: 12
Chagha Sefid—Hole 1977: 91–3
Chogha Mish—Delougaz and Kantor 1975: 94
Dalma—Young and Levine 1974: 11
Giyan—Contenau and Ghirshman 1935: 7, 38
Hajji Firuz—Voigt 1976: 216–284
Hakalan—VandenBerghe 1973
Jaffarabad—Dollfus 1971: 27; 1975: 22, 68
Jari—Egami et al. 1977: 7
Jowi—Dollfus personal communication; 1977: 171
Kozagaran—Stein 1940: 200
Parchineh—VandenBerghe 1975
Qabr Sheykheyn—Weiss 1972: 172–3
Seh Gabi B—Young and Levine 1974: 10, 13–14
Seh Gabi C—Hamlin 1974: 275
Susa—Morgan 1912; Mecquenem 1943: 5

Table 14. Largest Sites of the Middle/Late Village Period

Region	10–15 hectare	5–10 hectare	3–5 hectare	Total Sites	Phase
Deh Luran	0	0	2	12	Farukh
Susiana	1	0	0	77	Early Susa A
Hulailan	0	1	0	8	Early Chalcolithic
Saimarreh	0	0	1	?	Late Ubaid
Mahidasht	0	some	?	134 70	Ubaid J-Ware
Kangavar	0	0	0	23 17	Hosseinabad Seh Gabi
Nehavand	0	0	0	?	Late Ubaid (Giyan 2 ha)
Kur River	0	1	2	146	Bakun
Darab	0	1	0	25	Bakun
Fasa	?	?	?	42	Bakun
Ur-Eridu	1	1	1	7–11	Late Ubaid
Uruk	0	1	0	5–7	Late Ubaid

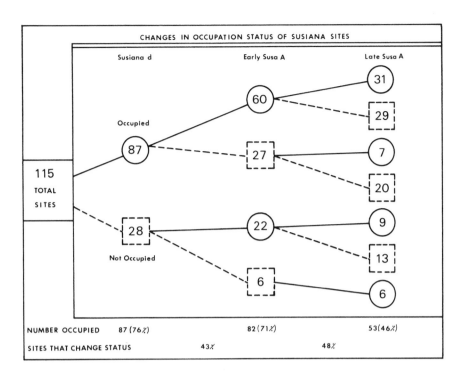

Figure 17. Tree diagram showing changes in occupation status of Late Village Period sites.

Chapter 4

The Changing Organization of Uruk Administration on the Susiana Plain

GREGORY A. JOHNSON

Introduction

Early state development and organization have again become a topic of intensive discussion as reflected by the recent spate of publications on the subject. (For examples see Cherry 1978; Claessen and Skalník ed. 1978; Cohen and Service ed. 1978; Friedman and Rowlands 1977; Jones and Kautz ed. 1981; Sanders and Webster 1978; Wright 1977; and Yoffee 1979.) This chapter reevaluates the available evidence for Uruk state formation on the Susiana Plain of southwestern Iran (figure 18).

The analysis presented here is based not so much on new data as on a modified framework for ordering the available evidence. This framework includes elements of organization and location theory which, while novel in the present context, have a long history elsewhere. Given the present state of research, one need not detail the extent to which this chapter sketches potential lines of research rather than provides an explanatory synthesis.

Most of the data as well as the interpretive background for this chapter are available in a series of publications including Johnson (1973, 1976); Wright (1977); Wright and Johnson (1975); and Wright et al. (1975). A very brief summary of our previous interpretation of Uruk developments should, therefore, provide sufficient introduction to the reevaluation that follows.

The collapse of the Susa A polity or polities during the Terminal Susa A (Terminal Ubaid) period of the early fourth millennium B.C. on the Susiana Plain was discussed in the previous chapter. It is sufficient to say

that this collapse involved a marked decrease in the population of the area. The succeeding Uruk period was one of economic and political reorganization. By Middle Uruk (ca. 3500 B.C.), the Susiana settlement system consisted of a four-tier settlement size hierarchy with direct evidence of resident administrative activity at its top and bottom levels. The presence of administrative function at the intervening levels of hierarchy, and of an overall four-level administrative organization seemed likely. In combination with evidence for the centralization of craft production as part of an administered local exchange system and the presence of an administered labor system, these features suggested the operation of a Middle Uruk state.

Initial state formation during the preceding Early Uruk was supported by the apparent similarities between Early and Middle Uruk institutions. The former appeared to be appropriately less complex and pervasive than the latter. Attempts to account for Early Uruk state formation in terms of the primary importance of processes such as population growth, warfare, expansion of irrigation systems or long-range trade were unsuccessful. We asserted that the immediate processes leading to state formation must have been complex and multiple, and collectively increasing the workload of regulatory institutions to the point where increased vertical complexity of organization was required.

The later Middle Uruk state appears to have been under considerable stress as evidenced by population decline and the fission of the system into two politically autonomous and hostile entities in Late Uruk (ca. 3200 B.C.). The causes of this decline were unknown but were presumed to involve the inability of Middle Uruk administrative organization to cope with an increasing regulatory workload.

With this interpretive sketch in mind, I will proceed directly with a reevaluation of the evidence. While the general picture of Uruk developments outlined below is consistent with the original interpretation in many respects, it also incorporates a number of significant changes which will be the focus of discussion.

Early Uruk

The Early Uruk settlement pattern is illustrated in figure 19. The almost 95 hectares of settlement are partitioned into a three-level settlement size hierarchy of villages, small centers, and a single large center, Susa (Johnson 1973:79). Designation of settlements as villages, centers, and so forth is based on the discontinuous frequency distribution of site sizes, supplemented by limited excavation data on functional differences between sites of different size classes. I originally suggested (Johnson 1973:101) that the absence of a large center on the eastern portion of the plain probably indicated that this area was something of an administrative vacuum. One way to evaluate the relationship between settlements in the eastern and western portions of the Susiana is to examine the rank-size distribution for the Early Uruk settlement pattern as a whole.

Rank-Size Distributions

A great many ancient and modern settlement systems are characterized by a frequency distribution of settlement population size such that the population of a settlement having rank r in a descending array of settlement sizes approximates $1/r$, the size of the largest settlement in the system. This relationship between settlement rank and size is linear with a slope of -1 in double logarithmic transformation. Analysis of rank-size distributions has long been a popular exercise among geographers and has recently become attractive to archaeologists, due in part to the increasing availability of regional settlement pattern data. (See Adams and Jones 1981; Blanton 1976; Blanton et al. 1982; Crumley 1976; Hodder 1979; Hodder and Orton 1976; Johnson 1977, 1980a, 1980b, 1981; Kowalewski 1982; Paynter 1982, 1983; Pearson 1980; Randsborg 1982; Upham 1982; and Weiss 1977).

This wide archaeological utilization of settlement rank-size distributions should not engender confidence that these distributions are well understood. I think it fair to say that we are presently unable to mathematically account for the linear form of the distribution when it is observed, despite numerous attempts involving: (a) introduction of stochastic variability in a basically Christallerian hierarchy (Beckmann 1958; Beckmann and McPherson 1970); (b) consideration of the linear form as a steady state of a stochastic growth process (Simon 1955); or (c) consideration of the determination of settlement size as a problem in conditional probability (Johnson 1981). It is not even clear that the "ideal" log-linear distribution is the appropriate baseline for comparison (Rapaport 1968; Voorrips 1981).

If our mathematical understanding of rank-size distributions is minimal, there is evidence of progress in stipulation of general nonmathematical conditions associated with the log-linear form and its major classes of deviations. General conditions associated with the presence of near "ideal" rank-size distributions have been reviewed by Richardson (1973) and C. A. Smith (1976) among many others. Posited associations, for example, of the ideal form with urbanization (Crumley 1976) and/or economic development (Berry 1961) have not been empirically convincing (Berry 1961; Richardson 1977:6), and considerable attention has shifted to examination of major classes of deviation from the linear model in the hope that their explication would be informative about processes generating the more frequently observed log-linear form.

Two major classes of deviations from log-linear rank-size distributions have been noted: concave (primate) and convex distributions. Primate distributions are those in which the size of settlements below the largest settlement in the system are markedly smaller than the log-linear model would predict. Primate distributions appear to be characteristic of systems in which economic competition is minimized (Blanton 1976:26; C. A. Smith 1976:32) and/or system boundary maintenance is the primary function of the primate center (Kowalewski 1982). Primacy may also indicate a situation in which the primate center is differentially articulated with a yet larger scale settlement system (Johnson 1977:498; Skinner 1977a:238; Vapnarsky 1969:585).

Convex distributions are those in which settlements below the size of the largest settlement in the system are markedly larger than the log-linear model would predict. Convex distributions are indicative of a relatively low degree of integration (interdependency) among the settlements being examined. This condition may be the product of pooling, the combination of two or more relatively autonomous settlement systems in the same analysis (Johnson 1981; Olsson 1965:21; Skinner 1977a:241), of an inherently open system (Kowalewski 1982:66), or of spatial marginality in a dendritic settlement system (Paynter 1982:152–56). Examples of historical settlement systems with convex rank-size distributions include Colonial America in 1750 (Green and Harrington

1932), China in 1843 (Skinner 1977a), and India in 1850 (Chandler and Fox 1974). All were characterized by low levels of system integration.

Decreasing convexity can, then, be taken as a measure of increasing integration. A numerical index of convexity would facilitate examination of changing patterns of integration. While a number of comparative rank-size measures have been suggested (El-Shakhs 1972; Malecki 1975), I use an index which I find more useful for descriptive purposes. This rank-size index (RSI) can be expressed by the following formula:

$$RSI = \frac{\sum\limits_{1}^{n} (log \, P_{obv} - log \, P_{rs})}{\sum\limits_{1}^{n} (log \, P_{cmax} - log \, P_{rs})}$$

where: RSI = rank-size index
n = number of settlements in the analysis
P_{obv} = observed settlement size
P_{rs} = expected settlement size: log-linear model
P_{cmax} = expected settlement size: maximum convex distribution

Here, the sum of deviations of an observed distribution from its associated, "expected" log-linear distribution is divided by the sum of deviations of that log-linear distribution from its associated "maximum convex" distribution. The "expected" distribution is calculated from the size of the largest observed settlement under analysis, and the "maximum convex" distribution is one in which all settlements in the system are the size of that largest observed settlement. As such, a very highly convex observed distribution would have an associated rank-size index value approaching 1.0, a log-linear distribution would have an index value approaching 0.0, and increasing primate distributions would be associated with increasingly negative index values.

Two additional matters require discussion before we can return to Early Uruk. First, the vertical axes of the rank-size graphs used later in this chapter indicate hectares of settlement. They assume that settlement area was directly proportional to settlement population. Further, the absolute values of population estimates will be analytically important. Archaeological population estimation, particularly from survey data, remains a difficult problem that has been reviewed recently by F. Hassan (1978), Kramer (1980), and Sumner (1979). The population estimates used here assume a settlement population density of 200 persons per hectare of settlement area. This figure is derived from data presented by Gremliza (1962) on fifty-three traditional villages on the Susiana. Settlement area and population exhibit a linear correlation of 0.855 (associated probability less than 0.01) with a mean density of 202 persons per hectare. At present, there is no direct way to evaluate the reliability of the use of these data for archaeological estimation. As is the case for many behavioral assumptions in archaeology, their reliability must be evaluated in terms of the degree to which they are consistent with patterning in independent data sets. The high degree of internal consistency among the disparate data sets examined in the following pages suggests that the present population estimates are relatively reliable.

A second issue involves a minor refinement in the calculation of the rank-size index. Most rank-size distributions show rapid falloff at very small settlement sizes. This "lower-limb" relationship (Haggett 1966:-106) probably relates to the size below which settlement economic viability decreases rapidly (Johnson 1977:501). Minimum settlement size for inclusion in calculation of an RSI in this study was set at one hectare, the point at which the Susiana survey rank-size curves begin rapid lower limb falloff. This point is indicated on the rank-size graphs as the "RSI cut point."

Definition of Administered Areas

The immediate problem is to evaluate the proposition that Early Uruk settlements on the eastern Susiana were either independent of, or only marginally related to, the administrative system centered on Susa in the western Susiana. If this were the case, the rank-size distribution for the plain should be convex, reflecting the relatively low degree of east/west interaction. Indeed the Early Uruk rank-size distribution (figure 20) was markedly convex and had a rank size index of 0.322.

Extending this line of reasoning, if the western portion of the plain was differentially integrated by an administrative system centered on Susa, the rank-size distribution for this area should be less convex than that for the plain as a whole. Comparative rank-size distributions for the entire plain and for the western area (between the present courses of the Diz and Karkheh rivers) are presented in figure 20. Note that, as predicted, the distribution for the western area alone shows a marked decrease in convexity from that for the plain as a whole. Deletion of the eastern sites reduces the rank-size index from 0.322 to 0.123.

It appears, then, that both the spatial distribution of settlements and spatial variation in rank-size distributions support the proposition that settlements in the western area of the Susiana were differentially integrated in a settlement system to which settlements in the eastern area were only marginally related. Further, the western system was probably divided into two major administrative areas.

Inspection of the Early Uruk settlement pattern map (figure 19) reveals a relatively regular distribution of sites in the immediate vicinity of the two centers of the western area, Susa and Abu Fanduweh (KS-59). Although villages in the western area seem to have obtained ceramics produced at both of these centers (Johnson 1973:92–94; 1976:210–12), the apparent spatial separation of these two emergent central place systems was probably related to factors of administrative separation. (See C. A. Smith 1976:20–23; Steponaitis 1978:427.)

Susa's relatively greater size doubtless assured its administrative control over the western Susiana in general, although I will suggest later that the degree of control exercised by Susa was relatively low. If the western Susiana, though dominated by Susa, was divided into two lower-level administrative districts, these districts should have been of approximately the same size. (This assumes that the work involved in administration of these districts was proportional to their sizes.) If hectarage of settlement is used as a measure of size, then these proposed districts were approximately equivalent with 22.25 hectares of settlement in the Susa area and 26.78 hectares in the Abu Fanduweh area. Given the fairly regular distribution of villages around centers, settlements north of KS-33 appear to have been associated with Susa, while those to the south (including KS-269) were associated with Abu Fanduweh. Having tentatively established the presence of two administrative districts in the western Susiana, it would be informative to consider their respective spans of control.

Span of Control

Span of control is an attribute of organizational structure that has been very extensively studied in modern cases by sociologists and other organization specialists. The literature on organizations and organization theory is much too large to even characterize here, and I will simply offer a few observations of immediate relevance. These are based on the standard literature as well as on recent applications work on more traditional anthropological and ethnographic cases.

I have suggested elsewhere (Johnson 1982b, 1983) that basic structural characteristics of archaeological, ethnographic, and contemporary organizations are heavily constrained by the information processing capabilities of individuals and groups in decision-making contexts (see also J. Moore 1983). Organizations from hunter-gatherer and egalitarian pastoral nomad camps to modern business firms, employment agencies, university committees, and nations are subject to what I have called "scalar stress," much akin to com-

munications stress as discussed by Meier (1972). Basically, as the number of organizational units—individuals, families, clans, departments, divisions, or whatever—engaged in either consensual decision making or under the supervision of a single, hierarchically differentiated individual or unit increases beyond the organizational size of six, decision performance degrades and the probability of structural alteration of the system concerned increases. This "magic number" of six appears to be related to basic, if poorly understood, characteristics of human neural organization (Johnson 1982b; Mayhew and Levinger 1976:1036; Miller 1956) and appears regularly as a structural transition point in laboratory studies of task-oriented small group dynamics in sociology and social psychology (see, for example, Cummings, Huber, and Arendt 1974).

Our interest here will be in span of control, or the number of individuals or organizational units that are immediately subordinate to a given individual or unit in a hierarchically structured organization.

Span is described as varying from "narrow" when few subordinates are involved to "wide" when many are involved. Urwick (1956:41) suggested some time ago that an optimum span of control in highly integrated organizations is somewhere around the familiar figure of six. This observation has been supported by a very wide variety of subsequent studies. Pugh et al. (1968:104), for example, report an average span for chief executives of fifty-two organizations in the area of Birmingham, England, to be 6.08 (range = 2–24, standard deviation = 3.08). Klatzky (1970:433) reports, in a study of fifty-three state and territorial employment agencies in the United States, that the average number of major subdivisions per agency is 6.6 (range = 2–13, standard deviation = 2.5). In a more anthropological example, Jones (1966:65) provides data on local communities controlled by subchiefs in the state organization of Basutoland in 1938. Subchiefs had an average span of control of 5.13 ($n = 18$, range = 2–11, standard deviation = 2.75).

Variability in span of control is another problem. While a relatively narrow span has been associated with a relatively wide scope of administrative responsibilities (Blau 1968:543), a narrow span is more often indicative of relatively close administrative supervision and control. Skinner (1977b:305) notes, for example, that span of control for prefectural level units in Late Imperial (Ch'ing) China ranged from 1 to 24 with a mean value of between 5 and 6. Wide spans were characteristic of regional cores where formal administration was concerned almost exclusively with tax collection, and other regulatory functions were exercised through informal political mechanisms (Skinner 1977b:336). Narrow spans were associated with regional peripheries where a high degree of control was required in areas of potential military disruptions (Skinner 1977b:321).

Elsewhere (Johnson 1983) I have summarized what we appear to know about scalar stress, and I will repeat those observations here.

1. Information processing overload is a mechanism that may constrain the operational size of consensual groups and span of control in hierarchical groups.
2. Information load and scalar stress are an exponential function of organizational size. (See Johnson 1982b for details.)
3. Organizational size is best measured in terms of basal organizational units which may vary in population size both within and between systems.
4. We can specify optimum mean organization size or span of control for decision-making purposes, as well as a rough potential range of variation for size and span.
5. We can predict stress points in organizational growth, beyond which there is an increasing probability of system response. (This is done for Terminal Susa A through Middle Uruk on the Susiana later in this chapter.)
6. We can identify a noninclusive list of types of potential system response to scalar stress that includes expansion of basal unit size, development of (or increase in complexity of) hierarchical organization, and group fission.

Given these considerations, it is clear that estimation of administrative span of control during Early Uruk on the Susiana would provide important information on the operation of the administrative system—most prominently on the relative degree of control exercised by center administrative elites over village populations.

Basal Administered Unit Size

The main problem in attempting to estimate administrative span of control for the Susiana Uruk is that we have no direct evidence of the size of the lowest-level organizational or administrative unit in the system. The best that I can do at this point is to evaluate the implications of a reasonable assumption about unit size. While this is not very satisfactory in an ideal sense, subsequent substantiation of those implications would then support the initial assumption of unit size.

One might well assume that the settlement was likely to have been the basic unit of administrative organization. The range of Uruk settlement sizes (less than 1 to about 25 hectares), however, makes this unlikely. One would expect that in a relatively simple system

such as this, basal level administered units would have been of roughly the same size.

An alternative is to take the size of the smallest viable settlement as the basic unit of organization and to consider larger settlements to represent multiples of this basic unit. A larger basal level unit would have necessitated frequent incorporation of spatially separated populations in the same unit and have reduced the potential degree of administrative control. A smaller basal level unit would have required a larger number of such units and have increased administrative workloads (Johnson 1978, 1982b).

The smallest viable settlement size is unlikely to have been the size of the smallest observed settlement in the system. I have suggested elsewhere (Johnson 1977:501) that the point at which a regional rank-size distribution undergoes rapid "lower-limb" falloff (Haggett 1966:106) probably represents the approximate threshold of minimum viable settlement size. This is the point at which the number of increasingly smaller settlements in the system decreases rapidly as seen on a log-normal rank-size plot. A number of variables were likely to have been involved in determination of this size threshold including agricultural productivity, degree of cooperative activity in agricultural production, degree of village articulation within a regional economic system, security, and administrative requirements.

Examination of the Early Uruk rank-size distribution (figure 20) suggests that this threshold value was approximately 1 hectare. This value was maintained in Middle Uruk and was, incidentally, the same as the threshold value for Early Uruk settlements in the Warka area of southern Iraq (Johnson 1980b).

Administrative Organization

While it seems reasonable to take 1 hectare of settlement area as the probable basal level administered unit, calculation of basal level span of control requires an estimate of organizational structure above the level of the basal unit. In the original analysis of the Susiana material, I argued for a three-level administrative hierarchy in Early Uruk on the basis of more detailed data suggesting a direct correspondence between levels of settlement hierarchy and levels of administrative hierarchy in Middle Uruk (Johnson 1973:141). I now suspect that neither of these propositions is correct.

The presence of large Early Uruk buildings on the Acropole of Susa (Wright 1978) can be taken as evidence of administrative activity in this center. The admittedly small excavation samples from two villages (KS-34 and KS-76, Johnson 1976) have not, however, produced similar evidence of resident administrative activity. (They show no evidence of major architecture or artifacts appropriate to resident administration.)

This suggests the possibility that administrative activity was limited to the two centers of Susa and Abu Fanduweh.

Figure 21 presents rank-size distributions for the Susa and Abu Fanduweh administrative districts defined earlier, as well as for the apparently unadministered eastern portion of the Susiana. Note that the distribution for the eastern area is quite convex (RSI = 0.402) as would be expected in an area of very low system integration.

The distribution for the entire western Susiana (figure 20) was relatively linear (RSI = 0.123). Within the western area, the Susa administrative district was highly primate (RSI = −0.547), while the Abu Fanduweh district was more linear (RSI = 0.247) though less so than I would have expected. As reviewed earlier, the primacy of the Susa district suggests that Susa was articulated with a settlement system beyond its immediate area. This local primacy in addition to the distributional linearity produced by combining the Susa and Abu Fanduweh districts and the status of Susa and Abu Fanduweh as large and small centers, respectively, all indicate that regional level administrative functions were located at Susa. If this were the case, one would expect district level administrative functions to have been located at Susa and Abu Fanduweh. Given the lack of evidence for resident administration at settlements smaller than centers, the foregoing analysis would indicate the operation of a two-level administrative hierarchy within a three-level settlement system.

If, as suggested earlier, 1 hectare of settlement represented a basal level administered unit, then the spans of control of district level administration at Susa and Abu Fanduweh would have been approximately equal to the total settlement area in each district of 22.25 (22) and 26.78 (27), respectively. The span of control for the regional administration at Susa would have corresponded to the number of administrative districts in the region, or two. Spans of control of 22 to 27 at the local level are wide and suggest that the degree of control exercised by district administrators on village populations was relatively low. Three classes of information are consistent with this proposition. These include estimates of center requirements for rural agricultural produce, spatial variation in administrative demand for labor, and spatial variation in rural utilization of centrally produced ceramics.

Tests of Organizational Implications

In an earlier analysis of settlement size and location in the immediate vicinities of Susa and Abu Fanduweh (Johnson 1973:94–98), the amount of agricultural land directly available to these centers was estimated. This analysis suggested that the immediate sustaining area available to Susa was 2.12 hectares per person

and to Abu Fanduweh was 2.19 hectares per person. Recent rural populations in the area that are involved in near maximum production utilize an average of 1.92 hectares per person, while Oates and Oates (1976b:120) cite Iraq Development Board figures of about 2 hectares per person as the maximum amount of land a family can cultivate with a traditional technology. These figures contrast sharply with those for land required for subsistence production. I estimated a figure of 0.5 hectares per person on the basis of the Early Uruk settlement pattern data (Johnson 1973:97), a figure that agrees well with estimates based on ethnographic data of 0.3–0.7 hectares per person (Kramer 1980:328) to 1.0 hectares per person (Oates and Oates (1976b:120) for similar agricultural areas.

It appears then that sufficient agricultural land was available in the immediate areas of Susa and Abu Fanduweh to permit maximum potential surplus agricultural production by their respective populations. Surplus is defined here as the agricultural production resulting from cultivation of more than 0.5 hectares of land per capita. If administrative demand for agricultural produce did not exceed the potential surplus productivity of center populations, Susa and Abu Fanduweh could have been largely independent of rural agricultural production. Potential independence would be consistent with the evidence presented earlier suggesting minimal center controls on village populations. The most important assumption here involves the level of administrative demand for surplus produce, a point to which I will return later.

A second line of evidence on administrative demand for surplus (in this case surplus labor) concerns the functional interpretation of a particular Uruk ceramic type, the bevel rim bowl. The bevel rim bowl is a common Uruk vessel which has been interpreted as a ration container for use in an administered labor system (Johnson 1973:129–39; Nissen 1970:137). This proposition along with previous functional interpretations of the type have been reviewed by Beale (1978) and LeBrun (1980). Beale views the type as a "presentation" bowl used in conjunction with religious activity; the very high densities of bevel rim bowls in lowland settlements would then imply a level of religiosity unprecedented among the world's archaic societies.

Wright, Miller, and Redding (1980:272) report bevel rim bowl discard rates at Tepe Sharafabad (KS-36, figure 19) to have been between 11 and 47 times those of other common Uruk ceramic types, with rim sherd densities of 235 to 3,621 per cubic meter in pit fill. As indicated in table 15, bevel rim bowls constitute 39 to 56 percent of the ceramic material in Middle and Late Uruk samples from the Susiana village site, KS-54 (figure 19).

In addition to very high bevel rim bowl densities,

Wright, Miller, and Redding (1980) present evidence for seasonal variability in bowl discard. Two years of winter/summer deposit are represented in the material recovered from a Middle Uruk pit at Tepe Sharafabad, with seasonality established on the basis of tooth eruption data from sheep-goat mandibles. One summer/winter sequence is especially well represented. The summer deposit (representing the agricultural "off-season," but the traditional period of intensive mud-brick construction) has an average bowl density of 2,098 rims per cubic meter. The winter deposit (representing the primary agricultural season) has an average bowl density of 956 rims per cubic meter. Administrative use of labor might be expected to be highest when that labor was not required for agricultural production, particularly if administrative demand for agricultural surplus was high. Further, recent textual evidence attests to the presence of ration issue at Tepe Yahya immediately after the Uruk (Beale 1978:313). Given these various lines of evidence, the ration bowl proposition still seems to account more fully for the available lowland bevel rim bowl data.

Of interest here is the observation (table 15) that Early Uruk bevel rim bowl density was only some 6 to 9 percent of Middle and Late Uruk densities from village deposits. Whatever the absolute level of center demand for Middle and Late Uruk village labor, Early Uruk demand was apparently very much less.

A low level of center demand for rural labor would be consistent with both low-level control of village populations and relative center agricultural autonomy. Center autonomy, however, would presumably have required actual rather than merely potential extraction of surplus production from center agricultural populations in support of other center functions. In this regard, Henry Wright (1979, personal communication) reports that some Early Uruk deposits at Susa contain nearly 700 bevel rim bowl sherds per cubic meter. This figure is roughly equivalent to those for densities in Middle and Late Uruk village deposits, but fully an order of magnitude greater than the available density from an Early Uruk village. This high level of labor demand on center, but not village, populations is consistent with the proposition of relatively low-level center control over villages.

If center administrators could extract little surplus labor from villagers, it seems likely that they could extract little surplus produce as well. This would have made them largely dependent on such surplus as could be generated by the agricultural populations of the centers themselves. On the other hand, if center administrators could extract a relatively large amount of surplus labor from center populations, it is likely that they could extract a relatively large amount of agricultural surplus as well. Given these data and the Early Uruk settlement locations around Susa and Abu Fan-

duweh indicating that center populations could have been engaged in near maximum surplus production, it would appear that administrative demand for center surplus was high but could be met by center populations.

The bevel rim bowl data are relevant to one additional aspect of the preceding analysis. Recall that the proposition that the eastern portion of the Susiana was only marginally related to a relatively integrated settlement system in the west was derived from spatial variability in rank-size distributions and the absence of a large center in the eastern area. Given the apparent function of bevel rim bowls in an administered labor system centered on Susa and Abu Fanduweh and their presence (in low density) in an associated village, one would expect that bowls should be either absent on eastern sites or exhibit much lower densities than on western sites.

While we do not have density data from the eastern area, bowl data are available from survey collections. Table 16 presents presence-absence data on Early Uruk bevel rim bowls (proto-bowls) from the eastern and western Susiana. While proto-bevel rim bowls are not restricted to the western Susiana, they are differentially associated with the western area. These results provide additional support for the proposition that eastern settlements were only marginally articulated with the west.

To return to the question of relatively low-level center control of Early Uruk villages on the western Susiana, a third source of data on Early Uruk center-village interaction deals with spatial variation in village demand for centrally produced ceramics.

In an earlier discussion of Early Uruk centralization of craft production (Johnson 1973:93–94), I made a case for the identification of workshop variability in neckless ledge rim jars, a common Early Uruk ceramic type. (For illustrations see Boehmer 1972: tables 54: 368–73; Johnson 1973: Plate III-b.) Two varieties were produced, apparently one at Susa and the other at Abu Fanduweh. The relative frequencies of these varieties in survey and excavation samples from six Early Uruk villages were reported earlier (Johnson 1973:183; 1976:212) and may be used to estimate relative interaction between the Early Uruk centers and these villages.

Archaeological interaction studies have increasingly used variants of a basic gravity model to examine the effects of variability in the size and spatial separation of interacting populations (Hallam, Warren, and Renfrew 1976:99–102; Hodder 1978; Johnson 1977:481–87). Wide application of gravity models in locational geography has produced the conclusion that the interaction of two populations is generally directly proportional to some function of the product of their sizes and inversely proportional to some function of the distance between them. Here, I will initially hold the size variable constant and focus on the distance variable and the expectation that center-village interaction should decline with increasing center-village distance.

In this case we are dealing with the interaction of villages with two centers. In the absence of adequate density data, I will consider the ratios of the two neckless ledge rim varieties present in collections from villages.

Let us begin with the simple proposition that interaction is inversely proportional to distance alone. If, for example, a village were twice as far from center B as from center A, its interaction with center B should be roughly one half of that with center A. If one aspect of this interaction involved acquisition of center products, one might expect products of centers A and B to occur in the village at a ratio of 2:1.

Table 17 presents data on center-to-village distance, as well as observed and expected ceramic frequencies (given sample size) for excavation samples from KS-34 and KS-76, and survey samples from KS-96, KS-108, KS-153, and KS-266. (See figure 19 for site locations.) It is evident that simple center-to-village distance is a reasonable predictor of center-village interaction as measured here. As illustrated in Figure 22, the correlation between the predicted and observed frequencies of the Abu Fanduweh variety at these six sites is 0.986. (Deletion of the comparatively high values for KS-34 reduces the coefficient to 0.980, p less than 0.01.) Not only are the predicted and observed values correlated, but they are identical in four of the six cases examined here.

It would appear then that village acquisition of center products was inversely proportional to center-village distance, or more accurately, center-village travel costs. This would imply both equivalency of "cost" of acquisition of ceramics at either locus of production and the absence of effective administrative constraints on the source from which villagers obtained center products. As such, this pattern of ceramic distribution is consistent with the proposition of relatively low-level administrative control of villages.

There are a number of other interesting aspects of these data. First, the samples under analysis are a mixture of excavation and judgment survey collections. That essentially identical results were obtained with both types of collection emphasizes the utility of survey data.

Second, there is some suggestion that the centers of Susa and Abu Fanduweh may have had a differential effect on villages in their immediate vicinities. Recall from table 17 that while distance-based predictions were accurate for KS-76 and KS-96 near Abu Fanduweh, they were slightly off for KS-34 near Susa where the relative frequency of the Susa-type neckless ledge rim was less than predicted and that of the Abu Fanduweh-type was more than predicted. This may indicate that villages in the administrative district of Susa were either differentially attracted to, or constrained by, Susa in comparison to villages in the Abu Fanduweh district. Given Susa's position as a regional as well as a district center, however, this minor distortion in interactional patterns would not be surprising.

Third, it is interesting that predictions of interaction are reasonably accurate for settlements on the eastern Susiana as well as for those in the west. I suggested earlier that Early Uruk settlements on the eastern Susiana were marginal to the more integrated system centered on Susa and Abu Fanduweh. The differential association of proto-bevel rim bowls with western sites supported this notion. Yet most of the ceramics in eastern survey collections are not obviously different from those in collections from the west. Early Uruk settlements on the eastern Susiana may have been marginal to the system in the west, but were by no means isolated from it. In currently fashionable terms, the distinction between core and periphery on the Early Uruk Susiana was probably clinal and incorporated much more variability than my discussion has suggested. The internal organization of the eastern system(s) and the form of its articulation with the west will be important problems for future work. The question of the impact of administrative relationships between western centers and eastern settlements on administrative workloads in the west will be particularly interesting.

The analysis of the three categories of data just reviewed—potential center requirements for rural agricultural produce, spatial variability in administrative demand for labor, and spatial variability in rural utilization of centrally produced ceramics—supports the proposition, derived from estimation of district level spans of control, that Early Uruk centers exercised relatively little control of rural populations. This low level of control apparently occurred in the context of a three-level settlement hierarchy and a two-level administrative hierarchy. Further, this system appears to have included primarily settlements on the western Susiana, while the eastern area was occupied by an undetermined number of smaller, relatively autonomous polities.

A major problem in this interpretation was originally noted by Sumner (1975:58). Centers are identified as being potentially autonomous, implying the anomalous concept of central places without hinterlands. Center control of rural populations appears to have been low, yet villages obtained at least some craft products from centers and were at least marginally involved in a centrally administered labor system. Further, the relatively regular distribution of villages around Susa and Abu Fanduweh suggests that center-

Gregory A. Johnson

village interaction had an important effect on village location.

The problem here is largely one of temporal resolution. The Early Uruk appears to have been a relatively long period, as well as one of rapid organizational change. I will suggest in the following section of this chapter that center control of rural populations was high during Middle Uruk. This degree of control is unlikely to have emerged overnight, but must have been achieved incrementally during Early and early Middle Uruk. We are simply unable to measure critical changes within periods in the absence of an improved internal chronology. Not only can we not measure change but the effects of change are likely to be superimposed on one another in a complex palimpsest that presents many analytical and interpretive problems.

Middle Uruk

The Middle Uruk settlement pattern of perhaps 3500 B.C. is illustrated in figure 23. The appearance of a major administrative center, Chogha Mish, on the eastern Susiana constitutes the most obvious change from the Early Uruk system. The population of the Susiana also increased by some 33 percent, and the system expanded from a three- to a four-level settlement hierarchy with the differentiation of a category of large villages (Johnson 1973:79).

I will suggest that Middle Uruk was also a period during which the proportion of the population of the Susiana that was articulated with a centralized administrative system increased markedly. As Blau (1970:-204–13) points out, increasing system size generates structural differentiation in organizations, which in turn enlarges the administrative component of organizations. His observation assumes that the internal administrative span of control remains constant. Structural differentiation and administrative component size would show even more marked increase in a situation in which span of control was being narrowed to increase effective control of the lower-order components of the system. I will attempt to show that the Middle Uruk on the Susiana was an example of just this sort of situation.

Spatial Constraints on Administrative Control

The preceding analysis of the Early Uruk settlement system indicated that center administrative control was, for the most part, spatially limited and only a portion of the settlements on the Susiana were closely articulated with a centralized administrative system. This section will examine the possibility of a similar situation during Middle Uruk.

As indicated above, Chogha Mish was probably founded (or grew very substantially) as an administrative center to control the eastern Susiana, and it is useful to maintain this east/west distinction. If the spatial range of Uruk administrative control from a given center was bounded, one might expect a decrease in settlement density as the bounds of this range were approached. As Adams (1974:11) has pointed out for later periods in Mesopotamia, centralized institutions capable of pooling and subsequent redistribution of subsistence commodities reduce the risk associated with agricultural production in an area of considerable spatial and temporal variability and uncertainty in agricultural yields. Figure 24 plots settlement density in hectares of settlement area per 10 square kilometer unit in 3 kilometer circular zones around Susa and Chogha Mish. The eastern and western portions of the plain are treated separately. Both plots indicate a decline in settlement density between 19 and 23 kilometers from these centers, suggesting the possibility that settlements beyond this approximate range may have been relatively independent of both center services and center controls.

The behavioral implications of distances of this magnitude may be clarified by transforming them to travel times. Movement cost transformations of linear distance have been very useful in locational geography (Olsson: 1965:57ff.), and transport cost or related travel time transformations have begun to appear in the archaeological literature (Hodder and Orton 1976:117; Johnson 1977:485–87). Table 18 presents data on travel times over relatively flat terrain in the Near East. The figures for distance traveled per day refer to linear distances. Briefly, the number of days spent in travel between named locations were extracted from nineteenth- and early-twentieth-century travel accounts. The straight line distances between these points were taken from maps of the relevant areas and divided by the number of days spent in travel between these points. The result is a measure of linear rather than total distance traveled per day. The average distance traveled per day according to these data is 39.44 (40) kilometers. This figure is roughly double that of the range (19 to 23 kilometers) beyond which settlement density falls off with distance from Susa and Chogha Mish.

I suggest that a 20-kilometer radius, or one-day roundtrip distance, may have been the maximum range of direct control from a given Uruk center. Indeed, this range may have been quite common in early systems. Renfrew (1975:14), for example, uses a concept of an "Early State Module" consisting of a central place and associated hinterland. He notes that these modules frequently had an area of about 1,500 square kilometers, with average distances between the central places of adjacent modules of about 40 kilometers. This would have placed the administrative boundary of adjacent systems at about 20 kilometers from their respective central places.

It is possible then that the Middle Uruk settlements on the Susiana located more than about 20 kilometers from a major administrative center were only marginally articulated with a central Susiana-administered settlement system. This would have placed the boundaries of an integrated settlement system including the major centers of Susa, Abu Fanduweh, and Chogha Mish within the Susiana rather than, as I have often assumed, between the Susiana and adjacent areas.

This proposition may be partially evaluated by examining the Middle Uruk rank-size distributions for the Susiana as a whole, and for the predicted administered portion of the plain. Figure 25 presents a rank-size plot for all Middle Uruk settlements in the survey area. This distribution is highly linear and has an associated rank-size index of 0.084. If, however, marginal settlements were effectively outside an integrated Susiana settlement system, their deletion from the analysis should further decrease the value of the rank-size index. Sites 7, 8, 99, 288, 173, 171, 197, 218, and 220 can be unambiguously deleted from the analysis since they are located more than 20 kilometers from a major center. Site 153 is 19.56 kilometers from Chogha Mish but is located on the opposite side of the Dizful anticline, well beyond a one-day roundtrip distance and can thus be deleted. Site 240 is 16.7 kilometers from Susa but is located on the opposite side of the present course of the Karkheh River and can also be deleted.

Figure 25 also illustrates the result of deletion of these sites. As expected, the rank-size index is reduced, from 0.084 to 0.012. This reduction is consistent with the proposition that the deleted sites were at least marginal to, if not outside, the major Susiana settlement system. These results parallel those discussed earlier for Early Uruk and support the proposition that a one-day roundtrip travel time was a significant factor in local administrative organization.

The implications of this rather restricted range of influence are difficult to evaluate at this time. Cherry (1978:425) attributes size restrictions on Early State Modules to the increasing costs of administration with increasing distance from a central place. I suspect, however, that this one-day roundtrip radius may have been more related to the ability of rural populations to avail themselves of center services than to the ability of center administrators to defray the cost of control of rural populations. It would be useful to examine this possibility more closely.

The relative centralization of Susiana Uruk craft production has been reasonably well demonstrated (Johnson 1973:90ff.; 1976:208–9). Both Henry Wright and I (Johnson 1973:159–60; Wright and Johnson 1975:283) have suggested that this cen-

tralization may have been, in part, an efficient system response to increasing seasonal demand by nomad populations. Rueschemeyer (1977) has pointed out that functional theories of differentiation in organizations are based on rather ephemeral efficiency considerations. The question is: efficiency for whom and for what? He suggests that the operational utility of such a functional approach may be enhanced by focusing on the interests or goals of those sectors of the system with access to disproportionate power. It seems reasonable that such disproportionate "power" (what I would call the differential ability to influence the behavior of others [Johnson 1978:100]) as it existed in the Uruk was controlled by center elites. It may be useful then to focus on potential elite goals.

While the importance of nomad demand remains to be ascertained, I now suspect that centralization was above all an explicit strategy of center administrators to more closely articulate rural populations with central economic activities. By subsidizing large-scale craft production, center administrators may well have been able to undercut rural producers and decrease the demand for rural craft products. Decreased demand for rural products would have led to decreased rural production and increased reliance on center workshops. The result of this process would have been an effective decline in the relative economic autonomy of rural villages and the increased articulation of their populations with centers.

It is possible that the circumstances of the Terminal Susa A population decline discussed in the preceding chapter may have favored opportunistic centralization of production in Early Uruk. Fifteen of the eighteen Terminal Susa A settlements in the area continued to be occupied in Early Uruk. Of these, Susa and Abu Fanduweh with estimated sizes of 5.0 and 5.16 hectares, respectively, were the largest settlements of the period, accounting for fully 34 percent of the total Terminal Susa A settlement area. Continued craft production at these two centers with Terminal Susa A abandonment of many villages having resident craftsmen may have markedly increased the proportional contribution of these centers to total craft output and facilitated centralization in Early Uruk.

Availability of craft products was not, of course, the only service attracting villagers to Early Uruk centers. Centers were also the loci of major religious ceremonial and, one supposes, numerous other central place functions.

If attracting rural populations into closer articulation with centers was a major Uruk concern, this would imply a considerable amount of freedom of action on the part of rural populations who, at least in Early Uruk, could largely decide whether or not to avail themselves of center services. Decisions to travel to centers, particularly to take advantage of available

Gregory A. Johnson

economic services, would have involved an element of cost-benefit calculation. The apparent one-day round-trip radius from major centers that apparently formed the boundary of the administered settlement system suggests that associated travel costs for longer distances were greater than most villagers were willing to assume—at least with any regularity. These costs may have included factors of food, housing, security, and time spent away from work at home.

There is, of course, another side to this story. It is unlikely that center administrators attempted to attract villagers for their decorative value. Increased rural dependence on center services was apparently associated with increased center economic and political control of rural populations, a topic I will address shortly. Recall that if Early Uruk administrators had relatively little control over rural populations, they were apparently able to extract considerable surplus produce and labor from center populations. Much of this surplus was undoubtedly invested in the kind of major construction projects (temples, etc.) which serve to both signal and reinforce elite status positions. Administrative subsidy of centralized craft production may then be viewed as another form in which surplus produce and labor could be invested. The result of this investment appears to have been twofold: some of the ugliest pottery in the Near East and a considerable increase in administrative control of rural populations.

Definition of Administrative Districts and Spans of Control

As was the case in Early Uruk, the Middle Uruk Susiana seems to have been divided into three major areas. The division of the western Susiana into the Susa and Abu Fanduweh areas continued, while the eastern Susiana came to be dominated by Chogha Mish. I noted earlier that at a given level of organizational hierarchy, organizational units can be expected to be of roughly the same size. Again taking settlement area as an indicator of population size and the areas defined above as functional administrative units, the latter should have contained roughly equivalent settlement areas.

If marginal settlements beyond the effective range of center administrative influence are deleted, the total hectarage of settlement for each of these three areas is as follows: Susa area, 33.19 hectares; Abu Fanduweh area, 32.56 hectares; and Chogha Mish area, 40.66 hectares. These figures are sufficiently close to support the proposition that the areas functioned as Middle Uruk administrative districts.

Figure 26 presents rank-size distributions for the three administrative districts discussed. The linearity of the distribution for the Chogha Mish area is particularly interesting. Recall that in Early Uruk, the east-ern portion of the Susiana did not contain a major administrative center and had a fairly convex rank-size distribution (RSI = 0.402). The appearance of Chogha Mish and the associated marked decrease in convexity of the rank-size distribution for the eastern area (RSI = 0.090) suggest a considerable increase in the integration of the settlement system in this area and lends further support to its identification as a major administrative district.

An increase in system integration is also indicated in the Abu Fanduweh area where the rank-size index decreased between Early and Middle Uruk from 0.247 to 0.106. The Susa area again shows a highly primate distribution (RSI = −1.264) consistent with the role of Susa in administration beyond its immediate district. Indeed the increase in primacy of the Susa district from an Early Uruk value of −0.547 can be partially related to increased administrative workload occasioned by the Middle Uruk extension of administrative functions to the eastern portion of the Susiana.

Earlier interpretations of Middle Uruk administrative organization appear to require revision. We have direct evidence of resident administrative activity at large centers such as Susa (Wright and Johnson 1975) and at apparently specialized villages such as Tepe Sharafabad, KS-36 (Wright and Johnson 1975; Wright, Miller and Redding 1980). I originally suggested that in view of direct evidence of resident administration at the top and bottom of a four-level Middle Uruk settlement hierarchy, the Middle Uruk administrative hierarchy was also likely to have had at least four levels above the general population (Johnson 1973:141). I am no longer confident that this was the case.

Inspection of the Middle Uruk settlement pattern map (figure 23) reveals that village-size administrative centers (marked by ceramic wall cones from survey and excavation collections) are distributed more or less linearly across the northern portion of the Susiana. Considering the evidence presented earlier for restriction of administrative influence to a 20-kilometer radius, it can be seen that these small administrative centers were located on the effective northern boundary of the administered Uruk settlement system. Indeed, none lie beyond 20 kilometers from either Susa or Chogha Mish, an observation lending further support to the importance of the 20-kilometer administrative radius.

If these small, specialized settlements exclusively represented the lowest level of the Susiana administrative hierarchy, one would expect them to be more uniformly distributed throughout the area rather than being restricted to the northern periphery of the administered settlement system. This northern concentration would have left the central and southern portions of the plain devoid of lowest-level administrative functions.

Note that with the exception of KS-153 (figure 23), which is located outside the probable area of the central Susiana system, the three remaining Middle Uruk small centers are restricted to the central and southern portions of the area. We have always assumed, although lacking direct evidence other than the presence of wall cones on KS-113, that these small centers were sites of resident administrative activity. If these three small centers were equivalent in administrative level to the smaller known administrative sites like Tepe Sharafabad, the spatial distribution of lowest level administration would appear much more uniform. A situation of settlements of different level in a settlement size hierarchy being of roughly equivalent status in an administrative hierarchy would parallel the China case described by Skinner (1977b:340), and possibly that of medieval Arab settlement systems described by Lapidus (1969:69–70).

Tentative acceptance of this proposition raises a number of problems, including the cause of the formal and spatial differences between small centers and administratively specialized villages. I noted earlier that specialized villages were restricted to the apparent northern boundary of the administered settlement system. As such, they might be expected to have been involved in some kind of boundary maintenance or boundary interaction among other functions. The question is one of interaction with whom—certainly not primarily with the scatter of small Uruk villages to the north. Although there are sedentary Uruk occupations in high valleys of the central Zagros (Wright ed. 1979), the most likely populations to have been important in boundary interaction with a lowland settlement system were the pastoral nomads for whom we have so little evidence. While the northern Susiana provided winter graze for historically known nomad groups (Pierre 1917) and Hole (1974) has excavated portions of a sixth millennium B.C. campsite in this area, we know virtually nothing about nomad populations for the Uruk time range.

The potential equivalency of specialized villages and small centers in administrative level has clear implications for overall administrative organization. It is reasonably clear that Susa dominated the Susiana in Middle Uruk and was the location of the highest level of administration in the area. As argued earlier, the Susiana was divided into three major administrative districts headed respectively by Susa, Abu Fanduweh, and Chogha Mish. The equivalency of specialized villages and small centers in administrative level would imply the operation of a three-level rather than a four-level (Johnson 1973:141) administrative hierarchy in Middle Uruk. As was the case for Early Uruk, the

vertical complexity of administrative organization may well have been less complex than I thought earlier.

Estimation of basal level span of control is again difficult. Let us first consider system level rural administration. On the reasonable assumption that rural administrative centers would have had no role in administration of the populations of regional or district centers, Susa, Abu Fanduweh, and Chogha Mish can be temporarily deleted from the analysis. This leaves 61.85 (62) hectares of settlement within the administered area of the Susiana as defined earlier. I assume again that 1 hectare of settlement represented the lowest-level Middle Uruk administered unit. (This is the point at which the Middle Uruk rank-size distribution [figure 25] undergoes rapid lower-limb falloff.) These sixty-two basal level units were distributed among nine rural administrative centers of which six were specialized villages and three were small centers. Average basal level span of control would thus have been about 7 (6.88). This span represented a very marked narrowing of the wide estimated spans of Early Uruk of 22 to 27 and suggests a considerable increase in the degree of administrative control exercised over rural populations.

This picture is somewhat modified if span of control is considered by district rather than on an aggregate level for the entire administered area of the plain. The Susa district had 8.19 hectares of settlement outside Susa and two specialized administrative villages for a basal span of 4 (4.10). This compares favorably with the figures for the Chogha Mish district. With 30.16 hectares of settlement outside Chogha Mish and six rural administrative centers (four specialized villages and two small centers), rural span would have been equal to about 5 (5.03).

The Abu Fanduweh district was apparently quite different. There were 23 hectares of settlement outside Abu Fanduweh with a single rural administrative site (a small center), suggesting a wide span of 23. This would have been comparable to the estimated Early Uruk spans of 22 to 27. The apparently wide basal level span of control in the Abu Fanduweh district might suggest that the district center was differentially involved in direct rural administration, that the number of administered activities was lower in the Abu Fanduweh district than elsewhere or that the degree of control of village populations was simply lower compared with elsewhere.

There is an intriguing parallel here with Skinner's China data. Recall that Skinner found wide spans of control in regional cores where administrators were primarily concerned with tax collection, and narrow spans in peripheral areas where military (boundary maintenance and social control) considerations were

Gregory A. Johnson

also important. I suggested earlier that the distribution of administratively specialized villages along the northern border of the administered Susiana settlement system might be indicative of their role in system boundary maintenance. Of the three Susiana administrative districts, those of Susa and Chogha Mish shared this northern boundary and had narrow estimated spans of control, while Abu Fanduweh was insulated in the southern portion of the plain and had an estimated wide span of control. This situation would suggest that the number of administered activities in the Abu Fanduweh district was lower than in the Susa and Chogha Mish districts.

These district-to-district variations aside, it seems clear that the overall decrease in basal level span of control between Early and Middle Uruk, along with an increase in the vertical complexity of the administrative hierarchy, would indicate increasing administrative control of rural populations.

Tests of Organizational Implications

The proposition of increasing Middle Uruk administrative control of rural populations may be partially evaluated from a number of different perspectives. Recall that given their respective population sizes, immediate sustaining areas, estimated demand for surplus agricultural produce and labor, and estimated low degree of control over rural populations, the Early Uruk centers of Susa and Abu Fanduweh were probably largely independent of village agricultural production. Given this suggestion of near maximum surplus production by Early Uruk center populations, substantial Middle Uruk increase in center sizes would have necessitated increased acquisition of agricultural produce and probably labor from surrounding villages. It appears that the population of Susa increased by some 2,600 persons and that of Abu Fanduweh by some 500 (528) during Middle Uruk.

It is instructive to examine probable Middle Uruk center requirements for rural agricultural products and potential rural surplus productivity more closely. Recall from the preceding discussion of Early Uruk centers that they had direct access to about 2 hectares of agricultural land per capita, and that this figure approximates both traditional per capita land use in the area today and maximum potential family productivity in Iraq. High administrative demand for labor from center populations plus a variety of other evidence for minimal center control of villages suggested that near maximum surplus production was being extracted from center agricultural populations. Given the figures also cited earlier indicating that approximately 0.5 hectares per capita were required for subsistence production, fallow, etc., maximum potential surplus production would amount to the yield of ap-

proximately 1.5 hectares of land per capita. As we are not able to monitor spatial variability in yields for relevant areas of the Susiana, I will assume that yields in these areas were equal.

If we assume that administrative demand for per capita surplus productivity in centers was constant between Early and Middle Uruk, the relationship between center demand and probable surplus production extracted from villages may be estimated. (This is a conservative assumption since it seems unlikely that demand for per capita surplus would decline during a period of increasing administrative complexity.) This estimate requires examination of the distribution of the Middle Uruk population in relation to immediately available agricultural land, or spatial variability in population density.

Figure 27 illustrates the imposition of a 5-kilometer interval grid on the central Susiana settlement pattern. Marginal settlements which appear to have been beyond the range of effective administrative control have been deleted from the analysis. Observed population density per square kilometer is tabulated for each grid square in table 19. Note from figure 27 (grid squares B7, C6, and F5) that agglomeration of the data in this fashion results in pooling the population estimates of two small centers (KS-96 and KS-113) with nearby villages (KS-94 and KS-4,5, respectively). The population of villages KS-54 and KS-98 are also pooled with that of Abu Fanduweh (KS-59). This pooling amounts to the assumption that the populations of these five villages near centers were engaged in maximum potential surplus production.

At maximum surplus production, involving the utilization of 2 hectares of agricultural land per capita, each grid square could have been occupied by about 50 people per square kilometer. It is evident that the populations of squares containing five of the six Middle Uruk large and small centers exceeded the density that could be locally supported at the levels of consumption discussed above. (These density figures are italicized in table 19.) Only the square (F5) containing the small center KS-113 could have been self-sustaining at a population density of 44 persons per square kilometer.

Table 20 contains two kinds of information. First, center surplus requirements in hectares of production beyond what would have been available locally are italicized. Consider the example of Abu Fanduweh (square C6). With a population of 102.72 persons per square kilometer in an area that would support 50 persons per square kilometer at estimated center surplus demand rates, the center population exceeded this maximum by 52.72 persons per square kilometer. This is equivalent to additional demand for 105.44 hectares of production (at 2 hectares per capita) per square kilometer in a 25 square kilometer unit, or 2,636 hectares of production.

One adjustment has been made to this form of calculation in the case of Susa (grid reference B4). With a unit population density of 200 persons per square kilometer, Susa would have required all of the land in its grid unit simply to support its population at subsistence level (0.5 hectares of production per capita). With estimated center demand of 2 hectares of production per capita, Susa required an additional 7,500 hectares of production from outside its immediate area. It seems probable, however, that Susa was also utilizing land available in adjacent unoccupied grid squares B3 and C4. If these were utilized to their fullest potential, they would have generated surplus of 1,875 hectares of production each or a total of 3,750. This would have reduced the unmet demand at Susa from 7,500 to 3,750 hectares of production (see table 20:B4.) With an estimated population of Susa of 5,000 persons, this model would allocate 3,750 or 75 percent to involvement in agricultural production. The actual size of the labor force would have been smaller than this as these figures were generated on a per capita basis.

This estimated population allocation is at least consistent with what little is known about the internal organization of Susa. The estimated 25 hectares of Middle Uruk occupation on the site was divided between the 9 hectares of the high Acropole and the 16 hectares of the lower Apadana area (Johnson 1973:69–71). The occupation of the Acropole contained a massive mud-brick platform surmounted by public architecture as well as areas of elite residences or smaller administrative buildings (Wright 1978). The Acropole, which occupies 36 percent of the Middle Uruk site by area, appears then to have been primarily devoted to ceremonial and administrative functions. If the larger Apadana which occupies 64 percent of the site was primarily devoted to lower status occupation, then the internal organization of Susa by area (64 percent "nonelite" and 36 percent "elite") would have approximated the population allocation figures suggested above of 75 percent food producers and 25 percent nonproducers. Interestingly, Oates and Oates (1976b:120) note that agriculturalists represent 75 percent of the population of modern Tell Afar in Iraq and comment that while this is a comparatively high figure, it probably approximates average conditions for later prehistoric towns.

Considering the adjustments of Susa's estimated demand for rural surplus discussed above, total center surplus requirements for the system amount to 8,858 hectares of production against a total potential rural surplus of 11,442 hectares. Estimated demand was thus about 77 percent of potential surplus. (Remember that this potential surplus was calculated on the basis of the number of people estimated to have been living in rural areas, not on some estimate of rural carrying capacity.)

While system level demand may have been at 77 percent of potential surplus, localized demand may have been even higher. If the plain was partitioned into eastern and western sectors along administrative district boundaries, center demand in the western area exceeded potential rural surplus production, while the opposite was the case in the eastern area (see table 21). This suggests that unmet demand in the western area may have been resolved by shipment of significant quantities of produce from the eastern Chogha Mish administrative district to the area of Susa and Abu Fanduweh.

The evidence of administrative technology including both commodity and message sealings (Wright and Johnson 1975:271; Wright, Miller, and Redding 1980) indicates that Middle Uruk administrators were involved in the storage and shipment of goods. This involvement perhaps encouraged the proliferation of Middle Uruk jar types, most of which have everted rims. Such rim forms are highly suitable for anchoring a cord-tied vessel cover, and I suspect that the marked variability in jar rim form during the Uruk represents intensive experimentation with methods of vessel closure associated with an increased volume of commodity storage and shipment.

The demand/potential surplus estimates made here are obviously very crude and probably overestimate both administrative demand and potential rural surplus. Spatial and temporal variability in potential productivity have not even been considered. The figures do, however, suggest a high level of center demand for rural produce and are consistent with the evidence of both administrative and ceramic technology. The figures are also consistent with the proposition of a marked increase in Middle Uruk administrative control of rural populations. Implications of these conclusions for the interpretation of Late Uruk developments on the Susiana will be examined later in this chapter.

Another line of evidence leads to much the same conclusions. Recall that the relatively low administrative demand for village labor in Early Uruk was established by comparing Early Uruk bevel rim bowl density at KS-34 (ca. 37 sherds/cubic meter) with Middle and Late Uruk densities at KS-54 (ca. 430–590 sherds/cubic meter). Of relevance here is the observation that not only were Early Uruk bowl densities low in villages, but Middle Uruk densities were high. This dramatic order-of-magnitude increase in what I would interpret as administrative demand for labor is consistent with both a narrowing of Middle Uruk basal span of control and the high level of center demand for rural surplus production indicated earlier.

Expansion of an administered labor system might well have advantages beyond simple increase in labor and surplus availability. Specifically, the operation of a regularized labor system might well allow administrators to monitor simultaneously changes in population size, composition, and spatial distribution. In other words, operation of such a labor system might allow maintenance of a rough continuing census of the administered population. Continuing census data could have been very important for projecting labor availability for agricultural production, public works construction, and so forth, and in general for increasing the reliability of the administered system.

Whether associated with the maintenance of census data or not, the effective operation of such an administered labor system would probably entail very regularized and frequent utilization of labor to ensure that the system would be operational when required. Considerable labor may then have been used not so much for acquisition of its immediate products, but to ensure its future availability. A portion of the intensive public building activity evidenced on Uruk sites and those of other periods may have been undertaken to absorb temporary labor surpluses which had to be used to maintain the regularity of the system, but were not required for more important economic activities.

More or less "monumental" construction projects had the obvious advantage of both signaling and reinforcing the position of local elites. This kind of labor intensive monumental construction or what might be called "piling behavior" has a very wide distribution in the world in early complex societies (mounds, pyramids, platforms, etc.), and I would simply suggest that the oft-cited advantages of elite aggrandizement may be insufficient in themselves to account for this frequently observed pattern of labor investment.

These admitted speculations aside, not only did Middle Uruk center growth require closer center articulation with villages, but the pattern of center growth within the Susiana system provides additional evidence of expanding center control of village populations. I suggested earlier that centralization of craft production was, in part, a strategy by center elites to increase village dependence on center services. This strategy appears to have been very successful. Table 22 presents grouped data on change in aggregate settlement size by size class and administrative district between Early and Middle Uruk. Large and small villages have been combined for this analysis. These data make it clear that the Middle Uruk increase in hectarage of settlement was restricted almost exclusively to centers despite the foundation, abandonment, and smaller size changes in village sites. Note that in all three Middle Uruk administrative districts, aggregate village area declined slightly, while aggregate center area increased markedly. Only in marginal areas be-

yond the range of center administration did aggregate village population increase. This rather striking pattern not only supports the proposition of increasing center control of villages but also lends additional credence to the identification of "marginal" settlements as beyond the effective range of regular participation in the central Susiana administered settlement system.

I suspect that during Middle Uruk, many villagers were shifting their residence to centers. It is possible, of course, that population growth was largely restricted to centers, while village populations remained stable. This possibility may be partially evaluated by examination of alternative population growth rates that would have been required to generate the observed pattern of population increase.

While we do not know the length of time over which the Early-Middle Uruk population increase occurred, it is unlikely to have been more than three hundred years. Table 23 presents growth rates that would have been required to account for the estimated Middle Uruk increase in twenty-five year intervals from three hundred to fifty years, under two alternative conditions: a uniform growth rate for the system as a whole with rural emigration to centers, and growth in centers only. The table also distinguishes growth in marginal settlements as they were defined earlier.

Cowgill notes that typical rates of population change prior to A.D. 1750 ranged from negative 7.0 to positive 7.0 persons per thousand per year (1975a:514), with average rates of 1.0 to 3.0 per thousand and surges over two hundred to three hundred years of 3.0 to 7.0 per thousand (1975b:218). Hassan (1975:42) cites figures with more positive variability, with an average "neolithic" growth rate of 1.0 per thousand and highs of 5.0 to 10.0 per thousand. Table 23 incorporates Cowgill's more conservative figures in comparing alternative growth models.

Table 23 contains two points of interest. Accounting for the Middle Uruk population increase solely in terms of population growth in centers would require improbably high rates if that growth occurred in less than 125 years and high rates for periods between 125 and 275 years. Growth in the system as a whole with rural emigration to centers, on the other hand, would require rates exceeding the average range only if that growth occurred in less than fifty years. While center populations may have had somewhat higher growth rates than those in villages, these figures strongly suggest that growth was relatively uniform in the system and that a significant proportion of the marked increase in center populations represented immigration from villages. This is consistent with the overall pattern of increasing center-village articulation suggested earlier.

The second point to note is that rates required to account for growth of settlements marginal to the central Susiana system are lower than rates required to account for growth within the system. Given the order-of-magnitude increase in administrative demand for Middle Uruk village labor and the potential importance of demand for labor in accounting for population growth (Blanton 1975:116–26; White 1973), the lower growth rate of marginal settlements was quite expectable. Beyond being expectable, these lower rates are yet another characteristic supporting the original "marginal settlement" classification and the concept of a 20-kilometer radius of effective Middle Uruk administrative influence.

The various classes of data reviewed here were relevant to center demand for surplus rural agricultural production, center demand for rural labor, and rural emigration to centers. All three were consistent with the proposition that the marked decrease in estimated Middle Uruk basal level span of control was associated with an increase in the degree of control exercised over rural populations.

Processes in Uruk State Formation

Table 24 presents a summary of estimated values for several system level variables during Early and Middle Uruk. The development of a three-level administrative hierarchy with substantial administrative influence over village as well as center populations suggests that the end of Early Uruk and the beginning of Middle Uruk was the immediate period of state formation on the Susiana. This operational criterion of vertical complexity of administrative organization has been discussed elsewhere (Claessen 1978:579; Johnson 1973:1–4; Wright 1977:383–58). It seems clear that the vertical specialization resulting in the emergence of a third level of administrative hierarchy in Middle Uruk was a response to an increased administrative workload involved in ensuring the integration of lower-level administered units.

In another discussion (Johnson:1978), I viewed vertical specialization as the addition of a new level to the top of an organization in response to an increasing workload required to provide integrative functions among an expanded series of equivalent highest-order administrative units. This model assumed that the level of integration in the system under analysis was both high and constant. The Susiana Uruk case was more complex than this since it involved change both in administrative organization and in the level of integration of the system.

High-level administration was present during Early Uruk and provided integration between administrative districts with wide spans of control and a relatively low degree of influence over village populations. Simple expansion of the size of the administered system during Middle Uruk with no change in degree of control would probably have resulted simply in a proliferation of district centers—at least up to a point. Uruk administrators, however, were concerned with increasing their level of control over village populations. This increased control required more direct local supervision beyond the capacity of district centers. The response to this problem was the addition of a level of local organization to the bottom rather than the top of the administrative hierarchy.

Lower-level vertical specialization was probably a response to marked increase in the scale of the administered system as well as to increase in the degree of control over village populations. As discussed earlier in this chapter, a large portion of the eastern Susiana was brought under centralized control during the Middle Uruk. This virtually doubled the spatial scale of the system. An additional increase in system population size was generated by population growth, probably in response to increased center demand for rural labor and surplus production. It should be explicitly pointed out, however, that while the population of the Susiana increased by some 33 percent between Early and Middle Uruk, the size of the population actually articulated with a centralized administrative system grew by 118 percent (see table 24).

An increasing number of scholars have stressed the importance of population growth relative to resource availability in the development of complex societies (Athens 1977; Carneiro 1970, 1981; Sanders and Webster 1978; Sanders, Parsons, and Santley 1979; Smith and Young 1972). Most such arguments are phrased in terms of aggregate population densities for relatively large areas. I have suggested here that expansion of the scale of the Early Uruk system was a significant factor in local political development, yet the aggregate population density for Susiana Uruk was comparatively very low. Total (center and rural) population densities, in persons per square kilometer, for the Susiana between Terminal Susa A and Late Uruk are estimated as follows: Terminal Susa A, 2.6; Early Uruk, 8.4; Middle Uruk, 11.2; and Late Uruk, 4.6. Compare these figures with those reported for only *rural* areas of the Near East with traditional agricultural systems: Lower Diyala, 28.9 (Adams 1965:-22); Susiana Diz pilot area, 46.3 (Gremliza 1962:2); Kur River basin Dorudzan project area, 18.9 (Sumner 1972:2,174–75); and the Gorgon region of Iran near Gombab-e Kavus, 28.8 (Daniel G. Bates 1978, personal communication).

There were simply very few people living on the Susiana during the Uruk and in terms of aggregate density, there was no apparent problem of land availability. Yet, I have argued for local resource shortages relative to demand, especially around large centers. The point here is that aggregate population figures often mean very little. The specific distribution of pop-

Gregory A. Johnson

ulation and differential demand for resources may, however, be of great importance irrespective of aggregate population density.

This is not to imply that growth is not important. The variables of greater interest, however, are probably system organizational scale and the degree to which that system is integrated. In presenting an admittedly tentative model of administrative system response to increase in system scale (Johnson 1978), I predicted that in very highly integrated systems, two levels of administrative hierarchy are likely to be present when about 24 basal organizational units are administered and three levels of hierarchy are likely to be present when about 70 basal units are administered. Although the 1978 model was based on assumptions that were unrealistic in the extreme, by simple accident that model generates organizational transitions when spans of control exceed six—a figure discussed above at some length. The formal characteristics of that model (not its assumptions) are thus in agreement with more recent work (Johnson 1982b, 1983) and may be evaluated with the Susiana data.

During the Terminal Susa A period there were four, largely autonomous enclaves of settlement on the Susiana (Johnson 1973:87–90). The largest of these was centered on Abu Fanduweh and contained about 12 hectares of settlement or, given my assumptions here, about 12 basal administered units. The administered settlement system of the western Susiana in Early Uruk contained about 49 administered units and that of the central Susiana in Middle Uruk about 107 administered units. Table 25 compares these values with those predicted for two- and three-level hierarchy formation. The values predicted for hierarchy transitions fit quite nicely between the estimated values for these three periods and provide additional support for the proposition that about 1 hectare of settlement functioned as the basal administered unit in these systems.

Increase in the scale and degree of integration of the Middle Uruk system also had an impact on the district level. The emergence of Chogha Mish to provide district-level administration in the eastern Susiana beyond the effective administrative ranges of Susa and Abu Fanduweh represented horizontal specialization at the district level of administrative organization.

Both horizontal and vertical specialization of the Middle Uruk administrative system were probably related to the continuing development of Uruk administrative technology. Prior to the appearance of numerical texts in Late Uruk (LeBrun 1971:179), administrative technology seems to have emphasized secure information transfer rather than information storage and as such is likely to have been more involved in maintaining activity coordination between levels of hierarchy than in aiding decision making within a

level of hierarchy. (See also Le Brun and Vallat 1978; Schmandt-Besserat 1979, 1980; and Wright, Miller, and Redding 1980.)

Figure 28 presents a partial flow chart of variable relationships for Early and Middle Uruk. It incorporates the variables in table 24 as well as centralization of craft production and other processes discussed here. Early Uruk administrative support functions provide the entry point to this chart. I have suggested elsewhere (Johnson 1978:101–3) that social status differentiation may often be functionally related to administrative organization in structuring or supplementing the differential social influence of administrative personnel that partially ensures general compliance with administrative decisions. (See also Sutherland 1975:290 and Udy 1970:48.) Such differentiation of elite administrators can be expected to be associated with the differentially high elite utilization of resources which serves to signal their status. In the virtual absence of burial data, the best available data on social differentiation come from architecture and its artifact associations. (See Johnson 1976:216–17 and Wright 1981a.) Related administrative support functions, in what was probably a theocratic society, would have involved temple construction and other public works which again serve to both signal and legitimize the position of administrative personnel (Webster 1976).

Administrative requirements for labor and surplus production were high in Early Uruk but could apparently be met largely by center populations. Expansion of the Middle Uruk system and apparently successful attempts to increase center control of village populations both ensured provision of various administrative support functions and ultimately amplified them.

Note that the genesis of Early Uruk administration has not been considered here. We do not yet understand the organization of the Susiana in Susa A or the reasons for its collapse in Terminal Susa A. The Early and Middle Uruk economic strategy to more closely articulate villages with centers may have been associated with a decline in the degree to which kinship relationships were manipulated for political (and economic) ends. This impression is reinforced by aspects of the marked stylistic change in the ceramic assemblage between Susa A and Uruk. Frank Hole (1977b) is engaged in an analysis of painted Susa A ceramics available in both survey collections from around the plain and from excavation samples from Susa, including the Susa A cemetery (Necropole) of perhaps 2,000 burials at Susa itself. He suggests that specific painted types may have been associated with elites at Susa and settlements in its hinterland. If these elaborately decorated types were used to signal affiliation with high status kin groups (see Wobst 1977), then the virtual absence of painted or other elaborate decoration in

Uruk ceramics may also indicate a substantial change in the organization of social relations. A major change in mortuary ritual in the Uruk, reflected by the great rarity of Uruk burials in comparison to earlier and later periods, suggests much the same conclusion.

Whatever the causes of the Susa A collapse, it is probable that Early Uruk integrative mechanisms (at least through most of the period) were significantly different from those operative during Susa A and not yet at the state level of organization of Middle Uruk. This gives Early Uruk a high priority for future research as a critical transitional period in complex society development on the Susiana.

Late Uruk

The Late Uruk Collapse

As outlined elsewhere (Johnson 1973:143–56), settlement on the Susiana declined markedly in Late Uruk to only about 53 hectares of occupied area (see figure 29). This decline was apparently accompanied by the emergence of major hostilities on the plain as suggested by two classes of evidence. First, military scenes appear on seal impressions from both Chogha Mish (Delougaz and Kantor 1969:25) and Susa (Amiet 1961:251, 312). Second, a regular band of area completely devoid of settlement and some 14 to 15 kilometers wide opened between the eastern and western portions of the plain. I suggested that hostilities in the area were generated when Chogha Mish was able to break away from administrative control by Susa and attempt (apparently successfully) to become the center of an independent polity. In 1973, I speculated that Middle Uruk administrative capacity had been exceeded, but was unable to suggest a mechanism that would specifically account for the collapse of the system.

The preceding analysis of probable Middle Uruk administrative demand for rural surplus production indicates that the eastern and western portions of the Susiana were very different in their estimated ratios of demand to supply. While center demand for rural surplus may even have exceeded potential rural production in the west, demand was only about 36 percent of potential production in the Chogha Mish administrative district (table 21). I would like to suggest that elites at Chogha Mish attempted to sever their subordinate political relationship with Susa in order to obtain exclusive control of the eastern Susiana with its relatively high potential for extraction of additional rural surplus. Such separation may have been viewed as especially desirable if the eastern Susiana had been providing a significant level of surplus productivity to the western area of Susa and Abu Fanduweh.

Administrative avarice may, however, not have been the only factor prompting Chogha Mish to try to separate itself from Susa. Shipment of significant quantities of agricultural produce (and perhaps labor) out of the Chogha Mish administrative district to meet administrative demand on the western Susiana might have been a source of considerable rural unrest in the eastern area. Separation from Susa would then serve to both reduce rural dissent and assure provision of labor and produce to Chogha Mish itself.

While this scenario provides a possible reason for Chogha Mish to have attempted to establish itself as the center of an independent polity, it does not account for the inability of Susa to retain control of its subordinate administrative center. Earlier in this chapter, I attempted to demonstrate that the spatial range of direct administrative influence during Middle Uruk was limited to about 20 kilometers, or a one-day roundtrip. It is interesting to note that while Late Uruk Susa retained control of Abu Fanduweh (12.27 kilometers away), it lost control of Chogha Mish which was 28.56 kilometers away. Note that Chogha Mish is 26.55 kilometers from Abu Fanduweh so that neither direct control from Susa nor indirect control through Abu Fanduweh was possible.

If the physical distance in excess of a one-day roundtrip between Chogha Mish and Susa/Abu Fanduweh contributed to the observed breakdown of political integration on the Susiana, there should be cases elsewhere in which regional political integration was maintained and distances between major administrative centers were equal to or less than a one-day roundtrip distance. The contemporary Late Uruk settlement system of the Warka area in southern Iraq provides a contrasting case. In a situation of similar topography, the Warka Late Uruk system appears to have been highly integrated and to have included five major administrative centers. The average first order nearest neighbor distance among these five centers was 18.16 kilometers with a range of 16.99 to 20.29 (Johnson 1975:317). This would appear to have been a nearly optimal spatial pattern for administration in that it would maximize the territory under control of a given center and thus minimize the number of high-order centers required in the system, while maintaining system political integration through linked control from one center to the next.

I would envision a situation in later Middle Uruk in which Susa was losing control of administration at Chogha Mish. As Chogha Mish became increasingly independent, it could be expected to have attempted to assert control over as many settlements within its 20-kilometer maximum administrative range as possible. That Chogha Mish was situated 28.56 kilometers from Susa and 26.55 kilometers from Abu Fanduweh means there would thus have been considerable overlap in the maximum administrative ranges

Gregory A. Johnson

of these centers. With Chogha Mish attempting to become the head of an independent polity, settlements located in this overlap zone would probably have been subject to conflicting administrative demands from Susa/Abu Fanduweh and Chogha Mish. This conflicting demand would most likely have taken the form of double assessments for agricultural produce and labor. It is not difficult to picture the plight of a villager in this overlap zone who, having discharged his labor (or military) responsibilities to the Susa administration, was confronted with identical demands from Chogha Mish. Recall that the average Middle Uruk center demand for surplus agricultural production was estimated to have been 77 percent of potential rural surplus. Doubling this demand would have created an obviously impossible situation and may account for the abandonment of numbers of villages located between Susa and Chogha Mish. Note that even if my original estimate of average center demand was substantially inflated, doubling that demand would probably have had the same effect as postulated here.

This hypothesis may be partially evaluated with the available settlement pattern data. Figure 30 indicates both the locations of Late Uruk and of abandoned Middle Uruk settlements. An administrative overlap zone has been superimposed on this map by drawing circles with 20-kilometer radii centered on Susa, Abu Fanduweh, and Chogha Mish. This theoretical administrative overlap zone corresponds closely to the observed band of settlement abandonment between the eastern and western portions of the plain. Indeed, of the fourteen Middle Uruk settlements in the overlap zone, eleven were abandoned by Late Uruk. Chogha Mish was apparently able to assert control over the remaining three settlements in this area. Two of these three settlements (KS-36 and KS-113) had been rural administrative centers within the Chogha Mish district in Middle Uruk and may then have been either more loyal to Chogha Mish in Late Uruk or better able to resist administrative demands from Susa.

It seems clear that the substantial conflict on the Susiana in Late Uruk postdates state formation. It is interesting that while this was a case of conflict within a society, it apparently originated within an administrative elite rather than between "classes" of markedly different social and economic characteristics. This view is supported by the rapid depopulation of the Susiana as seen primarily in the abandonment of smaller settlements. The aggregate area of large centers decreased by 22 percent from approximately 43 to 35 hectares. The aggregate area of smaller settlements, however, decreased by 68 percent from approximately 82 to 26 hectares.

The fate of the population represented by this decline is unknown. It is unlikely that a significant proportion of this population met its demise as the result of hostilities in the area. Most of the Late Uruk population decline can probably be attributed to emigration to other areas, despite clear evidence for local military activity. I once suggested that a portion of the Late Uruk population expansion in the Warka area of Iraq (Adams and Nissen 1972:11ff.) may have occurred at the expense of the Susiana (Johnson 1975:337). A similar suggestion of the impact of possible Susiana emigration has been made by Alden (1979b:79–81) for the Kur River basin of Iran. Whatever the destinations of these people, the differential pattern of depopulation by settlement size on the Susiana suggests that lower-status villagers were moving out of the area, while elites among whom Late Uruk conflict originated tended to remain.

Although these propositions remain to be evaluated, they do focus attention on the role of the relationship between the Susiana and other areas on local Susiana developments. External contacts have not been considered in this chapter despite ample evidence of their existence.

Susiana "Foreign Relations"

Fuller discussion of fourth millennium relations of the Susiana to other areas of greater Mesopotamia would involve an initial exercise in comparative relative chronology that is both a topic of little concensus (few C^{14} determinations are available) and one beyond the scope of this chapter. Therefore, I will sketch my view of sundry issues without recourse to the customary panoply of references to obscure artifact illustrations.

Small excavation samples of Early Uruk material are available from the Eanna deep sounding (von Haller 1932) and the vicinity of the Steingebäude (Boehmer 1972) at Warka in southern Iraq, from Tepe Farukhabad (Wright 1981a) on the Deh Luran Plain, Tall-i-Ghazir (Caldwell 1968) on the Ram Hormuz Plain, and Susa and nearby villages on the Susiana. The remainder of our data are largely from surface survey (Adams 1981; Adams and Nissen 1972; Johnson 1973; Wright 1981b).

Sufficient data are available, however, to note that Early Uruk was a period of increasing interaction of some undetermined sort between the Susiana and southern Sumer. This at least insofar as the conveniently nebulous process of "interaction" may be monitored by the degree of similarity of ceramic assemblages. Whatever the nature of this relation, the pattern of late fifth to early fourth millennium ceramic change on the Susiana virtually precludes Warkan population movement or political control as relevant mechanisms of interaction.

The spatial organization of the Warka area (Johnson 1980b) was quite different from that discussed earlier on the Susiana. Warka dominated an apparently dendritic settlement system with a four-level settlement hierarchy possibly indicating greater political complexity than is evident on the contemporary Susiana. This picture is complicated by the observation that the Nippur area north of Warka both dominated Warka demographically during Early Uruk and exhibited a distinct spatial structure (Adams 1981), implying a distinct and possibly yet more complex political organization.

Middle Uruk developments outside the Susiana and Deh Luran (Wright 1981a) have unfortunately received less attention, in part due to the difficulty of differentiating Late Uruk settlements from those occupied during Middle and Late Uruk on the basis of survey data. A Late Uruk population decline in the Nippur area (Adams 1981) made Middle Uruk occupations easily detectable in that area, as was the case on the Susiana. Massive Late Uruk expansion in the Warka area (Adams and Nissen 1972; Adams 1981) effectively obscures Middle Uruk developments in that critical area. Middle Uruk interregional data are then very limited, but the overall impression is one of an increasing relationship among a variety of local systems experiencing differential political development.

Late Uruk developments in greater Mesopotamia are better documented if even more poorly understood due to their complexity. Consider even the crude measure of aggregate population as indicated by hectares of occupation. Population of the demographically central Warka area increased by 121 percent (Adams 1981:69), while that of the nearby areas of Nippur (Adams 1981:69) and Ur/Eridu (Wright 1981c:325–27) decreased by 45 percent and 60 percent, respectively. The Late Uruk population on the Susiana declined 58 percent. Further decline in Uruk or Uruk-related settlement has been documented in the Izeh Valley of the Zagros (Wright 1979), on the Ram Hormuz Plain south of the Susiana, and probably in most of Luristan as well (Wright, this volume).

These peripheral population declines were approximately contemporaneous with a pattern of limited and apparently very specialized spatial expansion in a far periphery represented by classical Late Uruk occupations at Samsat, Habuba Kabira, and Jebel Aruda on the northern Euphrates (Alden 1982; Sürenhagen 1974/75; and van Driel and van Driel-Murray 1979), and perhaps slightly later at Godin in the Kangavar Valley of the Zagros (Weiss and Young 1975).

These demographic changes occur in the context of a very high degree of similarity of artifact assemblages, including both ceramics and administrative technology (seals and numerical tablets), that extends to very marked similarities in areas such as technique of building construction. The demographic changes indicated above would thus appear to have occurred during the period of highest interpolity interaction (and interdependence?) of the fourth millennium.

What happened? Fourth millennium specialists have a tendency to hide under their desks if they think that someone might ask them this question. There is some talk of colonies and trade emporia (Alden 1982; Kohl 1978; Lamberg-Karlovsky 1982; Weiss and Young 1975) that sometimes suggests a picture of expanding Warkan hegemony producing a greater Uruk coprosperity sphere. Yet there is little evidence for increasing long-range trade until the post-Uruk, Proto-Elamite period considered in Alden's contribution to this volume.

The interregional picture is thus opaque at best. The fourth millennium appears to have been one of emerging, complex polities, increasingly related to one another in an undetermined number of complex ways. How these large-scale relationships may have affected local developments such as that on the Susiana is an excellent question to which I have no answer. This is partially a problem of inadequate data, but is also one of inadequate theory. We simply have very little idea about what to expect of very large-scale interactions.

Conclusion

The conclusions presented in this chapter on the Susiana Uruk are tentative at best. As Henri Claessen remarked in his review of an earlier version, "It's like juggling with eggs—with all the risks of the game." The discussion has, however, highlighted a few of the problems in the development of this complex society.

The problem of variables involved in administrative control of rural populations is more than a little vexing. While the degree of control in Middle Uruk reflected by basal span of control, estimated administrative demand for labor, and estimated demand for surplus agricultural production was high, it was also spatially bounded. This limitation appears to have been engendered in part by the relative advantages to rural populations of participation in a centralized system rather than by the ability of administrative elites to impose control on those populations. Although many see physical force as central to the operation of early states (see Webb 1975, for example), there is an emerging view that early states functioned through a complex interaction of coercion and consensus (Claessen and Skalník 1978:640; Godelier 1978:767–768; Service 1975:266ff.). The apparent emigration of a significant portion of the rural population out of the Susiana in late Middle and Late Uruk suggests both that the advantages of rural participation in the system were declining rapidly and that administrative elites had access to insufficient force to prevent villagers from "voting with their feet."

The spatial limits on administrative control mentioned above raise another set of problems involving boundary phenomena. There appear to have been boundaries between administered settlement systems and marginal settlements on the Susiana in both Early and Middle Uruk. These boundaries were probably much more clinal than depicted here, being generated by a decline in rural interaction with centers over distance. Some boundaries were more sharply defined. The apparent northern boundary of the administered Middle Uruk settlement system was marked by a series of small, specialized administrative centers which surely must indicate administered boundary maintenance and interaction between the Susiana system and some other population(s), perhaps pastoral nomads. The boundary between the eastern and western Susiana in Late Uruk was the most clearly defined and appears to have been generated by competition and hostility between rival administrative centers. These various boundaries are very poorly understood. Problems of boundary formation, function, and relative permeability would certainly merit further investigation as boundaries may be more sensitive than core areas to processes of system change.

Another problem raised by this analysis involves the determinants of administrative span of control and especially how spatial variability in span may provide information on variability in degree of control and/or range of administered activities. Such questions will probably be most usefully addressed through formal organization theory which has been little used in archaeology.

A further problem is also related to the organization of administration. Throughout this chapter I have used the terms administrators and elites interchangeably although there is little reason to believe that the groups so designated were coterminous. For example, we have a fragment of an unusually heavily constructed building from the Late Uruk occupation of KS-54 near Abu Fanduweh. Copper implements and gold and lapis lazuli beads were found in a nearby pit (Johnson 1976:217). These are unlikely to have been the possessions of simple villagers. Yet (in a small sample) there was no evidence of resident administrative activity on the site. Perhaps this was the rural estate of an elite administrator from Abu Fanduweh, but perhaps not. We can probably expect that this complex society was in fact complex: that it was composed of a variety of noncoterminous groups of administrators of different grades, elites of different status, specialized craftsmen, simple laborers, agriculturalists, and so forth, all pursuing noncoterminous ends. The naiveté of models like that presented in figure 11 becomes ever more obvious.

Although most of the data used here have been available for some time and I thought that they had been wrung for about all they were worth, they have been useful in identifying a number of potentially productive lines of research. If I was wrong, it only illustrates the old point that the results obtained from the analysis of a data set are more than tangentially related to the questions asked.

Acknowledgments

This chapter has a history too long to relate here, but one that began at a School of American Research Seminar in 1977. For their comments on earlier versions of the manuscript, I would like to thank Robert McC. Adams, Daniel G. Bates, Henri J. M. Claessen, Gary Feinman, Frank Hole, Stephen A. Kowalewski, Carol Kramer, Nan Rothschild, Maurizio Tosi, Robert J. Wenke, Henry T. Wright, and several anonymous reviewers. Remaining sins of omission and commission are mine. Background research for this paper was supported by the Alexander von Humboldt-Stiftung and the Seminar für Vorderasiatische Altertumskunde of the Freie Universität Berlin during the academic year of 1980–81, and the CNRS project, Evolution des Sociétés Complexes du Sud-Ouest de l'Iran, during the summer of 1982. I would like to express my appreciation for the support of these institutions.

Table 15. Bevel Rim Bowl (BRB) Densities in Village Excavation Samples

Site	Period of Deposit	Type of Deposit	Vol. (m³)	BRB Sherd Count/m³	Non-BRB Sherd Count/m³	BRB Percent of Total Count
KS-54	Late	Arch.	17.04	429.87	665.66	39
KS-54	Middle	Pit	9.67	586.05	460.96	56
KS-34	Early	Pit	6.37	37.05	713.18	05

Table 16. Distribution of Proto-Bevel Rim Bowls on Early Uruk Sites (n = 49)

		Western Susiana	Eastern Susiana
Proto-Bevel Rim Bowls	Present	18	9
	Absent	7	15

Note: $x^2 = 5.87$, df = 1, p less than .02: Data Source—Johnson 1973: 39, 165–167.

Table 17. Distribution of Centrally Produced Early Uruk Neckless Ledge Rim Jars in Villages

Site	KS-34	KS-76	KS-96	KS-108	KS-153	KS-266
Type of Sample	excavation	excavation	survey	survey	survey	survey
Distance to Susa (km.)	5.14	21.49	17.48	25.31	47.96	22.21
Distance to Abu Fanduweh (km.)	7.10	11.20	7.67	22.76	45.68	19.25
Distance Ratio	1.50:1	.52:1	.43:1	.90:1	.95:1	.87:1
Neckless Ledge Rim Sample Size	30	8	8	6	3	4
Predicted Number of Susa Type	18.00	2.74-(3)	2.41-(2)	2.84-(3)	1.46-(1)	1.86-(2)
Observed Number of Susa Type	20	3	2	2	1	2
Predicted Number of Abu Fanduweh Type	12.00	5.26-(5)	5.59-(6)	3.16-(3)	1.54-(2)	2.14-(2)
Observed Number of Abu Fanduweh Type	10	5	6	4	2	2

Table 18. Distances Traveled per Day over Flat Terrain in the Near East

Traveler	Trip	Linear Distance (km.)	Days	Linear Distance per Day (km.)
Loftus (1857:306–310)	Shushtar-Dezful	55	2	27.5
Loftus (1857:288–89)	Mohammerah-Ahwaz	115	3	38.3
Loftus (1857:74)	Baghdad-Hilla	100	3	33.3
Heude (1817:215–16)	Erbil-Mosul	85	2	42.5
Heude (1817:220–25)	Mosul-Mardin	245	5	49.0
Soane (1908:109)	Erbil-Kirkuk	90	2	45.0

Table 19. Middle Uruk Population Density per Square Kilometer

	Western Susiana					Eastern Susiana			
	A	B	C	D	E	F	G	H	I
1†	0.00	5.44	0.00	0.00	0.00	0.00	0.00	0.00	0.00
2	0.00	12.08	0.00	8.32	0.00	0.00	0.00	0.00	0.00
3	12.16	0.00	4.80	6.40	3.04	0.00	80.00	9.60	0.00
4	0.00	200.00	0.00	0.00	12.00	33.92	16.00	0.00	16.00
5	0.00	34.72	18.56	2.88	24.64	44.00	0.00	0.00	0.00
6	0.00	8.96	102.72	5.12	6.00	0.00	6.72	0.00	0.00
7	0.00	60.80	18.24	18.56	20.96	0.00	58.64	0.00	0.00

Notes:
† Refers to grid in fig. 27.
n = densities higher than 50/km².

Table 20. Surplus Requirements and Potential Surplus Production (in Hectares)

	Western Susiana					Eastern Susiana			
	A	B	C	D	E	F	G	H	I
1†	0	204	0	0	0	0	0	0	0
2	0	453	0	312	0	0	0	0	0
3	456	1875	180	240	114	0	1500	360	0
4	0	3750	1875	0	450	1272	600	0	600
5	0	1302	696	108	924	0	0	0	0
6	0	336	2636	192	225	0	252	0	0
7	0	540	684	696	786	0	432	0	0

Notes:
† Refers to grid in fig. 27.
n = Potential Surplus Production
n = Center Surplus Requirements.

Table 21. Middle Uruk Surplus Requirements and Potential Surplus Production (in Hectares)

	System	Western Susiana	Eastern Susiana
Center Surplus Requirements	8858	6926	1932
Potential Rural Surplus Production	11442	6093	5349

Table 22. Patterns of Middle Uruk Population Growth: Change in Hectares of Settlement from Early to Middle Uruk

Administrative District	Large Centers	Small Centers	All Centers	Villages
Susa	13.00	0	13.00	−1.24
Abu Fanduweh	2.64	4.70	7.34	−1.96
Chogha Mish	10.00	2.30	12.30	−2.01
Marginal Areas	0	0	0	3.96
Totals			32.64	−1.25

Table 23. Alternative Middle Uruk Population Growth Rates

	Required Growth Rates per 1000 per Year		
Years over which Growth Occured	Marginal Settlements	Alternative (1): Administered System	Alternative (2): Centers Only
	Average Rates	Average Rates	Average Rates
300	0.701	0.989	2.595
275	0.773	1.058	2.831
			high rates
250	0.850	1.164	3.114
225	0.944	1.293	3.461
200	1.063	1.455	3.894
175	1.215	1.663	4.452
150	1.417	1.939	5.196
125	1.700	2.329	6.238
			improbably high rates
100	2.103	2.969	7.083
		high rates	
75	2.838	3.885	10.418
	high rates		
50	4.210	5.947	15.688

Table 24. System Level Changes from Early to Middle Uruk

Variable	Early Uruk	Middle Uruk	Change	Proportional Change
Levels of Administrative Hierarchy	2	3	1	.50
Basal Level Span of Control[a]	25	11	−14	−.56
Administered Population	9806	21382	11676	1.18
Proportion of Population in Centers	.39	.56	.17	.44
Population of the Susiana	19036	25338	6302	.33
Demand for Rural Labor(BRB/m^3)	37	510	473	12.78
Demand for Rural Surplus (Proportion of Potential Surplus)	.05[b]	.77	.72	14.40

Notes:

[a]These figures are administrative district averages. The Middle Uruk span, without consideration of district variability, is 7.

[b]I do not have a direct estimate of Early Uruk center demand other than it was "low." Assuming a close relationship between demand for produce and demand for labor, the Early Uruk figure of .05 is equal to village bevel rim bowl density as a proportion of center bevel rim bowl density.

Table 25. Observed and Predicted Number of Basal Administered Units in Two- and Three-Level Hierarchies

Period	Levels of Heirarchy	Observed Basal Administered Units	Predicted Basal Administered Units Required for Transition
Terminal Susa A	1	12	
			24
Early Uruk	2	49	
			70
Middle Uruk	3	107	

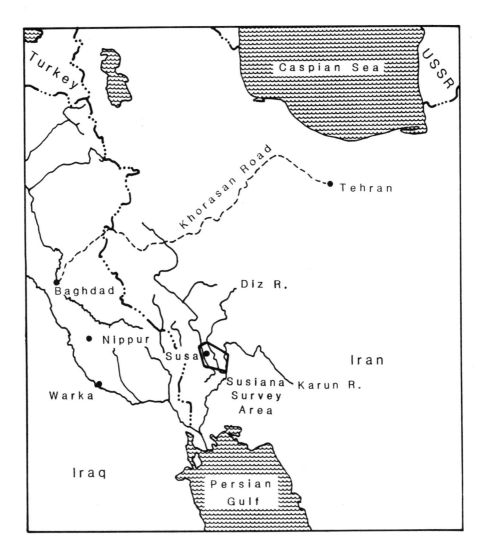

Figure 18. Location of the Susiana survey area.

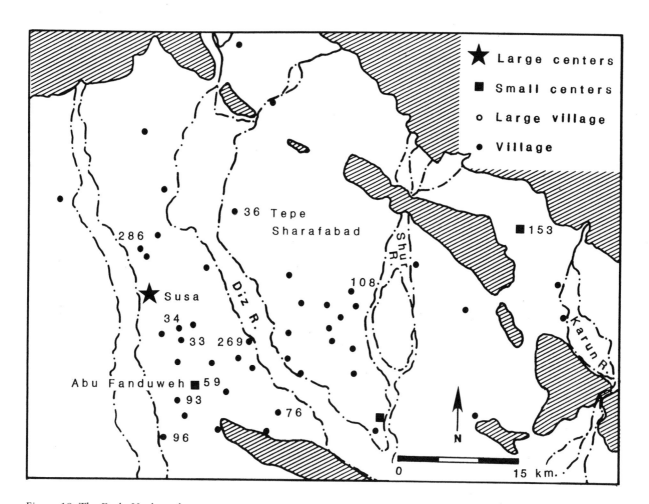

Large centers
Small centers
Large village
Village

286
36 Tepe
Sharafabad
Diz R.
Shur R.
Karun R.
153
108
Susa
34
33 269
Abu Fanduweh 59
93
76
96

N

0   15 km.

Figure 19. The Early Uruk settlement system.

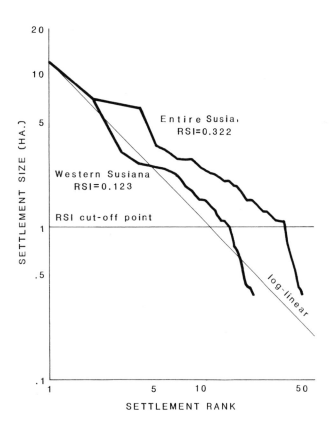

Figure 20. Early Uruk: Definition of the administered settlement system (rank-size distributions).

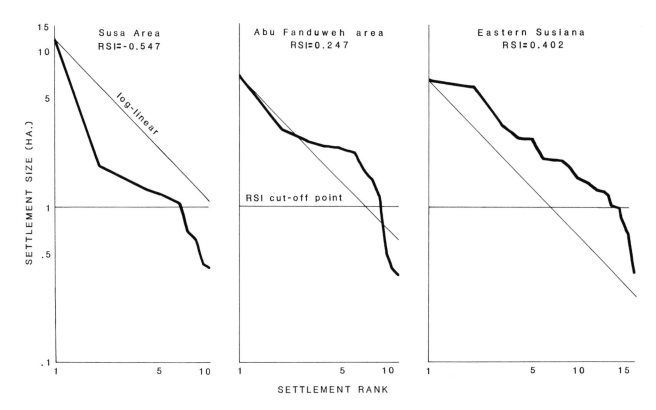

Figure 21. Early Uruk rank-size distributions: Administered districts and marginal area.

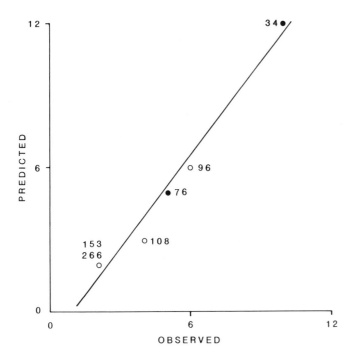

Figure 22. Early Uruk: Observed and predicted frequencies of Abu Fanduweh–type neckless ledge rim jars in villages (open circles = survey collections, filled circles = excavation collections); $r = 0.986$, $df = 4$, $p < 0.01$.

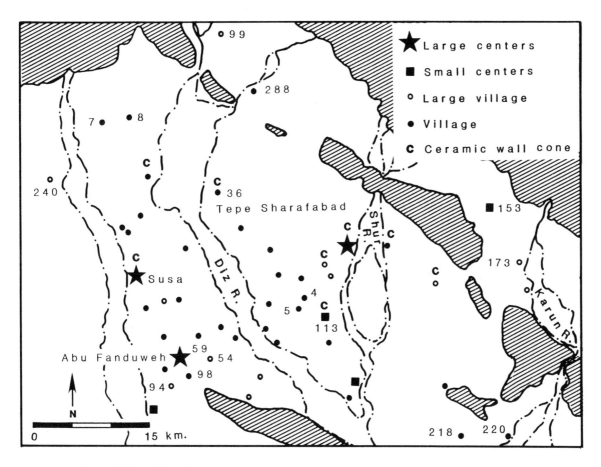

Figure 23. The Middle Uruk settlement system.

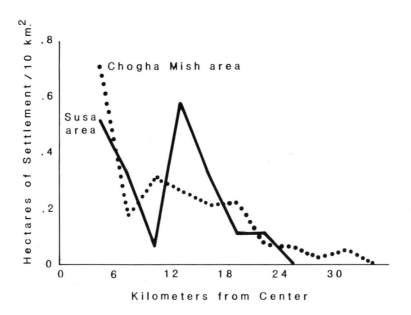

Figure 24. Settlement density in circular zones around Susa and Chogha Mish.

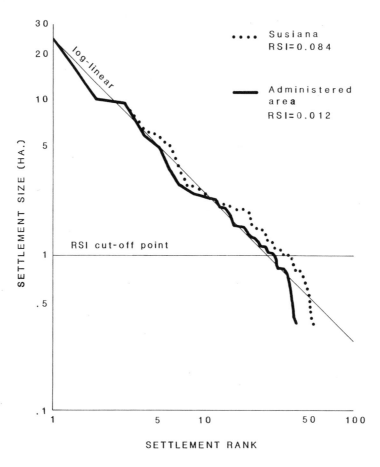

Figure 25. Middle Uruk: Definition of the administered settlement system (rank-size distributions).

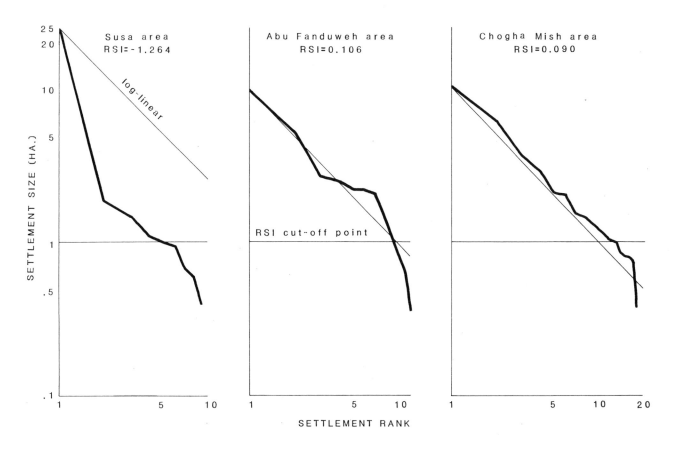

Figure 26. Middle Uruk rank-size distributions: Administrative districts.

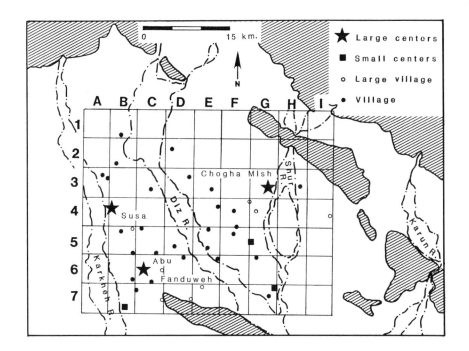

Figure 27. Grid system for analysis of Middle Uruk center demand and potential rural surplus productivity.

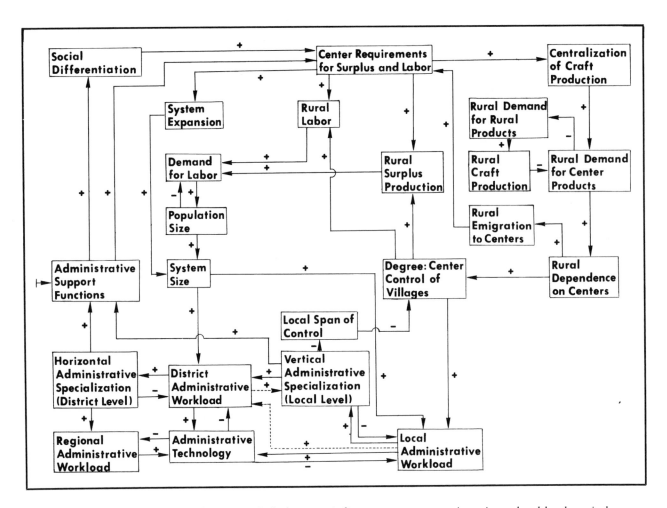

Figure 28. Processes in Uruk state formation (dashed arrows indicate processes operative prior to local-level vertical administrative specialization).

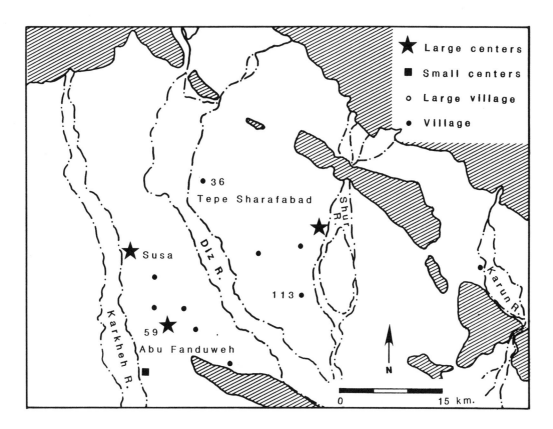

Figure 29. The Late Uruk settlement pattern.

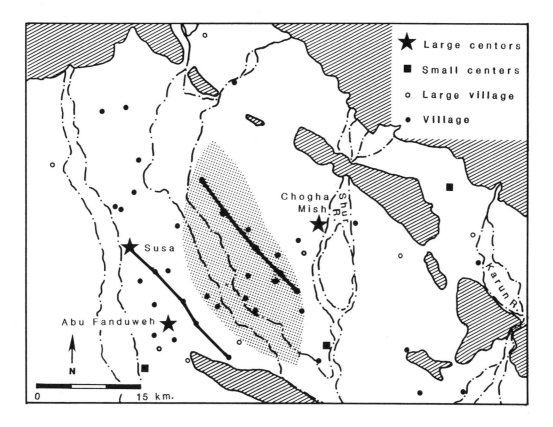

Figure 30. The Late Uruk administrative conflict zone and pattern of settlement abandonment.

Chapter 5

The Susiana Hinterlands during the Era of Primary State Formation

HENRY T. WRIGHT

Introduction

Anyone who visited the traditional centers of southwestern Iran in years past—for example Dizful or Shushtar (figure 3)—would have recognized that these towns depend upon the people of the surrounding villages both as sources of food and labor and as consumers of the towns' craft products and services. It would surprise no such visitor that archaeologists interested in the development of increasingly complex societies in the region have often viewed the settlements on the Susiana Plain as a single economic or political unit. Further observation of the traditional centers would have attested to relations with people of the more distant arid plains to the south and west and rugged hills to the north and east. Nomadic herders disposing of the products of their flocks were a common sight in the bazaars, particularly during the spring, before migration to upland summer pastures, and during the autumn, with the return. Though these migratory tribespeople have been politically dominated by the townspeople in recent decades, only a half century ago tribal leaders from the Susiana hinterlands were able to threaten the central government. These alternating, historically and ethnographically observed patterns must have arisen with the first towns. If archaeologists can recognize the remains of past migratory peoples at all—a question which must be dealt with first—then we can pose three questions relevant to the rise of traditional town-hinterland relations:

1. Was there a continuous occupation of the hinterlands, or did they serve as refuges for populations from the central areas who dispersed during times of overpopulation or of social crisis?
2. Did increases in transhumance and herding place economic and thus administrative demands on the developing central polities?
3. Could the emergent transhumant and nomadic social units pose a direct political challenge to the developing central polities?

Clearly, it is useful to assess the state of our knowledge about the mobile segments of society during the crucial era in human history when political states first came into being. Incomplete as our data may be, they may prove adequate for the evaluation of these questions.

Before discussing evidence from the Susiana hinterlands, it is worthwhile to define some terms. Following the rise of intensive agriculture, the emergence of sizable central towns, and the dominance of economic and political relations throughout Southwest Asia by the large populations on the bigger and richer tracts of agricultural land, it is convenient to think of "regions" composed of areas of differing potential to sustain these large populations. The richer tracts, such as the Susiana Plain, the Marv Dasht in Fars, the Mahidasht in the central Zagros, and the lower Euphrates alluvium of southern Mesopotamia, are "central" areas. (For a more detailed discussion of these regions, see chapter 2.) These areas are typically no more than a day's travel in radius, and they are separated from other similar areas by five to fifteen days of travel. Somewhat closer, within two to five days' travel time of the central areas, are small tracts of cultivable land, here termed "marginal" areas. The rugged—sometimes arid, sometimes forested—terrain separating these two types can be termed "interstitial" areas. According to this hierarchy of spaces, a "region" is defined as a set of areas related by exchange of goods or labor to a central area at a particular time. It will be shown later that the borders of regions can change and that whole regions can become fragmented or divided. Regions are thus to be seen as elements in "transregional" systems, but this larger sphere of cultural interaction is not the concern of this paper, as it would involve regions outside western Iran.

Inasmuch as we shall investigate the role of nomads and transhumant peoples, it is well to specify what archaeological features can be taken to characterize the degree of mobility of communities. We wish to distinguish differences along a continuum from (1) sedentary communities, most of whose inhabitants occupy solid immobile houses throughout the year; (2) transhumant groups that spend part of the year in solid houses and the remainder in movable housing such as tents; and (3) nomadic communities which make use of movable shelters only.

One criterion of sedentism is location, for the high mountain pastures are suitable only for nomadic or transhumant groups during the warm summers. Other locales are often favored by these mobile groups so that one can make reasonable inferences on the basis of geographic location and characteristics of topography and resources alone (Hole 1979; Digard 1975). Mounded accumulations usually mark the site of immobile houses, but such structures may be used seasonally by transhumant peoples so that other situational evidence such as the absence of water during the summer or lack of arable land must be used in any interpretation. Tent sites are sometimes marked by cobbles aligned with the tent walls, by hearths and pens, and by a range of pottery assemblages lacking the large storage jars that are often found in villages. In this chapter it is presumed that transhumants would maintain their constructed housing in lower winter pastures, and the evidence of camps with temporary housing in such areas implies nomads. Isolated cemeteries not associated with mound sites and other possible indications of the degree of mobility of marginal area peoples are discussed later. All statements should be considered suggestive rather than definitive, for only a program of multiple-site excavation in a number of areas can demonstrate the extent of patterns of mobility and the economic and political impact of the mobile communities.

The marginal areas of southwestern Iran were visited by archaeologists as early as the 1840s when both Austin Henry Layard (1846) and Henry Rawlinson (1840) recorded inscriptions and other features. Some early observations, such as those of Aurel Stein (1940)

and Erich Schmidt (1940), will prove useful in the following discussion. The question of transhumant and nomad impact on Susiana urban growth was posed elegantly by Robert McC. Adams (1962). However, it was only during the 1960s that improved understanding of local ceramic development and thorough examination of some marginal and interstitial areas began to produce the kind of information necessary for the present inquiry. Four marginal areas are the foci of the following discussion, two in the lowlands and two in smaller valleys nestled in the front ranges of the Zagros Mountains (figure 31).

1. As defined here, the Deh Luran Plain is an area of about 940 square kilometers centered 110 kilometers west-northwest of Susa on the historically preferred lowland route between the Susiana and Mesopotamia proper to the east. James A. Neely has kindly made available the collections and notes on the periods relevant to this discussion (Wright 1981b:63–70, 181–95).

2. The Ram Hormuz Plain, on the traditional route from the Susiana Plain southeast to Fars, centered 160 kilometers to the east-southeast of Susa, covered about 620 square kilometers but only the westernmost 445 square kilometers west of the Ala River have been surveyed. Data from this detailed survey which Elizabeth Carter and I conducted in 1969 but have not yet fully published, are used below.

3. The tiny Izeh Plain is an internally drained basin in the outer front ranges of the Zagros centered 155 kilometers east of Susa. It covers only 155 square kilometers and its floor averages about 750 meters above sea level. This plain is the last major area of winter grazing on the route going from Susa eastward toward modern Isfahan; a traveler can also step southwards down through the valleys of Qaleh Tol and Bagh Malik to reach the Ram Hormuz Plain. A detailed survey, in part an intensive survey on foot, was conducted by the Izeh Research Group of the Iranian Centre for Archaeological Research in 1976 (Wright 1979).

4. The Hulailan Plain is also in the front ranges of the Zagros, but is in inner Luristan, or Pish-i Kuh, centered 210 kilometers northwest of Susa. Indeed, it is only 70 kilometers from the center of Mahidasht, and dating and interpretation in the same terms used in dealing with the other marginal valleys will prove difficult. It covers only 167 square kilometers and its floor averages about 930 meters above sea level, low enough to provide some winter pasturage. Hulailan has been the object of an intensive walking survey directed by Peder Mortensen. His well-illus-

trated preliminary publications (1974b; 1976), combined with the broader observations of Clare Goff, the first researcher to ask explicit questions about mountain nomads during the period under consideration (Goff 1971:149), provide exceptional documentation relevant to the objective of this discussion.

These four plains constitute at best one-fifth of the marginal areas of southwestern Iran. Fortunately, it will be possible to refer to limited survey evidence from some of the other marginal and interstitial areas in order to assess the representativeness of the four areas for which detailed or intensive survey evidence is available (cf. Goff 1971; Zagarell 1975a, 1978, 1981).

In the following sections the consideration of each area in each period commences with an assessment of the settlements with permanent architecture: their total extent, their pattern of distribution, and the relation between this pattern and routes of transport and sources of water. Such relations may indicate the degree to which such settlement was only seasonal. Following this is an assessment of impermanent occupations—campsites and rock shelters—and of distributions of cemeteries indicative of such occupation. Where appropriate, evidence from various small excavations relevant to herding, local economic specializations, and local political control are mentioned.

The Later Fifth Millennium: Decline of the Hinterlands

Villages were ubiquitous in the smaller plains and valleys of southwestern Iran by the middle of the fifth millennium B.C. (roughly equivalent to the Late Ubaid in Mesopotamia; see chapter 2). Every area where a permanent spring or stream could be diverted to irrigate some portion of a few square kilometers of alluvial soil seems to have been occupied at this time. The evidence from both the Susiana Plain and the marginal valleys surveyed in detail, however, shows a consistent decline in settled area towards the end of the millennium, during the time of the later phases of the Susiana cultural tradition (table 26).

The Deh Luran Plain during the periods under consideration was not a valley with entrenched river channels as it is today. Though the basic vegetation pattern was similar (Woosley and Hole 1978:64–67), the rivers flowed more or less at plain level, probably in several shifting channels (Kirkby 1977:286–88). The extent of humid, easily irrigated soils was probably much greater (Redding 1981:259). Throughout the local sequence of later Susiana phases, the Deh Luran Plain (figure 32a) was dominated by the large, centrally located settlement of Musiyan, which cov-

ered about ten hectares (see chapter 2). Around the middle of the fifth millennium during the Farukh Phase (see chapter 3, table 12), there were subsidiary centers and small settlements of village and hamlet size both eastwards and westwards of this center (Wright 1981b:66–68, figure 32), all less than a kilometer from possible courses of river channels. Settlement declined during the succeeding centuries. The south half of Musiyan, the subsidiary center of Farukhabad, and the smaller communities northwest of Musiyan were abandoned. By the end of the fifth millennium, even the remnant settlement on the north portion of Musiyan and the smaller settlements to the east seem to have been deserted (Wright 1981b:70, figure 33). The only settlements perhaps occupied during this terminal phase in the Susiana tradition are two small communities near the sulphurous brackish spring on the north slopes of the plain on land today ill-suited for cultivation. These two settlements, which are close to the beginning of the route up to the high country of Pushti-Kuh (figure 6), have houses built on stone footings, a highland pattern not seen on the plain in almost a millennium (cf. Hole, Flannery, and Neely 1969:58–60, figure 17). They also had ceramics with crushed limestone and straw tempering and other features known from the Zagros (Wright et al. 1975:133–37, figures 7, 8). It is notable, however, that while these settlements may have been participants in montane household and craft patterns, only the locally limited cultivable land suggests transhumance. Throughout this long period of declining settlement, beginning with those areas most distant from the Susiana heartland (with eventual minor reoccupation), there are no indications of nomadic activities related to specialized herding, such as campsites or isolated cemeteries. However, the Deh Luran Plain has a heavy silt cover, partly of fifth millennium date (Kirkby 1977:280–83), which might well hide such sites. Furthermore, up the Mehmeh River in the foothills of the mountain Kabir Kuh (figures 12, 34), 45 and 75 kilometers, respectively, as the crow flies from Deh Luran, Vanden Berghe (1973b, 1974, 1975a, 1975b) reports the isolated cemeteries of Dum Gar Parchineh and Hakalan, certainly of the later fifth millennium.[1] In addition, near the later cemetery of Qaleh Nissar (35 kilometers northwest of Ilam), he found the stone footings of a complex of rooms with mud-brick walls, reported to have similar ceramics. The locations of these sites in an area poorly suited for grain cultivation suggests use by transhumants concerned primarily with herding, but this proposition remains to be tested with the evidence of fauna, flora, and nonceramic artifacts (Vanden Berghe 1973a:28, figure 1, plate 22).

Settlement on the Ram Hormuz Plain (figure 32b) shows changes throughout the later fifth millennium comparable to those discussed for the Deh Luran area. This plain is watered by a stream which is little entrenched and easily used for irrigation; furthermore, there are many large springs on the plain. The main settlement of the mid-fifth millennium seems to have been Sartoli, covering about 2.3 hectares, in the middle of the plain amid a nexus of small, hamlet-sized settlements. Later, however, during the Susa A phase, when this settlement was abandoned, Tal-i Ghazir—near a large spring at the west end of the plain—became the largest remaining settlement, covering at most 1.2 hectares. At the end of the millennium, it is the only site on the plain from which there is evidence of occupation (Caldwell 1968:349, figure 6–10). Thus, the second half of the fifth millennium in the Ram Hormuz area was a time of decline and abandonment, again beginning with the settlements most distant from the Susiana, as if communities were retreating toward the declining heartland. As in the Deh Luran area, there is no archaeological evidence of nomadism or transhumance; however, survey near Ram Hormuz has been less thorough than that on the other plains discussed here and such evidence could have been missed.

In contrast to the arid and steppe-covered marginal areas of the lowlands, those in the front ranges have high rainfall and excellent grazing, particularly during the early summer. Near the Izeh Plain (sometimes called Malamir) oaks cover the mountain slopes today, and no doubt oak forests were at least as extensive in the mid-fifth millennium B.C. During these times, the plain was dominated by the large central settlement of Sabz'ali Zabarjad, which probably covered about 3 hectares (figure 33a). This center and the small hamlets around it were soon abandoned, and only a few village-sized settlements near springs survived during the Susa A phase (Shahideh 1979:52–54, figure 23). A similarly isolated small settlement occurs on the Susan Plain 20 kilometers to the north of Izeh.[2] Apparently social conditions were such in this part of the front ranges that small social units could survive independently of nearby larger centers. By the turn of the millennium, however, these settlements were abandoned. At the same time at least one, and probably two, new settlements covering several hectares were founded in areas of the plain far from permanent springs. Rainy season streams and land ideal for grain cultivation are nearby, however. It is unlikely that such sites were fully occupied during the summer; rather they were probably the winter villages of transhumant communities with a major interest in herding. In spite of intensive walking survey of many parts of the Izeh Plain under conditions of good geological preservation of sites and land surfaces and of examination of many rock shelters, no indications of late fifth millennium campsites were found (Shahideh

1979:52–54, figure 24). However, on the Qaleh Tol Plain, 25 kilometers south of Izeh, an extensive scatter of fire-cracked stones, cobbles, and later Susiana ceramics has been exposed by plowing and erosion. Thus, while possible campsites do survive, they are apparently rare. In sum, during this period there is evidence in the Izeh area of population decline followed by settlement relocation with suggestions of seasonal transhumance and perhaps some nomadism.

As noted in the introduction, the valleys of inner Luristan are a considerable distance from Susa and are closer to the Mahidasht central area so they are not easily defined in the same terms used in the above discussions. Nevertheless, the area is important to processes in the southwestern lowland region, as indicated by the predominance of Zagros-related ceramics in the Deh Luran area at the turn of the fifth millennium. By the middle of the millennium, the Hulailan Plain (figure 33b) had a small central settlement covering about 2.3 hectares at Kazabad on its west, and a few small hamlet-sized dependencies, all near streams or springs (Goff 1971:137–39, figures 1–3; Mortensen 1974b:43–44; 1976:47, figures 4, 13). As in the Izeh area, in succeeding centuries, the center seems to have been abandoned and only a few of the smaller settlements appear to continue. By the turn of the millennium, only two of these settlements remained, but there was also occupation at two "open air" campsites in the nearby foothills, close to springs, suggesting increased nomadism (Mortensen 1974; 1976:47–48, figures 9, 12). It is important to note that the Hulailan Plain is a small tract at the juncture of two rivers, rather than an internally drained basin with only a few areas geologically suited for permanent springs like Izeh. Most locations in Hulailan are close to permanent water sources, and the criterion of inadequate summer water supply, taken to indicate transhumance in Izeh, cannot be used here.

Two general points can be made regarding the later fifth millennium. First, as table 26 illustrates, the general decline of settlements with more permanent architecture follows different patterns in the different parts of southwestern Iran. In the lowlands, the marginal areas of Deh Luran and Ram Hormuz decline to negligible population levels, while the central Susiana area declines to about one-third of its former density. In the front ranges of Izeh and Hulailan, some marginal areas show similar absolute declines and some do not, but in no case do they reach the negligible densities noted in lowland areas. Furthermore, the partial recovery documented in the Izeh area is probably paralleled in other marginal areas of the mountains—for example, Kuh-i Dasht in Inner Luristan (Goff 1971:40–42, figure 5) and Khana Mirza in the Bakhtiari Mountains (Zagarell 1975a)—at the end of the fifth millennium. Indeed, several populations politically allied and perhaps with nomad supporters might well have been able to threaten the social units of the Susiana Plain, whose fragmentation into four discrete settlement clusters during Terminal Susa A indicates considerable disorganization (Johnson 1973:87–90, figure 15). Second, while there are indications of nomadism and transhumance during the fifth millennium, patterns doubtless existing since the domestication of animals, the only indications of an increase in such activities are in the marginal areas of the front ranges at the end of the fifth millennium. The suggestion that transhumant occupation with winter use of established villages characterizes Izeh, while nomad use of winter campsites characterizes Hulailan, is provocative. But differences in the hydrology of the two areas and vagaries in the preservation of campsites both argue for cautious interpretation at the moment.

The Early Fourth Millennium: Local Consolidation and Growth

During the Early Uruk Period, the decline of the Susiana was reversed, and by the Middle Uruk Period, Susa had become a regional center larger than any seen before in southwestern Iran. Eventually covering about 25 hectares, it dominated the Susiana area through a hierarchy of mediating centers (Johnson 1973; chapter 4, this volume; Wright and Johnson 1975:270–73). In this crucial period, argued to be the era of state emergence, the four marginal areas under consideration had very different histories (figures 34, 35).

On the Deh Luran Plain (figure 34a), settlement proliferated on its long-abandoned western end, spreading from the northern edge of the plain during the Early Uruk Period and focusing on a small center of 5 hectares on the west bank of the Mehmeh River. During the Middle Uruk Period, the focus shifted eastward to the center of Farukhabad, covering perhaps 3 hectares, but the aggregate amount of settlement remained about the same. Throughout the period, all settlements are within a kilometer of likely sources of permanent water (Wright 1981b:182–83, figures 78, 79). The excavated materials from Farukhabad indicate that local ceramic production was predominantly in the Zagros traditions first recognized in the ceramics of Godin VII and VI (Young 1969a:3–10). There was increasing local exploitation of asphalt seeps, chert sources, and sheep herds, with increasing export of packaged bitumen, chert cores, and perhaps cloth. In return, other types of stone, marine shell, metals, and doubtless other exotic materials were received (Wright 1981b:265–75). In short, there seems to have been a relatively stable local society, agriculturally based and maintaining broader exchange

relationships. There are no local indications of either transhumance or nomadism during this period.

On the Ram Hormuz Plain (figure 34b), Tal-i Ghazir, the sole settlement of the turn of the millennium, continues to be occupied in the Early and Middle Uruk periods. There is at least one smaller subsidiary settlement on the southern edge of the plain, also adjacent to a permanent water source. Excavations at Ghazir indicate that the ceramic inventory was similar to that of contemporary Susa (Caldwell 1968:figures 11–27). There is also evidence of local carving of high-quality alabaster. presumably for export, and import of metal tools (Wright and Johnson 1975:278, table V). The existing excavation data are otherwise incomplete and the extent to which Ram Hormuz was a dependency of Susa, as suggested by the ceramic similarities and westerly clustering of settlement, in contrast to Deh Luran's evident independence, is difficult to evaluate. In any event, there is no evidence of transhumance or nomadism, although the relative incompleteness of survey in Ram Hormuz must be kept in mind.

The Izeh Plain (figure 35a), and nearby areas in the Zagros front range not far from Ram Hormuz, provide complementary evidence (Wright 1979, figure 26). During the Early Uruk Period, one of the village-sized settlements, far from a permanent spring, continues from the previous period. A similar village-sized settlement lacking an adequate summer water supply was founded on the nearby Qaleh Tol Plain. Between these two, dominating the crossroads giving access to the Inner Zagros and the Isfahan area, a center covering about 10 hectares was reestablished at Sabz'ali Zabarjad. By the beginning of Middle Uruk times, the villages were abandoned and the center had shrunk to a size of only 3 hectares. Samples from several tiny soundings indicate that the center had locally made ceramics similar to those of contemporary Susa and was the site of the external provisioning of supplies of chert and cattle (Wright and Redding 1979:64–93). Material evidence of local production for export is lacking, and it seems reasonable to propose that the Middle Uruk settlement was sustained to provide services for, or control over, transhumant communities established here since the turn of the millennium. Unfortunately, excavated samples are not available from Early Uruk levels. It is notable that, by the later Middle Uruk Period, even this settlement was abandoned, and a new center protected high on the rock of Qaleh Tol was founded. This is near a crossroads providing access to central Fars by an intermontane, rather than a lowland route and is immediately adjacent to a very large spring. The nearest contemporary site known at present is 115 kilometers to the west at Qaleh-i Rodeni, north of Shustar on the east bank of the Karun guarding this point of access to the Susiana Plain.[3] It seems reasonable to propose that the lonely outpost of Qaleh Tol guarded a strategic but little occupied frontier area, though there is also a possibility that it watched over local nomads whose remains have not yet been documented. Such propositions require testing with intensive surveys and soundings in the Qaleh Tol area.

As before, developments in inner Luristan are difficult to correlate with those to the south. However, for purposes of this discussion ceramics of Baba Jan V type can be equated with Middle Uruk, because of the presence of wheel-thrown cups and chaff-tempered trays (Goff 1971:144, figure 7:1) even though long, straight spouts and various jar rims (Goff 1971:figure 7:20, 30) have definite Early Uruk parallels. On the intensively surveyed Hulailan Plain (figure 35b), by the Middle Uruk Period there were two village-sized settlements, two "open air" campsites (all four near river channels), and two occupations in large rock shelters near springs in the foothills (Mortenson 1976:47). This settlement configuration seems only a quantitative expansion of that of the turn of the fifth millennium discussed previously. This modest development occurred only a day's journey from the larger centers such as Chia Pahan, covering about 12 hectares, on the Kuh-i Dasht or Chia Bal, about 4 hectares, on the Rumishgan Plain (Goff 1971:145, figure 5:30–60). To the south of this cluster of intermontane plains, the rugged interstitial areas of Bala Gariveh, the lower Saimarreh Valley, and the mountain ridge named Kabir Kuh must be crossed before reaching either the Deh Luran or Susiana areas. Isolated sites such as Afrineh Tepe (Goff 1971:132–33, and figures 4, 6:33–38) may have been outposts similar to Qaleh Tol near Izeh. Unfortunately, the limited information available from these settlements does not allow the specification of economic and social relations with other areas. The utilization of larger rock shelters, however, is elucidated by excavation data from Kunji Cave (Speth 1971; Wright et al. 1975:131–33, figure 6) near Khorramabad to the east of the Kuh-i Dasht area. Here, in a large shelter overlooking the Khorramabad Plain, were fourth millennium strata sealing a series of small oval enclosures built of rough stone blocks. Today, very young lambs and kids are hidden during the day in such structures, while the shepherds take the adult females out for grazing and afternoon milking (cf. Wright and Kossary 1979:14, figure 9, upper). The layers around and above these structures had much burned sheep or goat dung, and it is clear that the Kunji Cave evidence indicates not only impermanent settlement but also use by herders and their animals. This does not mean, however, that the herders in Middle Uruk Luristan were organized into large nomadic social units politically separate from the sedentary communities. Only the evidence of the broader settlement pattern, of cemeteries, and of fortified elite residences such as are known from the early first millennium B.C. (Goff 1968, 1969, 1970) could demonstrate this. Nevertheless, the evidence summarized here does indicate an increase in nomadism of some sort, whatever its relation to the settled communities.

In summary, during the first half of the fourth millennium B.C. there was some local growth in all of the marginal areas considered, as is shown in table 26. The marginal areas southeast and east of Susa, in both lowlands and front ranges, seem to have been closely related to the communities of the Susiana heartland, with local outposts appearing at key control points. To the northwest and north, in both lowlands and front ranges, development seems to have been local, with little evidence of Susa-related craft goods or of imposed control points. In both of the front-range areas under consideration, however, there are indications of a continuation, and perhaps an expansion, of patterns of transhumance and/or nomadism.

The Third Quarter of the Fourth Millennium: Regional Collapse

The Late Uruk Period is one of increasing, broad stylistic similarities and increasing indications of conflict throughout Greater Mesopotamia. In western Iran, many of the villages of the Susiana Plain were abandoned amid indications of conflict (Johnson 1973:143–56). The changing pattern of settlement in the marginal areas also suggests an era of instability.

On the Deh Luran Plain most of the smaller settlements were abandoned, although occupation continues at the former center on the high, defensible mound of Farukhabad, near one of the key crossings of the Mehmeh River. A new settlement was founded on the equally defensible mound of Chagha Sefid, abandoned since the end of the sixth millennium (Wright 1981b:185, figure 80). The excavated samples from Farukhabad indicate many changes from the previous period. In the ceramic inventory, sand-tempered vessels, visually and statistically indistinguishable from either Susa or Warka vessels, predominate. Part of the site exposed by the excavations was covered with nondomestic architecture, and bitumen working, chert core manufacture, and perhaps the organization of work gangs are concentrated around these constructions. Goats replace sheep as the more frequently slaughtered animal, and the evidence of local weaving in the form of possible loom weights becomes rare. There is little evidence of imported goods (Wright 1981b:185–88, 265–75). The sum of this evidence can most simply be understood as the result of the domination, and perhaps the dissolution, of local Middle Uruk communities and the emplacement of an outpost through which local resources are extracted, in unfinished form, in return for which little is received. The Deh Luran area thus seems to have been the object of direct exploitation by a larger lowland center elsewhere, perhaps Susa.

There is no evidence of occupation in the Ram Hormuz Plain, the Izeh Plain, or any other marginal area southeast of the Susiana Plain at this time. Neither Ghazir nor any other campsite or settlement in this area has the distinctive ceramics characteristic of the Late Uruk Period.[4] If the area was utilized, it was by groups using artifact inventories we are not yet able to recognize.

Similarly, there is little evidence of occupation in the valleys of inner Luristan. A few bevel rim bowls and a possible droop spout (Goff 1971:figures 19, 23; Mortenson 1976:figures 7, 8) on one of the campsites and one of the village sites of the Hulailan Plain are the sole possible indications of the Late Uruk Period, and they are not definitive.

Late Uruk abandonment of the marginal regions of southwestern Iran, coincident with the evidence of conflict and decline on the central Susiana area, seems to have been widespread. The inferred establishment of direct control over the Deh Luran area is also intelligible as a strategy pursued by a major center during the course of conflict within and between regions. While there are possible indications of continuing nomadism in Luristan, and while the exploitation of goat herds on the largely unsettled Deh Luran Plain implies the presence of nomads, there is no evidence of increase in the amount of nomadism or of the complexity of the organization of the existing nomad or transhumant groups.

The End of the Fourth Millennium and Commencement of the Third: Confrontation between Regions

Termed the Protoliterate c-d or Jemdet Nasr and Early Dynastic I periods in Iraq (Delougaz 1952; Hansen 1965) and the Proto-Elamite Period in southwestern and southern Iran (Whitcomb 1971; Alden 1982), this period in the area under consideration is generally one of limited occupation on the Susiana Plain with new patterns of development on some of the previously marginal plains (figures 36–37).

Late Uruk Susa seems to have been largely abandoned, if only for a short time, and subsequent settlement—at least on the southern part of the Acropole—has different brick forms, new kinds of hearths, and ceramics technically and stylistically unprecedented in this area (Le Brun 1971:202–5, 210–11, figures 33, 34, 60–64). All are similar to those that developed during the Banesh phase at Malyan in the high but fertile valleys of the Marv Dasht in southern Iran

(Sumner 1972; Alden 1979b; Nicholas 1980). Although Susa seems reduced in size, covering no more than the 10 hectares of the Acropole and a small fraction of the lower Ville Royale area, the existence of archives dealing with large quantities of items indicates that the site continued to be an important administrative center. The only other occupation of the plain consists of a few village-sized settlements next to abandoned Uruk communities strung out along the route leading eastward from Susa toward southern Iran, and a number of isolated finds suggesting shepherds' camps (see chapter 7).

Moving our focus eastwards, instead of westwards as in the discussion of previous periods, one can follow this route along the foot of the mountains toward the Ram Hormuz area. Here the small center of Tal-i Ghazir was reoccupied by an architectural complex with large storage chambers and indications of administrative activity (Whitcomb 1971). However, no contemporary sites are known in the surveyed portion of the Ram Hormuz Plain.

In the nearby mountain valleys, in contrast, settlement is much increased. Isolated settlements have been recorded at Tol-i Qir at the foot of Kuh-i Asmari near Masjid-i Soleyman, on the north end of the Qaleh Tol Plain, and even in the distant and tiny Susan Plain, apparently abandoned since the late fifth millennium.[5]

The Izeh Plain (figure 36) had a dense network of settlement at this time. The various communities had ceramics similar to those of contemporary Susa and of the Banesh phase of Malyan (Sajjidi 1979:93–94, figure 35). Just east of the old Early and Middle Uruk center of the earlier fourth millennium—and more poorly situated with respect to water supplies—was the large center of Sabz'ali Bagheri, covering at least 13 hectares. Located around the plain were four large village-sized settlements, one dominating each of the larger tracts of easily cultivable land, only one with easy access to a permanent spring (Sajjidi 1979: table 15, figure 36). All of these settlements have evidence of massive stone building foundations. There are in addition several smaller settlements, and five areas of scattered sherds and cracked rocks that were probably campsites. The total area of settlement is three times that of any time before the introduction of artificial tunnels that tap and concentrate the water table—qanats in modern Farsi—and is equalled only during the Seleuco-Parthian Period after the new hydraulic technology was available. It is most likely that this exceptional density of settlements, inconvenient to springs, was for use during the wet winter season, a possibility indicated as early as the turn of the fifth millennium but much expanded during the period under discussion. If so, the transhumant communities are populous—a settled area of 33 hectares indicating a population of 3,000 to 6,000 people (Kramer 1980:322–27; Schacht 1981:128–32)—and hierarchically organized. The normal rank-size distribution of site sizes (see chapter 4) and central, spatially dominant position (Wright and Johnson 1975:270) of Sabz'ali Bagheri indicate such organization. In addition to the indications of hierarchically organized transhumants, the number of campsites indicates the presence of nomads as well, although their population cannot be estimated from the extent of surviving artifactual debris.

Moving northwestward from Susa to the lowland Deh Luran Plain (figure 37) we find a florescence of settlement no less impressive than that just described for the intermontane Izeh Plain. The prototypes of its technology, however, are very different from those of Proto-Elamite Susa or Izeh, there having been a continuous development from Late Uruk technical and stylistic patterns. Wheel-made ceramics are more widely utilized and textural decoration declines while polychrome painting of jars is developed, perhaps from existing, though rarely used, monochrome and bichrome techniques. Building construction patterns, brick sizes, and internal features all continue, with individual buildings at Farukhabad being reconstructed continuously throughout the period.[6] The main center of the period, Musiyan, covered about 15 hectares at this time. Its impressive town wall may have been begun before the end of the period under consideration, and the walls of massive buildings of the period are visible in the sections of excavations opened on the site. Farukhabad and Baula were subsidiary centers on the western plain, each covering several hectares, and each with evidence of specialized production (Wright 1981b:188–94, figures 81, 82). Excavation at Farukhabad has produced evidence of both elaborate and simple residences, and indications that people associated with the more elaborate residences were involved in the production and exchange of processed asphalt, chert cores, and perhaps goat-hair products. The evidence for such production shows fluctuations during the period. The importation of exotic materials, principally to the more elaborate residences, also increases, and also shows fluctuations during this period. It is notable that the different elaborate structures have exotic cherts from different source areas, implying a return to the locally controlled production patterns of Middle Uruk times. Certainly during this later period, the evidence of the context of production and of the discard of imported materials indicate that exchange was under the control of the better-housed social units, each having somewhat different exchange networks (Wright 1981b:265–77, figure 99). Differentiation among the households of Farukhabad is paralleled at the level of areal settlement, where the primoconvex rank-size distribution of site sizes and spatial dominance of centrally located Musiyan indicate a well-organized hierarchy (figure 37). All sites, however, are close to spring-fed water sources or to the location of river channels at the time, and there is no reason why those sites could not have been occupied throughout the year. Nevertheless, harsh summer conditions on the Deh Luran Plain and easy access to the nearby higher and cooler Pusht-i Kuh might well have encouraged those not concerned with urban crafts and summer irrigation—the incidence of poplar in charcoal samples indicates such irrigation—to become summer transhumants. There is no evidence, direct or indirect, of transhumant or nomadic inhabitation of the Deh Luran Plain at this time. In Pusht-i Kuh to the north, however, Vanden Berghe has documented several cemeteries unassociated with settlements which may indicate such movement. At Mir Khair (Vanden Berghe 1979) the stone cist graves contain predominantly handmade gray-brown ware (a type used for a minority of the jars at Farukhabad) but with a few wheel-finished jars, some painted with designs close to those from the early part of the period under discussion at Farukhabad.[7] Several other cemeteries with large tomb chambers, such as Bani Surmah (Vanden Berghe 1968b), Kalleh Nissar (Vanden Berghe 1970a), and War Kabud (Vanden Berghe 1969), have material similar to that from Farukhabad representing the end of the period under discussion and later. Apparently these cemeteries became more common during the period and developed distinctive architectural features which differentiate them from the small, brick mortuary structures of lowland towns (Gautier and Lampre 1905:75–78). This suggests that transhumant or nomad communities were becoming more common and were also becoming socially differentiated from the contemporary lowland settlements by the early portion of the third millennium.

North of Kabir Kuh, in Pish-i Kuh or Inner Luristan, evidence of settlements with permanent architecture is limited. Chia Bal on the Rumishgan Plain (figures 12, 13) may have had continuing occupation into the third milennium (Goff 1971:149), but Hulailan was deserted; the major sites of Kuh-i Dasht also lack evidence of this period. Only Masur, a center of about 10 hectares on the Khorramabad Plain, has extensive occupation.[8] Most of the tombs discussed by Goff (1971:146–50) were, as she concludes, used during the later third millennium. However, two seem to date to the later part of the period under discussion. One of the stone cists at Mirvali on the Rumishgan Plain excavated by Schmidt had a jar duplicating the form, ribbing, and painted designs of vessels from Early Dynastic layers at Farukhabad (Pope 1936:127; Wright 1981b: figure 61i,j). Also, a set of larger tombs in Kunji Cave overlooking the Khorramabad Plain contains ceramics of Jemdet Nasr or Early Dynastic affinity (Speth 1971:173). However, the possibility that these tombs are associated with the nearby settlement at Masur rather than with nomads must be kept in mind.

The end of the fourth millennium and the beginning of the third is an unusual period in the history of southwestern Iran because the central area of the region is relatively depopulated. In a sense, what had been a culturally defined region centered on the Susiana since at least the later fifth millennium has become divided, and its component marginal regions have become joined with adjacent regions. Eastwards, on the southern part of the Iranian plateau, a supraregional network is centered on a widely separated set of towns, the largest presently known being Malyan (figure 31) (Sumner 1972; Alden 1979b). In the marginal areas of southern Iran are settlement groups or outposts, some such as Izeh probably articulated with transhumant or nomadic groups; others such as Tall-i Iblis (Caldwell 1968) or Yahya in southern Iran (Lamberg-Karlovsky 1971) associated with routes or sources of special materials. Susa was a small frontier town, perhaps important for its easy access to Mesopotamia proper. Masur to the north could have been a similar frontier point. Westwards, in alluvial Mesopotamia proper, another supraregional network is centered on the large towns along the lower Euphrates channels, among which Uruk was increasingly paramount during the period under consideration (Adams and Nissen 1972:17–28; Adams 1981:81–94). In the marginal areas at the foot of the Zagros front were smaller settlement clusters, such as the one on the Deh Luran Plain. In the front ranges of the Zagros, there are indications of increasing numbers of transhumant and nomadic communities. The progressive abandonment of the southern Zagros by Middle and Late Uruk communities and the integration of much of southwestern Iran with the plateau suggests conflict between these two great supraregional networks, but there is as yet no direct archaeological evidence of such conflict: no excavated late Uruk site in southwestern Iran has revealed evidence of destruction or fortification.

At present, it is most reasonable to conceptualize the changes of the later fourth millennium in southwestern Iran as a sequence of shifting commercial relations (Alden 1982), diplomatic realignments, military raids, and abandonments either under threat of raids or in response to more attractive circumstances elsewhere. Such circumstances may have varied as a result of ecological changes (Van Zeist and Bottema 1977), perhaps in part a result of herders' activities. Only if future research shows that the two networks were centralized polities or alliances of polities and that there are in fact repeated material indications of conflict

would one be justified in suggesting an interregional war. However, in the long term, interaction between the nomadic and seminomadic communities of the Zagros may well have been important. Indeed, future work on settlement systems such as those attested in the Izeh area may show that it was the close integration of transhumants in the plateau networks that gave plateau peoples an advantage over the peoples of Mesopotamia proper (Adams 1962). For purposes of this discussion, however, it suffices to say that there are widespread indications of an increase in the numbers and complexity of organization of transhumant and nomadic peoples in the mountains of southwestern Iran around the end of the fourth millennium.

Conclusion

It was my hope that more numerous and more intensive surveys of marginal and interstitial areas of southwestern Iran could be undertaken before an evaluation such as this was written. Regrettably, it will be some time before these often rugged and remote areas are again accessible to archaeological researchers, so one must make the best of what is currently available. It is heartening that a program of survey directed at questions of early nomads in the Inner Zagros to the north and east of Izeh has produced results broadly comparable to our own (Zagarell 1975a, 1978, 1981). It is unfortunate that the copious survey data from southern Iraq (Adams 1981) are relevant primarily to sedentary settlements.

But in spite of its limitations, the evidence reviewed above can be used to evaluate some of the propositions made regarding the importance of the marginal communities for the development of the central areas within the region. Three principal areas of inquiry arise:

1. Were the marginal areas refuges into which population dispersed in times of crisis in the more populous central areas? In fact, the settled population of the marginal areas declines when that of the Susiana declines during both the later Susiana and the Late Uruk phases. The indication of relative increases in the activities of transhumants and nomads comes not during these periods of decline but during the immediately succeeding phases, when nuclei of settled population are also beginning to grow again.

2. Did such increases in transhumance and nomadism, particularly during the early fourth millennium when the first state was developing in the Susiana area, place economic and thus administrative demands on the developing central polities? The indications of increasing transhumance and nomadism are few and localized in

places distant from the Susiana, but these observations do not permit a rejection of the importance of such demands because the absolute population of nomads and transhumants cannot be estimated from the evidence of campsites and cemeteries, even were survey coverage more extensive.

3. Could the emergent transhumant and nomadic social units pose a political challenge to the Susian state? Given that only a hierarchically organized polity could challenge even the relatively small Uruk Period polity centered at Susa, it is possible to answer this question. There is no indication of any degree of differentiation or hierarchy among the mountain transhumants and nomads of southwestern Iran until late in the fourth millennium and early in the third millennium when settlement variations in Izeh and tomb variations in Pusht-i Kuh indicate some degree of hierarchy. After the later fourth millennium, nomadic and transhumant peoples could have posed a direct military threat to the town dwellers of the larger mountain valleys and lowlands.[9] Before that time, such peoples could have exerted a political challenge only in combination with settled peoples. Alone, they would have been prey to exploitation by town-centered states, as seems to be indicated in the case of the Deh Luran area during Late Uruk times.

Notes

1. These ceramic assemblages can be compared with those of Tepe Farukhabad on the Deh Luran Plain, only 45 kilometers from Dum Gar Parchineh. There are differences, perhaps resulting from local stylistic preferences and/or from the selection of vessels with locally important symbolism for ritual deposition in the cemeteries. Nonetheless, one can correlate Dum Gar Parchineh, Sector A, with the Farukh phase of Farukhabad (cf. Vanden Berghe 1975a, figures 5:2, 5:7, 5:9, 5:10 with Wright 1981b, figures 23i and j, 20c and 21f, 20a, 22b, respectively). Sector B of the same site and the two sectors of Hakalan—all similar to each other and all largely distinct from Deh Luran assemblages—may be later than the Farukh phase and chronologically comparable to the Susa phase.

2. A visit to Qaleh Parsia near Deh Shaykh (first noted by Klaus Schippman), a site of about 0.2 hectare now cut by a canal to reveal a central mud-brick platform, produced bowl sherds with slash motifs and X-motifs identical to material from Susa A phase Jaffarabad (Dollfus 1971b: figure 11:4–7; figure 13:1, 3, 9).

3. Collections from Qaleh Tol made in 1969 and 1976, deposited in the Muzeh-ye Shush and the Muzeh Iran Bastan, contain beveled-rim bowls and trays of rough tempered ware and expanded and round lip jar rims and jar sherds with crosshatch motifs of a sandy ware duplicating that from Susiana Middle Uruk sites.

4. Caldwell (1968) suggested a Late Uruk occupation at Tal-i Ghazir, but examination of the sherds from the "Step Trench" now at the University of Chicago's Oriental Institute revealed no certain Late Uruk ceramics.

5. Collections from the Qaleh Tol area and from a site in a brick pit on the west edge of Deh Shaykh in Susan, made in 1976, were left in the Muzeh Iran Bastan. Those from Tol-e Qir, made in 1976 by Pierre de Miroschedji, were left in the Muzeh-ye Shush. Both collections contained jar rims and flaky slip sherds characteristic of this period.

6. Data from recent excavations in the Hamrin reservoir on the Diyala River indicate that only the period termed "Early Jemdet Nasr" in the Farukhabad report is even in part equivalent to "Jemdet Nasr" in the Northern Tigris-Euphrates alluvium. The period termed "Late Jemdet Nasr" is equivalent to Early Dynastic I and perhaps later. Precise recorrelation must await fuller publication of the Hamrin excavations. The following discussion, however, avoids this issue as much as possible.

7. The polychrome jar with horizontal curved lines and crosshatched triangles from Mir Khair (Vanden Berghe 1979:figure 17:1 [Tomb 58]) nearly duplicates examples from Farukhabad attributed to the Jamdet Nasr phases (Wright 1981b:figure 58g [Excavation B, Layer 28] and figure 58h [Excavation A, Layer 20]). A grayware jar from the same tomb (Vanden Berghe 1979:figure 17:6) duplicates examples of similar relative date from Farukhabad (Wright 1981b: figure 580 [Excavation B, Feature 18], figure 58p [Excavation A, Layer 16], figure 58q [Excavation B, Layer 27]). Interestingly, the copper bangles from Mir Khair (Vanden Berghe 1979:figure 18:4–6) are known from published stratified context only in Susa IIIa layers (Le Brun 1971:figure 67:18 [Acropole I, Layer 14b]), contemporary with Jemdet Nasr and Late-Middle Banesh phases elsewhere. These parallels indicate a date for Mir Khair considerably earlier than the later Early Dynastic date suggested by the excavator.

8. Masur is a mound of about 10 hectares in the center of the Khorramabad Plain. Examination of a construction site by the Izeh Research Group in 1976 revealed strata with beveled-rim bowls, heavy rim trays, and solid footed cups of rough chaff tempered ware as well as body sherds of wheel-thrown straw and crushed calcite tempered buff ware with painted dark bands. The items recovered and deposited with the Bastan Museum are paralleled in Banesh assemblages from Fars and the Godin V assemblage from northern Zagros.

9. This paper has profited from careful editorial readings and substantive comments by John Alden, Frank Hole, Gregory Johnson, Peder Mortenson, Susan Pollock, and Allen Zagarell. We are, however, not in complete agreement on the substantive issues, and the author bears full responsibility for the data, interpretation, and wording of the text.

Henry T. Wright

Table 26. Area Characteristics of Selected Plains in Southwestern Iran

	Susiana	Deh Luran	Ram Hormuz	Izeh	Hulailan
Elevation of Plain (meters above sea level)	80	120	150	750	930
Area in square kilometers					
Sloping rocky land	345	480	93	44	45
Low wet land	440	170	27	34	12
Level dry land	1,495	290	325	77	110
Total	2,280	940	445	155	167
Hectares of site area					
Susiana d	94.1	18.7	13.1	6.0	6.3
Susa A	59.3	8.0	3.2	4.4	1.8
Terminal Susa A	33.1	1.4	1.2	4.6	1.0
Early Uruk	97.1	9.0	1.8	12.6	2.0
Middle Uruk	127.1	9.6	3.8	3.0	
Late Uruk	53.0	3.0	1.8	———	1.0
Jemdet Nasr-Banesh	17.0	31.1	1.0	32.2	———
Average size in hectares of sites other than centers					
Susiana d	———	0.5	1.2	1.4	0.5
Susa A	———	———	———	1.5	0.3
Terminal Susa A	1.4	0.7	———	1.5	———
Early Uruk	1.4	0.7	———	1.5	0.5
Middle Uruk	1.3	0.8	1.4	———	
Late Uruk	1.8	———	———	———	———
Jemdet Nasr-Banesh	2.7	1.1	———	1.9	———
Mean distance from settlement to permanent water					
Susiana d		0.8	0.5	2.8	
Susa A		0.8	0.2	1.5	
Terminal Susa A		0.2	0.1	5.5	
Early Uruk		0.9	0.6	5.2	
Middle Uruk		1.2	0.5	3.0	
Late Uruk		0.4	0.6	———	
Jemdet Nasr-Banesh		0.9	0.1	4.1	

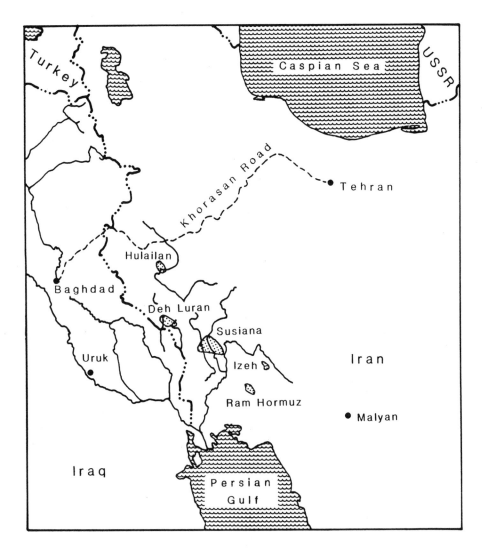

Figure 31. Southwestern Iran and surrounding regions showing the locations of the Susiana, Deh Luran, Hulailan, Izeh, and Ram Hormuz plains.

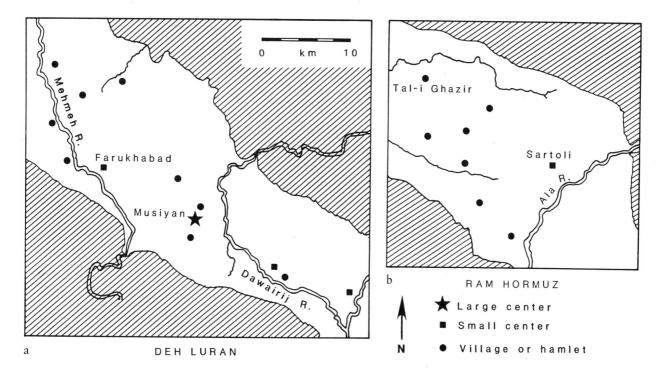

a
DEH LURAN

b
RAM HORMUZ

★ Large center

■ Small center

● Village or hamlet

N

Figure 32. Marginal lowland area settlement patterns of the late fifth millennium. Sources (a) Deh Luran Plain (Wright 1981b:Fig. 32); (b) Ram Hormuz Plain (field report and notes in files of the author).

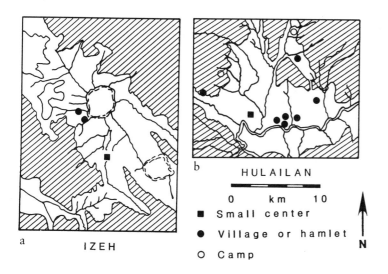

a
IZEH

b
HULAILAN

■ Small center

● Village or hamlet

○ Camp

N

Figure 33. Marginal highland area settlement patterns of the late fifth millennium. Sources: (a) Izeh Plain (Wright ed. 1979:Fig. 23); (b) Hulailan Plain (Mortensen 1976:Fig. 13).

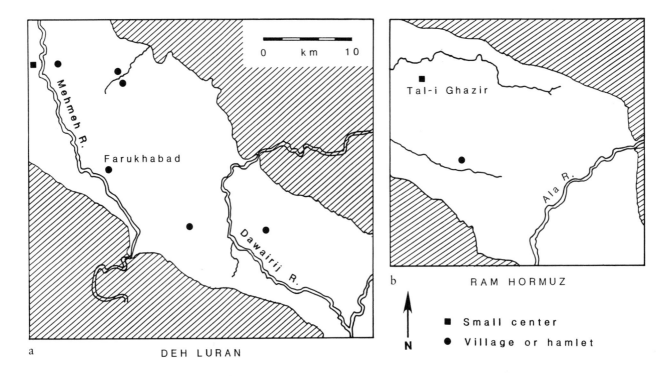

Figure 34. Marginal lowland area settlement patterns of the early fourth millennium. Sources: (a) Deh Luran Plain (Wright 1981b:Fig. 78); Ram Hormuz Plain (field report and notes in the files of the author).

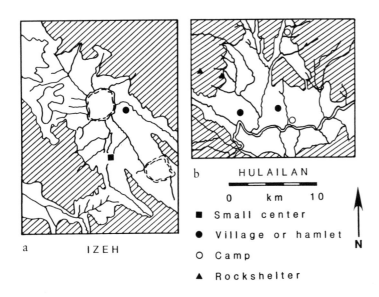

Figure 35. Marginal highland area settlement patterns of the early fourth millennium. Sources: (a) Izeh Plain (Wright ed. 1979:Fig. 26); (b) Hulailan Plain (Mortensen 1976:Fig. 12).

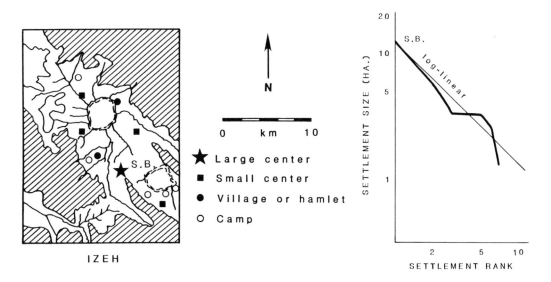

Figure 36. Marginal highland area settlement patterns of the end of the fourth millennium. Sources: Wright ed. (1979:Fig. 36 and site area figures from Table 15).

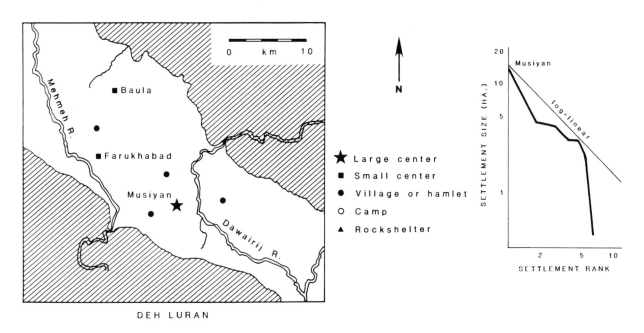

Figure 37. Marginal lowland area settlement patterns of the end of the fourth millennium. Sources: Wright (1981b:Fig. 81 and site area figures in the files of the author).

Chapter 6

The Susa III Period

JOHN R. ALDEN

Introduction

During the early third millennium B.C., the Susa III Period was marked by a population minimum in the Susiana Plain. Susa itself was only slightly more than 10 hectares in size, little more than a large village, and it represented over half of the total occupied area in the plain. Still, this region seems to have played an important role in geopolitical affairs. The Susiana Plain lay on the border between a Proto-Elamite sphere of influence centered in the highlands of the southern Zagros and the Jemdet Nasr/Early Dynastic polities of lower Mesopotamia (figure 38). Although at first glance it was merely a small town in a nearly empty region, Susa and the Susiana Plain were more significant than their sedentary populations would imply. (In chapter 5, the evidence for mobile populations is assessed.)

This period is rather poorly known, even though the enormous volume of material excavated at Susa during the first half of this century included a number of Susa III deposits (figure 39). However, in most of these excavations stratigraphic and contextual information was not adequately recorded. Consequently, the material from these early seasons is of little use except for stylistic and comparative purposes. Le Breton (1957) did about as much as possible in seriating these data, and in the years since his synthesis carefully controlled excavations have been carried out by the French Archaeological Delegation in Iran under the direction of Roman Ghirshman and, more recently, Jean Perrot (Stève and Gasche 1971; Le Brun 1971; and Carter 1981). This work provides a preliminary picture of the Susa III ceramic corpus. Although meticulously exca-vated and published, these excavations were quite limited in scope and the quantities of material recovered were small.

Data from regional surveys of the Susiana Plain are also limited and difficult to interpret unambiguously. In part this reflects the nature of the Susa III pottery and of typical Susa III settlements: several of the most diagnostic ceramic features are slips and painted decoration that tend to erode when exposed on the surface of sites, and most of the known Susa III settlements are small. In addition, undocumented surface collecting at many of the larger sites has removed a significant proportion, perhaps over 20 percent, of the diagnostic material present (Alden 1982: table 1). Nonetheless, enough careful, systematic surveying has been done to ensure that a reasonable proportion of the existing Susa III sites has been discovered. For the present, then, we can assume that the observed pattern of a few small villages and occasional sherds from a relatively small number of nearby sites represents the real nature of the Susa III settlement pattern and does not merely reflect the problems of identifying occupations of this era.

The chapter begins by reviewing what is known from the excavations at Susa and from regional surveys. I define the Susa III Period by specifying the archaeological deposits that contain unmixed materials from the era, and then examine the survey results in some detail, inferring from them the spatial organization during the Susa III Period. A comprehensive examination of the relationship between the Susiana Plain and the rest of the Middle East is beyond my purposes here, but I outline my understanding of that situation at the end of this chapter. For additional information and several conflicting interpretations, readers may refer to a number of other sources (Adams 1981; Alden 1982; Amiet 1979; Kohl 1978; Lamberg-Karlovsky 1978; Vallat 1980).

Excavated Susa III Material

Material of indisputable Susa III date was discovered at least as early as 1901, when the first Proto-Elamite economic-type tablets were unearthed (Brice 1962:15). Unhappily, inadequate vertical and horizontal control in the excavations and incomplete recording and publication of results led to extraordinary confusion in the Susiana ceramic sequence. Numerous schemes for organizing this material were devised, revised, and eventually rejected (Eliot 1950 presents a detailed discussion of Susa ceramic chronologies). It was not until 1957 that a reasonably accurate, widely available, and generally accepted chronological framework was published by Louis Le Breton, who had excavated at Susa in the mid-1930s and who had access to the materials from Susa in the Louvre. His Susiana a-e/Susa A-D sequence has been superseded by new terminology (Perrot 1971, 1978), but Le Breton was an astute scholar and observer and his work merits careful attention.

Le Breton (1957:104) used the appearance of Proto-Elamite writing as one of the principal characteristics defining the Susa C*b*, and he notes that this script continues in use until perhaps as late as the Susa D*d*. Although his pottery drawings show few details—for example, rim forms are typically impossible to determine (Le Breton 1957: figures 11–14, plate XXVI, and figures 35–36), they summarize the repertoire of forms, styles, and motifs used to distinguish the C and D periods and subphases. In his sequence, Susa C*b* through D*b* are equivalent to what we now call Susa III. Useful as Le Breton's observations have been, they were not based on material from carefully controlled excavations and should be used only with caution.

The first generally available publication of material from controlled stratigraphic contexts was that of Stève and Gasche, who reported on four seasons of excavation from 1965 to 1968. In 1965, M. J. Stève (as excavator) and Hermann Gasche (architect) opened a 20 meter by 10 meter sounding near the center of the western edge of the Susa Acropole (Stève and Gasche 1971:9–11). Figure 40 shows the location of this and other excavations that have yielded stratified Susa III remains. This initial sounding revealed the northern edge of the Susa A platform (chapters 2 and 3, this volume) and an important Jemdet Nasr period[1] addition to that structure, a thick wall or reconstructed facade made of *riemchen* brick.[2] These bricks are important because, as a distinctive feature of Sumerian building technology, their discovery indicates that Mesopotamian influence in the Susiana Plain continued after the Late Uruk Period, rather than ending with the abandonment of the Acropole I:17 occupation of Susa.

The *riemchen* wall covered a Late Uruk wall and a shallow deposit of associated material. Abutting the *riemchen* facade were two later strata of Jemdet Nasr period debris, the upper over one meter thick. These deposits were capped by a layer of Early Dynastic I debris some 60 to 75 centimeters thick. Stève and Gasche's Jemdet Nasr and Early Dynastic I periods are equivalent to what we now call Susa III; hence these deposits provide important evidence of the ceramic corpus defining this period. Later material from the northwest corner of the sounding and earlier debris from atop the Susa A platform were readily separable from the Susa III remains, and it seems safe to treat these deposits as generally unmixed and representative of the Susa III ceramic corpus. These and other good Susa III excavation units are listed in table 27.

In 1966, an area to the south of the 1965 sounding was opened, as "Chantier Ouest." To facilitate the disposal of the backdirt, the excavators dug a trench along the north edge of this operation to the western edge of the Acropole mound, and a Decauville railway was run through the trench. In 1968 the trench for the railway was extended to connect the sounding and "Chantier Ouest," and during the cleaning of the north face of the trench, two Proto-Elamite tablets were discovered in the Early Dynastic I stratum just described. These tablets confirm the relevance of the material from the sounding for the Susa III era. Sections B and C on Stève and Gasche's Plan 2 show the elevations and locations of these deposits.

In 1968, during operations designed to clarify the sequence of construction and occupation of the Susa A platform, Stève and Gasche (1971:25–41) excavated two late Jemdet Nasr units abutting the north face of the Susa A platform and atop the northern extension of the *terrasse* that is represented by the *riemchen* wall from the 1965 sounding. Quantities of ceramics and enough charcoal for two radiocarbon dates came from these deposits.[3] In addition, several areas containing Early Jemdet Nasr/Late Uruk ceramics were excavated in the northeastern sector of the "Chantier de la Terrasse," atop the Susa A platform. Because these were open surfaces, the associated ceramics cannot be considered closed depositional units even though several appear to be homogeneous groups (see table 27).

The more recent excavations at Susa that encountered Susa III Period strata, designated Acropole I (Le Brun 1971) and Ville Royale I (Carter 1979a, 1981),

John R. Alden

require less detailed discussion because they involve material that is clearly stratified. Acropole I, near the southern end of the Acropole and on the northern edge of Roland de Mecquenem's Sondage 2, met a major stratigraphic break between the Susa II (Uruk) layers 22–17 and the Susa III strata 16–14B (Le Brun 1971:210–11). Very little material was recovered from strata 14A and 13, although it was noted that these seem to represent a phase of the Susa III Period that should be distinguished from the earlier strata 16–14B. Fortunately, Ville Royale Chantier I overlaps chronologically with the latest strata of Acropole I. The Ville Royale excavation area, about 150 meters east-southeast of Acropole I, was first occupied at about the time of Acropole I strata 14A–13 (Carter 1981:20). Ville Royale I strata 18–16 represent a middle phase of the Susa III Period, and levels 15–13 define a late phase.

These excavations allow us to estimate the extent of occupation at Susa during the early third millennium B.C. Figure 40 shows the major areas of the site and my own judgment of the extent of Susa III Period settlement. The entire 9 hectares of the Acropole seem to have been occupied during this era, for Susa III material appeared in the south (Acropole I and Roland de Mecquenem's Sondage II), north (Roland de Mecquenem's Sondage I), and west central (Stève and Gasche excavations) areas of the mound. The Ville Royale I excavation, in the western corner of that mound, reveals evidence of occupation from the end of Early Susa III until the end of the Susa III Period. However, this occupation did not extend as far east as Ghirshman's Ville Royale B excavation. Amiet (personal communication) has drawn my attention to burials in the "Donjon," one of which contained two Proto-Elamite tablets (Mecquenem et al. 1943:103) and a number of which held pottery with general mid-third millennium B.C. parallels. These burials do not constitute evidence for habitation in that part of Susa during this era, but they do demonstrate that the "Donjon" area was being used. If the area of the Ville Royale settlement is set, rather arbitrarily, at 2 hectares, then Susa covered about 11 hectares during the Susa III Period. The area was probably somewhat less in the early part of the period and somewhat greater at the end, although such fine distinctions are of dubious merit when so little reliable information is available.

Susa III Settlement on the Susiana Plain

The Susiana Plain has been surveyed repeatedly, to locate sites for excavation, determine regional settlement patterns, and register sites for preservation. None of the surveys covered the entire plain but collectively they provide relatively complete information on visible archaeological remains. However, areas on the fringes of the plain were less thoroughly surveyed than the central portion, and only a few of the sites were mapped and systematically surface collected. Thus, the identification of minor occupations on large sites depends on the experience and visual acuity of individual surveyors. Still, although some sites were surely missed, survey coverage of the Susiana Plain is probably better overall than for any other major region in the Middle East. All in all, we can expect that a reasonable proportion of the existing Susa III sites has been discovered.

Figure 41 shows the locations of the reported Susa III sites. The lone large site is Susa, while to the east are two small sites: KS-308 (figure 43) and KS-396. The other twenty-nine sites are all significantly smaller, less than 1 hectare in size, and often indicated by only one or two sherds of Susa III date. When I resurveyed these sites in 1977, I found no diagnostic Susa III pottery on ten of the twenty-nine sites I visited; I got good collections from only KS-308 and KS-39. I was unable to locate KS-396, but Wenke's examination indicated that this should be considered a site on the scale of KS-308.

It is difficult to estimate the total area occupied on the plain during each phase of the Susa III Period. Most of the minor sites yielded so little diagnostic pottery that it seems they were probably occupied only sporadically or for very short times. Only KS-5, KS-39, and KS-49 produced enough diagnostic material to indicate continuing settlement, and the available sherds from those sites show parallels only with Early Susa III pottery (see figure 42). The deposits containing Susa III style pottery on KS-5 and KS-39 seem to be limited to small areas from the summits of these high mounds (see Johnson 1973: plates X and XIII for maps), from areas of about 0.2 hectare on each site. Site KS-49 (figure 43) seems to have had a slightly larger occupation, on the order of 0.5 hectare or so. In total, then, the minor sites probably represent little more than a total of a single hectare of permanent occupation.

Sites KS-308 and KS-396 are larger, covering 2.2 and 3.2 hectares, respectively. My systematic collections from KS-308 are unanalyzed and presently unavailable[4], but my notes on that material indicate that it fits into the Early/Middle or Middle Susa III. I have not examined the collections from KS-396 and can only speculate that it was occupied for most or all of the Susa III Period.

Table 28 summarizes our knowledge of the areas and phases of Susa III occupations in the Susiana Plain. Although other small or minor settlements assuredly remain undiscovered, and Susa certainly varied in size over these centuries, the basic demographic pattern of this era is clear. The settled population of the Susiana Plain was very small in size and concentrated in a single small town. Most of the other sites were small and were either occupied for brief periods or visited only sporadically.

Interpretations: The Susiana Plain

The observed pattern of settlement in the Susiana Plain is quite different from what is seen in either previous or subsequent eras. First, large parts of the region appear to be totally abandoned. Second, only a very few sites seem to have been continuously occupied. Third, no pattern of hierarchical spatial organization is evident. Together these features imply changes in both regional political organization and local subsistence patterns.

The most obvious feature of Susa III settlement is the abandonment of the eastern and northern edges of the plain. This depopulation began in the Late Uruk and resulted in a settlement pattern somewhat reminiscent of Terminal Susa A times (Johnson 1973:figures 15 and 32). A second feature becomes obvious when the minor sites are ignored: the permanent settlements are not clustered, but widely spaced along a line running eastward from Susa and roughly coincident with one of two proposed Middle Uruk exchange routes across the Susiana Plain (Johnson 1975:figure 23). Any statistical analysis involving only three locations would be fruitless, but this certainly does not look like a regional system where a small town dominates a pair of subordinate villages. The small town of Susa is separated from the two villages by the Diz River, the largest watercourse on the plain. With this distribution of sites, Susa appears to be the western terminus of a communication route running toward the Zagros Mountains. But if this is so, it was apparently not a route that was strongly controlled, for the small size and isolation of the settlements along the way make them look more like vulnerable outposts than thriving commercial hostelries.

The locations of the several dozen minor occupations may reflect practices of animal husbandry during the Susa III Period. These sites appear to have been inhabited only sporadically, and they can be divided into two distinct groups. The northern sites, in the triangular area bounded by the Diz and Shur rivers (figure 10) and south of the line between KS-308 and KS-396, all lie within 8 kilometers of a larger settlement. The other sites, including five of the seven minor occupations west of the Diz, are situated 11 to 21 kilometers from any permanent settlement. The closer sites are within range for a day trip with a herd of sheep or goats, but the more distant sites are a day's travel either way from each of the three villages. Perhaps the material found on the minor sites was deposited during short stays by shepherds managing the flocks of the villagers, a speculation that would accord with Wright's observations in the preceding chapter about the increasing importance of animals in the Jemdet Nasr Period.

It is significant that the sporadic occupations are concentrated in the area south of the two settlements between the Diz and Shur floodplains. Areas closer to the Zagros foothills are conspicuously avoided, which would be almost inexplicable if the occupants of KS-308 and KS-396 were engaged either in transhumant pastoralism or trading regularly with nomadic groups wintering on the Susiana Plain. The picture these data seem to indicate is one of isolation, with the residents of the Susiana Plain concentrated in a few relatively safe locations.

The Geopolitical Context of the Susa III Period

The Susa III Period is more or less contemporaneous with the use of Proto-Elamite script on the so-called economic tablets. This circumstance, along with a number of other ceramic and art historical parallels, allows us to crossdate Susa III with both the Iranian highlands and Mesopotamia. To the east, in the Zagros Mountains and on the Iranian central plateau (chapter 2, figures 12, 13), the era is generally designated as Proto-Elamite; in the plains of the Tigris and Euphrates rivers it has been divided into the Jemdet Nasr and Early Dynastic periods. These different names are more than arbitrary consequences of the history of excavation and modern political realities: they denote real differences in the archaeological assemblages from the two regions. In turn, these patterns of material culture reflect contrasts between the pre- and protohistoric societies that dominated the mountains of Iran and the lowlands of southern Iraq. The depopulation and isolation of the Susiana Plain can be understood only when viewed in this wider geopolitical context.

Table 29 outlines the data currently available on total occupation in each of the major regions around the Susiana Plain. These figures have been made as comparable as possible, but they must be used with caution. As investigators in each area have emphasized, the data are most useful as evidence of relative populations between different areas and eras. In particular, the surveys of Adams and Alden were more extensive than intensive, and both probably missed a significant proportion of existing sites in the 0–5 hectare size range in their surveys of the Mesopotamian alluvium and the Kur River basin in Fars (chapter 2, figure 16). Still, three major changes—doublings or halvings of total settlement area—are apparent in these data. First, the area of occupation in the Uruk region doubles between the Early/Middle and the Late

John R. Alden

Uruk. Both Adams (1981) and Johnson (1982a) have commented on this, remarking that ceramics are similar enough between the regions to indicate that the growth in the Uruk region may have resulted from migrations from the Susiana Plain, Nippur-Adab, and Ur-Eridu regions. Second, the doubling of settled area in the Kur River basin between Early and Late Middle Banesh times can be accounted for, as suggested in Alden (1982), by a migration from the Susiana Plain. Again, similarities in material culture between these regions support the suggestion of migrating populations. The third major change is a doubling in settled area in the Uruk region between the Jemdet Nasr and Early Dynastic I periods. Unlike the other two instances discussed here, this last increase is not accompanied by any significant decrease in settled area in a neighboring region. Adams (1981:82–84) explains this apparent change as artificial, a result of the unavoidable conflation of sequential occupations in the Early Dynastic. The picture these data suggest, then, is one of continuing emigration from the Susiana Plain to southern Mesopotamia during the Middle and Late Uruk periods, and to highland Iran during the Late Uruk and Jemdet Nasr.

These patterns are interesting, but their description tells us nothing about why the Susiana Plain—fertile, readily irrigable, and with easy access to the resources available in the western ridges of the Zagros Mountains—was being abandoned. Agricultural land was probably never a limiting resource during pre- and protohistoric times, but it is surprising to find that a location as attractive as the Susiana Plain was virtually depopulated. Clearly, we should examine the social and political situation in neighboring regions for an explanation of this apparently anomalous exodus.

During the Early/Middle Uruk, the Susiana Plain, along with several other areas neighboring the Uruk region, was home to a thriving society that used items of material culture typical of the Uruk region, but which may not have been ethnically "Uruk." All these areas suffered extensive depopulation during the Late Uruk, generally thought to be due to a breakdown in the internal sociopolitical structure of the society. At the same time, the city of Uruk attained new levels of population and religious and political supremacy by drawing people from the neighboring regions. It is possible that these changes resulted from Uruk's favorable location at the nexus of the Mesopotamian network of riverine transportation. Potential competing centers in the northerly Nippur-Adab region, like sites 1237 and 1306 (Adams 1981:figures 13 and 21), were reduced to insignificance by shifts in the major channels of the Tigris-Euphrates rivers. By Early Dynastic I times, Uruk was more than five times the size of the second largest city in Mesopotamia (Adams 1981:figure 20). But whatever the cause of this

growth, by the end of the Late Uruk the people of the Susiana Plain, separated from the Uruk region by extensive swamps and a distance of some 200 kilometers, ceased to have any close interaction with early Sumerian Mesopotamia.

During this same era, a new sociopolitical entity was developing to the east of the Susiana Plain. In highland Iran, the Late Uruk-Early Dynastic I Period spans the appearance, development, and demise of what I have called the Proto-Elamite hegemony (Alden 1982). "Hegemony" is a deliberately vague term, because the actual form of Proto-Elamite political organization is not clear. Indeed, we cannot even be certain of the kind of relationship that existed between the central area of Proto-Elamite development in the Kur River basin and the surrounding series of far-flung sites where Proto-Elamite tablets have been found. However, evidence from both surface surveys and excavations is compatible with the proposal that a single sociopolitical entity controlled long-distance trade in highland products across southwestern Iran. This Proto-Elamite hegemony gained power and influence when the northern route between Iran and the Mesopotamian alluvium was closed near the end of the Late Uruk Period by a southward migration of users of Transcaucasian gray wares of the types known from Yanik IV and Godin III. The fortifications recently discovered in the Hamrin (Gibson 1981) imply that the Early Dynastic inhabitants of the Diyala Plain had to protect their northeastern frontier from incursions by inhabitants of the north central Zagros. Although conflict need not have interdicted exchange, there are signs, particularly the dearth of lapis lazuli in Early Dynastic I contexts in sites on the Diyala Plain (Herrmann 1968:31), that long distance exchange along the Khorasan Road from Baghdad to Hamadan (chapter 2, figure 2) and across northern Iran never attained any significant level during the first centuries of the third millennium B.C.

However, let us return our attention to the region around Susa. With the competing attraction of the Early Sumerian and Proto-Elamite centers of political power and economic activity, the Susiana Plain continued to lose population between the Late Uruk and Jemdet Nasr periods. Lowland Mesopotamia and highland Iran have only infrequently been united by any common economic interests, and Proto-Elamite control over and restrictions on the flow of highland resources (Alden 1982) assuredly exacerbated the differences between the regions. Several pieces of the Sumerian epic literature, in particular *Enmerkar and the Lord of Aratta,* seem to refer to Jemdet Nasr/Early Dynastic I times and to the relationship between highlands and lowlands. A recent translation of this Enmerkar tale (S. Cohen 1973) indicates that while the two societies shared certain elements of religious and social ideology, the highlands were politically and economically fully independent of Sumer. Whether or not the Aratta of literature was a Proto-Elamite city, the relationship between lower Mesopotamia and the southern Zagros highlands during the early third millennium B.C. was certainly similar to what the epic describes.

According to Hinz (1971:645), "as early as this (the First Dynasty of Kish, 2700 B.C.) the historian can recognize the leitmotiv of relations between Elam and Mesopotamia, one of hereditary enmity, mitigated at the same time by equally persistent economic and cultural exchanges." If this were also the case in the preceding centuries it would help explain the status of Susa and the Susiana Plain during the Susa III Period. Life in the land between two competing polities often would have been distinctly unsafe. The highland peoples were not numerous enough to be a serious threat to the Sumerian heartland, and given the technological problems of supply and transportation faced by Jemdet Nasr/Early Dynastic I societies, any major incursion into the Zagros Mountains by the residents of Mesopotamia would probably have been impossible. Still, both sides could mount destructive raids into the lands between the two regions. With plenty of other land available, it is not surprising that the Susiana Plain, sitting directly on this border, was almost completely abandoned.

However, Susa itself remained occupied. In light of developments in Iran and Mesopotamia this seems curious, and it is something that must be explained. I would speculate that during this era Susa adopted a new role as a port of trade, a more or less neutral location where exchange between traders from the two neighboring polities could take place. This function would give the city a degree of protection as well as offering a profitable livelihood for many of its residents. The protection would come from mutual recognition that such a site was needed to facilitate the mechanics of trade, while the income would derive from the activities of middlemen: providing a market for large quantities of similar goods for importers, bulk-breaking and safe storage, and selection from a variety of goods for potential buyers. For neighboring polities the long-term costs of not having such a site would be greater than the short-term benefits to be gained from sacking it. The plethora of Proto-Elamite tablets at Susa, where they have been found in virtually every Susa III Period deposit recently excavated, might well reflect a pattern where most of the town's residents were engaged in some form of interregional exchange.

This port-of-trade hypothesis has been criticized on several counts. Vallat and Le Brun (1982) argue that such settlements ought to yield records from both sides participating in such trade. Because no tablets written in Early Sumerian have been found, it would follow that Mesopotamians were not coming to Susa in significant numbers. Lamberg-Karlovsky (1982) has argued that the small numbers of items and quantities apparently recorded on most Proto-Elamite tablets makes it unlikely that these were records of anything more than strictly local exchange. He also points out that the tablets recently excavated from Susa all seem to come from domestic contexts. Real middlemen at the nexus of trade between two major sociopolitical units ought to have large buildings for storage and their archives ought to reflect the quantities that they were presumably dealing in. Finally, Heskel (1982) suggests that if Susa were indeed a port of trade we would expect excavations at the site to have produced more high-status objects and greater quantities of rare materials. Although the location of Susa in an otherwise abandoned region between two distinct environmental zones and two separate polities seems to support the port-of-trade hypothesis, these three criticisms should be examined before that identification can be accepted.

The one-language problem, I suggest, results from a misconception of what a port of trade must be. It is a location where middlemen deal with both sides in a trading partnership. Records at such a site would reflect the cultural identity of the middlemen and not the identities of both sides in the exchange. If the middlemen came from both cultures we would find records in both languages; since we find records in only Proto-Elamite we can assume that the middlemen at Susa were all Proto-Elamite. The problem of small numbers might be explained in several ways. First, the scale of most exchanges could be small. Second, although the records that have been uncovered recently at Susa do record mostly small numbers, tablets from earlier excavations (and uncertain contexts) often show considerably larger numbers. The tablets with small numbers from domestic contexts may record local exchanges, but the other tablets could reflect the greater scale of activity of important traders. The scarcity of high-status objects that Heskel notes reflects recent excavations more than the sum of what has been found at Susa over the years. For instance, grave 576 from Level 17 or 18 in the Ville Royale I excavation, which contained two spouted copper pots, ten baskets, and seven ceramic vessels (Carter 1981:figures 5–8), is certainly not the tomb of a simple farmer. In short, none of these criticisms really controverts the port-of-trade interpretation. Although this hypothesis is certainly not yet proven, it merits serious consideration.

In sum, the Susa III Period cannot be dismissed simply as an era when events had passed over the Susiana Plain. To be sure, Susa was reduced to a small town and the surrounding plain was virtually depopulated,

John R. Alden

but that small town may have been an important link between the dominant societies of Mesopotamia and highland Iran. But in the long view this was only a brief anomalous phase in the long history of the region. Its productive land and strategic location were too important for the Susiana Plain to be neglected for long, and in subsequent centuries as in earlier ones, Susa was a major force in Middle Eastern history.

Notes

1. In their report Stève and Gasche used Mesopotamian chronological terms to refer to the somewhat different assemblages of material found at Susa. For the sake of simplicity, I use their terminology in reviewing their work and refer the reader to figure 39 for chronological equivalences.

2. *Riemchen* is the German name for a type of small rectangular brick, with a square or nearly square cross section, that is taken to mark what once was called the "Proto-Literate" Period.

3. Two dates were run from the same sample. SPr-43 gave a date of 2820 ± 218 B.C., and GrN-6051 indicated 3085 ± 40 B.C. A second carbon sample (GrN-6053), associated with ceramics dated to slightly earlier in the Jemdet Nasr period, yielded a date of 3065 ± 90 B.C. (Stève and Gasche 1971: footnotes 38 and 152). Both dates as given here use the Libby half-life of 5570 years; they are not MASCA-corrected.

4. These collections are stored in the Iran Bastan Museum in Teheran.

Table 27. Locations of Susa III Period Materials Excavated from Closed Stratigraphic Contexts at Susa

Period	Excavation Unit	Loci or Strata	Date Excavated
Late Susa II	Chantier de la Terrasse	Loci 282, 332, 334	1968
Early Susa III	Acropole I	Strata 16–14B	1969–71
	Chantier de la Terrasse	Loci 266 and 267	1968
Early/Middle Susa III	Stève and Gasche Sondage	Locus 376	1965
	Stève and Gasche Sondage	19.3 to 21.0 meters	1965
Middle Susa III	Ville Royale I	Strata 18 to 16	1972–75
	Acropole I	Strata 14A–12?	1969–71
	Chantier Ouest	Loci 101 & 102, 21.0–21.6 meters	1966, 68
	Stève and Gasche Sondage	21.0 to 21.6 meters	1965
	Stève and Gasche Sondage	Locus 374	1965
Late Susa III	Ville Royale I	Strata 15 to 13	1972–75

Table 28. Areas and Phases of Susa III Period Occupations on the Susiana Plain

	Period of Occupation		
Site	Early Susa III	Middle Susa III	Late Susa III
Susa	11 ha	11 ha	11 ha
KS-308	2.2 ha	2.2 ha	———
KS-396	3.2 ha	3.2 ha	3.2 ha
KS-5	0.2 ha	———	———
KS-39	0.2 ha	———	———
KS-49	0.5 ha	———	———
Total	17+ ha	16+ ha	14+ ha

Table 29. Total Areas of Occupation of Major Regions around the Susiana Plain during the Later Fourth and Earlier Third Millennia B.C.

	Southern Mesopotamia						Highland Iran	
	Ur-Eridu Region	Uruk Region[1]	Nippur-Adab Region[1]	Diyala Region[1]	Susiana Plain on the lowland steppe		Kur River Basin in Fars	
Early Dynastic I	34 ha [0]	690 ha [2, 1]	170 ha [2]	200 (?) ha [0][4]	Middle/Late Susa III	15 ha [0]	Late Banesh	57 ha [1]
Jemdet Nasr	53 ha [0]	328+ ha[2] [3]	142+ ha [1]	120 (?) ha [0][4]	Early Susa III	17 ha [0]	Late Middle Banesh	62 ha [1]
Late Uruk	18 (?) ha [0]	306 ha [1]	160 ha [1]	some growth	Late Uruk	62 ha [0]	Early Banesh	26 ha [0]
Early/ Middle Uruk	50 (?) ha [0]	138 ha [1]	290 ha [2]	very low	Middle Uruk	127 ha [0]	not related	
Source[3]	Wright	Adams	Adams	est.[4]	Johnson		Alden	

Notes:
[m, n] denotes number of small (40+ ha) and large (200+ ha) urban centers in each region.
[1]Areas reduced by 20 percent to correct Adams's method of estimation (Adams 1981: Chap. 3, note 6).
[2]From Adams and Nissen 1972: Figure 7, with the area of Uruk estimated at 100 hectares.
[3]From Wright 1981:325–27; Adams 1981:69–88; Johnson 1973:101, 145; Alden 1979b: Table 48.
[4]These data estimated from Adams (1965) are of dubious accuracy. In this 1957–58 survey, occupations were defined only as "Warka-Protoliterate" (Uruk-Jemdet Nasr) and "Early Dynastic" (I–III inclusive) and site areas were often exaggerated (Adams 1965:125, 183). Still, these estimates at least indicate the scale of occupation and growth. Since no town in the region was larger than 33 ha (Adams 1965:42), the Diyala had no urban centers comparable in scale to those found in other regions.

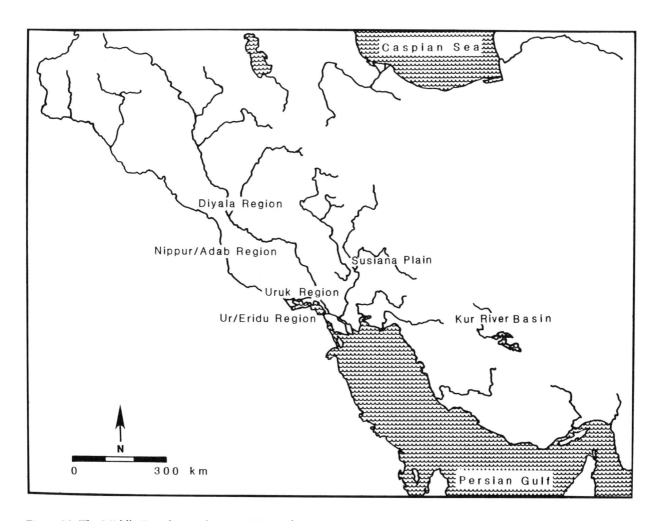

Figure 38. The Middle East during the Susa III Period.

Mesopotamia	Years B.C.	Susiana Period Le Breton	Susiana Period Perrot	Susa Excavations Acropole I	Susa Excavations Ville Royale I
	2600	Dc	———		13
Early Dynastic II			Late III	11?	
					15
———	2750	Db		12	16
Early Dynastic I			Middle III		
		Da		14a	18
———	2900				
				14b	
Jemdet Nasr		Cc	Early III		
		Cb		16	
———	3100		———	gap	
Late Uruk		Ca	Late II	17	
		Bd			

Figure 39. Archaeological chronology of the late fourth and early third millennia B.C. in southwestern Iran.

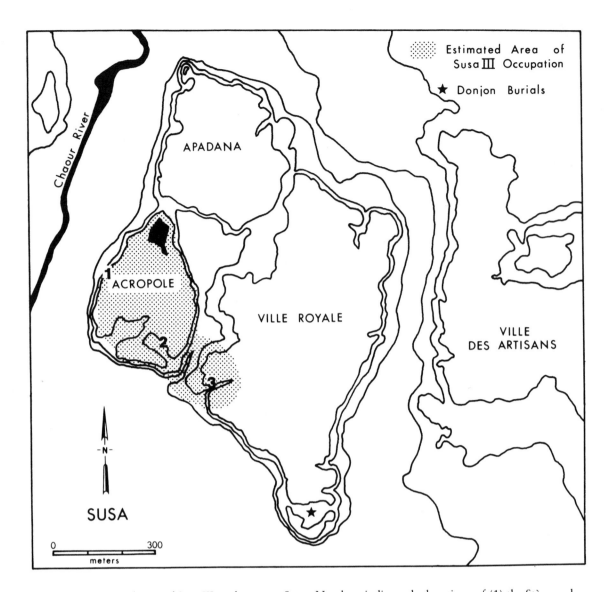

Figure 40. Estimated area of Susa III settlement at Susa. Numbers indicate the locations of (1) the Stève and Gasche sounding, (2) Le Brun's Acropole I excavation, and (3) Carter's Ville Royale I.

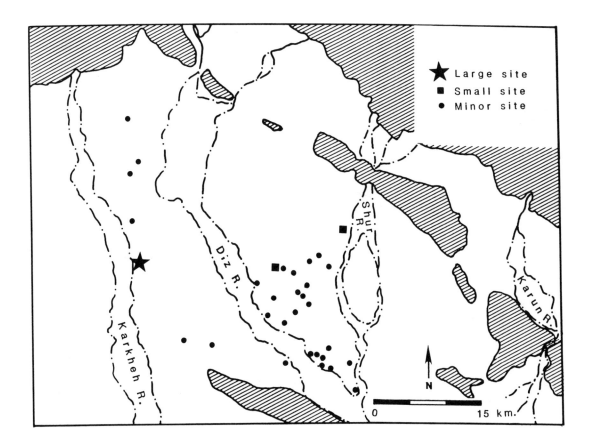

Figure 41. Sites on the Susiana Plain with surface finds of Susa III pottery.

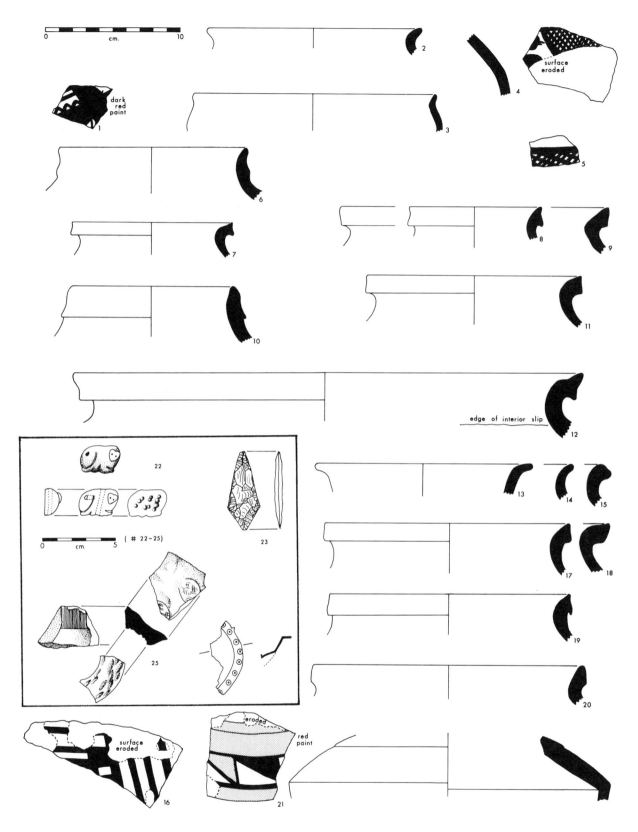

Figure 42. Pottery and small finds from the University of Michigan collections and the author's 1977 survey. Artifacts are listed as follows: number, item, site, size in centimeters, description; body color; density (heavy, medium, light), size (coarse, medium, fine), and type (grit, chaff) of temper; slip or paint Munsell color; parallels. (In the identifications that follow the asterisk indicates a comment made by Alain Le Brun when he examined these sherds.)

1. Painted body sherd, KS-308. Dusky red paint. Yellow with light fine grit, paint 10R3/2.

2. Small jar rim, KS-5. Outer Diameter (O.D.) 16, flakey reddish-black slip. Light yellow with medium medium coarse and very light fine grit, slip 10R2.5/1. Carter 1981:Fig. 10:3.

3. Small jar rim, KS-5. O.D. 18, fugitive reddish-brown slip. Light brown with light fine grit (dark red and black grits), slip 5YR5/4. Le Brun 1971:Fig. 65:20; Stève and Gasche 1971:Fig. 26:24; Carter 1981:Fig. 15:13.

4. Painted body sherd, KS-5. Fugitive dusky paint. Pinkish yellow with light very fine grit, paint 10R3/4. Paste and general motif paralleled by Le Brun 1971:Fig. 64:8; Stève and Gasche 1971:Fig. 31:23.

5. Painted body sherd, KS-5. Fugitive red paint. Light brown with medium fine grit, paint 10R4/6. Le Brun 1971:Fig. 64:5.

6. Jar rim, KS-308. O.D. 14, traces of fugitive dusky slip. Light yellow with medium very fine grit, slip 2.5YR3/2. Stève and Gasche 1971:Fig. 25:21.

7. Small jar rim, KS-49B. O.D. 12, thin flakey reddish-brown slip. Red body with dark brown core and light medium grit and chaff (dark red and black grits), slip 5YR5/4. Wright 1981:Fig. 44:h.

8. Small jar rim, KS-49. O.D. 10, thin flakey light red slip. Red with light fine grit (dark red and black grits), slip 2.5YR6/6.

9. Jar rim, KS-49A. O.D. 20, thin flakey dark reddish brown slip. Reddish yellow with medium medium chaff, slip 5YR3/2. Shape like Carter 1981:Fig. 8:1.

10. Jar rim, KS-15. O.D. 12, overfired green surface. Gray-green with medium medium grit and light medium chaff. Rim like Carter 1981:Fig. 16:4.

11. Jar rim, KS-49C. O.D. 16, thin flakey reddish-yellow slip. Light brown with medium coarse grit and medium medium chaff (dark red grits), slip 5YR6/6. Stève and Gasche 1971:Fig. 25:28; Carter 1981:Fig. 13:3.

12. Large jar rim, KS-39F. O.D. 38, thick reddish-yellow slip. Brown with gray core and light medium grit. Slip 5YR6/6. [Unusually large but right shape and slip for Acropole I:16–14b.*]

13. Bowl or jar rim, KS-39F. O.D. 16, thick flakey red slip. Red with gray core and light fine grit, slip 2.5YR4/6 interior and 2.5YR5/4 exterior. [This is the "rouge carmine" slip from Acropole I:16–14b.*]

14. Jar rim, KS-39A. O.D. 22, thick flakey dark reddish gray slip. Reddish brown with medium medium grit and chaff, slip 5YR4/2. Le Brun 1971:Fig. 61:20; Carter 1981:Fig. 10:3.

15. Jar rim, KS-39H. O.D. 28, thick flakey yellowish-red slip. Red with gray core and medium medium grit and light medium chaff, slip 5YR5/6. [Ware and slip like that found in Acropole l:16–15.*]

16. Painted body sherd, KS-39B. Fugitive black paint on flakey white slip, checkerboard and stripe pattern. Red with gray core and light medium grit, slip 10YR8/2 and paint 7.5YR3/2. [Like material from Acropole I:16–14b.*]

17. Jar rim, KS-39C. O.D. 18, thick flakey dark reddish-gray slip. Red with medium medium grit and chaff, slip 5YR4/2.

18. Jar rim, KS-39A. O.D. 24, thick flakey red slip. Red with medium medium grit and chaff, slip 2.5YR4/6. [This is the "rouge carmine" slip from Acropole I:16–14b.*]

19. Jar rim, KS-39C. O.D. 18, fugitive dark brown paint over white slip. Dark brown with light medium grit and chaff, paint 7.5YR3/2 and slip 5Y7/3.

20. Jar rim, KS-39B. O.D. 20, flakey reddish-brown slip. Red with gray core and light medium grit, slip 10R3/1 interior and 2.5YR6/4 exterior.

21. Painted carinated jar shoulder, KS-39. O.D. 21, flakey red and black paint on pale yellow slip. Greenish yellow with medium medium chaff, paint 10R4/6 and slip 5Y8/3.

22. Stamp seal, KS-108. Light green translucent alabaster, Late Uruk style.

23. Flint arrowhead, KS-108. Honey-colored brown flint. Date uncertain but found near item 22 among Uruk sherd scatter.

24. Copper-bronze fragment, KS-49. Date uncertain.

25. Burned clay door lock sealing, KS-308. Fabric impressions in exterior depressions and string and cane impressions on interior. Almost certainly of Susa III date.

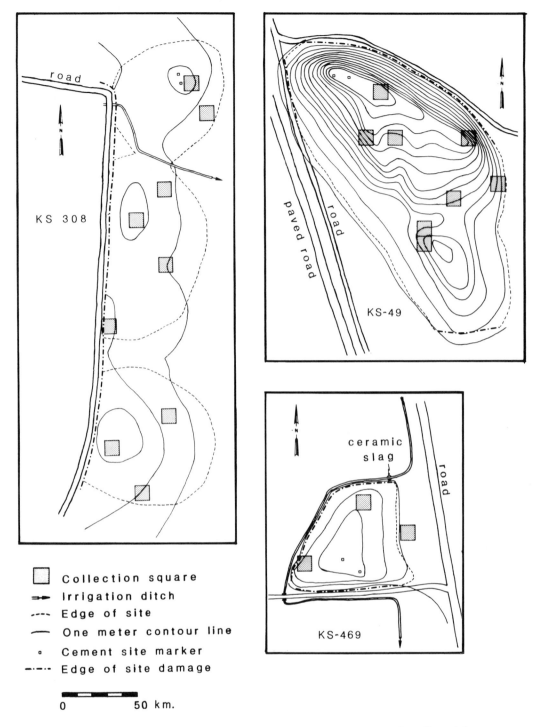

KS 308

☐ Collection square
⇒ Irrigation ditch
---- Edge of site
— One meter contour line
▫ Cement site marker
—·—·· Edge of site damage

0   50 km.

Figure 43. Maps of KS-308, KS-49, and KS-469 showing areas systematically collected during author's 1977 survey.

Chapter 7

Early Historic Cultures

ROBERT SCHACHT

Introduction

The archaeology of southwest Iran during the third and second millennia B.C., with special attention to the archaeological culture usually known as Elamite, is the broad subject of this chapter.[1] Its purpose is to examine the development of the settlement systems in southwest Iran during this time from a regional perspective, in the tradition inspired by Robert McC. Adams (1962, 1965). This is one line of evidence needed to understand the expanding scope and changing nature of the developing states in southwest Iran. This same period of time, seen from the perspective of ceramics from Level III at Godin Tepe is examined by Henrickson in chapter 8.

Table 30 illustrates the chronology for the third and second millennia. During this time, the nascent states described in the preceding chapters grew from barely recognizable local states into powerful, historically known nation states and empires transcending significant geographical and cultural barriers. The parallel evolution in Mesopotamia, the neighboring region to the west, profoundly influenced this process. The distinctive writing systems, which had begun in both regions with pictographic signs, evolved at comparable rates into more stylized and conventional written languages: Sumerian in Mesopotamia, and Proto-Elamite in Iran. Urbanism also developed during these millennia, although the largest Mesopotamian center was usually several times larger than the largest Iranian center.

The history of relations between the two regions is filled with trading, raiding, and conquests. Since these events have been chronicled elsewhere (e.g., Stolper 1984), it suffices here to make three points.

First, southwest Iran was a principal source of strategic natural resources coveted by Mesopotamia, such as metals, precious stones, and perhaps wood for construction. It was an intermediary for still other valued resources from regions farther to the east (Kohl 1978; Sarianidi 1971; Herrmann 1968).

Second, and to some extent as a result, parts of southwest Iran were repeatedly conquered and annexed by Mesopotamian rulers. Notable among these were the early Sargonids and the rulers of the Third Dynasty of Ur who directed conquests taking place during the last half of the third millennium B.C. One of the most tangible influences of the resulting Mesopotamian culture was expressed in the bureaucracy of southwestern Iran and its written records; for hundreds of years before and after 2000 B.C., most of the records used Akkadian, Sumerian, or Old Babylonian signs. In their format, these records are often nearly indistinguishable from those produced in Mesopotamia. Certainly many more subtle cultural influences were also present.

Third, qualitative changes in the nature of Mesopotamian state organization continued to occur throughout the early historic era (Larsen 1979).

Summary of Regional Surveys and Excavations

During the second and third millennia B.C., population concentrated in three principal areas in southwest Iran (cf. Young 1963b:12–13): the central Zagros, the lowland steppe, and the Marv Dasht region in Fars (figure 44). A more detailed description of these regions is presented in chapter 2. A summary of archaeological surveys within each of these regions follows.

The Central Zagros Region

Situated in the central Zagros around the town of Kermanshah, this region is about 170 kilometers long from east to west and 120 kilometers from north to south (figure 57). It can be subdivided into three adjacent areas: the Mahidasht Valley, the Kangavar Valley, and the south slopes of the Kuh-i Garin Mountains of the Kangavar Valley (see also chapter 2). Clearly, this region must have been of great historical importance. It has been identified previously as a coherent entity (Young 1963b:16–17; map I: "Population center D"), and associated, at least in part, with Parsua(sh) of the first millennium B.C. (Levine 1977a:138, 140). During the mid-second millennium B.C., the central Zagros region may have been the home base of the Kassites (cf. Goff 1968:129; Drower 1973:437). Before this time, some of this same region may have been called Shimashki (Stolper 1982:45–46; but see Vallat 1980:8–9 and 1985:6–16, who would locate Shimashki in Kerman), or possibly Awan (Vallat 1985:27).

We are also grouping in the central Zagros region other concentrations in Kangavar and in the various valleys along the south slopes of the Kuh-i Garin. To all of this might be added the settlements in the Borujerd Valley (see below). Consequently, the proposed identity of Shimashki might appear overly complex. Yet this complexity is supported in the historical sources which describe Shimashki as consisting of six "lands," at least five of which had their own local "governor" (ENSÍ) (Lambert 1972:footnote 71; but see Vallat 1985:7 for a different reading of the text). For the moment, it must be admitted that, despite the immense importance of the Kassite homeland and the country of Shimashki for understanding early Iran, we simply do not know where these historic entities were located. (On the difficulty of associating historic entities with archaeological assemblages, see Kramer 1977.) What we do know is that the central Zagros was the center of one of the principal ceramic traditions of early historic southwest Iran, exemplified by Giyan IV–II, Godin III, and Baba Jan IV (see chapter 8).

Archaeological surveys have catalogued some 166 sites dating to the second or third millennium B.C. in this region. We begin our review of the archaeology with the high valleys south of Kuh-i Garin and proceed down in altitude. This discussion is necessarily somewhat general, stressing patterns of distribution. A more detailed evaluation of the ceramic evidence is included in chapter 8.

The Kuh-i Garin (figure 57) rises to peaks of over 3,280 meters. Its south slopes contain a series of small valleys at elevations between 1,640 and 1,970 meters, including the Badawar, Khawa, and Alishtar plains (figures 13, 57). Goff (1971:147) reports about thirty-five "Bronze Age sites" scattered about these plains over an area some 80 kilometers long and 12 kilometers wide. She excavated one of these, Baba Jan (Goff 1976). Earlier, Stein (1940:277–311) excavated a number of these sites during his brief stay. The largest settlement found by Stein was Girairan, which has an area of about 13 hectares, but most of the sites are small, and many may be no more than cemeteries.

At 1,370 to 1,675 meters above sea level, the Kangavar Plain has been described as "a major hub of communications along the great High Road [the Khorasan Road] from Mesopotamia onto the Iranian plateau" (Young 1975:24). The Kangavar basin is shaped like a capital Y and encloses more than 1,000 square kilometers. This basin is well known for the excavations at Tepe Giyan in the Nehavand branch (Contenau and Ghirschman 1935), and at Godin Tepe near the town of Kangavar (Young 1969a; Young and Levine 1974; see Henrickson, chapter 8, for a discussion of the deposits at Godin Tepe). Archaeological surveys of this basin led to the discovery of fifty-six sites containing a total of about 84 hectares of occupation dating to the "Godin period" (Godin III). This was "the most populous period in the prehistory of the valley" (Young 1966, 1975a:26). Of this occupied area, 18 hectares are at Godin Tepe itself.

The Gamas Ab River leaves the Kangavar basin via a narrow valley 19 kilometers long and then enters the plain of Sahneh which is roughly 32 kilometers long and 10 kilometers wide. Young (1966) surveyed this valley in 1961, finding four sites of second or third millennium date.

The Sahneh Valley constitutes an eastward extension of the great plain of Kermanshah. This plain has not yet been systematically surveyed, but tracts totaling 1,062 square kilometers out of a planned survey area of 2,485 square kilometers have been examined. The result was seventy sites with Godin III material, "and many of the sites are substantial in both hectarage and depth of deposit" (Levine 1976a:289–290). Since the survey is about 40 percent complete, a total of 150 sites for the entire plain would not be unexpected. If so, this would be the largest concentration of second and third millennium B.C. sites anywhere in southwest Iran. Unfortunately, as yet we have no information about the sizes of these sites, but none is bigger than Godin Tepe (Young 1977:392, note 13).

We might include the Borujerd Valley in this region, as Young has done. He remarks that the great number of sites in the Borujerd region suggests that the area was more densely populated in the second and third

Robert Schacht

millennia B.C. than it is today (Young 1963b:12; cf. 1966:231–32). The Borujerd Valley is geographically distinct from the rest of this northwestern region, being at least 30 kilometers east of the closest parts of the Nehavand and Alishtar plains. Yet it appears closely tied to the Kangavar region during the early historic periods (Young 1966:230–35) and has been suggested as a possible location for ancient Shimashki (Stolper 1984:20).

The Lowland Steppe

The second great concentration of settlement in southwest Iran during the early historic periods lies in the lowland steppe (figures 6, 44). From northwest to southeast, the plains best known for settlements during the early historic periods are Deh Luran, Susiana, and Ram Hormuz (Carter 1971).

The Susiana Plain, on which the ancient urban center of Susa lies, had by far the largest concentration of settlement on the lowland plains. Besides Susa, which reached a maximum extent of 85 hectares during the second millennium B.C., a new 100-hectare settlement was built on a previously unoccupied locale now known as Chogha Zanbil. Some ninety settlements in the Susiana Plain scattered over an area of about 3,700 square kilometers have been dated to the early historic periods. Six more sites of these periods have been identified in the 643 square kilometers of the Deh Luran Plain; seven more lie in the 217 square kilometers of the Ram Hormuz Plain. The largest centers in Deh Luran were at Tepe Goughan (15 hectares) and Tepe Musiyan (13.5 hectares). In Ram Hormuz, the largest was Tepe Bormi (18 hectares).

Excavation at sites of the early historic periods on the plains has been in process for more than eighty years, particularly at Susa. (For a bibliographic summary, see Stève, Gasche, and Meyer 1980:107–16.) Important excavations have also been done in the Susiana Plain at Chogha Zanbil (Ghirshman 1966b, 1968), Haft Tepe (cf. Carter 1971:93–101), and Tepe Sharafabad (Schacht 1975a); in the Deh Luran Plain at Tepe Musiyan (Gautier and Lampre 1905) and Tepe Farukhabad (Wright 1981b); in the Ram Hormuz Plain at Tall-i-Ghazir (Caldwell 1968; Carter 1971:256–71); and on the Persian Gulf southwest of Shiraz at Bandar Bushehr (Pezard 1914).

These numerous and often extensive excavations have allowed the definition of a number of chronological subdivisions on the lowland plains, making it possible to analyze trends in population growth (Adams 1962; Carter 1971; Schacht 1973, 1976). These studies suggest that during the early historic periods, the aggregate population reached a total nearly twice that of any previous era (Schacht 1973). It may be that this relatively rapid population growth was in a large part due to the adoption of Mesopotamian administrative

and irrigation technology (Schacht 1976; Carter 1984:179).

The Marv Dasht Region in Fars

The third major concentration of settlement in southwest Iran was in the Fars province, in the Marv Dasht Plain northeast of Shiraz (figures 15, 44). Sumner (1972) found about eighty early historic sites (phases V and VI) scattered over an area of about 1,500 square kilometers at elevations between 1,500 and 1,675 meters. The largest of these settlements (up to 150 hectares) was Tepe Malyan (ancient Anshan), which was perhaps the largest urban center in all of southwest Iran during the early historic periods. Important excavations in Marv Dasht include Malyan (Sumner 1974, 1976) and Darvazeh (Nicol 1970; Jacobs 1980). On the basis of survey data, Sumner (1972:-193) has concluded that before the Islamic conquest, the population of Marv Dasht was greatest, by a substantial margin, during the Kaftari Period, circa 2000 B.C. (see figure 45).

Summary

Before the Islamic conquest, major concentrations of settlement were always localized in the following three major regions: the central Zagros, the lowland steppe, and Marv Dasht. These probably correspond, respectively, with Shimashki, Susa, and Anshan, the three most important historical entities in southwest Iran (Vallat 1980:6). Each major concentration of settlement contained at least one large urban center. In fact, Susa and Malyan grew to twice their previous maximum sizes. However, archaeologists familiar with the central Zagros do not know any comparably sized sites there (Levine and Henrickson, personal communication). Finally, where the archaeological evidence permits measurement—as in Kangavar, Susiana, and Marv Dasht—the regional population appears to be much larger than at any previous time. The available data on occupied hectares per period are summarized in figure 45.

History of Settlement

The following chronological review treats each of the three major regions of southwest Iran, insofar as data are available (table 30). In analyzing the settlement systems of each period, I employ two models borrowed from geography: the gravity model (Haggett 1965:35) and the rank-size model (Berry and Garrison 1958:84; Richardson 1973:240).

The Gravity Model

The gravity model[2] considers the sizes of settlements and the distances between them, on the assumption that interaction between settlements increases with size and decreases with distance. Johnson (1977:481–87) has reviewed the relevant literature with cautiously optimistic conclusions. Plog (1976:257) found that it appears valid for a wide range of types of human interaction. Also, Alden (1979a) has used the model in a study of Toltec sites in Mexico. These results are sufficiently encouraging to warrant our use of the model, but wherever possible, the analysis will be tested against other data such as historical records.

The Rank-Size Model

Johnson (chapter 4) discusses the rank-size model, which concerns the relationship between the rank of a settlement within a settlement system and the sizes of particular settlements. The rank-size model used here is a more general form, $P_i = KR_i^{-q}$, where R_i is the rank of settlement i, and P_i is its size.[3] The coefficient K and the exponent q can be statistically estimated for a given settlement system by log-log regression. The coefficient is the expected size of the largest settlement in the system, which takes into account all of the known settlements, not just the largest. If K is significantly smaller than the actual size of the largest settlement, then that center is called "primate," and it has special characteristics (Blanton 1976:255–57; Johnson 1977:496–500).

Previous archaeological studies have usually judged the "primate" status of settlements by more primitive methods than those used here. For example, they have sought visually a "concave" full-logarithmic graph of settlement size against settlement rank, or checked for a largest settlement which is more than twice the size of the next largest. The former requires a subjective assessment. The latter is ambiguous because it cannot differentiate the situation in which the biggest site is truly primate from the one in which the second largest site is smaller than expected.

The exponent q is an index of settlement size variability. If $q = 0$, all settlements are the same size. For many sedentary societies, $q = 1$ or nearly so. Because this case is common, many of those who are interested in the rank-size rule and who are reluctant to deal with exponents assume a priori that $q = 1$. This greatly simplifies the arithmetic but impoverishes the analysis, since as a settlement system becomes urbanized and centralized, the variability of settlement size, and therefore q, tends to increase (cf. Blanton 1976:254). Thus trends of change in K and q through time are linked to important changes in the nature and development of a settlement system. Consequently both K and q are useful variables in processual analysis.

Old Elamite I/Susa IV (ca. 2700–2200 B.C.)

Historical Background. By 3000 B.C., the urban revolution in Mesopotamia had produced the city of Uruk (Adams and Nissen 1972:18). At 400 hectares, this city was by far the largest in the world at the beginning of the third millennium B.C. By way of comparison, there were no cities anywhere in Iran larger than 80 hectares until after 2200 B.C. In Mesopotamia, urban architecture was already developing, including the construction of elevated temples and the earliest ziggurats, the architectural precursors of the Tower of Babel, and the earliest known palaces (Mallowan 1971:241, 273). Conflict was also growing in scale, forcing in Mesopotamia, at least, the abandonment of smaller settlements in favor of larger, fortified sites (Adams 1966:140; Adams and Nissen 1972:21) which formed the nucleus of at least eight organized city-states that were politically distinct (Adams 1972:742) or regional kingdoms (Jacobsen 1957:-125). This process was accompanied by "civil war" (S. Kramer 1959:35–44).

Although the state as a form of political organization had evolved perhaps a millennium earlier in Mesopotamia (Wright 1977:386), there is no convincing evidence for a centralized nation-state until the advent of Sargon of Akkad toward the end of this period (Larsen 1979:77–78). Before Sargon, an interesting but poorly understood Sumerian League had developed with a religious and cultic dimension that is difficult to describe in terms of familiar political realities (Westenholz 1979:109). Raiding or trading with the Iranian highlands is commemorated in the Sumerian epic, *Enmerkar and the Lord of Aratta* (Kramer 1959:17–28; Kohl 1978:468). It is also well documented archaeologically, with trade networks reaching as far east as the Indus Valley (Mallowan 1971:241, 254; Gadd 1971:453; Lamberg-Karlovsky 1972b).

Writing systems had been invented in both Iran and Mesopotamia in earlier periods. By the middle of the third millennium B.C., bureaucracy, as an indispensable instrument of statecraft, was born and thriving—at least in Mesopotamia (Lambert 1960, 1961).

A few hundred years later, Elam was subjugated by Sargonids, who left an Akkadian garrison at Susa and claimed lordship over all of Elam (Stolper 1984:10–16). Archaeological evidence for this form of subjugation includes a trend toward Mesopotamian ceramic styles and glyptic types, as well as the appearance of substantial numbers of tablets inscribed in Old Akkadian (Le Grain 1913; Amiet 1972:173–83; Carter 1980:25; 1984:135). At this time, the city may have become predominantly Semitic (Vallat 1980:3). Susa seems to have been the most important Elamite city and was associated during this period with the kings of Awan (Hinz 1971:644–54), the most conspicuous Elamite political center during this period (Stolper 1984:15). Little is known about the province of Fars during this time, apart from the cemetery at Jalyan (Miroschedji 1971; Carter 1984:136). The Marv

Robert Schacht

Dasht Plain appears to have been almost void of permanent settlements circa 2800–2200 B.C. (Carter 1984:152; Sumner 1985:21–22 and table I).

The Lowland Steppe. In central Khuzistan, the settlement system on the Susiana Plain is dominated by the urban center at Susa. During this period, it covered about 46 hectares. The rank-size distribution (figure 46) shows that Susa was larger than predicted by the settlements in the local system, and it was therefore "primate." The second largest settlement, Tepe Senjar, was smaller than predicted by the model. There were about 32 other sites ranging in size from 0.2 to 0.7 hectares. The gravity model for the interaction between sites shows that some of these sites fall into two major clusters or enclaves—one centered at Susa and the other at Chogha Pahn (KS-3) (figure 47). The rest of the sites can be considered as isolated, and they may have been relatively autonomous.

The gravity analysis points out several things about the Susa enclave. First, by comparison with later settlement systems, Susa is relatively weak. Small settlements within the northwest sector of the Susiana Plain (e.g., KS-17, KS-93) seem to have had a relatively low level of interaction with it. Second, the model takes into account only distance and settlement sizes. So, for example, we cannot assess how much of a barrier the Diz River was to the interaction between Susa and KS-37. Consequently, the status of KS-37 as a member of the Susa enclave is questionable.

West of Khuzistan, the Deh Luran Plain reached a peak of settlement in the early third millennium B.C. (Wright 1981b). Tepe Musiyan (13.5 hectares), Tepe Baula (5 hectares), and Tepe Farukhabad (3.5 hectares) all achieved their maximum size. In addition there was a settlement at Tepe Tenel Ramon (2 hectares; see Carter 1971:202–3, 226–31, 237).

The Central Zagros. Godin III:6–5 ceramics are scattered in the central Zagros (see chapter 8, and Henrickson 1984a:103–7 for more detail). Between Kuh-i Garin and Kuh-i-Sefid, the number of sites increases from only two in the Alishtar Plain during Godin III:6, to a scatter of sites throughout the neighboring valleys during Godin III:5. One of these is Baba Jan level 5 (Goff 1976). South of Kuh-i-Sefid, Godin III:6–5 ceramics are found primarily at Kamtarlan, Mirvali, and Surkh Dom in Rumishgan, and Dar Tanha in Pusht-i Kuh. Because of their isolation from the rest of the Godin III:6–5 sites, it may be that these southern sites are in the winter pasture areas of groups whose summer pastures lie on the southern fringes of the central Zagros region. Goff (1971:149) identifies Mirvali and Kamtarlan as large new settlements founded near springs at the western end of Rumishgan.

Polychrome pottery related to the Jemdet Nasr and other lowland developments not part of the Godin III tradition are found throughout Pusht-i Kuh and are more closely related to lowland Khuzistan (chapter 8). Bani Surmah is an important example, and Vanden Berghe (1968a:66; 1968b) has observed that the valleys in that region were more thickly populated then than they are today. Similar assemblages have been reported from a number of sites in Deh Luran (Gautier and Lampre 1905; Wright 1981b:111–25) and other nearby valleys (Carter 1984:141).

Historical Associations. A number of historical place names are associated with this general region during this period (Edzard, Farber, and Sollberger 1977:map 2 "Kerngebiet"). Nevertheless, the only entity located with certainty is Susa (Shushina). Elsewhere on the Susiana Plain was a place called Adamdun, known in several Sargonic texts from Girsu (Tello) in Mesopotamia, and Hupsana, known from an inscription from Susa of Puzur (=Kutik)-Inshushinak. Adamdun has been identified with Deh-No (KS-120) (Edzard, Farber, and Sollberger:4–5; Lambert 1972:74. Cf. Vallat 1985:25 who places Adamdun in the vicinity of Shushtar). In turn, Deh-No has been identified with ancient Hubshen on the basis of inscribed bricks found there, written in the late second millennium B.C. by kings of the Middle Elamite period (Stève 1968:300; Stève, Gasche, and Meyer 1980:101). Hupsana may simply be the ancestral form of the name Hubshen.

Deh-No does not appear to have been very large during the Susa IV period, but it is difficult to tell because of the extensive overburden of later occupations, possibly including a ziggurat (Carter 1984:162). Much of the pre-second millennium artifactual material recovered from the surface came from a series of erosion gullies on its east end (Carter 1971:144). The mound covers about 10 hectares, but because the third millennium B.C. artifacts are concentrated on one part of the exposed mound, an occupation area of only 3 hectares has been assigned to the site.

An even more important place during the third millennium, sometimes identified with a location near Dizful on the northern margin of the Susiana Plain, is Awan (Hinz 1971:647; Edzard and Farber 1974:20; Edzard, Farber, and Sollberger 1977:21). Dizful itself is a possibility, since Middle Elamite inscriptions have been found there (Stève, Gasche, and Meyer 1980:80). The most likely candidate among known archaeological sites of this area would be Tepe Charma (KS-100), a 4-hectare site between the modern towns of Dizful and Andimeshk. However, Dyson (1965:55–56) and Carter have made a good case for identifying Awan with Tepe Musiyan on the Deh Luran Plain, west of the Susiana Plain. Carter (1971:

229–30) observed that Musiyan appears to have reached its peak just before and during the dynasty of Awan, declining in importance in the late third and early second millennia. More recently, however, on the basis of Steinkeller (1982), Carter (1984:212, note 275) has identified Musiyan with ancient Urua, and Vallat (1985) has proposed that Awan consisted of the central Zagros region which in this chapter is identified with Shimashki.

An ancient text states explicitly that between Awan and Susa, on a river, is a place called Zahara (Sollberger and Kupper 1971:102, inscription of Rimush). It appears that Zahara must be Tepe Senjar (KS-7), the only currently known site larger than a village that fits the description.

Also problematical is the placement of Barahsum (Marhashi). It frequently is mentioned with Elam in conquest lists and is considered to be a northern neighbor of Awan and Zahara (cf. Edzard, Farber, and Sollberger 1977:24–25, map 2 "Kerngebiet"). It might therefore be located at Karieh Tepe, a high conical mound 180 meters in diameter about 100 kilometers northwest of Tepe Charma on the road to Khorramabad. This is a good location for a minor principality of the sort likely to rule the mountain districts between Dizful and Khorramabad (Goff 1971:132–33, 148). But Karieh Tepe seems too small for a place of such importance. Other possibilities include the "large" sites of Mirvali and Kamtarlan in Rumishgan, one of the two primary gateways from the ancient western highlands to the Susiana lowlands (chapter 8). It is even more likely that the location of Marhashi is to be sought north or east of Fars (Steinkeller 1982; Stolper 1984:11; Carter 1984:140, note 213; Vallat 1985:17–23).

The principal point to this excursion into historical geography is that the Susiana Plain appears in historical sources not as a unity, subordinate to Susa, but as a series of distinguishable entities—Susa, Zahara, Hupsana/Adamdun and perhaps Awan. At least Hupsana/Adamdun was semiautonomous: Mesopotamian sources treat it as an administrative district with its own governor distinct from Susa. Zahara, however, appears headed by a shakkanakkum, a political title applied at this time only "to vassals of foreign kings or of the Sargonic kings themselves" (Hallo 1957:100).

This interpretation of the historical geography of the plain is supported by the gravity model analysis, in which Tepe Senjar (Zahara?) is subordinate to Susa, but Chogha Pahn and Deh-No (Hupsana/Adamdun?) show less predicted interaction with Susa. It is also supported by cultural ecology, in that transhumant nomadism can be expected then, as now, to have exerted a divisive influence on Susiana: today, ethnic Lurs have winter pastures in the vicinity of Tepe Sen-

jar, and they seldom venture very far east of the Diz River. In contrast, ethnic Bahktiari winter their flocks in the eastern part of the plain and Arab peoples are among the inhabitants of the southern part (cf. Dez Irrigation Project 1958:figure II–2). Johnson (1973) has already demonstrated differences between ceramics from different parts of the plain in the fourth millennium B.C. Similar tests should be applied to the early historic periods. The point to which we shall return, however, is that previous investigations, perhaps overwhelmed by the volume of historical material from Susa, may have overestimated the control wielded by the inhabitants of that site over the rest of the plain.

The gravity model does not, however, show a basis for the historical relationship between Susa and Awan, regardless of whether Awan is identified with Musiyan, Tepe Charma, or some other site in or near Dizful. According to the model, a 5.5-hectare site underlying modern Dizful would have about the same amount of interaction with Susa as with Chogha Pahn. If such a site existed during Susa 4, the implied degree of interaction would support the historical sources and Hinz's assessment of the location of Awan. The association between Susa and Awan, as presently known, exists chiefly in the person of Kutik (Puzur)-Inshushinak. In one inscription from Susa, he is titled king of Awan, but elsewhere, in a number of other inscriptions, he is called "governor" (ENSÍ) of Susa and "viceroy" (GÌR.NITÁ) of Elam (Stolper 1984:15).

Susa V: Shimashki (ca. 2200–2000 B.C.)

Historical Background. The period which we are about to examine began with the decline of Akkadian influence in southwest Iran and the rise of a number of indigenous powers, particularly the Guti and the Shimashki. For our purposes, the decline of Akkadian influence took place with the ascendancy of the elusive Guti during the reign of the Akkadian King Shar-kalli-sharri, who reigned circa 2254–2230 B.C. (Middle Chronology) or circa 2352–2328 B.C. (Ultra-High Chronology). The Guti homeland may have been in the mountain valleys of Iran southwest of Kermanshah (Edzard and Farber 1974:71, map "Kerngebiet"; Edzard, Farber, and Sollberger 1977:65–66, map "Kerngebiet"), although a location farther to the north has also been suggested (Gadd 1971:444; see also Hallo 1979).

After a period of comparative anarchy, Mesopotamian military expeditions into southwest Iran resumed under Gudea of Lagash. They culminated with the annexation of Susa and its environs, including the unknown site of "Adamdun," by the Neo-Sumerian Dynasty. This annexation took place under Shulgi who reigned circa 2095–2048 (Middle Chronology) or circa 2232–2185 (Ultra-High Chronology). This subjugation is made abundantly clear not only in Mesopotamian sources but also at Susa, where administrative records from strata of this period are written in Sumerian and where Sumerian kings built temples (Stolper 1984:16–23).

Oppenheim (1967:27) regards the Neo-Sumerian state as essentially different from its predecessors. He notes that the Sumerians exercised control by governors and a centralized administration, whereas the kings of Akkad applied political and military coercion to support military garrisons in strategic locations (see also Larsen 1979:70; Westenholz 1979:113–41). This suggests that the Neo-Sumerians had a more highly evolved political system for effectively integrating new territories.

Mesopotamian hegemony over Khuzistan collapsed during the reign of Ibbi Sin (ca. 2029–2006 B.C. [Middle Chronology] or 2166–2143 B.C. [Ultra-High Chronology]). But Sumerian influence persisted in Khuzistan through the reign of the kings of Shimashki. Historical references to Shimashki begin near the end of Susa IV. They are common during the Third (Neo-Sumerian) Dynasty of Ur (Edzard and Farber 1974:181–82) and continue until at least the eighteenth century B.C. (High Chronology) in the Elamite royal titulary (cf. Kupper 1969). The period under consideration in this section continues until the end of the Shimashki Dynasty, at about the time of the reign of Gungunum of Larsa and Sumuabum of Babylon.

Marv Dasht Region in Fars. In Fars, sites contemporary with the Susa V (Old Elamite II) Period have not been systematically distinguished from those contemporary with the Old Elamite III Period, although a recent study by Nickerson (1983:194–200) demonstrating a temporal shift in the relative frequency of Kaftari Buff and Kaftari Red-Slipped wares indicates that a distinction might be possible (see also Sumner 1974:164–67). For the purposes of this study, however, we must be content with a consideration of the Kaftari settlement system which assumes the contemporaneity of all Kaftari sites; this study will be deferred to the next section.

The Central Zagros. In the central Zagros, the Godin III:4 assemblage dates to this period but is not found in the lowlands (chapter 8). The location of Shimashki (or Awan) is likely to be somewhere in this region. Candidates for the city of Shimashki—if indeed the name refers to a city and not a region—include Girairan in the Alishtar Plain just north of Khorramabad; Godin Tepe in the Kangavar Valley; and whatever other large sites of this period there may be in Mahidasht or elsewhere in the central Zagros region. Generally the distribution of sites in this region is somewhat more restricted and sparser than that of the previous phase, perhaps as a result of Sumerian military campaigns (R. Henrickson 1984b:107–11).

The Lowland Steppe. We are on firmer ground with respect to a reasonably well-dated settlement system in Khuzistan due to the work of Carter (1971:111–13 et seq.). The gravity model predicts a higher level of interaction than earlier (figure 49). The interaction coefficient between Chogha Pahn (KS-3) and Susa increases from 0.41 to 1.15. Unless the Diz River was a substantial obstacle to interaction, it would appear that Chogha Pahn was interacting a lot more with Susa and might have been subordinate to it. As a local center, however, the importance of Chogha Pahn did not suffer; it seems to have grown in size and is likely to have been a central place for KS-5 (as in Susa IV), KS-47, and KS-1 (Chogha Mish).

Tepe Charma (KS-100) (Awan?) and Deh No (Adamdun?) remained remote from the Susa and Chogha Pahn enclaves: their predicted interaction with sites in these enclaves is 0.31 or less. This conclusion agrees with historic records, which continue to treat Awan, Susa, and "Adamdun" as distinct entities. For example, the last Neo-Sumerian king claims to have suppressed an uprising in those three places by a military campaign lasting one day (Sollberger and Kupper 1971:158). "Adamdun" also appears frequently as a distinct administrative entity with its own "governor" (ENSÍ) in Ur III economic records. Awan, however, is rarely mentioned and no ENSÍ is recorded for it (Edzard and Farber 1974:3ff.; 20). In the southern sectors of the plain south of Haft Tepe ridge, only a few sites with late third millennium B.C. ceramics have been recognized; indeed, there may be important differences between the assemblages found there and those from Susa (cf. Carter 1971:165, KS-237).

The rank-size curve for Susa V (figure 48) shows the same pattern for large sites as observed earlier for Susa IV. Susa is much larger than expected, while the second largest site is much smaller than expected.

In economic texts of this period, the most common place name other than Susa is "Ashgupien" (Scheil 1908:tablets 28, 53, 60?, 64, 69?, 70, 73, 76?, 96?). Unless this is a part of Susa, the highest interaction coefficients from the gravity model suggest identifying Ashgupien with Tepe Kheif (KS-96), KS-57, or even Chogha Pahn (KS-3), for which coefficients with Susa are all between 1.15 and 1.46.

Old Elamite III (ca. 2000–1475 B.C.)

Historical Background. This period, often called "Sukkalmah," is contemporary with the First Dynasty of Babylon and the formative years of the Kassite rule in Mesopotamia. The Old Babylon dialect of Akkadian became the customary means of communication throughout the whole area (Postgate 1977:93), including Susa (Salonen 1962) and extending as far as Anshan (Tepe Malyan). Stolper (1976:91) has observed that a scribal school must have existed at Malyan in or before the Kaftari Period. He suggests that the school adopted pedagogical devices originating in Mesopotamia, but used wherever cuneiform script was taught. Correspondingly, Kaftari scribes at Malyan created administrative documents of Mesopotamian form and language.

Hammurabi, the most famous ruler of the time, promulgated a code of law that has fascinated generations of politicians and scholars. The principal surviving copy was written on a diorite stela which found its way to Susa, some 550 years later, presumably as one of Shutruk-Nahhunte's trophies of war (Hinz 1972:125). There it was discovered in the early twentieth century by French archaeologists who carried it to Paris as a trophy of archaeology (Pritchard 1958:138–39). But Hammurabi's Babylon was a one-man empire that faded soon after his death (Larsen 1979:75, 81).

Another one-man empire, that of Shamsi-Adad I, began the process of welding Assyria into a political unity, but this faltered under his successors due to Elamite and other pressures (Stolper 1984:30). Elam was ruled during most of the Old Elamite III period by a triumvirate: a *sukkal* or *sharrum* of Susa, a *sukkal* of Elam and Shimashki, and a *sukkalmah*, who was the highest official. The offices *sukkal* (minister or vizier) and *sukkalmah* (prime minister or grand vizier) originated as aides to the rulers of Mesopotamia, and sometimes Elam (cf. Hinz 1971:650) during the Early Dynastic III and Akkadian periods (Hallo 1957:112–21). Cameron (1936:71–72) showed that these offices were closely related and were often occupied by a succession of relatives. This provides a fascinating glimpse into the internal structure of the Elamite state, about which we still have much to learn (Hinz 1973:256; Vallat 1980:6; 1985:1–6). In any case, the minimum geographical dimensions of this Elamite state rank it as one of the largest polities of the early second millennium B.C. (Stolper 1984:31).

The Lowland Steppe. The Sukkalmah Period in central Khuzistan was a period of population growth (Carter 1971:101–11, 175, 182–5). During this period, probably more people were living on the Susiana Plain than ever before. The same was also true of the Marv Dasht Plain in Fars, although the maximum population size there may have been reached a little earlier.

In Khuzistan, Susa grew to an estimated 85 hectares. But more important, there was such an increase in the number and size of the local centers that Susa is no longer "primate," despite the fact that it is more than twice the size of the next largest settlement (fig-

ure 50). This surge in local centers is reflected in the gravity model analysis by a relatively high level of interaction. The overall morphology of the settlement system established in Susa IV remains the same: interaction centers are found at Susa and Chogha Pahn, which link together most settlements in the northwest and north central sectors of the plain. The southwest, southeast, and northeast sectors remain thinly settled by a scatter of isolated settlements. Despite their size of 7–8 hectares each, Tepe Charma (Awan?) and Deh No (Adamdun?) show only weak levels of predicted interaction with the centers of power. Several changes are worth noting:

1. Although they appear only weakly integrated, there is a significant increase in the number, size, and geographical range of settlements in the southwest plain. Perhaps this is a result of the development of the Shaur canal system (Schacht 1976, figure 11).
2. Chogha Pahn continues to grow as a regional center. It is now centrally located amid four other settlements with which it probably interacted: KS-5, 39, 47, and 111. This represents an increase from three interacting neighbors during Susa IV. The site has also doubled in size since Susa IV.
3. A dense cluster of larger-than-average sites develops in the southern part of the Susa enclave. It is centered at KS-53, a 13.5-hectare site that has recently been damaged by heavy earth-moving equipment (Carter 1971:123). Haft Tepe may have been occupied late in this period, but there is some uncertainty about this (Negahban 1969:177; 1972:162; Stève, Gasche, and Meyer 1980:63, note 15; 97, note 56).

Carter's analysis of ceramics (1971:104, 131ff.), both from the excavations at Susa and from surface survey from all parts of the plain, was unusually detailed, enabling a number of further observations. Large, shouldered stump-based jars (Type 5; cf. Gasche 1973:type 21b) were frequently found on the surface of small sites in the northern half of the northwest and north central sectors. A few types were found at more sites in the eastern and southern sectors than in the northwest quadrant (types 7, 8a, 8b, 12). Others were found only in the northwest quadrant (types 2, 5, 6, 11b, 13a, 13b). Of the seventeen types and subtypes, all but one were found on sites in the north central sector; ten on sites in the northeast; nine on sites in the southwest; and only five on sites in the southeast quadrant. In other words, the types of ceramics found on sites vary considerably from one part of the plain to another.

The average size of sites containing certain pottery types also varied. Painted wares (type 13) were found only on sites of at least 3.2 hectares. Fine ware button-base goblets (type 3), female figurines, and bed models are other examples of types which might be considered "elite" or "urban" in this sense.

West of central Khuzistan, data on settlement are not yet well controlled with the exception of Deh Luran. There the settlements of the early second millennium appear to be continuations on a smaller scale of sites which peaked in the final phases of the prehistoric and in the early third millennium (Carter 1971:240–42). Tepe Musiyan is still the principal center (13.5 hectares) with three other sites of 2.5 to 4 hectares.

On the Ram Hormuz Plain to the east, after an apparently lengthy abandonment, two small settlements are known (Carter 1971:282–85). About 65 kilometers north of Ram Hormuz, the Izeh Plain had five settlements ranging in size from 1.1 to 4.5 hectares during the Sukkalmah Period (Bayani 1979:-102). Not far from the Susiana-Anshan high road which passes through Kurangun is an impressive rock carving which lies 200 meters above the Fahlian Plain. On the basis of parallels with seal impressions of Susian rulers, it can be dated to the seventeenth century B.C. A similar relief, obscured by a Sasanian carving, has been found at Naqsh-i Rustam near Pasargadae (Carter 1984:154).

Marv Dasht Region in Fars. At this time, the Marv Dasht Plain in Fars became more populous than ever before. The Kaftari assemblage used to identify settlements of this period actually began earlier, during the preceding Susa V/Shimashki Phase in Khuzistan (table 32). But we assume that the population growth which began then did not crest until after 2000 B.C. By this time, Malyan (Anshan) had grown to at least 130 hectares, much larger than any other known settlement in southwest Iran up to that time. Malyan was certainly "primate" at that time in terms of the rank-size distribution of the settlement system. But even more impressive is the utter lack of intermediate-sized settlements (figure 52). It is also clear that the seventy Kaftari settlements were grouped into a number of distinct clusters (Sumner 1972:208; 1981:5–6, 10–11, 19; 1985:22). These clusters have been described as follows:

1. At the west end of the plain lies the Malyan cluster. Besides Malyan, the group contained nine other sites, several of which were 4–5 hectares in area. This cluster is separated from the next by about 7 kilometers distance.

2. In the central part of Marv Dasht are three adjacent clusters in an area corresponding to Sumner's Soon irrigation region which was probably begun prior to 4500 B.C. and has often supported a high population density.

a. The Charki group is located just east of the Malyan group. The chief settlements are Charki (6.3 hectares) and Kaftari (4.7 hectares). There are other sites ranging in size from 0.5 to less than 2.9 hectares.

b. Along the Kur River north of Charki is another group. The largest member, site 7H16, was 7.9 hectares. There are thirteen other sites in the group, ranging in size from 0.1 to 2.3 hectares.

c. East of Charki and downriver from group (b) is a third group containing several sites of moderate size: Ak (less than 8.1 hectares), Sureh (6.9 hectares), and Karatepe (10.5 hectares). These are situated fairly close to one another, and it seems unlikely that they were all fully occupied at the same time. There are seven other sites in this group, ranging from 1.0 to 2.4 hectares. These three groups are separated from each other by a massif more than 10 kilometers long, rising more than 800 meters above the valley floor.

3. Beginning 7.5 kilometers east of the large central cluster, along the Sivand River, is another group of settlements, the largest of which was probably Kamin (9.6 hectares). Ten other settlements ranged in size from 0.4 to about 3 hectares. Qaleh, the second largest Kaftari site at 15 hectares (Sumner, personal communication) lies 15 kilometers upstream in an isolated valley. This cluster is separated by about 6 kilometers from the nearest site in the next group. The site of Persepolis was subsequently built in this area.

4. The Tali Sabz (Sohz) cluster is located near the point at which the Kur and Sivand rivers merge (figure 15). Tali Sabz once covered 12 hectares, making it the third largest Kaftari site in the Marv Dasht. Between 1937 and 1972, it was leveled to make bricks. Cuneiform tablets and rich burials with bronze vessels and weapons were discovered there. The second largest site is Chel Burgi (6.2 hectares), and there are four other sites within 10 kilometers. This part of the valley is much more densely populated than it ever was before, leading Sumner (1981:7, 8, 19–22) to suspect that a new irrigation system might have been introduced at this time.

In addition to these clusters, there are a few isolated sites: two in the northwest along the upper Kur River, and four to the southeast downriver. The two sites in the extreme southeast are Teimuran and Darvazeh (figure 15). Other assemblages with Kaftari-style artifacts include Tell-i Nokhodi near Pasargadae, Liyan at Bushire on the Persian Gulf, and sites in the Fasa and Darab valleys southeast of Shiraz (figure 15; Carter 1984:154).

In terms of the gravity model, the Malyan cluster, the three adjacent clusters in the central part of Marv Dasht, and the Tali Sabz cluster (i.e., 1, 2, and 4 above) form the primary interaction network. Malyan is the principal center, linked to at least one of the 5–12 hectare centers in each of the three central clusters. These clusters all lie within 50 kilometers of Malyan and together occupy most of the Marv Dasht Plain. The Sivand River cluster and the large site of Qaleh, however, appear to be beyond the range of this primary interaction network. The same is true for the relatively isolated sites of Teimuran and Darvazeh, farther to the southeast. Two-thirds of the Kaftari sites are within 36 kilometers of Malyan, and most of those are linked into the primary network. In this context, the growth of the Tali Sabz cluster appears to represent an attempt by Malyan to assert control over the eastern half of the plain. In this sense, Malyan may have controlled more of Marv Dasht than Susa controlled of the Susiana Plain.

Sites with the Shogha and Teimuran assemblage may to some extent be contemporary with Kaftari (table 33). However, their distribution is not confined to the eastern end of the plain, although eleven of these sites are found east of the Sivand River and only six are to the west (Sumner 1972:209).

The Kaftari distribution is thus very different from that in central Khuzistan:

1. There are more sites. To some extent, this may reflect the fact that the Kaftari assemblage lasts longer. But even if we combine Old Elamite II (Susa V) and III settlements, there are still fewer sites in Susiana than there are Kaftari sites.
2. There are more clusters of sites.
3. There are fewer isolated sites.
4. Clusters are more evenly distributed across the plain.

An important underlying similarity between the two plains is that neither should necessarily be considered as culturally, politically, or economically uniform. A high priority for future work should be to determine the relationships within and between these clusters.

The Central Zagros. In Luristan, the Sukkalmah Period appears contemporary with Godin III:2 (chapter 8) and Giyan III as defined by Dyson (1973:694–97; 710). An expansion of the Giyan IV–III tradition took place at this time with wares of this type said to be found most frequently in the area that we have called the Kuh-i Garin district of the central Zagros region. Dyson has suggested that, relative to earlier periods, the number of sites tended to decrease as population grouped into "cities," the biggest of which was re-

ported to be Girairan in the Alishtar Plain. Girairan was probably fully occupied (13 hectares) during this period. Giyan was also large enough at this time to be called a large town (Carter 1984:155).

Henrickson (chapter 8) observes that Godin III:2 pottery is markedly more common, widespread, and uniform throughout its distribution in Luristan, Mahidasht, and into the Pusht-i Kuh than during any other phase of Godin III. From this, one might conclude that a population maximum was reached (Young 1977:393). This maximum may coincide with the maximum importance of historical Shimashki, first as an autonomous kingdom, and then as an integral part of Elam under the Sukkalmahs (Stolper 1982:48; R. Henrickson 1984b:108–13; cf. Vallat 1980:6–7).

Middle Elamite I (ca. 1475–1300 b.c.)

The Lowland Steppe. This period corresponds with the emergence of the Kassites as an international power (Brinkman 1972:274–75). It is defined archaeologically by characteristic pottery types found at Haft Tepe (Carter 1971:93–101) and Susa, and historically by the "Kidinuid" dynasty (table 34 and Vallat 1985:45–47). Because of the growth of Haft Tepe and its increasing importance as a regional center (conveniently summarized by Carter 1984:156–60), coinciding with an apparent decline at Susa, there would be ample justification for calling this the Haft Tepe Phase. Although Kassites, especially during the reign of Kurigalzu II (1332–1308 b.c., Middle Chronology), conquered Susa, Elam, and Marhashi, the extent and duration of Kassite domination over Elam are unknown and Kassite control of Susiana seems to have been only a brief episode (Stolper 1984:35).

Susa remained the largest center on the plain. But because of the growth at Haft Tepe and the continuation of many medium-sized sites established during the Sukkalmah Phase, Susa declined even further from the status of "primate" center that it had enjoyed in the third millennium. Despite the growth at Haft Tepe, it too is not as large as the model predicts from the rest of the settlement system (figure 53).

The gravity model analysis (figure 54) indicates that the northwest and north central sectors of the Susiana Plain were probably related by an interaction network. Susa (55 hectares), with one associated village (KS-23), was a central place for the following sites: (1) Haft Tepe (30 hectares, interaction coefficient with Susa = 10.0), which was a central place for KS-1x, 53, 59, 72, 90, 93, 96—sites of 1 to 6.5 hectares; (2) Chogha Pahn (20 hectares, interaction coefficient with Susa = 2.25), a central place for KS-39, 47, 111, and perhaps 37—sites of 3.5, 2.5, 3.5, 10.7 hectares, respectively; (3) Tepe Senjar (13 hectares, interaction coefficient with Susa = 1.64), a central place for

KS-11, 15—sites of 5 hectares each; (4) Tepe Galeh Bangoon/KS-37 (10.7 hectares, interaction coefficient with Susa = 2.40).

The settlement system morphology predicted by the gravity model is evidently essentially unchanged from what it was before, in the following regards:

1. The principal interaction network remains confined to the northwest and north central sectors of the plain, bypassing a few small settlements with low levels of interaction with other settlements (KS-18, 36, 79).

2. Susa remains the principal center, though in temporary decline. Chogha Pahn, Haft Tepe, and Tepe Senjar remain as local centers, growing in size.

3. The southern and eastern sectors of the plain continue to be occupied by a loose scatter of weakly interacting settlements.

   A new element is the emergence of several small clusters of settlements. These are predicted to interact with each other at the same level that interactions are postulated by the gravity model within the main interaction network in the northwest quadrant of the plain:

   a. KS-145 (5 hectares) and KS-146 (2 hectares) on the east bank of the Karkheh floodplain.

   b. The Ahu Dasht enclave: KS-233 (8.5 hectares), KS-234 (6 hectares), KS-235 (2 hectares). This area is subject to annual flooding. Each site may be completely surrounded by water for weeks at a time. An intensive study of this enclave would be worthwhile.

4. Tepe Charma (Awan?) and Deh No (Adamdun/Hubshen?) continue to be fully occupied at 9–9.5 hectares. The gravity model still postulates only a weak interaction between them and other settlements because of their remoteness and the relatively small size of their nearest neighbors. In addition, rivers and floodplains impose barriers which the gravity model does not take into account.

There are other ways of testing the results of the gravity model. Written records from Haft Tepe support both the ascendancy of Haft Tepe and the continuing primacy of Susa (Stolper 1984:32–35). The large number of tablets and other inscribed artifacts from Haft Tepe testify to its rank among the elite centers of the day. Nevertheless, although royal inscriptions and references to royalty are found at Haft Tepe (cf. Reiner 1973), royal titles proclaim "king of Susa and Anshan"—not king of Kabnak, the possible ancient name of Haft Tepe (Herrero 1976; Stève, Gasche, and Meyer 1980:97; but see Hinz 1972:123–24). In fact, the principal official of Kabnak is said to be subordinate to the king of Susa.

The distribution of pottery types is also of interest. Even within the northwest sector, there were relatively few examples of Haft Tepe types at Susa (Carter 1971:77, 94, 96–97, 100; Stève, Gasche, and Meyer 1980:76). Some Susa types are not known from Haft Tepe (Carter 1971:98). Several of the defining types of the Middle Elamite I (Carter's Transitional Phase types 1 and 2) are very rare outside the northwest sector. In contrast, the goblet forms are found on *more* sites outside the northwest sector (Carter 1971:93–95, 131–32, 147–48, 157–58, 166–67, 171, types 3 and 4).

We can also test the apparent isolation of the small villages through excavation. Our example in this case is Tepe Sharafabad, KS-36 (Schacht 1975a). If we had judged the extent of Elamite occupation at this site on the basis of sherd scatter, we would have concluded that the site was almost completely occupied. However, excavation revealed that the preserved built-up area was only about 0.2 hectare, plus several pits or refuse dumps on the margins of the site. Nevertheless, even if we used the larger area of surface scatter in the computations, Tepe Sharafabad is too small and far away from the nearest contemporary settlement to result in an interaction coefficient comparable to those between sites of the primary network.

The excavations at Sharafabad revealed an assemblage very similar to that found elsewhere in contemporary sites in the northwest quadrant of the plain, including an inscribed cylinder seal and an inscribed tablet fragment (Schacht 1975a:325–26). The cylinder seal has a presentation scene like others from Susa and bears names attested on tablets from this center. In fact, both names appear on a tablet from Susa, in which one of the individuals is called a canal inspector and scribe of Kabnak (Haft Tepe?). This tablet has been dated to an earlier period, Ur III/Old Akkadian, on the basis of spelling and script, so it is not likely that the same people are involved. However, it is possible that these artifacts are vestiges of a general process, which has been summarized in hypothetical form as follows:

> a combination of capital accumulation at Susa plus investment in the creation of an irrigated garden/orchard at Sharafabad by some unknown agency plus a general rise in population *created* a land rent (in the classical sense) on the garden/orchard and perhaps the adjacent fields, which led to the transformation of the community into a rural estate (Schacht 1973:110–11).

It is also possible that this "estate" was owned by a landlord with ties to Susa or other elite centers of the primary interaction network.

During this period, an important new settlement was established near Ahwaz at Chogha Haft Piran

(KS-2X). It lies on the Karun River, just south of the Golestan suburb of Ahwaz (Carter 1971:186–87). Although the entire site measures 500 by 700 meters, its second millennium area appears to have been between 5 and 10 hectares (Carter 1984:168). So far, this is the only known pre-Achaemenid site in Khuzistan south of Ahwaz. The nearest pre-Achaemenid site in the southwest Susiana Plain is located about 45 kilometers north of Chogha Haft Piran.

West of Khuzistan, in Deh Luran a significant change took place in the settlement system. The two largest sites were abandoned and replaced by two new large sites. Tepe Musiyan was replaced as the principal center by Tepe Goughan (15 hectares during this period), 3 kilometers to the northwest. Tepe Baula was replaced by the similarly sized Tepe Patak (Carter 1984:186). In Luristan, Giyan II pottery is concentrated in the Kuh-i Garin district. A few sites in the Hulailan Valley (e.g., Tepe Guran) seem to be all that remains of the Giyan tradition south of the Kuh-i-Sefid (Thrane 1970; Goff 1971:147). Unfortunately, the nature of the Godin III:1 assemblage does not permit definition of its distribution beyond Godin Tepe itself (chapter 8, this volume).

East of Khuzistan, in Ram Hormuz, settlement grew significantly. The assemblages there differ from those in central Khuzistan, and it has not yet been possible to differentiate middle from late second millennium settlements (Carter 1971:285–88). Tepe Bormi became the principal town, reaching a size of 18 hectares by the end of the second millennium. Tall-i Ghazir (7.5 hectares) remained an important center, and there were five villages as well. The geographical center of settlement shifted eastward with the growth of Tepe Bormi, located south of the modern city of Ram Hormuz on the Ala River. These two sites probably mark the position of the road between Susa and Fars (Carter 1984:168).

About 50 kilometers north of Tepe Bormi is the small valley of Qaleh Tol. At this site Stein (1940:-125–26) found an Elamite relief carved in stone at the main mound, which was covered with the crumbling remains of recent buildings, rising to a height of 20 meters above the surrounding ground. Pottery collected from this site ranges in date from late Susiana through Achaemenian, including a number of sherds of second millennium B.C. painted wares similar to those known from Ram Hormuz (Carter 1971:225). An old route connects Ram Hormuz and Qaleh Tol with Izeh, about 25 kilometers north of Qaleh Tol.

In the Izeh Plain the settlement system changed markedly (Bayani 1979:99–102). Although the total population probably changed little, four of the five Sukkalmah Phase sites were abandoned and replaced by three new sites. Two of these were relatively large (5.0–6.6 hectares). Here, too, the middle and late second millennia could not be distinguished. A small ex-cavation was made in the largest site, named Izeh (Wright et al., 1979:106–13). The ceramics closely resemble the contemporary assemblages from Ram Hormuz.

Marv Dasht Region in Fars. In the Marv Dasht Plain of Fars, most of the sites occupied during the Kaftari Phase were abandoned. Malyan was reduced to 50 hectares. There were two ceramic assemblages in the plain at this time, but neither has been found at many sites.

The Qaleh assemblage, which evolved from earlier Kaftari pottery, has been found only at Malyan and eight other sites scattered across the plain, in the Ram Hormuz and Izeh regions of eastern Khuzistan, and at Haft Tepe, where only a few sherds of this type have been found (Carter 1984:174). Most of the Marv Dasht sites are 3–9 hectares in extent, and Shogha-Teimuran ceramics are found on all of them (Jacobs 1980:132).

The dating of Shogha-Teimuran sites is not yet capable of distinguishing phases of second millennium settlement despite a stratified sequence of dates from Tepe Darvazeh (tables 32, 33). Nevertheless, there are only about fourteen possible habitation sites, mostly east of the Sivand River. At Malyan, only about a dozen Shogha-Teimuran sherds have been found; the other sites west of the Sivand have only a few sherds each, calling into question whether they should be regarded as settlements or merely as isolated occurrences, such as burials (Sumner n.d.:16, note 4). Sumner (1985:12) has identified twelve of these "special" sites in Marv Dasht. Jacobs (1980:125–28) was unable to discover any additional Shogha-Teimuran ceramics at these sites.

If we consider Qaleh and Shogha-Teimuran together, most of the sites, including five sites of 3–9 hectares, are located east of the Sivand River, in the eastern half of the plain. Only three sites, one of which is Malyan, lie in the western half. Obviously, there has been a drastic change since the Kaftari Period, and much remains to clarify the chronology of the Shogha-Teimuran assemblage and its relationship to the Qaleh ceramics.

Middle Elamite II (1300–1000 B.C.)

Historical Background. This period is characterized by a successful revolt against Kassite rule in Elam (Brinkman 1972:276–77) and the rise of Assyria and Elam as ambitious powers which plundered Babylonia. It may have been at this time that the Elamites carried Hammurabi's stela with the law code to Susa (Roux 1964:217). The construction of the huge site of Chogha Zanbil on an unoccupied ridge near the geographical center of the Susiana Plain illustrates the ambition of Elam at this time. This period begins historically with the rise of Ige-halki and his successors in the late fourteenth century B.C. (Stolper 1984:36, note 271).

Although the alliance between Susa and Anshan persisted in this period and was strengthened by the growth of towns in intermontane valleys such as Izeh and Ram Hormuz (Carter 1984:180), the archaeological assemblage at Malyan, with its ties to Khuzistan, differs from the Shogha-Teimuran ceramics that characterize the rest of the sites in the Marv Dasht at this time (Carter and Stolper 1976:37, 42). The only part of southwest Iran for which the settlement systems of this period can be distinguished from those of other periods are Khuzistan and Luristan.

The Lowland Steppe. In central Khuzistan, the most significant changes were the abandonment of many of the smaller settlements and the construction of a huge ceremonial center. Perhaps the center was intended to be the new capital of Khuzistan, in a centrally located position on top of Haft Tepe ridge. This site, Chogha Zanbil, is one of the most important landmarks on the entire Susiana Plain. An area close to 100 hectares is enclosed within an outer wall: inside many "public" buildings were constructed, including a number of temples and a ziggurat (Ghirshman 1966b, 1968).

In terms of the gravity model, it would appear that the primary effect of Chogha Zanbil would be to bring Deh No (Hubshen?)—at which the Shutrukids may have built a ziggurat (Carter 1984:162)—and the Ahu Dasht enclave (KS-233, 235) into the already established network linking settlements in the northwest quadrant of the plain. Nevertheless, Susa remained the primary center, growing once again to about 85 hectares. The settlement hierarchy is summarized in figure 56.

Susa interacted at a high level with three 13–20 hectare regional centers, evenly spaced at distances of 17–22 kilometers to the north (KS-7), east (KS-3), and south (KS-96). Susa interacted at the same level with the larger and more distant Chogha Zanbil.

Chogha Zanbil interacted with three smaller regional centers (8.5–10 hectares) spaced evenly to the west (KS-90), northeast (KS-120), and south (KS-233) at distances of 7–22 kilometers. Tepe Pomp (KS-221?) may also have been a subordinate center (Stève, Gasche, and Meyer 1980:82). If Chogha Zanbil is considered to have an effective occupied area (see below) of 50 hectares (Carter 1971:cf. 173, 177, 188–89), the interaction coefficients would be 1.9, 9.8, and 0.9, respectively. If Chogha Zanbil were double this size, each coefficient would be doubled.

Each of these six regional centers were long established as centers. Most of them appear to have reached their peak settlement during the Middle Elamite Phase.

At Chogha Zanbil, except for two mace heads of

Attar-Kittah (ca. 1310–1300 B.C.; for the inscriptions see Stève 1967:112–13), only inscriptions of Untash-Napirisha (ca. 1275–1240 B.C.) have been found. Parts of the site, however, may have continued in use several hundred years later, for example, the "palais hypogée" and the temple of Ishnikarab (Carter 1984:162–64, 184). Much of the site (20 hectares or more) was occupied by religious structures or "royal palaces" which appear to have been used only on ceremonial occasions. These gave the excavator the impression of a specially constructed religious center which, even though planned and executed on a large scale, was apparently never finished. The site did not become a large urban center in the same sense as Susa (Carter 1971:89, 92, 188–89; Ghirshman 1966b:1, 91–92; 1968:47–58, "Avant propos"). In any event, it seems likely that if Chogha Zanbil ever acquired the function of a major administrative center, it ceased that role by 1200 B.C. The site was abandoned with the collapse—perhaps brought about by Tukulti Ninurta—of the dynasty founded by Ige-halki, not more than 150 years earlier (Hinz 1972:120–21, 184; Labat 1963:12–13). Although the Elamite wars of Nebuchadnezzar I (1125–1104 B.C.) ended this phase of Elam's written history, there is no indication of any long-term Babylonian control of Elamite territory, and the effects of Nebuchadnezzar's victory are obscure and do not necessarily imply a sudden and utter collapse of Elamite power (Stolper 1984:43–44).

The rank-size distribution of central Khuzistan at this time (figure 55) shows a continuation of the second millennium pattern. Susa remains smaller than expected given the sizes of the rest of the sites on the plain. Counted as a 50-hectare site, Chogha Zanbil is of the expected size. If, however, we count it as 100 hectares, it would be the largest site and it, too, would fit the pattern of being smaller than predicted by the rank-size model. In this case, however, Susa is the second largest site and would be larger than expected (figure 56).

West of central Khuzistan, significant changes occurred in cultural development. Deh Luran may have been substantially abandoned (Carter 1971:202, note 1), becoming part of a buffer zone between Elam and Mesopotamia (Stolper 1984:42; Carter 1984:169,-180). In Luristan, the "Bronze Age" tradition of Godin III and Giyan IV–II was replaced by a new assemblage of Iron Age I gray ware cultures, representing a reorientation of cultural ties toward the north (Young 1965b:70–71, 78–79; 1966:236; 1967a:22; Goff Meade 1968:127; Dyson 1973:712–15).

Historical Evidence. Middle Elamite II royal inscriptions have been found from Susa to Bandar Bushehr on the Persian Gulf southwest of Fars. They provide some of the best available evidence for an administrative geography of the Middle Elamite state (Stolper 1978:93). The ties of the Elamite kings to Bandar Bushehr were repeatedly restated by a succession of Elamite kings from Humbannumena I (ca. 1300–1275 B.C.) to Shilhak-Inshushinak (ca. 1150–1120 B.C.). (See Konig 1965:8–13 for a catalog of inscriptions and their proveniences.) Bushehr has been identified with Liyan or Bashime by Steinkeller (1982).

Inscriptions from different parts of the Susiana Plain indicate that perhaps for the first time a serious attempt was made to bring the entire plain under a centralized administration. Two copies of an inscription of Ige-halki (ca. 1320 B.C.) found at Deh-No, a major site near the center of the Susiana Plain, may indicate the beginning of this process. The unification of the plain received major impetus beginning with Untash-Napirisha (ca. 1275–1240 B.C.). He had the site of Chogha Zanbil constructed at a strategic spot near the center of the plain, perhaps intending that it serve as the administrative center for the unified plan (cf. Stolper 1984:37–38). He also sponsored building projects where his inscriptions have been found at KS-102,[4] Deylam (KS-47), and Gotvand (KS-172), near Shushtar in the northeast quadrant of the Susiana Plain (Stève, Gasche, and Meyer 1980:80–81) and at Tepe Bormi in Ram Hormuz (Vallat 1981).

This eastward policy was reaffirmed under Shilhak-Inshushinak (ca. 1150–1120 B.C.). His inscriptions have been found at Dizful, Chogha Pahn (KS-3), Tepe Pomp, and Shustar in the northeast Susiana Plain (Stève, Gasche, and Meyer 1980:80–81), and at Tulaspid (Herzfeld 1929:82ff.) in western Fars.

Shustar and Tepe Gotvand are located in the northeast corner of the Susiana Plain on the principal route taken by modern Bakhtiari nomads into the mountains. These nomads currently winter their flocks in that part of plain. The building inscriptions might be part of an attempt to gain some measure of control or influence over the northeastern plain and its nomadic inhabitants.

However, the uneven success of these attempts at centralization can be seen in the possible variation in the distribution of ceramic types across the Susiana Plain: several types from Susa are not known from Chogha Zanbil and vice versa. There are also "certain small differences" between the Middle Elamite types found at Deh-No (KS 120) and Chogha Zanbil and other principal sites of this period (Carter 1971:90–91, 145, 189). Of the six Middle Elamite types defined by Carter, only types 3 and 6 were found at sites outside the northwest quadrant (i.e., the northwest and northcentral sectors of the Susiana Plain).

The evidence suggests that an attempt to incorporate more areas of Elam under a central administration was combined with an aggressive policy toward the rest of the world (Labat 1975:384–85, 482–83;

Stolper 1984:35–41). In fact, the title "expander of the kingdom" is used on more than half of the inscriptions of the Shutrukids (ca. 1205–1100 B.C.) (Vallat 1978:102). The internal consolidation and the military successes in the borderlands suggest that this imperial ideology was no empty boast. This later Middle Elamite II Phase has been depicted as "The Glory of an Elamite Empire" (Cameron 1936:113–37). In some respects, it invites comparison with the Third Dynasty of Ur (cf. Larsen 1979:79, 90–91).

Conclusion

The early historic periods span the two millennia between the origins of the state and the rise of the Assyrian and Achaemenid empires in Greater Mesopotamia and southwest Iran. It was the era during which the social, political, and economic foundations of these empires evolved. An essential element in understanding the process of political development in this area is the development of regions that combined city rule with leadership of tribal federations and their interurban territories (Stolper 1984:27) and the role played by nomads and the elites of nomadic societies (Rowton 1973a, 1973b, 1974, 1976a, 1976b, 1976c, 1980). From this perspective, one finds that the appropriate unit of analysis is not a large valley plain (such as the Susiana Plain) or even a section of mountains (such as Luristan) but a connected series of altitudinally and geographically diverse microenvironments incorporating parts of large plains (cf. Coe and Flannery 1964). Contrary to what one might expect, the major centers on the plains are displaced to one side, leaving large portions of the plain beyond the reach of the primary interaction network—at least this is the pattern with Susa in the Susiana Plain and Malyan in Marv Dasht; on a smaller scale, we could also cite Musiyan in Deh Luran during the third millennium B.C. and perhaps Tepe Bormi in Ram Hormuz during the second millennium B.C. An explanation for this locational bias may have to do with an association between the principal urban center and the currently most powerful nomadic chiefdom (to use Rowton's terminology). This might be seen, for example, as the context of the relationship between Susa and Luristan during the early and middle third millennium B.C. and perhaps the relationship between Tepe Bormi, Qaleh Tol, and Izeh during the middle and late second millennium B.C. Once entrenched, these asymmetrical settlement patterns may have become quite durable, outliving their original raison d'être.

The development of rival centers on the same plain in territory associated with other nomadic groups may have been actively suppressed. So for example, over a period of two millennia, no settlements larger than 12 hectares are found in southern or eastern Susiana or in eastern Marv Dasht. This hypothetical interpretation of relationships between parts of the major plains needs to be tested by a detailed distributional analysis of ceramic types and design attributes, perhaps along the lines of Johnson (1973:27ff., 87–156), supplemented where possible by evidence from contemporary written sources. At the same time, we need much better control over the basic data of each region such as chronology and sizes of sites.

Population growth is another factor in the development of southwest Iran. Although the data are far from complete, present indications (illustrated in figure 45) suggest population growth in the three major regions of southwest Iran during the early historic periods reached a peak in all three regions at about 2000 B.C. During the second millennium B.C., the settled population of the highland plains seems to have declined, if the available data are representative. Settlement in Khuzistan under the Elamites, however, remained at a high level until the first millennium B.C., when the Assyrian invasions under Assurbanipal in the seventh century devastated the area (Adams 1962:115; Miroschedji 1981c:171–72). It is also of interest that the three most populous parts of southwest Iran—the central Zagros, the lowland steppe of Khuzistan, and Marv Dasht of Fars—seem to correspond directly to three of the most significant historical entities during early historic times: Shimashki, Susiana, and Anshan (cf. Vallat 1980:6).

If we review the trends in rank-size organization in Khuzistan—the only place for which we have data from enough periods to speak usefully about trends— we find that although Susa doubles in size during the early historic period, it nevertheless declines in status from a "primate" center during the third millennium to a center which is smaller than expected during the second millennium. This apparent decline is caused mostly by a great increase in the number and size of sites of medium size.

Reviewing the trends in the parameters of the rank-size distributions, we find evidence of increasing urbanization—not merely of the principal urban center, but of the entire settlement system:

1. The coefficient K, which is an estimate of the size of the largest settlement, increases almost sixfold over the course of the two millennia we have examined. At first Susa exceeds this estimate, but during the second millennium, it falls behind because it does not grow as fast as the rest of the settlement system. This suggests that the construction of Chogha Zanbil may not have been a mere whim but a reasoned response to a growing need, as well as a part of a political strategy to unify Khuzistan under a central administration.

2. The exponent q increases from 1.03 to 1.43, indicating an increasingly "top-heavy" rank-size distribution—i.e., one of increasing urbanization. This can

also be seen in the monotonically increasing number of settlements of at least 8.5 hectares and in the proportion of total settlement area taken up by these sites, which steadily increases from 32 percent in Susa IV to 82 percent in Middle Elamite (Chogha Zanbil is considered as 50 hectares) of the aggregate area of contemporary settlements. The nearest neighbor statistics for the early historic periods of Susiana show remarkably little variation. The statistic varies from a maximum of 1.39 in Susa V to a minimum of 1.17 in Middle Elamite, with a slight tendency to decrease over time from 3000 to 1000 B.C. The implication is that the distribution is a little more regular than random—not a surprising result. Not unexpectedly, the average distance to nearest neighbor is smallest during the Sukkalmah and Middle Elamite I periods, during which the largest number of sites are distributed over the same area. Perhaps most significant is that the variance of distance to nearest neighbor is also lowest during the Sukkalmah and Middle Elamite I periods— a variance only half the size of that during the Susa IV and Middle Elamite II periods. If the nearest neighbor analyses were repeated leaving out the eastern and southern sectors with their relatively small and isolated sites, however, a different result might emerge.

Finally, we have frequently referred to "interaction" between settlements in a way which, although sometimes mathematically precise, may seem of questionable meaning in cultural terms. We have also implicitly referred to the amount of interaction as measured by number of artifact types in common, proportion of common artifact types in the assemblage as a whole, presence of administrative artifacts or elite artifacts, and so on. And, we have referred to relatively "isolated" sites which, nevertheless, shared artifact types and other aspects of culture with sites in a "primary interaction network." To develop the knowledge of interactions between settlements and between regions necessary for understanding the processes of growth and development in early historic cultures, it will be necessary to utilize every available form of evidence—archaeological and historical—from every kind of site. Furthermore, to utilize these larger masses of data effectively, it will be necessary to use models that can transform these data into coherent results. The character of a civilization cannot be judged by the examination, however thorough, of one site, or even one set of historical contexts.

Appendix

Chronology

The chronology for southwest Iran during the second millennium B.C. is based on a combination of cross-dating of artifact types, fitting of historical sources to a broader Near Eastern historical framework, and radiocarbon dating. Moreover, this Near Eastern historical framework cannot be regarded as proven (Brinkman 1972:271, note 2; 1977:335; Labat 1975:379–80). Although this is not the place to undertake an exhaustive review of the alternatives (see Rowton 1967, 1970; Güterbock 1967:963–64, among others), ignorance of them can lead to confusion. For example, when trying to establish the date of the Elamite occupation at Tepe Sharafabad (Schacht 1975a), I did not realize that although a majority of scholars in the 1970s favored a "Middle Chronology" dating the region of Hammurabi as 1792–1750 B.C., two of the sources I was depending on to date seals and inscribed materials (Salonin 1962; Borker-Klahn 1970) advocated a "Low Chronology" dating the reign of Hammurabi sixty-four years later. This followed a scheme long advocated by Albright (see most recently Albright 1973) and Cornelius (1958) and favored by a generation of biblical scholars (e.g., Bright 1972:48, note). By scrutinizing radiocarbon dates, Mellaart (1979) has revived the argument for a "High" (see previously Goetze 1964) or even an "Ultra High" chronology (Strommenger 1964), placing the accession of Hammurabi 56 to 138 years earlier than the Middle Chronology. In consequence, in the extreme positions, there is a difference of some two hundred years in the date of Hammurabi. This variance enhances the importance of a critical evaluation of calibrated radiocarbon dates, which have been compiled for tables 31–35. Although limitations of space prevent an exhaustive use of the dates in the following tables to test the alternative chronologies, it is my impression that, while far from conclusive, the results would favor a higher chronology than the Middle Chronology favored today.

The collection of radiocarbon dates that follows has provided a guide to the periodizations used in this chapter, but it is not intended to be definitive. There are now so many dates that the task of evaluating them all, using a procedure such as that outlined by Wright (1980), is impossible here. Instead, I have selected for inclusion in the tables those dates which seem most reliable, relegating others to footnotes. Many radiocarbon dates have been removed from the main body of each table because they seem to be too old or too young for their context. These rejected dates include many which, considered individually, would appear within the expected general range for assemblages of the same type, but which appear out of stratigraphic order when compared with other samples from the same site. Some dates have been rejected as a result of cross-dating with more reliably dated assemblages. For a more thorough discussion of most of these dates and their comparative stratigraphy, see Dyson and Voigt (in press).

The radiocarbon age in the following tables is given after the lab number in years B.P. using the Libby half-life. These dates are calibrated using an unpublished supplement to Klein et al. (1982) providing calibration ranges with 67 percent confidence intervals. Assemblages with several dates may be pooled according to the procedure suggested by Ward and Wilson (1978) and Wilson and Ward (1981).

Although there is insufficient space here to offer a detailed evaluation of the various historical chronologies referred to above, a recent controversy (Stève, Gasche, and Meyer 1980:54–68 contra Carter 1979a; Young 1978) regarding the comparative stratigraphy of Khuzistan cannot be ignored. First, it must be noted that there is a wide area of agreement on many important aspects of the problem: both groups accept the Middle Chronology and more or less agree on how to date the main occupation at Haft Tepe and Chogha Zanbil. They also agree on the date of Ville Royale A XIII–XV and B V–VII at Susa. Their disagreement on the dating of A XII–IX was due to the fact that pottery in the reserves at Susa was marked with the level of origin, whether intrusive or not, and published by Gasche (1973) without any indication of which deposits were intrusive. Now that these deposits have been identified (Stève, Gasche, and Meyer 1980), the main outlines of the comparative stratigraphy are agreed upon (Carter, personal communication). The principal remaining problem is the typological definition of the beginning of the Middle Elamite I ("Transitional") Phase, now placed at 1475 B.C. on the basis of epigraphic evidence and equated with the Late phases of Level A-XII associated with Kidinu at Susa (Stève, Gasche, and Meyer 1980:-78,98). The assemblage at Tepe Sharafabad (Schacht 1975a) is critical in this regard, but a new assessment of its chronological significance requires a more lengthy study. (See Carter 1984:156, 163, and figure 15.)

Comparative Stratigraphy

The Susa IV or Old Elamite Period (table 31) is defined by a stratigraphic sequence at Susa Ville Royale I (Carter 1979b, 1980) equivalent to Susa Dc-De (Le Breton 1957) and Acropole Couche 1–4 (Stève and Gasche 1971). It is dated by ceramic and epigraphic evidence to ED III-Akkad in Mesopotamia. Henrickson (chapter 8) has shown that Godin III:6 has the strongest parallels with early Susa IV and Early Dynastic III in Mesopotamia, which makes the radiocarbon dates for late Godin IV (table 31) appear several hundred years too young. Similarly, Godin III:5 finds its closest parallels with late Susa IV and Akkadian assemblages, making it appear that the radiocarbon dates for Godin III:5 are several hundred years too young. The radiocarbon date for Sagzabad A II provides additional evidence for an earlier beginning date for Godin III, if it really is associated with ceramics resembling those of Godin III (as reported in *Radiocarbon* 14[2]:458–59, citing Negahban 1971). The Susa V (Shimashki) or Old Elamite II Period is defined by a stratigraphic sequence at Susa including Ville Royale I levels 3–6 (Carter 1979b; 1980) and Ville Royale B VII–VI (Gasche 1973) and dated by ceramic and epigraphic evidence to the Ur III and early Isin-Larsa periods in Mesopotamia (Carter 1979b:120–22; 1984:148). Unfortunately, few reliable radiocarbon dates from related assemblages are available for this period (table 32). One date for a basal Kaftari deposit at Malyan (Sumner 1976:88, note 4) suggests a plausible beginning date for that type of assemblage, but not enough has been published about its earliest phases to be sure. Selenkahiyeh 4, from a site near Aleppo in Syria, has artifacts tentatively dated to the Ur III Period (Van Loon 1969:276).

The Old Elamite III A (Sukkalmah) Period is defined by the archaeological assemblage from Ville Royale B V and A XV–XIII at Susa (Gasche 1973). It is dated by ceramic and epigraphic evidence to the period roughly equivalent to the First Dynasty of Babylon in Mesopotamia (Gasche 1973; Stève, Gasche, and Meyer 1980:88–91; Stolper 1984:26–27). This makes it contemporary with the Khabur ware horizon (cf. Hamlin 1971; Dyson 1973:708), which is well-represented at Dinkha Tepe in Iranian Azerbaijan in Period IV from which a good series of radiocarbon dates is available (table 33). This assemblage has a small number of parallels with Godin III:1 (table 34) and Giyan II–III (Hamlin 1971:141–46, 192; Henrickson chapter 8, this volume), and perhaps Darvazeh Ic (Nicol 1970:20, "Darvazeh II"), an early Shogha-Teimuran assemblage in Fars. Information on the unpublished radiocarbon dates from Darvazeh is available in Jacobs (1980:48–52), whose phase designations are adopted in the following tables. Old Elamite III A is also related to the Kaftari assemblage of Fars (Carter 1979b:122–23). The early group of dates from Kaftari deposits at Malyan (table 33) are from wells, at least one of which is associated with building level I. The second group of dates (TUNC 28, 29, 30) are from above building level I. The date from Tell Rimah II is associated by Mellaart (1979:12) with the Assyrian king Shamsi-Adad I. Old Elamite III B (table 34) is defined by the archaeological assemblages from Ville Royale A XII at Susa (Ghirshman 1964; Stève, Gasche, and Meyer 1980:74–75) and from Tepe Sharafabad (Schacht 1975a) and corresponds with the formative years of Kassite rule in Mesopotamia, a period of scarce documentation and uncertain dynastic sequences in Mesopotamia (Brinkman 1972:274; Gadd 1973:224–25) and in Khuzistan (cf. Stève, Gasche, and Meyer 1980:91; Stolper 1984:32–33). Be-

cause of its historical context, this subdivision of the Old Elamite III deserves special attention in order to elucidate an otherwise poorly known period. The radiocarbon sample from Tell al Rimah is associated with an assemblage with ceramic and other parallels with Nuzi and Mitannian materials estimated to date circa 1500 B.C. (Stukenrath and Ralph 1965:190) and provides an acceptable date for the beginning of this subdivision of Old Elamite III.

Middle Elamite is defined primarily by the assemblage from Haft Tepe Transitional Phase (cf. Carter 1979b:115–9; 1984:163–64) and Ville Royale A XI at Susa (Stève, Gasche, and Meyer 1980:75–76, 91–100). It is linked to Aqar Quf by goblets of Groups 19a, 19c, and 20b (Gasche 1973:38–40; Stève, Gasche, and Meyer 1980:75–76 and figure 7) and button-base bowls or "lids" (Carter 1971:100). Susa's political relationship with Anshan (Tepe Malyan) is revived (Stève, Gasche, and Meyer 1980:92–95). Table 34 provides data from Aqar Quf, the Kassite capital of Dur Kurigalzu. When calibrated, the Aqar Quf date agrees well with the date of circa 1400 B.C. expected on archaeological grounds (Burleigh, Matthews, and Amber 1982:248).

Middle Elamite II is defined by the assemblages from Chogha Zanbil (Ghirshman 1966b, 1968), Ville Royale A X at Susa (Gasche 1973; Stève, Gasche, and Meyer 1980:76–77, 100–106; figures 9, 10), and Malyan (Carter and Stolper 1976). At the same time, an Iron Age I "gray pottery culture" was gathering strength in the north, represented by assemblages such as Hasanlu V, which would influence Giyan I and other sites in Luristan (Dyson 1973:712–13), although perhaps at a later date. A good series of radiocarbon dates (table 35) from Hasanlu V and Malyan Middle Elamite helps provide a framework to which to tie sites lacking adequate written materials to a relatively well-defined historical context.

Acknowledgments

I would like to thank Frank Hole and all of the other members of the seminal 1977 Advanced Seminar at the School of American Research for their encouragement and assistance with this manuscript and their critical examination of its earlier versions. I am particularly grateful in this regard to Elizabeth Carter and William Sumner, who in their roles as original participants in the seminar and as critical readers have contributed much to this manuscript even though their names do not appear as coauthors. I also thank Robert Henrickson, a late contributor, for his helpful suggestions and patient responses to my inquiries, and from whose contributions to this volume I have learned much. Significant substantive and editorial contributions have also been made to this manuscript by Matthew Stolper, Robert Dyson, Mary Voigt, John Alden, Richard Meadow, Bonnie Hole, and many others. I particularly wish to thank Bonnie Hole and Heidi Fogel for redrafting the figures and Bonnie Hole for typing the several versions of this manuscript. This chapter thus owes much to the cooperation and help of all these people. Of course, I alone am responsible for any errors of fact or judgment which remain in the manuscript.

Notes

1. For the purposes of this study, Carter's (1984:103) inclusive definition will be used:

> The terms *Elam* and *Elamites* . . . in their broadest sense . . . describe the western and southern areas of the modern Iranian state and the peoples who occupied them from the early third millennium B.C. to the middle of the first millennium B.C. In modern geographic terms, ancient Elam corresponded to Khuzistan, Fars, and parts of the Kerman, Luristan and Kurdistan provinces.

For the definition of these terms see also Amiet (1979:197–98), Miroschedji (1980:137–38), Vallat (1980; 1985:1–6), and Stolper (1984:4), whose definitions are more narrow than those used here.

2. Interaction coefficients from the gravity model were used as the basis for a simple cluster analysis. We used the standard version of the gravity model from Haggett (1965:35), for which the interaction coefficient is

$$M_{ij} = A_i A_j / (d_{ij})^2$$

where A_i and A_j are the areas of settlements i and j and d_{ij} is the distance between them, measured in hectares and klommeters, respectively.

3. Cf. Berry and Garrison (1958:84) and Richardson (1973:240). They express the rank-size distribution in terms of R rather than P, so that K is an estimate of P_1 only if q equals *1*. Without changing the form of the rank-size distribution, I have redefined K and q so that K always approximates P_1, regardless of the value of q.

4. Inscribed brick fragments gathered by the 1971 survey of the University of Michigan. See also Stolper (1984:37).

Robert Schacht

Table 30. Summary of Regional Chronologies, Third through Second Millennia B.C.

Absolute Date B.C.	Mesopotamia	Lowland Steppe: Khuzistan	Central Zagros: Luristan	Fars and Kerman; Marv Dasht		Related table in this book
	Early Dynastic I–II	Susa III	Godin IV	Banesh Yahya IVB/early		Table 31
2700						
	Early Dynastic III	Susa IVa (Old Elamite I)	Godin III/6 Baba Jan 5	Jalyan		
	Akkadian	Susa IVb	Godin III/5	Yahya IVB/late		
2200						Table 32
	Ur III	Susa V	Godin III/4			
	Isin-Larsa	(Old Elamite II)	Giyan IVA		Early	
2000				Kaftari;	Shogha-Teimuran	
	Old Babylonian Old Assyrian	Old Elamite IIIA	Giyan IVC,III Godin III/2			Table 33
1650						
		Sharafabad (OE IIIB)	Godin III/1		Middle	
1475	Kassite		Giyan II	Qaleh;	Shogha-Teimuran	Table 34
		Haft Tepe (ME I)				
1300						
	Middle Assyrian	Chogha Zanbil (Middle Elamite II)	Giyan I	Middle Elamite;	Late Shogha-Teimuran	Table 35
1000						
	Neo-Assyrian	Neo-Elamite				

Note: See the appendix on Chronology (at the end of this chapter) for a discussion of dates and interregional comparisons.

Table 31. Radiocarbon Dates for Late Proto-Elamite and Contemporary Assemblages, 3100–2700 B.C.

Provenience	Lab Number	Libby Age B.P.	Calibrated Age B.C.
Yahya IVB/5–4	GX-1727	4430±360	3380–2890
Malyan, Late Middle Banesh	P -2335	4390± 90	3355–2910
	P -2333	4320± 90	3165–2880
Yahya IVB/4	GX-1734	4320±170	3180–2855
Yanik E.B.I/HX6	P -1250	4315± 59	3108–2892
Malyan, Late Banesh	P -2982	4260± 70	3025–2870
	P -3072	4179±260	3054–2535
Nippur Early Dynastic I/Inanna IXA high	P - 819	4272± 65	3030–2875
	P - 800	4157± 62	2900–2650
Shahr-i-Sokhta I/10–9	P -2543	4200± 60	2925–2780
Shahr-i-Sokhta I/ 9–8	R - 629	4200± 50	2925–2780
	R - 633a	4170± 50	2905–2760
Yanik E.B.I/L5	P -1247	4204± 60	2925–2780
	P -1248	4149± 76	2908–2642
Nippur Early Dynastic I/Inanna IXB low	P - 798	4145± 59	2898–2647
Shahr-i-Sokhta II/7	P -2076	4160± 60	2900–2650
	P -2076A	4080± 60	2870–2545
	P -2086	4080± 60	2870–2545
	P -2541	4080± 70	2870–2545
Nippur Early Dynastic I/Inanna VIII	P - 807	4090± 64	2875–2620

Notes:

Dates rejected as too old for their context:
Yahya IVB: WSU-876 (5395±465);
Susa, Jemdet Nasr: GrN-6051 (5035±40); GrN-6053 (5015±90); Brux-SPr 43 (4770±218);
Malyan, Late Banesh. P-2981 (4780±60); P-2984 (4770±290);
Nippur E.D.I: P-799 (8472±102); E.D.I/Inanna IXB low: P-803 (4221±53); E.D.II/Inanna VIIB high: P-806 (4345±66); P-804 (4095±52)
Shahr-i-Sokhta II/7: P-2085 (4270±60); II/7–6: P-2546 (4170±70).

Dates rejected as too young for their context:
Yahya IVC/IVB2: TF-1136 (4130±85);
Nippur Early Dynasty I/Inanna IXA high: P-820 (4090±62); E.D.I/Inanna IXB low: P-809 (3945±62); E.D.II/Inanna VIIB high: P-805 (4006±62)
Godin IV/late: SI-4908 (3880±50); GaK-1071 (3803±120); Tepe Farukhabad, late Jemdet Nasr: M-2151 (3990±180); M-2419 (3800±160)

Table 32. Radiocarbon Dates for Susa IV–V (Old Elamite I–II) and Contemporary Assemblages, 3700–2000 B.C.

Provenience	Lab Number	Libby Age B.P.	Calibrated Age B.C.
Sagz-Abad A II	TUNC- 8	4086± 66	2875–2620
Nippur Early Dynastic II–III/Inanna V	P -810	4074± 64	2805–2545
Mari Early Dynastic IIIA	Gif-496	4100±150	2910–2530
	Gif-497	4075±150	2900–2525
	Gif-498	4040±150	2885–2400
Yahya IVB1	TF-1143	4150±130	2930–2535
	TUNC-39	3859± 61	2423–2267
Ur, Royal Cemetary	BM- 70	4030±150	2880–2395
	BM- 76	3990±150	2805–2315
	BM- 64	3920±150	2655–2185
	P -724	3959± 59	2640–2395
Abu Salabikh Early Dynastic IIIA	BM-1365A-D*	3912± 65*	2545–2315
	BM-1366	3869± 56	2425–2295
Selenkahiye Phase 1 (Early Dynastic III?)	P -1788	3900± 60	2435–2310
	P -1789	3860± 70	2426–2244
Yanik E.B. II	P -1251	3918±101	2640–2305
	P -1252	3656± 61	2180–1925
Sagz-Abad A III	TUNC-13	3696± 62	2645–2450
Malyan Basal Kaftari	P -2186	3670± 60	2185–1950
Darvazeh Ic	GX-1522	3660±106	2205–1890
Godin III/5	QU-1041	3660± 80	2192–1926
	QU-1043	3580±100	2150±1770
Selenkahiye Phase 4(Ur III?)	P -1794	3620± 50	2155–1890

*Weighted mean of four samples from same locus

Notes:

Dates rejected as too old for their context:
Sagz-Abad A I: TUNC-9 (4426±69);
Godin III/5: Gak-1070 (4173±101);
Abu Salabikh E.D.IIIA: P-2050 (4850±50); P-2053 (4390±60); P-2052 (4330±60); P-2051 (4100±60); BM-1390 (4267±85)
Susa "Proto-Imperial": Brux-SPr-46 (4096±140)
Gasur Akkadian: P-1468 (4002±61);
Nippur Ur III: C-752 (3943±106);
Warka Ur III: H 141-120/166 (3825±85);
Selenkahiye Phase 4: P-1792 (3970±70); P-1793 (3970±60)

Dates rejected as too young for their context:
Abu Salabikh E.D.IIIA: HAR-1877 (3830±70);
Yahya IVB1: TF-1140 (3560±110);
Godin III/4: SI-4902 (3405±80)

Table 33. Radiocarbon Dates for Old Elamite IIIA and Comtemporary Assemblages, 2000–1650 B.C.

Provenience	Lab Number	Libby Age B.P.	Calibrated Age B.C.
Malyan ABC/B.L.1(Kaftari)	P -3070	3590± 60	2130–1870
	P -3071	3560± 60	2035–1855
	P -2062	3560± 60	2035–1855
Dinkha IV/basal?	P -1429/31	3598± 66	2148–1873
	P -1692	3576± 70	2125–1825
Darvazeh IIa?	GX-1512	3573±130	2176–1715
Dinkha IVc	P -1690	3539± 59	1995–1765
	P -1452	3522± 63	1985–1740
	P -1430	3468± 59	1915–1700
	P -1233	3458± 59	1905–1695
Malyan ABC/above B.L.1	TUNC-30	3531± 63	2010–1746
(Kaftari)	TUNC-29	3526± 61	2000–1745
	TUNC-28	3510± 63	1977–1730
Tepe Hissar III/late	TUNC-20	3486± 65	1950–1710
Tell Rimah II	P -1117	3480± 60	1940–1705
Darvezeh IIb	GX-1514	3384± 95	1875–1580
	GX-1517	3354±105	1785–1560
	GX-1518	3345±105	1780–1555
Dinkha IVd	P -1450	3435± 83	1910–1670
	P -1232	3403± 52	1870–1665
	P -1231	3285± 52	1695–1540

Notes:

Dates rejected as too old for their context:
Malyan, Kaftari: P-3064 (4260±250); P-3067 (4150±210); P-3068 (3980±80); P-3069 (4090±200);
Darvazeh IIb: GX-1515 (3573±95);
Godin II/2: QU-1044 (3980±110);
Susa Ville Royal A-XIII: Gif-182 (3920±250)
Malyan, late? Kaftari: P-3065 (3550±70); P-3066 (3560±60)

Dates rejected as too young for their context:
Malyan, Kaftari: P-2063 (3428±62);
Dinkha IV/basal?: P-1721 (3458±66); IVb: P-1720 (3395±70);
Susa Ville Royale A-XIII: Gif-183 (1750±150); Gif-184 (2730±200);
Darvazeh IIa: GX-1510 (2893±115); GX-1530 (3359±180);
Darvazeh IIb: GX-1519 (2607±85);
Darvazeh II "mixed": GX-1616 (3121±95); GX-1511 (3000±85);
Tepe Guran C: K-856 (3170±120)
Godin III/2: SI-4900 (2655±70)

Table 34. Radiocarbon Dates for Assemblages of the Mid-Second Millennium, 1650–1300 B.C.

Provenience	Lab Number	Libby Age B.P.	Calibrated Age B.C.
Tell al Rimah 5	P-844	3291± 57	1700–1545
Godin III/1	P-1469	3203± 50	1655–1405
Sharafabad IIIB	TUNC-35	3200±188	1690–1345
Aqar Quf	BM-1477	3110± 35	1490–1345

Notes:

Dates rejected as too old for their context:
Sharafabad III: P-2209 (4260±330)

Dates rejected as too young for their context:
Godin III/1: P-1470 (2742±41)
Sharafabad IIIA: TUNC-34 (3172±125);
Sharafabad III: P-2281 (2770±270)

Table 35. Radiocarbon Dates for Middle Elamite II and Contemporary Assemblages, 1300–1000 B.C.

Provenience	Lab Number	Libby Age B.P.	Calibrated Age B.C.
Hasanlu V	P-2390	3130± 60	1550–1360
	P-2155	3110± 60	1535–1340
	P- 198	3083±122	1555–1230
	P-2156	3020± 50	1395–1230
	P-2161	3010± 50	1385–1230
	P- 185	3000±120	1415–1075
	P-2393	3000± 60	1385–1200
	P-2391	2950± 50	1335–1095
	P-2392	2950± 50	1335–1095
Malyan, Middle Elamite	P-2061	3060± 60	1420–1245
	P-2330	2980± 95	1390–1085
	P-2332	2950± 60	1340–1085
	P-2331	2830± 60	1115– 875

Notes:

Dates rejected as too old for their context:
Malyan, Middle Elamite: P-2060 (3170±50)

Dates rejected as too young for their context:
Hasanlu V: P-418 (2899±49); P-419 (2880±45)

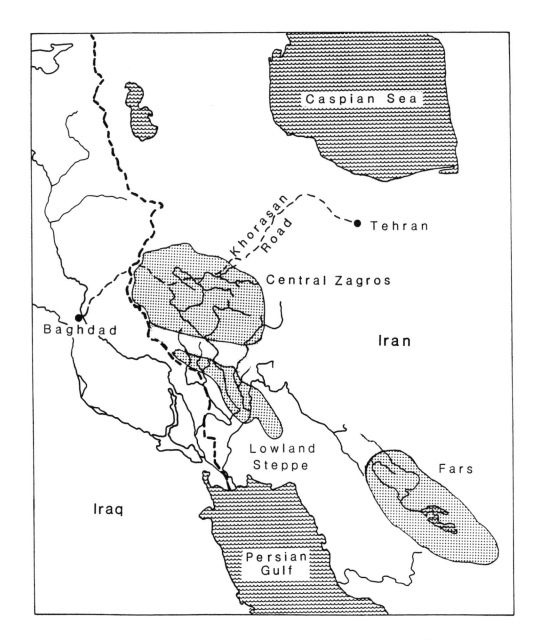

Figure 44. Map of western Iran indicating major areas of occupation discussed in the chapter.

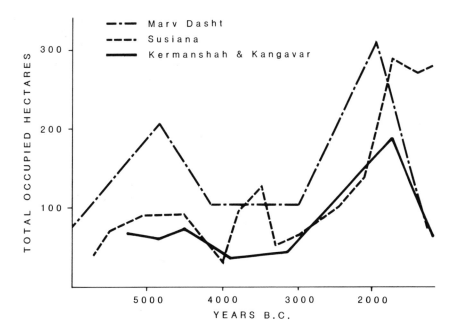

Figure 45. Occupied hectares per period in Marv Dasht in Fars, in Susiana in Khuzistan on the lowland steppe, and in the Kermanshah region of the central Zagros. Data on Kangavar in the central Zagros are from Young (1977:391); on Susiana, from Schacht (1973:52, 135); on Marv Dasht from Sumner (1972:190, 193).

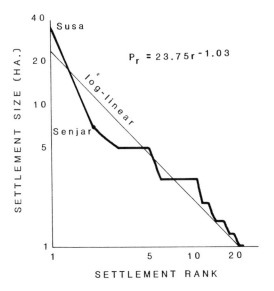

Figure 46. Rank-size graph of Susa IV (Old Elamite I). Plotted on two-cycle logarithmic paper.

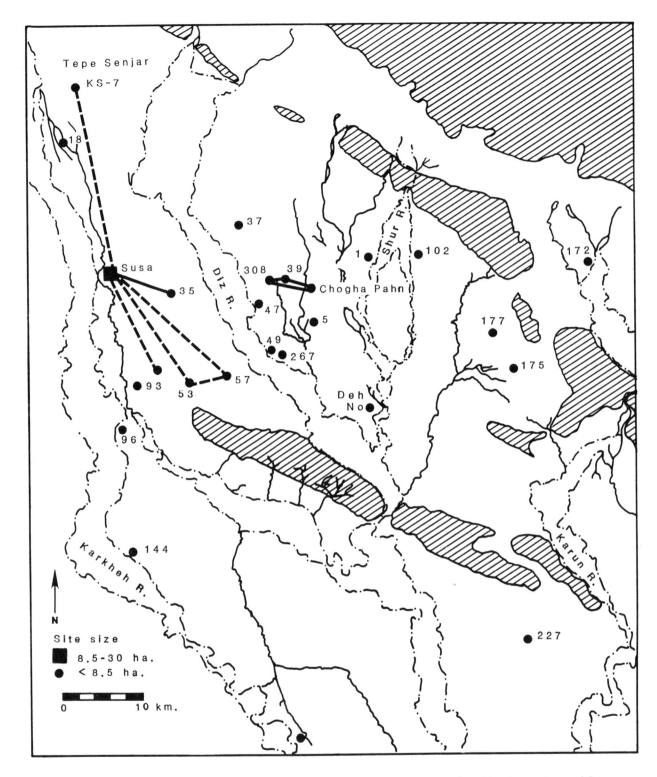

Figure 47. The Susiana Plain during Susa IV (Old Elamite I) showing interactions predicted by the gravity model.

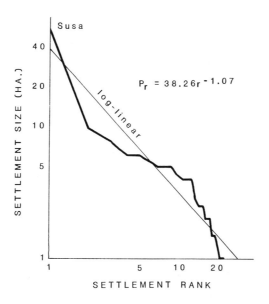

Figure 48. Rank-size graph of Susa V (Old Elamite II).
Plotted on two-cycle logarithmic paper.

Figure 49 may be found on the overleaf.

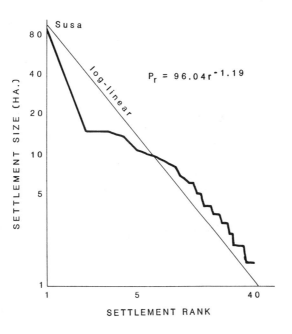

Figure 50. Rank-size graph of Sukkalmah (Old Elamite
III). Plotted on two-cycle logarithmic paper.

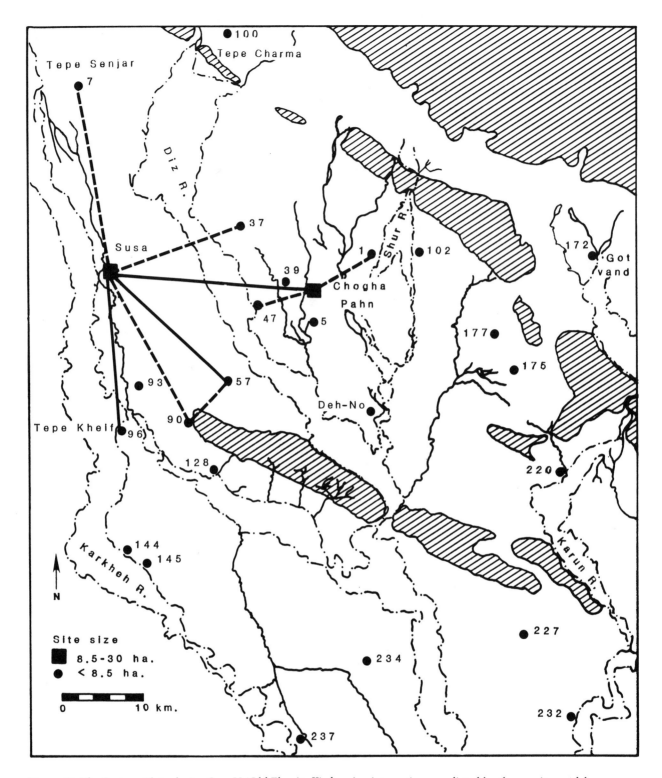

Figure 49. The Susiana Plain during Susa V (Old Elamite II) showing interactions predicted by the gravity model.

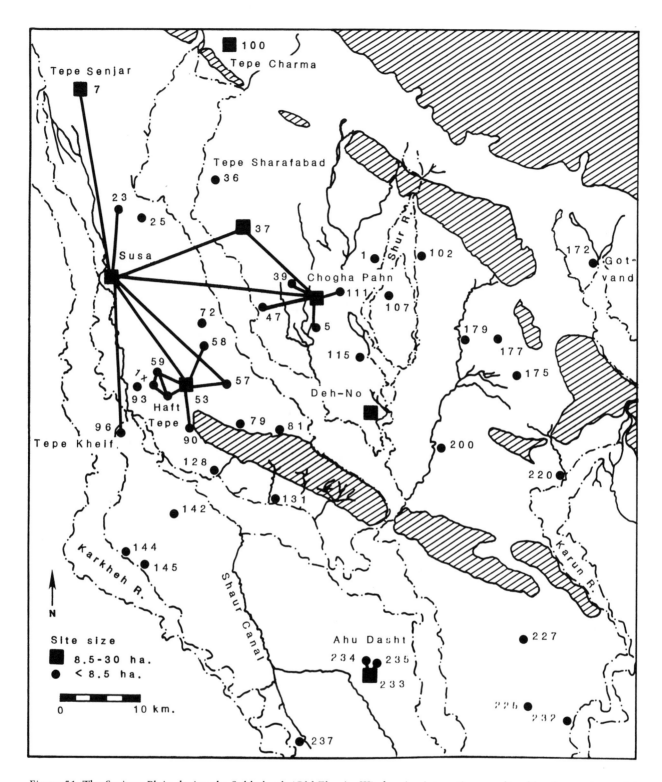

Figure 51. The Susiana Plain during the Sukkalmah (Old Elamite III) showing interactions predicted by the gravity model.

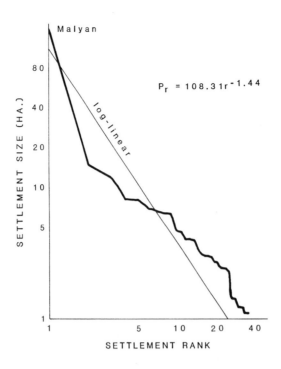

Figure 52. Rank-size graph of Kaftari. Plotted on two-cycle logarithmic paper.

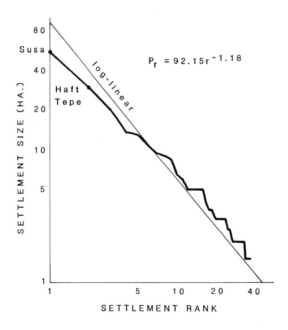

Figure 53. Rank-size graph of Middle Elamite I (Haft Tepe Phase). Plotted on two-cycle logarithmic paper.

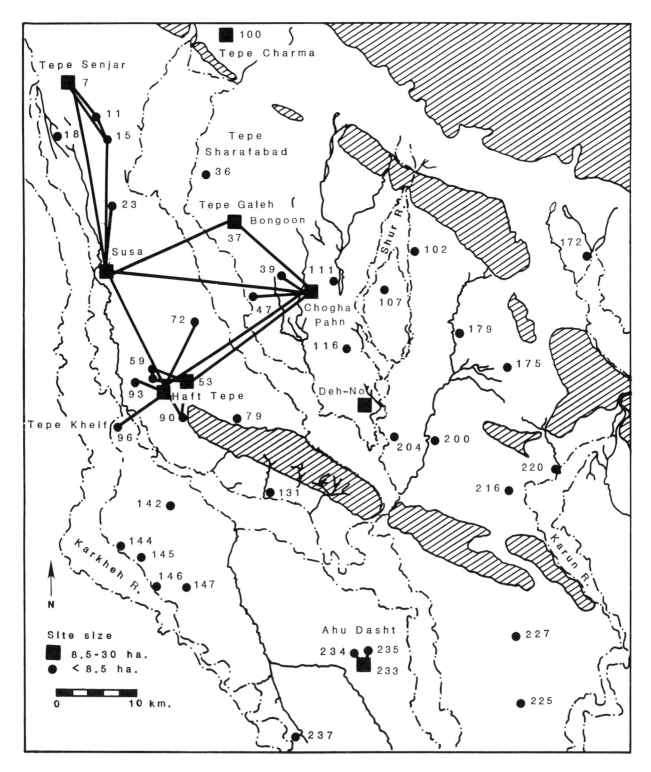

Figure 54. The Susiana Plain during the Middle Elamite I (Haft Tepe Phase) showing interactions predicted by the gravity model.

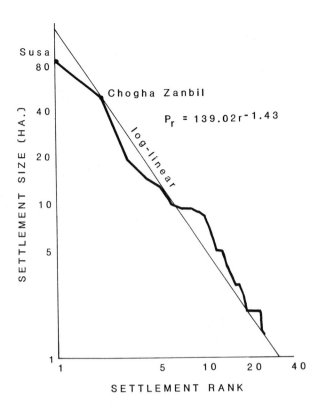

Figure 55. Rank-size graph of Middle Elamite II (Chogha Zanbil Phase). Plotted on two-cycle logarithmic paper.

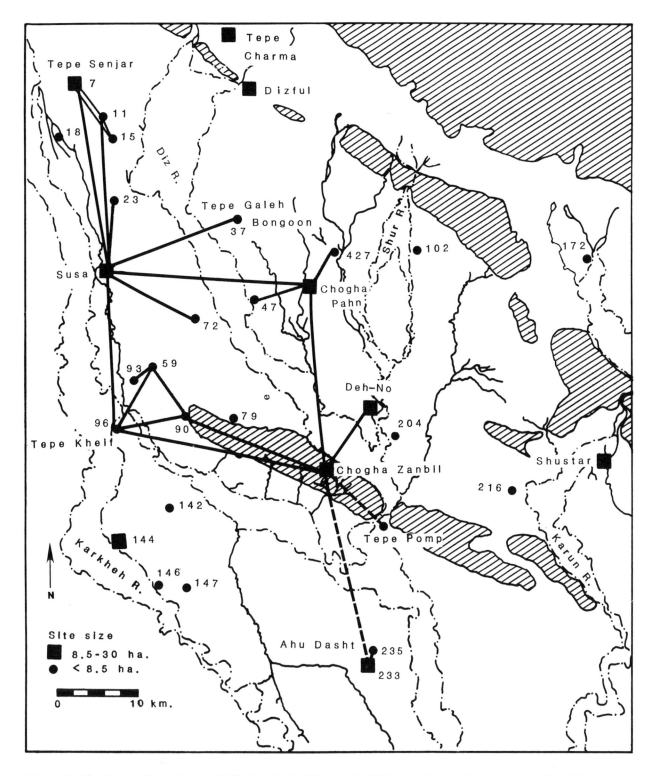

Figure 56. The Susiana Plain during Middle Elamite II (Chogha Zanbil Phase) showing interactions predicted by the gravity model. Effective area of Chogha Zanbil assumed to be 50 hectares.

Chapter 8

Godin III and the Chronology of Central Western Iran circa 2600– 1400 B.C.

ROBERT C. HENRICKSON

Introduction

For almost fifty years, the ceramic chronology of the mid-third to mid-second millennium B.C. in the central Zagros (modern Luristan) has depended on the results of excavations at Tepe Giyan in the Nehavand Valley (figure 57). Giyan levels IV–II were characterized by a distinctive monochrome painted buff ware tradition (Contenau and Ghirshman 1935). The data, however, consist essentially of graves whose stratigraphic positions and relationships are uncertain. Although the Giyan sequence has been variously construed (Nagel 1964, 1969; Dyson 1965a, 1973; Young 1965b; R. Henrickson 1983–84, 1984a, 1986b-c), all assessments rest primarily on typology for which the published drawings provide poor documentation (Contenau and Ghirshman 1935: plate 8–34; R. Henrickson 1983–84:197, appendix B). Moreover, Giyan IV–II represents only the latter half of the period to be considered here.

The stratigraphic excavations in Level III at Godin Tepe, hereafter Godin III, in the Kangavar Valley (figure 57) now enable reliable definition of phases of development in this monochrome painted pottery tradition and associated plain wares. Work on Godin III concentrated on clearance of 500–700 square meters in the Deep Sounding through a depth of 9 meters. Limited excavation in the cemetery area on the southern edge of the site (Operations M and O) and at other points on the mound (e.g., Operations R, AA5-AA10, and EEE) also yielded Godin III material (Young 1969a; Young and Levine 1974; R. Henrickson 1984a).

This chapter is intended as an overview of Godin III,

complementing other chapters in this volume. It consists of a summary of the Godin III sequence (figures 58–65) and its relationship to Giyan IV–II; assignment of dates to this sequence (figure 64); and a review of the distribution of pottery of each phase, with brief comments from a cultural and historical perspective. Examples of distinctive pottery types associated with each phase are illustrated in figures 58–63. I have treated elsewhere the definition of the phases of Godin III as well as the development of the ceramic assemblage, chronology, and detailed historical interpretation of the site (R. Henrickson 1983–84, 1984a-b, 1986a-c).

Before proceeding to the main discussion, several terms and problems should be explained. The principal stratigraphic phases within Godin III, referred to as "levels," have been defined by reference to the architectural remains in the Deep Sounding. A "level" is a coherent occupational episode whose beginning and end are defined by discontinuities across the entire area of excavation. Within a level there must be at least a thread of stratigraphic and occupational continuity, although there may be any number of localized interruptions. Considerable architectural development and change may occur. These levels provide a convenient series of stratigraphic subdivisions of the Godin III sequence, each of which is culturally (i.e., in its ceramic remains) distinctive. The levels are numbered 1–6, from top to bottom. The phases of Godin III are thus numbered III:6 to III:1, from earliest to latest. An additional phase, consisting of graves stratified between Levels III:2 and III:1, is designated Post-III:2.[1] "Level III:n" will be used to refer to material at Godin Tepe itself; "Godin III:n" will denote regional phases of the culture contemporary with individual levels at Godin Tepe.

Near Eastern villages and towns, ancient and modern, are not static entities, permanently limited to a specific size and position on the landscape. Settlements grow and decline, and within them a mosaic of evolving uses of space is found. Areas may be abandoned and later reoccupied. The intensity of use and nature of areas vary in both space and time (e.g., C. Kramer ed. 1982:86–148). This phenomenon, which I have referred to as "patchwork stratigraphy" (R. Henrickson 1984a:chapter 4) and Young has described as "spiral stratigraphy" (Young and Levine 1974:18–20), is clear in the Godin III occupation at Godin Tepe.

Although there was a settlement at Godin Tepe through most of the Godin III Period, the area of the Deep Sounding was at various times an important component of the settlement, on the periphery, or abandoned while occupation may have continued on other parts of the site. This is to be expected since the area of the Deep Sounding was the summit of the site throughout Godin III and previous periods. When modern villages in this region are built on large and relatively steep mounds, the summit is often left unoccupied.

The earliest Godin III occupation at Godin Tepe probably lay on the perimeter or lower slopes of the abandoned Period IV mound. In early level III:6 the settlement seems to have expanded up the slope, ultimately entering the area of the Deep Sounding from the southeast. In time an important part of the settlement was here, but eventually the area was abandoned. In Level III:5 the settlement seems to have lain on the north slope of the mound so that only part of the Deep Sounding, the very summit, was occupied. Later, in Level III:4, the area was a prosperous neighborhood within the settlement. The following Level III:3 village seems to have been on the southern slope of the mound, outside the area of the Deep Sounding. In Level III:2 the area was again part of a wealthy neighborhood. After its abandonment, Post-III:2 graves were dug into the summit of the mound. The remains of Level III:1 seal the Post-III:2 graves but are badly disturbed by weathering due to prolonged abandonment and construction activity of the Period II occupation. The Deep Sounding thus yields data on several discrete phases within the Godin III occupation(s) at Godin Tepe (R. Henrickson 1984a: chapter 5).

Several general technical comments on Godin III pottery are in order. Methods of manufacture, basic wares, and essentials of decoration were consistent throughout the range of distribution of each phase. Nonetheless, interregional, and even intervalley variability, particularly in decoration, is evident within individual phases. Plain wares were handmade, generally by sequential slab construction (Vandiver 1985), and probably finished on a *tournette* (turntable). Only small- to medium-size carinated painted vessels (maximum diameter <20 centimeters) were thrown on a true potter's wheel. Larger vessels were made using a combination of sequential slab construction and tournette. Most pottery seems to have been produced by specialist craftsmen, at least until the latest phases of Godin III (R. Henrickson 1986a). Vessel forms were simple and persistent; carinated restricted vessels in various forms were made for almost a millennium. Shapes usually are diagnostic for individual phases only in combination with specific wares and style of decoration. Rims, particularly on pots and jars, are usually simply rounded. (For a brief description of the basic wares of Godin III see Young 1969a:16–17). Figure 65 presents the changing frequencies of major ware groups.

Definition of the geographical distribution of Godin III pottery is based on limited data (R. Henrickson 1984a; 1986b) and must be considered within the context of the physical geography of the region (figure 57). In the central Zagros highlands the successive ridges isolate intermontane valleys from one another. The Kabir Kuh, the westernmost major ridge of the Zagros, separates the Mesopotamian lowlands from the highland valleys of western Luristan. In the center of Luristan, the Kuh-i Sefid is a major barrier, especially toward the north. To the east the Kuh-i Garin forms a lesser but still significant barrier. Few major routes pass into or through the region. The High Road (or Great Khorasan Road), the best east-west route through central western Iran to the lowlands of central Mesopotamia, runs through the Kangavar and Mahidasht valleys. Within Luristan itself, the few good routes run southeast-northwest, parallel to the mountain ridges, or follow the river valleys. Two important routes run northward from the Susiana lowlands to the High Road on either side of the Kuh-i Garin. A third route runs northward along the eastern face of the Kabir Kuh.

The distribution of sites may be discussed in terms of six geographical areas:

1. East of the Kuh-i Garin (Kangavar, Asadabad, Sahneh, Nehavand, Malayer, and Borujerd valleys);
2. Eastern Pish-i Kuh between the Kuh-i Garin and Kuh-i Sefid (Kakawand, Chawari, Khawa, Alishtar, and Khorramabad valleys);
3. Western Pish-i Kuh (Hulailan, Kuh-i Dasht, Rumishgan, Tarhan, and Saimarreh valleys);
4. Mahidasht Valley;
5. Pusht-i Kuh; and
6. Khuzistan and the Mesopotamian lowlands.

Robert C. Henrickson

Stein (1940), Young (1966), and Goff (1966, 1971) conducted reconnaissances in Luristan, but only Goff (1966) and Stein illustrated pottery from a number of sites. More intensive surveys have since been done in Kangavar (Young 1975a), Malayer (Howell 1979), Hulailan (Mortensen 1979), and the Mahidasht (Levine 1975), but little has yet been published on Godin III.[2] Sites have been recorded and reported to be "Giyan IV–II" or "Godin III," but these terms lack precision in many cases when considered in the light of the Godin III sequence. The northern edge of the distribution, north of the Mahidasht and Kangavar valleys, is even less well known archaeologically and will not be discussed (see Swiny 1975). Table 36 provides gross distribution information for each phase of Godin III; the number of sites in each of the regions is based on occurrences of pottery datable by reference to the Godin III sequence.

Godin III:6

Architecture

The Level III:6 occupation lasted longer than any other at Godin Tepe. The architecture underwent gradual modification, with independent rebuilding or replacement of separate units or components. No structure built early in the phase survived even in highly modified form until the end. The eastern half of the Deep Sounding provides a long stratified sequence of domestic architectural contexts which yield subphases of Level (and thus Godin) III:6. The western portion of the Deep Sounding yielded the remains of a long-lived massive complex, perhaps a "public building," which was ultimately replaced by modest domestic architecture. The earliest Godin III occupation at Godin Tepe which probably lay on the lower slopes of the site was not reached by the excavations (R. Henrickson 1984a:chapter 5.2 and figures 7–18; see Young and Levine 1974:figure 20 for a preliminary plan).

Pottery

The pottery of Level III:6 is characterized by carinated pots and jars (and related forms with rounded profiles) in a wide variety of proportions and sizes (figure 58:1–3, 8–11, 13–16). The relatively simple painted decoration is concentrated in the main register, just above the carination or maximum diameter. Several trends in decoration of this register may be noted. Combinations of straight and wavy vertical lines tend to be early (figure 58:2, 11). "Shark's teeth" (figure 58:3, 16) and other such motifs are more characteristic of the middle to late subphases of Level III:6. "Bull's eyes" are late and continue into Level III:5 (figures 58:14; 59:10). In middle to late Level III:6 a characteristic motif on jars consists of a series of three arcs in the main register which form a triangle when seen from above; this basic layout may be embellished (figure 58:15).

Large ovoid jars with ridges around their necks and shoulders, similar in shape to jars of Susa Dc-d (e.g., Stève and Gasche 1971:plate 17.5; R. Henrickson 1984a:figures 59–62), are present but rare. Some appear to be imports at Godin Tepe. Well-made ovoid pithoi have "cable" decoration interspersed with bands of paint on the shoulders and finger-impressed bases (Young and Levine 1974:figures 25.18; R. Henrickson 1984a:figures 65–66); these continue into Level III:5 (R. Henrickson 1984a:figure 104). A distinctive jar form, found in both buff common and red-slipped wares, has an inset conical rim which extends to well below where the body joins the collar, thus forming a slosh-proof jar (figure 58:7). This is found in earliest Level III:6 and perhaps late Godin IV.

Medium and large bowls (rim diameter greater than circa 15 centimeters) with enlarged or modelled rims, usually painted, and carinations or complex profiles are characteristic of Level III:6. A wavy line is sometimes incised below the rim on both the interior and exterior (figure 58:4–6). Beakers with straight or curvilinear profiles are also found (figure 58:20).

A handmade burnished gray-black ware is found throughout Level III:6 (figure 65). Characteristic shapes include shallow carinated bowls (figure 58:2–19), tankards (figure 58:18), and large concave-sided cylindrical vessels (R. Henrickson 1984a:figures 85.12–14; 88.7, 23; Young 1969a:figure 23.15).

Godin III:6 is absent at Tepe Giyan (R. Henrickson 1986b).

Distribution

Godin III:6 pottery is found in the major southern and eastern valleys, particularly in the valleys east of the Kuh-i Garin. Too little material is available, however, to determine whether the full range of material known from Godin Tepe is found throughout the region. Between the Kuh-i Garin and Kuh-i Sefid, few Godin III:6 sites are known. Godin III:6 pottery is found in the Mahidasht, although the characteristic triple-arc motif on the shoulder is lacking. In the southwestern Pish-i Kuh only the excavations in the Rumishgan Valley have yielded Godin III:6 pottery in quantity.[3] In the southern Pusht-i Kuh, Dar Tanha has yielded a version of the triple arc (Vanden Berghe 1970b;1972:22–33, plates IX–X). Thus the documented distribution of Godin III:6 pottery is rather "hollow," given its almost total absence in central Luristan (areas 2 and 3 above) (table 36). The low intensity of survey effort there and the limited amount of pottery published may, however, accentuate or even create this pattern.

Susa Dc-d (Le Breton 1957) or Susa IVA (Carter 1980) monochrome pottery in the Susiana lowlands is clearly of the same tradition as Godin III:6. At Susa, recent excavations on the Acropole (Stève and Gasche 1971) and the Ville Royale (Carter 1980) have yielded stratified material comparable to Godin III:6 pottery (R. Henrickson 1986b:table 3). A limited number of sherds of imported monochrome painted pottery similar to Godin III:6 and Susa monochrome have also been found in well-dated context at al-Hiba (ancient Lagash) in Mesopotamia (Hansen 1973:figures 14–15 and personal communication).[4] The monochrome painted pottery traditions of Susiana and Luristan seem to have developed from the various interrelated early third millennium polychrome traditions of the Zagros piedmont zones (Carter n.d.; Haerinck n.d.). The main areas are Deh Luran (Gautier and Lampre 1905; Wright 1981b), Pusht-i Kuh (Vanden Berghe 1968b, 1970a-b, 1972, 1973d, 1979), and the Jebel Hamrin basin (Thuesen 1981).

Date

At al-Hiba the monochrome painted pottery is associated with sealings and tablets with the names of Enannatum, Eannatum, and Lummatur (son of Enannatum), thus providing a firm Early Dynastic III date (figure 64; Hansen 1973:68–69). This Early Dynastic III date is corroborated by material from the Acropole (Stève and Gasche 1971:plates 16–23) and Ville Royale I (Carter 1980:figures 25–29) which provide numerous parallels in both shapes and motifs to Godin III:6 (R. Henrickson 1986b). In Carter's sounding in the Ville Royale it is noteworthy that while the strata characterized by Susa IVA (Susa Dc) monochrome painted pottery (strata 9–12 [Carter 1980:figures 25–29]) provide numerous parallels to Godin III:6, the preceding strata (13–15) which are characterized by the use of a red wash on bowl and jar rims also provide good parallels to Godin III:6 (Carter 1980:figure 15). Susa IVA monochrome painted pottery seems to have flourished in Early Dynastic III and disappeared during the Akkadian period (Carter 1980:15–26, table 1).

The evidence from the Mahidasht also tends to support an Early Dynastic III date for Godin III:6, perhaps even extending back into Early Dynastic II. At Chogha Maran, 20 kilometers northwest of Kermanshah, roughly a dozen sherds of Godin III painted pottery, several identifiably Godin III:6, were found stratified in trash strata characterized by an assemblage of burnished red-slipped vessels in basic simple shapes (Maran Red-Slipped ware). All of these shapes have parallels in early Godin III:6 red-slipped wares at Godin Tepe (R. Henrickson 1984a:figures 168–72; 1986c). The most distinctive shape in the

Maran Red-Slipped assemblage was the slosh-proof jar found in earliest Level III:6 (cf. figure 58:7) and perhaps late Godin IV. A second common vessel form at Chogha Maran is a small, shallow hemispherical cup in burnished gray ware with a carination or ridge somewhat below the rim (R. Henrickson 1984a:figure 169). Occasionally, a line of incisions, in rare cases retaining a white filling, were cut into the carination. Godin III:6 gray ware provides generic shape parallels (figure 58:17) and Godin IV burnished gray pottery often has incised white-filled decoration (Young 1969a:figure 11). Found together with the Maran Red-Slipped pottery and the associated few Godin III:6 sherds in trash strata were almost two hundred sealings. Most were executed in a local style, but several may be dated to Early Dynastic II or III based on glyptic parallels to material from the Sin Temple at Khafajah (H. Pittman, personal communication, 1981). Thus, in at least the central portion of the Mahidasht, we find an assemblage contemporary with, but distinct from, early Godin III:6.

Godin III:6 therefore dates to Early Dynastic III times, perhaps as early as Early Dynastic II. Two radiocarbon dates from late Godin IV strata at Godin Tepe (Gak-1071 and SI-4908 [table 37]) suggest that Godin III:6 began by the mid-third millennium.

Cultural Developments

Godin III:6 is contemporary, but not coterminous, with the Early Dynastic III Period in southern Mesopotamia. The rather meager historical records reveal a number of independent or semiautonomous polities in the western Iranian highlands and lowlands (see Schacht, chapter 7, this volume; Stolper 1984).

This contrasts strongly with the widespread overall similarity of contemporary monochrome painted wares in the western Iranian highlands (Godin III), Susiana (Susa IV or Susa Dc [Carter 1980: 1984]), and Fars (Late Banesh [Sumner 1985:figure 3.J-O]). All three regional traditions are stylistically interrelated (R. Henrickson 1986b). This widespread similarity of monochrome painted traditions during a period of political fragmentation becomes more noteworthy when patterns in later periods are considered. Even when interregional political confederation is achieved later (see the discussion of Godin III:2 below), ceramic assemblages remain regionally distinct.

Developments east of the Kuh-i Garin may reflect the spread of the Godin III pottery tradition into the region, where the Godin III:6 assemblage replaces that of Godin IV. A measure of continuity from one to the next may be marked by early Godin III gray-black ware. Godin IV is characterized by a distinctive burnished gray-black ware (cf. "Yanik ware" [Burney 1961]). In central western Iran the Godin IV assemblage penetrated only into the valleys east of the Kuh-i Garin (Asadabad, Kangavar, Nehavand, Borujerd, Malayer, and the Hamadan Plain [Young 1966; Howell 1979; R. Henrickson 1986b]). With the sole exception of the very poorly known Hamadan Plain, only these valleys also have Godin III:6 monochrome painted and gray-black wares. Thus Godin III:6 gray-black ware is found only in valleys with Godin IV occupations. Although there is no direct continuity in forms from Godin IV to Godin III:6 gray-black wares, related forms are found (R. Henrickson 1986b). The Godin IV ceramic tradition seems to have been assimilated into the Godin III:6 assemblage as a minor component ware in this region. Rather than a "replacement" of one "ceramic people" by another, a measure of acculturation and continuity is manifest.

The spread of the Godin III:6 and related monochrome painted pottery traditions may reflect growing spheres of economic interaction since contemporary historical sources document an absence of political unity within Iran at this time. Widespread contemporary similarities in style suggest some form of interregional contact. This may be related to the contemporary, Early Dynastic III intensive importing of metals, minerals, and other materials best exemplified in the Early Dynastic III Royal Cemetery at Ur.

Godin III:5

Architecture

As the Level III:6 occupation in the area of the Deep Sounding drew to an end, almost the entire area was abandoned except for a small structure in the northwest quadrant. Thick layers of debris and wash covered the ruins of late Level III:6 architecture to the east. Only about 40 percent of the area of the Deep Sounding, just the flat summit of the mound, was built on at that time. The Level III:5 settlement lay farther to the north and east, in the area now lost to the erosion of the north slope of the mound. Level III:5 is characterized by small two- or three-room units, some separated from others by unroofed passageways or small courtyards. All of the buildings were destroyed in a single event, perhaps by an earthquake. Rooms and courtyards were filled with half a meter or more of collapse material. This debris covered a large number of complete or restorable pottery vessels, as well as the bodies of several persons apparently killed in the destruction. The area of the Deep Sounding then remained abandoned for some time (R. Henrickson 1984a:chapter 5.3, figures 19–21).

Pottery

Carinated pots and jars continue to be the most common vessel form in the painted pottery. Two basic types of decoration are used in the main register: (1) a band of solid or crosshatched diamonds; or (2) paired waterfowl, eagles, goats, "stingrays," or nested diamonds alternating with chevrons (figure 59:1, 2, 4, 8–11). The characteristic vessel forms of Level III:6 gray-black ware continue in use in Level III:5 (figure 59:5–6, 9). A well-made burnished red-slipped ware first appears in Level III:5 (figure 59:7, 9, 12, and figure 9); hemispherical bowls with a grooved rim are the most characteristic shape (figure 59:7).

Only grave 102 at Tepe Giyan (Contenau and Ghirshman 1935:plate 30) belongs to this horizon and is thus the earliest grave at that site.

Distribution

Godin III:5 pottery is found in most valleys east of the Kuh-i Sefid and in the Mahidasht (table 36 and figure 57). Level 5 at Baba Jan in Khawa (Goff 1976) is a typical Godin III:5 assemblage. In the western Pish-i Kuh, Godin III:5 is found in the Rumishgan and Hulailan valleys. None is known from the Pusht-i Kuh itself. A number of pieces are known from previous work at Susa, but little has come from the recent better-controlled excavations on the Acropole and Ville Royale (e.g., Stève and Gasche 1971:plates 16.12 or 75.8; R. Henrickson 1986b:table 3).

Date

At Susa this material is found only in the later contexts yielding monochrome pottery, which are dated to the Akkadian period (e.g., Stève and Gasche 1971:plates 16.10, 12; Carter 1980:figure 29.10; R. Henrickson 1986b:table 3). Two radiocarbon dates from Godin Tepe (QU-1043 and QU-1041) agree with this or a slightly lower date (see table 37). An Akkadian date, 2400–2200 B.C., is thus appropriate for Godin III:5 (figure 64).[5]

Cultural Developments

This phase is contemporary with the Akkadian and post-Akkadian periods. Susa had fallen under the control of the Akkadian dynasty which conducted numerous campaigns into the outer highlands, but no attempts at long-term control of these areas seem to have been made. Highland polities, ill-defined in our historical sources, were probably autonomous, except perhaps in the outermost valleys (Stolper 1984). The assemblages from Fars (Kaftari [Carter 1984]) and Susiana (Susa IVB [Carter 1980, 1984]) are distinctly different from Godin III:5 which is found only in the central Zagros highlands (R. Henrickson 1986b). The political isolation from the highlands is reflected in the pottery of Susa, which is increasingly Mesopotamian in character (Carter 1980); few Godin III:5

vessels or sherds are known from Susa (R. Henrickson 1986b:table 3).

Godin III:4

Architecture

After the destruction of Level III:5, the area of the Deep Sounding remained unoccupied for some time. The Level III:4 occupation may have begun within a decade or two, before the ruins of Level III:5 architecture had decayed to a featureless surface, since several new walls were built on top of previous ones. Considerable time and effort was invested in the Level III:4 construction which involved extensive cutting and terracing with stone retaining walls or revetments and stone pavements and steps. Far more stone was used in construction during this level than any other. Contigious buildings filled most of the area of the Deep Sounding, and a road ran through the southeast corner, following the same course it had since midway through Level III:6. This in itself is a good indication that occupation at Godin Tepe was continuous even though the area of the Deep Sounding was sometimes abandoned. In Level III:4 most of the nine complete or partial contemporary architectural units which were recovered seem to have been houses. Some modification, rebuilding, and expansion of the structures took place during the occupation. At least the central area was destroyed in an intense fire. In a room to the west the sprawled body of a person crushed under the bricky collapse lay on a stone pavement (Young and Levine 1974:plate XIX). Deep deposits of bricky collapse found in the rooms suggest that this destruction may have been general, perhaps due to an earthquake (R. Henrickson 1984a:chapter 5.4, figures 22–26; see Young and Levine 1974:figure 21 for a preliminary plan). An elaborate Godin III:4 burial was found in Operation EEE on the southwestern edge of the mound (R. Henrickson 1984a:figures 132–33).

Pottery

Level III:4 pottery clearly continues the tradition of the previous phases. Carinated pots and jars remain the characteristic shape for painted vessels (figure 60:1–3, 8–14). Ridges applied to the carination become more frequent and are integrated into the curve of the shoulder, providing a clear antecedent to the bag-shaped jars and pots with shoulder ridges typical of Godin III:2 (figure 60:3). Although simpler decoration in the style of Godin III:5 is found, the tendency is toward more elaborate decoration. Painted decoration exhibits a considerable amount of regional variability. The other characteristic ware in the assemblage is a well-made burnished red-slipped ware (figure 65). Simple hemispherical bowls and carinated

pots and jars are common (figure 60:4–7). The early Godin III(:6–5) gray-black ware no longer appears as part of the assemblage; cast-ups from earlier levels are rare (figure 65).

Godin III:4 corresponds to Giyan IVA (figure 64).

Distribution

Godin III:4 pottery has approximately the same distribution as that of Godin III:5 (table 36 and figure 57). Two basic areas may be distinguished within this region on the basis of differences in style of decoration: (1) valleys east of the Kuh-i Garin (Nehavand and Kangavar); and (2) valleys between the Kuh-i Garin and the Kuh-i Sefid and the Mahidasht.

The Kangavar and Nehavand valleys, east of the Kuh-i Garin, yield the most elaborately painted pottery. The decoration tends to be finely drawn, using large numbers of lines to build up rather complex patterns, particularly in borders. Elaborate motifs such as the "oiseau peigne" (comb animal) and a star in a circle, both found on Giyan IVA vessels, are extreme examples, but simpler geometric designs, such as rows of hatched diamonds or lozenges, are common (R. Henrickson 1986b:figures 19–23). Even within this region, however, there is perceptible variability from valley to valley. For example, the large carinated jars with the "oiseau peigne" at Tepe Giyan are more elaborately painted than those at Godin Tepe. Paired ducks, longer and thinner than those in Godin III:5, are found only at Godin Tepe. Low ridges used to decorate the lower portions of these large jars are found at both Godin and Giyan (cf. R. Henrickson 1984a:figures 119–20; 1986b:figures 12.3, 19.6–7, 20.7). In the region between the Kuh-i Garin and Kuh-i Sefid and in the Mahidasht the same basic assemblage is found, but the painted pottery has the simpler geometric types of decoration (e.g., Jamshidi IV [Contenau and Ghirshman 1935:plates 79–81, graves 11–19]).

Date

With little direct evidence available for the date of Godin III:4, the dates of the preceding and following phases provide the best indication (figure 64). However, the duration of the hiatus between Godin III:5 and III:4 is uncertain and although the architectural evidence might be taken to suggest that the interval is relatively brief, the pottery appears to indicate the opposite. It should be remembered that the occupation could have lasted more than a generation, particularly given the quality of construction, and that the best stratified pottery derives primarily from the end of the Godin III:4 phase. Typologically and stylistically there is considerable difference between the pottery of Godin III:5 and III:4. Godin III:4 may well begin very late in the third millennium, close to 2000 B.C. The one

Robert C. Henrickson

radiocarbon date from Godin III:4 (SI-4902 [Table 2]) is low, even when calibrated. A terminal date for Godin III:4 must be based on Godin III:2 for a terminus ante quem. As will be argued below, Godin III:2 probably begins 1900 B.C. Godin III:4 must therefore end very early in the second millennium.

Cultural Developments

Godin III:4 is contemporary with the Ur III and early Isin-Larsa periods in Mesopotamia. From the reign of Shulgi into that of Ibbi-Sin, Susa was a province of the Ur III state. Contact with highland polities, both peaceful and military, is documented by the Ur III "messenger texts" and year names (Stolper 1982, 1984). This political separation between the highlands on the one hand, and Susa and the lowlands on the other, is seen in the pottery assemblages. The notable local stylistic variability within the Godin III tradition in the highlands may mark separate ethnic or political groups (R. Henrickson 1984a, 1986b). Stylistic differentiation of material culture may represent an attempt to preserve distinct group identities in the face of pressure toward unification (e.g., Hodder 1982). This interpretation is compatible with the historical data which document numerous highland polities resisting strong lowland political and military action.

Godin III:3

Level III:3 was defined stratigraphically but little deposit lay within the area of the Deep Sounding (see strata 10A-10C and 11D-11H in the Master Section [Young and Levine 1974:figure 18]; these extended no more than 6 meters into the area of excavation). The duration of this phase is uncertain (R. Henrickson 1984a:chapter 5.5, figure 27). Little pottery was recovered from well-stratified architectural contexts. Since the pottery of this phase cannot be properly defined, it is impossible to discuss the distribution of contemporary material on other sites (cf. figure 65).

Godin III:2

Architecture

The relationship of Level III:2 to Level III:3 is unclear, but there was probably a hiatus in occupation between the two. Most of two large, well-built structures and parts of several other smaller ones were found in Level III:2. One was clearly the home of a relatively wealthy person. Some levelling had been done in preparation for the construction; later, part of the house was rebuilt in more modest fashion. Ambiguous evidence, primarily deep bricky collapse and a displaced wall, suggest that the final abandonment of this level may have been due to a severe earthquake (R. Hen-

rickson 1984a:chapter 5.6, figures 28–30; see Young and Levine 1974:figures 22–23 for preliminary plans).

The tomb in Operation O on the southern edge of Godin Tepe dates to Godin III:2, judging from typological and stylistic criteria (R. Henrickson 1984a:figures 154–57).

Pottery

By the time of Godin III:2, the carinated pots and jars which had characterized earlier phases became much more bag-shaped as the maximum diameter moved lower on the vessel. The former carination is replaced by a ridge on the shoulder. The painted decoration centered on this ridge tends to become simpler, consisting primarily of horizontal straight and wavy lines (figure 61:1, 2, 11–15, 22). Small vessels often have handles (figure 61:22). Both deep and shallow tripods with simple geometric painted decoration, in red-slipped and plain buff wares, are diagnostic of this phase (figure 62:9, 24). Conical buff bowls with pendant garlands painted below the rim and istakans, both ceramic and bronze, are also found (figures 61:9, 24). Several closely interrelated varieties of a well-made burnished gray ware are found in this phase and later (figure 65).[6] Most vessels in this gray ware are bowls with enlarged or grooved rims, although jars, pots, and even tripods are also found, a few with pattern burnishing (figure 61:21, 23, 24; R. Henrickson 1984a:figures 151–52). The common plain buff ware pottery which constitutes the majority of the assemblage is, however, handmade and often quite irregular in shape. Bowls and pots tend to have simple sinuous profiles and bevelled rims (figure 61:3–5, 7, 8).

Godin III:2 corresponds to Giyan III, Giyan IVC, and graves 108 and 110 of Giyan IVB (figure 64) (Dyson 1965b:233–34; 1973:692–97).[7]

Distribution

Godin III:2 pottery is markedly more common and widespread through Luristan and the Mahidasht than that of any other phase of Godin III, although there is regional stylistic variability (table 36 and figure 57). Sherds from ridged-shoulder jars are the single most common diagnostic for Godin III:2 in surface survey collections. Pieces of tripods are rare in survey collections, but are ubiquitous in graves (e.g., Operation O Tomb at Godin Tepe [Young 1969a:figure 30–31]; Giyan III graves at Tepe Giyan [Contenau and Ghirshman 1935:plates 25–29]; graves at Chigha Sabz and Kamtarlan II).

On the basis of various distinctive aspects of style and ware, at least two groups of valleys may be suggested: (1) Kangavar, Sahneh, and the Mahidasht; (2) Nehavand, Mirbeg (Baba Jan), and Rumishgan. Godin III:2 gray ware at present is known only in the

Kangavar Valley, although elsewhere it may not have been recognized as such. Red-slipped painted ware is rare in Level III:2 at Godin Tepe in comparison to further south and west in graves at Giyan (Nehavand), Chigha Sabz, and Kamtarlan II (both Rumishgan) (R. Henrickson 1986b). In the Mahidasht it seems to be entirely absent. Several varieties of bichrome painted decoration are found, primarily in the northern portion of the distribution. For example, simple and sparse bichrome linear decoration is found in the Mahidasht, Kangavar, and Hulailan. Red bands integrated within more complex dark decoration are found at Godin Tepe, Jamshidi, and Giyan (e.g., Contenau and Ghirshman 1935:plates XXIII.5 and 77.6; Young 1969a:figure 20.1; R. Henrickson 1986b). These stylistic differences may reflect ancient sociopolitical groupings within the overall Godin III:2 tradition.

Date

Several pieces of data may be used to establish the date of Godin III:2 (figure 64). Although there is relatively little similarity between the assemblages of Godin III:2 and contemporary Susa, some parallels may be noted, all dating to 1900–1600 B.C. Much of the Godin III:2 gray ware has shape parallels in the gray wares found in Khuzistan in the second quarter of the second millennium B.C. (Ville Royale Chantier B VII–V and A XV–XI, especially A XV–XIV [Gasche 1973:plates 28; 10.3,5,7–9; 12.1–4,7,21; 13.1,2]; Sharafabad [Schacht 1975:figures 6.e,o; 7.a,f,h]). Vessels of shape Groupe 14a from Ville Royale A XV–XIV (Gasche 1973:plate 16) are a good parallel to the body of deep tripods (e.g., figure 61:6,10,21).

Parallels to Mesopotamian material also suggest an early second millennium B.C. date. The classic form of the istakan, with a concave cylindrical body and sharp carination near the flat disk base, dates to the first half of the second millennium B.C. (R. Henrickson 1983–84).[8] A bronze tripod found in the Sin-kashid palace at Warka dates to no later than the eighteenth century B.C. (Strommenger 1962:38,plate 18a). Aside from its long legs, it is an excellent shape parallel to Godin III:2 deep tripods.[9]

A hematite seal found at Tepe Jamshidi in Grave 3 is dated to the seventeenth century B.C. (Schaeffer 1948:461; Dyson 1973:693). Young considers a globular gray ware jar in Tomb O at Godin Tepe (Young 1969a:figure 33.7) to be Hissar IIIC gray ware. At Tepe Hissar, Period IIIC has yielded a radiocarbon date of 1641 ± 65 B.C. (5730 half-life) (TUNC-20 [Bovington et al. 1974:1981]).

Charcoal from twigs and branches in a pot apparently placed on the roof slabs of Grave 11 at Tepe Guran yielded a date of 1220 ± 120 B.C. (5570 half-life;1500–1400 ± 134 B.C., MASCA-corrected)—

(Meldgaard, Mortensen, and Thrane 1963:133). This latter date is low and the standard deviation large. Since the pot was found outside the grave proper, on a roof slab, its contents need not date the tomb.[10] The two radiocarbon dates from Level III:2 at Godin Tepe are useless (table 37).

Based on these data, a date of 1900–1600 B.C. for Godin III:2 is appropriate.

Cultural Developments

The broad distribution and relative homogeneity of the Godin III:2 pottery suggest an unprecedented degree of regional integration. Survey data indicate that in some valleys the number of smaller sites declined, while central sites in large valley systems, such as Girairan in Alishtar, attained considerable size (Goff 1971:150).

This phase is contemporary with the Sukkalmah Period at Susa (for which see Stolper 1982:54–56; 1984; Carter 1984). The culmination of the regional integration seen in the pottery distribution is contemporary with the political consolidation of the Shimashki lands reflected in texts of the early second millennium. Historical data suggest that Shimashki lay in the highlands north of Susiana and/or Fars, but little certainty is possible. I have argued elsewhere (1984b) that Luristan is the most probable location of the Shimashki lands (cf. Vallat 1980 for another view; see Stolper 1982:45–46 for a review of discussion of the location). Whether it is proper to identify this archaeological phenomenon of ceramic homogeneity and apparent increase in settlement with historical "Shimashki" cannot be answered definitively using nontextual data. Nonetheless, by the early second millennium B.C. much of central western Iran had achieved a notable degree of socioeconomic, and perhaps political, integration. This suggests that the developments traced in the archaeological data from central western Iran may indeed represent Shimashki (R. Henrickson 1984b).

The confederated nature of the Elamite "state" both as a whole and in its component parts, such as the Shimashki lands, is an essential characteristic. The loose political cohesion corresponds quite well with the regional variation in the material cultures of components of the Elamite "state" outlined above.

Post-III:2

Architecture

This phase is defined stratigraphically by two graves cut through an irregular stretch of stone paving in the southeast corner of the Deep Sounding into the ruins of Level III:2. Typologically related material was found in eight other graves elsewhere at Godin Tepe

(R. Henrickson 1984a:chapter 5.7, figures 31, 158–62).

Pottery

Since the pottery of this phase comes only from graves at Godin Tepe, the corpus is limited in both size and variety. Two varieties of footed goblets or craters are diagnostic of this phase: (1) curvilinear profile and finely painted decoration ("Bird and Sun" [Goff 1966:107])—(figure 62:1–3); and (2) carinated with simple painted band decoration (so-called Habur) (figure 62:7, 10–12).[11] Footed bowls with a softly carinated or sinuous profile and decoration consisting of simple painted bands are another characteristic form (figure 62:5, 8). Other pottery associated with these goblets in graves consists of simple, irregular, handmade vessels (figure 62:4, 6, 9). Although a few sherds of these goblets are found in the latest strata of Godin III and others are illustrated in the sherd plates of the Giyan report (Contenau and Ghirshman 1935:plates 61a-c), none have been excavated in situ in habitation contexts.

The ware group frequencies in figure 65 are notably odd in comparison to the prior and succeeding phases. This can probably be attributed to the comparatively small sample size and the differing proveniences of the material. Pottery of Level III:2 and III:1 comes from domestic contexts, while all Post-III:2 material consists of grave goods.

Post-III:2 corresponds to Giyan IIa-b (figure 64)—(Dyson 1973:708–12).

Distribution

This pottery has a more restricted and sparser distribution than that of Godin III:2 (table 36 and figure 57). The "Habur" banded goblets are found throughout this range; the "Bird and Sun" goblets seem restricted more the the Kangavar/Nehavand region in the northeast (Goff 1966:site catalogue and plates 95–106; Dyson 1973:711). The pottery has been found in Giyan II graves excavated at Tepe Giyan, 64–65, 71, 73–77, 79–81); Tepe Jamshidi, Khawa Nehavand (Contenau and Ghirshman 1935: Graves (Contenau and Ghirshman 1935: Graves 1–2); Baba Jan, Khawa (Goff 1976:figure 11.20); Tepe Guran, Hulailan (Thrane, personal communication); Godin Tepe, Kangavar (Young 1969a:figure 35); and Bad Khoreh, Asadabad (Contenau and Ghirshman 1935:Graves II–III).

Post-III:2 pottery is relatively uncommon in survey (Young 1966; Goff 1966, 1971). Goff found sherds primarily in the northeastern Pish-i Kuh between the Kuh-i Garin and Kuh-i Sefid, although some was found farther to the west. A single tomb at Sarab Bagh, near Qabr Nahi in the south, yielded comparable material (Vanden Berghe 1973d:28, 34–35).

Date

It is difficult to date this assemblage due to the lack of good parallels (figure 64). Generic resemblances of the goblets with band decoration and the shallow flat-rimmed bowls with painted decoration on the rims to Habur ware (as found in the Habur assemblage of Dinkha Tepe) suggest a date somewhat before the middle of the second millennium B.C. (Hamlin 1974a:129–31; Dyson 1973:708). Parallels to the metal artifacts suggested a date of 1500–1400 B.C. for the "Bird and Sun" goblet graves (Dyson 1973:709). Generic parallels to the goblets are also found at Susa in Ville Royale Chantier A XIV–XIII (Gasche 1973:plate 16 [Groupe 14b]).

At Godin Tepe the two graves of this phase were sealed by courtyard surfaces of Level III:1. A radiocarbon sample from Level III:1 yielded a date of 1253 ± 50 B.C. (P-1469; 5570 half-life; 1520–1590 ± 62 B.C., MASCA-corrected).

A date of 1600–1400 B.C. is appropriate for the Post-III:2 phase.[12]

Cultural Developments

The pronounced uniformity and wide distribution of the Godin III:2 phase is notably diminished in Post-III:2 times. Only the goblets and bowls are useful index fossils for this later phase. The former widespread political or economic integration seems to have broken down. The distribution pattern suggests the annual migrations of transhumant pastoralists in the light of ethnographic data. The eastern group of valleys corresponds to modern summer pastures, the western to winter pastures (R. Henrickson 1986b; cf. Goff 1971:133–34; E. Henrickson 1985). If Post-III:2 is in fact contemporary with late Godin III:2 (see footnote 11; Dyson 1973:710–11; R. Henrickson 1986b), then the distribution of Post-III:2 pottery may reflect the pastoralist component of the vigorous Godin III:2 regional economy characterized by large and abundant sites.

Godin III:1

Architecture

Architectural remains of Level III:1 were found only in the eastern portion of the Deep Sounding. The cut for the large columned hall of Period II had removed the deposit in the west. A single multiroom house with substantial stone foundations and surrounded by several courtyards and passageways was the only coherent structure recovered. The area had suffered severely from erosion so that little mudbrick remained on the foundations (R. Henrickson 1984a:figures 32–33, 37; for a preliminary plan, see Young 1969a:figure 16).

Pottery

There is little pottery from contexts in Level III:1, although several smashed pithoi and smaller vessels were found in situ. Painted pottery is rare (figure 63:1, 2). The majority of the assemblage consists of irregular handmade vessels (figures 63:3–13).

Distribution

Given our inability to assemble a proper corpus of material from primary or secondary contexts and the nondescript nature of the pottery we do have, it is not possible to define the distribution of pottery of this phase beyond Godin Tepe itself.

Date

The sole evidence for the date of Godin III:1 is radiocarbon date P-1469, which suggests circa 1500 B.C. is appropriate (figure 64).[13]

Cultural Developments

The evidence from Godin Tepe suggests that by the middle of the second millennium the earlier integration, which had peaked in the Godin III:2 phase, had completely broken down. Even the quality of the pottery is inferior to earlier phases. The second half of the second millennium in the central Zagros is very poorly understood; what was happening is not at all clear (see R. Henrickson 1983–84 for a summary based on data from Tepe Giyan).

Late Unstratified

A number of burials, pits, patches of stone pavement, and bits of surfaces were not stratified within the Godin III deposit. The burials were either dug into or lay above the latest coherent Godin III remains in their particular areas. Pottery from these graves consists of irregular hemispherical cups with vertical loop handles and sinuous sided bowls. Both are difficult to date and not distinctive.

Given the absence of reliable stratified contexts and distinctive material, it is impossible to discuss regional distribution. Nor is there anything from these unstratified contexts on which to base a date.

Conclusion

The Period III sequence at Godin Tepe has provided a firm chronological basis for analysis of cultural development in the central Zagros from the mid-third to mid-second millennium B.C. This, in turn, facilitates investigation of synchronic and diachronic socioeconomic problems on both the regional and settlement levels. Combined with historical data, the archaeological material will aid in reconstruction of the sociocultural development of the region and definition of its role in the contemporary Elamite and Mesopotamian world.

Acknowledgments

This paper, a revision of a manuscript completed in May 1983, was originally intended as a preliminary report on my (then) unfinished dissertation (R. Henrickson 1984a). I have dealt elsewhere with questions of regional distribution (1984b, 1986b), chronology (1983–84, 1986c), and pottery production (1986a). The results of the Kangavar and Mahidasht surveys for the Godin III Period and the final report on Period III at Godin Tepe are being prepared.

I would like to thank T. Cuyler Young, Jr., Louis D. Levine, E. F. Henrickson, and E. Haerinck who read and commented on various drafts of this paper. I owe particular thanks to F. Hole for the invitation to contribute to this volume and his editorial comments. I have benefited from many suggestions: the errors, omissions, and matters of interpretation remain my responsibility. I would like to thank the West Asian Department of the Royal Ontario Museum, particularly Carole Gilbert, for assistance in preparation of the illustrations.

Notes

1. In the course of my analysis of the data, a new level was defined (R. Henrickson 1984a:chapter 5). This necessitated renumbering the early levels. The relationships between the revised designations and those used by Young (Young and Levine 1974) are summarized below:

Revised	Young and Levine 1974
III:1	III:1
Post-III:2	- - -
III:2	III:2
III:3	III:3
III:4	III:4
III:5	- - -
III:6	III:5(-6)

Post-III:2 is not an especially felicitous designation, but phases of Godin III at Godin Tepe were defined with reference to the architectural remains. The numbering of the levels had been fixed when Post-III:2 was established as a separate phase on the basis of distinctive pottery unlike that of either Level III:2 or III:1. (See also footnote 12.)

2. The limited Godin III pottery available from Young's 1961 reconnaissance in Sahneh, Asadabad, Nehavand, Borujerd, Khorramabad, and Ali Gudarz (Young 1966) has now been published (R. Henrickson 1986b:figures 18, 24–27), as have Royal Ontario Museum sherd reference collections from Tepe Giyan and Kazabad A (Hulailan [R. Henrickson 1986b:figures 19–23, 28]). Godin III pottery from the Kangavar (Young 1975a) and Mahidasht (Levine 1975a) survey projects is much more abundant and is being prepared for publication.

3. See also the "Susa D" site at Chemeshk, 30 kilometers east of Pol-i Dukhtar (Goff 1971:figure 8). Pope (1936) published only eight Godin III vessels or sherds from the Holmes Luristan Expedition excavations in the Rumishgan Valley. A travel grant from the Associates of the University of Toronto in 1981 enabled me to examine collections of unpublished material from Kamtarlan, Mirvali, Chigha Sabz, and Dumavizeh at the Oriental Institute (University of Chicago), the University Museum (University of Pennsylvania), and the Metropolitan Museum of Art (New York).

4. D. Hansen kindly sent me copies of unpublished drawings of this material from al-Hiba (see R. Henrickson 1986c for more detailed discussion of this material).

5. A third radiocarbon date from Godin III:5 (Gak-1070) is too high and must be rejected (see table 37). Two cylinder seals have been used to date this phase. The one from Grave 102 at Tepe Giyan was dated by Schaeffer to 2000 B.C. (1948:462), citing parallels to Ras Shamra. H. Pittman doubts this date (personal communication, 1981). Porada has suggested an ED III–Akkadian date (personal communication, 1984, citing Moortgaat [1966: No. 145] as a motif parallel). At Kamtarlan a "Gutian" seal is reported (Dyson 1973:693–94) to have been found with pottery comparable to Giyan Grave 102 (i.e., apparently Godin III:5).

6. In figure 65 it has been necessary to present Godin III:6–5 Gray-Black and Godin III:(4-)2 Gray ware in a single group. This was unavoidable because all were considered "gray-black ware" in field sherd counts. All of the gray-black pottery in Levels III:6–5 is what I now refer to as "Godin III(:6–5) Gray-Black ware." In Level III:2 all of the sherds would be "Godin III(:2) Gray ware," aside from a few inevitable upcasts of the early Gray-Black ware. The situation in Level III:4 is less certain. Having handled all of the sherds, I can say that most of the gray pottery in Level III:4 is related to Godin III:2 Gray ware, but upcasts of the early Gray-Black ware are found. Since the frequencies are based on material from both primary ("floor") and secondary (trash strata) contexts, some out-of-place sherds were probably included in the figures on which figure 65 is based.

7. In Grave 108 pots 1 and 3, and probably 2 and 6, are Godin III:2. Pot 7, however, looks rather like Godin III:4, but the quality of the illustration leaves considerable uncertainty (Contenau and Ghirshman 1935:plate 31).

8. See the bronze istakan with a handle inscribed with the name of Atta-hushu, a contemporary of Sumu-abum of Babylon (Sollberger 1968); unfortunately it was not found in a properly supervised excavation.

9. The reported association between Giyan III:2 pottery (tripods and vessels with shoulder ridges) and a bronze Gilgamesh standard at Cheshmeh Mahi (Maleki 1964) has been treated with scepticism (Porada 1965b:86,235, note 12; Moorey 1971:125).

10. The pottery and metal objects from this grave (Thrane 1968) have Godin III:2 parallels (R. Henrickson 1986b [contra Dyson 1973:710]; cf. Tomb O at Godin [Young 1969a:figures 30–33], or graves of Giyan III [Contenau and Ghirshman 1935:plates 25–29]).

This radiocarbon date may serve as a rough terminus ante quem for Godin III:2.

11. Dyson (1973:708–9) postulated two chronological phases at Tepe Giyan based on the two types of goblets: 1) Giyan IIa (the banded or "Habur" goblets); and 2) Giyan IIb (the "Bird and Sun" goblets). The distinction of two discrete chronological phases is difficult to support, particularly with the evidence from Giyan. Given the appreciable co-occurrence of the two types, they may instead reflect regional or social variability.

Goblet Type	Giyan	Godin
"Bird and Sun" (IIb)	1	1
Banded or "Habur" (IIa)	3	6
Both	7	2
Totals	11	9

Compare, for example, the diversity in shape and decoration of the pottery from the Godin III:4 graves at Tepe Giyan (figure 64) (Contenau and Ghirshman 1935:plate 31–34) or from Level III:4 houses at Godin Tepe (R. Henrickson 1984a:figures 110–21) and the two distinctive styles of decoration used on slightly different vessel forms (slightly different proportions) found together on floors of Level III:5 (R. Henrickson 1986a).

Dyson postulated a third phase, Giyan IIc, at Tepe Giyan (1973:709–10) which is characterized by tall carinated pedestal-based goblets, usually with painted decoration. A characteristic motif is the crosshatched triangle. I have assigned these to a "carinated pedestal-based goblet" phase which is more related to Iron I than late Godin III (R. Henrickson 1983–84). These are not found at Godin Tepe, and their chronological relationship to Godin III:1 is unknown.

12. Several ambiguous bits of evidence suggest that Post-III:2 (Giyan II) may have been contemporary with later Godin III:2 (Giyan III)—(Dyson 1973:710–11; R. Henrickson 1986b,c). At Bad Khoreh in Tombs 1–3, several Giyan II-like vessels are found in predominantly Giyan III groups (Contenau and Ghirshman 1935:plate 82). At Godin Tepe a large piece of a tripod was found in Level III:1, but its context is uncertain. If it indeed belongs in Level III:1 which sealed the Post-III:2 graves, it would provide evidence for the contemporaneity of later Godin III:2 and the Post-III:2 assemblage.

13. Another sample, P-1470, attributed to Godin III:1 context yielded an unacceptably low date (see table 37).

Table 36. Gross Distribution of Phases of Godin III

				Godin III		
Region	6	5	4	2	Post-2	1
East of the Kuh-i Garin	8	4	3	10	4	1
Eastern Pish-i Kuh	6	12	8	29	5	
Mahidasht	X	X	X	X		
Western Pish-i Kuh	4	5	2	12	5	
Pusht-i Kuh	2				2	

Notes:
X = found but number of sites not yet available.
All totals are *minimum* figures (for details, see Henrickson 1986b: Tables 2–4).

Table 37. Godin III and Late Godin IV Radiocarbon Dates from Godin Tepe

	Godin III					
Lab Number	Level	Area	Libby B.P.	Libby B.C.	5730 B.C.	Masca B.C.†
P-1469*	III:1	1028	3203±50	1253±50	1349±52	1520-1590±62
P-1470*	III:1	1012	2742±41	792±41	874±42	940- 980±52
QU-1044	III:2	2016	<3980±110	<2030±110	<2149±113	<2590±123
SI-4900	III:2	2014	2655±70	705±70	785±72	850- 890±82
SI-4902	III:4	4003	3405±80	1455±80	1557±82	1770-1870±92
GaK-1070+	III:5	5004	4173±101	2223±101	2348±103	2920±113
QU-1043	III:5	5019	3580±100	1630±100	1737±103	2090±113
QU-1041	III:5	5004	3660±80	1710±80	1820±82	2140±92
GaK1071+	Late Godin IV		3803±120	1853±120	1967±124	2190-2300±134
SI-4908	Late Godin IV		3880±50	1930±50	2046±52	2440-2480±62

Notes:
* *Radiocarbon* 12:580.
+ Young 1969a:49, note 37: based on reanalysis of stratigraphy, GaK-1071 is now assigned to late Godin IV.
† (Ralph, Michael, and Han 1973)
All other dates are previously unpublished.

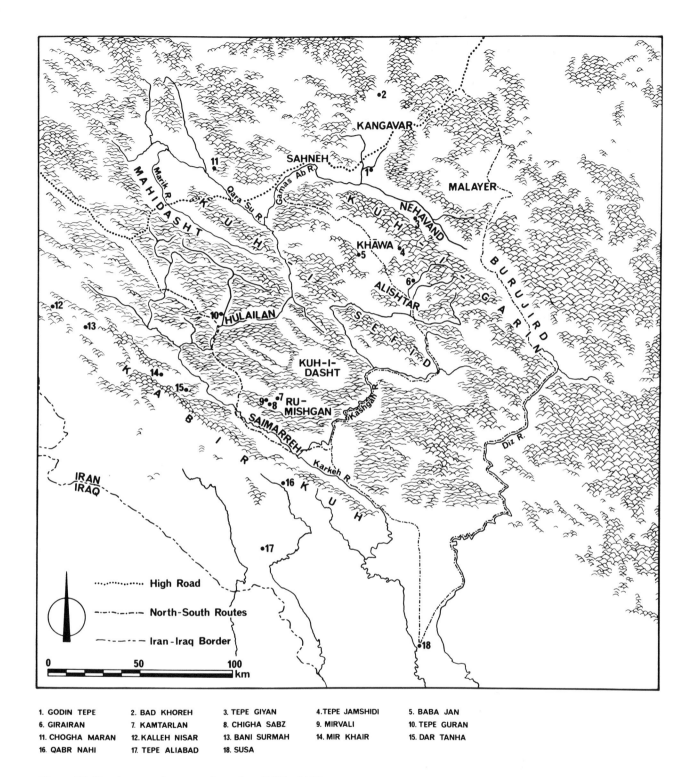

Figure 57. Sites in central western Iran circa 2600–1400 B.C.

1. GODIN TEPE
2. BAD KHOREH
3. TEPE GIYAN
4. TEPE JAMSHIDI
5. BABA JAN
6. GIRAIRAN
7. KAMTARLAN
8. CHIGHA SABZ
9. MIRVALI
10. TEPE GURAN
11. CHOGHA MARAN
12. KALLEH NISAR
13. BANI SURMAH
14. MIR KHAIR
15. DAR TANHA
16. QABR NAHI
17. TEPE ALIABAD
18. SUSA

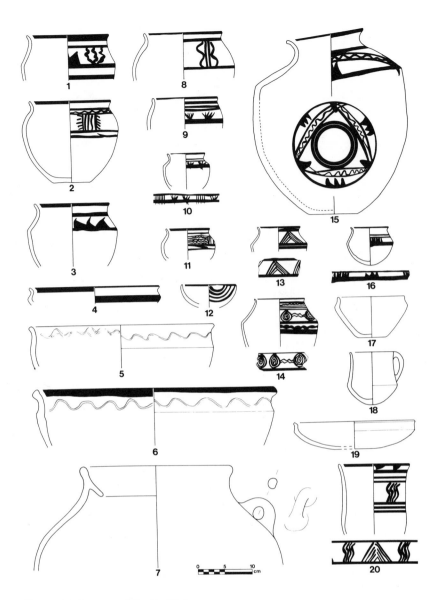

Figure 58. Pottery of Godin III:6

Key	Object Number	Locus	Description
1	73-2133	6050/6043	Buff common; wheelmade; dark gray paint.
2	73-2044	6032/9944	Buff common; tournette; dark brown paint.
3	73-2005	6025/6027	Cream-slipped common; wheelmade; dark red paint.
4	73-2072	6039/6031	Buff common; wheelmade; dark red-brown paint.
5	73-2099	6043/6050	Buff common; tournette; incised decoration.
6	73-2100	6028	Buff common; handmade; dark red paint and incised decoration.
7	73-2045	6030/9944	Buff common; handmade.
8	73-2115	6033	Buff common; wheelmade; red-brown paint.
9	71-2571	6129	Buff common; wheelmade; dark red-brown paint.
10	73-2007	6025/6027	Buff common; wheelmade; dark brown paint.
11	73-2118	6050/6043	Buff common; wheelmade; dark brown paint.
12	71-2546	6153	Buff common; wheelmade; dark brown paint.
13	71-2572	6153	Buff common; wheelmade; dark brown paint.
14	71-2545	6153	Buff common; wheelmade; dark brown paint.
15	71-348	6085	Cream-slipped common; tournette; brown paint.
16	71-35	6134	Cream-slipped common; wheelmade; dark red-brown paint.
17	71-135	6163/6162	Gray-black common; handmade; burnished.
18	67-86	M, Area 1	Gray-black coarse; handmade; burnished.
19	73-2022	6049	Gray-black common; handmade; burnished.
20	71-2051	6114	Buff common; wheelmade; dark red-brown paint.

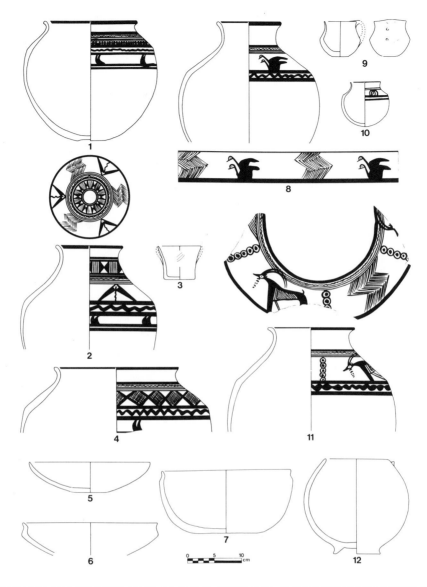

Key	Object Number	Locus	Description
1	71-37	5004	Buff common; tournette; dark red-brown paint.
2	69-2002	5016/5014	Buff common; tournette; dark brown paint.
3	71-113	5020	Gray-black coarse; handmade; burnished.
4	71-2040	5006	Cream-slipped common; tournette; dark brown paint.
5	71-59	5006	Gray-black coarse; handmade; burnished.
6	71-2080	5006	Gray-black common; handmade; burnished.
7	69-2503	5028	Red-slipped common; handmade.
8	71-2001	5004	Cream-slipped common; tournette; dark brown paint.
9	71-63	5006	Red-slipped common; tournette.
10	71-87	5006	Buff common; wheelmade; dark brown paint.
11	71-2003	5003	Buff common; tournette; dark brown paint.
12	71-319	5006	Buff coarse; tournette.

Figure 59. Pottery of Godin III:5

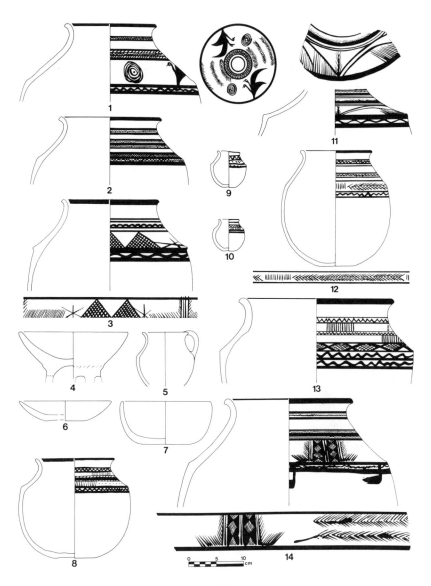

Key	Object Number	Locus	Description
1	69-2005	4009	Cream-slipped common; tournette; dark brown paint.
2	69-2027	4003	Cream-slipped common; tournette; dark brown paint.
3	67-417	4070	Buff common; tournette; dark brown paint.
4	69-2038	4002	Red-slipped coarse; handmade.
5	69-2556	4005/4026	Red-slipped coarse; handmade.
6	69-2569	4040	Red-slipped coarse; handmade.
7	69-2036	4003	Red-slipped coarse; handmade.
8	73-389	EEE, grave	Cream-slipped common; tournette; dark brown paint.
9	73-394	EEE, grave	Cream-slipped common; wheelmade; dark brown paint.
10	73-393	EEE, grave	Cream-slipped common; wheelmade; dark brown paint.
11	69-2516	4048	Buff common; tournette; dark brown paint.
12	71-2432	4043	Buff common; tournette; dark brown paint.
13	69-2008	4006	Cream-slipped common; tournette; dark brown paint.
14	71-2111	4005/4004	Buff common; tournette; dark brown paint.

Figure 60. Pottery of Godin III:4

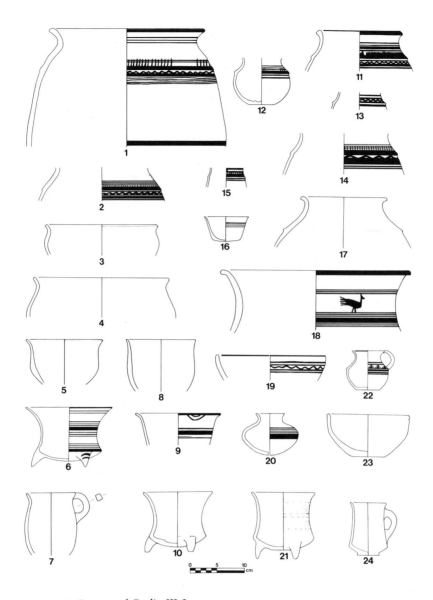

Figure 61. Pottery of Godin III:2

Key	Object Number	Locus	Description
1	69-2011	2040	Cream-slipped common; tournette; dark brown paint.
2	69-2494	2053	Buff common; tournette; dark brown paint and incised decoration.
3	69-2443	2039	Buff common; handmade.
4	67-2133	2035/2036	Buff coarse; handmade.
5	67-2171	2049	Buff coarse; handmade.
6	69-199	2200	Buff common; wheelmade; dark brown paint.
7	67-2169	2048/2049	Buff-slipped coarse; handmade.
8	67-2172	2049	Buff-slipped coarse; handmade.
9	69-2318	2200/2016	Buff common; handmade; dark brown paint.
10	69-200	2078	Red-slipped coarse; wheelmade.
11	69-2413	2049/2047	Buff common; tournette; dark brown paint.
12	69-2707	AA6	Red-washed common; wheelmade; dark brown paint.
13	67-2126	2037/2038	Red-washed common; wheelmade; dark brown paint.
14	69-2491	1811/2076	Red-washed common; tournette; dark brown paint.
15	69-2439	2039	Buff common; wheelmade; dark brown paint.
16	69-2238	2052	Red-washed common; wheelmade.
17	69-2479	2064	Buff coarse; tournette.
18	67-2124	2037/2038	Red-washed coarse; tournette; dark brown paint.
19	67-2125	2037/2038	Buff-slipped coarse; handmade; dark brown paint.
20	67-370	2024/2025	Buff common; wheelmade; dark brown paint.
21	67-213	O, Tomb, Burial B	Gray common; wheelmade (?); pattern burnished.
22	67-152	2030/2031	Red-slipped common; wheelmade; dark brown paint.
23	67-234	O, Tomb, Burial B	Gray common; wheelmade (?); burnished.
24	67-251	O, outside tomb	Gray common; wheelmade (?); burnished.

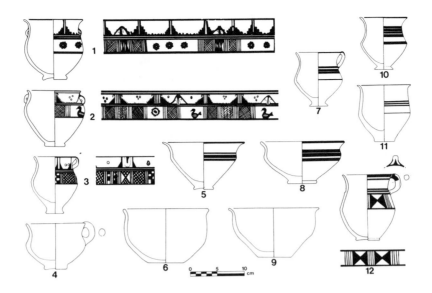

Key	Object Number	Locus	Description
1	69-662	R, Burial 1	Buff common; wheelmade; brown paint.
2	69-668	R, Burial 1	Buff common; wheelmade; brown paint.
3	67-396	AA2, Burial 1	Buff common; wheelmade; dark brown paint.
4	69-676	R, Burial 2	Buff coarse; handmade.
5	69-464	C3, Burial 1	Cream-slipped common; wheelmade; dark brown paint.
6	69-666	R, Burial 1	Buff coarse; handmade.
7	67-400	AA2, Burial 2	Buff common; wheelmade; dark brown paint.
8	67-402	AA2, Burial 2	Buff common; wheelmade; dark brown paint.
9	69-665	R, Burial 1	Buff coarse; handmade.
10	67-401	AA2, Burial 2	Buff common; wheelmade; dark brown paint.
11	69-660	R, Burial 1	Buff common; wheelmade; dark brown paint.
12	69-678	R, Burial 2	Buff common; wheelmade; dark brown paint.

Figure 62. Pottery of Post-III:2.

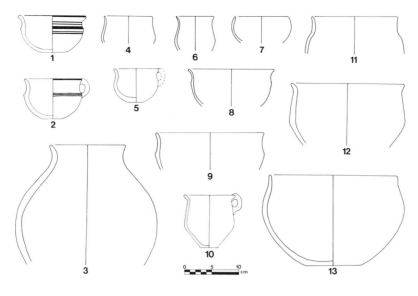

Key	Object Number	Locus	Description
1	67-311	1030	Buff common; wheelmade (?).
2	67-437	1010	Buff common; wheelmade (?); dark brown paint.
3	67-2067	1010	Buff coarse; handmade.
4	67-2060	1100	Buff common; handmade.
5	67-342	1009	Buff coarse; handmade.
6	67-2061	1012	Buff common; handmade.
7	67-2070	1006	Gray common; handmade; burnished.
8	67-2068	1008	Buff-slipped coarse; handmade; burnished.
9	67-2047	1022/1023	Buff coarse; handmade.
10	67-145	1100	Buff coarse; handmade.
11	67-2063	1014	Buff coarse; handmade; burnished.
12	67-2046	1022/1023	Buff coarse; handmade.
13	67-2073	1030/1031	Buff heavy coarse; handmade; burnished.

Figure 63. Pottery of Godin III:1.

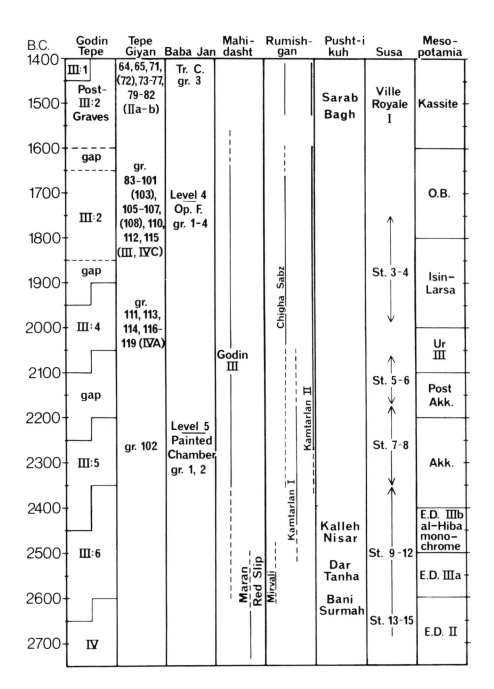

Figure 64. Chronology of central western Iran circa 2600–1400 B.C.

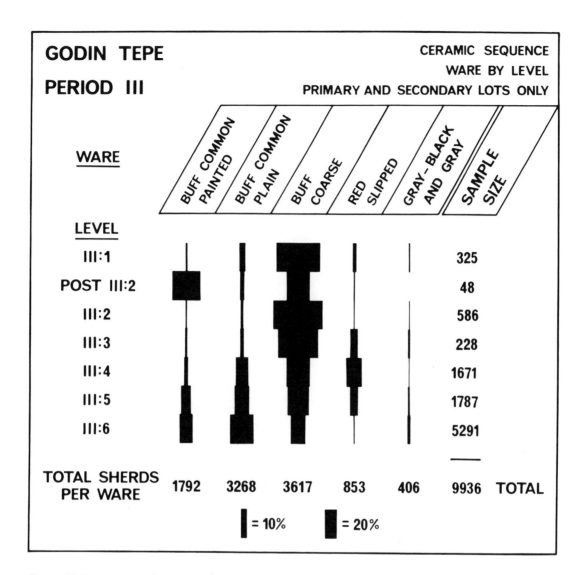

Figure 65. Frequencies of major Godin III ware groups at Godin Tepe.

Chapter 9

The Iron Age

LOUIS D. LEVINE

Introduction

The first two-thirds of the first millennium B.C. witnessed changes in western Iran as dramatic as any the area had undergone since the Neolithic. At the turn of the millennium, the three great historical rivals in lowland Mesopotamia—Elam, Babylonia, and Assyria—were still playing out a drama that had begun almost two thousand years before. By the end of the period, not only had these three powers disappeared, but the Achaemenid Empire was in the hands of the Macedonian Alexander, bringing the last of the great oriental empires of antiquity to its conclusion. The periods that followed are overlain by a Hellenistic veneer that often obscures the structures developed during the first seven centuries of the first millennium. The focus of this chapter is to outline what we presently know about western Iran in the first millennium B.C.

The chapter differs from others in this volume in a number of essential features. From post-Neolithic times through the end of the second millennium, with the exception of short intervals, the historical center of gravity for western Iran was the Khuzistan Plain. When the Zagros and the western Iranian plateau figured in the picture, they did so as parts of Elamite civilization, or as independent but less influential cultural areas interacting with Elam or Mesopotamia. From the start of the first millennium, this changed, slowly at first, but with ever-increasing rapidity. Early in the millennium, the written sources record the appearance of previously unknown groups in the highlands; with the demise of Elam as a major power, the focus of western Iran shifted decisively to these other groups. The Zagros first replaced Khuzistan at center

stage and then shared that position with it until the Seleucid Period. Thus, the major concern of this chapter is perforce the mountains, not the lowland plain of Khuzistan.

Another circumstance alters the shape of this chapter as well. Unlike Khuzistan, and Susa in particular, which have been intensively researched for almost a century, the archaeological study of the Zagros is a relatively recent development. Until the late 1950s virtually the entire corpus of excavated material bearing upon the Iron Age of this extensive highland area came from a cemetery at Tepe Sialk, on the eastern periphery of our area, and a few graves at Tepe Giyan. The Achaemenids were known only from the two imperial sites of Persepolis and Pasargadae.

Furthermore, the approach to the archaeology of the Iron Age, even after World War II, has differed in kind from that used in other periods considered in this book. Basic to this approach has been an orientation toward excavation. Until the very end of the 1960s, no intensive survey was done in the highlands of Iran, and the few (mostly unpublished) highland surveys done are still first-generation efforts. This contrasts with Khuzistan, where a second and third generation of survey work has built upon Adam's initial effort in 1960–61 (Adams 1962). But even in Khuzistan, the two periods falling within the chronological compass of this book that have not advanced substantially beyond Adam's initial attempt are the Iron Age and the Achaemenid period.

This chapter surveys what is known about Iron Age and Achaemenid western Iran and introduces the historical data as a framework around which the archaeological edifice can be built. After discussing the sequences of Iron Age sites, suggestions will be made for their periodization. The survey data from western Iran can then be considered before moving to some general observations about the Iron Age of western Iran.

The Historical Framework

Viewed from the perspective of western Iran, the period dealt with in this chapter can be divided into three broad historical subdivisions. The first covers the initial 350 years of the first millennium, and is largely, although not exclusively, dominated by Assyria. This is followed by the rise to power of the Medes after the fall of Assyria in 612 B.C. The third period, that of the Achaemenid kings, begins with Cyrus's accession to the throne in 559 B.C. and ends with the defeat of Darius III by Alexander the Great in 330 B.C. A period of political fragmentation serves as an epilogue to the story.

The Neo-Assyrian Period

Although Assyria was the predominant power during much of this period, Babylonia and Elam in the south and Urartu in the north at times also played important roles in western Iran (figure 66). In the Zagros proper, however, there were no geopolitical units which could rival their power. Rather, a profusion of geographical names is found, representing polities of varying size.

The most important source for the reconstruction of the political picture during this period is the corpus of Neo-Assyrian royal inscriptions. These are contemporary with the events themselves, but derive from an area adjacent to, rather than from, western Iran itself. Inscriptions relating to Iran begin in the reign of Shalmaneser III (858–824 B.C.) and extend into the reign of Ashurbanipal (668–627 B.C.). The most abundant information comes from the reigns of Shalmaneser III, Tiglath-pileser III (745–727 B.C.), and Sargon II (722–705 B.C.); otherwise, the royal inscriptions only rarely touch on western Iran. In addition to the royal inscriptions, we have other documents including letters from or to the royal court, treaties and historical omens—all from Assyria—chronicles from Babylon, and occasional Elamite texts.

The geopolitical situation of the Zagros can be described in terms of four areas.[1] In the far north, the area south and west of Lake Urmia is under the control of Urartu by about 800 B.C. and continues under its control until the rise of the Medes. Prior to this eastward expansion of Urartu, the area seems to have been divided into small units, although we infer this only by reading backward from later references (figure 66).

To the south of Lake Urmia, in Iranian Kurdistan, the sources refer to a kingdom called Mannea. The extent of this polity and details about its governance

are unclear, but a hereditary king seems to have ruled a number of provinces which were under the control of governors. Both Urartu and Assyria meddled in Mannean affairs.

In Luristan, a second Zagros kingdom, Ellipi came to power. Here a provincial system is less in evidence, although occasional references to such provinces appear in the sources. Kingship is hereditary, as in Mannea. Elam, rather than Urartu, serves as the counterfoil to Assyrian hegemony in this area, and Ellipi is found allied with one or the other at different points during the period.

In contrast with Mannea and Ellipi, the valleys of the Khorasan Road which lie between Kurdistan and Luristan are not organized into a single political unit. Instead, numerous small principalities are found, each one under the control of what the Assyrians call a "city chief" (bēl āli). Along the western stretch of the road, the most important of these "cities" is Harhar. Farther east, starting approximately at Bisitun, the many groups encountered are collectively identified as Medes by the Assyrians, although more specific names are usually used. As with so many of these terms, it is impossible to know precisely what is meant by "city chief" or even "Mede."

At the beginning of the Neo-Assyrian Period, Assyrian relations with Mannea and the area adjacent to the Khorasan Road seem to have been aggressive. Shalmaneser III repeatedly raided the area but established no lasting control. Nor is there any evidence that such control was envisaged as part of Assyrian strategy. Ellipi is hardly mentioned in the sources. In any event, Babylonia had experienced a brief resurgence in the ninth century, and it is unlikely that Assyria could have exerted much influence over the area that borders on Babylonia. Whatever goods and products Assyria needed from the Zagros and points east seem to have been obtained from the Urmia region, although there is little textual evidence to support this view (Levine 1977a). This contact was severed by the incorporation of the Urmia region into the Urartian kingdom at the turn of the eighth century.

Beginning in the reign of Tiglath-pileser III (744–727 B.C.), a significant political change occurred in the central western Zagros. Harhar, which is probably located in the Kermanshah Valley or the eastern Mahidasht, was turned into an Assyrian province, with the express purpose of serving as a base to control the Medes. Thus, for the first time, Assyria imposed its imperial administrative structure on western Iran.

It is difficult to judge just how long this control lasted. Little is heard of the areas along the Khorasan Road after the reign of Sargon II (721–705 B.C.), perhaps indicating a loss of control. But it is equally true that once an area became part of the Assyrian Empire, it normally fell from view in the royal inscriptions,

Louis D. Levine

unless trouble brought in the army. The few hints that we have about the situation there are contradictory. On the one hand, some of the groups appear as enemies, or potential enemies, in the records of Sargon II and Sennacherib. On the other, the vassal treaties of Esarhaddon are with Median principalities. This would seem to imply continued control of the area, including the Kermanshah Valley.

To summarize, the geopolitical map of western Iran up to approximately 650 B.C. can be roughed in as follows. In the far north and far south, two major states controlled territory; Urartu was in the Lake Urmia basin, Elam in Khuzistan and the adjacent mountains. Sandwiched between these states were two extensive, but presumably less populous and less powerful kingdoms, Mannea in Kurdistan and Ellipi in Luristan. These in turn flanked the valleys of the Khorasan Road, which were not organized into an extensive political unit.

It should be stressed that the static picture presented here is overly simplified and only an approximation of the historical reality. Occasionally we see in the sources that parts of one unit are detached and added to another and that alliances are constantly shifting. But the general outlines of the geopolitical picture remain relatively stable, and unless the geographical reconstruction is substantially revised in the light of new information, it will need only relatively fine tuning in the future.

Before considering the next two periods, it is useful to sketch yet another kind of distributional data available to us from the Assyrian sources, the data derived from personal and geographical (especially "city" and "tribal") names. Here, too, the discussion must be prefaced with cautionary remarks. The personal names represented in the texts reflect only that part of the population which the Assyrians thought worth recording, namely the ruling personages. Thus, these names do not necessarily represent a cross-section of the local population. Moreover, we still only imperfectly control the Assyrian system of transcribing foreign names, and, thus, ascriptions to language groups are often tenuous.[2]

With geographic names, we look for other information. Significant changes in the geographical terminology would indicate changes in the population base, as geographical names are notoriously conservative. To measure such change or continuity, the same areas need to be recorded in both earlier and later documents. This presupposes opportunities for contact with these areas in earlier periods, however indirect. But in many cases, no clearly demonstrable prior contact can be proven.

Nonetheless, we can make certain statements. Much of the terminology used in the cuneiform sources of the late third and second millennia for de-

scribing areas to the north and east of Babylonia has changed by the first millennium. Subar(t)u, Guti, Simurrum, and Hurri do not occur in the later texts, and even Lullu(bi) is rarely used. Only a few names survive and these usually in areas where contact with the lowlands is most probable—those immediately adjacent or of easy access, such as along the westernmost flanks of the Zagros or the Khorasan Road.

The new geographical names are found at a greater distance from Mesopotamia, either farther into the mountains of Luristan and Kurdistan, or farther east along the Khorasan Road. These names have not been subjected to a thorough linguistic analysis. S. Brown, however, has recently observed that many names which are compounded with an initial *Gin* or *Kin* are restricted to central western Iran. He has suggested that this element be compared with Iranian and Sanskrit *kantha* (town), pointing to an Indo-European language base for these names (1979: 68). Other "native" geographical names should be noted. Some begin with the Semitic *bīt*, usually a "tribal" designation in first millennium Mesopotamia, while other names form groups that cannot be identified as to language family. Thus, new geographical names figure, but some older names persist in areas adjacent to the lowlands.

Personal names show an equally diverse mosaic pattern. For the first time, names that can be analyzed as Iranian are found. Such names, however, appear not only in areas that can be identified as Iranian, such as Media and Parsua, but also in areas such as Ellipi. Other linguistic groups are also identified by onomastic analysis. Hurrian names, or names that occur in the heavily Hurrian environment of Nuzi around 1500 B.C., are found in our texts (Boehmer 1964). Semitic names are used, but it might be argued that they are purposefully imitative of those used in the perceived "superior" Mesopotamian culture area. Finally, members of the same family can use names from a number of these language groups.

The one major exception to the picture drawn here is Elam. While we do have new cities serving as "capitals," Elam and the Elamite language survived the upheavals of the transition from the Bronze Age to the Iron. Furthermore, the name Anshan, which is intimately linked with Elam also survives in the texts.

When the evidence from personal and place names is taken together, certain conclusions seem inevitable. New groups have moved into western Iran. As unfashionable as *Volkserwanderungen* are in modern archaeological literature, I know of no other vehicle for the introduction of language. That part of this movement is connected with the arrival of Iranians in western Iran cannot be doubted. In the first half of the second millennium, we have no evidence of Iranian names. For the Neo-Assyrian Period, the evidence of such names is widespread. What remains unclear is the scale of this movement, and the levels of society that were affected.

The picture, however, is not monolithic. While there is no doubt that Iranians are present, many of the areas discussed reveal a mosaic of different language groups. As yet, we cannot control these data quantitatively, and so statements must be impressionistic, but the onomastics seem to indicate that the more easterly reaches of the Great Khorasan Road are more heavily Iranian, while the western Zagros are more polyglot. The northern and southern areas, on the other hand, betray fewer or no Iranian elements.

The Median Period

The collapse of the Assyrian Empire led to major changes in the geopolitical structure of western Iran. Two successor states divided much of the Assyrian Empire, after collaborating in its overthrow. The Neo-Babylonians acquired the Tigris-Euphrates Valley and the territories in the west, while the Zagros kingdoms and provinces apparently became part of the Median kingdom. Elam regained a precarious and short-lived independence (Miroschedji 1982:62: Carter and Stolper 1984:54–55).

The circumstances surrounding the rise of the Median state are obscure. An account is preserved in Herodotus, but as Helm (1981) has shown, the story is replete with folkloristic elements. S. Brown (1985) has recently tried to salvage parts of the account, and while his arguments are plausible, they lack confirmation. Thus, we must either accept Herodotus's account in part or in whole, or be left with little to say about the Median kingdom.

Whatever the historical circumstances surrounding the fragmented Medes visible a century earlier in the records of Sargon II had been forged into a unit strong enough to contest the Assyrian heartland. It is usually assumed, combining the attack on Assyria reported in the *Babylonian Chronicle* with the chronology of Herodotus and subsequent events, that by this time a Median state had emerged. This position has recently been challenged by Sancisi-Weerdenburg (1985), who would see a refragmentation after the initial success against the Assyrians, without any enduring state structure.

Unfortunately, our written sources for the period, aside from Herodotus, are virtually nonexistent. The collapse of Assyria left a power vacuum in the Iranian highland areas, but the presence of a successor Median state, to say nothing of its territorial extent, is moot. By the end of the period, however, when Cyrus usurped the throne, there is some evidence for more than a loose confederation of Zagros polities. First, Astyages founded a royal city at Hamadan. Second,

there is no evidence for the plethora of small political groupings that marked the Neo-Assyrian Zagros. Finally, all of western Iran seems to have passed to Achaemenid rule. Thus, it appears that sometime in the Median Period, a kingdom formed in Media, incorporated the native states of western Iran, and was in turn incorporated as one of the component parts of Cyrus's empire.

The administrative and political structures of this Median kingdom are poorly known. The king apparently ruled from Hamadan; subordinate royal lines ruled in other centers. Marriages between these royal lines are documented (Cameron 1936:223–24), and the rise of the Achaemenids can be seen as the replacement of one line by another. The economic base of the state is totally unknown from the written records.

The Achaemenid Period

With Cyrus's assumption of the throne of Media and his subsequent conquests, the empire of the Medes and the Persians was reorganized. Among the lists of satrapies, three, and possibly four, refer to western Iran. Persia, Elam, and Media must have covered most of Khuzistan and the Zagros, but the eastern boundaries of Persia and Media, while poorly defined, lay beyond "western Iran" proper. The region around Lake Urmia, which was earlier part of Urartu, may have been part of Armenia, although the later name for the area, Media Atropatene, suggests its inclusion in Media.

Three imperial centers were located in the three major satrapies just named: Hamadan in Media, Pasargadae and then Persepolis in Persia, and Susa in Elam. Other place names are recorded in the Bisitun inscription and the Persepolis fortification tablets, but little else is known of them.

The population of the imperial centers was polyglot. This is apparent not only from the tablets found at Persepolis but also from biblical references. The nature of the population in the countryside is unknown, although one must assume that it, too, contained diverse ethnic elements, including Medes, Persians, Elamites, and remnants of the autochthonous groups encountered in the earlier Assyrian records.

Aside from this paltry collection of data, we have only the accounts of the Greek historians. These are largely concerned with the political history of the empire, and in particular with the west. They add little to our understanding of the situation in the Zagros and Khuzistan. We are thrown, therefore, onto the evidence of material culture, to which I now turn.

The Archaeological Evidence

In 1965, T.C. Young, Jr., and R.H. Dyson, Jr., each published articles reviewing the evidence available for the Iranian Iron Age. While differing in approach and in some details, they were in general agreement as to conclusions. Young divided the Iron Age into three units, labelled the "Early Western Gray Ware Horizon," the "Late Western Gray Ware Horizon," and the "Late Western Buff Ware Horizon." Dyson replaced Young's somewhat cumbersome but useful names, calling the first two Iron I and II, and dividing the "Late Western Buff Ware Horizon" into the Iron III and Historic periods. Both authors relied heavily on the sequence from Hasanlu in the Solduz Valley, Azerbaijan, for the framework of their arguments.

In the two decades since these articles were published, a number of new sites throughout western Iran have been excavated, and we can no longer generalize the Solduz Valley sequence over all of western Iran. Instead, starting with the end of the second millennium, we must construct a series of independent regional ceramic sequences, linking them where the data permit. Four areas will each be considered in turn: Azerbaijan and Kurdistan; the Khorasan Road and Luristan; Khuzistan; and Fars.[3] Only those sites which contribute to the chronological framework will be considered in these discussions. The reviews of the regional sequences will be followed by a suggested relative and absolute chronology for the Iron Age. Finally, I will sketch the distributional patterns in each of the subphases of Iron Age western Iran.

Azerbaijan and Kurdistan

The basic sequence for Azerbaijan still rests upon the excavations at Hasanlu, although the more fully published sites of Dinkha, Agrab, and Bastam must be used to gain a clear picture of the sequence.

Hasanlu Tepe is a large mound located in the Solduz Valley on the southwest corner of Lake Urmia. Excavations have concentrated on the citadel, although the lower town has been tested in a number of places, especially in areas known to have been used for cemeteries in the Iron Age. The sequence for the Iron Age comes from the citadel and consists of Periods V–III. Period V, which falls entirely in the second millenium, will only be touched on briefly. Period II may also belong in the pre-Parthian sequence, although there is almost no information published about it.

Hasanlu V is important to our discussion because it represents a complete break with the earlier Hasanlu VI assemblage and is the beginning of the material culture tradition seen in Hasanlu IV. Young (1965b) described the typical ceramics for periods V and IV, and Dyson (1977a) has shown that architectural links between these levels are present. The best published corpus of pottery from this period is from the burials at Dinkha Tepe near Hasanlu (Muscarella 1974).

Hasanlu IV is a major architectural complex on the citadel mound at Hasanlu.[4] It consists of at least four large buildings surrounding a courtyard in the southwest corner, as well as other smaller buildings both in this area and in the northern sector of the citadel. The entire level was destroyed by fire at the end of the ninth century B.C. The number and range of goods found in these buildings is staggering. The ceramics from this level, and from grave groups thought to be contemporary with it, represent Young's Late Western Gray Ware Horizon. In manufacture they carry on the tradition of the Early Western Gray Wares, although at Dinkha, again the best published corpus, a larger percentage of the vessels are oxidized red rather than reduced gray. The horizon marker of this pottery is the bridged spouted pot or jar, which appears at many of the Azerbaijan sites of the period.

Hasanlu III, Young's Late Western Buff Ware Horizon, follows Hasanlu IV after a short gap. It is more complex and difficult to deal with, both because the evidence from Hasanlu itself has not been fully published, and because the discussions of Young and Dyson differ considerably in their evaluation of the evidence. This situation has been partially alleviated by the excavations at Bastam, at Agrab Tepe, and at two sites in Iranian Kurdistan, Ziwiyeh and Zendan-i Suleiman.

Located north of the northwest corner of Lake Urmia in the Aq Chai Valley, Bastam is a large Urartian site built at the base and on the slope of a rock spur. The site itself exhibits little stratigraphy, but Kroll was able to identify three groups of "Urartian" period pottery, one early, one later, and one that appeared with both the early and the late groups (Kroll 1976:151–56). In addition, a small corpus of post-Urartian "Median" pottery was found at the site (Kroll 1979). Agrab Tepe is a small fortified site just southwest of Hasanlu that was completely excavated during the 1964 season of the Hasanlu project (Muscarella 1973). While the radiocarbon determinations indicate a long occupation, both the pottery assemblage of red-slipped and buff wares, as well as the stratigraphy, point to a single period site. Ziwiyeh is a fortified site located atop a mountain in central western Kurdistan. The finding of a treasure there led to commercial excavations which disturbed large areas and produced no scientific results (Muscarella 1977). In 1964, Dyson conducted a three-week season with a small staff at the site and was able to outline some of its characteristics (Dyson 1963; 1965b: 205–6). The ceramics were buff, with finer examples characterized by cream slipping. Since then, an Iranian team has resumed work at the site, but results are not yet known. The Zendan-i Suleiman is a site built around a high calcareous sinter in central Kurdistan. At least two periods of construction are recorded, but the earlier has almost no associated material. The ceramic assemblage is much like that of Ziwiyeh.

Among these sites, Hasanlu has the longest stratified sequence. Dyson has indicated recently (personal communication) that a re-examination of Period III shows the sequence to be more complex than previously realized. Hasanlu IIIB, the earliest level, has at least two phases. In one area, early IIIB walls collapsed, sealing lower IIIB deposits. These contained Urartian red-slipped wares, but no painted wares. The upper IIIB deposits seem to contain some painted sherds which Dyson has called "classical triangle ware." The IIIA deposits, which overlie upper IIIB, contain buff ware, and later forms of triangle ware which differ qualitatively in paint and fabric from the earlier classical triangle ware.[5]

This reappraisal of the Hasanlu sequence corresponds more closely with what is known from the other sites in the region. Agrab Tepe contains no painted ware, nor does Urartian Bastam, but both have Urartian red-slipped wares. Thus, they appear to be roughly contemporary with lower Hasanlu IIIB. Indeed, until Hasanlu III is more fully published, one must rely on Agrab and Bastam to define the nature of the ceramic assemblage for this subperiod.

This suggestion is further supported by Kroll's study of Urartian ceramics based on the Bastam assemblage and other assemblages from known Urartian sites in Iran (1976). Using his catalogue of all published (and some unpublished) parallels to the Urartian forms, it has been possible to prepare figure 67.[6]

Figure 67 must be used with caution, as it is based on comparing forms from Urartian sites with those from other sites, rather than comparing total assemblages. Furthermore, the size of the samples from the various sites was highly varied, with few published examples available from Hasanlu III, and references to the unpublished material from Hasanlu III coming before the reappraisal of the stratigraphy referred to above.

Despite the shortcomings in the data, the figure points up the high number of shared forms between the three "Urartian" sites of Hasanlu IIIB, Agrab, and Bastam. Further, it shows a relatively low number of parallels between these sites and post-Urartian Bastam, and between them and Hasanlu IIIA.[7] Thus, it would seem that we have here a discrete regional ceramic assemblage temporally bounded by the earlier Hasanlu IV ceramics, and the later materials from post-Urartian Bastam and upper Hasanlu IIIB.

Equally interesting is the way in which the two Kurdistan sites of Ziwiyeh and the Zendan fit into the picture. These contain closely related buff ware ceramic assemblages. At Ziwiyeh, painted wares like the "classical triangle ware" from upper Hasanlu IIIB were found on the surface, but not in the excavations conducted by Dyson (1965b: 206). At the Zendan,

there are "imported" incised sherds like those from Ziwiyeh, but no painted wares. Given the little that is known about the stratigraphy at Ziwiyeh, it is impossible to determine if the Zendan fits wholly within its lifetime, but it is clear that the two sites overlap. It is also probable that the painted wares from Ziwiyeh are part of a later component. Neither the Zendan nor Ziwiyeh assemblage is the classic Urartian red-slipped ware, indicating a different technological (and aesthetic?) approach to pottery manufacture. Yet the high number of parallels between these sites and the Urartian assemblage indicates that all of the sites share a repertoire of specific shapes which is different from that which follows it. Unfortunately, we have no information about the preceding phase in Kurdistan, one which would correspond with Hasanlu IV.

In summary, the Iron Age sequence of Azerbaijan and Kurdistan proves to be considerably more complex than previous attempts at its characterization would indicate. The early part of the sequence, with its Early and Late Western Gray Wares (Dyson's Iron I and II), continues to be valid for the Urmia region, although these wares are not attested in Kurdistan. The later part of the sequence (Dyson's Iron III and Historic, Young's Late Buff Ware) should be subdivided. At first, we have a period with plain buff wares in Kurdistan, and contemporary with them Urartian red wares in Azerbaijan. This period has no associated painted pottery. It is followed by another period, where the Urartian ceramics are replaced by an unpainted buff ware assemblage at Bastam. At Hasanlu, we apparently have two periods in which a buff ware tradition includes two painted wares. These painted wares are called by Dyson "classical triangle ware" and "late triangle ware."

The Khorasan Road and Luristan

There are four key sites for the sequence in the central west: Baba Jan, Godin, Nush-i Jan, and Jameh Shuran. The first is located in Luristan-i Kuchik, while the other three are found in valleys that are part of the Khorasan Road. For our period, only Baba Jan and Jameh Shuran have stratified sequences.

Baba Jan consists of two main mounds and a saddle between them. The east mound contains a sequence for the Iron Age. The lowest level reached had a large "painted chamber" attached to a building called a fort (Goff 1977). The material from this level was contemporary with the uppermost material from the central mound, where a small fortified manor was excavated. This earliest Iron Age Period found, termed Baba Jan III by Goff, is characterized by the handmade painted ceramics that are commonly known as Genre Luristan wares (Goff 1978). Over the burnt ruins of Baba Jan III, Goff found a squatter occupation of some duration. The Genre Luristan wares continued during this

Baba Jan II Period, but a new type of buff, unpainted wheel-made pottery, called "micaceous buff ware" by S. Brown (1979), appeared alongside the older type. By Baba Jan I, the latest of the periods at the site, the squatter occupation was replaced by a series of poorly understood house remains on the east mound and in the saddle (Goff 1985). The pottery associated with this period was a later form of the wheel-made ceramics of Baba Jan II. The Genre Luristan wares had completely disappeared.

Nush-i Jan is located atop a rock spur in the middle of the Malayer Valley. Basically a single period site, it consists of a small number of specialized structures (a fort, two shrines, and a columned hall), all surrounded by a fortification wall (Stronach and Roaf 1978).[8] The site has a highly uniform assemblage of buff unpainted wheel-made pottery, closely paralleled by the Baba Jan II wheel-made ceramics. The range of shapes thus far published from Nush-i Jan is restricted and the pottery seems to represent a short period of time, apparently coincident with the end of occupation of the Iron Age structures (R. Stronach 1978).

Godin II is the latest period found atop the large mound called Godin Tepe in the Kangavar Valley. The occupation comprises a single large fortified building showing a long history of additions and alterations to the basic structure and remarkable architectural parallels with Nush-i Jan. The ceramic assemblage is similar to Baba Jan II/Nush-i Jan and Baba Jan I buff wares and shares many shapes with both, although parallels to the later Baba Jan I material predominate. While the assemblage probably represents the end of the Godin II occupation for the most part, the long history of the building and the sealing off of parts of it before the final abandonment would account for the apparent chronological range represented by the pottery. In addition to the buff wares from the fortress atop the mound, a small number of graves with characteristic Early Western Gray Ware shapes were found on the southern flat extension of the mound.

The fourth site in this area, Jameh Shuran, has not yet been discussed in the literature. It is a large site lying just south of the town of Mahidasht and just east of the Marik River. Surface survey of the site in 1975, and again before excavation in 1978, revealed a chronological range from "Genre Luristan" to at least Parthian times. Two small sondages were cut into the east slope of the mound; neither reached virgin soil. On preliminary analysis, the material from the two sondages can be divided into three ceramic assemblages, which we label Assemblage I to III, starting from the top (Levine n.d.).

Assemblage III was found only in a very restricted area in Operation 2. It is characterized by a coarse, straw-tempered hand- and wheel-made white ware. Shapes are few (the total sample was just over fifty diagnostic sherds) and simple. One characteristic shape is a goblet like the Elamite and Kassite goblets of the end of the second millennium.

Assemblage II is marked by ceramics that are part of the "micaceous buff ware" tradition. In Operation 2, it is present in a number of successive levels in respectable quantity. In Operation 1, it was found only at the bottom of the sondage in a restricted area. On initial analysis, it appears that this assemblage can be divided into an earlier and later phase. The earlier phase, IIB, included bowls with horizontal handles and goblets with two opposed handles, similar to shapes found at Baba Jan II and Nush-i Jan. No painted ware is associated with this phase.

The later phase, Assemblage IIA, has parallels to Godin II and Baba Jan I. It has a wide range of shallow bowl shapes in fine and common wares, a feature which seems to characterize this period. Assemblage IIA also contained the earliest painted ceramics found in excavation at Jameh Shuran. The painted forms were almost exclusively shallow, flat, or slightly convex rimmed bowls with decoration restricted to the rim. The motifs varied widely, but included triangles, parallel lines, bow ties, and the like.

Assemblage I was the best represented at the site. It too was basically a buff ware assemblage with a great variety of shapes. Among these were flat bowls (so-called fish plates), pitchers with trefoil rims, a number of thin-bodied cups, tulip bowls, and canteen fragments. A large number of painted sherds were found with the paint usually on the visible surface of the vessel—the exterior on closed shapes, the interior on open shapes. The painting occurred on both highly burnished and smoothed surfaces. While some of the Assemblage II painted bowls and other forms continued to appear in Assemblage I, they did so in small quantities, and the assemblages are markedly different.

At Jameh Shuran, neither Genre Luristan nor Clinky Ware appeared in the sondages, although both were present on the surface. Given the limited size of the excavation, such lacunae may be disappointing but are hardly unexpected. Nevertheless, the presence of the Genre Luristan material on the surface leads us to postulate a gap in occupation in the excavated areas between Assemblage III and II. The absence of Clinky Ware is perhaps fortunate, for it provides an approximate terminus ante quem for Assemblage I at the site (Levine n.d.). One last observation needs to be made, not about Jameh Shuran, but about the Mahidasht, where classical Early Western Gray Ware was found on survey. Thus, this material occurs throughout the region.

The four major sites under discussion yield a coherent picture for the sequence in central western Iran. The earliest stratified material is found in the Mahidasht and is represented by the Assemblage III corpus at Jameh Shuran, with its "Elamite/Kassite goblets." This material is apparently absent in the Kangavar and Malayer valleys. At Godin, however, we have the Early Western Gray Ware found in the cemetery. The contemporaneity of these will be discussed below. The Genre Luristan wares of Baba Jan III appear next, although these are absent in Kangavar and more easterly areas. It remains unclear what, if any material fits this time range there. The early "micaceous buff wares" are then introduced, appearing by themselves along the Khorasan Road, both at Nush-i Jan and Jameh Shuran IIB, but mixing with the Genre Luristan material at Baba Jan in Baba Jan II times. Some of the "early" Godin II material may fit here as well. A later buff ware phase is represented by Baba Jan I and most of Godin II. It seems that Jameh Shuran IIA is contemporary with this material or slightly later. Finally, the assemblage of Jameh Shuran I appears, and while it is still the only such excavated assemblage in the central western Zagros, it occurs on survey throughout central western Iran.

Khuzistan

Despite our relative lack of information about Khuzistan, Miroschedji's recent work at Susa forms the kernel from which all future analysis of this region must proceed (1981a, 1981b). Miroschedji tentatively divides his material into four groups. The earliest group (Levels 13–10) begins in the late second millennium and continues into the beginning of the first. This material contains, inter alia, the "Elamite" goblet. After a possible hiatus, a second group (Levels 9–8) is dated to the eighth and seventh centuries. A third group, represented only by material from burials, is placed in the period after the destruction of Susa by Assurbanipal in 646 B.C. and before the Achaemenid reoccupation between 550 and 520 B.C. (Levels 7–6). The fourth group is late Achaemenid in date (Levels 5–4). Of special note here is Miroschedji's discussion of Ghirshman's work in the Achaemenid Village (Girshman 1954b; Miroschedji 1981a). He demonstrates that the painted ware in Achaemenid Village I must be out of place, thereby solving one of the outstanding problems in the relative chronology of western Iran.

Finally, a small group of sherds found at Chogha Mish must be noted. These are wheel made, buff, and virtually indistinguishable from the late "micaceous buff wares" of the central west (Young 1978). They must be integrated into the sequence of Iron Age material for Khuzistan.

Fars

Fars remains a mystery for the first half of the first millennium. At the turn of the millennium, there is

evidence of occupation in the Middle Elamite building at Malyan (Carter and Stolper 1976), and Jacobs (1980) has suggested that the Qaleh period materials may continue into the first millennium. While the first datum seems secure, there are many problems with the end date of Qaleh, and it seems best at the present to suspend judgment. Thus, when the Achaemenids appear at the midpoint in the millennium, they do so with no apparent antecedents.

The two principal sites for our understanding of Achaemenid and post-Achaemenid Fars are Persepolis and Pasargadae. The former produced few ceramics, mostly from immediately predestruction contexts (i.e., ca. 330 B.C.), and none of them painted. Pasargadae which continued as a settlement after the fall of the Achaemenids, is more problematic (D. Stronach 1978). The contexts from which the pottery derive are often obscure, and the nature of the published sample is not defined. But from the published plans and the accompanying text, none of the pottery need predate Period II on the Tall-i Takht, and the terminal date assigned to this level by Stronach is circa 280 B.C.

In sum, the data for Fars are meagre. It would appear that aside from the Middle Elamite building at Malyan there is no material to fill the pre-Achaemenid Period and that even the Achaemenids are only well represented by material from the very end of the period. The unpainted tradition of Persepolis is succeeded at Pasargadae by one that included such typical shapes as the "tulip bowl," the pitcher with trefoil spout, "fish bowls," and thin-walled cups, some of which are painted.

The Relative and Absolute Chronology

Having reviewed the regional sequences, it is now possible to establish, however tentatively, a relative and absolute chronology for western Iran in the Iron Age (figure 68). In this discussion, I will employ the terms Iron I through Iron IV to set the assemblages into a sequence. In so doing, I intend the terms to represent nothing more than loosely defined chronological periods. No cultural or evolutionary baggage should be attached to these labels. All of them subsume a number of distinct ceramic assemblages or forms which are roughly contemporary, nothing more.

Late Iron I

Although falling outside the limits of this discussion, Iron I serves as a baseline for discussion of the later material (Young n.d.). Two basic index fossils mark the period: the button or pedestal based Early Western Gray Ware goblet, and the "Elamite" or "Kassite" goblet. Both are part of larger ceramic complexes, which will not be described here.

The relative position of Early Western Gray Ware is

Louis D. Levine

most clearly defined in Azerbaijan, where it overlies the painted assemblage of the first half of the second millennium represented by Hasanlu VI and Dinkha Tepe (Hamlin 1974a). At other sites in Azerbaijan, the relationship of this material to earlier assemblages is less well defined. At Haftavan, it seems to overlie the painted assemblage of Haftavan VIB (M. Edwards 1981), but the date of this transition is unclear. In other places where Early Western Gray Ware is found, the relative position of the assemblage is less certain, although a reanalysis of the graves at Tepe Giyan adds some clarity to the question for central western Iran (R. Henrickson 1983–84).

The relative position of the "Elamite" goblet is best known from Susa, where the form is found in levels 12–10 of the Ville Royale II sounding and in associated Middle Elamite II assemblages. The "Kassite" goblet is well known from a number of Mesopotamian sites, especially from the recent excavations at Nippur (Gibson 1975). Unfortunately, the assemblages connected with this index marker are still, for the most part, poorly published, so it is not known how many other vessel forms are shared. Carter, however, notes a close correspondence between the Malyan and Khuzistan assemblages (Carter and Stolper 1984: 164–65).

The contemporaneity of the Early Western Gray Ware and the "Elamite" or "Kassite" goblets hangs on slim threads of evidence. First, both have been assigned dates in the late second millennium on independent grounds. Second, at Tepe Giyan, both Early Western Gray Ware forms and what seem to be miniature "Elamite" goblets appear in the same set of graves from Level I, and in one case, they appear in the same grave (Contenau and Ghirshman 1935: Grave 47).

Absolute dates for the end of Iron I are generally fixed by radiocarbon determinations from Hasanlu V and from structural members in the Hasanlu IV buildings (*Radiocarbon* 1:49–50; 5:85–88; 8:349–50; 19:243; 20:219–23), from Malyan (Carter and Stolper 1976: 41), and from historically associated material at Susa (Carter and Stolper 1976:41). All of these point to the last few centuries of the second millennium for the late Iron I material.

Iron II

The relative chronological position of the Iron II assemblages and their interrelationships are more difficult to establish. In the northwest, Late Western Gray Ware follows on the Early Western Gray Ware. This material is most fully published for Dinkha Tepe (Muscarella 1974), although the corpus from Hasanlu IVB will ultimately prove crucial in defining the assemblage.

The date of the transition from Early to Late West-

ern Gray Ware is uncertain. It has generally been assumed that Early Western Gray Ware is chronologically coterminous with Hasanlu V, while Late Western Gray Ware is coterminous with Hasanlu IV, and that these two assemblages define Iron I and Iron II, respectively. Although it is impossible for the moment to improve on these assumptions, it should be noted that the ceramics from Level V come from relatively small excavated areas while those from Level IV date to the end of the major occupation of the Burned Buildings. The three hundred years represented by the architecture of Level IV are ceramically undocumented in stratified architectural contexts, and the contemporary graves from Hasanlu and Dinkha are not firmly linked to this architectural sequence. Thus, it is possible that the Early Western Gray Ware forms continued in use during part of Period IV. This may eventually lead to a reorganization of the periodization in Azerbaijan.

For the central west, the Genre Luristan wares have yet to be found in a clear stratigraphic position relative to the earlier Iron I assemblages. At Jameh Shuran, Genre Luristan material was found on the surface, but not in the excavation proper. At Baba Jan, the Genre Luristan assemblage of Baba Jan III rests on deposits dating to the Godin III Period (Henrickson, chapter 8), indicating a hiatus in settlement at the site. Thus, it is only in the reconstructed sequence of graves from Tepe Giyan that we have anything approaching a sequence, and even there the evidence is tenuous at best (R. Henrickson 1983–84). In the areas east of the Genre Luristan distribution, we do not even know what material fits the Iron II time range. S. Brown (1979) has suggested that the early "micaceous buff wares" should be pushed back to fill the gap, but at present there is no evidence to support such a proposition.

In Khuzistan, the developments are local and best represented by Miroschedji's Neo-Elamite I Phase at Susa. The nature of the occupation in Fars is unknown.

The Iron II Period in the Zagros and Khuzistan is, therefore, characterized by a number of relatively distinct and nonoverlapping ceramic assemblages, which are considered to be contemporaneous because they fit between earlier and later periods where better interregional correlations are possible. The absolute dates are largely determined by the extensive series of radiocarbon assays from Hasanlu IV, which range from circa 1100 B.C. to 800 B.C.

Iron III

In the succeeding Iron III Period, the picture becomes more complex. Figure 69, which combines the data presented by Kroll (1976) and R. Henrickson (1977), is far from ideal. Kroll concentrated on ceramics with parallels to Urartian shapes. Thus, for example, shape parallels between Ziwiyeh and Godin II that do not also occur in the Urartian corpus would usually not be noted. Henrickson's work compared only Godin, Nush-i Jan, and Baba Jan and did not include the most recent publications of Baba Jan (Goff 1978,1985).[9] Perhaps most important, the pottery of Ziwiyeh, Hasanlu III, and Nimrud remain only partially published, and the corpora from Pasargadae, Susa, Jameh Shuran, and Baba Jan I are excluded from the chart. Nevertheless, the chart allows us to move away from a relative chronology based upon specific index fossils and toward a more quantified approach, however crude that may be at present.

Figure 69 demonstrates graphically the close interrelationship among many of the Iron III sites. Thus, Bastam shares a large number of forms with Agrab, Hasanlu IIIB, Ziwiyeh, and Zendan-i Suleiman, as discussed above, but it also shares many with Godin II and Persepolis. When we check these other sites against one another, the number of corresponding forms remains high in each matched pair (Godin/Zandan; Ziwiyeh/Persepolis, etc.) despite the fact that only shapes occuring on Urartian sites are considered. The exception, Hasanlu IIIB, probably results from the limited publication.

Henrickson's figures are equally interesting (the underlined numbers on figure 69). If Kroll's figures had been used instead, a very different picture would have emerged. Thus, the pairs would have been Baba Jan I/Godin-6; Baba Jan II/Godin-1; Nushi-i Jan/Godin-2; Nush-i Jan/Baba Jan I-2; and Nush-i Jan/Baba Jan II-2. This seems to demonstrate a regionalization in the pottery at the same time that a large number of forms are interregional. This observation, based upon analysis of shape, is also reflected in type of ware. Thus, the red-slipped "Urartian" wares appear in the northwest, the cream-slipped wares in Kurdistan, the "micaceous buff wares" in the central west, and the coarse wares in Khuzistan, although these wares are hardly exclusive to these areas.

Finally, it is clear that within Iron III we have subphases in the different regions, but these seem to be local, rather than reflecting interregional events or trends. Along the Khorasan Road, the earlier Iron III assemblage found at Nush-i Jan is succeeded by the later Godin II material, although some of the earlier forms persist in the Godin II assemblage. The Nush-i Jan assemblage also penetrates Luristan, where it is found alongside the late Genre Luristan pottery of Baba Jan II. By later Iron III, this mixture disappears at Baba Jan, replaced by material closely resembling Godin II. Thus for the central west, we might divide Iron III into an early phase, the Nush-i Jan/Baba Jan II horizon, and a late phase, the Godin II/Baba Jan I horizon. Such a division is purely chronological, as the

early Iron III Phase contains two distinct ceramic assemblages, early "micaceous buff ware" and late Genre Luristan.

The picture for Iron III is further complicated in central western Iran by the sequence at Jameh Shuran. On preliminary analysis, Jameh Shuran IIB appears to be contemporary with the material from Nush-i Jan and Baba Jan II, although it lacks the Genre Luristan wares of Baba Jan II. This may be the result of the more inaccessible geographical position of Baba Jan where the local painted pottery tradition would have had a higher chance of surviving. Jameh Shuran IIA, which overlays Jameh Shuran IIB, has many characteristics of the late Iron III assemblage of Godin II and Baba Jan I, but it also contains the bowls with painted rims. In this case, it is unclear if Jameh Shuran IIA is contemporary with the late Iron III assemblages of Godin II and Baba Jan I, representing a regional variant, or if it is post-Godin II and thus represents a still later phase of Iron III. For the present, since no painted Jameh Shuran IIA bowls have been found on survey in the Kangavar Valley, I would argue for its being a regional phenomenon contemporary with Godin II. This is the working hypothesis adopted here. Unfortunately, the parallel painted pottery from Hasanlu IIIB and Ziwiyeh does not allow us to clarify this problem because of the uncertainties in the stratigraphy at both those sites.

In Azerbaijan, there is again indication for a subdivision of the Iron III Period. At Bastam, the earlier "Urartian" ceramics of the main occupation are replaced by the "post-Urartian" ceramics from the latest phase of the Hallenbau. These are related to the Iron III ceramics of the central west, although it is unclear where these fit into the central western sequence because of the relatively small sample published. At Hasanlu, a two-part division is also evident. The earliest IIIB material corresponds to the Urartian assemblage at Bastam, while the so-called classical triangle ware of upper Hasanlu IIIB appears to be linked to the Jameh Shuran IIA material. Again, however, we have a problem. Are the later materials from Bastam contemporary with or earlier than the "classical triangle ware"? Since both seem to be traditions imported from the south, one could argue that the "triangle ware" and the late Bastam material are temporally distinct. But it could also be argued that different distribution patterns are at work, or that sample sizes are inadequate for any measure of certainty. In either event, at least two phases are present in the Iron III of Azerbaijan, an early and a late, but their temporal relationship with the early and late phases in central western Iran remains uncertain.

In Khuzistan, a similar situation obtains. Two groups, Neo-Elamite II and Achaemenid, have been defined by Miroschedji. They are distinct one from the other, with the latter having some links with late Iron III from the central western area. There are no painted wares, however, in Miroschedji's Achaemenid material from Khuzistan. In Fars, it is not yet possible to define an earlier and later group for Iron III, although the material from Persepolis seems to fit better with the late Iron III range described above.

The beginning and end dates of Iron III, to say nothing of the dates of the subdivisions in each region, are difficult to establish. In Azerbaijan, the destruction of Hasanlu IV provides a terminus post quem for the beginning of the period. The radiocarbon determinations for this destruction fall in the last quarter of the ninth century B.C., and correlate well with the textual information, which shows an Urartian presence along the south shore of Lake Urmia by the first quarter of the eighth century B.C. Six dates from Agrab Tepe (Muscarella 1973: 71) exhibit a very wide spread, ranging from MASCA-corrected midpoints of 850–900 to 420 B.C. As noted in the discussion of Agrab Tepe, the stratigraphy is difficult and the meaning of this spread uncertain. Two of the dates, P-895 (MASCA 850–900 ± 56 B.C.) and P-980 (MASCA 790 ± 58 B.C.), both from low in the desposit, fit the range of immediately post-Hasanlu IV dates well, as does one other date, P-894 (MASCA 800 ± 57 B.C.). Since there is no apparent Hasanlu IIIA material at the site, the later dates are probably contaminated. At Hasanlu, Period IIIA has three radiocarbon dates (570–560 or 500–420; 460–440; 470–440 B.C.), but it is hard to determine what ceramics go with the dates. Dyson notes pottery links to Charsada and Ai Khanum, which would make the material early third century and comparable with that from Pasargadae (Dyson 1977b).

In the central west, the situation is far less happy. One radiocarbon date from Godin Tepe (Young 1969a: 31) underlies the earliest part of the Period II building and has an uncorrected determination of 2750 ± 100 B.P. (GaK-1069: 5570 half life). When corrected, this date seems to be too high for association with the founding of the building, and as the site seems to have been abandoned for some time prior to the founding, the date can only be viewed as anomalous. No other radiocarbon determinations are available from the area. All other dates suggested thus far are based upon the comparison of single index fossils with material from dated sites such as Nimrud or Persepolis. Since the chronological range of any of these index fossils has not been determined, this is a highly dangerous procedure when attempting to achieve a fine-grained chronological picture.

For Khuzistan, Miroschedji suggests a date in the second half of the eighth century for the start of the Neo-Elamite II (1981a: 39). This date, like the end date of the period at circa 520 B.C., is based on little

evidence, as he readily admits. The end of the Achaemenid Period is set by him at circa 330 B.C., corresponding to the political life of the dynasty.

In Fars, we again have almost no material. The pottery from Persepolis represents the very end of its occupation and must lie close to the end of Iron III. No other information on the span of the material is available.

Iron IV

The term Iron IV was originally proposed by Young to describe material in the Kangavar Valley postdating the Godin II assemblage, and predating the material that could be clearly labelled Parthian (1975b). In this chapter, I propose to extend that term over all of western Iran and to identify it with what Haerinck has called "early Parthian" (1983).

The most remarkable feature of the Iron IV ceramic assemblage is the introduction of a widespread painted tradition. This tradition is well documented at Jameh Shuran I and at Pasargadae. These two sites also share much in ceramic production techniques, and in their shape repertoire as well, and the overlap between the two assemblages is significant (Levine n.d.). Similar material is found in other areas of western Iran, but its date must be determined by reference to Jameh Shuran I and Pasargadae.

The absolute dates of the period are also difficult to determine. Based on the coin evidence from Pasargadae, the assemblage falls in the post-Achaemenid Period, with the earliest good contexts from circa 280 B.C. Kroll has shown that this material cannot begin earlier than the Achaemenid Period, but he has little indication that it might not be later still (Kroll 1975, 1976: 165). The end of the period has been arbitrarily linked to the appearance of Clinky Ware, although the painted tradition may continue for a short time thereafter (Stronach 1974). At present, there is no clear date for the introduction of this distinctive pottery, but it does occur in early levels at Seleucia, giving a terminus ante quem in the mid-second century B.C.

This discussion of the relative and absolute chronology makes a number of points clear. First, the chronology stands on very shaky ground. Not enough stratified sequences have been excavated, and even those are poorly published and poorly dated. Second, it is evident that there is considerable change from the beginning to the end of the period. Often, the change is regional, and even within regions there are significant differences between sites. Thus, it is difficult to correlate the interregional sequences with any precision, and my use of the terms Iron I–IV for all of western Iran, implying a unity not present in the data, is fraught with danger. Finally, organizing the data in this way betrays a highland bias. If one were to start in Khuzistan, as is the norm in this volume, the divisions would lie elsewhere, as Miroschedji's terminology implies. Yet without such terms and without the choice of a focal area, it would be impossible to discuss the distributional data, to which we now turn.

The Distributional Data

As poor as the chronological data are, they appear excellent when compared with the distributional data. This set of data can be studied on two levels: the gross distribution of certain ceramic types in western Iran, and the results of systematic regional surveys. Since the latter can be disposed of quickly, we will begin with a discussion of these surveys.

Within western Iran, a series of discrete and discontinuous valleys and plains comprising less than 5 percent of the total area has been systematically surveyed. The most important of these are the north Khuzistan Plain, the Marv Dasht in Fars, and the Malayer, Kangavar, and Mahidasht valleys along the Khorasan Road. This list, however, gives a false impression of what we know. For the Iron Age, none of these surveys has yet been published in any detail. Furthermore, each area surveyed has its own history, and the areas are often separated by many miles of difficult mountainous terrain. Thus, each area needs a separate investigation of changes in settlement patterns and demographic trends before they can be tied together into a meaningful picture. Given the many uncertainties in the chronological framework and our inadequate grasp of the historical situation, the results from any one area cannot be generalized over all of western Iran.

Khuzistan has recently profited from some work by Miroschedji, the first serious effort to deal with the Iron Age in this region (1981c). Unfortunately, after an initial month's survey in 1977, the long-range program was interrupted by the onset of the Iranian revolution. Miroschedji notes that in northwestern Khuzistan, the general trend during the first millennium is one of population decline, and that this reaches its nadir during the Achaemenid Period. But he also notes the difficulties in identifying the Achaemenid assemblage. This decline is reversed in the Seleucid and early Parthian periods, when an unprecedented increase in the number of sites occurs. Other areas of Khuzistan are little known or poorly reported for this period.

In Fars, the Marv Dasht has been systematically surveyed by Sumner, but the first half of the first millennium is invisible, and the second half, the Achaemenid and Iron IV periods, is only lightly touched upon in the literature. Nevertheless, the evidence indicates some settlement during the Achaemenid Period, as one would expect of an area that was one of the centers of imperial Iran, although the site density is modest. The following Iron IV Period, according to Sumner is invisible again, although it may be confused with the previous and following periods (1972:269).[10]

Along the Khorasan Road, three valleys, Malayer, Kangavar, and the Mahidasht, have been systematically surveyed. Malayer is published only in a short notice (Howell 1979). No "Early Iron Age" sites were located, but eighty-four Iron III sites were found. Iron IV was apparently not recognized. Kangavar is also published only in a preliminary note (Young 1975b). Here, all of the Iron Age periods were found, with twenty-three sites in the Iron I/II range totalling 30 hectares, thirty-three sites in Iron III totalling 38 hectares, and seventeen sites in the Iron IV Period totalling 16 hectares.[11] For the Mahidasht, which is also virtually unpublished, most of the survey work was done prior to the fine-grained analysis of the sequence which we now have. Consequently, initial statements (Levine 1975b; 1976b) will have to be reassessed in the light of this better information. In addition, the geomorphological history of the area indicates that there has been a great deal of site burial and destruction in post-Iron Age times (Brookes, Levine, and Dennell 1982). Thus, even with a more detailed analysis, it is unclear how much of the past settlement patterns can be recovered. In sum, despite the amount of survey done in the central Zagros, we cannot yet make general statements about population trends in the area.

For the northern Zagros, including Kurdistan and Azerbaijan, no systematic work has been carried out. Kleiss has conducted and published his extensive searches for Urartian sites, but these do not have the time depth needed for settlements studies.

The discouraging picture just outlined is somewhat ameliorated by the long tradition of reconnaissance-type survey in Iranian archaeology. In the Zagros, this approach was pioneered by Stein (1940), and added to for the Iron Age by Young (1966), Goff (1968), Swiny (1975), and Kleiss (Kleiss and Hauptmann 1976). In these wide-ranging trips, many sites were examined, but no attempt was made at detailed coverage of an area. Thus, the major contribution of these reconnaissances lies in providing indications of the geographical extent of certain index fossils.

The resulting distribution data are best portrayed by a series of maps (figures 70–73) showing the geographical extent of the assemblages described above. It is impossible to document here all of the occurrences of ceramics from these assemblages, but it should be noted that at times we are dealing with minimal evidence, often a single index fossil. Thus, the areas outlined on the maps cannot yet be said to represent a large shared repertoire of ceramic forms, to say nothing of other cultural traits. Furthermore, the periods and subperiods are treated as contemporaneous on the maps, but this is certainly not assured.

Iron I

The map for the Iron I Period shows that there are large areas for which no data exist (figure 70). Early Western Gray Ware is well documented in the Lake Urmia basin, and the assemblages are well defined at the type sites of Hasanlu and Dinkha Tepe. This same assemblage has clear connections with areas to the east that fall beyond the map, both at Khorvin/Chandar in the Alburz Mountains and at Tepe Sialk. Sporadic finds are also reported on survey in the central west. At Godin Tepe and Tepe Giyan, the Iron I material derives from graves, and there do not seem to be associated settlements. Whether this holds true for other sites in central western Iran with such material is yet to be determined.

The distribution of Early Western Gray Ware is complemented by the distribution of the "Elamite" or "Kassite" goblets. Sites in Khuzistan and Malyan in Fars share many items in their ceramic inventory, reflecting the linkage between these two centers. The "Elamite" goblet is but one of these shared forms. In the central west, both in the Mahidasht and at Tepe Guran in the Hulailan Valley (Thrane 1970), there are settlement sites with goblets, although it is difficult to determine if they compare with the "Elamite" or "Kassite" form. At various times, the valleys along the Khorasan Road exhibit either a southern (Elamite) or a western (Babylonian) orientation, and the present evidence does not allow us to decide which is the more likely during the Iron I Period. Politically, either a resurgent Middle Elamite kingdom or a resurgent Second Dynasty of Isin could have penetrated the area in some fashion.

The mixture of the Early Western Gray Ware and the "Elamite/Kassite" goblets in the central west is more difficult to explain. The idea that the Gray Ware burials represent transhumant groups from the north who were interacting with the settled population represented by the "Elamite" goblets has little evidence to support it. Until more is known about the nature of the settlements in the central west associated with these ceramic markers and of the Iron I Period in Kurdistan, little can be said of this interaction.

Iron II

The Iron II map presents the distribution of assemblages early in the first millennium (figure 71). It, too, is appallingly empty, but the limited information that we have is coherent. Three distinct assemblages are present. In the north, around Lake Urmia, Late Western Gray Ware predominates. Again, the published corpora are too small to make any firm statements, but the impression is one of reasonable uniformity. This material does not have strong ties with other areas. Young noted this already in his 1965 survey of the material, characterizing the Iron II Period as "fragmented into individual ceramic traditions" (1965: 78).

A second assemblage, early Genre Luristan (Baba Jan III), is found in Luristan, with particularly strong representation in the valleys south of the Khorasan Road and east of the Kuh-i Sefid. This material is found sporadically as far east as the Kangavar Valley and as far west as the Mahidasht, Hulailan, and Rumishgan valleys. In the core area, it is clearly associated with settlements such as Baba Jan III. Its appearance on survey outside the core area is more difficult to assess, as the occurrences are rare. Furthermore, the lack of other material attributable to Iron II times in the valleys along the Khorasan Road makes understanding the cultural dynamics of the region difficult.[12]

The lack of material in other regions has already been noted. The Neo-Elamite I assemblage at Susa is in part contemporary with the material just discussed, but it is isolated and seems to be restricted to Khuzistan. The nature of the period in Kurdistan and Fars is unknown.

The Iron II assemblage distributions correspond with the little we know of the Zagros from the written sources of the period. These present a picture of fragmented groups in Kurdistan, along the Khorasan Road and in Luristan. In the last area, we may have evidence of a nascent Ellipi in the Genre Luristan distribution, assuming that ceramic distribution is a measure of social and, in this case, political integration. The apparent lack of settlement along the Khorasan Road may be traced to Assyrian political and military policy, which can be seen as an attempt to keep the area as unsettled as possible (Levine 1977a). This, however, would account only for the end of the period, and the reasons for lack of settlement in the tenth century remain unexplained. In the far north, the sites around Lake Urmia do not show any influence of an expanding Urartu.

Iron III

The map of the Iron III period is the most complex of the four maps which we present (figure 72). Not only are there more ceramic assemblages in this period than in any other, but we can also discern at least two phases in each of the regions. Since we cannot as yet set the temporal boundary between the earlier and later phase in each region with precision, the map presents all of the Iron III data. Despite the chronological problems, we can assume with some certainty that the early Iron III assemblages in all of the various regions overlap temporally at least part of the time, and that the same can be said for late Iron III.

Early Iron III in Azerbaijan is synonymous with Urartian control, and it is possible to draw a line representing the limits of Urartian expansion in Iran (Kleiss and Hauptmann 1976). This expansion, however, represents a process that took some time to accomplish. In Kurdistan, Iron III settlements are found, but we cannot distinguish an early and late phase. Only at Ziwiyeh, where Jameh Shuran IIA painted ware occurs, can we be sure of a late Iron III component. Thus, the distribution pattern must represent, at least in part, early Iron III. However, the absence of clear late Iron III material on the survey may not be significant, because the painted wares are both rare and seem to have a restricted distribution.

In central western Iran, early Iron III "micaceous buff wares" are distributed from the Malayer Valley to the Mahidasht and into northern Luristan. They may also extend into the Hamadan Plain, but this distinction was made after Swiny conducted his survey. Throughout the area, we seem to have a significant increase in the settled population at this time, although this observation is impressionistic rather than based on hard numbers.

Associated with this apparent increase in settlement is another phenomenon deserving notice. An assemblage unrelated to the "micaceous buff ware" tradition is found in some quantity in the low-lying areas of the Pusht-i Kuh, but thus far it is always associated with burial sites (VandenBerghe 1977, 1978). The only other place where it has been found is at Chogha Maran in the Mahidasht, also in burials. Both the association of this assemblage exclusively with burial sites and its geographic distribution suggest that we may be dealing with the pottery and related artifacts of a transhumant group that spent the winter in the Pusht-i Kuh and the summer in the higher areas around Kermanshah. The location of Chogha Maran at one of the access points to the high grazing grounds of the Kuh-i Parau lends further strength to the suggestion.

Finally, we must note the situation in Khuzistan. Here, Miroschedji has called the early Iron III material Neo-Elamite II (1978). It is marked by a local assemblage with parallels to Assyria and to Luristan, but without marked connection to other highland regions.

Early Iron III largely corresponds to the period of Urartian and Assyrian (and Neo-Babylonian?) supremacy in the affairs of Western Asia. The gross distribution of ceramic assemblages in western Iran seems to reflect the situation known from the texts, with each assemblage corresponding to one of the major groups that can be identified. Thus, in the north we have Urartu (red-slipped ware), in Kurdistan Mannea (cream-slipped ware), and in Media along the Khorasan Road (micaceous buff ware). The mixture of late Genre Luristan and "micaceous buff wares" in Luristan may reflect Ellipi, while the Khuzistan assemblage, which is so different, can be equated with Elam.

While various ceramic assemblages have distinct distributions, the great overlap in forms points to the high degree of interaction hinted at in the textual record. The sharing of many shapes with both Urartean and Assyrian ceramics may well reflect an emulation, conscious or not, of styles from the perceived higher culture areas.

The late Iron III distribution is more difficult to discuss, because the data are fewer. The starting point is the area of the Khorasan Road, where the picture is clearest. The early Iron III traditions of Nush-i Jan are replaced by those of Godin II in the eastern reaches, while the Jameh Shuran IIA assemblage finds a home in the west. Both ceramic assemblages share much technically and in terms of shape repertoire, although Jameh Shuran has a painted component in the assemblage which is absent at Godin.

There are a number of interesting phenomena associated with these late Iron III materials of central western Iran. First, we have the appearance of the Jameh Shuran IIA painted ware in Kurdistan at Ziwiyeh (in the surface material, not the excavation by the University Museum) and at Hasanlu in the post-Urartian materials. This pottery has not been reported from areas in eastern Kurdistan, and thus may be restricted to the far western parts of the central and northern Zagros, extending as far north as the southern shore of Lake Urmia. The eastern and northern shores of the lake seem to have the unpainted Godin II-like version of late Iron III, if the small assemblage at Bastam is any indication. Second, unpainted late Iron III material like that found in central western Iran occurs at still other sites widely removed from the "source" area: at Chogha Mish, at other sites in Khuzistan, and probably at Persepolis. Thus, while there is still considerable variety among regions, it seems to be far less than in early Iron III.

If early Iron III is the period of Urartian and Assyrian domination, then late Iron III is in some way connected with the events following the fall of Assyria. Unfortunately, we cannot precisely date the transition from early to late Iron III, and thus do not know whether its start is associated with the expansion of Media or with the rise of the Achaemenids. The earlier starting date may be indicated by the widespread occurrence of forms that seem to develop from the earlier "micaceous buff wares," with their center in and around "Media," but this is an admittedly weak argument. In either case, it seems likely that the distribution of these wares should be seen as reflecting the scope of Iranian imperial expansion, be that Median or Achaemenid.

The evidence for the end date of Iron III is contradictory. On the one hand, the lack of Iron IV pottery at Persepolis seems to imply that Iron IV is a post-Achaemenid phenomonen, and would extend Iron III into the fourth century B.C. On the other hand, however, the association of Iron IV painted ware with shapes that seem to be Achaemenid (Kroll 1975) would argue for an earlier terminus ante quem.

Iron IV

The map of the distribution of Iron IV painted wares reflects a phenomenon not previously attested in the Iron Age (figure 73). (See also Haerinck 1983: 242.) The range of this phenomenon, from the Araxes River in the north to Pasargadae and Tepe Yahya (not on the map) in the south, and its appearance in all of the areas that had previously exhibited varying degrees of regionalism is difficult to explain. Most of the sites noted on the map are known from the presence of one or two diagnostics. More important, however, is the uncertainty surrounding the starting date of the Iron IV. If this is to be set in the Achaemenid Period, then the distribution probably reflects an imperial style spread throughout western Iran, a style which survived the collapse of the empire itself and continued on into the early Parthian Period. If, on the other hand, the starting date is post-Achaemenid, then the ceramic distribution indicates a stylistic unity in the face of political fragmentation which is not easily explained.

Conclusion

This review of the Iron Age highlights a number of important points. The ground-breaking syntheses of the Iron Age presented by Young and Dyson in 1965 established the framework for much of the subsequent work. Questions of chronology, of defining the nature of the periods within the Iron Age, of the relationship between texts and material culture, and of appropriate strategies to advance the inquiry can all be traced back to the intellectual climate established by those two studies.

In the past two decades, however, a vast amount of new information has radically altered many of our perceptions of the period. Instead of an outline based upon a half dozen sites, we now have one that is far more complete and infinitely more complex. The vast, previously empty territories separating the few original sites have begun to be filled by excavation and survey, providing data that must be added to the picture and allowing us to take advantage of older materials that were previously of limited use. But we are still dealing with a data set that is inadequate in many fundamental ways, particularly in the extent of publication.

Nonetheless, the data now at our disposal have allowed me to put forward a new, if provisional synthesis of the Iron Age in western Iran. In this, I have retained Dyson's basic scheme of assigning numbers to the periods of the Iron Age, and expanded it following Young to include a component called Iron IV. But these terms have been defined to carry only chronological meaning. They cannot be made into bearers of "cultural" meaning without doing serious violence to the archaeological record.

Within each period of the Iron Age, western Iran can be seen as a mosaic of cultural patterns. Both the nature and configuration of the tesserae in the mosaic shift through time. These shifts can at times be correlated with sociopolitical developments known from the textual sources. The most obvious overall correlation is the spread of stylistically similar "fossil markers" on an ever-widening geographical horizon as the integration of western Iran into a single large political unit progresses during the first millennium.

Perhaps most important is that after the collapse of political unity following the death of Alexander the Great the pattern of apparent integration persists. Were it not for the written sources about this period, we would be hard pressed to posit such political fragmentation based on the archaeological materials currently available. Indeed, just the opposite would be suggested.

This last observation points up one of the major avenues of future research. In Iranian (and Near Eastern) archaeology, ceramics are our most abundant artifact, and their study will continue to be the foundation on which all of our other structures are built. The theoretical frameworks within which we interpret this ceramic evidence, both for chronological purposes and for understanding cultural processes and patterns, are just beginning to be elaborated. These need to be made explicit and tested against the available evidence.

Similar points can be made about the written sources. These are complex documents that need to be treated with all of the caution and skill available to the historian. Only then will they serve as the counterfoil for the archaeologically generated data.

Implicit in all of this is the need for better and more data. Since the current political situation makes it impossible to collect further information in the field, we must turn to publishing the vast amounts of data already in hand from both excavation and survey. This will bring the picture presented here into sharper focus and allow greater precision in our cultural and chronological statements. Only then will we be able to deal with the kinds of processual questions addressed in other chapters of this book.

The rewards of such a pursuit promise to be considerable, for no other period in the ancient history of western Iran has a better balance of written documentation and material remains. The systematic integration of these disparate sources can lead to insights about the processes of cultural change that are otherwise denied to us in the absence of one or the other. Survey, excavations, and textual study will allow us to address the question of the relationship between material-cultural remains and political systems; to document the nature of change in the face of new political realities; to examine the continuities in adaptive strategies that characterize this diverse region of the Near East; and to describe and understand the innovations that lead from small fragmented polities to world empire.

Acknowledgments

I would like to thank Oscar White Muscarella and Remy Boucharlat for reading and commenting on early drafts of this chapter. T. Cuyler Young, Jr., Irene Winter, and Bob Hunt read more recent drafts and proffered suggestions, which were sometimes wisely accepted. Special thanks are due to Robert C. Henrickson for many hours of help in all stages of preparing this manuscript. The maps and figures were prepared by Carol Gilbert of the West Asian Department, Royal Ontario Museum. The Mahidasht Project was supported by the Social Sciences and Humanities Research Council of Canada.

Notes

1. In this chapter, I follow the geographical scheme outlined in my work on the Neo-Assyrian geography of the Zagros (Levine 1972, 1973–74, 1977b), accepting the modifications introduced by S. Brown (1979). For an alternate position, see Reade (1978), but note Brown's comments on Reade's position.

2. For a brilliant discussion of this issue and the problems involved in relation to a much better understood corpus, that of West Semitic names, see Fales (1977).

3. The bibliography for Iranian archaeological sites and surveys is extensive. I have refrained from cluttering the text with long lists of references to general discussions of the sites. For these, the reader is referred to Vanden Berghe (1979), which is complete through 1978. Specific references will be cited. I have omitted two groups of sites

from discussion. The first consists of the sites in the Bakhtiari region recently published by Zagarell (1982). While tantalizing, the small amount of information retrieved makes dealing with these sites difficult. The second group consists of the cemetery sites in the Pusht-i Kuh excavated by Vanden Berghe. These are a major source of information, but require a study in and of themselves. Furthermore, they are not "settlement" data in the strict sense of the term and seem to form a quite distinct subgroup that will eventually need to be integrated into the larger picture we are drawing here.

4. The architectural history of Hasanlu IV is complex and has been discussed briefly by Dyson (1977b). Since virtually all of the published artifacts associated with the architecture of Period IV are also associated with the destruction of Period IVB, the level which is represented by all of the major buildings in their final form, I have treated Period IV as a single unit in this discussion.

5. For earlier discussions of some of the problems associated with the Period III sequence, see Dyson (1977b: 549), and Kroll (1975; 1977: 105).

6. Kroll cites parallels to Hasanlu III, IIIA, and IIIB, without quoting a source. Presumably, he examined the Hasanlu collections in Philadelphia and discussed the assignments with Dyson. Muscarella informs me that his own parallels to Hasanlu IIIB and IIIA cited in the Agrab Tepe report are derived from records in Philadelphia, which were so labelled. In this study, the parallels cited by Kroll (1976) were taken as published, without rechecking each citation.

7. The low number of parallels between Hasanlu IIIA and post-Urartian Bastam may be due to the Urartian bias in the data base referred to above.

8. There is a small Parthian Period occupation overlying the main period at the site.

9. The pottery published by R. Stronach (1978) was available to Henrickson thanks to the generosity of the Stronachs. I have used Henrickson and Kroll because the data were readily available. While it would be useful and desirable to bring these studies up to date, any such undertaking is beyond the limits of this paper.

10. Sumner is well aware of the problem and has expressed puzzlement at the lack of relevant material, but cannot as yet offer a solution to these problems. An important article by Sumner (1986) arrived too late to be incorporated into this study. Inter alia in this article, Sumner tries to wrestle with some of the problems addressed here, and it is good to have this up-to-date summary of his thinking. His suggestions as to the Achaemenid ceramic corpus of Fars still leave many questions outstanding, without materially affecting the argument made in the article.

11. The Iron IV figures were kindly supplied by Young.

12. The presence in central western Iran of Late Western Gray Ware, which in some forms is easily confused with Godin III:2 gray wares, has yet to be conclusively documented.

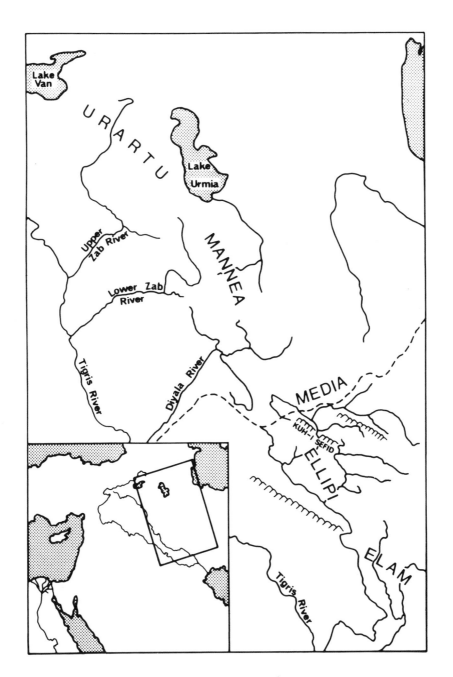

Figure 66. The Zagros in the Neo-Assyrian Period.

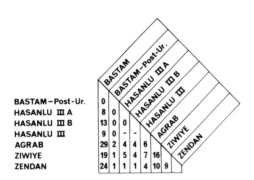

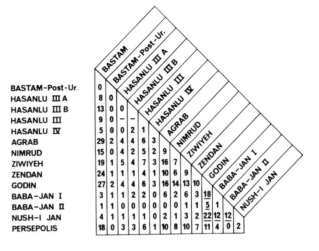

Figure 67. Shared ceramic shapes for Iron III sites in Azerbaijan and Kurdistan.

Figure 69. Shared ceramic shapes for Iron II/III sites in western Iran.

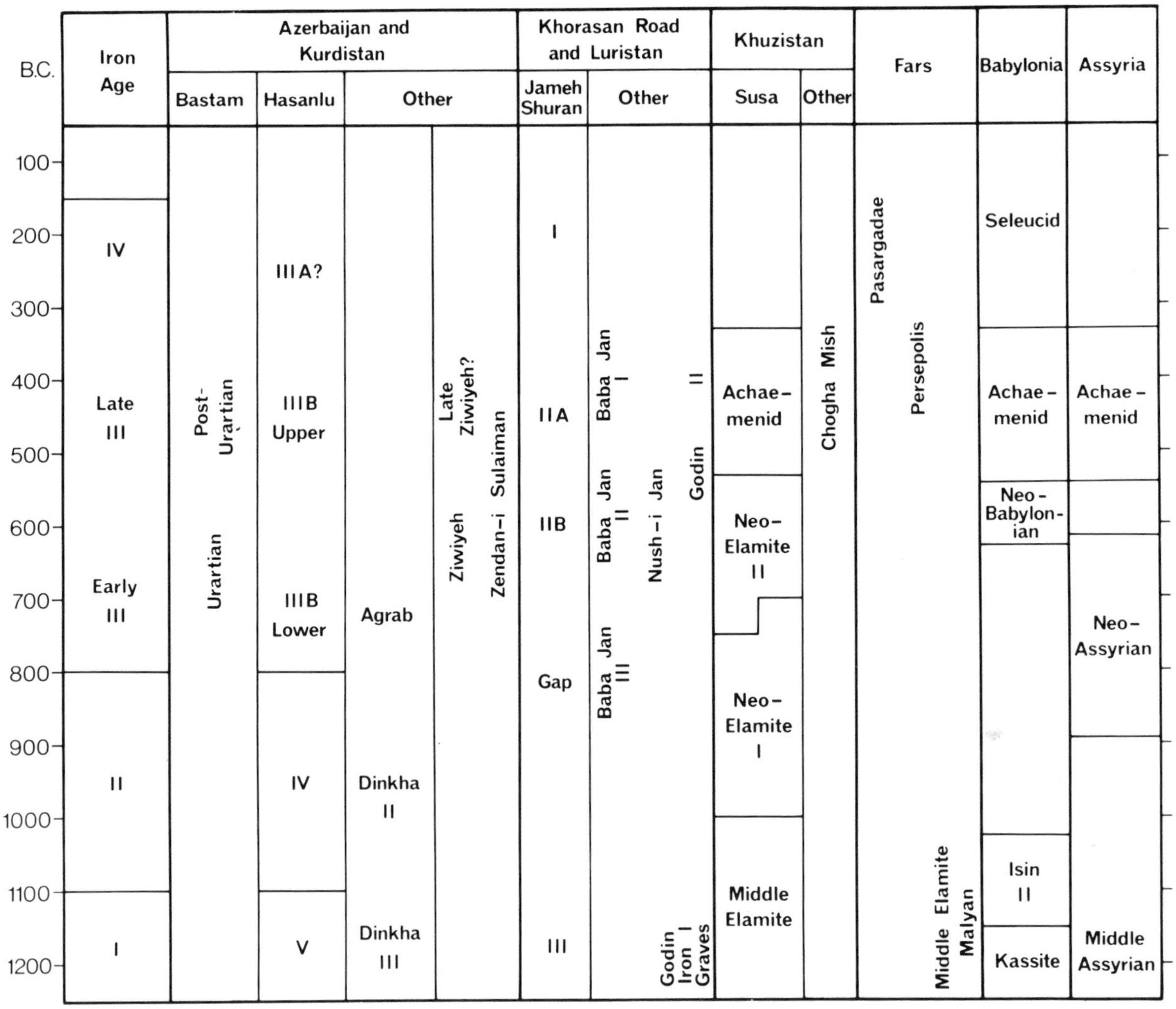

	BASTAM	BASTAM-Post-Ur.	HASANLU III A	HASANLU III B	HASANLU III	AGRAB	ZIWIYE
BASTAM–Post-Ur.	0						
HASANLU III A	8	0					
HASANLU III B	13	0	0				
HASANLU III	9	0	–	–			
AGRAB	29	2	4	4	6		
ZIWIYE	19	1	5	4	7	16	
ZENDAN	24	1	1	1	4	10	9

	BASTAM	BASTAM-Post-Ur.	HASANLU III A	HASANLU III B	HASANLU III	HASANLU IV	AGRAB	NIMRUD	ZIWIYEH	ZENDAN	GODIN	BABA-JAN I	BABA-JAN II	NUSH-I JAN
BASTAM-Post-Ur.	0													
HASANLU III A	8	0												
HASANLU III B	13	0	0											
HASANLU III	9	0	–	–										
HASANLU IV	5	0	0	2	1									
AGRAB	29	2	4	4	6	3								
NIMRUD	15	0	4	2	5	2	9							
ZIWIYEH	19	1	5	4	7	3	16	7						
ZENDAN	24	1	1	1	4	1	10	6	9					
GODIN	27	2	4	4	6	3	16	14	13	10				
BABA–JAN I	3	1	1	2	2	0	6	2	6	3	18			
BABA–JAN II	1	1	0	0	0	0	0	0	1	1	5	1		
NUSH–I JAN	4	1	1	1	1	0	2	1	3	2	22	12	12	
PERSEPOLIS	18	0	3	3	6	1	10	8	10	7	11	4	0	2

Figure 68. Relative chronology of archaeological sites in western Iran in the first millennium B.C.

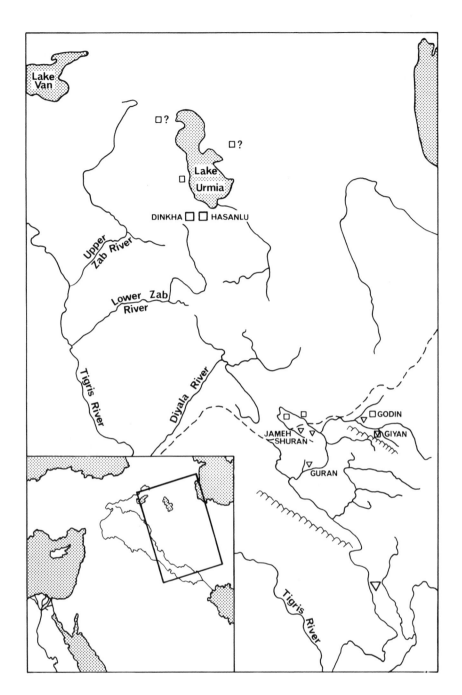

Figure 70. Distribution of Iron I sites in western Iran.
    ☐ Early western gray ware sites
    △ Elamite/Kassite goblets
    ––– Great Khorasan Road

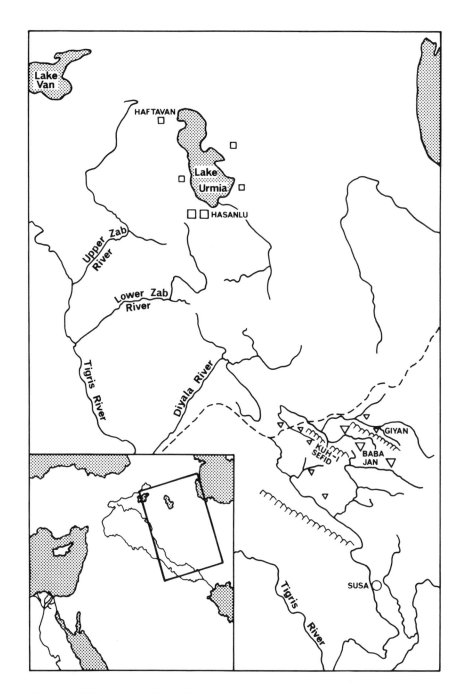

Figure 71. Distribution of Iron II sites in western Iran.
    □ Late western gray ware sites
    △ Genre Luristan sites
    ——— Great Khorasan Road

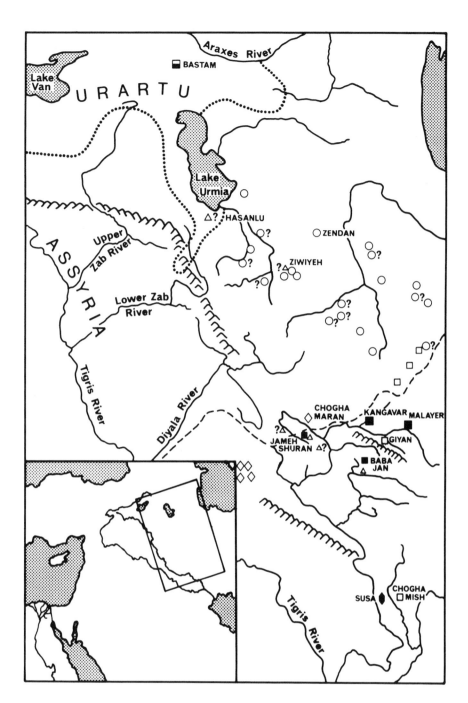

Figure 72. Distribution of Iron III sites in western Iran.

■ Early and late micaceous buff ware sites
□ Indeterminate micaceous buff ware sites
◇ Pusht-i Kuh wares
△ Jameh Shuran IIA painted wares
○ Cream-slipped buff wares
◆ Neo-Elamite II wares
———Great Khorasan Road

Urartian wares are spread throughout the area
marked Urartu.

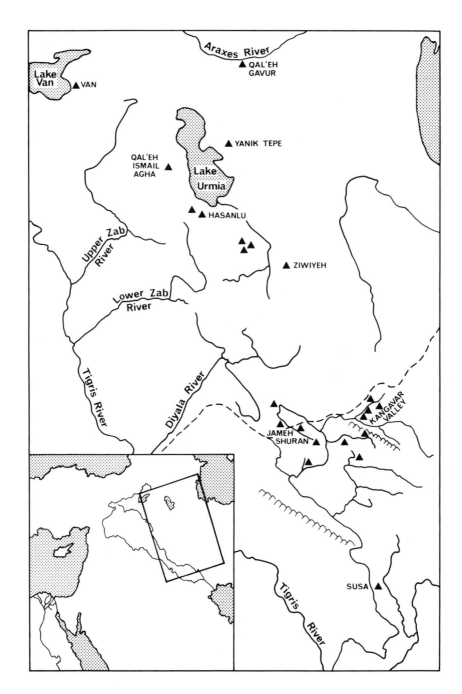

Figure 73. Distribution of Iron IV painted wares in western Iran.

Chapter 10

Western Iran in the Partho-Sasanian Period: The Imperial Transformation

ROBERT J. WENKE

Introduction

With the death of Alexander in 323 B.C., western Iran and the whole of Southwest Asia entered a century of political fragmentation and conflict. Between about 210 B.C. and A.D. 640, however, two successive empires—the Parthian (ca. 210 B.C.–A.D. 225) and the Sasanian (ca. A.D. 225–A.D. 640)—developed in highland Iran and eventually brought much of Southwest Asia under political and economic control.

By conventional standards of cultural complexity, Sasanian political, economic, and social institutions were much more complex and powerful than those of the Parthians, but both can be viewed as representative of a general class of *imperial* sociocultural formations (labelled "pre-industrial empires" by Eisenstadt [1963]). Other representatives of this social type appeared in ancient China, Peru, Mexico, and elsewhere.

As a purely descriptive label, "pre-industrial empire" has no necessary or sufficient definitions, but most of the political systems of this type had hundreds of different occupational specializations; administrative hierarchies with five, ten, or even more levels; military force sufficient to implement central government policies over areas thousands of kilometers in extent; and settlement patterns marked by unprecedented levels of urbanization and extreme differentiation of settlement function.

Scholarly interest in the Parthians and Sasanians has focussed on their antagonistic relationship with Imperial Rome (e.g., Debevoise 1938), their art (e.g., Porada 1965a), and, particularly in the case of the Sasanians, the influences of their political and economic systems on their Islamic successors (e.g., Mo-

rony 1984). There have also been several archaeologically based attempts to compile regional Partho-Sasanian culture histories (Adams 1962, 1965, 1981; Keall 1967, 1975; Adams and Nissen 1972; Wenke 1975–76, 1982; Maurer n.d.). Nevertheless, the Partho-Sasanian archaeological record remains poorly known, and most of our interpretations of these cultures are based on early Arab geographies and histories that are in many respects incomplete and inaccurate (Pyne 1982).

In this chapter I shall summarize both the documentary and the archaeological evidence for the Partho-Sasanian Period and then consider the Partho-Sasanian archaeological record from the perspective of an important question of archaeological method and theory. Specifically, given the awesome size of the Partho-Sasanian archaeological record and our ultimate dependence on surface sampling for much of what we know about it, how best can we sample and analyze Partho-Sasanian archaeological sites?

My other objective here is to set studies of the Parthians and Sasanians within the general inquiry about the evolution of cultural complexity in Southwest Asia. Although the Parthians and Sasanians were far removed in time from the first "complex" societies in this area, I argue that they are significant for understanding the overall evolutionary pattern of Southwest Asian cultural complexity. Of particular relevance here is the question of evolutionary tempo and mode: are the Parthians and Sasanians best viewed as predictable continuations of evolutionary processes already evident at the period of the origins of cultural complexity, with cycles of expansion and collapse that were simply extensions of the scale on which these evolutionary processes operated (Wenke 1975–76)? Or can patterns of cultural evolution in Southwest Asia usefully be viewed in terms of "punctuated equilibria," where cultural change is not gradual, but marked by periods of rapid, radical change? Or is the notion of cultural evolutionary tempo and mode appropriate here at all?

Partho-Sasanian Culture History

Reconstructions of Partho-Sasanian culture history can draw on archaeological and documentary evidence, but both are of highly variable quality. Partho-Sasanian occupations were encountered at many major sites during excavations early in this century (at Susa, Kish, Uruk, Hatra, Babylon, Nippur), yet in most cases the research objectives were much earlier occupations, and all too often Partho-Sasanian levels were removed with little care and less analysis. In excavating Parthian and Sasanian levels at the great city of Susa, for example, Morgan devised the following plan:

> A general excavation (in five meter levels) was therefore called for without taking into account the natural levels, which are imperceptible and which it would be childish to try to distinguish . . . experience [showed] that if the workmen threw the dirt into the wagons from a height of five meters the materials would not suffer (Morgan 1906, quoted in Huot 1965: 54).

Some Partho-Sasanian occupations in western and southern Iran have been systematically excavated, including Susa (Ghirshman 1952, 1953, 1954b; Rosen-Ayalon 1971, 1974; Labrousee and Boucharlat 1974); Bishapour (Ghirshman 1956); Ivan-i Karkhah (Ghirshman 1952); Jundishapur (Adams and Hansen 1968); Tepe Yahya (Lamberg-Karlovsky 1970); Siraf (D. Whitehouse 1971, 1972, 1975); Qasr-i Abu Nasr (Frye ed. 1973); Bisitun (Kleiss 1970); Qaleh-i Yazdigird (Keall 1967, 1975, 1977b); and Shahr-i Oumis (Hansman and Stronach 1974). But generally these excavations have been limited in scale, directed mainly at other occupational periods, or conducted on atypical or urban sites. And in most cases the excavated samples have not been used to construct regional Parthian or Sasanian ceramics seriations.

Much of our archaeological evidence, in fact, comes not from excavations but from systematic regional surveys of the Susiana Plain (Adams 1962; Wenke 1975–76; Schacht 1975b); the Plain of Izeh (Wright ed. 1979); Ram Hormuz (Wright ed. 1979); the Deh Luran Plain (Neely 1974); Fars province (Vanden Berghe 1961); the Gulf coast (Whitcomb 1979); the Arak Plain (Thompson personal communication); Ira-

nian Kurdistan (Keall 1977b); and in east-central Iran, the Damghan area (Maurer 1978, 1981).

Partho-Sasanian sites in Soviet Asia have been excavated, but publication in Russian has lessened the impact of this research.

With few exceptions the seriations of ceramics in these various areas have not been sufficiently precise to allow rigorous analyses of settlement patterns.

Our documentary evidence of the Parthians and Sasanians includes only a few contemporary texts, but numerous coins and seals (Wroth 1903; Le Rider 1965) and several major rock inscriptions (all reviewed in Christensen 1944). Some contemporary references to the Parthians and Sasanians are to be found in Greek, Roman, Armenian, Hebrew, and Chinese literature (R. Miller 1957; Christensen 1944). The paucity of Sasanian written documents is attributed by some (e.g., Spuler 1954:54–55) to the intentional destruction of these texts by the Arabs and Turks.

Our most detailed written sources on Partho-Sasanian Iran, however, are the historians and geographers of early Islam (reviewed in Schwarz 1896; Pyne 1982). Collectively these sources are imprecise about many important demographic, economic, and political aspects of these empires, and there are numerous conflicts and evident inaccuracies (Pyne 1982). However, they do provide a vast amount of information about political strategies, tax systems, dynastic succession, religious rituals, and the (supposed) exploits of kings.

The historical texts, coins, and other historical data pertaining to Partho-Sasanian studies have occasioned an extensive secondary literature containing extended debates on such topics as the accuracy of applying stage classifications (e.g., "feudalism") to these cultures (e.g., Widengren 1956; Pigulevskaja 1963; Neusner 1963; Ziegler 1964:15–17) and determining connections between historically documented macropolitical events and specific segments of the archaeological record (e.g., Debevoise 1938; Hansman 1967; Keall 1975; Wenke 1982).

Some issues in analyzing these various categories of evidence and combining them with the archaeological data are discussed below.

The Ecological Context

Because of their greater size and complexity, Parthian and Sasanian cultures interacted with their ecological environment in a manner different from that of their more simply organized predecessors. Yet there is still much about the Parthians and Sasanians that we can understand on the basis of their ecological setting.

First, western Iran consists for the most part of foothills and mountains. The alluvial plains and mountain valleys on which much of the archaeological attention

Robert J. Wenke

has been lavished constitute only a small fraction of the total area. But an important element in understanding Partho-Sasanian imperial dynamics may be the extent to which the farmers and herdsmen who exploited the highlands were brought into lowland economies and political systems (Hole 1980). Thus, additional research in highland areas is required, particularly in the form of surveys, to estimate population density and distribution changes during Partho-Sasanian culture history.

Second, the western Iranian lowlands, especially northwest Khuzistan, include extraordinarily rich agricultural zones where high average temperatures, fertile soil, and adequate water munificently rewarded investments in irrigation systems, roads, and efficient agricultural administration. Rice, sugarcane, orchard crops, and other "exotic" or expensive and exportable crops that grow well in few other areas of Southwest Asia flourish in Khuzistan. As discussed below, it is Khuzistan's great agricultural productivity—and the *tax* potential of this productivity—that has been a major force in the area's political history.

A third geographical factor of importance is that western Iran during the Parthian and Sasanian eras was crisscrossed by many important trade routes over which caravans carried jewels, oil, cloth, metals, woods, dyes, spices, glassware, and other products between Persian Gulf ports, India, China, Mesopotamia, and the Mediterranean world. Obviously, then, analyses of imperial dynamics in this region cannot be conducted in isolation; the Parthians and Sasanians of Khuzistan were part of a much larger economic and political matrix, and their archaeological record must be viewed in this context.

A fourth important ecological consideration is that during the Parthian and Sasanian periods the physical landscape of western Iran was much different from that of earlier and later epochs. The major rivers in Khuzistan had begun down-cutting at least by the second millennium B.C. (Kirkby 1977), and by the Parthian and Sasanian periods they had reached nearly their present levels. Irrigation for the Parthians and Sasanians was a much more ambitious and costlier venture than it had been for previous occupations. Raising great volumes of water to plain level required locating dams and barrages farther up the river courses, as well as constructing larger and longer primary canals. Moreover, there is some evidence that the extension of pastoral nomadism and vastly increased lumbering activities during the Parthian and Sasanian periods altered permanently the ecological conditions in much of the highlands as well as the flow characteristics of the rivers dependent on these large upland watersheds (Kirkby 1977). The extent of these changes remains largely unknown.

Finally, we must consider the possibility that the size and complexity of the settlements of the Parthian and Sasanian periods are so much greater than those of earlier occupations in this area that their essential ecological operations were different.

To take one epidemiological example, a great problem for metropolises on the flat, hot plains of Southwest Asia is that they frequently cannot protect their water supplies from sewage contamination, either as the water is introduced through canals or qanats, or as it is stored and used. Scores of diseases, many of them fatal and contagious, can be transmitted in this fashion, with dramatic impact on every aspect of life including fertility rates.

Partho-Sasanian Settlement Patterns in Northern Khuzistan

Because of the great political and economic importance of Khuzistan in Partho-Sasanian history, this province should not be considered representative of many other, less-developed areas belonging to these empires. The Parthian and Sasanian empires were truly international political systems that cannot be fully analyzed on the basis of small isolated segments of their components. Nonetheless, Khuzistan is the only area in western Iran for which we have reasonably precise settlement pattern studies, and it will therefore be the focus of the present analysis. Aside from Khuzistan, the primary source of comparative data on the Parthians and Sasanians is from the Tigris-Euphrates and Diyala floodplains (Adams 1965, 1981).

Elsewhere I have described the methods and most of the results of our 1973 archaeological survey of the Susiana Plain (Wenke 1975–76, 1982). Briefly, we used aerial photographs and surveys in an attempt to locate all occupations of all periods. The aerial photographs were sufficiently precise that, in my opinion, we missed fewer than 5 percent of such occupations.

Each site located was measured in its maximum dimensions and height, and artifact samples were collected from its surface. Although these samples were "informal," in the sense that they were not probabilistically designed or collected, we tried to make a representative collection of "diagnostic" bases, rims, and decorated sherds. On many sites "block" samples were done by collecting every such "diagnostic" in a 5 by 5 or 10 by 10 meter square. On topographically complex sites, several such block samples and general samples were retrieved.

Estimates of population size during different periods were made on the basis of these type frequencies and by estimates of the distribution of specific ceramic types on a given site.

Almost every Middle Eastern archaeologist has catalogued the potential and problems of this general archaeological survey approach (reviewed in Adams 1981). And, as I discuss below, there remain significant questions about the extent to which we can estimate anything beyond broad chronological groupings of sites with such data. Nonetheless, on the basis of relative ceramics seriations, coin and figurine associations, and other evidence (Wenke 1975–76), I have reconstructed settlement patterns on the northern Susiana Plain during the following periods: Achaemenid (ca. 521–325 B.C.), Seleuco-Parthian (ca. 324–25 B.C.), Elymean (ca. 25 B.C.–A.D. 125), Terminal Parthian (ca. A.D. 125–A.D. 250), Early Sasanian (ca. A.D. 250–400), Late Sasanian (ca. A.D. 400–640), and Early Islamic (ca. A.D. 640–1000) (see figures 74–79). I have also computed rank-size plots for several of these periods, and these are presented in figures 80–82.

It should be noted, however, that, on the basis of excavations at Susa after my 1973 survey, Miroschedji (1981a) and Boucharlat (n.d.) have persuasively argued that my reconstruction of the Achaemenid settlement pattern on the Susiana included some sites that belonged to the Neo-Elamite Period. If they are right, the Achaemenid Period seems to have had lower rural population densities and more limited agricultural productivity than was previously thought. As various scholars have remarked (Adams 1962; Wenke 1975–76), it is somewhat surprising that so few Achaemenid towns and villages existed on the Susiana Plain in an era when Susa was supposedly the capital of a great empire.

During the Seleuco-Parthian Period (ca. 324–25 B.C.), Susa was apparently at first the center of a rich province of the Seleucid state and incorporated most of the northern Susiana Plain. Strabo, Diodorous, and other classical commentators recorded that "Susis" was an exceptionally fertile area, producing rice, vegetables, dates, and many other crops, and several contemporary texts record the efforts of the city's administration to increase production by constructing irrigation canals. But the major source of wealth for the Susiana may have been its role as "middleman" and supplier to the lucrative trade routes connecting the Persian Gulf to markets in the north and west (Le Rider 1965). Analyses of coins found at Susa at this time indicate rising commerce with Seleucia-on-the-Tigris and other cities (Le Rider 1965). With its strategic position and great agricultural productivity, the Susiana may have been the wealthiest province within the Parthian sphere of influence.

Compared to the Achaemenid occupation of the Susiana Plain (figure 74), the Seleuco-Parthian population densities (figure 75) were somewhat higher, but the rate of population growth during these periods was apparently very slow. Seleuco-Parthian settlements are considerably smaller, on the average, than Achaemenid settlements (Wenke 1975–76), perhaps

indicating greater internal security, in that few if any of these smaller settlements appear to be fortified. The comparatively small size of Seleuco-Parthian settlements may also indicate changing agricultural strategies. In contrast to dry-farmed wheat and barley, the cultivation of rice and other labor-intensive crops—which appear to have been produced in increasing quantities in the Seleuco-Parthian Period—has elsewhere been associated with reduced settlement size (Geertz 1963). Major new canal systems were built on the Susiana Plain during the Seleuco-Parthian Period, probably to irrigate rice and orchard crops, as well as vegetables, wheat, barley, and other produce.

Generally, the Seleuco-Parthian settlement pattern closely follows that of the preceding Achaemenid Period: areas of the plain largely uninhabited during the Achaemenid Period remained so during the Seleuco-Parthian Period, and the areas of densest settlement during the two periods were approximately the same. Approximately 33 percent of the Achaemenid sites were occupied in the Seleuco-Parthian Period. Toward the end of the period of Seleucid control, Susa and its environs probably became a semiautonomous political entity, although when the first powerful monarchs attacked the Seleucid ruler (ca. 139 B.C.), Susa fought with the Seleucids against the Parthians (Debevoise 1935).

The Elymean or Middle Parthian Period (ca. 25 B.C.–ca. A.D. 125) (figure 76) coincides with the rise of an autonomous *Elymean* state, incorporating Susa and most of the Susiana Plain. It is also apparently the period when Susa reached its zenith as an economic power. Coins dated to this period and minted at Seleucia and other major cities are frequently found at Susa, and Susa's own coinage is well represented at most large nearby cities (Le Rider 1965). During the 1973 survey, we found many coins of this era, even on tiny sites on the plain's periphery.

Rural Susiana settlement patterns at this time indicate a considerable increase in population densities, vastly greater investments in irrigation systems, and the emergence of a ring of substantial settlements around Susa itself. Large investments were made to irrigate and cultivate marginally productive areas of the plain, and in a few locations the limits of traditional agricultural productivity were probably approached.

In the Terminal Parthian Period (A.D. 125–250) (figure 77), literary and numismatic evidence suggests that Susa was slowly losing some of its share of the wealth generated by long-distance trade. Keall (1975) has argued that Vologases I, a Parthian monarch, tried in about A.D. 70 to strengthen central Parthian control of western Iran and southern Iraq by diverting to the imperial treasury trade revenues from Susa (then part of the satrapy of Elymais) and from Characene (a satrapy centered around the ports of the Shatt al-Arab). According to Keall, in about A.D. 60 Vologases founded a new city, Vologasias, near Seleucia-on-the-Tigris, as a competitor to that rich and often insubordinate city; he imposed in about A.D. 73 a Parthian governor on Characene; and, to strengthen his western flank, he came to terms with Rome about control of Armenia.

The political history of the second century A.D. was greatly complicated by Trajan's invasions in A.D. 116, after which provinces in western Iran and adjacent areas entered into various political and economic relationships with either Rome or the Parthians, or both. At times in this era, Susa and Elymais were probably autonomous in most activities.

In terms of changes in settlement patterns on the Susiana during the Elymean and Terminal Parthian periods, perhaps the most significant development was the growing number and size of unwalled sites, composed of many small buildings laid out apparently without regard to any overall plan. This same type of settlement has also been observed by Adams in the Parthian and Sasanian occupations of the Diyala region of Iraq:

> With very few exceptions, Sasanian sites are low and sprawling, with irregular shapes and indefinite contours. Not infrequently, occupational remains extend in thin bands for considerable distances along old canal levees or crop up sparsely at intervals separated by apparently uninhabited areas. While surface evidence alone must remain inconclusive, all of this is not suggestive of a "feudal" society, with peasant villages hugging the flanks of high, fortified seats of a landed nobility. Instead it seems to imply a considerable degree of internal peace and central control (Adams 1965:73).

Such settlements were already common on the Susiana in the Middle and Terminal Parthian periods, and they were particularly numerous in the Sasanian (A.D. 250–640) era.

While rural population densities apparently reached their premodern peaks during the Parthian Period, it was during the Sasanian Period that the most drastic reshaping of settlement and subsistence on the Susiana Plain apparently occurred. Many smaller irrigation canals appear to have lost their importance, but other larger canals were built elsewhere and massive stone weirs were erected at several points on the Diz, Karkheh, and Karun rivers. Qanats several kilometers long were built to bring water underground to larger Sasanian settlements, and roads linked the Susiana Plain to other centers of the empire.

Building on the accomplishments of the Parthian Period, the Sasanians fundamentally reshaped the settlement patterns of the Susiana. Few other areas of the ancient world witnessed the scale of planned urbanism reached on this plain. In an area of hardly 1,600 square kilometers, at least three large cities (Ivan-i Karkhah, Jundishapur, Shushtar—and perhaps Susa) existed contemporaneously, with a combined population of possibly several hundred thousand. Jundishapur was a polyglot city inhabited by Persians, Arabs, Jews, Christians, Greeks, Indians, and other groups. Coins of this period and early Arabic accounts reflect a vibrant money-based economy in which a flourishing textile and silk industry centered at Shushtar apparently played a major economic role. Roman engineers captured by Shapur I are recorded as having designed the irrigation systems necessary to support these large populations (Schwarz 1896: 346–47). Although the exterior walls of Ivan-i Karkhah enclose about 5 square kilometers, and those of Jundishapur about 9 square kilometers, we do not know the occupied extent of either city at any particular time.

An interesting aspect of the construction of Ivan-i Karkhah and Jundishapur is that neither seems to be particularly well located in relation to the economic resources of the Susiana Plain. Supplying Jundishapur with water, for example, required construction of expensive canals and qanats to bring water far greater distances than would have been necessary if the settlement was built elsewhere. Ivan-i Karkhah, aside from difficulties in water supply, was located many kilometers from the agricultural areas that must have supported the city. Both Ivan-i Karkhah and Jundishapur are today deserted, and their areas of the plain are the least densely settled.

Perhaps the best location on the plain—at least in relation to water supply, agricultural areas, and transport routes—is occupied today by the city of Dizful and the areas immediately south of it, but persistent searching of excavations carried out there has yet to yield Sasanian remains. The large area extending several kilometers south of the city also seems to have been almost uninhabited during both the Parthian and Sasanian periods.

Thus, it is tempting to accept the tradition that both Ivan-i Karkhah and Jundishapur were located and constructed by imperial fiat—perhaps without much regard for economic realities (Nöldeke 1973:40–41)—and that the failure of these cities to reach the dimensions set out by their walls is a reflection of this unrealistic urban planning.

Rural Sasanian settlement patterns on the Susiana Plain can be divided into an Early Period (ca. A.D. 240–A.D. 400) and a Late Period (ca. A.D. 400–A.D. 640) (figures 78 and 79), although the problem of reoccupied sites and the imprecisions in the ceramic seriations require that this distinction be treated as a very rough approximation.

Generally, the urbanization of the Susiana Plain

throughout the Sasanian Period appears to have been reflected directly in declining rural population densities and migration to the cities, perhaps as a result of rising agricultural productivity stimulated by government investments. Much of the population of Ivan-i Karkhah, Jundishapur, and Shushtar was probably composed of immigrants to the Susiana, but it is also likely that many villagers and townsmen from the Susiana emigrated to the cities. Adams noted much the same pattern in the Diyala area during the Sasanian Period (1965:115–16), and similar processes of urbanization are thought to have been common in Aztec Mesoamerica and elsewhere (Cowgill 1975a). In this context it is interesting to note that movements of agricultural workers and peasants in ninth-century Iraq were manipulated by entrepreneurs who promised them larger shares of the harvests, thereby drawing large numbers of people to their domains (Jabbar 1973:16). A similar system might have prevailed in Partho-Sasanian Khuzistan, but more important in this migration process was probably the rise of an important textile and silk industry in Shushtar (and perhaps Jundishapur) during the Sasanian Period. The production of glass, metalwork, and many other crafts (Tafazzoli 1974) under imperial control required thousands of craftsmen, administrators, and other specialists whose activities could most effectively be coordinated in large cities.

On the other hand, the emigration to the cities of thousands of peasants poses some problems, given the Sasanians' massive investments of labor and money in agricultural production on the plain. Archaeological as well as textual evidence suggests that the Sasanian agricultural strategy on the Susiana probably involved intensive cultivation of rice, sugarcane, and orchard crops—all of which require enormous amounts of labor and precisely controlled irrigation systems (however, rice is specifically listed as absent in Persia by at least one Chinese traveler ca. A.D. 630 [R. Miller 1957:15]). Yet one can see in figures 77–79 that many areas of the plain which were densely occupied and intensively irrigated during Parthian times were, during the Sasanian Period, apparently abandoned, with no evidence of salinization or other calamity. And although many inhabitants of the cities no doubt traveled each day to labor in the fields, the extremely low population densities of some areas of the plain during Sasanian times and the apparent abandonment of many smaller irrigation systems do not accord well with the labor- and water-intensive requirements of rice, sugarcane, and orchard crops. Perhaps, as Adams (1962) suggests, most of the plain was still planted in wheat and barley.

At this point it is not possible to judge the effect on Susiana settlement patterns of interregional political developments, such as the reported devastation of Khuzistan by Arab tribes during the minority of Shapur II, circa A.D. 309–325 (Rawlinson 1875:144). This problem underscores again the difficulty of understanding rural Sasanian settlement patterns and agricultural systems without being able to connect them with specific time periods and events—a problem for which the only remedy is more surveys and better ceramic seriations.

At least some of the rural depopulation on the Susiana during the Sasanian Period may have resulted from environmental changes. For example, major alterations in the regime of several perennial streams crossing the Susiana probably occurred during the Sasanian Period. These watercourses seem to have fed a complex of irrigation systems during the Parthian Period, but most of these canals seem to have fallen out of use in Sasanian times (Wenke 1975–76:136). Although one of the streams apparently supplied much of Jundishapur's water requirements for at least part of the year, large qanats and canals were apparently constructed to bring water from the Diz to the city in the Late Sasanian Period.

Parthian and Sasanian Settlements on the Deh Luran Plain

In western Iran, the only region beside the Susiana Plain for which we have systematic survey data is the Deh Luran Plain, lying about 125 kilometers northwest of Susa.

Neely (1974) has provided tentative settlement pattern maps for the period between circa 530 B.C. and A.D. 226 (the Achaemenid, Seleucid, and Parthian periods) and for the period between about A.D. 226 and 800. Despite the rather gross scale of this information, there are some interesting aspects. First, it is apparent that, in contrast to developments on the Susiana Plain, the most impressive increases in population density and agricultural investments took place on the Deh Luran Plain during the Sasanian Period rather than during the Parthian Period. The possibility of error in assigning population settlements to various periods is great here, but comparison of some of the Deh Luran ceramics with the more firmly dated ceramics from the Susiana Plain suggests that, indeed, the Sasanian Period was the era of maximum population increase in Deh Luran. Neely found eleven sites apparently having occupations spanning the Achaemenid through the Parthian periods (1974:26). All were quite large (average 16 hectares) relative to contemporary occupations on the Susiana. Neely estimates that at any one time there were about thirty-five people per square kilometer, that irrigation was accomplished through relatively simple and short canals, and that population densities generally remained far below the level supportable through simple mixed farming and herding.

Robert J. Wenke

In the Sasanian and Early Islamic periods, however, population densities rose to about seventy-five people per square kilometer—close to the supposed maximum under traditional farming strategies—and considerable investments were made to intensify agriculture. Many qanats, some of them nearly 2 kilometers long, were built to bring water underground from the Mehmeh and Dawairij rivers to the center of the plain, and in the northern part of the plain numerous check dams and terraces were built to divert and collect runoff from rainfall. Although quite simple, these check dams and canalized wadis greatly increased the productivity of some of the higher, drier areas and may also have augmented the available pasturage for the farmers' livestock or for the sheep and goats of the pastoral nomads who wintered in this area (Neely 1974:30). In addition, scores of masonry "drop-towers" were built to transfer water from spring-fed canals to lower areas, and which also provided water power for mills to grind wheat and barley.

The considerable investments made in the Deh Luran Plain during the Sasanian and Early Islamic periods may have been part of the national developmental program of the stronger Sasanian monarchs, such as Shapur II or Chosroes, as well as the Early Islamic caliphs such as Hisham (d. A.D. 743). But they also could quite easily have been accomplished with local initiative and resources.

Neely has suggested that the florescence of Deh Luran during the Sasanian and Early Islamic periods was a " . . . direct result of processes of planned expansion and growth promoted by the Sasanian government" (1974:39). Yet relatively few Parthian or Sasanian coins have been recovered from the Deh Luran area, suggesting that the economic transactions in Deh Luran during these periods were different from those on the Susiana at the same time. Perhaps Deh Luran was somewhat marginal to the flourishing regional economies in Mesopotamia and in Media. It does not appear probable that Deh Luran was on a major trade route during either the Parthian or Sasanian periods—at least given the reconstructions of these trade routes based on the distribution of coinage and other evidence (Keall 1975; Le Rider 1965:267–71). The major routes in both these periods apparently ran north from Susa through the mountains to Hamadan by way of Khorramabad, while routes connecting Susa to the Mesopotamian alluvium apparently went directly west, joining the Tigris at Amara and following the river north to the major metropolises (Le Rider 1965:268). Other routes went south from Susa to Ahwaz and then west to Basra and Kufa (during Early Islamic times at least). The old Achaemenid royal highway did, however, pass close to the current village of Deh Luran. Also, Deh Luran was only a few days' journey from the large, important

Sasanian cities of Jundishapur, Ivan-i Karkhah, and Shushtar, and it was relatively close to other major Sasanian cities including Ctesiphon and Seleucia. Thus, although possibly not an important trade center, it is not at all unlikely that Deh Luran was chosen for imperially directed development schemes.

Deh Luran settlements during the Sasanian Period apparently were both much smaller and less frequently walled than those of the Achaemenid through the Parthian eras, indicating perhaps greater internal security. Yet few if any of the larger settlements were constructed in a planned, rectangular layout similar to that of Ivan-i Karkhah or Jundishapur.

Once Umayyid power was established, Deh Luran seems to have been the focus of agricultural developments and intensive exploitation of its natural tar seeps and naptha reserves. These products, known to have been extensively exploited in Ram Harmuz under Caliph Hisham (ca. A.D. 724–43) (Bari 1972:299), may also have been a commercially important commodity much earlier. Examination of large "torpedo" storage jars—which occur in the hundreds at most Partho-Sasanian sites—reveals them to be almost always coated on the interior with a tarry substance, possibly bitumen.

Having summarized some of the data about the Partho-Sasanian occupations of western Iran, I will now consider some attempts to interpret and explain Partho-Sasanian culture history in general. I will also relate the Khuzistan data to comparative materials from the Partho-Sasanian heartland in central Mesopotamia.

Population Growth and Cultural Change

Much has been written about the supposed role of population growth in causing cultural changes, but basic disagreements remain. Regardless of the correctness or incorrectness of individual positions on this issue, it is nonetheless still the case that: (1) we do not fully understand the relationship between demographic variation and many major ancient cultural transformations, and (2) there is at least a strong statistical relationship between such demographic variations and developments such as the rise of urbanism in ancient Southwest Asia and the cycles of ancient empires (Smith and Young, 1972; Gibson 1973).

Despite the long-term increases in human population densities in Southwest Asia between about 700 B.C. and A.D. 640, evidence from the Susiana Plain, the Diyala region, the Deh Luran area, and the environs of Uruk indicates relatively stable and low rates of population growth. Population estimates and growth rate inferences based on archaeological data are inherently suspect, but given the population estimate of the Susiana Plain during the Achaemenid Period (figure 74), for example, the increased population density there during the Terminal Parthian and Early Sasanian periods could be accounted for by an average annual increase of only one or two people per thousand, a much lower rate than for some contemporary societies (Cowgill 1975). In addition, throughout the period of maximum settlement density and agricultural productivity on the Susiana Plain, the carrying capacity—even broadly defined—was rarely, if ever, reached in most areas. Regions of the Susiana Plain that today support relatively successful farming with only minimal irrigation were largely uninhabited during the peak periods of population density and agricultural exploitation, and similar situations seem to have existed in Deh Luran, the Diyala Plain, and all other areas where Parthian and Sasanian remains have been intensively surveyed. In short, it seems a reasonable inference that land shortages, or the threat of such shortages, were rarely if ever the major direct or indirect cause of significant national political and social changes in these areas between 700 B.C. and A.D. 640. Nor do some of the most significant technological, social, and political changes observed in post-Achaemenid western Iran and Southwest Asia correlate well with presumed "population pressures." Wet-rice cultivation, massive irrigation systems, transport routes, changes in agricultural strategies, and major reformulations of administrative systems all appeared on the Susiana at times when large areas of the plain were unexploited, or only marginally exploited, and when the population-to-agricultural land ratio was comparatively low. And even when the Susiana landscape was drastically changed by the construction of two, and perhaps three, extremely large cities, these cities were probably populated, not by people squeezed off an over-populated plain, but by the precipitous abandonment of large tracts of the plain and the emigration of their populations to these urban centers.

The Partho-Sasanian demographic pattern in Mesopotamia proper (Adams 1981:179–85) seems to have been quite similar to that of the Susiana, although there were some interesting differences. As on the Susiana, already by Partho-Sasanian times there were state-sponsored irrigation and urbanization projects in central Mesopotamia (Adams 1981:179). In both areas it appears that the central government chose specific sub-areas for intensive development, but nowhere is there evidence that the government was forced into massive agricultural investment projects by rapidly increasing population densities.

Adams concludes (1981:183) that the climax of Sasanian economic growth and political integration in central Mesopotamia was in the sixth century A.D., whereas corresponding developments on the Susiana apparently occurred earlier. But this is in line with the Sasanian pattern of shifting economic investments from one zone to another.

Hydraulic Agriculture and Imperial Cycles

Despite repeated criticisms (e.g., Adams 1966, 1981), Karl Wittfogel's (1957) analysis of imperial developmental patterns as functions of the needs and products of irrigation-based, intensive agriculture has been forcefully revived by Marvin Harris (1977), among others. Harris argues that imperial cycles and the strong parallels among early empires, as well as some of the variations to be found among them, can be explained by analyzing the similarities and differences of their hydraulic agricultural systems in combination with the stresses caused by what Harris considers a somewhat constant pressure of human population increase. Harris explains the apparent "stationary" nature of ancient empires, that is, their somewhat unchanging social, legal, and technological forms throughout long cycles of imperial political expansions and collapses, as functions of the relatively stable productivity of irrigation agriculture. When a central political authority collapsed, the new leaders had only one choice: they had "to clean out the canals, rebuild the levees, and restore the hydraulic mode of production" (Harris 1977). Differences in the lengths of dynastic cycles, Harris implies, are the result of local variations in fertility rates and hydraulic potential. The overall similarity of early empires in following developmental cycles, and the factors which limited the length of time any single political entity could stay in power, depended on population growth rates, inevitable increases in governmental corruption and inefficiency over time, foreign invasions, and natural disasters. Harris follows Wittfogel's basic thesis in arguing that a highly centralized despotic government was the only practical administrative system for these early hydraulic political systems because of the requisites of coordination and administration of the massive labor forces necessary to make these systems operate effectively.

The intimate connection between irrigation systems and Partho-Sasanian culture history presents a test case of many aspects of the "hydraulic hypothesis." While there can be no doubt that many characteristics of Partho-Sasanian culture history were directly determined in part by the nature of this irrigation agriculture economy, at the same time there appears to have been great variability over time and through the component regions of the Parthian and Sasanian empires that does not seem to be connected to changes in the conditions of irrigation agriculture. As Adams notes in the case of central Mesopotamia:

> Irrigation seems to have had relatively little direct influence on the growth, powers, forms, or legitimization of the institutions of centralized authority. A more indirect influence in this realm as well is not to be denied, of course, since it is difficult to imagine the existence of any of those institutions

except in the politically unstable, stratified, urban context that in southern Mesopotamia irrigation was primarily responsible for making possible (1981:248).

A primary point of departure for understanding and explaining Partho-Sasanian history is to investigate the nature of its irrigation systems, but, to the extent that we can talk about historical causes, we must also address political, social, and even ideological factors, in addition to the basics of environment and agriculture, in order to have a comprehensive understanding of Partho-Sasanian cultures and histories.

Partho-Sasanian Administrative Institutions

Most of what we know about Partho-Sasanian administrative institutions comes from early Islamic documents (Morony 1984) and concerns the late Sasanian Period. Pyne (1982) has documented many contradictions and inaccuracies in these documents as they pertain to Khuzistan, but these sources do provide some apparently reliable information. As they are summarized in Schwartz (1896) and Pyne (1982), these documents suggest the Sasanians greatly altered and elaborated traditional administrative institutions in Southwest Asia. They apparently concentrated silk-making, textile and glass production, and other crafts in large urban centers and carefully administered their production; they taxed individual farmers very efficiently through representatives of the imperial government (rather than collecting taxes from provincial authorities); and they established an enormous bureaucracy to channel imperial power down to the level of the individual citizen. Subsistence agricultural systems in many areas gave way, under imperial direction and funding, to the cultivation of sugar, rice, orchard crops, and other commodities whose major value could be realized only with a centralized system of management, transport, distribution, and, especially, taxation. Texts and archaeological evidence suggest that the Sasanians moved tens of thousands of people, sent engineering missions into the most undeveloped parts of their empire, and literally reshaped the land surface of their country. They were, in short (again, if we accept the documentary evidence), more successful administrators than any previous and many later Southwest Asian political systems. Part of this success was engendered by improved communications. Road building was a continual effort in Sasanian times, and there apparently was remarkably swift transit for goods, people, and information by caravan and ship (Christensen 1936: 122–23). More important than communications, perhaps, was administrative reorganization (Pigulevskaya 1963:168–69).

One of the tactics used in this reorganization, according to early Islamic commentators, was the creation by the Sasanian imperial authorities of a class of nobles that was encouraged to compete with and thus check the authority of the "Great Families," the hereditary aristocracy that controlled much of the country and which in previous periods had constantly sought to undermine imperial authority. By directly appointing high officials of state, ministers, economic administrators, and royal officials, the Sasanians were able to establish a link, independent of the "Great Families," to the economic and social base of the country.

According to Mas'udi, one of the most innovative Sasanian administrators was Chosroes I (Nushirvan) (ruled A.D. 531–579) who came to power at a time of governmental stagnation and corruption and effected major reforms. Chosroes, according to early Islamic authorities, formed four great satrapies out of the many rival provinces within the empire and appointed a powerful governor to administer directly the affairs of each—maintaining his own power over the governors by his personal military detachment and an intricate system of spies. When Chosroes first came to power the taxation system was such that the government confiscated most production beyond a subsistence level, and many crops were wasted because they could not be harvested until a tax-collector determined the state's share. Chosroes substituted a system whereby taxes were fixed and paid regularly, but individual farmers were allowed to profit greatly from increased output.

Far from simply reacting to the stresses caused by overpopulation, Chosroes apparently promoted the growth of population densities by resettling captured foreigners and by compelling the marriage of all eligible women, underwriting the expense of both the dowry and any resulting children (Nöldeke 1973:163–64). He is also reported to have supported the construction of irrigation canals, funded road-building projects, and reorganized the army into a much more efficient form (Nöldeke 1973).

How accurate these "histories" are remains a source of debate, but the agreement of Roman, Chinese, Jewish, and other historical traditions on Sasanian administrative efficiency is reasonably compelling, even if the exploits of individual kings like Chosroes I are somewhat inflated.

Analysts of the evolution of cultural complexity have frequently noted that organized national religions offer supremely effective agents of secular authority and control (White 1949:383; Eisenstadt 1963:257–58; Marx 1965:9–10). With only moderate investments in personnel, temples, and ritual paraphernalia, the mass of the populace can be motivated to cooperate economically and militarily for the "good" of the state, even to the point of personal death. The Sasanians, as well as the Egyptians, the Inca, the Chou, and other early states and empires, provide examples of the correlation between the rising power of the state and the rise of state churches. It should be noted, however, that Zoroastrianism, the Sasanian's state religion, was not always an effective social adhesive. The Mazdakite revolts were suppressed with great bloodshed, and it has been suggested that the spread of Islam in Iran was greatly facilitated by the dissatisfaction of the lower classes with what may have been an effete Zoroastrianism that was supported primarily by the rich and powerful (Spuler 1954:54–55).

Several authors (e.g., Benet 1963; R. Hassan 1969) have argued that an important element of the great urbanization programs that followed the Muslim conquest was the effectiveness of Islam in superseding kinship ties; that is, religion became a powerful organizing principle through Koranic injunctions to achieve "sedentarization" and urbanization (R. Hassan 1969:234).

Politically and socially, one of the most potent developments in later Sasanian and Early Islamic times was the increasing segmentation of Southwest Asian societies through religious transformations that created "a society composed of religious communities which amounted to social corporations with their own legal institutions which gave sanction to matters of personal status such as marriage, divorce, and inheritance" (Morony 1974:8). Jews, Nestorian and Monophysite Christians, Magians, and—with the Arab conquests—Muslims, all developed community structures in which previous ties among members based on language, occupation, or geographical origins were replaced in large part by "primary identification based on membership in a religious community" (Morony 1974). Morony, in fact, ascribes a major role in the rapid spread of Islam to the formation in early Sasanian times of these essentially self-contained religious communities.

Through a national religion, organized taxation, and other bureaucratic mechanisms, the imperial Sasanian government tied the people more closely to the central government than did most previous empires, but this also had its negative aspects. By linking even the peasant agriculturalists and artisans directly to the imperial government, shock waves caused by foreign invasions of imperial territory or internal revolts affecting the top of the administrative pyramid were transmitted directly down to the agricultural and industrial base. Tax revenues lost through military reverses or the insurgencies of vassals no doubt meant on many occasions a marked reduction in funds available for the upkeep of irrigation systems. Also, as Adams notes (1965:69), the imperial government tried to check the power of its vassals by constructing large cities and forcibly relocating thousands of citizens, but the economic, social, and political disruption occasioned by these drastic measures may, in some cases, have crippled regional economies, partic-

ularly in view of the continuing demands placed on imperial resources by the hostilities with Rome. Although the military successes of some Sasanian kings made possible the establishment of a standing army—thereby circumventing the power of the nobility (Adams 1965:70–71)—military expenditures ate deeply into the Sasanian revenues.

Another problem resulting from the extension of Sasanian administrative institutions was that, for perhaps the first time, the imperial government's monetary requirements apparently were often so great that large areas were "tax farmed" to the point of widespread environmental deterioration. Adams notes (1965:81–82), for example, that several key canal systems in the Diyala area may have been so mismanaged that dependent fields became highly salinized. Similar events may have occurred on the Susiana Plain, particularly in the rich, easily irrigated areas just north of the Haft Tepe anticline.

The problem of relating the above discussion of Sasanian administrative history to the archaeological record is, to repeat, severely limited by the quantity and quality of available archaeological evidence. Archaeologically, settlement patterns are the most accessible reflections of the administrative and economic forces that shaped ancient cultures. Simple regional surveys without extensive accompanying excavations can tell us much about population densities, the organization of economic systems, and other important matters. But the application of mathematical locational models to archaeologically reconstructed settlement patterns like those of the Parthian and Sasanian periods involves many problems: samples are small and biased toward larger sites, the contemporaneity of settlements is difficult to establish, and sweeping assumptions must be made about population densities and "functional size." The problem is especially complicated for the Sasanian occupations of the Susiana Plain, because it is not presently possible to estimate with any precision the populations at any given time of Ivan-i Karkhah, Jundishapur, or Shushtar, its three largest settlements. These settlements, while no doubt occupied contemporaneously at some times, were at any given moment probably vastly different in population size (Wenke 1975–76:152–53).

One approach to the analysis of archaeological settlement patterns is the construction of rank-size plots (Berry 1967), which are produced by graphing settlement population (or, in this case, size) against rank (from largest to smallest) on a full logarithmic scale. Repeated studies have shown that such plots can vary greatly in degree of convexity or concavity and that, under some conditions, a straight line is produced. Many, often contradictory, interpretations of these empirical results have been advanced, some arguing for example that a linear rank-size relationship is indicative of a high degree of integration among settlements in economically developing countries (Richardson 1973, 1977), others asserting that it is characteristic of a "steady state" settlement system whose settlement sizes have been influenced by a large number of essentially stochastic variables (Simon 1955). Another variant of the rank-size plot is the "primate" distribution, in which a markedly concave distribution is produced, suggesting that "large settlements are larger than expected or small settlements are smaller than expected" (Johnson 1977:496). Interpretations of primate distributions range from the view that they reflect concentration of economic growth in the largest settlements as a consequence of abundant low-cost labor (Berry 1973) to the interpretation that they are indicative of a system in which political administration of the economy has increased to the point that economic competition among communities has been minimized (C. A. Smith 1976).

In a purely experimental spirit, rank-size plots have been calculated for six post-Elamite occupations of the Susiana Plain (figures 80–82) and despite the arguable equation of settlement size with settlement population and other strictures on these types of reconstructions, it is evident that these rank-size plots reflect considerable change over the centuries represented here. Little reliability can be accorded to either the lower third of the curve or, in this case, the upper ends of these plots because it is not possible to estimate the population of Susa, Ivan-i Karkhah, and Jundishapur, except to note that they were at times very large. The logarithmic scale here fortunately compresses these errors of estimation, and we can at least interpret these results on the speculative assumption that these estimates are close to the actual distributions. Given this, we can note the following:

1. The cut-off settlement size is quite constant. About one-half hectare is a minimum below which there are few settlements in any period, and this apparent size limitation does not change significantly through time.
2. The "primate" distribution of the Seleuco-Parthian Period may reflect the rising commercial importance of Susa during this period (Le Rider 1965:278–79), but the minor convexity of the overall plot may not be significant here, given the extreme difficulties of estimating settlement sizes under the much heavier and later Parthian and Sasanian deposits that often covered Seleuco-Parthian occupations.
3. The linear plot of the Elymean Period would be expected on "steady state" grounds, since numismatic evidence demonstrates that even small rural hamlets were participating in the monetary economy centered at Susa. The cultivation of

rice and sugarcane is strongly suggested for this period on the basis of textual sources and other evidence (Wenke 1975–76:114–23), and both crops require the kinds of intensive labor, well-managed water supplies, and organized processing, transport, and administration networks likely to produce such plots (Berry 1961). The productive, relatively peaceful trade relationships of the Susiana with adjoining regions is amply documented by the presence at Susa of many coins minted at cities elsewhere in the Mesopotamian heartland.

4. The increasing convexity of the Terminal Parthian Period (relative to the previous period) may have originated in declining systems' growth rates (Vining 1974), for we know from varieties of evidence that this period was one of political instability, cessation of local coinage at Susa, and other degenerative processes culminating in the Sasanian takeover at the end of the period. Alternatively, Johnson suggests that convexity should appear when the distribution of the settlement system "actually approaches the discontinuous hierarchy posited by central place theory, at least in cases with multiple highest order central places," or in cases where discrete adjacent systems of approximately equal size are being "pooled" (1977:498), or where there is decreasing integration of the system. The Terminal Parthian settlement pattern has not been determined with sufficient precision to allow application of any of these conflicting interpretations of this rank-size plot.
5. The unusual shape of the rank-size plot of the Early Sasanian Period may be a result of the fact that we have essentially no idea of the population of the four major settlements in this period. Perhaps the most conservative inference at this point is that Jundishapur, Ivan-i Karkhah, Susa, and Shushtar were not substantial settlements at the same time. Fragmentary evidence exists that Susa was destroyed at one point during the Late Sasanian Period, that Jundishapur was occupied by and built for prisoners of war, that Shapur I built Jundishapur for more or less whimsical reasons (see Nöldeke 1973:40–43), that neither Jundishapur nor Ivan-i Karkhah ever achieved the population necessary to inhabit fully their impressive intramural areas—in short, that these large cities were not occupied by large populations at the same time. The definition of the boundaries of the Sasanian political and economic systems, however, must be approached with some caution. As Johnson notes (1977), when dealing with archaeological data there is always the possibility that the region studied may be smaller or larger than the settlement sys-

tem of interest. Thus, the scale at which the rank-size distribution of Sasanian settlements in western Iran may be most useful may extend far beyond the boundaries of northwest Khuzistan.

Finally, it is of some interest to compare the rank-size plot of the Sasanian occupations of the Susiana with the moderately convex plots Adams constructed (1981:figure 38) for the Sasanian Period in central Mesopotamia. Adams (1981:241) raises the possibility that his plot reflects a situation in which smaller centers grow and increase in number in a pattern "unaffected by centralized imperial policy." Adams's plot and those for the Sasanian Susiana are not directly comparable, given the different time periods incorporated in each, but they do suggest that the administrative organization of central Mesopotamia and the Susiana were quite different.

Highland-Lowland Economic Integration in Parthian and Sasanian Times

Currently, there is not sufficient evidence, either archaeological or historical, to evaluate changing patterns of highland-lowland economic integration during the Parthian and Sasanian periods. However, the few fragments of information we do possess generally suggest highland-lowland relationships may have been crucially important in determining cultural change in these periods. We have already noted the possible environmental degradation brought about by increasing population densities among nomad and other highland groups, and it is probable that the Sasanian government was able to extend taxation and other administrative institutions to many smaller highland communities and perhaps even to nomads. Rowton (e.g., 1976b) argues that the antagonistic relationships among lowland agriculturalists and nomadic herdsmen from the arid Zagros-Taurus steppe and foothills were keys to the "oscillations," or imperial cycles, that dominated Southwest Asian culture history for most of the last five millennia. He notes that sometimes the activity of nomadic herdsmen has brought whole empires into collapse after long periods of warfare among lowland-based states—an event he exemplifies with the case of the ten thousand Arab nomads who were able to overthrow a Sasanian empire weakened by years of warfare with the Byzantines. Even when no organized warfare was waged between highland and lowland groups, the highlands probably sheltered brigands and insurgents of various kinds, many of whom may have preyed on trade routes and resources of lowland communities (for a possible example, see Keall 1977). Recent relations between nomads and agriculturalists have at times been so antagonistic that for long periods there were few if any agricultural communities in highland areas (Black-Michaud 1974). This may have

been true at times in the Partho-Sasanian Period as well. On the other hand, Cahen argues that the Arab conquest of Iran resulted in significantly increased interaction between nomad and sedentary groups and that the Bedouin heritage of the conquerors brought nomadism to areas that previously had been unexploited (1970). Additional information on these important aspects of Parthian and Sasanian administration and economy must, however, await further research on the archaeology of nomads (Hole 1975a) and on the irrigation systems, sites, and other features distributed in great numbers throughout the highlands.

Methodological Approaches to Partho-Sasanian Archaeological Data

The analyses of Partho-Sasanian occupations discussed above are based mainly on documentary sources. These records, primarily of early Islamic provenience, do not contain the kinds of systematic, statistical, diachronic data required for even simple statistical description of Partho-Sasanian occupations (e.g., rank-size plots), and they are wholly inadequate as a basis for a truly explanatory approach to this archaeological record. When we consider the problem of an *archaeological* analysis of the Parthians and Sasanians, it is apparent that much of what we can hope to know about these periods must be derived from surface collections of artifacts. This situation results from a convergence of theoretical and practical considerations. As scholars have formulated increasingly complicated explanations of Southwest Asian cultural change (e.g., Johnson 1975; Wenke 1975–76; Redman 1978), they have come to recognize that many of the processes and events they are trying to analyze are more directly and accessibly measurable at a regional scale, using data from many points in a regional settlement pattern, than by means of data retrieved through extended excavations at one or a few sites. Moreover, even where multiple excavations are possible or necessary, the resources of modern archaeology are such that we shall never be able to excavate more than a tiny fraction of the Parthian and Sasanian occupations. Sample "fraction" is not always a primary concern in statistical testing of archaeological hypotheses, but the archaeological records created by the later complex societies of Mesopotamia are typically so heterogenous, and current explanatory "models" so complex, that without currently unfeasible sampling intensities and sample stratification (Asch 1975), many models and hypotheses cannot be tested with convincing statistical reliability if we rely primarily on excavated data (Ammerman and Feldman 1978; Kintigh and Ammerman 1982).

In the face of this situation, many archaeologists have resorted to the same strategy: they concentrate

Robert J. Wenke

most of their resources on making extensive surface collections, often in a somewhat "informal" statistical sampling design; they use excavated data to test relative seriations and to retrieve categories of evidence not available from surface deposits; they then combine these data from the surface and excavations with historical and ecological information to reconstruct regional settlement histories (Willey 1953; Adams 1965, 1981; Parsons 1971; Gibson 1972; Johnson 1973; Wenke 1975–76; Blanton 1978).

This approach has been productive, particularly when the objective has been to reconstruct regional culture histories by measuring broad shifts in population density, land-use strategies, and settlement patterns.

But in recent years the analytical demands placed on surficial data have greatly increased, as they have come to be treated as the primary data base for such quantitatively sophisticated forms of analyses as information and hierarchy theory (Johnson 1973, 1975, 1977; Wright and Johnson 1975), mathematical locational models (reviewed by Johnson 1978; Hodder and Orton 1976), mathematical models of exchange (Plog n.d.; Alden 1979b), and quantified models of cultural change (Alden 1979b).

Such applications of complex statistical procedures to the archaeological records of the Parthians and Sasanians cannot be accomplished with good effect in the absence of precise settlement pattern reconstructions. It is here that the scale problem is most severe. By way of illustration, Johnson, in his reconstruction of Uruk settlement patterns on the Susiana (1973:26)—which are not even a tenth of the extent of the Partho-Sasanian patterns—estimates that it would require a crew of ten working eight hours a day, six days a week, almost two years just to pick up the artifacts in a systematic, stratified, unaligned, random, 10 percent surface collection from the approximately sixty small sites directly involved in the evolution of early complex states in this small area of the Mesopotamian alluvium.

Yet in view of multicomponent occupations, imprecise relative seriations, and many other factors, even a 10 percent sample may be far from adequate for a reliable statistical test of some of the most important hypotheses about this case of cultural evolution. And when one raises one's perspective to take in the rest of the Mesopotamian alluvium, the problem is even more daunting.

Thus, in the case of the Parthians and Sasanians, we must ask what are we trying to measure with surface collection of artifacts, what kinds of questions can we hope to answer, and what can we do to improve our sampling procedures so that we increase our ability to answer important archaeological questions.

In analyzing surficial evidence archaeologists have encountered the same fundamental problems posed by excavated data, specifically, questions about unit formation and statistical adequacy. That is, how can we partition or arrange surficial data to answer important questions and what kinds of samples do we need to answer these questions? Although specific problems and theoretical perspectives dictate the kinds of analytical units to be created and the method of their collection, all archaeological analyses of surface collections are bound together by the fact that all must confront the problem of defining and measuring stylistic and functional variability in the archaeological record.

Stylistic Variability

Traditionally, archaeologists have used stylistic variability in the archaeological record for three purposes: relative seriations, (reviewed in Marquardt 1978; Dunnell 1970, 1981), description of regional interaction patterns (e.g., Plog n.d.; Upham, Lightfoot, and Feinman 1981; Johnson 1973), and description of community patterning (Cowgill 1974). Stylistic variability can be defined as variability that does not directly affect the Darwinian fitness of the populations in which it occurs (Sahlins and Service 1960; Binford 1968; Gould et al. 1977; Dunnell 1978:199).

Although relative seriations are perhaps usually thought of as involving the contents of excavated units, recently there has been considerable effort to construct seriated ceramic sequences on the basis of surface collections of ceramics (Johnson 1973; Wenke 1975–76; Le Blanc 1975). It has even been suggested that seriations constructed mainly on surface-collected data are superior to most of those done on excavated data because surface collections, by virtue of their ease of recovery in quantity, tend to give a more complete picture of contemporaneous assemblages than the more limited exposures of excavations (Dunnell 1981).

Recent reviews of the seriation process (Dunnell 1970, 1981; Marquardt 1978) have focused on two major questions: (1) How can we create units that are maximally sensitive to temporal variability?, and (2) How can we best test these units against the expectations of the seriation model and thereby infer accurate relative seriations?

Before we examine various aspects of these questions in the context of Partho-Sasanian surficial data, let us consider the parallel problem of measuring functional variability, for it is likely that solutions to problems of dealing with these two kinds of variability will overlap considerably.

Functional Variability

Many anthropologists, beginning at least with White (1949:379–93), have argued that important aspects of ancient cultural complexity can be defined and analyzed in terms of functional redundancy and interdependence. For example, all Southwest Asia Neolithic communities apparently were functionally redundant in the sense that each community organized and conducted almost all the activities necessary for its survival, and almost all communities comprised the same range of activities, with only minor specializations. In early complex societies, however, not only did individuals within communities specialize in certain activities, but communities themselves, and even regions, became functionally interdependent in the sense that continued operation of these systems required complicated exchanges of goods and services. If we assume that from a cultural evolutionary perspective the major difference between, for example, the Akkadians and the Sasanians was in the greater development in the latter of administrative hierarchies, and if we are to use archaeological data to analyze exchange networks, administrative hierarchies, and similar phenomena (e.g., Johnson 1973, 1978; Earle and Ericson ed. 1977; Blanton 1978; Plog n.d.), we must find reflections of these essentially functional forms of variability in surface data. Site location and configuration will be important in this regard, but it is likely that our most accessible category of functional evidence will be variability in functional attributes of ceramics and other kinds of artifacts. While the equation between increasing functional complexity and increasing complexity of functional attributes in artifacts cannot be presumed to be exact, it is difficult to imagine a situation in which the range of functions performed at a settlement is not reflected in its artifacts.

We must at least examine the possibility that we can define operationally the concept of function on the basis of artifacts. Then we must test the hypothesis that surficial remains in any specific case represent a sufficient sample of the artifact assemblage of an occupation to serve as a way of estimating functional diversity. There are many models that attempt to describe the distribution of functional variability through space and time in the archaeological record, ranging from Central Place Theory (e.g., Berry 1967) to hybrid Marxian-ecological models (e.g., Orlove 1980).

But whatever the model appealed to for an explanation of the distribution of functional variability through time and space, one must, in the end, deal with the same questions noted in connection with analyzing stylistic variability: specifically, how do we create the proper analytical units, what models can we test them against, and how much confidence can we have in the conclusions generated from these units and tests?

A problem inherent in many archaeological studies involving stylistic and functional variability, including the Susiana Plain studies considered here, is that the analytical units employed—specifically, artifact "types"—are constructed by blending what must be assumed to be stylistic and functional variability such as the "Uruk Beveled Rim Bowl" or the "Middle Formative Decorated Olla."

Most such types are so highly loaded with stylistic variability that they work well as "index fossils" (Adams 1965:121), and in most areas of the world their usefulness in chronological seriation has been confirmed through excavations. But it must be assumed that units defined partly in terms of size, vessel shape, and other such characteristics vary to some degree in the record in response to functional factors. And if so, it seems obvious that more powerful analytical units could be constructed if stylistic and functional variability were separated.

Several methods have been proposed to differentiate stylistic and functional variability. Dunnell (1970, 1978, 1980) has argued that the proper units for chronological seriation should be paradigmatically defined classes created through intentional definitions and that these units should be tested against the assumptions of the seriation method (that the units are of equivalent duration in time, with unimodal and continuous distributions through time, etc.). He specifically rejects in this context the units produced by numerical taxonomic methods (1970, 1981). Elsewhere Dunnell (1978) has attempted to measure some aspects of functional variability in lithic assemblages by constructing a paradigmatic classification of wear and breakage patterns and assessing the distribution of these wear classes across different environments.

A different approach to the problem of partitioning functional and stylistic variability has been taken by Drennan (1976), Close (1977, 1980), Marquardt (1978), and others who have used multivariate statistics of attribute combinations to "factor out" stylistic and functional variability.

As a basis for analyzing stylistic variability, however, we have simply a set of empirical generalizations suggesting stylistic behavior can be found which is continuously and unimodally distributed through time and that stylistic similarity seems to follow a distance-decay function across space. Both these generalizations are subject to exceptions and distortions of various kinds (Deetz and Dethlefsen 1965).

The same problem afflicts the use of empirical generalizations about the distribution of functional variability through time and space. For example, some of the most plausible evaluations of spatial patterning in the archaeological record have come through the application of locational geographic models (reviewed in Johnson 1978). It is possible, using this approach, to predict spatial patterning in the archaeological record and to "confirm" that prediction through research. Yet even the proponents of this approach recognize its many limitations: that a given pattern can be the product of different—and different combinations of—factors. Moreover, such explanations rely heavily on ethnographic analogies that may not be particularly appropriate, and they incorporate questionable inferences, such as the equation of settlement size and functional complexity. It is, of course, far easier to list the problems of spatial analysis in archaeology than to offer alternatives, and locational analysis of archaeological data have been shown to be remarkably informative.

Even with the best of sampling programs, however, the analysis of complex societies mainly on the basis of their surficial archaeological records presents formidable problems. The formation processes of archaeological sites (reviewed in Lewarch and O'Brien 1981) are such that we expect many sampling difficulties; artifacts of different sizes and shapes are differentially deposited and moved by postdepositional factors; the determination of subsurface features at thick, multicomponent sites on the basis of surface remains is a complex problem; and other depositional and postdepositional factors affect the sampling of surficial data.

A particularly important difficulty in archaeological sampling involves the definition of spatial relationships. Just because we have sampled with sufficient precision to estimate, say, numbers of sites in an area, we cannot conclude that our sampling procedures have been sufficient to estimate the spatial relationships obtaining among these sites. This is a different kind of sampling problem, one for which geographers have developed a variety of tactical approaches, but for which there is no standard solution.

Generally, experiments (reviewed in Jermann 1981) have shown that the use of such tactics as quadrant sampling to estimate Nearest Neighbor Indices or other expressions of element clustering requires awesome sampling intensities, if traditional standards of statistical reliability are observed. Even if we abandon these standards and work heuristically, we must recognize that all of the commonly used measures of element clustering can easily be uninformative or misleading, given what in archaeological contexts are modest degrees of sampling bias, differential preservation, heterogenous distributions and variances, and boundary problems (Speth and Johnson 1976; Jermann 1981).

In summary, then, archaeologists face various difficulties in working with surficial data. Much of the evidence we do have is published in terms of type frequencies that are of undemonstrated significance in terms of their spatial and temporal variability; there are few, if any, valid theoretical precepts that explain how the archaeological record is distributed stylistically and functionally through time and space; and,

even for relatively simple questions of spatial analysis, archaeological sampling is of unproven efficiency.

A Test of Susiana Surface Collections for Functional and Chronological Studies

In trying to assess the usefulness of standard kinds of surface surveys of sites on the Susiana and elsewhere, especially in dealing with the extensive remains of the later complex societies in this area, I will consider both Johnson's analysis (1973) of the Uruk Period (ca. 3800–3200 B.C.) and my own study (Wenke 1975–76, 1982) of the Parthian and Sasanian periods (ca. 240 B.C.–A.D. 640).

In explaining his surface sampling procedures, Johnson noted (1973:table 12) that to take a 10 percent random sample of surface artifacts from sites of the periods immediately prior to, during, and just after state formation was far beyond his resources. He compromised by taking a random 10 percent sample from one site, a 2 percent sample from another, and "areal pickups" from the other sixty-five sites with occupations in the relevant periods. These latter collections were made simply by dividing each site into rough topographic zones and collecting one or more bags of diagnostic sherds from the surface of each zone.

As in many similar types of surveys, Johnson tabulated type frequencies in these samples, and then used these frequencies to determine periods of occupation and some aspects of site function. He noted (1973:26), however, that the research design did not call for detailed studies of functional variability within sites, but that he wanted to retrieve sufficient samples of ceramics to estimate all periods of Uruk occupation at each site and to collect sufficiently large samples of certain types of ceramics to study local exchange patterns.

As noted above, I used a similar strategy in my survey, except that I relied entirely on nonprobabilistic sampling, and my major goal in forming a pottery typology was to create a relative chronological seriation.

It should be noted that both Johnson and I used ceramic "types" in part because only with this kind of analytical unit could we compare our results directly with previous research in this area, for, almost without exception, earlier studies have been reported in terms of a traditional ceramic typology, usually without any kind of tabulation of type frequencies.

Despite the statistical "informality" in collecting these data and the type-based nature of their classification and tabulation, these ceramics collections from the Susiana represent the largest, most systematically retrieved samples from anywhere in Iran. Moreover, they are not atypical of collections made in other areas (e.g., Parsons 1971).

For all their limitations, then, we can at least test the null-hypothesis that variability in type frequencies in these samples is reflective of unpatterned random variation. The alternative hypothesis is that this variability reflects nonrandom, perhaps stylistic and/or functional variability.

Let us consider first the problem of analyzing stylistic variability in these samples. Both Johnson and I constructed artifact typologies designed mainly to measure temporal variability, but until these types and their frequencies can be shown to be in accordance with the seriation model and with stratigraphically retrieved data, we cannot accept them as accurately and exclusively reflective of the passage of time. Indeed, we must suspect substantial contamination of the data in the form of functional variability by virtue of the fact that many of Johnson's and my types were based on attributes of vessel size and shape. Our sampling procedures, too, would make one expect substantial random error variance.

How best can we evaluate such tables of type frequencies as a basis for chronological seriations? Both Johnson and I gathered surface samples, constructed a similarity matrix expressing the spatial co-occurrence of types, ordered the matrix, and from that defined groups of types that presumably circulated at about the same time. These groups were found to be in substantial agreement with sequences worked out on the basis of excavations. Samples from individual sites were then evaluated against these groups of types to determine in what periods the site was occupied (i.e., what groups of types were found in the samples).

This type-based, rather than provenience unit-based, approach was required because most of the surface samples were from multicomponent sites and contained elements from different time periods. They were therefore unsuitable for the usual kinds of frequency-based, sample-unit orderings normally relied upon to produce chronological seriations.

One way to test the adequacy of the units used in our surveys is to assume that the period assignments of the various groups of types are substantially correct and then see if stylistic variability within these periods matches expectations based on empirical generalizations about stylistic behavior. For example, if we compare the "Middle Uruk" ceramic type frequencies for, say, thirty sites assigned to the Middle Uruk Period, we would expect these type frequencies *not* to fit the Fordian bar-graph model, since, presumably, we have "factored out" temporal variability by looking only at stylistic elements of a single short-term period. Indeed, if our samples within these periods did fit the seriation model, we would conclude that the periodization of these data could be substantially refined.

Comparing thirty sites on perhaps fifteen stylistic variables directly in the form of Fordian bar-graphs

would be rather tedious, (there are 30! permutations), so we might employ some less exact and exacting way of getting a testable seriation. The statistical tool used here to do this is multidimensional scaling, hereafter MDS (Kruskal and Wish 1978). MDS analyses usually begin with a set of elements (e.g., archaeological surface samples) that have been measured on a set of variables such as pottery types. The similarity of these elements could be perfectly expressed as a spatial distance by representing the elements in a space with a number of dimensions equal to the number of variables on which the elements have been measured. In MDS the measurements of elements on a set of variables are expressed as a similarity measure, and then the matrix of these similarity scores is analyzed for "structure": the assumption is that if there is some single factor that is determining the similarity of these units to one another, it should be possible to express the proximity of these units to one another (as derived from their similarity coefficients) on a single axis, or dimension. MDS analyses usually express the location of the elements with respect to each other in a space of many dimensions, and then, through an iterative process of moving the points around, the number of dimensions is reduced while trying to maintain the distance relationships among the elements. Obviously, if more than one factor determines the structure of the similarity matrix, it will not be possible to maintain exactly the proximity of each element to every other element in a space of one dimension. Departures from a perfect one-dimensional "solution" to a similarity matrix are expressed in terms of a "stress" coefficient. Since stress in this sense is dependent upon the number of elements being scaled, there is no absolute scale for its interpretation.

There are several versions of MDS, the major distinction being whether the algorithm attempts to maintain the exact proximity (as expressed in the numerical value of the similarity coefficients) of the elements being scaled, or simply the rank-order of their proximities (a technique known as nonmetric multidimensional scaling).

Let us consider the stylistic variability in the two Susiana surveys from the perspective of an MDS analysis. The periods of interest here are the Early, Middle, and Late Uruk, and the Elymean (figures 83–86, and Chapter 4, figure 19), the former being Johnson's chronological divisions between 3900 and 3300 B.C. and the latter being mine for the period between about A.D. 25 and A.D. 150. As noted above, if these period designations and the pottery types used to define them really represent approximately contemporaneous groupings of types, we would have certain expectations about the distribution of these type frequencies through time and, perhaps, space. If we calculate a similarity measure among the sites of any of these time periods on the basis of the frequencies of the stylistic types determined to be in circulation in that period (to avoid the problem of multiple-period sites), we might expect that MDS analysis of this matrix would indicate no single dimension of variability that correlates strongly with some measure of time; for presumably, we are holding time constant by grouping our artifacts into contemporaneous units. We might expect that the similarity coefficients based on presumably stylistic variables would express to some degree the spatial distance between these sites, since the gravity model tells us that stylistic similarity usually is inversely related to distance; but here we would also have to expect that it is degree of interaction, not just straight line distance, that is important. And to the extent that there is functional contamination of our samples, we might expect that sites of similar size (which are presumed to have similar functions in applications of spatial models to archaeological data) would be similar to each other.

A TORSCA (described in Kruskal and Wish 1978) nonmetric multidimensional scaling analysis was performed on matrices of Spearman's rho coefficients expressing the supposed stylistic and functional similarity among sites in the Early, Late, and Middle Uruk periods, and in the Elymean Period. There are many statistical qualifications one would have to make concerning these scalings, including the problems posed by inequalities of sample sizes, the questionable virtues of rho as a similarity measure, and so on, but these figures at least offer a starting point from which to consider the possibilities of this form of analysis.

Uruk Stylistic Variability

Using Johnson's type frequencies for most of the Susiana Uruk Period sites, I performed an MDS analysis in 1, 2, 3 dimensions. These scalings are illustrated in figures 83–85, and if we compare them to the geographic maps of the Uruk settlements, several points can be made. First, there is a slight but significant correlation between the MDS plots of these sites and their geographic positions. The Early and Late Uruk Period scalings in particular show some similarity to the actual spatial relationships among these sites—the Middle Uruk Period less so (in fact, if the Brainerd-Robinson coefficient is used, the MDS "map" of the Late Uruk Period is a much more vivid expression of these spatial relationships). The strongest pattern here is the division between Late Uruk sites east of the Diz River and those to the west.

If we have any confidence in the relative degree with which MDS can retrieve the spatial configuration of these settlements from counts of their presumably stylistic elements, we might consider the relative accuracy of these "maps" for successive periods to be significant. In the Early Uruk Period, for example, we

are apparently dealing with a prestate society in which there may have been some degree of functional interdependence and hierarchically arranged administrative institutions, but we would expect these characteristics of cultural complexity to be less developed than in the Middle and Late Uruk periods. If so, it is unclear what we would expect in the spatial distribution of stylistic elements. Perhaps interaction rates would be lowest in the Early Uruk, when villages were presumably most similar functionally, and thus we might expect greater success in retrieving spatial patterning in the Late Uruk, when Johnson (1978) suggests administrative institutions were moving ceramics from central kilns to settlements in their immediate service area. This expectation seems to have some modest degree of support in the apparent east-west separation of Late Uruk sites (figure 85).

It is thus difficult to understand the Elymean data where there is no more approximation to the actual spatial patterning than would be expected by chance. We might conclude that, because the Elymean period settlements were probably parts of highly integrated economic systems that were centrally administered and dominated by the capital at Susa, we would find very little overlap between stylistic similarity and spatial distribution: most settlements in this 40-by-40 kilometer area would be using the same mass-produced, centrally distributed wares.

It is of interest, however, that for none of these MDS plots of these periods is there any evidence of a low stress solution to the data in just one or two dimensions. This indicates that there is not just one major factor determining the structure in these similarity matrices, perhaps because temporal variability has been effectively factored out of these samples by their periodizations. It might also mean that these frequencies tap so many other sources of variability, from sample size to site size to functional differences, that no clear one- or two-dimensional solution can be found. Yet the solutions for most of these samples are much "better" (i.e., lower stress) than if the data were random. The problem is in interpreting the pattern.

Uruk Functional Variability

As previously noted, most of the applications of locational models to archaeological data make an equation between site size and functional complexity because there is seldom any basis on which to measure the range of social, economic, and political functions that an unexcavated site offered when it was an operating society.

Ceramic and lithic artifacts would seem to offer our only realistic way to measure functional variability on the basis of data derived from the surface of Middle Eastern sites, since other kinds of artifacts that might be useful in this context are quite rare (e.g., cylinder seals, inscribed bricks, semiprecious stones, etc.) and are also subject to more postdepositional disturbance than pottery sherds.

We might test, then, the possibility that we can construct units that are sensitive to functional kinds of variability from samples of Susiana ceramics and that these functional units would be differentially distributed through time and space. Larger sites in periods of relatively great cultural complexity, for example, might be expected to have a more diverse functional complement of artifacts than smaller sites of the same period, or than sites of similar size in a period of less cultural complexity.

To examine such possibilities, I first reduced Johnson's fifty-four types (which he constructed to be heavily "loaded" stylistically) to twelve different "functional types," consisting of small bowls, large bowls, small jars, large jars, spouts, trays, bottles, cups, sickles, and so forth. I used Johnson's estimates of the periods in which these types were used, and then correlated site size during the three subdivisions of the Uruk Period with the number of functional types of each time period present at each site during that time period. I also correlated site size with numbers of his own fifty-four types for each of the periods.

The results of this analysis, although subject to many statistical qualifications, have some interesting aspects. Johnson argues that the period spanned by the Early and Late Uruk periods saw the evolution of the first true states in this area, and indeed we see that the correlation between site size and number of functional types (table 38) increases over this period. If this relationship could be securely established, it would show that in this case, at least, we may be measuring a significant change in functional complexity by analyzing relatively small and unsystematic collections of ceramics.

But the statistical picture presented by table 38 is not at all clear. The greater number of functional types at larger sites may be a product of the fact that larger samples were taken at larger sites. Analysis of regression residuals was used to evaluate the possibility that variability in the number of functional ceramic classes present at these sites correlates not with the size of the collection taken but rather with site size. The results were inconclusive: there *may* be a relationship between site size and the functional complexity of its ceramic assemblages (as this complexity is defined here), but we cannot be certain on the basis of these data.

One lesson to be drawn from this aspect of table 38, then, is that to examine questions of this nature we must have samples that can be compared, while holding size of sample constant. If such samples were collected in units of uniform size and shape, for example, it would be possible to establish the relationship of site size, collection size, and numbers of functional types.

This should not be construed as criticism of either Johnson's or my own collection strategies, since in both cases the main priority was to construct relative seriations for chronological, not functional, purposes, and any greater systematizing of the collection procedures would probably have made it difficult to complete the surveys with the time and resources available.

With no significant (0.05 level) correlation between site size and number of functional types present at the Elymean sites, questions must be raised about reasoning from surficial ceramic samples to the notion of cultural complexity. Compared to the Uruk samples, the Elymean samples are larger, more securely dated, and more variable in both site size and spatial distribution. Moreover, there is good reason to believe that the Elymean economy was considerably more complex than the Uruk; for example, there are documents describing a large export trade and considerable craft production. Two qualifications must be noted, however. First there is some suggestion (Wenke 1982) that Elymean sites approximated a "primate" rank-size distribution, with the capital at Susa dwarfing all other occupations. Many or even most of the functional variability of this system may have been between Susa and one or two other centers on the one hand, and all the rest of the communities on the other. Thus, without the Susa data (not available) no correlation between site size and number of functional ceramic types would be demonstrable. Second, instead of expression primarily in ceramics, functional variability in these "industrial" economies may have been expressed in coinage, glass, metal, and other kinds of artifacts that were not adequately sampled in the course of our survey.

Here, too, surface data collected in regular size units—even if not distributed strictly according to a random sampling design—would allow closer, more meaningful comparisons on these points. And it must be stressed that all artifacts, not just ceramics, should be inventoried in these collections, if some form of functional analyses is anticipated.

But it is by no means apparent that, even with improved samples, it would be possible to find gross differences in the numbers and percentages of functional types, if the idea of function is defined in these terms. It may be necessary to define "function" operationally in terms other than these traditional ceramic "types," in which different kinds of variability can be presumed to be combined.

Working with these traditional types, however, there are some aspects of functional variability that we may be able to examine. Consider, for example, table 39. Here a statistical measure (a distance coefficient produced by a two-dimensional MDS analysis) has been computed to express the similarity of individual collections at several sites. The premise is that if larger

Robert J. Wenke

sites represent loci for the performance of a broader range of economic activities than smaller sites, then surface samples taken from different areas of larger sites should be less similar to each other than surface samples taken from smaller sites are similar to each other. It may well be, for example, that size variability in early agricultural communities on the Susiana is only a reflection of variability in agricultural productivity of adjacent areas, not of different levels of functional complexity. Thus, collections from any of these early sites, regardless of size, may be expected to be more similar to each other than collections from later, functionally more complex settlements are to each other.

Table 39 shows that the "functional distance" between collections from small sites tends to be less than that at larger sites, although the pattern is weak statistically. One must hurriedly add the numerous statistical caveats here. We have little basis on which to conclude that this relationship would hold with other samples from the Susiana or elsewhere, and there are many problems in assuming that the functional types were contemporary, that earlier occupations are not obscuring later ones, that sample units are of equal size, etc.

Still, the figures in table 39 are in line with expectations, supporting hopes that this sort of unsystematic surface sampling can measure this kind of variability. Such comparisons, too, would be more meaningful if surface collections are made in units of standard size and shape, even when these units cannot be positioned on the basis of a probabilistic sampling design.

A more complex problem than simply correlating site sizes and numbers of pottery types is to use surface collections of artifacts to group settlements into functionally similar classes. The essence of archaeological settlement pattern analyses to date has been to infer the functional significance from variability in site size and location, and these kinds of analyses would be extended if it could be shown that surface collections could reliably be used to group sites by functional significance.

In attempting to do this with the present data set, I collapsed Johnson's fifty-four types into nine Early Uruk functional types, seven Middle Uruk functional types, and nine Late Uruk functional types. I also reduced the Elymean data to ten functional types. I then did an MDS analysis of the similarity matrices, expressing the similarity of sites to one another within these various time periods. The two-dimensional solutions are reproduced in figures 87–90.

We might expect that an MDS analysis of these settlement patterns would require several different dimensions to define these proximities, since presumably these ceramics reflect varied activities, ranging from food preparation to regional commodity transport. We might also expect that settlements of similar

size would be grouped closely together on the most important dimensions, in line with the assumption that settlement size is a good predictor of functional significance.

If we examine figures 87–90 with these expectations in mind, we can see that in most cases there is no single dimension of variability on which all the settlements can be placed with little "stress." The pattern of reduction in stress for most of the periods indicates that there is considerable "noise" in these data, but the sharp reductions in "stress" in the first two dimensions of some of these plots suggest the data are not random.

In the Early Uruk Period (figure 87) for example, there is a weak clustering by site size, if we read around the "horseshoe," beginning with 288 and ending with 94; but the "fit" here is not dramatic. One interesting point about this scatter, though, is that every site that increased substantially in size in the Middle Uruk Period (#96, #165, #108) is located in the same general area and is somewhat separated from sites that lost substantial size in the Middle Uruk (#49, #4, #64). In addition, there is some reasonable resemblance to the exchange system Johnson recreated on the basis of artifact measurements (1973:95).

How do these vague patterns compare with our expectations? First, since the Early Uruk is the period just prior to state formation, one might expect relatively low level of functional differentiation with most of the size variations being insignificant functionally, since they might reflect only different levels of agricultural productivity. Second, we might expect that at least a faint representation of the spatial map would be recovered by MDS because the plain is not uniform with respect to access to irrigation water and other natural resources, so that sites close together were probably more similar in agricultural practices than sites far apart (for example, dry farming was probably more common on the eastern edge of the plain than in the neighborhood of Susa). Thus, there is nothing in the MDS graph of the Early Uruk functional data that contrasts greatly with expectations.

In the succeeding Middle Uruk Period (figure 88) we would expect to see somewhat different patterns, because population densities were higher, functional differentiation was presumably greater, and interaction rates between the populations of different settlements may have been increased. Johnson (1973) identifies this as the period when the first "state" administrative systems appeared on the Susiana.

Overall, the Middle Uruk MDS graph does not show much structure. There is minimal clustering by size, although the exceptions to the pattern are severe (e.g., sites #153, #79). Stress reduction figures indicate that there is no simple and elegant one-dimensional solution to these data, and certainly nothing that factors out neatly in accordance with Johnson's settlement hierarchy. One interesting aspect of this graph, however, is the relatively tight clustering of those sites that persisted into the Late Uruk Period; but this may be mainly a function of site size, since the larger sites persisted into the Late Uruk Period more frequently than did smaller settlements (although note that neither #153 or #79 did). There is almost no similarity between the spatial patterning of these settlements and their relative position on the MDS plot, although the significance of this is obscure.

In the Late Uruk Period (figure 89) there is also some grouping by site size, but here too no clear pattern in two dimensions is evident. Sites #54, #59, #32, and #96 are clustered approximately as they are spatially arranged, and there are other resemblances between the spatial map and the MDS plot—here, too, perhaps a result of the spatial autocorrelation associated with different kinds of agricultural strategies on the plain. Since this is a period of population loss and apparent administrative reorganization, we might expect random factors to camouflage the functional organization of these communities. If we read around the parabola of the MDS plot, beginning with #36 and ending with #96, the strongest trend seems to be settlement size, although geographic position may influence this configuration somewhat.

The Elymean Period data show very little apparent patterning except, perhaps, a rough ordering of site size on dimension 1. The stress values (figure 90) suggest that this is a complex situation, not reducible to a single dimension and perhaps not even reducible to two dimensions. There are several possible interpretations of this. It is possible, for example, that most of these settlements, even though they vary considerably in size, are essentially functionally redundant because this was a period when the economic life of the plain was heavily concentrated at Susa. Yet this would not seem likely: not only did these settlements differ sharply in their internal architecture and arrangements (Wenke 1975–76), it is also likely they were involved in very different kinds of economic production. Some were situated in dry-farming areas with no apparent canals near them, others were in heavily canalized regions.

It may be that the economic functions of these sites are not being adequately measured by these samples. Sites of this period usually have large amounts of glass, metal, and other nonceramic artifacts, and it is possible that much of the functional variability is reflected in these categories, rather than in ceramics.

Summary of Multidimensional Scaling Analyses

The argument according to which the above MDS analyses were conducted is this: (1) the notion of function is a critical concept in the analysis of cultural evolution; (2) most forms of settlement pattern analysis and other locational techniques make rather crude inferences about function, using primarily site size and location as evidence; (3) the size and complexity of most archaeological records are such that our primary sources of evidence about many aspects of functional variability will have to come from surface collections; and (4) MDS represents one way of evaluating and interpreting both functional and stylistic variability in surface collections of artifacts.

Although the above scalings are not in themselves remarkably revealing about functional variability in the Uruk and Elymean periods on the Susiana, they at least raise the possibility that—with appropriate data—the general kinds of analyses illustrated here might be useful. The appropriate data would likely include samples that can be dated securely to period, that are categorized in a way maximally sensitive to functional and stylistic variability, and that are collected in units of standard size and in large enough numbers to permit intensive numerical analysis.

One of the limitations of this approach is the fact that many important aspects of functional variability will likely not be expressed in pottery sherd frequencies. But some aspects of functional variability in ancient communities like those of the early Susiana will be expressed to some extent in ceramic type frequencies, and if this kind of information can be combined with evidence about site size, location, topography, and other kinds of artifacts, and then related to excavated materials from a sample of sites, it may be possible to improve our general analysis of cultural change.

The Parthians and Sasanians in Evolutionary Perspective

Most of this chapter has been devoted to answering two questions: what do we know about the culture history of the Parthians and Sasanians in western Iran, and what is the most effective way to analyze their archaeological records?

Left unanswered, however, is the more fundamental question of what the Parthians and Sasanians can tell us about the general nature of cultural evolution. Recent controversies among biological evolution theorists (e.g., Gould 1977), as well as increasing scepticism about the applicability of "physical science" kinds of models of explanation to archaeological data (Dunnell 1982), have revived interest in using evolutionary concepts to understand cultural data. The faults of traditional attempts to draw analogies between biological and cultural evolution seem widely recognized (reviewed in Dunnell 1981), but various scholars have suggested that these faults can be avoided or remedied by different methods of unit formation and by divorcing the concepts of inheritance, mutation, drift, flow, and natural selection from a genetic basis (e.g., Alexander 1975; Cohen 1981; Dunnell 1981). Evident in many of these reworkings of evolutionary theory is the idea that there are two kinds of explanations possible with cultural data: functional explanations, which attempt to account for the presence of a characteristic or trait by identifying the role that characteristic or trait plays in perpetuating the organism or system; and, evolutionary explanations, which attempt to use general principles to account for the variability exhibited in the developmental history of the organism or system. From a functional point of view, for example, we might try to explain the appearance in the Partho-Sasanian periods of the first widespread bronze coinage in this area by reference to the role this coinage played in facilitating local trade. Similarly, we could adduce functional explanations for expansion of irrigation systems, urbanization, and other characteristics of Parthian and Sasanian cultures. But these functional explanations would not necessarily involve any general principles that account for the overall history of the Parthians and Sasanians, or that would relate them to their predecessors and successors.

Is there anything in recent reworkings of evolutionary theory and concepts of explanation that may help us understand the archaeological record of the Parthians and Sasanians and their place in overall culture history of Southwest Asia in terms of such general evolutionary principles?

Much of the recent debate among biological evolutionists has focused on the tempo of evolutionary change. The "phyletic gradualists" propose that in any biological evolutionary sequence for which we have a complete record, we would discover a finely graded series of forms progressively more similar through time to descendant species and less and less similar to ancestral species. Those forms intermediate in time would also be intermediate in morphological characteristics (Cronin et al. 1981). The alternative view is that much of the evolutionary change evident in the record of any biological form has been concentrated in relatively brief periods and in marginal areas of the form's range, and that the apparent "gaps" in fossil records are real. The importance of these debates goes beyond simple rates of evolutionary change, for the ultimate goal of evolutionists is to understand the *mechanisms* of evolutionary changes.

Tests of these contrasting views about evolutionary tempo are relatively simple, conceptually, when dealing with the biological phenomena, such as hominid cranial capacities (Cronin et al. 1981), since all that is required is sufficient data to construct the relevant time functions. But the gradualist versus punctuated equilibria distinction would seem in some ways irrelevant to cultural phenomena, because cultures do not change primarily through mechanisms affecting their genetic constituents.

Yet the gradualist/punctuated equilibria dispute has been expressed in very similar terms for many years in analyses of cultural complexity (Adams 1966). Whether one sees the period from the first settlement of the Mesopotamian alluvium to the Islamic invasion as a history of gradual, cumulative change, or of long periods of stability punctuated by brief periods of rapid change, depends on the variables measured:

> It should be stressed that the same paradigm is not necessarily the most fitting for all aspects of a particular historical sequence; different curves of growth may be applicable to different criteria of study. With respect to both Mesopotamia and Mexico, the "step" simile applies the best if we focus on such qualities as monumentality of architecture, artistic achievement, and style. . . . The "ramp" simile . . . requires a different focus: the emergence of increasingly autonomous, differentiated sectors of social activity—socioeconomic classes; military, political, and administrative elites; economic networks of tribute, trade, and redistribution (Adams 1966:171–172).

Adam's choice of variables here raises various questions. Monumental architecture can usually be measured to some extent, but to what inferential limits should we go if we are trying to graph the emergence of administrative elites, and such? If evolutionary mode and tempo are our concern, inference of administrative elites, except from the historical literature, may not be appropriate: we can at least try to scale variability in the archaeological record directly against time, without the intervening assumption that what we are measuring is something like administrative elitism.

But even strict concentration on the material archaeological record would not solve our scale and unit problems. In the case of monumental architecture, for example, if we view this phenomenon as mainly an expression of, say, "waste" (Dunnell 1978), and we wish to measure the mode and tempo of change in this form of variability in the archaeological record, we would have to ensure that we measure all forms of "waste" and that we could control for allometric relationships. Thus redefined and controlled, we may find that the apparent explosive appearance of monumental architecture in Mesopotamia represents a predictable segment in a gradual trend in societal waste in this region.

In a similar fashion, the appearance of great population peaks in the Parthian and Sasanian periods could, when treated as growth curves, be the result of stable growth rates, and the extension of irrigation canals in this period could be a local expression of a long-term gradual pattern of economic intensification that elsewhere may have been expressed in expanded craft production or shorter fallowing cycles.

It seems clear from the preceding that there is no generally valid standard for cultural evolution, only criteria that an investigator defines as important for understanding some aspect of cultural change. How then can we best approach the Southwest Asia archaeological record from the point of view of evolutionary tempo and mode?

To begin with, the problem of applying cultural evolutionary models to the Partho-Sasanians requires some redefinition. When we note the end of the Parthian Empire at such and such a date and the commencement of the Sasanian at another, the distinction between the two may lose much of its importance in an evolutionary sense. For when we examine what is involved in this transition, we see that it is mainly superficial elements of ethnic identification—the players in a game, not the game itself. In demography, governmental organization, economics, and many other fields there are strong patterns of continuity be-tween the Parthians and the Sasanians, and the point at which we should divide this continuity may not be where there is a formal change of government, but rather where architectural changes are most rapid, fertility rates change, and so forth.

In the absence of a clear formulation of the guiding principles of cultural evolution, then, a productive analytical step in this direction may be to try to construct accurate time series graphs of many different kinds of variables, region by region, and for progressively larger areas. Of course archaeologists have been trying to do just this for many years (e.g., Adams 1981), and the difficulties are widely recognized. But there seems no alternative to continuation of the recent emphasis on site surveys coupled with surface collections and precisely designed excavations—a point argued at length above.

Table 38. Correlation between the Size of Sites in Different Periods and the Numbers of Functional and "Original" Types

Period	Functional Types	Original Types
Early Uruk	.26 N=37 Sig.=.11	.11 N=37 Sig.=.26
Middle Uruk	.47 N=37 Sig.=.002	.51 N=37 Sig.=.001
Late Uruk	.60 N=12 Sig.=.029	.61 N=12 Sig.=.018

Note: The correlation (Spearman's rho) is between the size of sites in different periods and the numbers of functional and "original" (as defined by Johnson 1973) types of ceramics at these sites.

Table 39. Average Interpoint Distance of Surface Samples from Various Middle Uruk Sites

Site Number	Size (ha.)	Number of Samples	Mean Interpoint Distance in 2 Dimensions
059	9.56	7	.260
108	2.80	6	.352
079	2.32	4	.083
165	2.00	3	.480
039	1.50	6	.084
036	1.04	6	.099
052	.96	3	.135
064	.64	3	.262

Note: Values in italics are those from sites with largest samples.

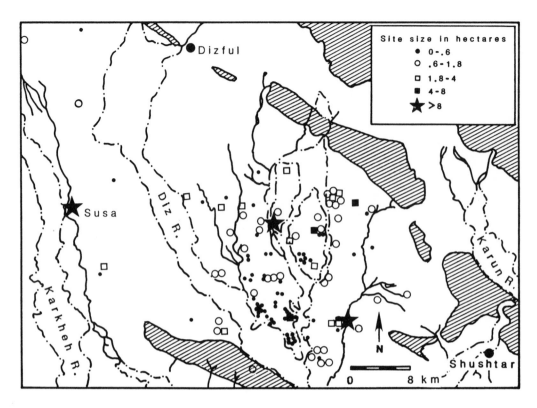

Figure 74. The Achaemenid settlement pattern on the Susiana Plain.

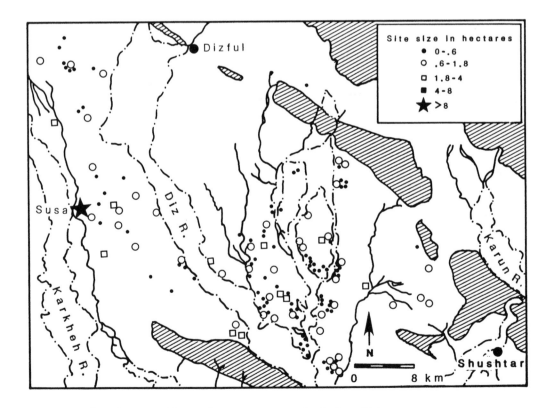

Figure 75. The Seleuco-Parthian settlement pattern on the Susiana Plain.

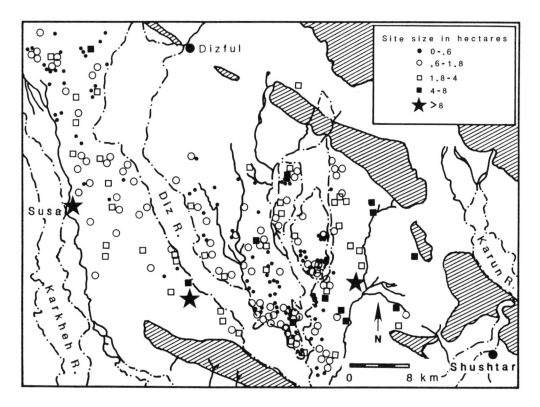

Figure 76. The Elymean settlement pattern on the Susiana Plain.

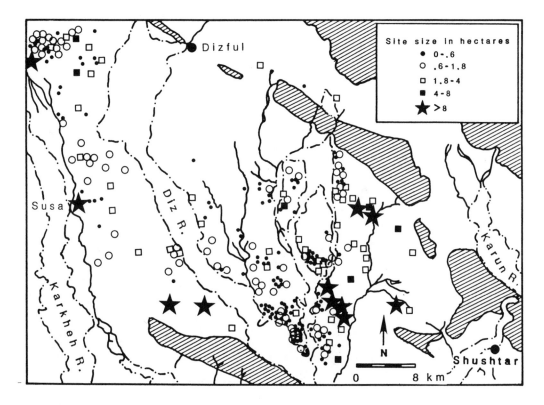

Figure 77. The Terminal Parthian settlement pattern on the Susiana Plain.

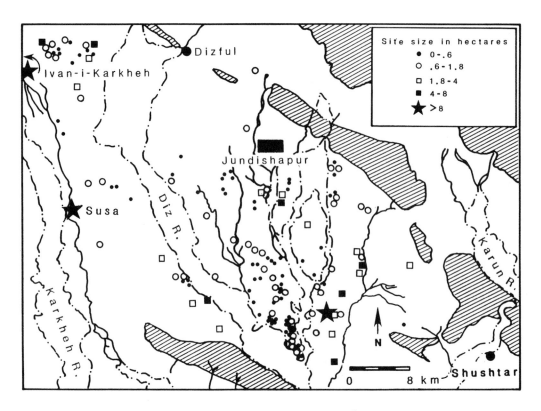

Figure 78. The Early Sasanian settlement pattern on the Susiana Plain.

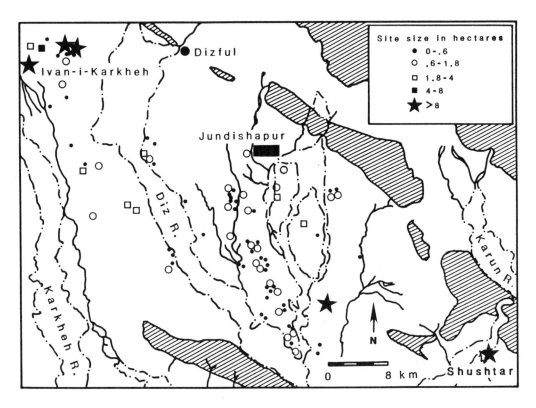

Figure 79. The Late Sasanian settlement pattern on the Susiana Plain.

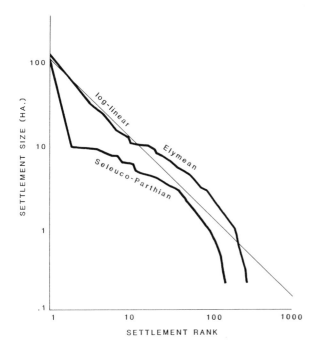

Figure 80. Rank-size plots of Seleuco-Parthian and Elymean settlements on the Susiana Plain.

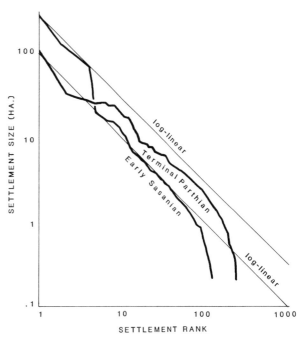

Figure 81. Rank-size plots of Terminal Parthian and Early Sasanian settlements on the Susiana Plain.

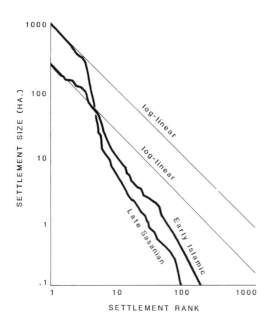

Figure 82. Rank-size plots of Late Sasanian and Early Islamic settlements on the Susiana Plain.

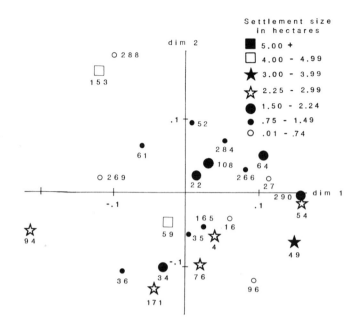

Figure 83. A TORSCA multidimensional scaling of twenty-five Early Uruk sites in two dimensions on the basis of a "stylistic" ceramics typology (similarity coefficient = Spearman's rho; number of stylistic types = 14; stress: 1 dimension = 0.40, 2 dimensions = 0.23, 3 dimensions = 0.13).

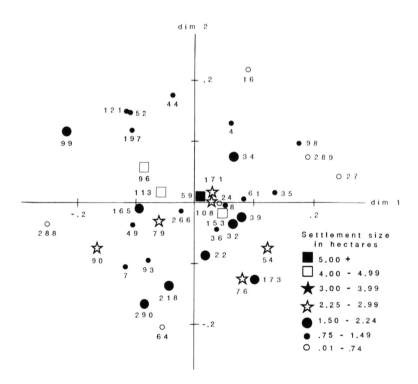

Figure 84. A TORSCA multidimensional scaling of thirty-nine Middle Uruk sites in two dimensions on the basis of a "stylistic" ceramics typology (similarity coefficient = Spearman's rho; number of stylistic types = 11; stress: 1 dimension = 0.44, 2 dimensions = 0.24, 3 dimensions = 0.14).

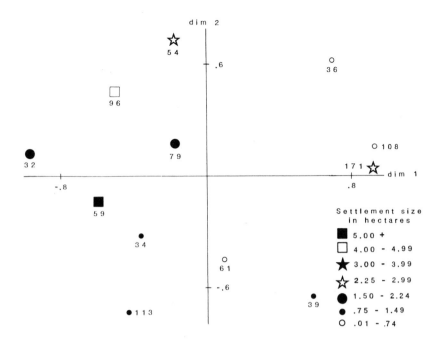

Figure 85. A TORSCA multidimensional scaling of twelve Late Uruk sites in two dimensions on the basis of a "stylistic" ceramics typology (similarity coefficient = Spearman's rho; number of stylistic types = 15; stress: 1 dimension = 0.38, 2 dimensions = 0.12, 3 dimensions = 0.06).

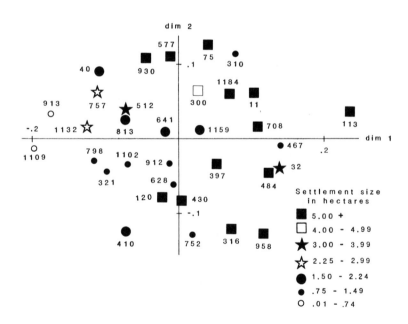

Figure 86. A TORSCA multidimensional scaling of thirty-three Elymean sites in two dimensions on the basis of a "stylistic" ceramics typology (similarity coefficient = Spearman's rho; number of stylistic types = 34; stress: 1 dimension = 0.38, 2 dimensions = 0.23, 3 dimensions = 0.26).

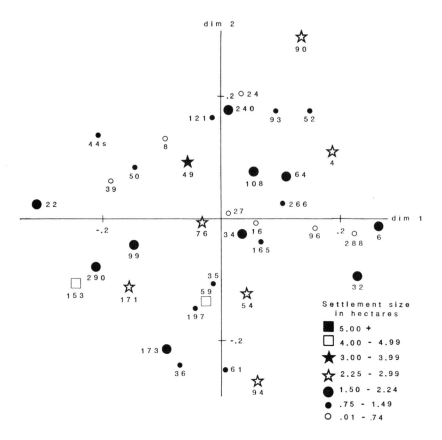

Figure 87. A TORSCA multidimensional scaling of thirty-seven Early Uruk sites in two dimensions on the basis of a "functional" ceramics typology (similarity coefficient = Spearman's rho; number of functional types = 9; stress: 1 dimension = 0.38, 2 dimensions = 0.21, 3 dimensions = 0.14).

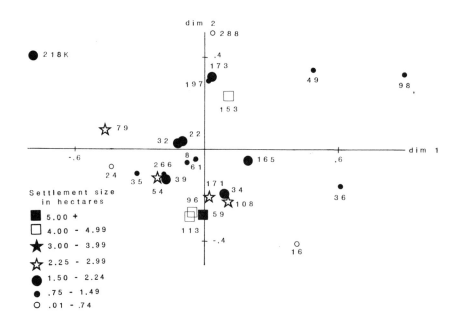

Figure 88. A TORSCA multidimensional scaling of twenty-six Middle Uruk sites in two dimensions on the basis of a "functional" ceramics typology (similarity coefficient = Spearman's rho; number of functional types = 7; stress: 1 dimension = 0.38, 2 dimensions = 0.15, 3 dimensions = 0.08).

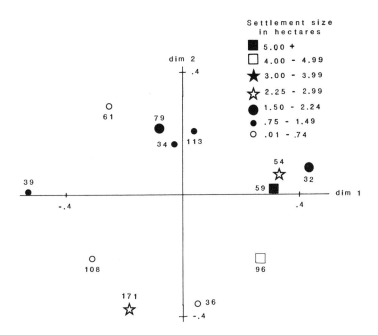

Figure 89. A TORSCA multidimensional scaling of twelve Late Uruk sites in two dimensions on the basis of a "functional" ceramics typology (similarity coefficient = Spearman's rho; number of functional types = 9; stress: 1 dimension = 0.32, 2 dimensions = 0.13, 3 dimensions = 0.05).

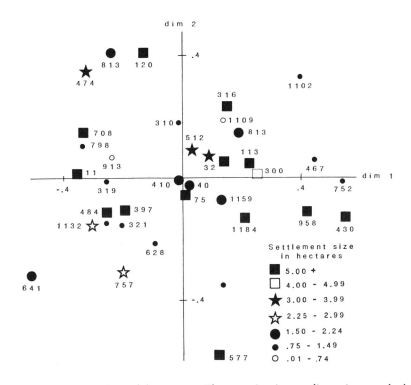

Figure 90. A TORSCA multidimensional scaling of thirty-seven Elymean sites in two dimensions on the basis of a "functional" ceramics typology (similarity coefficient = Spearman's rho; number of functional types = 10; stress: 1 dimension = 0.35, 2 dimensions = 0.17, 3 dimensions = 0.10).

Chapter 11

Nine Thousand Years of Social Change in Western Iran

GREGORY A. JOHNSON

I suspect that the nonspecialist reader who has endured the technicalities of the foregoing chapters may well have been unable to retain an overall impression of social change in western Iran. By way of summary, I will draw on the interpretive efforts of my co-contributors to offer a narrative of developments over some nine millennia. I refer the reader to individual chapters for more complete areal coverage, data presentation, detailed argumentation, academic qualification, explication of methodology, theoretical introspection, doubts, and a plethora of references to relevant literature.

The Village Period

Hole (chapter 2 and 3) assumes the considerable task of reviewing our knowledge about western Iran to the end of the fifth millennium. That the isolated plains and rugged mountains of this region were long occupied by Paleolithic hunter-gatherers is clear. Unfortunately, we know little else about them. Hole speaks of low-density, highly mobile occupation utilizing a variety of base camps, transient camps, and special-purpose sites. Hunter-gatherer material from Asiab on the Mahidasht Plain dates to perhaps the ninth millennium. This camp contained at least one temporary circular shelter of about 75 square meters. Two individuals stained with red ochre were buried beneath its floor. Associated debris contained beads, pendants, bracelet and figurine fragments as well as flint implements and faunal remains. Iran may have had its fairly complex hunter-gatherers in some areas.

Food-producing villages appeared widely by the seventh millennium and bore an unknown rela-

tionship to earlier (or contemporary) hunter-gatherer groups. Small clusters of Initial Period villages occupied widely separated agricultural plains including Deh Luran, Susiana, Mahidasht, Hulailan, and Solduz.

In Deh Luran the initial occupation employed a mixed subsistence strategy. Farming and animal husbandry were essentially a supplement to hunting and gathering. Both plants and animals were in the early morphological stages of domestication. In the course of the Initial Village Period, the domesticates became well developed and dependence on wild resources declined. Social organization in these small communities was egalitarian. Burials of individuals of both sexes and all ages were placed within or beneath the floors of nuclear family residences. Burial goods were restricted to a few simple personal ornaments. This pattern also occurs in the Initial Period village of Hajji Firuz far to the north near Lake Urmia. Extra-plain contacts were rare in Deh Luran and restricted to exchange for minor amounts of obsidian or other materials unavailable locally.

Elsewhere there were several Initial Period villages (locally Archaic) on the Susiana Plain, though little information about them is available. Chogha Mish and two nearby communities may have been quite large, but perhaps not more complex than settlements known in other areas. Ganj Dareh in the Kangavar region of the central Zagros highlands was early indeed. A camp or small village of the mid-eighth millennium, where archaeologists found a single sherd from a secure context, was succeeded by a small village of mud-walled houses. Cultivated barley is present from the beginning and crude ceramics appear in level D.

This may have been an area that witnessed initial domestication and sedentarization.

The overall impression of the Iranian material is one of egalitarian simplicity in small, widely separated clusters of communities that slowly developed reliable techniques of food production. Considerably greater complexity existed elsewhere in the Near East at sites like Çatal Hüyük or Çayönü, but was seemingly absent in Iran.

Hole's Early Village Period covers developments of the mid-sixth to early fifth millennium. Techniques of food production had become sufficiently reliable to permit substantial population growth in still virtually empty agricultural plains. Hole notes two patterns of expansion, one much more rapid than the other. He suggests that rapid increase associated with a marked discontinuity in ceramic assemblages in Mahidasht and Kangavar was the result of population movements from northern Mesopotamia and Azerbaijan.

A smaller scale intrusion of nonlocal folk occurred on the Deh Luran Plain where intensive agriculturalists, originally from the Mandali Plain of eastern Iraq, appeared amid the local population in about 5400 B.C. Irrigated six-row, hulled barley; free-threshing hexaploid wheat; lentils; and flax were introduced along with domestic cattle and dogs. This intrusion did not involve displacement of the local population as may have been the case in other areas.

By the earlier fifth millennium, population density on the Deh Luran Plain was the highest for any region in western Iran. Note, however, that each small Khazineh Phase community had access to some 1,500 hectares of agricultural land. This was an amount probably sufficient to support some three thousand people at subsistence level. Comparative density in the Early Village Period was low indeed.

Only sixteen communities, not all contemporaneous, are known from the Susiana Plain. The largest village covered no more than 1.5 hectares and contained closely spaced residential structures of large rooms surrounded by smaller storage facilities. Although increasing community size may have caused problems of interhousehold activity integration and dispute resolution, there was little if any specialized leadership or ascribed status differentials. These difficulties were probably resolved through an increase in household size, thereby reducing household numbers, and through increasing emphasis on the community as a social group. The latter may have been indicated by a shift in mortuary ritual in which adults were only rarely buried within residence units, but were probably interred in community cemeteries of the sort known from later periods. (Infants and children continued to be buried in the traditional household context.) An increasing emphasis on communal interests

may also have been responsible for construction of a 48-square-meter mud-brick platform at Chogha Mish that suggests community level activities.

Other areas with Early Village occupation reviewed by Hole exhibited features similar to those of the Deh Luran and Susiana plains. Exchanges among regions are documented in occasional ceramics and decorative materials including obsidian, copper, dentalium, cowrie shells, and various types of stone such as turquoise and carnelian. While these may have originated very far indeed from their ultimate locations of use, exchange was probably among adjacent populations and volume was low.

The Early Village Period of western Iran was contemporaneous with initial agricultural occupation of the southern alluvium in Mesopotamia. Thus the stage was set for the shifting and often unfriendly relation between Iran and Mesopotamia that would be so important in latter millennia. A considerable increase in social complexity was necessary, however, before these regions would have a significant impact on one another.

I suspect, though Hole would not agree, that critical components of this requisite complexity were developed in the Middle Village Period of the fifth millennium. Occupation of major agricultural plains continued to expand, with the exception of Deh Luran, which may have undergone slight decline. Evidence of the use of irrigation becomes widespread while advantage is made of dry farming in some other areas. Many areas reached the highest population levels they would attain before the onset of general decline in sedentary settlement in the late fifth and early fourth millennium.

In sharp contrast to the pervasive smaller villages of the Initial and Early Village periods, Chogha Mish on the Susiana Plain covered an area of some 15 hectares by 4300 B.C. Most architecture consisted of residences and associated ceramic kilns. The community also contained at least one monumental building, perhaps more. This 10-by-15-meter structure had walls of between 1 and 2 meters thick and contained several interior rooms. One of these rooms was stacked with storage jars, while another was apparently used in working flint. A substantial mud-brick platform stood nearby. This period in Susiana and elsewhere saw the introduction of formalized closure of containers using clay sealings that often carried the impression of a decorated seal. This practice is ordinarily associated with problems of security in materials storage or shipment.

Differentiated small occupations included simple villages and specialized production sites like Jaffarabad on the western Susiana Plain which seem to have been utilized exclusively in ceramic production. A high degree of uniformity in ceramics across the plain suggests that production may not have occurred in all communities. The flint working room at Chogha Mish suggests comparable specialization in lithic tool production. Flint blades were being imported into Deh Luran at this time, and a specialized tool production was undertaken at the site of Murian on the Mahidasht Plain. Other crafts may have been pursued by specialists as well.

Infants and children continued to be buried within communities, as occasionally were adults. These inhumations were increasingly in mud-brick tombs and associated with fine ceramics. Cemeteries for adults are presumed to have been in use, but have not been located for this period.

Architecturally specialized areas of contemporary Farukhabad in Deh Luran were distinguished by light versus heavy construction. Refuse associated with a thick walled building atop a mud-brick platform contained a differentially large number of gazelle bones, while that associated with simpler structures revealed mostly equids. The implication is one of differential elite access to preferred foods.

All of this strikes me as indicative of a hierarchically organized social system with some degree of influence over labor and resource allocation. The fact that the known major architecture at Chogha Mish was destroyed by fire and the community abandoned at the end of the Middle Village Period suggests that elite influence over the population in general was less than elites might have wished. I summarize Hole's position on fifth millennium social organization in the following discussion of late fifth millennium developments.

The Late Village Period on the Susiana Plain (locally Susa A and Terminal Susa A) spanned the last two centuries of the fifth millennium. After the abandonment of Chogha Mish as a large center, a new center of some 15 hectares was established at Susa on the far western side of the plain. Much of a declining rural population also shifted westward, residing in generally small villages not exceeding 2 hectares in area.

Hole identifies several types of settlements. Susa stood alone in several respects. Occupation focused on a massive platform constructed from more than 50,000 cubic meters of mud brick. This structure was surmounted by a major architectural feature, presumably a temple, perhaps with associated priestly residences. A large cemetery containing more than one thousand burials in mud-brick tombs was located at the foot of the platform along with a variety of domestic architecture.

Goods associated with the Susa burials ranged from simple cooking vessels to the very finely made and elaborately painted ceramics for which the period is famous. Some elaborate graves also contained hoards of copper in the form of large axes and discs. On the basis of his most recent work, Hole (1984) has shown that beakers common in graves had a fairly tight design structure occurring in six or seven varieties. A few examples of a type otherwise distinguished by a band of long-necked birds at the vessel rim also incorporated a variety of centrally placed motifs that resemble emblems.

Seals and seal impressions were present in some numbers, implying specialized closure of containers for shipment and/or storage. Rare seal designs illustrated elaborately dressed individuals engaged in presumably ceremonial activity.

Rural agricultural settlements like that at Jaffarabad near Susa contained domestic rooms around courtyards. Elaborate ceramics and other scarce goods were present, as were the burials of infants in mud-brick tombs. Burial ceramics of the type found at the Susa cemetery are known from some, but not all rural settlements.

A second type of rural settlement exemplified by the last occupation of Gabr Sheykeyn on the eastern Susiana Plain consisted of a single elaborate residence on the highest portion of the site. Hole proposes that this was an elite residence of the leader of a rural kin group. He expects that specialized craft production locations, such as existed in the Middle Village Period, and the ephemeral camps of pastoralists would complete this fairly complex settlement picture.

Hole uses the comparatively rich record from Susiana to characterize Late Village society. Though differences in social status were present, he sees no convincing evidence of the operation of political or economic hierarchies. With no shortage of agricultural land and no nearby neighbors as sources of competition, he envisions a loose organization of economic specialization and cooperation. Organic interdependence or "pluristic collectivism" within a basically egalitarian society was based on periodic exchange of specialized products and on common ideological bonds.

Susa was a cult center, its monuments and sacred personnel voluntarily supported by the rural populace in deference to supernatural forces of fertility and rejuvenation. Social standing was acquired with age, experience, and perhaps by special relationship with the gods. Decision making was consensual, probably mediated among groups by elder kin and religious specialists. Political office, systematic coercion, and exploitation existed neither in practice nor concept. Peace and tranquility reigned upon the land, to be broken only by an intrusion of an alien political organization and ideology from Mesopotamia in the early fourth millennium.

Although I hesitate to mar this Apollonian vision with dispute, I feel constrained to note that Hole's interpretation of late fifth millennium society is a minority view. Others, including myself, view Susa

A as a complex, hierarchically organized, and kin-based society. Hereditary inequality and positions of power and privilege were legitimized in sacred terms, signaled in architecture and material possessions, and supported by the sweat of a sometimes restive population. This population presumably gained intercession with the gods, pride in association with great enterprise, and occasional aid in time of need. Serious consideration has been given only recently to late fifth millennium sociopolitical organization in Iran; it will be interesting to see the findings.

However organized, the society on the Susiana Plain was the most complex of its time in western Iran. This complexity occurred in the context of very widespread decline in settlement. A small center with Susa A ceramics and elaborate architecture dominated four small villages in Deh Luran. Of the other areas reviewed by Hole, only the Marv Dasht contained a hierarchy of settlement, but center size did not exceed 5 hectares. Other regions were occupied by a declining number of small villages. Cemetery and architectural evidence from highland Kurdistan and Luristan suggest the presence of largely self-sufficient populations emphasizing pastoralism.

By the end of the fifth millennium this pattern of decline had become one of collapse in many areas. During the Late Village Period at Susa, a large fire took place atop the great temple platform. A portion of the decorated facade of the platform collapsed, crushing at least one unfortunate person at its base. Whether this event was the result of conflict or carelessness is unknown, but the damage was repaired. Conflict may be implicated by the collapse of Susiana in Terminal Susa A. Susa was reduced to not more than 5 hectares. Most villages were abandoned, leaving four small enclaves of settlement along local watercourses. Similar collapse characterized many other areas including the Deh Luran Plain where the center of Musiyan and its associated villages were abandoned. Only two small settlements with distinctive highland-related ceramics remained on the plain.

The causes of late fifth millennium social fragmentation are obscure at best. Even at its fifth millennium peak, population density in most areas was remarkably low. Yet there was no shortage of agricultural land and climatic conditions were stable if not improving throughout the millennium. The conjunction of favorable climate and abundant land does not add up to subsistence shortages as a source of social stress. There is no evidence that pastoralist populations were either large enough or sufficiently organized to harass the occupants of large sedentary settlement systems out of existence. (See Johnson 1983 for group size constraints on nonhierarchically organized pastoralists.)

The disappearance of painted ceramic decoration was one aspect of the Terminal Susa A collapse. This millennia-old tradition probably functioned in signaling social position and affiliation (see especially Pollock 1983). Its disappearance suggests a fundamental transformation of social relations. I suspect that the causes of decline and collapse in the later fifth millennium are to be sought in unresolved problems of social organization rather than in strictly economic or subsistence affairs.

A parallel transformation of social relations was occurring at this time in Mesopotamia where ceramic painting also declined rapidly in Terminal Ubaid. Though Ubaid population density and probably social system size were even lower than that of Susa A, the rapid political change of the fourth millennium was not presaged by the same demographic collapse.

The Uruk Period

Following the poorly understood Terminal Susa A, developments of the Uruk period on the Susiana Plain proper are reviewed by Johnson (chapter 4), while Wright (chapter 5) considers the Susiana hinterlands.

During Early Uruk on the Susiana, settlement increased to a total of 95 hectares. A three-level settlement size hierarchy was dominated by Susa with an occupation covering about 12 hectares. While new ceramic forms are similar to those appearing at this time in Mesopotamia, there is no evidence of an intrusion of Mesopotamian population into the Susiana Plain. The evidence rather suggests increasing contact among a series of rapidly changing lowland polities.

Johnson's analysis indicates the presence of a two-level administrative hierarchy on the western Susiana. Clusters of communities around Susa and Abu Fanduweh apparently constituted territorially defined administrative districts with highest-level controls located at Susa itself. Developing administrative elites exercised considerable control over the residents of centers, but were much less influential in the countryside. Initiation or elaboration of a corvée labor system and initial centralization of craft production were used to gradually increase rural articulation with center economies. Increasing rural dependence on center services was paralleled by increasing central control of rural hinterlands.

The disappearance of the elaborate Susiana tradition of ceramic painting, with its apparently heavy burden of social information encoded in stylistic variation, and of inhumation in mortuary ritual (except for infants) both suggest an attempt to deemphasize kinship and kin obligations as an organizing framework of economic and political affairs. Administrative technology involving counters and perhaps simple numerical invoices in conjunction with an increasing practice of official sealing of containers for storage and shipment indicate an increasing administrative involvement in day-to-day transactions.

The eastern Susiana Plain was marginal to the developing system of the west in Early Uruk. Secondary areas of settlement considered by Wright (chapter 5) exhibited different trends in this period. Settlement increased on the Deh Luran Plain where a distinctive ceramic assemblage was in use. The Ram Hormuz Plain, apparently more closely related to the Susiana, increased slightly in population. Greater increase occurred in highland Izeh, where a new 10-hectare center dominated the local, perhaps transhumant, communities, as well as access routes to the inner Zagros and the Isfahan area.

The Susiana Plain was one of three major areas of Early Uruk settlement; the other two were located in the Warka and Nippur regions of Mesopotamia. These three areas shared an increasingly similar material culture but quite different spatial organization of their settlement systems. Early Uruk demographic predominance was held by the Nippur region, an attribute it would lose by the later fourth millennium. Whatever the nature of interaction among these three areas, it was to increase significantly in subsequent centuries.

The Early Uruk system had been substantially transformed by 3500 B.C. Efforts to bring the countryside under administrative control had been facilitated by the establishment of a major center at Chogha Mish on the eastern Susiana Plain and of a series of small rural administrative centers. A four-level settlement hierarchy contained a three-level administrative system in which Susa exercised overall control of three administrative districts. Rural populations, with the probable exception of those more than a one-day roundtrip from a district center, had been fully incorporated into the corvée labor system. Labor utilization was highest in the summer months when construction work was undertaken. Administrative extraction of rural surplus reached an estimated 70 percent of potential production given the size of the rural population. Aggregate center size had increased from Early Uruk, apparently the product of both systemwide population growth at a modest rate and substantial rural migration into centers.

Administrative technology became more complex, presumably in response to an increasing frequency and/or volume of official transactions. Many modifications in the ceramic assemblage appear to have been motivated by the search for an improved system of vessel closure, again for storage and shipment. I estimate substantial movement of agricultural products from the Chogha Mish administrative district to the Susa and Abu Fanduweh districts on the western side of the plain.

Middle Uruk appears to mark the development of state-level organization on the Susiana Plain. This political transition was associated with a 33 percent increase in population of the plain, but a 118 percent increase in administered population. The latter was due to expansion of the area under administrative control. Administrative utilization of rural labor increased more than 1,000 percent over Early Uruk, as did extraction of rural surplus.

Elsewhere in Iran (Wright, chapter 5), a stable population on the Deh Luran Plain shifted its focus to the small center of Farukhabad where bitumen, chert cores, and probably cloth were exported in exchange for exotic stone, metals, marine shell, and other products. Tal-i Ghazir on the Ram Hormuz Plain probably exported locally carved alabaster in return for metals and other products. The large Early Uruk center in highland Izeh declined from 10 to about 3 hectares, while its associated, perhaps transhumant, communities were abandoned. Other highland areas, however, show local increases in occupation that suggest an expansion of transhumance and/or nomadism. Nowhere, however, is there evidence that these more mobile populations were hierarchically organized in a fashion that could pose a potential threat to lowland population centers.

Interaction among Middle Uruk polities on the Susiana Plain and those in the Warka and Nippur areas of Mesopotamia was more intense than in Early Uruk. This is suggested by an increased degree of similarity in their ceramic assemblages and other aspects of material culture. I suspect that the Mesopotamian systems will be shown to have been more complex than that in Susiana, but there is still no evidence of imposition of Mesopotamian power on affairs in Susiana.

Late Uruk developments in Mesopotamia and Susiana were rapid and dramatic. On the Susiana Plain, conflict broke out between elites of the Susa/Abu Fanduweh districts versus those in the Chogha Mish area. These apparently found their source in an attempt of Chogha Mish to sever its dependent relationship with longer established elites in western Susiana. Scenes of violence appeared on cylinder seals, many villages and small centers were abandoned, and a no-man's land separated the contending parties east and west. Settled population declined rapidly, a process that would continue into the third millennium.

While engaged in apparently extensive neighborly dispute, the trappings of administration became more complex. Numerical tablets came into use for the first time, presaging the introduction of lexical texts. Long-range trade increased in its spatial scope, with lapis lazuli appearing from presumably Afghan sources. Gold and copper, marine shell, and exotic stone were acquired from distant sources. Elites enjoyed higher living conditions than ever before while villagers, who formed the agricultural base of Susiana society, were being forced to flee demands for surplus and labor they could no longer meet.

Late Uruk was also a period of instability in the Susiana hinterlands (Wright, chapter 5). Most smaller communities in the Deh Luran area were abandoned, with settlement continuing only at defensible locations. Wright contends that the Deh Luran Plain had lost its previous considerable autonomy and was being directly controlled and exploited from elsewhere, perhaps Susa. Middle Uruk communities in Ram Hormuz, Izeh, and other areas southeast of the Susiana Plain were totally abandoned, and there is little evidence of a Late Uruk presence in inner Luristan.

Local collapse is also evident in the Nippur and Ur/Eridu areas of Mesopotamia, with settlement abandonment roughly proportional to that on the Susiana Plain. Simultaneously, settlement flourished in the Warka area with a very substantial increase in occupied area. Warka itself, with an area of 100 hectares, was the largest and probably most complex center of the Late Uruk world.

This already complex pattern was further elaborated by the implantation of what were most probably fortified Uruk colonies on the northern Euphrates, and somewhat later, in the Kangavar Valley of the central Zagros. These colonies endured for perhaps a century and were then abandoned as well.

What all this means in terms of culture process is unclear. For the moment we might say that by the mid-fourth millennium, state-level organization had been achieved by a number of increasingly interactive polities. A chaotic situation of differential cooperation, growth, expansion, competition, decline, and eventual marked regionalization were the result.

The Proto-Elamite Period

Late Uruk population decline continued into the early third millennium on the Susiana Plain. The Susa III or Proto-Elamite Period is discussed by Alden (chapter 6). More than half of the much reduced population of Susiana resided at Susa itself, the rest occupying a few small villages vaguely aligned in the direction of a new center of power (Tall-i Malyan) in the Kur River basin of southern Iran in Fars. Most of Susiana must have presented a fairly grim picture: long-abandoned and crumbling towns and villages, irrigation systems filling with silt, fields and orchards reverting to natural vegetation.

The relative desolation of the countryside was in sharp contrast to Susa itself which continued as an important if peripheral center. Scribes were now recording lexical as well as numerical information on texts that may have documented occasionally substantial transactions. Local elites continued to enjoy the privileges of position. Painted ceramic decoration and inhumation in mortuary ritual reappear after a hiatus of some seven hundred years.

The former close relationship of Susiana with southern Mesopotamia in Late Uruk had been largely transformed. Indeed the period was one of wide-ranging regionalization (see especially Alden 1982). The inhabitants of the Susiana Plain found themselves on the frontier of two major spheres of influence: the Proto-Elamite centered in southern Iran and the Early Sumerian in southern Mesopotamia. Alden suggests that Susa was important in mediating exchange between these powerful and possibly antagonistic regions.

Wright (chapter 5) notes that this was a period characterized by isolated clusters of agricultural settlement along the foot of the Zagros, with evidence of an expanding presence of now hierarchically organized transhumant and possibly nomad communities in intermontane valleys such as Pusht-i Kuh and Izeh. Increasing mobility may then have been one common response to the political instability of the later fourth millennium, a response that was to have continuing importance in highland/lowland relations.

Political and economic realignment was associated with a resurgence of long-distance trade. Centers such as Tall-i Iblis and Tepe Yahya were involved in specialized production and/or transshipment of elite commodities in a Proto-Elamite network which extended nearly to the border of Afghanistan. Many products reached Mesopotamia where early records document not only transactions, but an elaborate organization of specialized labor.

From about 2700 B.C., southwest Iran emerges historically as Elam, a diversified region containing three principal concentrations of population: the Kur River basin of Marv Dasht in Fars, the Susiana Plain on the lowland steppe, and the Kermanshah area of the central Zagros. As reviewed by Schacht (chapter 7), these correspond to the historical geographical units of Anshan, Susa, and, perhaps, Shimashki. Early Elamite (Old Elamite–Susa IV) developments were contemporaneous with an early if ill-defined association of at least eight Sumerian polities in Mesopotamia. These were characterized by a high degree of population aggregation, by increasing bureaucratic organization, and by conduct of extensive trading, raiding, and generalized neighborly dispute.

The population of the Susiana Plain had grown substantially since its Proto-Elamite nadir. Susa, associated with the kings of Awan, expanded to 46 hectares and may have been the most important Elamite city. Schacht uses a combination of settlement pattern and historical records to suggest, however, that Susa's control of the countryside was less complete than many have assumed.

Whatever the specific nature of political relations either within Susiana or between Elamite polities in other areas, the general pattern was one of increasing political unification. This process in Iran was more than matched by what happened in Mesopotamia under Sargon of Akkad, generating in the late third millennium a clearly recognizable nation state. One consequence of the Sargonid organizational transformation was a territorial expansion that left the inhabitants of Susa as the ungrateful hosts of an Akkadian garrison, and diverse Elamite polities the subjects of Akkadian rule.

The Akkadians and After

Akkadian fortunes on the Susiana Plain (and elsewhere) declined as the third millennium progressed. The Susa V Period saw the rise of the Guti and somewhat later the Shimashki, perhaps originally in the general area of Kermanshah. The Susiana Plain, however, was not long free of meddlesome Mesopotamians and soon had to endure the incursions of Gudea of Lagash. These led to eventual reannexation of the Susiana by the Neo-Sumerian Dynasty under Shulgi. An increasingly sophisticated Mesopotamian political organization is implied by Neo-Sumerian control through a centralized bureaucracy rather than through the military garrison so favored by the earlier Akkadians.

Mesopotamian control of the Susiana Plain ended with the overthrow of the Ur III (Neo-Sumerian) state, an event that involved the participation of highland Iranian kingdoms of the Shimashki (Henrickson, chapter 8). Mesopotamian influence on the plain continued through the reign of Shimashki kings. Susa was again marginalized and appears to have coexisted in increasing interaction with two or three administratively equivalent neighbors.

With the rise of the First Dynasty of Babylon, the Old Babylonian dialect of Akkadian became the international language of commerce and administration in Elam as well as Mesopotamia. Old Elamite III (Sukkalmah) begins at the turn of the second millennium on the Susiana Plain and marks a period of local political control as well as population growth, both there and on the Marv Dasht Plain to the south.

Sukkalmah political organization was headed by a triumvirate in which the *sukkal* of Elam and Shimashki was subordinate only to the overall head of the Elamite state, the *sukkalmah*. These holders of high office were regularly successful in passing their positions on to one or another of their relatives. Susa grew to some 85 hectares, dominating an expanded assort-

ment of lower-order centers, although Schacht's analysis (chapter 7) suggests that Susa may have exercised less control over its hinterland than did Malyan in the Marv Dasht.

The Sukkalmah Period saw an unprecedented degree of economic integration in the highlands of central western Iran, the presumed location of the Shimashki. Henrickson (chapter 8) notes that archaeological data on interaction parallel the textual record of an integrated Shimashki as an important component of the Elamite state. In the absence of definitive highland textual material, he suggests that highland ceramics and lowland texts monitor the same phenomena.

The rapid population expansion of the first half of the second millennium is widespread if unexplained. This was the possible period of a transition in lowland river systems from aggrading to degrading regimes. Such a transition would have required a substantial investment of labor in reorganization of irrigation. Perhaps the population increase that we see in this period can be attributed to an increasing demand for irrigation labor in the context of a political system able to use that labor effectively.

While the Sukkalmahs pursued their own ends in Iran, important processes were underway in Mesopotamia. These are seen historically as continuing refinements in political control and spatial scope of political systems. This was the period of Hammurabi and his law code of Babylon, and Shamsi-Adad I with similar imperial ambitions in Assyria. In the middle of the second millennium, Babylonia came under the control of the expanding Kassites. This expansion soon reached Elam, large portions of which fell under Kassite domination.

On the Susiana Plain in Middle Elamite I, Susa remained the largest community, but its degree of preeminence declined with the growth of Haft Tepe (probably the ancient Kabnak). Royal inscriptions from Haft Tepe refer to the "king of Susa and Anshan," indicating Susa's continuing if eroding dominance of the plain. Schacht's analysis shows that many medium-size Sukkalmah communities continued to be occupied and, as earlier, the plain contained differentiated clusters of highly interacting settlements. Marked ceramic distinctions bewtween the Susa and Haft Tepe areas suggest that overall Susian political control did not involve close day-to-day interaction.

The impact of Kassite control is seen in other areas of Elam. In Marv Dasht most Sukkalmah (locally Kaftari) settlements were abandoned and Anshan (Malyan) was reduced from 150 to 50 hectares. Sukkalmah communities in the Deh Luran region were abandoned and others founded in new locations, a process repeated on the highland Izeh Plain. The high degree of economic integration in highland western Iran (Shimashki) under the Sukkalmahs gave way to a period of regionalization (Henrickson, chapter 7).

The last three centuries of the second millennium witnessed a successful Elamite revolt against the Kassites and the emergence of Elam as an international power capable of pillaging Babylonia. It was perhaps at this time that the principal known copy of the law code of Hammurabi (a diorite stela) was brought to Susa from the Babylonian heartland.

Schacht considers that it was only in the last quarter of the second millennium that the Susiana Plain was brought under a unified Elamite administration. This was marked, in part, by the construction of Chogha Zanbil, a walled ceremonial/religious complex of nearly 100 hectares at the summit of the Haft Tepe anticline. Although this center was apparently never finished or occupied by a substantial resident population, it did reflect an aggressive policy of internal consolidation that was paralleled in peripheral expansion.

Historical developments of the late second and much of the first millennium are taken up by Levine (chapter 9). Many of these were to be dominated by Neo-Assyrians whose influence on Mesopotamian affairs had been increasing with Kassite decline. It is during this period that the focus of western Iran shifts from Susiana and the lowlands to the highland valleys of the Zagros. By 824 B.C., the area around Lake Urmia in Azerbaijan had come under control of Urartu, an expanding Anatolian state centered at Van on Lake Van in eastern Turkey. The local polities evidenced in Levine's earlier Iron II Period in the Zagros are followed by a series of larger, historically known groups in Iron III. These developments were associated with changes in personal and place names in the Zagros that Levine contends can only be explained by the movement of peoples speaking different languages into western Iran. Iranians were among these groups.

The kingdom of Mannea appears in Iranian Kurdistan, pressed on the north by Urartians and on the west by Assyrians. A similar kingdom of Ellipi in Luristan was contested by Assyria and the still powerful Elam.

The intervening mountain valleys along the Great Khorasan Road were occupied by a variety of polities referred to by the Assyrians as the Medes. In the eastern portion of this area, Iranian personal and place names are most heavily concentrated. This critical trade route fell under Assyrian control in the mid-eighth century when it was incorporated into the Assyrian Empire as a province centered in Kermanshah or eastern Mahidasht. Levine discusses the difficulties involved in relating these historical events—known from royal Neo-Assyrian inscriptions and a variety of other sources—to the sparse and uneven archaeological record of the Zagros at this time. Still, the spatial distribution of Iron IIIA ceramic assemblages roughly corresponds to the locations of historically known polities.

The conflicting interests of Assyria and Elam led to sporadic confrontation and ultimately a full-scale Assyrian invasion of Elam. Led by Assurbanipal, Assyrian forces devastated much of southwestern Iran, including the Susiana Plain in 646 B.C., an action that may have left the Susiana devoid of sedentary occupation.

Assyrian occupation of the highland territory of the Medes was short lived, for by 614 B.C., the previously fragmented Medes appear as a state strong enough to threaten the Assyrian heartland and to contribute to the collapse of its empire. Median affairs are known almost totally through the account of Herodotus, but it seems that provincial royal descent lines were subservient to the Median king who ruled from Hamadan.

One of the royal lines, the Achaemenids, succeeded in putting Cyrus, one of their own rulers, on the throne and subsequent military expansion brought about the reorganization of the kingdom of Medes and Persians. The Achaemenids under Darius I reoccupied Susa in 521 B.C., making it the capital of the satrapy of Elam. Other imperial centers were located at Hamadan in Media and Pasargadae, followed by Persepolis in Persia. Aside from depictions used as decoration on imperial architecture, we know from the Persepolis tablets and biblical references that these imperial centers were occupied by a variety of peoples, including Medes, Persians, and Elamites.

That the Achaemenids went on to dominate Mesopotamia (Nineveh fell in 612 B.C. followed by Babylon in 539 B.C.) and become a world power is well known. Susa was an especially prominent royal center, site of the great place of Darius I, and apparently still home to Achaemenid royalty when Xerxes' northern ambitions were halted by troublesome Greeks in 480 B.C. Late Achaemenid political infighting was stopped with the defeat of Darius III by Alexander in 330 B.C. Power at Susa, as at Persepolis, was abruptly Greek.

Wenke (chapter 10) considers the Susiana and Deh Luran plains from the death of Alexander in 323 B.C. to the Arab invasion of A.D. 640. The Seleucid successors of Alexander established their capital at Seleucia-on-the-Tigris, and the Susiana Plain was an important province of the Seleucid state. Susa flourished as a mediator of trade between the Persian Gulf and markets to the north and west. Irrigation systems were expanded considerably as agricultural production was increasingly oriented to production of rice, vegetables, dates, and other labor-intensive crops. Rural settlement size declined as labor was more evenly distributed over the intensively cultivated area of the plain. Overall population increased slightly over Achaemenid levels.

Seleucid control deteriorated in the second century, in part under pressure from Parthians expanding westward from the Iranian plateau. Seleucid provinces such as Susiana became semiautonomous, engaging in shifting patterns of cooperation and conflict with Seleucia. Though Susa had attacked the Seleucid ruler in 139 B.C., its forces fought beside Seleucid troops against the encroaching Parthians.

While Parthians replaced Seleucids as the dominant power in Mesopotamia and Iran, many "provinces" of the Parthian "empire" operated with considerable autonomy. Direct Parthian control at Susa was finally replaced in about 45 B.C. by the Elymeans whose original kingdom lay south of Susiana. An Elymean state of varying autonomy from Parthian control that incorporated Susa and most of the Susiana Plain lasted from circa 25 B.C. to A.D. 125. Susa was a trading center of vast wealth during this period, and rural Susiana underwent very substantial development. Irrigation systems were expanded and cultivation was extended to even marginally productive areas of the plain. Rural communities grew in number and size; they were mostly unwalled and consisted of a disorganized scatter of small buildings. These developments were associated with rapid population growth. The limits of traditional agricultural productivity were probably reached in some areas of the plain.

The Parthians would, no doubt, have had greater influence on Susiana affairs had their attention not been occupied by conflict with Rome and on other fronts. After Trajan's invasions of A.D. 116, the Susiana and other "Parthian" provinces of western Iran engaged in intricate political maneuvers, allying themselves with Rome, the Parthians, or both. Widespread political disruption in the first century and first half of the second century A.D. may have led to some decline in rural settlement on the Susiana Plain, but no major abandonment. The proportion of open, sprawling rural communities increased, though a decline in the number of coins found on rural sites may indicate a decline in intercommunity rural exchange.

While Parthian fortunes were in decline, a vassal dynasty of Persians in Fars province of southern Iran was consolidating its local control. A confrontation between Parthians and these Sasanians led to the death of the Parthian king in A.D. 224. Sasanian forces seized the Parthian capital at Ctesiphon and through a combination of administrative cleverness and military might, went on to found a Persian empire that ultimately reached from Syria to northwest India.

Population may have peaked on the Susiana Plain during the Parthian Period, but it was imperial Sasanian investment that radically transformed settlement and subsistence in the area. Kilometers of qanats, large new canals, and massive stone weirs were constructed to ensure and expand cultivation and to supply new urban centers. Much design work on the hydrological system was apparently done by captured Roman engineers. Extensive agricultural investment was also made in the Deh Luran area where population reached unprecedented levels.

The Susiana Plain became the site of extensive planned urbanism with the construction of three large towns (Jundishapur, Ivan-i Karkheh, and Shushtar) possibly occupied simultaneously with Susa. The combined population of these centers was perhaps several hundred thousand and included Persians, Arabs, Jews, Christians, Greeks, Indians, and others. Rural settlement declined as villagers moved into these new cities while agricultural productivity probably increased due to imperial investment in water works. Commerce flourished in a money-based economy. Shushtar was a major center of textile and silk production.

The Sasanian achievement was being threatened, however, by Arab incursions. The Susiana Plain apparently suffered severe damage early in the fourth century. By the mid-seventh century, Sasanian rule had been replaced by the Arab Umayyids of the Early Islamic Period.

The advent of Islamic control in western Iran marks the conclusion of the nearly nine millennia considered in this volume. The dominant impression of this long period is one of continuing flux at differing spatial scales in population, organization, and political fortunes. This local, regional, and interregional variability should not be masked by the long-term trend of increasing complexity. Little has been explained, but we have a better idea of the processes in ancient western Iran for which we need to account.

We leave "recent" developments in western Iran to others. I might simply note that, following the internal collapse of the Pahlavi dynasty in Iran, the current (late second millennium A.D.) conflict between Iran and Iraq had produced depredations on both sides like those that have occurred so often in the past. Susa has come under artillery attack and the town at the foot of the ancient settlement has been abandoned. Human affairs can be depressingly repetitive.

References

The form [q.v.] is used to signal the location of the full reference in this list.

Adams, R. E. W., and Richard C. Jones
1981   Spatial Patterns and Regional Growth among Classic Maya Cities. *American Antiquity* 46(2):301–22.

Adams, Robert McC.
1962   Agriculture and Urban Life in Early Southwestern Iran. *Science* 136:109–22.
1965   *Land behind Baghdad: A History of Settlement on the Diyala Plain.* Chicago: University of Chicago Press.
1966   *The Evolution of Urban Society: Early Mesopotamia and Prehispanic Mexico.* Chicago: Aldine.
1972   Patterns of Urbanism in Early Southern Mesopotamia. In *Man, Settlement and Urbanism,* ed. P. J. Ucko, R. Tringhaus, and G. W. Dimbleby. London: Duckworth.
1974   The Mesopotamian Social Landscape: A View from the Frontier. In *Reconstructing Complex Societies,* Supplement to the Bulletin of the American School of Oriental Research no. 20, ed. Charlotte B. Moore.
1975   The Emerging Place of Trade in Civilizational Studies. In *Ancient Civilization and Trade,* ed. J. Sabloff and C. C. Lamberg-Karlovsky. Albuquerque: University of New Mexico Press.
1978   Strategies of Maximization, Stability, and Resilience in Mesopotamian Society, Settlement, and Agriculture. *Proceedings of the American Philosophical Society* 122:329–35.
1981   *Heartland of Cities.* Chicago: University of Chicago Press.

1983   Natural and Social Science Paradigms in Near Eastern Prehistory. In *The Hilly Flanks and Beyond,* ed. T. C. Young, Jr., Philip E. L. Smith, and Peder Mortensen [q.v.], 369–74.

Adams, Robert McC., and D. P. Hansen
1968   Archaeological Reconnaissance and Soundings in Jundi Shahpur. *Ars Orientalis* 7:53–73.

Adams, Robert McC., and Hans Nissen
1972   *The Uruk Countryside.* Chicago: University of Chicago Press.

Albright, William Foxwell
1973   The Historical Framework of Palestinian Archaeology between 2100 and 1600 B.C. *Bulletin of the American School of Oriental Research* 209:12–18.

Alden, John
1979a   A Reconstruction of Toltec Period Political Units in the Valley of Mexico. In *Transformations: Mathematical Approaches to Culture Change,* ed. K. Cooke and C. Renfrew. New York: Academic Press.
1979b   Regional Economic Organization in Banesh Period Iran. Ph.D. diss., University of Michigan.
1982   Trade and Politics in Proto-Elamite Iran. *Current Anthropology* 23(6):613–40.

Alexander, R. D.
1975   The Search for a General Theory of Behavior. *Behavioral Science* 20:77–100.

Allchin, F. R., and N. Hammond, eds.
1979   *The Archaeology of Afghanistan from Earliest Times to the Timurid Period.* New York: Academic Press.

Al-Tha, Alibi
1963   *Histoire des rois des Perses*. Trans. H. Zotenberg. Paris: Imprimerie Nationale.

Amiet, Pierre
1961   *La glyptique mésopotamienne archaique*. Paris: Centre National de la Recherche Scientifique.
1966   *Elam*. Auvers-sur-Oise: Archee Editeur.
1972   *Glyptique susienne. Mémoires de la Délégation archéologique française en Iran* no. 43. 2 vols. Paris: Paul Geuthner.
1979   Archaeological Discontinuity and Ethnic Duality in Elam. *Antiquity* 53:195–204.
1980   *La glyptique mésopotamienne archaique*. 2d ed. Paris: Centre National de la Recherche Scientifique.
n.d.   Les importations exotiques à Suse. Paper presented at the CNRS-NSF Joint Seminar on the Development of Complex Societies of Southwest Iran, 24–29 June 1985, Bellevaux, France.

Ammerman, A. J.
1981   Surveys and Archaeological Research. *Annual Review of Anthropology* 10:63–88.

Ammerman, A. J., L. L. Cavalli-Sforza, and D. K. Wagener
1976   Toward the Estimation of Population Growth in Old World Prehistory. In *Demographic Anthropology*, ed. Ezra B. W. Zubrow. Albuquerque: University of New Mexico Press.

Ammerman, A. J., and M. W. Feldman
1978   Replicated Collection of Site Surfaces. *American Antiquity* 43(4):734–40.

Ammianus, Marcellinus
1911   *The Roman History*. Trans. C. Yonge. London: G. Bell.

Asch, David
1975   On Sample Size Problems and the Uses of Non-probabilistic Sampling. In *Sampling in Archaeology*, ed. J. W. Mueller. Tucson: University of Tucson Press.

Athens, Stephen J.
1977   Theory Building and the Evolutionary Process in Complex Societies. In *For Theory Building in Archaeology*, ed. Lewis R. Binford. New York: Academic Press.

Bari, Abdul
1972   Economic Aspects of the Muslim State during Caliph Hisham (A.H. 105–125, A.D. 724–743). *Islamic Culture* 46:297–305.

Barker, Harold, and John Mackey
1968   British Museum Natural Radiocarbon Measurements V. *Radiocarbon* 10:1–7.

Bayani, Mohammed Ismael
1979   The Elamite Periods on the Izeh Plain. In *Archaeological Investigations in Northeastern Xuzistan, 1976*, ed. Henry T. Wright [q.v.].

Beale, Thomas W.
1973   Early Trade in Highland Iran: A View from a Source Area. *World Archaeology* 5:133–48.
1978   Beveled Rim Bowls and Their Implications for Changes and Economic Organization in the Later Fourth Millennium B.C. *Journal of Near Eastern Studies* 37:289–313.

Beckmann, M. J.
1958   City Hierarchies and the Distribution of City Size. *Economic Development and Cultural Change* 6:243–48.

Beckmann, M. J., and J. McPherson
1970   City Size Distributions in a Central Place Hierarchy: An Alternative Approach. *Journal of Regional Science* 10:25–33.

Benet, F.
1963   Ideology of Islamic Urbanization. *International Journal of Comparative Sociology* 4(2):211–26.

Berlinski, David
1976   *On Systems Analysis*. Cambridge, Mass.: MIT Press.

Berry, B. J.
1961   City Size Distributions and Economic Development. *Economic Development and Cultural Change* 9:573–87.
1967   *Geography of Market Centers and Retail Distribution*. Englewood Cliffs, N.J.: Prentice Hall.
1973   *The Human Consequences of Urbanization*. New York: St. Martin's.

Berry, B. J., and W. L. Garrison
1958   Alternate Explanations of Urban Rank-size Relationships. *Annals of the Association of American Geographers* 48:83–91.

Bertanlanffy, Ludwig von
1968   *General Systems Theory*. New York: Braziller.

Bevan, B., and J. Kenyon
1975   Ground-Penetrating Radar for Historical Archaeology. *MASCA Newsletter* 11(2):2–7.

Binford, Lewis R.
1968   Archeological Perspectives. In *New Perspectives in Archeology*, ed. Sally R. Binford and Lewis R. Binford. Chicago: Aldine.

Birdsell, J. B.
1973   A Basic Demographic Unit. *Current Anthropology* 14:337–56.

Black-Michaud, Jacob
1974   An Ethnographic and Ecological Survey of Luristan, Western Persia: Modernization in a Nomadic Pastoral Society. *Middle East Studies* 10(2):210–28.

Blalock, Hubert M.
1972   *Social Statistics*. 2d ed. New York: McGraw-Hill.

Blanton, Richard E.
1975   The Cybernetic Analysis of Human Population Growth. In *Population Studies in Archaeology and Biological Anthropology: A Symposium. American Antiquity* 40:2:2, Memoir 30, ed. Alan C. Swedlund.
1976   Anthropological Studies of Cities. *Annual Review of Anthropology* 5:249–64.

1978   *Monte Alban: Settlement Pattern at the Ancient Zapotec Capital.* New York: Academic Press.

Blanton, Richard E., Stephen A. Kowalewski, G. Feinman, and Jill Appel
1981   *Ancient Mesoamerica.* New York: Cambridge University Press.
1982   *Monte Alban's Hinterland. Part 1: The Prehispanic Settlement Patterns of the Central and Southern Parts of the Valley of Oaxaca, Mexico.* Memoir no. 15. Ann Arbor: University of Michigan Museum of Anthropology.

Blau, Peter M.
1968   The Hierarchy of Authority in Organizations. *American Journal of Sociology* 39(4):453–67.
1970   A Formal Theory of Differentiation in Organizations. *American Sociological Review* 35(2):201–18.

Boehmer, Rainer M.
1964   Volkstum und Städte der Männaer. *Baghdader Mitteilungen* 3:11–24.
1972   *Die Keramikfunde im Bereich des Steingebäudes.* XXVI und XXVII vorläufiger Bericht über die von dem Deutschen Archäologischen Institut und der Deutschen Orient-Gesellschaft aus Mitteln der Deutschen Forschungsgemeinschaft unternommenen Ausgrabungen in Uruk-Warka 1968 und 1969. Berlin: Gebr. Mann Verlag.

Bökönyi, Sandor
1977   *Animal Remains from the Kermanshah Valley, Iran.* British Archaeological Reports Supplementary Series no. 34. Oxford: Oxford University Press.

Borker-Klahn, Jutta
1970   Untersuchungen zur Altelamischen Archäologie. Inaugural diss., Free University of Berlin.

Boucharlat, R.
n.d.   Suse, marché agricole ou relais du grand commerce. Paper presented at the CNRS-NSF Joint Seminar on the Development of Complex Societies of Southwest Iran, 24–29 June 1985, Bellevaux, France.

Boulding, Kenneth E.
1968   *Beyond Economics.* Ann Arbor: University of Michigan Press.

Bovington, Charles, Robert H. Dyson, Jr., Azizeh Mahdavi, and Roghiyeh Masoumi
1974   The Radiocarbon Evidence for the Terminal Date of the Hissar IIIC Culture. *Iran* 12:195–99.

Bovington, Charles, Azizeh Mahdavi, and Roghiyeh Masoumi
1973   Tehran University Nuclear Centre Radiocarbon Dates II. *Radiocarbon* 15:592–98.

Bovington, Charles, and Roghiyeh Masoumi
1972   Tehran University Nuclear Centre Radiocarbon Date List I. *Radiocarbon* 14:456–60.

Braidwood, L. S., R. J. Braidwood, B. Howe, C. A. Reed, P. J. Watson, eds.
1983   *Prehistoric Archeology along the Zagros Flanks.* Oriental Institute Publications 105. Chicago: University of Chicago Press.

Braidwood, Robert J.
1952   *The Near East and the Foundations for Civilization.* Condon Lecture Series. Eugene: University of Oregon.
1958   Near Eastern Prehistory. *Science* 127:1419–30.
1960a   Seeking the World's First Farmers in Persian Kurdistan. *Illustrated London News* Oct. 22:695–97.
1960b   Preliminary Investigations Concerning the Origins of Food-Production in Iranian Kurdistan. *British Association for the Advancement of Science* 17:214–18.
1961   The Iranian Prehistoric Project, 1959–1960. *Iranica Antiqua* 1:3–7.
1973   The Early Village in Southwestern Asia. *Journal of Near Eastern Studies* 32:34–39.

Braidwood, Robert J., and L. Braidwood
1953   The Earliest Village Communities of Southwestern Asia. *Journal of World History* 1:278–310.

Braidwood, Robert J., Halet Çambel, Charles L. Redman, and P. J. Watson
1971   Beginnings of Village-Farming Communities in Southeastern Turkey. *Proceedings of the National Academy of Sciences* 68:1236–40.

Braidwood, Robert J., B. Howe, et al.
1960   *Prehistoric Investigations in Iraqi Kurdistan.* Oriental Institute of the University of Chicago, Studies in Ancient Oriental Civilization no. 31. Chicago: University of Chicago Press.

Braidwood, Robert J., B. Howe, and Ezat O. Negahban
1960   Near Eastern Prehistory. *Science* 131:1536–41.

Braidwood, Robert J., B. Howe, and Charles Reed
1961   The Iranian Prehistoric Project. *Science* 133:2008–10.

Braidwood, Robert J., and Charles Reed
1957   The Achievement and Early Consequences of Food Production. *Cold Spring Harbor Symposia on Quantitative Biology* 22:19–31.

Brice, William C.
1962   The Writing System of the Proto-Elamite Account Tablets of Susa. *Bulletin of the John Rylands Library* 45(1):15–39.

Bright, John
1972   *A History of Israel.* 2d ed. Philadelphia: Westminster.

Brinkman, J. A.
1972   Foreign Relations of Babylonia from 1600 to 625 B.C. *American Journal of Archaeology* 76(3):271–81.
1977   *Mesopotamian Chronology of the Historical Period: Ancient Mesopotamia.* Chicago: University of Chicago Press.

Brookes, I. A., L. D. Levine, and R. W. Dennell
1982   Alluvial Sequence in Central West Iran and Implications for Archaeological Survey. *Journal of Field Archaeology* 9:285–99.

Brown, A. B.
1981   Bone Strontium and Human Diet at Tepe
        Farukhabad. In *An Early Town on the Deh Luran
        Plain,* Memoir no. 13, ed. Henry Wright. Ann Ar-
        bor: University of Michigan Museum of
        Anthropology.

Brown, Stuart C.
1979   Kinship to Kingship: Archaeological and Historical
        Studies in the Neo-Assyrian Zagros. Ph.D. diss.,
        University of Toronto.
1985   The Meditcos Logos of Herodotus and the Evo-
        lution of the Median State. Papers of the Fifth
        Achaemenid History Workshop, 31 May–1 June
        1985. Forthcoming in *Achaemenid History 3:
        Problems of Method and Theory,* ed. E. Kuhrt and
        H. Sanuisi-Weerdenburg.

Buccellati, Georgio
1977   "Apiru and Munnabtutu"—The Stateless of the
        First Cosmopolitan Age. *Journal of Near Eastern
        Studies* 36:146–47.

Buck, R.
1956   On the Logic of General Systems Theory. In *Studies
        in the Philosophy of Science,* ed. M. Feigl and H.
        Scriven. Minneapolis: University of Minnesota
        Press.

Burleigh, R., K. Matthews, and J. Ambers
1982   British Museum Natural Radiocarbon Measure-
        ments XIV. *Radiocarbon* 24(3):247–48.

Burney, C. A.
1958   Eastern Anatolia in the Chalcolithic and Early
        Bronze Age. *Anatolian Studies* 8:157–209.
1961   Excavations at Yanik Tepe, North-west Iran. *Iraq*
        23:138–53.
1962   Excavations at Yanik Tepe, Azerbaidjan, 1961.
        Iraq 24:134–49.
1964   The Excavations at Yanik Tepe, Azerbaidjan, 1962:
        Third Preliminary Report. *Iraq* 26:54–61.
1977   *From Village to Empire: An Introduction to Near
        Eastern Archaeology.* Oxford: Phaidon Press.

Burney, C. A., and D. M. Lang
1971   *The Peoples of the Hills.* London: Weidenfeld and
        Nicolson.

Burton-Brown, T.
1950   Archaeological News. *American Journal of Archae-
        ology* 54:66.
1951   *Excavations in Azerbaidjan, 1948.* London:
        Murray.

Butzer, Karl W.
1975   Patterns of Environmental Change in the Near East
        during the Late Pleistocene and Early Holocene
        Times. In *Problems in Prehistory: North Africa and
        the Levant,* ed. Fred Wendorf and A. E. Marks.
        Dallas: Southern Methodist University Press.

Cahen, C.
1970   Economy, Society, Institutions. In *The Cambridge
        History of Islam,* vol. 2, ed. P. M. Holt, Ann K.
        Lambton, and Bernard Lewis. Cambridge: Cam-
        bridge University Press.

Caldwell, Joseph R.
1968   Tell-i Ghazir. In *Reallexikon der Assyriologie und
        Vorderasiatischen Archäologie,* vol. 3:349–55.

Caldwell, Joseph R., ed.
1967   *Investigations at Tal-i Iblis.* Illinois State Museum
        Preliminary Reports no. 9. Springfield: Illinois State
        Museum.

Calmeyer, Peter
1976   Some of the Oldest "Lorestan Bronzes." In *Pro-
        ceedings of the Annual Symposium on Archae-
        ological Research in Iran* 4:368–79. Tehran: Ira-
        nian Centre for Archaeological Research.

Çambel, Halet, and Robert J. Braidwood
1970   An Early Farming Village in Turkey. *Scientific
        American* 222:50–56.

Cameron, George G.
1936   *History of Early Iran.* Chicago: University of Chi-
        cago Press.

Canal, D.
1978   La Haute Terrasse de l'Acropole de Suse. *Paléorient*
        4:169–76.

Carneiro, Robert L.
1970   A Theory of the Origin of the State. *Science*
        169:733–38.
1981   The Chiefdom: Precursor of the State. In *Transition
        to Statehood in the New World,* ed. Grant D. Jones
        and Robert R. Kautz. Cambridge: Cambridge Uni-
        versity Press.

Carter, Elizabeth
1970   Second Millennium Sites in Khuzistan. *Iran* 8:200–
        02.
1971   Elam in the Second Millenium B.C.: The Archaeo-
        logical Evidence. Ph.D. diss., University of Chicago.
1976   Suse—Ville Royale I, campagne 1975. *Proceedings
        of the Annual Symposium on Archaeological Re-
        search in Iran* 4:232–39. Tehran: Iranian Centre
        for Archaeological Research.
1978   Suse, Ville Royale I. *Paléorient* 4:197–211.
1979a   The Susa Sequence—3000–2000 B.C.: Susa, Ville
        Royale I. *American Journal of Archaeology*
        83:451–54.
1979b   Elamite Pottery, ca. 2000–1000 B.C. *Journal of
        Near Eastern Studies* 38(2):111–28.
1980   Excavations in Ville Royale I at Susa: The Third
        Millennium B.C. Occupation. *Cahiers de la Déléga-
        tion archéologique française en Iran* 11:11–134.
1984   Archaeology. In *Elam: Surveys of Political History
        and Archaeology.* University of California Publica-
        tions in Near Eastern Studies, vol. 25.
n.d.a   Elam (Archaeology). Unpublished manuscript.
n.d.b   The Piedmont and the Pusht-i Kuh in the Early
        Third Millennium B.C. Paper presented at the CNRS
        Colloquium "La préhistoire de la Mésopotamie du
        Vième millénaire av. J.C., 17–19 Dec. 1984, Paris.
1976   Middle Elamite Malyan. *Expedition* 19:33–43.

Carter, Elizabeth, and Matthew W. Stolper
1976   Middle Elamite Malyan. *Expedition* 18:33–42.
1984   *Elam: Surveys of Political History and Archae-*

ology. University of California Publications in Near Eastern Studies, vol. 25.

Cauvin, J.
1972 Nouvelles fouilles à Tell Mureybet (Syria): 1971–1972, Rapport préliminaire. *Annales archéologique arabe syrien* 22:105–15.
1977 Les Fouilles de Mureybet (1971–1974) et leur signification pour les origines de la sédentarisation au Proche Orient. *Annual of the American Schools of Oriental Research* 44:19–48.

Chandler, Tertius, and Gerald Fox
1974 *Three Thousand Years of Urban Growth.* New York: Academic Press.

Chaumont, M. L.
1973 Etudes d'histoire parthe: (II) Capitales et résidences des premiers Arsacides IIIe–Ier S. av. J.C. *Syria* 13:197–222.

Cherry, John F.
1978 Generalization and the Archaeology of the State. In *Social Organization and Settlement: Contributions from Anthropology, Archaeology and Geography,* British Archaeological Reports International Series (Supplementary) no. 47, ed. David Green, Colin Haselgrove, and Matthew Spriggs.

Childe, V. Gordon
1946 *What Happened in History.* New York: Penguin Books.
1951 *Man Makes Himself.* New York: The New American Library.
1952 *New Light on the Most Ancient East.* 4th ed. London: Routledge and Kegan Paul.

Chisolm, B. S., D. E. Nelson, and H. P. Schwarcz
1982 Stable-carbon Isotope Ratios as a Measure of Marine versus Terrestrial Protein in Ancient Diets. *Science* 216:1131–32.

Christensen, A.
1936 *L'Iran sous les Sassanides.* Copenhagen: Levin and Munksgaard.
1944 *L'Iran sous les Sassanides.* 2d ed. Copenhagen: Levin and Munksgaard.

Claessen, Henri J. M.
1978 The Early State: A Structural Approach. In *The Early State,* ed. J. M. Claessen and Peter Skalnik. [q.v.].

Claessen, Henri J. M., and Peter Skalnik
1978 The Early State: Models and Reality. In *The Early State,* ed. Henri J. M. Claessen and Peter Skalnik [q.v.].

Claessen, Henri J. M., and Peter Skalnik, eds.
1978 *The Early State.* The Hague: Mouton.

Close, A.
1977 The Identification of Style in Lithic Artifacts from Northeast Africa. *Mémoires de l'Institut d'Egypte* 61.
1980 A Study of Stylistic Variability and Continuity in the Nabta Area. In *Prehistory of the Eastern Sahara.* New York: Academic Press.

Coe, Michael, and Kent V. Flannery
1964 Microenvironments and Mesoamerican Prehistory. *Science* 143:650–54.

Cohen, R.
1981 Evolutionary Epistemology and Human Values. *Current Anthropology* 22(3):201–18.

Cohen, R., and E. Service, eds.
1978 *The Origins of the State: The Anthropology of Political Evolution.* Philadelphia: ISHI Publications.

Cohen, Sol
1973 Enmerkar and the Lord of Aratta. Ph.D. diss., University of Pennsylvania.

Colledge, M.
1967 *The Parthians.* London: Thames and Hudson.

Contenau, J.
1939 La Susiane dans une inscription palmyrenienne. *Mélanges Dussaud* 1:277–79.

Contenau, J., and R. Ghirshman
1935 *Fouilles de Tepe Giyan.* Paris: Paul Geuthner.

Cook, Sherburne, and R. Heizer
1968 Relationships among Houses, Settlement Areas, and Population in Aboriginal California. In *Settlement Archaeology,* ed. K. C. Chang. Palo Alto, Calif.: National Press Books.

Coon, Carleton S.
1951 *Cave Explorations in Iran.* Philadelphia: University Museum, University of Pennsylvania.

Copeland, Lorraine
1979 Observations on the Prehistory of the Balikh Valley, Syria, during the 7th to 4th Millennium B.C. *Paléorient* 5:251–75.

Cornelius, F.
1958 Chronology, eine Erwiederung. *Journal of Cuneiform Studies* 12:101ff.

Cowgill, George L.
1974 Quantitative Studies of Urbanization at Teotihuacan. In *Mesoamerican Archaeology: New Approaches,* ed. N. Hammond. Austin: University of Texas Press.
1975a On Causes and Consequences of Ancient and Modern Population Changes. *American Anthropologist* 77(3):505–25.
1975b Population Pressure as a Non-Explanation. In *Population Studies in Archaeology and Biological Anthropology: A Symposium, American Antiquity* 40(2):2, Memoir 30, ed. Alan C. Swedlund.

Crawford, Harriet
1978 The Mechanics of the Obsidian Trade: A Suggestion. *Antiquity* 52:129–32.

Crawford, Vaughn E.
1963 Excavations in Iraq and Iran. *Archaeology* 16:290–91.
1972 Excavations in the Swamps of Sumer. *Expedition* 14(2):12–20.

Cronin, J. E., N. T. Boaz, C. B. Stringen, and Y. Rak
1981 Tempo and Mode in Hominid Evolution. *Nature* 292:113–22.

Crumley, Carol L.
1976 Toward a Locational Definition of State Systems of Settlement. *American Anthropologist* 78:59–73.

Cummings, L. L., G. P. Huber, and E. Arendt
1974 Effects of Size and Spatial Arrangement on Group Decision Making. *Academy of Management Journal* 17:460–75.

Cumont, F.
1932 Nouvelles inscriptions grecques de Suse. *Comptes rendus de l'Académie des inscriptions* 271–86.

Dalton, George
1969 Theoretical Issues in Economic Anthropology. *Current Anthropology* 10:63–102.

David, N.
1972 On the Life Span of Pottery, Type Frequencies, and Archaeological Influence. *American Antiquity* 37:141–42.

Davidson, T. E., and H. McKerrell
1976 Pottery Analysis and Halaf Period Trade in the Khabur Headwaters Region. *Iraq* 38:45–56.

De Boer, W. R., and D. W. Lathrap
1979 The Making and Breaking of Shipibo-Conibo Ceramics. In *Ethnoarchaeology: Implications of Ethnography for Archaeology*, ed. C. Kramer, New York: Academic Press.

Debevoise, Neilson C.
1934 *Parthian Pottery from Selucia on the Tigris.* Ann Arbor: University of Michigan Press.
1938 *A Political History of Parthia.* Chicago: University of Chicago Press.

Deetz, J. A., and E. Dethlefsen
1965 The Doppler-effect and Archaeology: A Consideration of the Spatial Aspects of Seriation. *Southwestern Journal of Anthropology* 21:196–206.

Delougaz, Pinhas P.
1952 *Pottery from the Diyala Region.* Oriental Institute Publications 63. Chicago: University of Chicago Press.

Delougaz, Pinhas P., and Helene J. Kantor
1969 New Light on the Emergence of Civilization in the Near East. *The UNESCO Courier,* Nov. 1969:22–25, 28.
1971 The Fourth Season of Excavations at Chogha Mish in Khuzestan (1969–70), Preliminary Report. *Bastan Chenassi va Honar-e Iran* 7/8:36–41.
1972 The 1971 Season of Excavation of the Joint Iranian Expedition. *Bastan Chenassi va Honar-e Iran* 9/10:88–96.
1974 The Čoqa Miš Excavations—1972–1973. *Proceedings of the 2nd Annual Symposium on Archaeological Research in Iran* 2:15–22. Tehran: Iranian Centre for Archaeological Research.
1975 The 1973–74 Excavations at Čoqa Miš. *Proceedings of the 3rd Annual Symposium on Archaeological Research in Iran* 3:93–102. Tehran: Iranian Centre for Archaeological Research.

De Niro, Michael J., and Samuel Epstein
1978 Influence of Diet on the Distribution of Carbon Isotopes in Animals. *Geochemica et Cosmochemica* 42:495–506.
1981 Influence of Diet on the Distribution of Nitrogen Isotopes in Animals. *Geochemica et Cosmochemica* 45:341–51.

Dez Irrigation Project
1958 *Report on the Dez Irrigation Project: Agricultural and Civil Technical Analyses Cost and Benefit Appraisal.* Arnhem: Nederlandsche Heidemaatschappij.

Digard, Jean-Pierre
1975 Campements Baxtyari. *Studia Iranica* 4(1):117–129.

Dixon, Wilfred J., and Frank J. Massy, Jr.
1969 *Introduction to Statistical Analysis.* 3d ed. New York: McGraw-Hill.

Dollfus, Geneviève
1971a Djaffarabad 1969–1970. *Syria* 48:61–84.
1971b Les fouilles à Djaffarabad de 1969 à 1971. *Cahiers de la Délégation archéologique française en Iran* 1:17–162.
1975 Les fouilles à Djaffarabad de 1972 à 1974, Djaffarabad, Périodes I et II. *Cahiers de la Délégation archéologique française en Iran* 5:11–62.
1977 Tepe Djowi. *Iran* 15:169–72.
1978 Djaffarabad, Djowi, Bendebal: Contribution à l'étude de la Susiane au 5e millénaire et au début du 4e millénaire. *Paléorient* 4:141–67.
1981 Prospections archéologiques au Khuzistan en 1977. *Cahiers de la Délégation archéologique française en Iran* 12:169–92.
1983 Tepe Djowi: Contrôle stratigraphique, 1975. *Cahiers de la Délégation française en Iran* 13:17–131.
1983a Tepe Bendebal, Travaux 1977, 1978. *Cahiers de la Délégation archéologique française en Iran* 13:133–275.
1983b Remarques sur l'organization de l'espace dans quelques agglomerations de la Susiane du 5e millénaire. In *The Hilly Flanks and Beyond* ed. T. Cuyler Young, Jr., P. E. L. Smith, and Peder Mortensen [q.v.], 283–313.
n.d. Peut-on parler de "Choga Mami Transitional" dans le sud-ouest de l'Iran? Paper presented at the CNRS Colloquium "La préhistoire de la Mèsopotamie du Vième millénaire av. J.C.," 17–19 Dec. 1984, Paris.

Dollfus, Geneviève, and P. Encreve
1982 Marques sur poteries dans la Susiane du Vième millénaire: Réflexions et comparaisons. *Paléorient* 8(1):107–15.

Drennan, R. D.
1976 A Refinement of Chronological Seriation Using Nonmetric Multidimensional Scaling. *American Antiquity* 41(3):290–302.

Drews, R.
1973 *The Greek Accounts of Eastern History.* Center for

Hellenic Studies, Washington, D.C. Cambridge, Mass.: Harvard University Press.

Driel, G. van, and C. van Driel-Murray
1979   Jebel Aruda 1977–1978. *Akkadica* 12:2–28.

Drower, Margaret S.
1973   Syria c. 1330–1400 B.C. In *Cambridge Ancient History*, II/1:417–525, ed. I. E. S. Edwards, C. J. Gadd, N. G. L. Hammond, and E. Sollberger. Cambridge: Cambridge University Press.

Dunnell, Robert
1970   Seriation Method and Its Evaluation. *American Antiquity* 35(3):305–19.
1978   Style and Function: A Fundamental Dichotomy. *American Antiquity* 43:192–202.
1980   Evolutionary Theory and Archaeology. In *Advances in Archaeological Method and Theory*, vol. 3, ed. M. B. Schiffer. New York: Academic Press.
1981   Seriation, Groups, and Measurements. Paper given at the Union Internacional de Ciencias Prehistoricas y Protohistoricas, Coloquio Manejo de Datos y Metodos.
1982   Science, Social Science and Common Sense: The Agonizing Dilemma of Modern Archaeology. *Journal of Anthropological Research* 38(1):1–24.

Dyson, Robert H., Jr.
1961   Excavating the Mannaean Citadel of Hasanlu and New Light on Several Millennia of Azerbaidjan. *Illustrated London News* Sept. 30:534–37.
1963   Archaeological Scrap: Glimpses of History at Ziwiye. *Expedition* 5:32–37.
1965a Problems in the Relative Chronology of Iran, 6000–2000 B.C. In *Chronologies in Old World Archaeology*, ed. R. W. Ehrich. Chicago: University of Chicago Press.
1965b Problems of Protohistoric Iran as Seen from Hasanlu. *Journal of Near Eastern Studies* 24:193–217.
1966   Excavations on the Acropolis at Susa and Problems of Susa A, B and C. Ph.D. diss., Harvard University.
1967   Early Cultures of Solduz, Azerbaijan. In *A Survey of Persian Art, XVIV,* ed. A. U. Pope and P. Ackerman. London: Oxford University Press.
1969   A Decade in Iran. *Expedition* 11:39–47.
1973   The Archaeological Evidence of the Second Millennium B.C. on the Persian Plateau. In *Cambridge Ancient History*, II/1:686–715, ed. I. E. S. Edwards, C. J. Gadd, N. G. L. Hammond, and E. Sollberger. Cambridge: Cambridge University Press.
1977a Architecture of the Iron I Period at Hasanlu. In *Le plateau iranien et l'Asie Centrale des origines à la conquête islamique*, 155–70. Paris: Editions du CNRS.
1977b The Architecture of Hasanlu: Periods I to IV. *American Journal of Archaeology* 81:548–52.

Dyson, Robert H., Jr., and Mary Voigt
       Problems in the Relative Chronology of Iran, 600–1500 B.C. In *Chronologies in Old World Archaeology*, 3d ed., ed. Robert W. Ehrich. Chicago: University of Chicago Press. In press.

Dyson, Robert H., and T. Cuyler Young
1960   The Solduz Valley, Iran: Pisdeli Tepe. *Antiquity* 34:19–27.

Earle, T. K., and J. E. Ericson, eds.
1977   *Exchange Systems in Prehistory*. New York: Academic Press.

Edwards, I. E. S., C. J. Gadd, and N. G. L. Hammond
1970   Prolegomena and Prehistory. In *Cambridge Ancient History*, I/1, ed. I. E. S. Edwards, C. J. Gadd, and N. G. L. Hammond. Cambridge: Cambridge University Press.
1971   Early History of the Middle East. In *Cambridge Ancient History*, I/2, ed. I. E. S. Edwards, C. J. Gadd, and N. G. L. Hammond. Cambridge: Cambridge University Press.

Edwards, I. E. S., and E. Sollberger
1973   The Middle East and the Aegean Region c. 1800–1380 B.C. In *Cambridge Ancient History*, II/1, ed. I. E. S. Edwards, C. J. Gadd, N. G. L. Hammond, and E. Sollberger. Cambridge: Cambridge University Press.

Edwards, Michael R.
1981   The Pottery of Haftavan VIB (Urmia Ware). *Iran* 19:101–40.

Edzard, Dietz O., Gertrud Farber, and E. Sollberger
1977   Die Orts- und Gewässernamen der präsargonischen und sargonischen Zeit. *Répertoire géographique des textes cunéiformes* 1. Wiesbaden: Dr. Ludwig Reichert.

Edzard, Dietz O., and Gertrud Farber
1974   Die Orts- und Gewässernamen der Zeit der 3. Dynastie von Ur. *Répertoire geographique des textes cunéiforms* 2. Wiesbaden: Dr. Ludwig Reichert.

Egami, Namio
1967   Excavations at Two Prehistoric Sites: Tepe Djari A and B in the Marv-Dasht Basin. In *A Survey of Persian Art XVIV*, ed. A. U. Pope and P. Ackerman. London: Oxford University Press.

Egami, Namio, Sei-Ichi Masuda, and Takeshi Gotoh
1977   Tal-i Jarri A: A Preliminary Report of the Excavations in Marv Dasht, 1961 and 1971. *Orient* 13:1–7.

Egami, Namio, and Sei-Ichi Masuda
1962   *Marv-Dasht I. The Tokyo University Iraq-Iran Archaeological Expedition Report 2*. The Institute of Oriental Culture. Tokyo: University of Tokyo.

Egami, Namio, and Toshihiko Sono
1962   *Marv-Dasht II, The Excavations at Tall-i Gap, 1959. The Tokyo University Iraq-Iran Archaeological Expedition Report 3*. The Institute of Oriental Culture. Tokyo: University of Tokyo.

Ehmann, Dieter
1975   *Bahtiayaren, Persische Bergnomaden im Wandel der Zeit*. Wiesbaden: Reichert.

Eiseley, Loren
1970   *The Invisible Pyramid*. New York: Charles Scribner's Sons.

Eisenstadt, S.
1963   *The Political Systems of Empires.* New York: The Free Press of Glencoe.
1967   *The Decline of Empires.* Englewood Cliffs, New Jersey: Prentice-Hall.

Eliot, Henry Ware
1950   *Excavations in Mesopotamia and Western Iran.* Special publication of the Peabody Museum. Cambridge, Mass.: Harvard University.

Epstein, Samuel, and Crayton J. Yapp
1976   Climatic Implications of the D/H ratio of Hydrogen in C-H Groups in Tree Cellulose. *Earth and Planetary Science Letters* 30:252–61.

Evans, J. G.
1978   *An Introduction to Environmental Archeology.* London: Paul Elek.

Fales, Frederick M.
1977   On Aramaic Onomastics in the Neo-Assyrian Period. *Oriens Antiquus* 16:41–68.

Field, Henry
1939   *Contributions to the Anthropology of Iran.* Anthropological Series, Field Museum of Natural History, vol. 29, no. 2. Chicago: Field Museum of Natural History.

Fischer, Thomas
1970   Untersuchungen zum Partherfeldzug Antiochos' VII im Rahmen der Seleukidengeschichte. Ph.D. diss., University of Munich.

Flannery, Kent V.
1965   The Ecology of Early Food Production in Mesopotamia. *Science* 147:1247–56.
1972a   The Origins of the Village as a Settlement Type in Mesoamerica and the Near East: A Comparative Study. In *Man, Settlement and Urbanism,* ed. P. J. Ucko, R. Tringhaus, and G. W. Dimbleby. London: Duckworth.
1972b   The Cultural Evolution of Civilizations. *Annual Review of Ecology and Systematics* 3:399–426.
1973   The Origins of Agriculture. *Annual Review of Anthropology* 2:271–310.

Flannery, Kent V., ed.
1976   *The Mesoamerican Village.* Academic Press: New York.

Flohn, H.
1981   Tropical Climate Variations during the Late Pleistocene and Early Holocene. In *Climatic Variations and Variability: Facts and Theories,* ed. A. Berger. Boston: D. Reidel Publishing Co.

Ford, James A.
1962   *A Quantitative Method for Deriving Cultural Chronology.* Technical Manual 1. Washington, D.C.: Pan American Union.

Frankfort, Henri
1948   *Kingship and the Gods.* Chicago: University of Chicago Press.
1950   Town Planning in Ancient Mesopotamia. *Town Planning Review* 21:98–115.

Fried, M. H.
1967   *The Evolution of Political Societies.* New York: Random House.

Friedl, Ernestine
1962   *Vasilika: A Village in Modern Greece.* New York: Holt, Rinehart and Winston.

Friedman, J., and M. J. Rowlands
1977   Notes toward an Epigenetic Model of the Evolution of "Civilizations." In *The Evolution of Social Systems,* ed. J. Friedman and M. J. Rowlands. London: Duckworth.

Fry, Robert E.
1980   *Models and Methods in Regional Exchange.* SAA Papers no. 1. Washington, D.C.: Society for American Archaeology.

Frye, Richard
1963   *The Heritage of Persia.* London: Weidenfeld and Nicolson.

Frye, Richard, ed.
1973   *Sasanian Remains from Quasr-i Abu Nasr: Seals, Sealings, and Coins.* Cambridge, Mass.: Harvard University Press.

Fukai, Shinji, Kiyoharu Horiuchi, and Toshio Matsutani
1973   *Marv Dasht III: The Excavations at Tall-i Mushki, 1965.* Institute of Oriental Culture. Tokyo: University of Tokyo.

Gabl, R.
1973   *Der sasanidische Siegelkanon, Handbuch der Mittelasiatischen Numismatik,* vol. 4. Braunschweig: Klinkhardt and Biermann.

Gadd, C. J.
1971   The Cities of Babylonia: The Dynasty of Agade and the Gutian Invasion, Babylonia *c.* 2120–1800 B.C. In *Cambridge Ancient History,* I/2, ed. I. E. S. Edwards, C. J. Gadd, and N. G. L. Hammond. Cambridge: Cambridge University Press.
1973   Hammurabi and the End of his Dynasty. *Cambridge Ancient History* II/1:176–227, ed. I. E. S. Edwards, C. J. Gadd, N. G. L. Hammond, and E. Sollberger. Cambridge: Cambridge University Press.

Gasche, Henri
1973   La poterie élamite du deuxième millénaire A.C. *Mémoires de la Mission archéologique en Iran* 47. Paris: Paul Geuthner.

Gautier, J. E., and G. Lampre
1905   Fouilles de Moussian. *Mémoires de la Délégation en Perse* 8:59–149. Paris: Ernest Leroux.

Geertz, Clifford
1963   *Agricultural Involution: The Processes of Ecological Change in Indonesia.* Berkeley: University of California Press.
1964   Tihingan: A Balinese Village. *Bijdragen* 120:1–33.

Genouillac, H. de
1924   *Premières recherches archéologiques à Kich.* Vol. 1. Paris: Librairie Ancienne E. Douard Champion.

Ghirshman, Roman

1952 Cinq campagnes de fouilles à Suse, 1946–1951. *Révue d'assyriologie* 46:1–18.

1953 Mission archéologique en Susiane en hiver, 1952–1953. *Syria* 30:222–33.

1954a *Iran.* Baltimore: Penguin Books.

1954b Village Perse-Achémenide. *Mémoires de la Mission archéologique en Iran* 34. Paris: Presses Universitaires de France.

1956 *Bichapour II: Les mosaiques sassanides.* Musée de Louvre, Départment des Antiquités Orientales, Série Archéologique, vol. 7. Paris: Paul Geuthner.

1962 *Persian Art: The Parthian and Sassanian Dynasties, 249 B.C.–A.D. 651.* Trans. Stuart Gilbert and James Emmons. New York: Golden Press.

1964 Susa, campagne de fouilles 1962–1963, Rapport préliminaire. *Arts Asiatiques* 10:3–10.

1966a Excavations at Bard e Nechandeh. *Illustrated London News* July 16.

1966b Tchoga Zanbil (Dur-Untash): La Ziggurat. *Mémoires de la Mission archéologique en Iran* 39. Paris: Paul Geuthner.

1968 Tchoga Zanbil (Dur Untash): Temenos, temples, palais, tombes. *Mémoires de la Mission archéologique en Iran* 40. Paris: Paul Geuthner.

1970 Masjid-i Solaiman. *Iran* 8:183–85.

Gibson, McGuire

1972 *The City and Area of Kish.* Miami: Field Research Publications.

1973 Population Shift and the Rise of Mesopotamian Civilization. In *The Explanation of Culture Change,* ed. Colin Renfrew. London: Duckworth.

1974 Violation of Fallow and Engineered Disaster in Mesopotamian Civilization. In *Irrigation's Impact on Society,* Anthropological Papers of the University of Arizona no. 25, ed. T. E. Downing and M. Gibson. Tucson: University of Arizona Press.

1975 *Excavations at Nippur: Eleventh Season.* O.I.C. 22. Chicago: University of Chicago.

1981 Summation. In *Uch Tepe I: Tell Razuk, Tell Ahmed al-Mughir, Tell Ajamat,* ed. McGuire Gibson. Chicago: Oriental Institute of the University of Chicago.

Gilbar, G. G.

1976 Demographic Developments in Late Qajar Persia, 1870–1906. *Asian and African Studies* 11(2):125–56.

Godard, Andre

1931 Les bronzes du Luristan. *Ars asiatica: Etudes et documents* 17. Paris: G. Van Oest.

Godelier, Maurice

1978 Infrastructures, Societies, and History. *Current Anthropology* 19(4):763–71.

Goetze, Albrecht

1964 The Kassites and Near Eastern Chronology. *Journal of Cuneiform Studies* 18:97–101.

Goff, Clare L. (Meade)

1963 Excavations at Tall-i-Nokhodi. *Iran* 1:43–70.

1964 Excavations at Tall-i-Nokhodi, 1962. *Iran* 2:41–52.

1966 New Evidence of Cultural Development in Luristan in the Late Second and Early First Millennia. Ph.D. diss., Institute of Archaeology, University of London.

1968 Luristan in the First Half of the First Millennium B.C. *Iran* 6:105–34.

1969 Excavations at Baba Jan, 1967. *Iran* 7:115–30.

1970 Excavations at Baba Jan, 1968. *Iran* 8:141–56.

1971 Luristan Before the Iron Age. *Iran* 9:131–52.

1976 Excavations at Baba Jan: The Bronze Age Occupation. *Iran* 14:19–40.

1977 Excavations at Baba Jan: The Architecture of the East Mound, Levels II and III. *Iran* 15:103–40.

1978 Excavations at Baba Jan: The Pottery and Metal from Levels III and II. *Iran* 16:29–66.

1985 Excavations at Baba Jan: The Architecture and Pottery of Level I. *Iran* 23:1–20.

Goff, Clare, and J. Pullar

1970 Tepe Abdul Hosein. *Iran* 8:199–200.

Gotch, Paul

1968 A Survey of the Persepolis Plain and Shiraz Area. *Iran* 6:168–69.

1969 The Persepolis Plain and Shiraz: Field Survey 2. *Iran* 7:190–92.

1971 Bakun A IV Pottery—A History and Statement of Possibilities. *Bulletin of the Asia Institute of Pahlavi University* 2:72–90.

Gould, R., et al.

1977 The Shape of Evolution: A Comparison of Real and Random Clades. *Paleobiology* 3(1):23–40.

Green, Evarts B., and Virginia D. Harrington

1932 *American Population before the Federal Census of 1750.* New York: Columbia University Press.

Gremliza, F. G. L.

1962 *Ecology and Endemic Diseases in the Dez Irrigation Pilot Area.* A Report to the Khuzistan Water and Power Authority and Plan Organization of Iran. New York: Development and Resources Corporation.

Guterbock, Hans G.

1967 Babylonia and Assyria, III: History. *Encyclopedia Britannica* 2:960–68.

Haerinck, E.

1983 La céramique en Iran pendant la période parthe. *Iranica Antiqua,* supplement 2.

n.d. The Chronology of Luristan, Pusht-i Kuh in the Late Fourth and First Half of the Third Millennium B.C. Paper presented at the CNRS Colloquium "La préhistoire de la Mésopotamie du Vième millénaire av. J.C., 17–19 Dec. 1984, Paris.

Haggett, Peter

1965 *Locational Analysis in Human Geography.* London: Edward Arnold Ltd.

1966 *Locational Analysis in Human Geography.* Reprinted from the 1965 edition. London: Edward Arnold.

Hallam, B. R., J. E. Warren, and Colin Renfrew
1976   Obsidian in the Western Mediterranean: Characterization by Neutron Activation Analysis and Optical Emission Spectroscopy. *Proceedings of the Prehistoric Society* 42:85–110.

Hallier, U. W.
1974   Eine parthische Stadt in Ostpersian. *Archäologische Mitteilungen aus Iran* n.s. 7:173–90.

Hallo, W. W.
1957   *Early Mesopotamian Royal Titles: A Philologic and Historical Atlas.* New Haven: American Oriental Society.
1979   Gutium. *Reallexikon der Assyriologie und vorderasiastischen Archäologie* 3/9:709–20.

Hamlin, Carol (Kramer)
1971   The Habur Ware Ceramic Assemblage of Northern Mesopotamia: An Analysis of Its Distribution. Ph.D. diss., University of Pennsylvania.
1973   The 1971 Excavations at Seh Gabi, Iran. *Archaeology* 26:224–27.
1974a   The Early Second Millennium Ceramic Assemblage of Dinka Tepe. *Iran* 12:125–53.
1974b   Seh Gabi, 1973. *Archaeology* 27:274–77.
1975   Dalma Tepe. *Iran* 13:111–27.

Hansen, Donald P.
1965   The Relative Chronology of Nippur from the Middle Uruk to the End of the Old Babylonian Period (3400–1600 B.C.). In *Chronologies in the Old World*, ed. Robert Ehrich. Chicago: University of Chicago Press.
1973   Al-Hiba, 1970–1971: A Preliminary Report. *Artibus Asiae* 35:62–78.

Hansman, John
1967   Charax and the Karkheh. *Iranica Antiqua* 7:21–58.

Hansman, John, and David Stronach
1974   Excavations at Shahr-i Qumis, 1971. *Journal of the Royal Asiatic Society of Great Britain and Ireland* 1:8–22.

Harris, David R.
1977   Settling Down: An Evolutionary Model for the Transformation of Mobile Bands into Sedentary Communities. In *The Evolution of Social Systems*, ed. J. Friedman and M. J. Rowlands. London: Duckworth.

Harris, Marvin
1977   *Cannibals and Kings.* New York: Random House.

Hassan, Fekri A.
1975   Determination of the Size, Density and Growth Rate of Hunting-Gathering Populations. In *Population, Ecology and Social Evolution*, ed. Steven Polgar. The Hague: Mouton.
1978   Demographic Archaeology. In *Advances in Archaeological Method and Theory*, vol. 1, ed. M. B. Schiffer. New York: Academic Press.
1979   Demography and Archaeology. In *Annual Review of Anthropology* 8:137–60.
1981   *Demographic Archeology.* New York: Academic Press.

Hassan, Riaz
1969   The Nature of Islamic Urbanization—An Historical Perspective. *Islamic Culture* 43(3):233–37.

Heinz, Gaube
1973   *Die südpersische Provinz Arragan von der arabischen Eroberung bis zur Safawidenzeit: Analyse und Auswertung literarischer und archäologischer Quellen zur historischer Topographie.* Wien: Österreichschen Akademie der Wissenschaften.

Helbaek, Hans
1969   Plant Collecting, Dry Farming, and Irrigation Agriculture in Prehistoric Deh Luran. Appendix in *Prehistory and Human Ecology of the Deh Luran Plain*, Memoir no. 1, ed. Frank Hole, Kent V. Flannery, and James Neely. Ann Arbor: University of Michigan Museum of Anthropology.

Helm, Peyton R.
1981   Herodotus' *Mêdikos Logos* and Median History. *Iran* 19:85–90.

Henning, Hans, and Rudolf Nauman
1961   Takht-i Suleiman. *Tehraner Forschungen* 1. Berlin: Gebr. Mann.

Henrickson, Elizabeth F.
1983   Ceramic Styles and Cultural Interaction in the Early and Middle Chalcolithic of the Central Zagros, Iran. Ph.D. diss., University of Toronto.
1985   An Updated Chronology of the Early and Middle Chalcolithic of the Central Zagros Highlands, Western Iran. *Iran* 23:63–108.
1985b   The Early Development of Pastoralism in the Central Zagros Highlands (Luristan). *Iranica Antiqua* 20.

Henrickson, Robert C.
1977   Iron III and Central Western Iran. Unpublished paper.
1983–   Giyan I and II Reconsidered. *Mesopotamia* 18–
84   19:195–220.
1984a   Godin III, Godin Tepe, and Central Western Iran. Ph.D. diss., Department of Near Eastern Studies, University of Toronto.
1984b   Šimaški and Central Western Iran: The Archaeological Evidence. *Zeitschrift für Assyriologie* 74:98–122.
1986a   Workshops and Pottery Production in the Central Zagros (Iran), ca. 2300 B.C. In *Ceramics and Civilization*, ed. D. Kingery. American Ceramic Society.
1986b   A Regional Perspective on Godin III Cultural Development in Central Western Iran. *Iran* 24.
1986c   The Godin III Revised Chronology for Central Western Iran 2600–1400 B.C. *Iranica Antiqua* 21.

Herrero, Pablo
1976   Tablettes administratives de Haft Tepe. *Cahiers de la Délégation archéologique française en Iran.* 6:93–116.

Herrmann, Georgina
1968   Lapis Lazuli—The Early Phases of Its Trade. *Iraq* 30:21–56.

Herzfeld, Ernst

1929 Drei Inschriften aus persischem Gebiet. *Mitteilungen der altorientalischen Gesellschaft* 4:81–85.

1932 *Iranische Denkmaler: Steinzeitlicher Hügel bei Persepolis.* Berlin: Dietrich Reimer/Ernst Vohsen.

Heskel, Dennis

1982 Comment on Alden (1982). *Current Anthropology* 23:628–29.

Hesse, A.

1975 Note sur la forme et la dimension des houes de pierre. *Cahiers de la Délégation archéologique française en Iran* 5:63–66, appendix 1.

Hesse, Brian

1978 Evidence for Husbandry from the Early Neolithic Site of Ganj Dareh in Western Iran. Ph.D. diss., Columbia University.

1979 Rodent Remains and Sedentism in the Neolithic: Evidence from Tepe Ganj Dareh, Western Iran. *Journal of Mammalogy* 60:856–57.

1982 Slaughter Patterns and Domestication: The Beginnings of Pastoralism in Western Iran. *Man* 17:403–17.

Heude, William

1819 *A Voyage Up the Persian Gulf and Overland from India to England in 1817.* London: Longman, Hurst, Rees, Orme and Brown.

Higgs, E. S., ed.

1972 *Papers in Economic Prehistory.* Cambridge: Cambridge University Press.

1975 *Palaeoeconomy.* Cambridge: Cambridge University Press.

Higgs, E. S., and C. Vita-Finzi

1972 Prehistoric Economies: A Terrestrial Approach. In *Papers in Economic Prehistory,* ed. E. S. Higgs [q.v.]

Hinz, Walther

1971 Persia, c. 2400–1800 B.C. In *Cambridge Ancient History* I/2, ch. 23, ed. I. E. S. Edwards, C. J. Gadd, and N. G. L. Hammond. Cambridge: Cambridge University Press.

1972 *The Lost World of Elam.* Trans. Jennifer Barnes; originally published in West Germany as *Das Reich Elam,* 1964. London: Sidgwick and Jackson.

1973 Persia c. 1800–1550 B.C. In *Cambridge Ancient History,* II/1:256–88, ed. I. E. S. Edwards, C. J. Gadd, N. G. L. Hammond, and E. Sollberger. Cambridge: Cambridge University Press.

Hodder, Ian

1978 Some Effects of Distance Patterns of Human Interaction. In *The Spatial Organisation of Culture,* ed. Ian Hodder. Pittsburgh: University of Pittsburgh Press.

1979 Simulating the Growth of Hierarchies. In *Transformations: Mathematical Approaches to Culture Change,* ed. Colin Renfrew and Kenneth L. Cooke. Academic Press: New York.

1982 *Symbols in Action.* Cambridge: Cambridge University Press.

Hodder, Ian, and Clive Orton

1976 *Spatial Analysis in Archaeology.* Cambridge: Cambridge University Press.

Hoffman, M. A.

1979 *Egypt before the Pharoahs.* New York: A. A. Knopf.

Hole, Bonnie L.

1980 Sampling in Archaeology: A Critique. *Annual Review of Anthropology* 9:217–34.

Hole, Frank

1962 Archeological Survey and Excavation in Iran, 1961. *Science* 137:524–26.

1969a Report on the Survey of Upper Khuzistan. In *Preliminary Reports of the Rice University Project in Iran, 1968–1969,* ed. Frank Hole. Houston: Rice University Department of Anthropology.

1969b Evidence of Social Organization in Western Iran: 8000–4000 B.C. In *New Perspectives in Archeology,* ed. L. Binford and S. Binford. Chicago: Aldine.

1970 The Paleolithic Culture Sequence In Western Iran. *Proceedings: VIIth International Congress on Prehistoric and Protohistoric Sciences, Prague, 1966.* Prague: Institut d'archéologie de l'Académie tchéchoslovaque des sciences à Prague, 286–292.

1971 Comments on "Origins of Food Production in Southwestern Asia: A Survey of Ideas," by G. Wright. *Current Anthropology* 12:472–73.

1974 Tepe Tula'i, an Early Campsite in Khuzistan, Iran. *Paléorient* 2:219–42.

1975a Ethnoarchaeology of Nomadic Pastoralism: A Case Study. Mimeographed manuscript.

1975b The Sondage at Tepe Tula'i. *Proceedings of the 3rd Annual Symposium on Archaeological Research in Iran* 3:63–76. Tehran: Iranian Centre for Archaeological Research.

1977a *Studies in the Archeological History of the Deh Luran Plain.* Memoir no. 9. Ann Arbor: University of Michigan Museum of Anthropology.

1977b Social Implications of the Prehistoric Ceramics of Khuzistan. Paper presented at the 6th Annual Symposium on Archaeological Research in Iran, Tehran.

1978a Pastoral Nomadism in Western Iran. In *Explorations in Ethnoarchaeology,* ed. Richard A. Gould. Albuquerque: University of New Mexico Press.

1978b The Early Prehistoric Periods. *Proceedings of the 6th Annual Symposium on Archaeological Research in Iran.* Tehran: Iranian Centre for Archaeological Research.

1979 Rediscovering the Past in the Present: Ethnoarchaeology in Luristan, Iran. In *Ethnoarchaeology,* ed. C. Kramer. New York: Columbia University Press.

1980 The Prehistory of Herding: Some Suggestions from Ethnography. In *L'Archéologie de l'Iraq du début de l'époque néolithique à 333 avant notre ère: Perspectives et limites de l'interprétation anthropologi-*

que des documents. Colloques Internationaux du Centre National de la Recherche Scientifique no. 580, ed. Marie-Thérèse Barrelet. Paris: Editions du Centre National de la Recherche Scientifique.

1983   Symbols of Religion and Social Organization at Susa. In *The Hilly Flanks and Beyond*, ed. T. C. Young, Jr., Philip E. L. Smith, and Peder Mortensen [q.v.].

1984   Analysis of Structure and Design in Prehistoric Ceramics. *World Archaeology* 15:326–47.

1985   A Reassessment of the Neolithic Revolution. *Paléorient* 10:49–60.

Hole, Frank, ed.
1969   *Preliminary Reports of the Rice University Project in Iran, 1968–1969.* Houston: Rice University Department of Anthropology.

Hole, Frank, and K. V. Flannery
1962   Excavations at Ali Kosh, Iran, 1961. *Iranica Antiqua* 2:97–148.

1968   The Prehistory of Southwestern Iran: A Preliminary Report. *Proceedings of the Prehistoric Society for 1967* 33:147–206.

Hole, Frank, K. V. Flannery, and J. A. Neely
1969   *Prehistory and Human Ecology of the Deh Luran Plain.* Memoir no. 1. Ann Arbor: University of Michigan Museum of Anthropology.

Howe, Bruce
1983   Karim Shahir. In *Prehistoric Archeology along the Zagros Flanks.* Oriental Institute Publications 105, ed. L. S. Braidwood, R. J. Braidwood, B. Howe, C. A. Reed, and P. J. Watson. Chicago: Oriental Institute of the University of Chicago.

Howell, Rosalind
1979   Survey of the Malayer Plain. *Iran* 17:156–57.

Huot, Jean Louis
1965   *Persia.* Volume 1, *From the Origins to the Achaemenids.* Trans. H. B. S. Harrison. New York: World Publishing Co.

Huxley, Sir Julian
1932   *Problems of Relative Growth.* London: Methuen. Reprint Dover, 1972.

Ibn Khaldoun
1958   *The Muquaddimah: An Introduction to History.* 3 vols. New York: Pantheon.

Invernizzo, Antonio
1976   Ten Years' Research in the Al-Mada'in Area [sic] Seleucia and Ctesiphon. *Sumer* 32(1–2):167–75.

Izeh Research Group
n.d.   Archaeological Survey on the Plain of Izeh, 1976. Manuscript. Tehran: Iranian Centre for Archaeological Research.

Jabbar, Muhammed A.
1973   Agricultural and Irrigation Labourers in Social and Economic Life of Iraq during the Umayyad and Abbasid Caliphates. *Islamic Culture* 47(1):15–31.

Jacobs, Linda
1979   Tell-i-Nun: Archaeological Implications of a Village in Transition. In *Ethnoarchaeology*, ed. Carol Kramer. New York: Columbia University Press.

1980   Darvazeh Tepe and the Iranian Highlands in the Second Millennium B.C. Ph.D. diss., University of Oregon.

Jacobsen, Thorkild
1957   Early Political Development in Mesopotamia. *Zeitschrift für Assyriologie* 52:91–140.

1976   *The Treasures of Darkness. A History of Mesopotamian Religion.* New Haven: Yale University Press.

Jermann, J.
1981   Archaeological Space and Sampling: Methods and Techniques in the Study of Pattern in Past Cultural Activity. Ph.D. diss., University of Washington.

Johnson, Gregory A.
1973   *Local Exchange and Early State Development in Southwestern Iran.* Anthropological Papers no. 51. Ann Arbor: University of Michigan Museum of Anthropology.

1975   Locational Analysis and the Investigation of Uruk Local Exchange Systems. In *Ancient Civilization and Trade.* School of American Research Advanced Seminar Series, ed. Jeremy Sabloff and C. C. Lamberg-Karlovsky. Albuquerque: University of New Mexico Press.

1976   Early State Organization in Southwestern Iran: Preliminary Field Report. *Proceedings of the 4th Annual Symposium on Archaeological Research in Iran* 4:190–223. Tehran: Iranian Centre for Archaeological Research.

1977   Aspects of Regional Analysis in Archaeology. *Annual Review of Anthropology* 6:479–508.

1978   Information Sources and the Development of Decision-Making Organizations. In *Social Archeology: Beyond Subsistence and Dating*, ed. Charles Redman et al. New York: Academic Press.

1980a Rank-Size Convexity and System Integration: A View from Archaeology. *Economic Geography* 56(3):234–47.

1980b Spatial Organization of Early Uruk Settlement Systems. In *L'Archéologie de l'Iraq du début de l'époque néolithique à 333 avant notre ère: Perspectives et limites de l'interprétation anthropologique des documents.* Colloques Internationaux du Centre National de la Recherche Scientifique no. 580, ed. Marie-Thérèse Barrelet. Paris: Editions du Centre National de la Recherche Scientifique.

1981   Monitoring Complex System Integration and Boundary Phenomena with Settlement Size Data. In *Archaeological Approaches to Complexity.* Albert Egges van Giffen Instituut voor Prae- en Protohistorie, CINGVLA VI, ed. S. E. van der Leeuw. Amsterdam: University of Amsterdam.

1982a Comment on Alden (1982). *Current Anthropology* 23:629–30.

1982b Organizational Structure and Scalar Stress. In *Theory and Explanation in Archaeology: The Southampton Conference*, ed. Colin Renfrew, Michael J. Rowlands, and Barbara Abbott Segraves. New York: Academic Press.

1983   Decision-Making Organization and Pastoral Nomad Camp Size. *Human Ecology* 11:175–99.

n.d.   Scalar Stress and Pastoral Nomad Camp Size. Unpublished manuscript.

Jones, G. I.
1966   Chiefly Succession in Basutoland. In *Succession to High Office,* ed. J. Goody. Cambridge: Cambridge University Press.

Jones, Grant D., and Robert R. Kautz, ed.
1981   *The Transition to Statehood in the New World.* Cambridge: Cambridge University Press.

Kantor, Helene J.
1974   The Čoqa Miš Excavations. *Proceedings of the 2nd Annual Symposium on Archaeological Research in Iran* 3:15–22. Tehran: Iranian Centre for Archaeological Research.
1976   The Excavations at Čoqa Miš, 1974–1975. *Proceedings of the 4th Annual Symposium on Archaeological Research in Iran* 4:23–41. Tehran: Iranian Centre for Archaeological Research.

Keall, E.
1967   "Qal'eh-i Yazdigird: A Sassanian Palace Stronghold in Persian Kurdistan. *Iran* 5:99–122.
1975   Parthian Nippur and Vologases' Southern Strategy: A Hypothesis. *Journal of the American Oriental Society* 94(4):589–91.
1977a   Qal'eh-i Yazdigird: The Question of Its Date. *Iran* 15:1–9.
1977b   Political, Economic, and Social Factors on the Parthian Landscape of Mesopotamia and Western Iran. *Bibliotheca Mesopotamica* 7:81–89.

Kearton, Regnar
1969   Survey in Azerbaijan. *Iran* 7:186–87.
n.d.   *A Study of Settlement in the Salmas Valley, West Azerbaijan, Iran.* Unpublished manuscript.

Kenyon, K. M.
1960   Excavations at Jericho, 1957–1958. *Palestine Exploration Quarterly* 92:1–21.

Khaduri, M.
1947   The Nature of the Islamic States. *Islamic Culture* 21:327–31.

Khwand, Mir
1832   *History of the Early Kings of Persia.* Trans. D. Shea. London: Oriental Translation Fund.

Kigoshi, Kunihiko, and Kunihiko Endo
1963   Gakushuin Natural Radiocarbon Measurements II. *Radiocarbon* 5:109–17.

Kintigh, K. W., and A. J. Ammerman
1982   Heuristic Approaches to Spatial Analysis in Archaeology. *American Antiquity* 47(1):31–63.

Kirkbride, Diana
1966   Five Seasons at the Pre-Pottery Neolithic Village of Beidha in Jordan. *Palestine Exploration Quarterly* 98:8–274.
1972   Umm Dabaghiyah 1971: A Preliminary Report. *Iraq* 34:3–19.

1974   Umm Dabaghiyah: A Trading Outpost? *Iraq* 36:85–92.

Kirkby, Anne, and Michael J. Kirkby
1976   Geomorphic Processes and the Surface Survey of Archaeological Sites in Semi-Arid Areas. In *Geoarchaeology: Earth Science and the Past,* ed. D. A. Davidson and M. L. Shackley. London: Duckworth.

Kirkby, Michael J.
1977   Land and Water Resources of the Deh Luran and Khuzistan Plains. In *Studies in the Archaeological History of the Deh Luran Plain,* Memoir no. 9, ed. Frank Hole. Ann Arbor: University of Michigan, Museum of Anthropology.

Kirkby, Michael J., and A. V. T. Kirkby
1969   Provisional Report on Geomorphology and Land Use in Deh Luran and Upper Khuzistan. In *Preliminary Reports of the Rice University Project in Iran 1968–1969,* ed. Frank Hole. Houston: Rice University Department of Anthropology.

Klatzky, S. R.
1970   Relationship of Organizational Size to Complexity and Coordination. *Administrative Science Quarterly* 15:428–38.

Klein, Jeffrey, J. C. Lerman, P. E. Damon, and E. K. Ralph
1982   Calibration of Radiocarbon Dates: Tables Based on the Consensus Data of the Workshop on Calibrating the Radiocarbon Time Scale. *Radiocarbon* 24:103–50.

Kleiss, Wolfram
1970   Zur Topographie des "Partherhanges" in Bisitun. *Archäologische Mitteilungen aus Iran* n.s. 3:133–68.

Kleiss, Wolfram, and Harold Hauptmann
1976   *Topographische Karte von Urartu.* Archäologische Mitteilungen aus Iran Ergänzungsband 3. Berlin: Dietrich Reimer.

Kohl, Philip L.
1974   Seeds of Upheaval: The Production of Chlorite at Tepe Yahya and an Analysis of Commodity Production and Trade. Ph.D. diss., Harvard University.
1978   The Balance of Trade in Southwestern Asia in the Mid-Third Millennium B.C. *Current Anthropology* 19:463–92.

Kohl, Philip L., and R. P. Wright
1977   Stateless Cities: The Differentiation of Societies in the Near Eastern Neolithic. *Dialectical Anthropology* 2:271–83.

Konig, Fredrich Wilhelm
1965   Die elamischen Königsinschriften. *Archiv für Orientforschung* 16. Graz: E. Weidner.

Kowalewski, Stephen A.
1982   The Evolution of Primate Regional Systems. *Comparative Urban Research* 9(1):60–78.

Kramer, Carol
1977   Pots and People. In *Mountains and Lowlands: Es-*

says in the *Archaeology of Greater Mesopotamia*, ed. Louis D. Levine and T. Cuyler Young, Jr. Malibu: Undena.

1979   An Archaeological View of a Contemporary Kurdish Village: Domestic Architecture, Household Size, and Wealth. In *Ethnoarchaeology: Implications of Ethnology for Archaeology*, ed. C. Kramer. New York: Columbia University Press.

1980   Estimating Prehistoric Populations: An Ethnoarchaeological Approach. In *L'archéologie de l'Iraq du début de l'époque néolithique à 333 avant notre ère: Perspectives et limites de l'interprétation anthropologique des documents*. Colloques Internationaux du Centre National de la Recherche Scientifique no. 580, ed. Marie Thérèse Barrelet. Paris: Editions du Centre National de la Recherche Scientifique.

1983   Spatial Organization in Contemporary Southwest Asian Villages and Archaeological Sampling. In *The Hilly Flanks and Beyond*, ed. T. C. Young, Jr., Philip E. L. Smith, and Peder Mortensen [q.v.], 347–68.

Kramer, Carol, ed.
1979   *Ethnoarchaeology: Implications of Ethnography for Archaeology*. New York: Columbia University Press.

1982   *Village Ethnoarchaeology: Rural Iran in Archaeological Perspective*. New York: Academic Press.

Kramer, Samuel N.
1959   *History Begins at Sumer*. New York: Doubleday.

Krinsley, Daniel B.
1970   *A Geomorphological and Paleoclimatological Study of the Playas of Iran, Parts I and II*. AFCRL-70-0503. Washington, D.C.: Geological Survey, U.S. Department of the Interior.

Kroll, Stephan
1975   Eine Schüssel der *Triangle Ware* aus Azarbaidschan. *Archäologische Mitteilungen aus Iran* n.s. 8:71–74.

1976   *Keramik urartaischer Festungen in Iran*. Archäologische Mitteilungen aus Iran Ergänzungsband 2. Berlin: Dietrich Reimer.

1977   Urartaische Plätze in Iran: B. Die Oberflächenfunde des Urartu-Surveys 1976. *Archäologische Mitteilungen aus Iran* n.s. 10:83–118.

1979   Meder in Bastam. In *Bastam I*, Teheraner Forschungen 4, ed. Wolfram Kleiss, 229–34. Berlin: Gebr. Mann.

Kruskal, J. B., and M. Wish
1978   *Multidimensional Scaling*. Beverly Hills: Sage Publications.

Kupper, J. R.
1969   Le pays de Simaski. *Iraq* 31:24–27.

Kutzbach, John E.
1981   Monsoon Climate of the Early Holocene: Climate Experiment with the Earth's Orbital Parameters for 9000 Years Ago. *Science* 214:59–61.

Labat, René
1963   Elam *c.* 1600–1200 B.C. *Cambridge Ancient History* II, facsimile of Chapter 29. Cambridge: Cambridge University Press.

1975   Elam and Western Persia. *Cambridge Ancient History* II/2. Cambridge: Cambridge University Press.

Labrousse, A., and R. Boucharlat
1974   La fouille du Palais du Chaour à Suse en 1970 et 1971. *Cahiers de la Délégation archéologique française en Iran* 2:61–168.

Lamberg-Karlovsky, C. C.
1970   *Excavations at Tepe Yahya, Iran, 1967–1969, Progress Report No. 1*. President and Fellows of Harvard College. Cambridge, Mass.: Harvard University.

1971   The Proto-Elamite Settlements at Tepe Yahya. *Iran* 9:87–96.

1972a   Tepe-Yahya—Mesopotamia and the Indo-Iranian Borderlands. *Iran* 10:89–100.

1972b   Trade Mechanisms in Indus-Mesopotamian Inter-Relations. *Journal of the American Oriental Society* 92(2):222–30.

1975   Comments on Professor Adams' Paper. In *Reconstructing Complex Societies*, Supplement to the Bulletin of the American School of Oriental Research no. 20, ed. Charlotte Moore.

1976   The Third Millennium of Tappeh Yahya: A Preliminary Statement. *Proceedings of the 4th Annual Symposium on Archaeological Research in Iran* 4:71–84. Tehran: Iranian Centre for Archaeological Research.

1978   The Proto-Elamites on the Iranian Plateau. *Antiquity* 52:114–20.

1982   Comment on Alden (1982). *Current Anthropology* 23:631–33.

Lambert, Maurice
1960   La naissance de la bureaucratie. *Revue historique* 224:1–26.

1961   La première triomphe de la bureaucratie. *Revue historique* 225:21–46.

1972   Hutelutush-Inshushinak et le pays d'Anzan. *Revue d'assyriologie* n.s. 66:61–76.

Langdon, S.
1934   The Excavations at Kish and Barghuthiat in 1933: Sassanian and Parthian Remains in Central Mesopotamia. *Iraq* 1:113–23.

Langsdorff, Alexander, and D. E. McCown
1942   *Tall-i-Bakun A: Season of 1932*. Oriental Institute Publications 54. Chicago: University of Chicago Press.

Lapidus, Ira M.
1969   Muslim Cities and Islamic Societies. In *Middle Eastern Cities: Ancient, Islamic, and Contemporary Middle Eastern Urbanism: A Symposium*, ed. Ira M. Lapidus. Berkeley: University of California Press.

Larsen, C. E.
1975   The Mesopotamian Delta Region: A Reconsideration of Lees and Falcon. *Journal of the American Oriental Society* 95(1):43–57.

Larsen, Mogens T.
1979   The Tradition of Empire in Mesopotamia. In *Power and Propaganda*, ed. Mogens T. Larsen. Copenhagen: Akademisk Forlag.

Lattimore, Owen
1951   *Inner Asian Frontiers of China*. Boston: Beacon Press.

Lawn, Barbara
1970   University of Pennsylvania Radiocarbon Dates XIII. *Radiocarbon* 12:577–89.
1974   University of Pennsylvania Radiocarbon Dates XVII. *Radiocarbon* 16:219–37.

Lawrence, B.
1982   Principal Food Animals at Çayönü. In *Prehistoric Village Archaeology in South-eastern Turkey*, Ed. Linda S. and Robert J. Braidwood. Oxford: British Archaeological Reports, International Series 138.

Layard, Austen Henry
1846   Description of the Plain of Khuzistan. *Journal of the Royal Asiatic Society* 16:78–86.

Le Blanc, Steven A.
1971   An Addition to Naroll's Suggested Floor Area and Settlement Population Relationship. *American Antiquity* 36:210–11.
1975   Microseriation: A Method for Fine Chronological Differentiation. *American Antiquity* 40:22–38.

Le Blanc, Steven A., and P. J. Watson
1973   A Comparative Statistical Analysis of Painted Pottery from Seven Halafian Sites. *Paléorient* 1:117–32.

Le Breton, Louis
1947   Note sur la céramique peinte aux environs de Suse et à Suse. *Mémoires de la Mission archéologique en Iran* 30:120–219. Paris: Presses Universitaires de France.
1957   The Early Periods at Susa, Meospotamian Relations. *Iraq* 19(2):79–124.

Le Brun, Alain
1971   Recherches stratigraphiques à l'Acropole de Suse (1969–1971). *Cahiers de la Délégation archéologique française en Iran* 1:163–216. Paris: Paul Geuthner.
1978   Suse, Chantier "Acropole 1". *Paléorient* 4:177–92.
1980   Les écuelles grossières: Etat de la question. In *L'archéologie de l'Iraq du début de l'époque néolithique à 333 avant notre ère: Perspectives et limites de l'interprétation anthropologique des documents*. Colloques Internationaux du Centre National de la Recherche Scientifique no. 580, ed. Marie-Thérèse Barrelet. Paris: Editions du Centre National de la Recherche Scientifique.
n.d.   A propos de l'architecture domestique et des documents comptables du niveau 18 de l'Acropole de Suse. Paper presented at the CNRS-NSF Joint Seminar on the Development of Complex Societies of Southwest Iran, 24–29 June 1985, Bellevaux, France.

Le Brun, Alain, and F. Vallat
1978   L'origine de l'écriture à Suse. *Cahiers de la Délégation archéologique française en Iran* 8:11–59.

Lees, G., and N. Falcon
1952   The Geographical History of the Mesopotamian Plains. *Geographical Journal* 118(1):24–39.

Le Grain, Leon
1913   Tablettes de comptabilité . . . de l'époque de la Dynastie d'Agade. *Mémoires de la Mission archéologique de Susiane* 14:62–126. Paris: Ernest Leroux.

Legros, Dominique
1977   Chance, Necessity, and Mode of Production: A Marxist Critique of Cultural Evolutionism. *American Anthropologist* 79(1):26–41.

Lepper, F. A.
1948   *Trajan's Parthian War*. London: Oxford University Press.

Le Rider, Georges
1965   Suse sous les Seleucides et les Parthes: Les Trouvailles Monétaires et l'histoire de la ville. *Mémoires de la Mission archéologique en Iran* 30. Paris: Paul Geuthner.

Lerner, Judith A.
1976   Sasanian Seals in the Department of Medieval and Later Antiquities of the British Museum. *Journal of Near Eastern Studies* 35(3):183–87.

Levine, Louis D.
1972   *Two Neo-Assyrian Stelae from Iran*. Toronto: Royal Ontario Museum.
1973–   Geographical Studies in the Neo-Assyrian Zagros.
74   *Iran* 11:1–27; *Iran* 12:99–124.
1974   Archaeological Investigations in the Mahidasht, Western Iran, 1975. *Paléorient* 2:487–90.
1975a   The Mahidasht Project. *Iran* 14:160–61.
1976a   Survey in the Province of Kermanshah 1975: Mahidasht in the Prehistoric and Early Historic Periods. *Proceedings of the 4th Annual Symposium on Archaeological Research in Iran* 4:284–297. Tehran: Iranian Centre for Archaeological Research.
1976b   The Mahidasht Project. *Iran* 14:160–61.
1977a   Sargon's Eighth Campaign. In *Mountains and Lowlands: Essays in the Archaeology of Greater Mesopotamia*, ed. Louis D. Levine. Malibu: Undena.
1977b   East-West Trade in the Late Iron Age: A View from the Zagros. In *Le plateau iranien et l'Asie Centrale des origines à la conquête islamique*, 171–86. Paris: Centre National de la Recherche Scientifique.

Levine, Louis D., and Carol Hamlin (Kramer)
1974   The Godin Project: Seh Gabi. *Iran* 12:211–13.

Levine, Louis D., and Mary A. McDonald
1977   The Neolithic and Chalcolithic Periods in the Mahidasht. *Iran* 15:39–50.

Lewarch, Dennis E.
1977   Locational Models and the Archaeological Study of Complex Societies. Paper presented at the 76th Annual Meeting of the American Anthropological Association, 1 Dec. 1977, Houston.

Lewarch, Dennis E., and Michael J. O'Brien
1981 The Expanding Role of Surface Assemblages in Archaeological Research. In *Advances in Archaeological Method and Theory*, vol. 4, ed. M. B. Schiffer. New York: Academic Press.

Lloyd, Seton
1947 The Oldest City: A Pre-Sumerian Temple Discovered at Prehistoric Eridu. *Illustrated London News* May 31:581–83.
1948 The Oldest City of Sumeria: Establishing the Origins of Eridu. *Illustrated London News* Sept. 11:303–5.

Lloyd, S., and F. Safar
1947 Eridu: Preliminary Communication on the First Season's Excavations: January–March 1947. *Sumer* 3:84–111.

Loftus, William Kennett
1857 *Travels and Researches in Chaldaea and Susiana.* New York: Robert Carter and Bros.

Malek Shamirzadeh, Shapour
1977 Tepe Zagheh: A Sixth Millennium B.C. Village in the Qazvin Plain of the Central Iranian Plateau. Ph.D. diss., University of Pennsylvania.

Malecki, Edward J.
1975 Examining Change in Rank-Size Systems of Cities. *The Professional Geographer* 27(1):43–47.

Maleki Yolande
1964 Une fouille en Luristan. *Iranica Antiqua* 2:1–35.

Mallowan, M. E. L.
1971 The Early Dynastic Period in Mesopotamia. In *Cambridge Ancient History* I/2:238–314, ed. I. E. S. Edwards, C. J. Gadd, and N. G. L. Hammond. Cambridge: Cambridge University Press.

Mallowan, M. E. L., and J. C. Rose
1933 Excavations at Tall Arpachiyah, 1933. *Iraq* 2:1–178.

Markwart, Josef
1901 Eranshahr nach der Geographie des Ps. Moses Xorenac'i. *Abhandlungen der Kön. Gesellschaft der Wissenschaften zu Göttingen, Philhist. Klasse*, n.s. 3, no. 2.
1931 *A Catalogue of the Provincial Capitals of Eranshahr*, ed. Giuseppe Messina. Rome: Pontificio Instituto Biblico.

Marquardt, W. H.
1978 Advances in Archaeological Seriation. In *Advances in Archaeological Method and Theory.* Vol. 1, ed. M. B. Schiffer. New York: Academic Press.

Marx, Karl
1965 *Pre-Capitalist Economic Formations.* Trans. and ed. Jack Cohen. New York: E. J. Hobsbawon, International Publishers.
1973 *Grundrisse. Foundations of the Critique of Political Economy* [1857–58]. New York: Vintage Books.

Maurer, K. R.
1978 *Final Report on an Archaeological Survey of the Damghan Area.* Mimeographed manuscript.

1981 The Partho-Sassanian Frontier: Settlement in Northeast Iran. Paper presented at the Annual Meeting of the Society for American Archaeology, Philadelphia.
n.d. Rural Economic Integration in Sassanian Iran. Mimeographed manuscript.

May, D. A., and D. M. Heer
1968 Son Survivorship, Motivation and Family Size in India: A Computer Simulation. *Population Studies* 22:199–210.

Mayhew, Bruce H., and R. L. Levinger
1976 On the Emergence of Oligarchy in Human Interaction. *American Journal of Sociology* 81:1017–49.

McCown, D. E.
1942 *The Comparative Stratigraphy of Early Iran.* Studies in Ancient Oriental Civilization no. 23, Oriental Institute. Chicago: University of Chicago Press.

McDonald, Mary M. A.
1979 An Examination of Mid-Holocene Settlement Patterns in the Central Zagros Region of Western Iran. Ph.D. diss., University of Toronto.

Meadow, R. H.
1983 The Vertebrate Faunal Remains from Hasanlu Period X at Hajji Firuz Tepe. In *Hajji Firuz Tepe, Iran: The Neolithic Settlement*, University Museum Monograph 50, appendix G:369–422. University Museum, University of Pennsylvania.

Mecquenem, Roland de
1910 Compte-rendu sommaire des fouilles à Suse 1909–1910. *Bulletin de la Délégation en Perse*, Facs. 1. Paris: Ernest Leroux.
1912 Catalogue de la céramique peinte susienne conservée à Musée du Louvre. *Mémoires de la Délégation en Perse* 13:105–58. Paris: Ernest Leroux.
1928 Notes sur la céramique peinte archaique en Perse. *Mémoires de la Mission archéologique Perse* 20:99–132. Paris: Ernest Leroux.
1935 Fouilles préhistoriques en Asie Occidentale: 1931–1934. *L'Anthropologie* 45:93–104.
1938 Fouilles préhistoriques en Asie Occidentale: 1934–1937. *L'Anthropologie* 48:55–71.
1943 Fouilles de Suse, 1933–1939. *Mémoires de la Mission archéologique en Iran* 29:1–161. Paris: Ernest Leroux.

Mecquenem, Roland de, G. Contenau, R. Pfister, and N. Belaiew
1943 Archéologie Susienne. *Mémoires de la Mission archéologique en Iran* 29. Paris: Presses Universitaires.

Meier, R. L.
1972 Communications Stress. *Annual Review of Ecology and Systematics* 3:289–314.

Meldgaard, J., P. Mortensen, and H. Thrane
1963 Excavations at Tappeh Guran. *Acta Archaeologica* 34:97–133.

Mellaart, James
1967 *Catal Hüyük: A Neolithic Town in Anatolia.* New York: McGraw-Hill.

1975a *The Neolithic of the Near East.* New York: Charles Scribner's Sons.

1975b The Origins and Development of Cities in the Near East. In *Janus Essays in Ancient and Modern Studies,* ed. L. L. Orlin. Ann Arbor: University of Michigan.

1979 Egyptian and Near Eastern Chronology: A Dilemma? *Antiquity* 53:6–18.

1980 James Mellaart Replies to His Critics. *Antiquity* 54:225–27.

Merpert, N. Y., and R. M. Munchaev

1971– Early Agricultural Settlements in Northern Meso-
72 potamia. *Soviet Anthropology and Archaeology* 10:203–52.

1973 Early Agricultural Settlements in the Sinjar Plain, Northern Iraq. *Iraq* 35:93–113.

1976 Evidence about Ancient Farming Settlements in North Mesopotamia Obtained by the Soviet Expedition. *Proceedings of the 9th International Congress of Prehistoric and Protohistoric Sciences.* Reports and Communications by Archaeologists of the USSR, 58–67. Prepublication multilith.

Merpert, N. Y., R. M. Munchaev, and N. Bader

1976 The Investigations of the Soviet Expedition in Iraq, 1973. *Sumer* 32:25–61.

Middleton, John, and David Tait

1958 *Tribes Without Rulers.* London: Routledge and Kegan Paul.

Miller, George A.

1956 The Magical Number Seven, Plus or Minus Two: Some Limits on Our Capacity for Processing Information. *Psychological Review* 63:81–97.

Miller, Naomi

1977 Preliminary Report on the Botanical Remains from Tepe Jaffarabad, 1969–1974 Campaigns. *Cahiers de la Délégation archéologique française en Iran* 7:49–53.

1983 Paleoethnobotanical Results from Bendebal and Jaffarabad. *Cahiers de la Délégation archéologique française en Iran* 13:277–84.

Miller, Naomi, and T. L. Smart

1984 Intentional Burning of Dung as Fuel: A Mechanism for the Incorporation of Charred Seeds into the Archaeological Record. *Journal of Ethnobiology* 4:15–28.

Miller, Roy Andrew

1957 *Accounts of Western Nations in the History of the Northern Chou Dynasty.* East Asian Studies, Institute of International Studies, University of California, Chinese Dynastic Histories Translations no. 6. Berkeley and Los Angeles: University of California Press.

Miroschedji, Pierre de

1971 Poteries élamites du Fars oriental. *Bastan Chenassi va Honar-e Iran* 7/8:60–67. Tehran: Iranian Centre for Archaeological Research.

1973 Prospections archéologique dans les vallées de Fasa et de Darab. *Proceedings of the 1st Annual Symposium on Archaeological Research in Iran, 1972*

1:1–7. Tehran: Iranian Centre for Archaeological Research.

1974 Tepe Jalyan, une necropole du IIIe millénaire av. J.C. au Fars oriental (Iran). *Arts Asiatiques* 30.

1978 Stratigraphie de la période néo-élamite de Suse (c. 1110–c. 540). *Paléorient* 4:213–27.

1980 Le dieu élamite Napirisha. *Revue d'assyriologie* 74:129–43.

1981a Fouilles du chantier Ville Royale II à Suse (1975–77). I. Les niveaux élamites. *Cahiers de la Délégation archéologique française en Iran* 12:9–136.

1981b Observations dans les couches neo-élamites au nord-ouest du Tell de la Ville Royale à Suse. *Cahiers de la Délégation archéologique française en Iran* 12:143–68.

1981c Prospections archéologiques au Khuzistan en 1977. *Cahiers de la Délégation archéologique française en Iran* 12:169–92.

1982 Notes sur la glyptique de la fin de l'Elam. *Revue d'assyriologie* 76:51–63.

Moore, A. M. T.

1975 The Excavation at Tel Abu Hureyra in Syria. *Proceedings of the Prehistoric Society* 41:50–77.

1982 Agricultural Origins in the Near East: A Model for the 1980's. *World Archaeology* 14:225–37.

1985 The Development of Neolithic Societies in the Near East. *Advances in World Archaeology* 4: 1–69.

Moore, James A.

1983 The Trouble with Know-it-alls: Information as a Social and Ecological Resource. In *Archaeological Hammers and Theories,* ed. James A. Moore and Arthur S. Keene. New York: Academic Press.

Moorey, P. R. S.

1971 Towards a Chronology for the "Luristan Bronzes". *Iran* 9:113–30.

Moortgat, A.

1966 *Vorderasiatische Rollziegel: Ein Beitrag zur Geschichte der Steinschneidekunst.* Berlin: Gebr. Mann Verlag.

Morey, R. M.

1974 *Continuous Subsurface Profiling by Impulse Radar.* Proceedings of Engineering Foundation Conference on "Subsurface Exploration for Underground Excavation and Heavy Construction," August 1974, Henniker, New Hampshire, American Society of Civil Engineers.

Morgan, Jacques de

1895a Etudes géologiques, géologie stratigraphique. *Mémoires de la Délégation en Perse* 3.

1895b Cartes des rives méridionales de la Mer Caspienne du Kurdistan, du Moukri et d'Elam. *Mission Scientifique en Perse* 1:750.

1900 Etude géographique sur la Susiane. *Mémoires de la Délégation en Perse.* Paris: Ernest Leroux.

1906 *Les recherches archéologiques.* Paris: Ernest Leroux.

1912 Observations sur les Couches profondes de l'Acropole de Suse. *Mémoires de la Délégation en Perse* 13:1–25. Paris: Ernest Leroux.

1913 Feudalism in Persia: Its Origin, Development, and

Present Condition. *Smithsonian Institute Report for 1913,* 579–606.

1927   *La Préhistoire Orientale.* Vol. 3, *L'Asie Antérieure.* Paris: Paul Geuthner.

Morony, Michael Gregory
1972   Transition and Continuity in Seventh-Century Iraq. Ph.D. diss., University of California, Los Angeles.
1974   Religious Communities in Late Sasanian and Early Muslim Iraq. *Journal of the Economic and Social History of the Orient* 17(2):113–45.
1984   *Iraq after the Muslim Conquest.* Princeton: Princeton University Press.

Mortensen, Peder
1963   Early Village Occupation: Excavations at Tepe Guran, Luristan. *Acta Archaeologica* 34:110–21.
1964   Additional Remarks on the Chronology of Early Village Farming Communities in the Zagros Area. *Sumer* 20:28–36.
1972   Seasonal Camps and Early Villages in the Zagros. In *Man, Settlement and Urbanism,* ed. P. Ucko, R. Tringham, and G. W. Dimbleby. London: Duckworth.
1974a   A Survey of Early Prehistoric Sites in the Holailan Valley in Lorestan. *Proceedings of the 2nd Annual Symposium on Archaeological Research in Iran* 2:34–52. Tehran: Iranian Centre for Archaeological Research.
1974b   A Survey of Prehistoric Settlements in Northern Luristan. *Acta Archaeologica* 45:1–47.
1975   Survey and Soundings in the Holailan Valley, 1974. *Proceedings of the 3rd Annual Symposium on Archaeological Research in Iran* 3:1–12. Tehran: Iranian Centre for Archaeological Research.
1976   Chalcolithic Settlements in the Holailan Valley. *Proceedings of the 4th Annual Symposium on Archaeological Research in Iran* 4:42–62. Tehran: Iranian Centre for Archaeological Research.
1979   *The Holailan Survey: A Note on the Relationship between Aims and Method.* Akten des VII Internationalen Kongresses für Iranische Kunst und Archäologie, Munich, 7–10 Sept. 1976, Archäologische Mitteilungen aus Iran, Ergänzungsband 6. Berlin: Dietrich Reimer.
1983   Patterns of Interaction between Seasonal Settlements and Early Villages in Mesopotamia. In *The Hilly Flanks and Beyond* ed. T. C. Young, Jr., Philip E. L. Smith, and Peder Mortensen [q.v.], 207–30.

Mortensen, Peder, and Kent V. Flannery
1966   *En af Verdens Aeldste Landsbyer.* Copenhagen: Nationalmuseets Arbejdsmark.

Mueller, James W., ed.
1975   *Sampling in Archaeology.* Tucson: University of Arizona Press.

Munn-Rankin, Margaret
1980   Mesopotamian Chronology: A Reply to James Mellaart. *Antiquity* 54:128–29.

Munnich, K. O.
1957   Heidelberg Natural Radiocarbon Measurements I. *Science* 126:194–99.

Muscarella, Oscar White
1973   Excavations at Agrab Tepe. *Metropolitan Museum Journal* 8:47–76.
1974   The Iron Age at Dinkha Tepe, Iran. *Metropolitan Museum Journal* 9:35–90.
1977   "Ziwiye" and Ziwiye: The Forgery of a Provenience. *Journal of Field Archaeology* 4:197–219.

Nagel, Wolfram
1964   Djamdat Nasr Kulturen und Früh-Dynastische Buntkeramiker. *Berliner Beiträge zur Vor- und Frühgeschichte* 8. Berlin: Bruno Hessling.
1969   Giyan Tepe. *Reallexicon für Assyriologie* 3:405–7.

Naroll, Raoul
1956   A Preliminary Index of Social Development. *American Anthropologist* 58:687–715.
1962   Floor Area and Settlement Population. *American Antiquity* 27:587–89.

Naroll, Raoul, and Ludwig von Bertanlanffy
1956   The Principle of Allometry in Biology and the Social Sciences. *General Systems* 1:76–89.

Neely, James A.
1969   Preliminary Report on the Archaeological Survey of Deh Luran. In *Preliminary Reports of the Rice University Project in Iran, 1968–1969,* ed. Frank Hole. Houston: Rice University Department of Anthropology.
1970   The Deh Luran Region. *Iran* 8:202–3.
1974   Sassanian and Early Islamic Water-Control and Irrigation Systems on the Deh Luran Plain, Iran. In *Irrigation's Impact on Society,* ed. T. E. Downing and M. Gibson. Tucson: University of Arizona Press.

Negahban, Ezat O.
1969   Haft Tepe. *Iran* 7:173–77.
1971   Excavations at Sagz-Abad and Zaghe. Symposium, Tehran University, June 1971.
1972   Brief General Report of the Third Season of Excavation at Haft Tepe. *Fifth International Congress of Iranian Art and Archaeology* 1:153–62.
1979   A Brief Report on the Painted Building of Zaghe. *Paléorient* 5:239–50.

Neusner, Jacob
1963   Parthian Political Ideology. *Iranica Antiqua* 3(1):40–59.

Nezam-Mafi, M.
1962   *Une région agricole de l'Iran, le Khouzistan.* Lausanne: Librairie Payot.

Nicholas, Irene
1980   A Spatial/Functional Analysis of "Proto Elamite" Occupations at the TUV Operation, Tall-i Malyan, Iran. Ph.D. diss., University of Pennsylvania.

Nickerson, John L.
1983   Intrasite Variability during the Kaftari Period at Tal-e Malyan (Anshan). Ph.D. diss., Ohio State University.

Nicol, Murray B.
1970   Excavations at Darvazeh Tepe: A Preliminary Report. *Bastan Chenassi va Honar-e Iran* 5:19–22.

Nissen, H. J.
1970   Grabung in den Quadraten K/L XII in Uruk-War-ka. *Baghdader Mitteilungen* 5:102–91.
1974   Südbabylonien in parthischer und sasanidischer Zeit. *Baghdader Mitteilungen* 6:79–86.
1983   Political Organization and Settled Zone: A Case Study from the Ancient Near East. In *The Hilly Flanks and Beyond,* ed. T. C. Young, Jr., Philip E. L. Smith, and Peder Mortensen [q.v.], 335–45.

Nissen, H. J., and A. Zagarell
1976   Expedition to the Zagros Mountains, 1975. *Proceedings of the 4th Annual Symposium on Archaeological Research in Iran* 4:159–89. Tehran: Iranian Centre for Archaeological Research.

Nodelman, S. A.
1960   A Preliminary History of Characene. *Berytus* 13:83–121.

Nöldeke, T., trans. and ed.
1973   *Geschichte der Perser und Araber zur Zeit der Sasaniden: Aus der Arabischen Chronik des Tabari.* Reprint of the 1879 edition, E. J. Brill: Leiden. Graz: Akademische Druck- und Verlagsanstalt.

Norbeck, Stig
1971   Urban Allometric Growth. *Geografiska Annaler 53* (B#1):54–67.

Oates, David, and Joan Oates
1976a   *The Rise of Civilization.* Oxford: Elsevier-Phaidon.
1976b   Early Irrigation Agriculture in Mesopotamia. In *Problems in Economic and Social Archaeology,* ed. G. Sieveking, I. H. Longworth, and K. E. Wilson. London: Duckworth.

Oates, Joan
1968   Prehistoric Investigations near Mandali, Iraq. *Iraq* 30:1–20.
1969   Choga Mami 1967–68: A Preliminary Report. *Iraq* 31:115–52.
1972a   A Radiocarbon Date from Choga Mami. *Iraq* 34:49–53.
1972b   Prehistoric Settlement Patterns in Mesopotamia. In *Man, Settlement and Urbanism,* ed. P. J. Ucko, R. Tringham, and G. W. Dimbleby. London: Duckworth.
1973   The Background and Development of Early Farming Communities in Mesopotamia and the Zagros. *Proceedings of the Prehistoric Society* 39:147–81.
1983   Ubaid Mesopotamia Reconsidered. In *The Hilly Flanks,* ed. T. C. Young, Philip E. L. Smith, and Peder Mortensen [q.v.], 251–81.

Oates, Joan, T. E. Davidson, D. Kamilli, and H. McKerrell
1977   Seafaring Merchants of Ur? *Antiquity* 51:221–34.

Oberlander, Theodore
1965   *The Zagros Streams.* Syracuse Geographical Series no. 1. Syracuse: Syracuse University Press.

Olsson, Gunnar
1965   Distance and Human Interaction: A Review and Bibliography. *Bibliography Series No. 2.* Philadelphia: Regional Science Institute.

Oppenheim, A. L.
1967   *Letters from Mesopotamia.* Chicago: University of Chicago Press.

Orlove, Benjamin S.
1980   Ecological Anthropology. *Annual Review of Anthropology* 9:235–73.

Parsons, Jeffrey R.
1971   *Prehistoric Settlement Patterns in the Texcoco Region, Mexico.* Memoir no. 3. Ann Arbor: University of Michigan Museum of Anthropology.

Paynter, Robert
1982   *Models of Spatial Inequality: Settlement Patterns in Historical Archaeology.* New York: Academic Press.
1983   Expanding the Scope of Settlement Analysis. In *Archaeological Hammers and Theories,* ed. James A. Moore and Arthur S. Keene. New York: Academic Press.

Pearson, Charles E.
1980   Rank-Size Distributions and the Analysis of Prehistoric Settlement Systems. *Journal of Anthropological Research* 36(4):453–62.

Pecirkova, Jana
1975   Recent Views on the Emergence and Character of the Earliest States in Southern Mesopotamia. *Archiv Orientalni* 43:131–45.

Perrot, Jean
1971   Les recherches à Djaffarabad et dans les couches profondes de l'Acropole de Suse. *Cahiers de la Délégation archéologique française en Iran* 1:13–15. Paris: Paul Geuthner.
1978   Introduction to the Susa Conference. *Paléorient* 4.

Pezard, Maurice
1914   Mission à Bender-Bouchir. *Mémoires de la Délégation en Perse* 15:1–103.

Pierre, L.
1917   Map of the Dizful-Shushtar-Shush Area. Prepared by the Basrah Survey Party, Indian Expeditionary Force D.

Pigulevskaja, Nina
1963   *Les villes de l'état iranien aux époques parthe et sassanide.* Ecole Pratique des Hautes Etudes, Sorbonne VI Section, Documents et Recherches no. 6. Paris and The Hague: Mouton.

Piperno, Marcello
1972   Jahrom: A Middle Palaeolithic Site in Fars, Iran. *East and West* n.s. 22(3/4):183–97.
1974   Upper Palaeolithic Caves in Southern Iran: Preliminary Report. *East and West* n.s. 24(3/4):9–13.

Pires-Ferreira, Jane Wheeler
1975   Table of Identification of Bone Tools. *Cahiers de la Délégation archéologique française en Iran* 5:67, appendix 2.
1977   Tepe Tula'i: Faunal Remains from an Early Campsite in Khuzistan, Iran. *Paléorient* 3:275–80.

Plog, Stephen
1976   Measurement of Prehistoric Interaction between

Communities. In *The Early Mesoamerican Village*, ed. Kent V. Flannery. New York: Academic Press.

n.d.   The Evolution of Social Networks in the American Southwest. Paper presented at the 45th Annual Meeting of the Society for American Archaeology, Philadelphia, 1980.

Polgar, Steven, ed.
1975   *Population, Ecology and Social Evolution*. Ninth International Congress of Anthropological and Ethnological Sciences, Chicago, 1973. The Hague: Mouton.

Pollock, Susan
1983   Style and Information: An Analysis of Susiana Ceramics. *Journal of Anthropological Archaeology* 2(4):354–90.

Polybius
1959   History. In *The Portable Greek Historians*. New York: Viking Press.

Pope, Arthur Upham
1936   A Note on Some Pottery from the Holmes Luristan Expedition of the Institute. *Bulletin of the American Institute of Persian Art and Archaeology* 4(3):120–25.

Porada, Edith
1965a   *The Art of Ancient Iran: Pre-Islamic Cultures*. New York: Crown Publishers.
1965b   *Ancient Iran: The Art of Pre-Islamic Times*. London: Methuen.

Postgate, Nicholas
1977   *The First Empires*. Oxford: Elsevier.

Potts, Thomas P.
1982   The Zagros Frontier and the Problem of the Relations between the Iranian Plateau and Southern Mesopotamia in the Third Milennium B.C. In *Mesopotamien und seine Nachbarn*, ed. H-J. Nissen and J. Renger, Berliner Beiträge zum Vorderen Orient 1.

Price, B. J.
1982   Cultural Materialism: A Theoretical Review. *American Antiquity* 47:709–41.

Pritchard, James B., ed.
1958   *The Ancient Near East: An Anthology of Texts and Pictures*. Princeton: Princeton University Press.

Protsch, R., and R. Berger
1973   Earliest Radiocarbon Dates for Domesticated Animals. *Science* 179:235–39.

Pugh, D. S., J. J. Hickson, C. R. Hinings, and C. Turner
1968   Dimensions of Organization Structure. *Administrative Science Quarterly* 13:65–105.

Pullar, Judith
1975   The Neolithic of the Iranian Zagros. Ph.D. diss., University of London.
1977   Early Cultivation in the Zagros. *Iran* 15:15–37.

Pyne, Nanette
1982   The Impact of the Seljuq Invasion on Khuzestan: An Inquiry into the Historical, Geographical, Numismatic, and Archaeological Evidence. Ph.D. diss., University of Washington.

Ralph, Elizabeth K.
1959   University of Pennsylvania Radiocarbon Dates III. *Radiocarbon* 1:45–58.

Ralph, Elizabeth K., H. N. Michael, and M. C. Han
1973   Radiocarbon Dates and Reality. *MASCA Newsletter* 9(1).

Randsborg, Klaus
1974   Social Stratification in Early Bronze Age Denmark. *Prähistorische Zeitschrift* 49:38–61.
1982   Theoretical Approaches to Social Change: An Archaeological Viewpoint. In *Theory and Explanation in Archaeology: The Southampton Conference*, ed. Colin Renfrew, Michael J. Rowlands, and Barbara Abbott Segraves. New York: Academic Press.

Rapaport, Anatol
1968   Rank-Size Relations. In *International Encyclopedia of the Social Sciences*, 13:319–23, ed. David Sills. New York: Macmillan.

Rawlinson, Henry C.
1839   Notes on a March from Zohab . . . to Khuzistan, and Thence through the Province of Luristan to Kermanshah. *Journal of the Royal Geographical Society* 9:26–116.
1875   *The Seventh Great Oriental Monarchy*. vol. 1. New York: Dodd, Mead and Co.

Reade, Julian
1978   Kassites and Assyrians in Iran. *Iran* 16:137–43.

Redding, R. W.
1981   The Faunal Remains. In *An Early Town on the Deh Luran Plain*. Memoir no. 13, ed. Henry Wright. Ann Arbor: University of Michigan Museum of Anthropology.

Redman, Charles
1978   *The Rise of Civilization*. San Francisco: W. H. Freeman.

Redman, Charles, and Patty J. Watson
1970   Systematic, Intensive Surface Collection. *American Antiquity* 35:279–91.

Reed, C. A., ed.
1977a   *Origins of Agriculture*. The Hague: Mouton.

Reed, C. A.
1977b   A Model for the Origins of Agriculture in the Near East. In *Origins of Agriculture*, ed. C. A. Reed. The Hague: Mouton.

Reiner, Erica
1972   Tall-i-Malyan, Inscribed Material. *Iran* 10:210.
1973   Inscription from a Royal Elamite Tomb. *Archiv für Orientforschung* 24:87–102.

Renfrew, Colin
1973   *Before Civilization*. New York: Knopf.
1974   Beyond a Subsistence Economy: The Evolution of Social Organization in Prehistoric Europe. In *Reconstructing Complex Societies*, ed. Charlotte Moore. Boston: MIT Press.
1975   Trade as Action at a Distance: Questions of Integration and Communication. In *Ancient Civilization*

and Trade, ed. Jeremy Sabloff and C. C. Lamberg-Karlovsky. Albuquerque: University of New Mexico Press.

1977   The Later Obsidian of Deh Luran: The Evidence of Chagha Sefid. In *Studies in the Archaeological History of the Deh Luran Plain*. Memoir no. 1, ed. Frank Hole. Ann Arbor: University of Michigan Museum of Anthropology.

1978   Space, Time and Polity. In *The Evolution of Social Systems*, ed. J. Friedman and M. J. Rowlands. Pittsburgh: University of Pittsburgh Press.

1982   Socio-economic Change in Ranked Societies. In *Ranking, Resource and Exchange*, ed. C. Renfrew and S. Sherman. Cambridge: Cambridge University Press.

Renfrew, Colin, and J. E. Dixon
1976   Obsidian in Western Asia—A Review. In *Problems in Economics and Social Anthropology*, ed. I. H. Longworth, G. Sieveking, and K. E. Wilson. London: Duckworth.

Renfrew, Colin, and S. Shennan, eds.
1982   *Ranking, Resource and Exchange*. Cambridge: Cambridge University Press.

Ricciardi, R.
1973–   Trial Trench of Tell Baruda. *Mesopotamia* 7–
74   9:15–20.

Richardson, Harry W.
1973   Theory of the Distribution of City Sizes: Review and Prospects. *Regional Studies* 7:239–51.

1977   City Size and National Spatial Strategies in Developing Countries. *World Bank Staff Working Paper* 252.

Roggen, M. van
1905   Notice sur les anciens travaux hydrauliques en Susiane. *Mémoires de la Délégation en Perse* 7:166–207.

Rosen-Ayalon, M.
1971   Islamic Pottery from Susa. *Archaeology* 24(3):204–8.

1974   Niveaux islamiques de la Ville-Royale. *Cahiers de la Délégation archéologique française en Iran* 2:169–201.

Rostovtzeff, M.
1932   *Seleucid Babylonia: Bullae and Seals of Clay with Greek Inscriptions*. Yale Classical Studies no. 3. New Haven: Yale University Press.

Roux, George
1964   *Ancient Iraq*. Cleveland: World Publishing Company.

Rowton, Michael B.
1967   Chronology IV: Babylonian and Assyrian. *Encyclopaedia Britannica* 5:724–25.

1970   Chronology: Ancient Western Asia. In *The Cambridge Ancient History*, I/1, ed. I. E. S. Edwards, C. J. Gadd, and N. G. L. Hammond. Cambridge: Cambridge University Press.

1973a   Autonomy and Nomadism in Western Asia. *Orientalia* 42:247–58.

1973b   Urban Autonomy in a Nomadic Environment. *Journal of Near Eastern Studies* 32:201–15.

1974   Enclosed Nomadism. *Journal of the Economic and Social History of the Orient* 17:1–30.

1976a   Dimorphic Structure and the Tribal Elite. *Studia Instituti Anthropos* 28:219–57.

1976b   Dimorphic Structure and Topology. *Oriens Antiquus* 15:17–31.

1976c   Dimorphic Structure and the Problem of the 'Apiru-'Ibrim. *Journal of Near Eastern Studies* 35:13–20.

1977   Dimorphic Structure and the Parasocial Element. *Journal of Near Eastern Studies* 36:181–98.

1980   Pastoralism and the Periphery in Evolutionary Perspective. In *L'Archéologie de l'Iraq du début de l'époque néolithique à 333 avant notre ère: Perspectives et limites de l'interprétation anthropologique des documents*. Colloques Internationaux du Centre National de la Recherche Scientifique no. 580, ed. Marie-Thérèse Barrelet. Paris: Editions du Centre National de la Recherche Scientifique.

Rueschemeyer, Dietrich
1977   Structural Differentiation, Efficiency and Power. *American Journal of Sociology* 83:1–25.

Safar, Fuad, M. A. Mustafa, and Seton Lloyd
1981   *Eridu*. Baghdad: Republic of Iraq Ministry of Culture and Information, State Organization of Antiquities and Heritage.

Sahlins, Marshall
1972   *Stone Age Economics*. Chicago: Aldine.

Sahlins, Marshall, and Elman Service
1960   *Evolution and Culture*. Ann Arbor: University of Michigan Press.

Sajjidi, Mansur
1979   The Proto-Elamite Period on the Izeh Plain. In *Archaeological Investigations in Northeastern Xuzistan, 1976*, ed. Henry T. Wright [q.v.].

Salmon, M.
1978   What Can Systems Theory Do for Archaeology? *American Antiquity* 43(2):174–83.

Salonen, Erkki
1962   *Untersuchungen zur Schrift und Sprache des Altbabylonischen von Susa*. Studia Orientalia 27, no. 1. Helsinki: Edidit Societas Orientalis Fennica.

Sancisi-Weerdenburg, H.
1985   What about the Median Empire? *Papers of the Fifth Achaemenid History Workshop*. London, 31 May–1 June 1985.

Sanders, William T., Jeffrey R. Parsons, and Robert S. Santley
1979   *The Basin of Mexico: Ecological Processes in the Evolution of a Civilization*. New York: Academic Press.

Sanders, William T., and David Webster
1978   Unilinealism, Multilinealism, and the Evolution of Complex Societies. In *Social Anthropology: Beyond Subsistence and Dating*, ed. Charles E. Redman et al. New York: Academic Press.

Santley, R. S.
1974 The Painted Pottery from Tepe Siahbid: A Study in Ceramic Technology and Ecology. M.A. thesis, Department of Anthropology, Penn State University.

Sarianidi, V. I.
1971 The Lapis-Lazuli Route in the Ancient East. *Archaeology* 24:12–15.

Sato, Jun, Tomoko Sato, Yasuki Otomori, and Hisashi Suzuki
1969 University of Tokyo Radiocarbon Measurements II. *Radiocarbon* 11:509–14.

Schacht, Robert M.
1973 Population and Economic Organization in Early Historic Southwestern Iran. Ph.D. diss., University of Michigan.
1975a A Preliminary Report on the Excavations at Tepe Sharafabad, 1971. *Journal of Field Archaeology* 2:307–29.
1975b Population Changes in Early Southwest Iran. Paper presented at AAA meeting, 1975; revised March 1976.
1976 Some Notes on the Development of Rural Settlement on the Susiana Plain. *Proceedings of the 4th Annual Symposium on Archaeological Research in Iran, 1975* 4:446–62. Tehran: Iranian Centre for Archaeological Research.
1981 Estimating Past Population Trends. *Annual Review of Anthropology* 10:119–40.
n.d.a The Contemporaneity Problem. Unpublished manuscript.
n.d.b Susiana Site Survey Index. Computer data file available from the author.

Schaeffer, Claude F. A.
1948 *Stratigraphie comparée et chronologie de l'Asie Occidentale (IIIe et IIe millénaires).* London: Oxford University Press.

Scheil, Vincent J.
1908 Textes élamites-semitiques, Quatrième Série. *Mémoires de la Délégation en Perse* 10. Paris: Ernest Leroux.
1929 Inscription d'Adda-Baksu. *Revue d'assyriologie* 26:1–7.
1939 Melanges epigraphiques. *Mémoires de la Mission archéologique Perse* 28. Paris: Ernest Leroux.

Schippmann, Klaus
1971 *Die iranischen Feuerheiligtümer.* Berlin: Walter de Gruyter.

Schmandt-Besserat, Denise
1977 An Archaic Recording System and the Origin of Writing. *Syro-Mesopotamian Studies* 1:31–70.
1979 An Archaic Recording System in the Uruk-Jemdet Nasr Period. *American Journal of Archaeology* 83(1):19–48.
1980 The Envelopes That Bear the First Writing. *Technology and Culture* 21:357–85.

Schmidt, Eric F.
1940 *Flights over Ancient Iran.* Chicago: University of Chicago Press.

Schwarz, Paul
1896 *Iran im Mittelalter nach den arabischen Geographen.* Vol. 1. Leipzig: Wilhelm Heims.
1921 *Iran im Mittelalter nach den arabischen Geographen.* Vol. 4. Leipzig: Wilhelm Heims.

Sellwood, David G.
1971 *Introduction to the Coinage of Parthia.* London: Spink and Son.
1976 The Drachms of the Parthian "Dark Age". *Journal of the Royal Asiatic Society* 1:2–25.

Service, Elman R.
1962 *Primitive Social Organization.* New York: Random House.
1975 *The Origins of the State and Civilization.* New York: W. W. Norton.

Shahideh, Elaheh
1979 The Archaic Period on the Izeh Plain. In *Archaeological Investigations in Northeastern Xuzistan,* ed. Henry T. Wright [q.v.].

Shakhs, Salah El-
1972 Development, Primacy, and Systems of Cities. *Journal of Developing Areas* 7:11–35.

Simon, H. A.
1955 On a Class of Skew Distribution Functions. *Biometrika* 42:425–40.

Skinner, G. William
1977a Regional Urbanization in Nineteenth-Century China. In *The City in Late Imperial China,* ed. G. William Skinner. Stanford: Stanford University Press.
1977b Cities and the Hierarchy of Local Systems. In *The City in Late Imperial China,* ed. G. William Skinner. Stanford: Stanford University Press.

Smith, C. A.
1976 Regional Economic Systems: Linking Geographic Models and Socioeconomic Models. In *Regional Analysis.* Vol. 1, *Economic Systems,* ed. C. A. Smith. New York: Academic Press.

Smith, Philip E. L.
1967 Ghar-i Khar and Ganj-i Dareh. *Iran* 5:138–39.
1968 Ganj Dareh Tepe. *Iran* 6:158–60.
1970 Ganj Dareh Tepe. *Iran* 8:174–76.
1971 Iran, 9000–4000 B.C.: The Neolithic. *Expedition* 13:6–13.
1972a Ganj Dareh Tepe. *Iran* 10:165–68.
1972b Prehistoric Excavations at Ganj Dareh Tepe in 1967. The Memorial Volume, 5th International Congress of Iranian Art and Archaeology 1968, 1:183–93.
1972c Land-use, Settlement Patterns and Subsistence Agriculture: A Demographic Perspective. In *Man, Settlement and Urbanism,* ed. P. J. Ucko, R. Tringham, and G. W. Dimbleby. London: Duckworth.
1974 Ganj Dareh Tepe. *Paléorient* 2:207–9.
1975 Ganj Dareh Tepe. *Iran* 13:178–80.
1976a *Food Production and Its Consequences.* Menlo Park, Calif.: Cummings.
1976b Reflections on Four Seasons of Excavations at Tap-

peh Ganj Dareh. *Proceedings of the 4th Annual Symposium on Archaeological Research in Iran* 4:11–22. Tehran: Iranian Centre for Archaeological Research.

Smith, Philip E. L., and P. Mortensen
1980 Three New "Early Neolithic" Sites in Western Iran. *Current Anthropology* 21:511–12.

Smith, Philip E. L., and T. Cuyler Young, Jr.
1972 The Evolution of Early Agriculture and Culture in Greater Mesopotamia: A Trial Model. In *Population Growth: Anthropological Implications,* ed. B. B. Spooner. Cambridge, Mass.: MIT Press.
1983 The Force of Numbers: Population Pressure in the Central Western Zagros 12,000–4500 B.C. In *The Hilly Flanks and Beyond,* ed. T. C. Young, Jr., Philip E. L. Smith, and Peder Mortensen [q.v.], 141–62.

Soane, E. B.
1912 *To Mesopotamia and Kurdistan in Disguise.* Boston: Maynard.

Solecki, R. L., and R. S. Solecki
1973 Tepe Seavan: A Dalma Period Site in the Margavar Valley, Azerbaijan, Iran. *Bulletin of the Asia Institute* 3:98–116.

Solecki, R. S.
1969 Survey in Western Azerbaijan. *Iran* 7:189–90.

Sollberger, Edmond
1968 A Tankard for Atta-Hushu. *Journal of Cuneiform Studies* 22:30–33.

Sollberger, Edmond, and Jean-Robert Kupper
1971 *Inscriptions royales sumeriennes et akkadiennes.* Paris: Editions du Cerf.

Sollberger, J. B., and L. W. Patterson
1983 A Pressure Method for Microblade Manufacture. *Lithic Technology* 12:25–31.

Sono, Toshihiko
1967 Recent Excavations at Tepe Gap, Marv-Dasht. In *A Survey of Persian Art,* 14:2940–46, ed. A. U. Pope and P. Ackerman. London: Oxford University Press.

Spaulding, Albert
1973 Archaeology in the Active Voice: The New Anthropology. In *Research and Theory in Current Archeology,* ed. C. L. Redman. New York: John Wiley and Sons.

Spear, Percival
1961 *India: A Modern History.* Ann Arbor: University of Michigan Press.

Spencer, H.
1883 *Social Statics.* New York: D. Appleton.

Speth, John
1971 Kunji Cave. *Iran* 13:172–73.

Speth, John, and Gregory A. Johnson
1976 Problems in the Use of Correlation for the Investigation of Tool Kits and Activity Areas. In *Culture Change and Continuity,* ed. C. Cleland. New York: Academic Press.

Spooner, B., ed.
1972 *Population Growth: Anthropological Implications.* Cambridge, Mass.: MIT Press.

Spüler, B.
1952– Geschichte der islamischen Länder. *Handbuch der*
54 *Orientalistik* vol. 6, nos. 1–2.
1954 Iran and Islam. In *Studies in Islamic Cultural History* ed. G. E. von Grunebaum; trans. I. Lichtenstadter. Menasha, Wisconsin: American Anthropological Association.

Statistical Center of Iran
1971 *Village Gazetteer.* Vol. 26, *Khuzistan.* Tehran: Iranian Statistical Center, Imperial Government of Iran.

Steel, Robert G. D., and James H. Torrie
1980 *Principles and Procedures of Statitics: A Biometrical Approach.* 2d ed. New York: McGraw-Hill.

Stein, Sir Aurel
1936 An Archaeological Tour in the Ancient Parsis. *Iraq* 3:111–230.
1937 *Archaeological Reconnaissances in North-western India and South-eastern Iran.* New York: Macmillan.
1940 *Old Routes of Western Iran.* New York: Greenwood Press.

Steinkeller, Piotr
1982 The Question of Marhashi: A Contribution to the Historical Geography of Iran in the Third Millennium B.C. *Zeitschrift für Assyriologie und Vorderasiatischen Kunst* 72:237–65.

Steponaitis, Vincas P.
1978 Location Theory and Complex Chiefdoms: A Mississippian Example. In *Mississippian Settlement Patterns,* ed. Bruce D. Smith. New York: Academic Press.

Stève, M. J.
1967 Tchoga-Zanbil (Dur Untash). Vol. III, *Textes élamites et accadiens de Tchoga Zanbil. Mémoires de la Délégation en Perse* 41.
1968 Fragmenta elamica. *Orientalia* n.s. 37:290–303.

Stève, M. J., and H. Gasche
1971 L'Acropole de Suse. *Mémoires de la Délégation archéologique en Iran* 46. Paris: Paul Geuthner.

Stève, M. J., H. Gasche, and L. de Meyer
1980 La Susiane au deuxieme millénaire: A propos d'une interprétation des fouilles de Suse. *Iranica Antiqua* 15:49–154.

Steward, Julian
1949 Cultural Causality and Law: A Trial Formulation of the Development of Early Civilizations. *American Anthropologist* 51:1–27.

Stolper, Matthew J.
1976 Preliminary Report on Texts from Tal-e Malyan. *Proceedings of the 4th Annual Symposium on Archaeological Research in Iran* 4:89–97.
1978 Inscribed Fragments from Khuzistan. *Cahiers de la*

Délégation archéologique française en Iran 8:97–108.

1982 On the Dynasty of Šimaški and the Early Sukkalmahs. *Zeitschrift für Assyriologie* 72:42–67.

1984 Political History. Part 1 in *Elam: Surveys of Political History and Archeology*, ed. E. Carter and M. W. Stolper, Near Eastern Studies 25:3–100. Berkeley: University of California Press.

Street, F. A., and A. T. Grove

1979 Global Maps of Lake Level Fluctuations Since 30,000 Years B.P. *Quaternary Research* 12:83–118.

Strommenger, Eva

1962 *Die Kleinfunde aus dem Sinkasid-Palast: Vorläufiger Bericht über die von dem Deutschen Archäologischen Institut und der Deutschen Orient-Gesellschaft aus Mitteln der Deutschen Forschungsgemeinschaft unternommenen Ausgrabungen in Uruk-Warka* 18:30–38.

1964 *5000 Years of the Art of Mesopotamia*. Trans. Christina Haglund. New York: Henry N. Abrams.

Stronach, David

1965 Excavations at Pasargadae, Third Preliminary Report. *Iran* 3:9–40.

1974 Achaemenid Village I at Susa and the Persian Migration to Fars. *Iraq* 36:239–48.

1977 Shahr-i Qumis. *Iran* 15:179.

1978 *Pasargadae*. Oxford: Clarendon Press.

Stronach, David, and Michael Roaf

1978 Excavations at Tepe Nush-i Jan: Part 1, a Third Interim Report. *Iran* 16:1–11.

Stronach, Ruth

1978 Excavations at Tepe Nush-i Jan: Part 2, Median Pottery from the Fallen Floor in the Fort. *Iran* 16:11–24.

Stuckenrath, Robert, Jr.

1963 University of Pennsylvania Radiocarbon Dates VI. *Radiocarbon* 5:82–103.

Stuckenrath, Robert, Jr., W. R. Coe, and E. K. Ralph

1966 University of Pennsylvania Radiocarbon Dates IX. *Radiocarbon* 8:348–85.

Stuckenrath, Robert, Jr., and B. Lawn

1969 University of Pennsylvania Radiocarbon Dates XI. *Radiocarbon* 11:150–62.

Stuckenrath, Robert, Jr., and Elizabeth K. Ralph

1965 University of Pennsylvania Radiocarbon Dates VIII. *Radiocarbon* 7:187–99.

Sumner, William M.

1972 Cultural Development in the Kur River Basin, Iran: An Archaeological Analysis of Settlement Patterns. Ph.D. diss., University of Pennsylvania.

1974 Excavations at Tall-i Malyan, 1971–72. *Iran* 12:155–80.

1975 An Investigation of Uruk Settlement Patterns in Susiana. *Reviews in Anthropology* 2(1):55–60.

1976 Analysis of Material from Tal-e Malyan: 1975. *Proceedings of the 4th Annual Symposium on Archaeological Research in Iran* 4:85–88.

1977 Early Settlements in Fars Province, Iran. In *Mountains and Lowlands: Essays in the Archaeology of Greater Mesopotamia*, Biblioteca Mesopotamia 291–305, ed. L. D. Levine and T. C. Young, Jr. Malibu: Undena.

1979 Estimating Population by Analogy: An Example. In *Ethnoarchaeology: Implications of Ethnography for Archaeology*, ed. Carol Kramer. New York: Columbia University Press.

1981 The Development of an Urban Settlement System in the Kur River Basin, Iran. Paper presented at the Joint U.S.S.R. Academy of Sciences/U.S. National Academy of Science Exchange Program on Central Asia.

1985 The Proto-Elamite City Wall at Tal-i Malyan. *Iran* 23:153–61.

1986 Achaemenid Settlement in the Persepolis Plain. *American Journal of Archaeology* 90:3–31.

n.d.a Early Settlements in Fars Province, Iran. Mimeographed manuscript.

n.d.b Settlement in the Kur River Basin, Iran. Mimeographed manuscript.

n.d.c Full Coverage Regional Archaeological Survey in the Near East: An Example from Iran. Paper presented at the 50th Annual Meeting, Society for American Archeology, 5 May 1985, Denver.

Sürenhagen, Dietrich

1974– Untersuchungen zur Keramikproduktion innerhalb
75 der Spät-Urukzeitlichen Siedlung Habuba Kabira-Süd in Nordsyrien. *Acta Praehistorica et Archaeologica* 5–6:43–164.

Sutherland, John W.

1975 *Systems: Analysis, Administration and Architecture*. New York: Van Nostrand-Reinhold.

Swiny, Stuart

1975 Survey in Northwest Iran, 1971. *East and West* 25(1–2):77–96.

Sykes, P.

1921 *A History of Persia*. 2d ed. London: Macmillan.

Tafazzoli, A.

1974 A List of Trades and Crafts in the Sassanian Period. *Archäologische Mitteilungen aus Iran* n.s. 7:191–96.

Tarn, W.

1951 *The Greeks in Bactria and India*. Cambridge: Cambridge University Press.

Tauber, Henrik

1968 Copenhagen Radiocarbon Dates IX. *Radiocarbon* 10:295–327.

Thomas, David Hurst

1976 *Figuring Anthropology*. New York: Holt, Rinehart and Winston.

Thrane, Henrik

1964a Archaeological Investigations in Western Luristan. *Acta Archaeologica* 35:153–69.

1964b [Tepe Guran:] The Bronze Age Occupation and Graves. *Acta Archaeologica* 34:121–33.

1968 Bronzerne fra Luristan—og et Dansk Pionerarbejde. *Nationalmuseets Arbejdsmark*, 5–26.

1970 Tepe Guran and the Luristan Bronzes. *Archaeology* 23:27–35.

Thuesen, I.
1981 Early Dynastic Pottery from Tell Razuk. In *Uch Tepe I*, ed. McG. Gibson, 28–87. Chicago: Oriental Institute.

Tobler, Waldo
1969 Satellite Confirmation of Settlement Size Coefficients. *Area* 1:30–34.

Ucko, P. J.
1969 Ethnography and Archaeological Interpretation of Funerary Remains. *World Archaeology* I(2):262–80.

Udy, Stanley H., Jr.
1970 *Work in Traditional and Modern Society*. Englewood Cliffs, New Jersey: Prentice-Hall.

Upham, Steadman
1982 *Politics and Power: An Economic and Political History of the Western Pueblo*. New York: Academic Press.

Upham, Steadman, K. G. Lightfoot, and G. M. Feinman
1981 Explaining Socially Determined Ceramic Distributions in the Prehistoric Plateau Southwest. *American Antiquity* 46(4):822–33.

Urwick, L. F.
1956 The Manager's Span of Control. *Harvard Business Review* 34:39–47.

Vallat, François
1974 Les briques inscrites de Deylam. *Proceedings of the Second Annual Symposium on Archaeological Research in Iran* 2:63–65 (Persian section).

1978 Une brique élamite de Hutelutush-Inshushinak. *Cahiers de la Délégation française en Iran* 8:97–107.

1980 *Suse et l'Elam: Recherche sur les grandes civilisations*. Mémoire no. 1. Paris: Editions ADPF.

1981 Un fragment de brique de Tepe Bormi inscrit en elamite. *Cahiers de la Délégation archéologique française en Iran* 12:193–196.

1985 Elements de géographie élamite. First draft of a paper circulated at the Joint Seminar on the Development of Complex Societies of Southwest Iran, 24–29 June 1985, Bellevaux, France.

n.d. Haft Tepe et les tablettes de Malamir. Unpublished manuscript.

n.d.a Elements de géographie élamite. Paper presented at the Joint Seminar on the Development of Complex Societies of Southwest Iran, 24–29 June 1985, Bellevaux, France.

Vallat, François, and Alain Le Brun
1982 Comment on Alden (1982). *Current Anthropology* 23:633.

Vanden Berghe, Louis
1952 Archaeologische Opzoekingen in de Marv Dasht-vlakte. *Jaarbericht Ex Oriente Lux* 12:211–20. 20.

1954 Archaeologische Navorsingen in de Omstreken van Persepolis. *Jaarbericht Ex Oriente Lux* 13:394–408.

1959 *Archéologie de l'Iran Ancien*. Leiden: E. J. Brill.

1961 Récentes découvertes de monuments sassanides dans le Fars. *Iranica Antiqua* 1:163–98.

1963 Le relief Parthe de Hung-i Nauruzi. *Iranica Antiqua* 3(2):155–68.

1965 La céramique préhistorique du Fars dans son contexte culturel avec le Proche-Orient ancien. In *Ceramics and Man*, Viking Fund Publications in Anthropology no. 41, ed. F. R. Matson. New York: Wenner-Gren Foundation.

1968a *On the Track of the Civilizations of Ancient Iran*. Memo from Belgium no. 104–5. Brussels: Ministry of Foreign Affairs and External Trade.

1968b La nécropole de Bani Surmah. *Archeologia* 24:53–63.

1969 Recherche archéologique dans le Luristan. *Iranica Antiqua* 9:1–48.

1970a La nécropole de Kalleh Nisar. *Archeologia* 32:64–73.

1970b Prospections archéologiques dans la région de Badr. *Archeologica* 36:10–21.

1971 Kalleh Nisar. *Iran* 9:170–72.

1972 Prospections dans le Pusht-i Kuh central, Rapport préliminaire. *Iranica Antiqua* 9:1–48.

1973a Excavations in Luristan at Kalleh Nissar. *Bulletin of the Asia Institute* 3:25–56. Shiraz: Pahlevi University.

1973b La nécropole de Hakalan. *Archeologia* 57:49–58.

1973c *De Iconografische Betekenis van het Sassanidisch Rotsrelief van Sarab-i Qandil (Iran)*. Mededelingeq van de Koniklijke Academie Voor Wetenschappen, Lettern en Schone Kunsten van Belgie 35 (1).

1973d Le Luristan à l'Age du Bronze: Prospections archéologiques dans le Pusht-i Kuh central. *Archeologia* 63:24–36.

1974 La nécropole de Dum Gar Parchinah, Rapport Préliminaire. Ghent: Mission archéologique de le Pusht-i Kuh, Luristan.

1975a Fouilles au Lorestan: La nécropole de Dum Gar Parchinah. *Proceedings of the 3rd Annual Symposium on Archaeological Research in Iran* 3:45–62. Tehran: Iranian Centre for Archaeological Research.

1975b La nécropole de Dum Gar Parchinah. *Archeologia* 79:46–61.

1977 La nécropole de Chamzhi Mumah. *Archeologia* 108:52–63.

1978 Les fibules provenant des fouilles au Pusht-i Kuh, Luristan. *Iranica Antiqua* 13:35–74.

1979 La nécropole de Mir Khair au Pusht-i Kuh, Luristan. *Iranica Antiqua* 14:1–37.

Vandiver, P.
1985 Sequential Slab Construction: A Near Eastern Pot-

tery Production Technology, 8000–3000 B.C. Ph.D. diss., MIT.

Van Driel, G., and C. Van Driel-Murray
1983 Jebel Aruda 1982: A Preliminary Report. *Akkadica* 33:1–26.

Van Loon, Maurits
1969 New Evidence from Inland Syria for the Chronology of the Middle Bronze Age. *American Journal of Archaeology* 73(3):276–77.

Van Roggen/Graadt, D. L.
1905 Notice sur les anciens travaux hydrauliques en Susiane. *Mémoires de la Délégation en Perse*, 2d series, 7:166–208.

Van Zeist, Willem
1967 Late Quaternary Vegetation History of Western Iran. *Review of Paleobotany and Palynology* 2:301–11.

Van Zeist, Willem, and S. Bottema
1977 Palynological Investigations in Western Iran. *Paleohistoria* 19:19–95.
1982 Vegetational History of the Eastern Mediterranean and the Near East during the Last 20,000 Years. In *Palaeoclimates, Palaeoenvironments and Human Communities in the Eastern Mediterranean Region in Later Prehistory*, British Archaeological Reports International Series 133:277–321, ed. J. L. Bintliff and W. Van Zeist.

Vapnarsky, Cesar A.
1969 On Rank-Size Distributions of Cities: An Ecological Approach. *Economic Development and Cultural Change* 17:584–95.

Vickers, R. S., and L. T. Dolphin
1975 A Communication on an Archaeological Radar Experiment at Chaco Canyon, New Mexico. *MASCA Newsletter* 11/1.

Vining, D. R., Jr.
1974 On the Sources of Instability in the Rank-size Rule: Some Simple Texts of Gibrat's Law. *Geographical Annual* 4:313–29.

Vita-Finzi, Claudio
1968 Late Quaternary Alluvial Chronology of Iran. *Geologische Rundschau* 58:951–73.
1978 *Archeological Sites in Their Setting*. London: Thames and Hudson.

Vita-Finzi, Claudio, and E. S. Higgs
1970 Prehistoric Economy in the Mount Carmel Area of Palestine: Site Catchment Analysis. *Proceedings of the Prehistoric Society* 36:1–37.

Voigt, M. M.
1976 Hajji Firuz Tepe: An Economic Reconstruction of a Sixth Millennium Community in Western Iran. Ph.D. diss., University of Pennsylvania.
1977 The Subsistence Economy of a Sixth Millennium Village in the Ushnu-Solduz Valley. In *Mountains and Lowlands: Essays in the Archaeology of Greater Mesopotamia*, ed. Louis D. Levine and T. Cuyler Young, Jr. Malibu: Undena.

1983 *Hajji Firuz Tepe, Iran: The Neolithic Settlement*. University Museum Monograph 50. Philadelphia: University Museum, University of Pennsylvania.

Von Haller, A.
1932 Die Keramik der archaischen Schichten von Uruk. In *Vierter Vorläufiger Bericht über die von der Notgemeinschaft der Deutschen Wissenschaft in Uruk Unternommenen Ausgrabungen*. A. Nöldeke et al. Berlin: Walter de Gruyter.

Voorrips, A.
1981 To Tailor the Inflected Tail: Reflections on Rank-Size Relationships. In *Archaeological Approaches to the Study of Complexity*. Albert Egges van Giffen Instituut voor Prae- en Protohistorie, CINGVLA VI, ed. S. E. van der Leeuw. Amsterdam: University of Amsterdam.

Wailly, Faisal El-, and Benham Abu Es-Soof
1965 The Excavations at Tell Es-Sawwan: First Preliminary Report. *Sumer* 21:17–32.

Wallace, A. F. C.
1972 Paradigmatic Processes in Culture Change. *American Anthropologist* 74:467–78.

Ward, G. K., and S. R. Wilson
1978 Procedures for Comparing and Combining Radiocarbon Age Determinations: A Critique. *Archaeometry* 20(1):19–31.

Watson, Patty Jo
1979 *Archaeological Ethnography in Western Iran*. Viking Fund Publications in Anthropology no. 57. Tucson: University of Arizona Press.

Webb, Malcolm C.
1975 The Flag Follows Trade: An Essay on the Necessary Interaction of Military and Commercial Factors in State Formation. In *Ancient Civilization and Trade*, ed. Jeremy A. Sabloff and C. C. Lamberg-Karlovsky. Albuquerque: University of New Mexico Press.

Weber, Max
1963 *The Sociology of Religion*. Trans. E. Fischoff. Boston: Beacon Press.

Webster, David L.
1976 On Theocracies. *American Anthropologist* 78(4):812–28.

Weiss, Harvey
1972 Qabr Sheykheyn, Excavation Report. *Iran* 10:172–73.
1976 Ceramics for Chronology. Ph.D. diss., University of Pennsylvania.
1977 Periodization, Population and Early State Formation in Khuzistan. In *Mountains and Lowlands: Essays in the Archaeology of Greater Mesopotamia*. Bibliotheca Mesopotamica 7, ed. L. D. Levine and T. Cuyler Young, Jr.

Weiss, Harvey, and T. Cuyler Young, Jr.
1975 The Merchants of Susa: Godin V and Plateau-Lowland Relations in the Late Fourth Millennium B.C. *Iran* 13:1–17.

Wells, Robert V.
1975   *The Population of the British Colonies in America before 1776: A Survey of Census Data.* Princeton: Princeton University Press.

Wendorf, Fred
1976   The Use of Ground Grain during the Late Paleolithic of the Lower Nile Valley, Egypt. In *Origins of African Plant Domestication,* ed. Jack R. Harlan, J. M. J. de Wet, and A. B. L. Stemler. Chicago: Aldine.

Wenke, Robert John
1975–   Imperial Investment and Agricultural Development
76   in Parthian and Sassanian Khuzestan: 150 B.C. to A.D. 640. *Mesopotamia* 9–11:31–221.
1977   Human Population Growth and Evolving Cultural Complexity in Ancient Southwestern Iran. Paper presented at a symposium on "Patterns of Settlement and Cultural Development in Western Iran," School of American Research.
1981a   Explaining the Evolution of Cultural Complexity: a Review. In *Advances in Archaeological Method and Theory,* vol. 4, ed. M. Schiffer. New York: Academic Press.
1981b   Elymeans, Parthians, and the Evolution of Empires in Southwestern Iran. *Journal of the American Oriental Society* 101(1):303–15.

Westenholz, Aage
1979   The Old Akkadian Empire in Contemporary Opinion. In *Power and Propaganda,* ed. Mogens T. Larsen. Copenhagen: Akademisk Forlag.

Whallon, Robert, and S. Kantman
1969   Early Bronze Age Development in the Keban Reservoir, East Central Turkey. *Current Anthropology* 10:128–33.

Whitcomb, Donald
1971   The Proto-Elamite Period at Tall-i Ghazir. M.A. thesis, University of Georgia.
1979   Trade and Tradition in Medieval Southern Iran. Ph.D. diss., University of Chicago.

White, Benjamin
1973   Demand for Labor and Population Growth in Colonial Java. *Human Ecology* 1(3):217–36.

White, Leslie
1949   *The Science of Culture.* New York: Grove Press.

Whitehouse, D.
1971   Excavations at Siraf: Fourth Interim Report. *Iran* 9:1–18.
1972   Excavations at Siraf: Fifth Interim Report. *Iran* 10:63–88.
1975   Siraf. *Iran* 13:187.

Whitehouse, Ruth
1977   *The First Cities.* Oxford: Phaidon Press.

Wildegren, George
1956   Recherches sur le féodalisme iranien. *Orientalia Suecana* 5:79–189.

Willey, Gordon R.
1953   *Prehistoric Settlement Patterns in the Viru Valley,*

Peru. Bureau of American Ethnology Bulletin 155. Washington, D.C.: Smithsonian Institution.

Wilson, S. R., and G. K. Ward
1981   Evaluation and Clustering of Radiocarbon Age Determinations: Procedures and Paradigms. *Archaeometry* 23(1):19–39.

Wittfogel, K.
1957   *Oriental Despotism: A Comparative Study of Total Power.* New Haven: Yale University Press.

Wobst, H. M.
1974   Boundary Conditions for Paleolithic Social Systems: A Simulation Approach. *American Antiquity* 39:147–78.
1975   The Demography of Finite Populations and the Origins of the Incest Taboo. *Society for American Archaeology,* Memoir no. 30:75–81.
1977   Stylistic Behavior and Information Exchange. In *For the Director: Research Essays in Honor of James B. Griffin.* Anthropological Papers no. 61, ed. Charles E. Cleland.

Wolski, Jozef
1965   Le role et l'importance des mercenaires dans l'état parthe. *Iranica Antiqua* 5(2):102–15.
1967   L'Aristocratie parthe et les commencements du féodalisme en Iran. *Iranica Antiqua* 7:133–43.

Woosley, Anne, and Frank Hole
1978   Pollen Evidence of Subsistence and Environment in Ancient Iran. *Paléorient* 4:59–70.

Wright, Henry T.
1969a   Tepe Farukhabad, Excavation Report. *Iran* 7:172–73.
1969b   *The Administration of Rural Production in an Early Mesopotamian Town.* Anthropological Papers no. 38. Ann Arbor: University of Michigan Museum of Anthropology.
1972   A Consideration of Inter-Regional Exchange in Greater Mesopotamia, 4000–3000 B.C. In *Social Interaction and Exchange.* Anthropological Papers no. 46, ed. E. Wilmsen.
1975   Archaeological Survey on the Plain of Izeh. Mimeographed manuscript. Tehran: Iranian Centre for Archaeological Research.
1977   Recent Research on the Origin of the State. *Annual Review of Anthropology* 6:379–97.
1978   *Preliminary Excavations of IVth Millennium Levels on the Northern Acropole of Suse: 1978.* Technical Report in the Archives of the Délégation archéologique française en Iran.
1980   Problems of Absolute Chronology in Protohistoric Mesopotamia. *Paléorient* 6:93–98.
1981a   The Development of Settlement in the Area of Ur and Eridu. In *Heartland of Cities,* ed. Robert McC. Adams. Chicago: University of Chicago Press.
1981b   *An Early Town on the Deh Luran Plain: Excavations at Tepe Farukhabad.* Memoir no. 13. Ann Arbor: University of Michigan Museum of Anthropology.
1981c   The Southern Margins of Sumer. In *Heartland of*

Cities by Robert McC. Adams. Chicago: University of Chicago Press.

n.d.   Archeological Survey in the Areas of Ram Hormuz, Shushtar and Gutvand. Mimeographed manuscript, 1969.

Wright, Henry T., ed.
1979   *Archeological Investigations in Northeastern Xuzistan, 1976.* Technical Reports no. 10. Ann Arbor: University of Michigan Museum of Anthropology.

Wright, Henry T., and Gregory A. Johnson
1975   Population, Exchange, and Early State Formation in Southwestern Iran. *American Anthropologist* 77:267–89.

Wright, Henry T., and Yahya Kossary
1979   Archaeological Survey on the Dast-e Gol, February 1975. In *Archaeological Investigations in Northeastern Xuzistan, 1976,* ed. Henry T. Wright.

Wright, Henry T., Yahya Kossary, Ismail Yaghma'i, and Mansur Sadjadi
1976   Archaeological Survey in the Middle Karun Valley. *Proceedings of the 4th Annual Symposium on Archaeological Research* 4:430–45. Tehran: Iranian Centre for Archaeological Research.

Wright, Henry T., Naomi Miller, and Richard Redding
1980   Time and Process in an Uruk Rural Center. In *L'Archéologie de l'Iraq du début de l'époque néolithique à 333 avant notre ère: Perspectives et limites de l'interprétation anthropologique des documents.* Colloques Internationaux du Centre National de la Recherche Scientifique no. 580, ed. Marie-Thérèse Barrelet. Paris: Editions du Centre National de la Recherche Scientifique.

Wright, Henry T., J. A. Neely, G. A. Johnson, and J. Speth
1975   Early Fourth Millennium Developments in Southwestern Iran. *Iran* 13:129–48.

Wright, Henry T., and R. Redding
1979   Test Excavations at Tappeh Sabz 'Ali Zabarjad. In *Archaeological Investigations in Northeastern Xuzistan, 1976,* ed. Henry T. Wright.

Wright, Henry T., and Ismail Yaghma'i
1976   Test Excavations at Reza Qoli Abad Sangi: An Epipaleolithic Site in Southwestern Iran. Mimeographed manuscript.
1979   Archaeological Survey in the Vicinity of Iveh, January 1976. In *Archaeological Investigations in Northeastern Xuzistan, 1976,* ed. Henry T. Wright.

Wroth, W.
1903   *Catalogue of the Coins of Parthia.* London: Trustees of the British Museum.

Wüstenfeld, F.
1864   Jacut's Reisen, aus seinem geographischen Wörterbuche. *Zeitschrift der Deutschen Morgenländischen Gesellschaft* 18.

Yapp, Crayton J., and Samuel Epstein
1977   Climatic Implications of D/H Ratios of Meteoric Water over North America as Inferred from Ancient Wood Cellulose C-H Hydrogen. *Earth and Planetary Science Letters* 34:333–50.

Yoffe, Norman
1979   The Decline and Rise of Mesopotamian Civilization. *American Antiquity* 44(1):5–35.

Young, T. Cuyler, Jr.
1962   Taking the History of the Hasanlu Area Back Another 5000 Years. *Illustrated London News* 241:707–9.
1963a   Dalma Painted Ware. *Expedition* 5:38–39.
1963b   Proto-Historic Western Iran: An Archaeological and Historical Review Ph.D. diss., University of Pennsylvania.
1965a   Iran Project. *Archaeological Newsletter* n.s. 4, Sept. 1965, University of Toronto. Toronto: Royal Ontario Museum.
1965b   A Comparative Ceramic Chronology for Western Iran, 1500–500 B.C. *Iran* 3:53–85.
1966   Survey in Western Iran, 1961. *Journal of Near Eastern Studies* 25:228–39.
1967a   The Iranian Migration into the Zagros. *Iran* 5:11–34.
1967b   Godin Tepe. *Iran* 5:139–40.
1969a   *Excavations at Godin Tepe.* Occasional Papers 17, Art and Archaeology. Toronto: Royal Ontario Museum.
1969b   The Chronology of the Late Third and Second Millennia in Central Western Iran as Seen from Godin Tepe. *American Journal of Archaeology* 73(3):287–91.
1975a   An Archaeological Survey of the Kangavar Valley. *Proceedings of the 3rd Annual Symposium on Archaeological Research in Iran* 3:23–30.
1975b   Kangavar Valley Survey. *Iran* 13:191–93.
1977   Population Dynamics and Philosophical Dichotomies. In *Mountains and Lowlands: Essays in the Archaeology of Greater Mesopotamia,* Bibliotheca Mesopotamica, vol. 7. Malibu: Undena.
1978   The Comparative Stratigraphy of Second and First Millennium Khuzistan. *Paléorient* 4:237–38.

Young, T. Cuyler, Jr., and L. D. Levine
1974   *Excavations of the Godin Project: Second Progress Report.* Occasional Papers no. 26, Art and Archaeology. Toronto: Royal Ontario Museum.

Young, T. Cuyler, Jr., and Philip E. L. Smith
1966   Research in the Prehistory of Central Western Iran. *Science* 153:386–91.

Young, T. Cuyler, Jr., Philip E. L. Smith, and Peder Mortensen, eds.
1983   *The Hilly Flanks and Beyond: Essays on the Prehistory of Southwestern Asia, Presented to Robert J. Braidwood, November 15, 1982.* Studies in Ancient Oriental Civilization no. 36. Chicago: Oriental Institute of the University of Chicago.

Zagarell, Allen
1975a   An Archaeological Survey in the Northeast Baxtiari Mountains. *Proceedings of the 3rd Annual Symposium on Archaeological Research in Iran* 3:145–

56. Tehran: Iranian Centre for Archaeological Research.

1975b Nomad and Settled in the Bakhtiari Mountains. *Sociologus* n.s. 25:127–38.

1977 The Role of Highland Pastoralism in the Development of Iranian Civilization. Ph.D. diss., Free University of Berlin.

1978 Baxtiari Mountain Survey, 1978. *Proceedings of the 6th Annual Symposium on Archaeological Research*. Tehran: Iranian Centre for Archaeological Research.

1981 Indigenous Development and External Integration: The Baxtiari Mountains. Paper presented at the Joint U.S.S.R. Academy of Sciences/U.S. National Academy of Science Exchange Program on Central Asian Archaeology.

1982a *The Prehistory of the Northeast Bahtiyari Mountains, Iran*. Beihefte zum Tübinger Atlas des Vorderen Orients no. 42. Wiesbaden: Reichert.

1982b The First Millennium in the Bakhtiari Mountains. *Archäologische Mitteilungen aus Iran* n.s. 15:31–52.

Ziegler, K.
1964 *Die Beziehungen zwischen Rom und dem Partherreich*. Wiesbaden: Franz Steiner.

Zotenberg, H.
1871 *Chronique de Tabari*. Paris: Imprimerie Nationale.

Zubrow, Ezra B. W.
1975 *Prehistoric Carrying Capacity: A Model*. Menlo Park, Calif.: Cummings.

Zubrow, Ezra B. W., ed.
1976 *Demographic Anthropology: Quantitative Approaches*. Albuquerque: University of New Mexico Press.

Notes on Contributors

JOHN ALDEN, who received his Ph.D. in anthropology from the University of Michigan, has specialized in the Proto-Elamite civilization of western Iran and conducted a number of surveys in that country. He currently holds a nonacademic position in Ann Arbor, Michigan.

ROBERT HENRICKSON recently completed his Ph.D. degree at the University of Toronto in West Asian archaeology. His field research, on which his dissertation was based, deals with the culture history of the central Zagros of Iran during the third and second millennia B.C.

FRANK HOLE holds positions as professor of anthropology and curator of archaeology at the Peabody Museum, Yale University. His research has centered on the early stages of the domestication of animals and plants in Southwest Asia and the social changes that ensued. Following extensive fieldwork in Iran, he is now engaged in surveys and excavations in northern Mesopotamia.

GREGORY JOHNSON has specialized in developing models derived from geography and from informational and organizational theory concerning changes in levels of organizational complexity relating to emerging statehood in prehistoric times. A professor at Hunter College, New York, he has carried out excavations and surveys in Iran, Pakistan, and Italy.

LOUIS D. LEVINE is curator of West Asian archaeology at the Royal Ontario Museum, Toronto. His fieldwork has been concentrated in Iran where he has conducted both excavations and surveys. His primary research interest currently involves historical questions concerning interregional relations during the Iron Age in Greater Mesopotamia.

ROBERT SCHACHT, currently living in Albuquerque, is a graduate of the University of Michigan where he received his Ph.D. degree in anthropology with a specialization in Near Eastern archaeology. His principal field research was in Iranian Khuzistan. His current interests include the development of methods and theories in archaeological demography and the study of economic and administrative organizations using ancient cuneiform records from the Middle East.

ROBERT WENKE is engaged in field research in Egypt, where he served for two years as director of the American Research Center. Currently professor of anthropology at the University of Washington, he has been chiefly concerned with the archaeological study of empires of the first millennium. He is the author of a widely used introductory text, *Patterns in Prehistory*.

HENRY WRIGHT, professor of anthropology and curator of Old World Civilizations, Museum of Anthropology, University of Michigan, has focused his research on the origins of state-level polities, on which he has written a number of theoretical articles. His fieldwork includes surveys and excavations in Iraq, Iran, Madagascar, Mexico, and the United States.

Index

Index entries have been arranged under the following headings:

Archaeological Sites

*Archaeological
Periods and Phases*

Individuals
Named in Text

Ceramic Wares

Historical Individuals

Historical Peoples